BUNNY MELLON

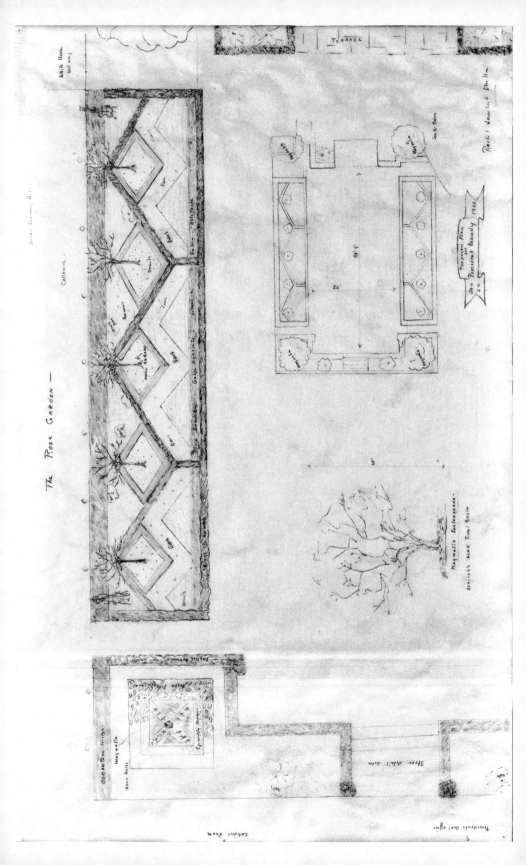

BUNNY MELLON

THE LIFE OF AN AMERICAN STYLE LEGEND

MERYL GORDON

GRAND CENTRAL
PUBLISHING

NEW YORK   BOSTON

Grand Central Publishing
Hachette Book Group
1290 Avenue of the Americas, New York, NY 10104
grandcentralpublishing.com
twitter.com/grandcentralpub

First Edition: September 2017

Grand Central Publishing is a division of Hachette Book Group, Inc. The Grand Central Publishing name and logo is a trademark of Hachette Book Group, Inc.

The publisher is not responsible for websites (or their content) that are not owned by the publisher.

The Hachette Speakers Bureau provides a wide range of authors for speaking events. To find out more, go to www.hachettespeakersbureau.com or call (866) 376-6591.

Endpapers copyright © Gerard B. Lambert Foundation.
Title page and chapter illustrations by Bunny Mellon, copyright © Gerard B. Lambert Foundation.

Print interior book design by Thomas Louie.

Library of Congress Cataloging-in-Publication Data

Names: Gordon, Meryl, author.
Title: Bunny Mellon : The Life of an American Style Legend / Meryl Gordon.
Description: First edition. | New York : Grand Central Publishing, 2017. |
Includes bibliographical references and index.
Identifiers: LCCN 2017016493| ISBN 9781455588749 (hardback) | ISBN
9781478976905 (audio download) | ISBN 9781455588732 (ebook)
Subjects: LCSH: Mellon, Paul, Mrs. | Upper class women—United
States—Biography. | Gardeners—United States—Biography. | Women
gardeners—United States—Biography. | Philanthropists—United
States—Biography. | Women philanthropists—United States—Biography. |
BISAC: BIOGRAPHY & AUTOBIOGRAPHY / Rich & Famous. | HISTORY / United
States / 20th Century. | BIOGRAPHY & AUTOBIOGRAPHY / Political.
Classification: LCC CT275.M469122 G67 2017 | DDC 361.7/4092 [B] —dc23
LC record available at https://lccn.loc.gov/2017016493

ISBNs: 978-1-4555-8874-9 (hardcover); 978-1-4555-8873-2 (ebook)

Printed in the United States of America
LSC-C

10 9 8 7 6 5 4 3 2 1

To Walter
Time After Time

Contents

All Illustrations by Bunny Mellon

Chapter One

President Kennedy Has a Request

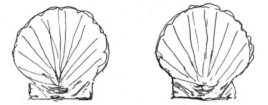

Bunny Mellon would always remember where she was—and how she felt—when she got the phone call that transformed her life. The year was 1961, and on that sunny August morning, Bunny was sitting in her four-poster bed at her summer home on the privately owned island of Oyster Harbors in Cape Cod, gazing at the water and looking forward to the day ahead.

The estate that she shared with her second husband, Paul Mellon, the heir to the Pittsburgh banking and oil fortune, served as an impressive showcase for the couple's passions. As president of the National Gallery, Paul consumed art, buying troves of paintings by British artists (Stubbs, Turner); Impressionists (Renoir, Degas, Cézanne, Monet); and American artists (Sargent, Homer). The Cape Cod house had such a deceptively cozy money-whispers ambience—wooden ship models, antique duck decoys, quilts on the beds—that visitors were often startled to see the masterpieces on the walls.

An ardent gardener, Bunny had tamed the property with so many cultivated plots of flower beds and vegetables that it took nine employees to tend them. Walking amid the colorful landscape, Paul would indulgently joke with the gardeners, "Is this one of my $1,000 tomatoes?"

His wife had fallen in love with flowers as a child, drawn to the gardens and fields of wildflowers at her wealthy family's properties, which included beachfront rentals in the Hamptons, a New Hampshire farm, and a sprawling two-hundred-acre estate in Princeton, New Jersey.

Bunny's paternal grandfather had licensed and named Listerine, and her advertising genius father, Gerard Lambert, popularized the antiseptic as the cure to the social malady that he invented, halitosis. Born in 1910, the oldest of three children, Bunny found refuge in nature from a household with bickering parents, hovering servants, and an excruciating sibling rivalry with her gorgeous younger sister. Bunny read her father's gardening books and was given her own land to tend. "I always had a garden," she recalled, "first a very small square with an enormous sundial that I had spent all my allowance on."

Now, at age fifty-one, slender and perfectly groomed, Bunny reveled in creating magnificent outdoor landscapes and unusual floral arrangements. Her Cape Cod property paled in comparison to the couple's full-time residence, a nearly five-thousand-acre Virginia horse farm with football-field-sized gardens and gigantic greenhouses filled with exotic plants. "The greenhouses went on and on and on," says Lee Radziwill, the younger sister of Jackie Kennedy. "Flowers from Sicily, flowers from South America, she sent her top gardener everywhere, she told me."

Bunny prowled the grounds at her homes in couture Balenciaga gardening clothes, pruning shears in hand. She knew the Latin names of flowers and plants and collected rare books on horticulture. On Cape Cod, she banned the local hardy favorite, hydrangea, in favor of blue salvia, achillea, and sweet peas. Paul Mellon would later admiringly say of his wife, "The thing I envy about Bunny is that from the age of five or six, her entire life has been occupied by horticulture, by one consuming thing."

Described in society columns as a style-setter, she embraced such discreet I'm-so-rich-I-don't-have-to-flaunt-it trends as wearing a gabardine coat lined with mink and customizing her Christian Dior handbags with gold Schlumberger clasps and a hidden gold monogram. Bunny could slip into couture gowns and adorn herself with formidable jewelry—Schlumberger, Verdura, Van Cleef & Arpels, Tiffany's—to play the perfect hostess. Just a few years earlier, she and Paul had entertained the Queen of England and Prince Philip at the farm.

Yet she was happiest outdoors, gardening or sketching. In her journals and letters, she wrote lyrically about the fragile opening of a flower petal, seeing the dew at dawn and the change of seasons. In a typical note to her daughter, Eliza, Bunny included a whimsical sketch of wildflowers stretching upward, with a description: "This is how I feel the flowers feel on the first day of summer. It is hot and the air is filled with insect songs. The day stays light and the colors come together like a summer mist."

She savored imperfect perfection. At her behest, trees were pruned into rounded shapes, yet she wanted her grounds to reflect the seasons. Woe to the gardener who raked up apples lying on the ground. The errant staffer was ordered to empty the barrels and put the fruit back. The flagstones on her Cape Cod garden terrace were spaced to allow weeds to artfully spring up. "On any of her properties, anything you'd see would be perfect but it wouldn't seem manipulated, it would seem natural," says Sam Kasten, a master weaver who produced fabrics for the Mellons' homes. Bunny wanted to exert control over her environment yet give the illusion that everything was effortless. Her favorite saying was: "Nothing should be noticed."

Bunny started her mornings on Cape Cod with breakfast in bed delivered by her maid, with a typical menu of coffee, a poached egg, and kedgeree (an Anglo-Indian dish, made from fresh fish caught by her staff off her dock). Even the trays were pleasing to the eye: Her carpenters had crafted butterfly-shaped wooden trays, at her instruction, and each morning a freshly plucked wildflower was placed in a tiny inkwell as decoration. "Her tray had to be perfect," says Linda Evora, one of many generations of Cape Cod housekeepers. "We used silver and good china. If she ate in her room at night, she wanted a red rose on her tray, she asked for other flowers earlier in the day."

Bunny would linger in her second-floor bedroom, looking at the enticing view: the sailboats traversing the saltwater Seapuit River, the sandy sliver of Dead Neck Island, an uninhabited pristine barrier island owned by the Mellons, and beyond, the Atlantic Ocean. She enjoyed the morning quiet, a time to read the newspapers, write letters, plan menus, or just daydream. Bunny and her husband had adjoining rooms—and, some gossiped, adjoining lives—and while the couple usually shared lunch and dinner, Paul was an early riser and they ate breakfast apart.

Bunny had divorced her first husband, country newspaper publisher Stacy Lloyd Jr., with whom she had two children, to marry the widowed Paul Mellon in 1948. The son of Treasury Secretary Andrew Mellon, Paul had been ranked by *Fortune* magazine in 1957 as the fifth-wealthiest man in America. A horse-breeding and racing aficionado, a reserved gentleman with a wry sense of humor, Paul had spent years in analysis to deal with the debris from his wrenching childhood and his parents' bitter divorce. (Able to afford the best, he was analyzed by Carl Jung and consulted Anna Freud.)

Paul had been in the public eye his entire life. As a student at Yale, when he turned down an invitation to the secret society Skull and Bones to join rival Scroll and Key instead, this momentous decision merited an article in the *New York Herald Tribune*. Paul Mellon was a great catch, but he was also an introspective and moody man who had learned to deflect emotions behind a facade of good manners.

At Cape Cod, the couple had a daily routine: Bunny went sailing in the morning with local boatbuilder Chet Crosby while Paul would test the waters in the afternoon in his own boat, also accompanied by Crosby. Paul's horses frequently raced at Saratoga during the summer, and he would fly up on his private plane for an afternoon at the races.

Bunny's reverie on that August morning in 1961 was broken by the sound of excited conversation and laughter coming from the industrial-sized kitchen on the ground floor. The staff was keyed up since special guests were coming for lunch: President John F. Kennedy and his wife, Jackie. This was not the first time that Bunny's cook had made corn soup for JFK—in fact, he would often request it in advance—but each occasion was memorable in this heady first year of the Kennedy administration.

Just four years earlier, a mutual friend had introduced Bunny to Jackie Kennedy. Even though Bunny was nineteen years older than Jackie—and only four years younger than Jackie's formidable mother, Janet Auchincloss—the two women bonded as if they were contemporaries, each thrilled to have found a trustworthy confidante. Asked whether Bunny was like a best friend, sister, or mother to Jackie, Lee Radziwill replied "More sister."

Bunny and Jackie both loved art and fashion and ballet and all things French. They could tease each other and tell each other the truth. "God, you can't imagine what a funny girl, she would make you laugh," Bunny later said of Jackie. "She's very, very bright." In the seven months since the Kennedys had been in residence at the White House, Bunny had been a frequent visitor, advising Jackie on redecorating the white elephant of a mansion and arranging flowers for state dinners.

For seven weekends during the summer of 1961, the president and Jackie had escaped Washington for his father's compound in Hyannis Port. The couple and their toddlers, Caroline and John Jr.— accompanied by the Secret Service—would frequently take the family motorboat, the *Marlin*, to cruise the short distance to the Mellon estate for swimming, sailing, and lunch.

This was a fraught summer for the new president as he grappled with a Cold War crisis. Soviet premier Nikita Khrushchev was belligerently threatening to upend the postwar status quo in Europe by dividing Berlin in half with a barbed-wire fence. Reporters staked out the Kennedys' Cape Cod estate, anxiously noting which advisers had come to brief the president. Determined to be perceived as confident and unflinching, President Kennedy decided on Sunday, August 13, to carry on with such carefree activities as sailing and going to lunch at the Mellons' rather than flying back to Washington.

Bunny had the amenities at hand for a formal meal: delicate china, monogrammed silver, and the large dining room table that had once held pride of place on her father's racing yacht, the *Atlantic*. But what she thought would please the president instead was a simple picnic at her modest beach house, an open-air shack on the water with a small kitchen and a wooden-lattice-covered deck furnished with wicker chairs.

That morning, she was reviewing her plans for the lunch when the phone rang. Jackie Kennedy was on the line and confided in a rushed conversation about her husband's new idea. "Jack's going to ask you to do something for him, promise me that you will do it," she told Bunny. "He wants you to design a garden for him at the White House."

"Where?" Bunny asked.

"Outside his office."

As Bunny later recalled, "She was breathless and in a hurry. Before I could answer, she had hung up."

The request from the president was simultaneously unnerving and exhilarating. Bunny projected aloof self-confidence but she was, at the core, deeply insecure. She had longed to attend college but her autocratic father had turned her down, urging her to focus instead on finding a suitable husband. She compensated by becoming voraciously well-read.

She had spent her life in the shadow of two famous and accomplished men, her father and her husband, and lately she had become known as the woman standing beside Jackie Kennedy. Here was Bunny's chance to step into the spotlight and do something that would, indeed, be noticed.

"I was sitting in my bed looking out at the sea. How could I cope with a garden of this size?" she wrote in an unpublished reminiscence. "Technical things like drains, water pipes, etc. must be considered and drawings made...I had never had any formal schooling in landscape design, which would have helped now."

She worried that she wasn't up to it—but of course, she had to do it. She roused herself with thoughts of her maternal grandfather, Arthur Lowe, a Massachusetts cotton mill owner who had encouraged her interest in gardens and paid more attention to her than her parents. He had served as the mayor of Fitchburg and had taken Bunny, at a young age, to meet Calvin Coolidge, then the governor of Massachusetts.

"A voice from my childhood began to speak," she recalled as she sat in bed and considered Jackie's request. She remembered her grandfather's solemn advice: "We are all part of this country and if we have something, however small, to contribute to it we must."

That morning, the president and the First Lady attended the 10 a.m. Mass at St. Francis Xavier Roman Catholic Church in Hyannis. "Mrs. Kennedy wore a checked beige princess dress and beige kerchief," reported the *Boston Globe*, noting that after the church services, "under a sparkling blue sky fleeced with light clouds," the couple and their daughter, Caroline, headed by boat to the Mellons' for a two-hour lunch. During the seaside picnic, the president asked Bunny to join him for a private chat, and broached the subject of the White House garden.

Even in the midst of a world crisis, Kennedy was thinking about the atmospherics surrounding his presidency. After pioneering and mastering presidential television debates—his handsome, energetic demeanor contrasting with Richard Nixon's sweaty countenance—the former Massachusetts senator was aware that appearances mattered.

He had just returned from a state visit to Europe with stops in France, Austria, and England, where he had admired the historic gardens. He wanted Bunny to create the perfect outdoor stage set as the backdrop for his presidency, and for every president to come. He envisioned not just a garden, but rather an American symbol that would be an elegant and welcoming vista.

"As an amateur, I questioned my ability to design a garden of such importance," Bunny later wrote. "Paying little attention to that doubt, he bubbled with enthusiasm, with fascinating details of how he wanted a garden to appeal to the most discriminating taste, yet a garden that would hold a thousand people for a ceremony. What gardener could resist? I agreed, on the spot, to meet in September."

Five years later, as a Christmas gift, Jackie Kennedy gave Bunny an oversized scrapbook commemorating her work on the Rose Garden with photographs, letters, dried flowers, and humorous and touching commentary. In calligraphy-style handwriting, Jackie described Bunny's adventures toiling on the project, such as the moment that the gardeners, following Bunny's design plans, accidentally cut the cable to the Strategic Air Command and briefly put the country on nuclear war alert.

The photos in the scrapbook ranged from candid family snapshots of the president playing with his children in the flowering garden to grave photos showing JFK solemnly walking through the plot with Defense Secretary Robert McNamara during the Cuban missile crisis.

Jackie marveled over the beauty of the Rose Garden and stressed that her husband's happiest times in the White House had been spent there. She wrote that "he will always be remembered" for creating such a scenic spot.

And on the next page, Jackie added to her dear friend Bunny: "As you will be too."

Chapter Two

Fifty Summers Later

The voice on the phone was frail but clear, with a hint of Southern gentility. "I have to tell you, my dear, I hate publicity," Bunny Mellon told me. "I don't know what I've done that has made people so interested in me, more than anyone else."

It was the summer of 2011, a half century after President John F. Kennedy had asked Bunny Mellon to design his garden. Now one hundred years old, she had long since faded into genteel obscurity. It had been decades since society columnists breathlessly chronicled her every move. Her intimates were gone: Jackie Kennedy Onassis died in 1994 and Paul Mellon passed away in 1999.

Suffering from macular degeneration, Bunny had been leading a quiet life on her Virginia farm, rarely venturing out in public.

But now she had become front-page news, enmeshed in a scandal. An enthusiastic supporter of North Carolina senator John Edwards's 2008 presidential campaign, she had not only given the former trial lawyer more than $3 million for his issue advocacy organizations but circuitously routed him $725,000 for his personal use. On June 3, 2011, Edwards had been indicted by federal prosecutors and charged with violating campaign-finance laws, using Bunny's money to conceal his extramarital affair with Rielle Hunter and the existence of their daughter. News helicopters buzzed over Bunny's farm and the FBI had interviewed her. The case was headed for trial.

I had written to Bunny to request an interview for *Newsweek*, mentioning that I knew John Edwards in the hope that might break the ice. In 2001, I had written the first major magazine profile about Edwards, and after the story appeared, he and his wife, Elizabeth, invited my husband, political columnist Walter Shapiro, and me to dinner in Washington. Other private dinners and drinks followed in the capital and on the campaign trail in New Hampshire, Iowa, and Wisconsin. Elizabeth and I had become closer after she was diagnosed with breast cancer, and she mentioned our friendship in her autobiography, *Saving Graces*. We had e-mailed back and forth the night that her husband had gone on ABC News to publicly admit to his affair with Rielle Hunter. Elizabeth died in December 2010, six months before her husband's arrest.

Bunny Mellon's penchant for privacy was well known. While awaiting her reply to my interview request, I spoke with her friend Bryan Huffman, a North Carolina decorator. They had talked on the phone every night at 9 p.m. for the past decade. Bryan had arranged for Bunny to meet John Edwards and was directly involved in her money transfers to the politician. "It's been like falling down the rabbit hole with Alice in Wonderland," he told me. "Bunny and I were the last people on earth who knew about the girlfriend and the baby." The gregarious Huffman, who had not been accused of any wrongdoing and was scheduled to be a key prosecution witness at the trial, offered to put in a good word with Bunny on my behalf.

Nonetheless, when my phone rang and Bunny introduced herself, I was startled. "Well, I'll tell you, dear," she said, "with all these scary people around who want to know this and know that, it makes my life a misery." But she had decided to take a chance and call me. She sounded pleased, saying, "Well, this is very nice that we're talking one-on-one."

It quickly became evident that Bunny was eager to chat with someone who knew and liked John Edwards—as I had—and could understand their friendship. News accounts had depicted Edwards as exploiting her for financial gain, but she didn't see it that way. "He would have been a great president," she enthused. "He and I were great friends. Every time he'd go on a debate against Hillary, he'd call and we'd talk." She was drawn to him, Bunny added, because of his "very deep intelligence. He was wise, he was clear, he was a very good person. I don't like complicated people."

Explaining her interest in presidential elections, she referred to her maternal grandfather, Arthur Lowe, who had inspired her to take on the White House Rose Garden. "I'm not politically minded but I want to help. My grandfather told me, 'If there's anything you can do for your country, Bunny, do it.' So I get involved with strange political people, it's very interesting. I don't know [Barack] Obama well, but people like John. Am I helping you or hindering you?"

"You are helping me a lot," I replied.

As our conversation meandered over a variety of topics, she kept expressing surprise that anyone was interested in her life, asking, "What have I done that is so unusual?" I brought up the work she had done at the White House and added, "You've been a living witness to history." She replied, with warmth in her voice: "That's true."

She complained that her vision had been failing for several years, a source of great frustration. "I'm happy to talk to you because I can't put it in letters. It's hard being one hundred and blind, I don't mind being one hundred, I can cope with that, but not seeing is scary. I gave something to a friend this morning, I gave it to her upside down." Bunny asked my age, and when I replied, "Sixty," she laughed and said, "You're not too far away."

Despite her age, she told me that she kept active with projects and was currently building a "Memory House" on her property to honor her deceased daughter, Eliza, featuring Eliza's paintings and photographs and a room replicating her art studio. Bunny was now selling some of her properties since she no longer traveled and the maintenance costs were prohibitive. "I'm very busy," she insisted. "I can't write but I dictate, I talk to people. I have so much to do. I have a house in Antigua I have to sell, I have lived there for sixty years."

She urged me not to write a story about her, suggesting that we get to know each other instead. "My dear, if you want to be a friend to me, let's stay telephone friends and I won't talk about my life and what's going on. I don't like publicity that way, that's the way I grew up. I'm so glad to talk to you... What can I do to be your friend and not publish?"

After I explained that if I turned down the assignment, the magazine would just put another journalist on it, she relented. "If you can't stop it, then do the best you can, high in attitude, low in knowledge," she said. With her 101st birthday approaching on August 9, she added, "I may not be here a year from now."

"That's why I want to do the story now," I replied.

She laughed, a mellifluous sound. "Oh you're bad. Just plain bad. We'll talk again."

And we did, several months later. She liked my *Newsweek* article; I had sent her my biography of Brooke Astor, whom she knew, and I suggested that Bunny's life would make for a compelling book. Bunny had been contemplating writing an autobiography for years, jotting down notes in her spidery handwriting on scrap paper, legal pads, and daily calendars. But she had put it aside, unwilling to be public during her lifetime. She still wondered whether anyone would care. I assured her that they would indeed.

She had closed our initial phone conversation by issuing instructions, words that I would take to heart as I began work on this biography.

"I'll have to put trust in you and God, write it nice, friendly, nongossipy. I'm simple, here I am, do it like that. Be kind. Calm it down, Calm it down."

Chapter Three

The Auction of the Decade

The glossy Sotheby's catalogues landed on doorsteps in October 2014 with a thunk, sixteen pounds and 1,556 pages worth of lushly photographed objects. This four-volume set depicted the ultimate lifestyle of a bygone era, made possible by a Gilded Age fortune. Sent gratis to valued customers and on sale for $300 by the auction house, supplies quickly vanished and sets began going for $600 on eBay. The catalogue itself had become a collectible.

The curated contents of seven luxurious homes owned by one family—in Paris, Manhattan, Nantucket, Antigua, Cape Cod, Washington, and Virginia—were for sale, with art (works by Rothko, Seurat, Picasso, O'Keeffe, Diebenkorn); Giacometti tables; more than 160 pieces of serious jewelry (including a rare 9.75-carat blue diamond, a 1925 platinum-and-diamond watch, a white-gold-and-ruby necklace); and enough antique silver and porcelain to entertain the entire Social Register.

"Property from the collection of Mrs. Paul Mellon" was the title spelled out in blue lettering on the catalogues. But the newspapers—and everyone even remotely in the know—referred to this extravaganza as "the Bunny Mellon auction." The *New York Times* pronounced it to be "among the most highly anticipated sales from a fabled family collection."

Rachel Lowe Lambert Lloyd Mellon, nicknamed Bunny by her childhood nurse, had died early Monday morning, March 17, 2014, at her snow-dusted estate, Oak Spring Farm, in the tiny village of Upperville, Virginia. Cogent until the end, the 103-year-old widow had conducted fond farewell phone conversations with friends during her final weekend. "We talked two days before she died," Hubert de Givenchy, the French fashion designer, told me. "About flowers, about a book, about the nice time we had on a boat trip."

Unwilling to acknowledge the inevitable, that weekend she urged her friend, the actor Frank Langella, to "call again, soon." A framed photograph of former North Carolina senator John Edwards remained on her nightstand; she spoke to him one last time. Bunny was comforted by the reassuring voice of Beverly Newton, the psychic whom she had been consulting for more than three decades. "I spoke to her a few hours before she died," Newton recalls. "I told her to go in peace and that I loved her."

During the final twenty-four-hour bedside vigil at her home, Bunny bestowed a frail but loving smile on her irrepressible six-year-old great-granddaughter, Fiona Lloyd, who came skipping into Bunny's bedroom, bearing a bouquet of just-picked crocuses.

Shortly thereafter, when informed of the family matriarch's death, Fiona solemnly pronounced, "She heavened."

For Caroline Kennedy, who had been a baby when Bunny befriended her mother, Jackie Kennedy, the news marked the end of a powerful emotional connection. "I can't imagine the world without Bunny," Caroline wrote in the days shortly after the death. "She is the last of the great trees that held up the sky of my childhood—tall and strong and graceful—spreading shade and sunlight—and protecting us always with love and strength.

"She and Mummy were the best of friends and it was a friendship that nurtured and sustained them both through the hardest times. They were like a pair of twins with their own special language, their own love of mischief, and their own special combination of respect for tradition masking a complete disregard for convention."

Now, Bunny Mellon's earthly possessions were to be auctioned off as specified in her will, with the proceeds benefiting the botanical library foundation located on her farm, housing ten thousand rare books and named after her father, Gerard B. Lambert. The photographs in the Sotheby's catalogues had been chosen to highlight the heiress's unique twentieth-century history and give the objects price-boosting provenance.

A candid 1961 snapshot showed Bunny conducting a private chat with President Kennedy at her Cape Cod beach shack. (She is wearing a cotton T-shirt, skirt, and hat; the president is in a short-sleeved white shirt, white slacks, and sunglasses.) A few years later, carrying a distinctive Dior handbag now for sale, Bunny was photographed on the street, looking protectively at Jackie. In a 1966 sketch from *Women's Wear Daily*, she is at lunch at the restaurant Lafayette with Truman Capote the day after his famous Black and White Ball.

In Washington party pictures, she stands posture perfect beside her husband Paul Mellon at National Gallery galas graced by Lady Bird Johnson, Ronald and Nancy Reagan, and George and Barbara Bush. At her Antigua home, she is wearing a straw hat and is sitting barelegged as she relaxes outdoors with her houseguest, Hubert de Givenchy. The embroidered tablecloths that they designed together for Bunny's exclusive use were now on the market, too.

One blurry photo looked out of place in the perfectly produced tome: Bunny and Jackie joining their patrician executor, Alex Forger, the now ninety-one-year-old attorney who had chosen Sotheby's as the auctioneer for both sought-after estates. He had been their mutual champion: negotiating a sizable settlement for Jackie from her estranged husband Aristotle Onassis's estate, handling four decades of legal work for Bunny, including the fallout of her late-in-life involvement in the John Edwards imbroglio. Bunny had continued to rely on the former Milbank, Tweed, Hadley & McCloy chairman even as he passed traditional retirement age. She had teased him in recent years that given his age and hers, they "were racing for the grave." Determined to protect her legacy, Forger was supervising Sotheby's proceedings.

The upcoming sale of Bunny's possessions received glowing media coverage as magazine and newspaper articles stressed two themes: her exquisite taste and how much she abhorred attention. "She was fiercely private and rarely opened her home to visitors," wrote Carol Vogel in the *New York Times*. The *Telegraph* in London stated that she "rarely gave interviews and shunned the public eye." The *Financial Times* pronounced, "Before her death, few things were known about Bunny Mellon," and quoted Forger's remark, "She was more interested in climbing trees than in climbing the social registers."

The *Pittsburgh Tribune-Review*, which closely followed Mellon news because the family fortune was founded in that city, described her as "one of America's most reclusive socialites." An article that I wrote for *Town & Country* was given the title "Inside the Auction of the Decade." The *New York Social Diary*'s Jill Krementz wrote approvingly that "she and her husband placed great significance on their privacy."

Paul Mellon had frequently praised his wife for influencing his taste and helping build his art collection. But at the National Gallery of Art in Washington, which had received hundreds of paintings and sculptures from the couple, the plaques credited "Mr. and Mrs. Paul Mellon." Other prominent female donors were listed by their own names, such as Agnes Meyer, the mother of *Washington Post* publisher Katharine Graham, or Pamela Harriman, the widow of statesman Averell Harriman. Yet Bunny preferred to remain offstage as the unheralded "Mrs."

A consummate shopper with a discerning eye and an unlimited budget, Bunny had taken great pleasure in furnishing and updating her homes. She employed a rotating staff of decorators, often housing them rent-free at Mellon properties. She perused auction catalogues, visited art galleries, and made expeditions to antiques stores in Paris, London, Manhattan, Virginia, and Cape Cod. She allowed her gardens and her library to be photographed for magazines such as *Vanity Fair*, the *New York Times Magazine*, and *Country Life*. But only select friends had been inside her homes. "Bunny did not receive many people in Virginia," Givenchy says in his lilting, French-accented English. "She doesn't like to know too many people, she's discreet, she likes privacy."

More than five thousand people flocked to Sotheby's during the week before the auction to experience the six floors featuring Bunny's possessions. Even the elevators were decorated with replicas of the handsome trompe l'oeil painting in her gardening shed, featuring plants, baskets, and tools. On the top floor, Sotheby's re-created— with flowing fabric panels—the allée of crab apple trees at Bunny's farm, a leafy, U-shaped canopy framing a path. The room resembled a secret garden, but the flowers on display were made of gold and precious stones, such as a gold tree-shaped brooch with ruby apples and diamond leaves, a floral spray of cabochon amethysts, and bee-shaped brooches with ruby eyes.

For celebrity spotting, Sotheby's was one of the best venues in town that week. The boldfaced names who attended the cocktail previews and the auction itself included Lee Radziwill; designers Valentino, Ralph Rucci, and Tory Burch; and such influential writers as *Vanity Fair*'s Amy Fine Collins and *Vogue*'s Marina Rust, an heiress to the Marshall Field fortune.

This retro-glamour display created an instant trend: Bunny mania. Home décor blogs on Pinterest and Instagram embraced the centenarian as a lifestyle inspiration, and the Internet was flooded with photos and commentary about Bunny's quirky juxtaposition of extremely valuable and shabby chic finds. *Architectural Digest* labeled it a "breathtaking private collection."

To glide up the escalators at Sotheby's from one floor to the next was visually overwhelming, due to the sheer quantities of possessions. If Bunny liked an object, she bought obsessively: There were dozens of antique porcelain tureens and serving dishes shaped like cabbages, cauliflowers, sunflowers, pineapples, melons, grapes, and asparagus. "She may not have even known what she had," says Beverly Newton, her friend and psychic, who attended the auction. Setting the table at Bunny's homes required multiple decisions: She owned 47 pieces of Georgian silverware, 149 pieces of "Trefid" pattern flatware, a 215-piece set of French porcelain and silverware dating back to 1740, 249 pieces of blue-and-white Tournai and Loosdrecht china, a 134-piece set of 1820 Worcester and Derby Imari porcelain, a 55-piece dinner set of Coalport porcelain, and a 51-piece Meissen dinner set with studies of fruits and berries.

It went on and on: the myriad of goblets; silver candlesticks; silver coffee and tea sets; ornamental gold, lapis, and enameled snuffboxes; a rug merchant's bazaar of Aubusson and English needlepoint carpets; and humble Americana hooked rugs. The furniture included a Louis XVI writing table, an eighteenth-century Regency chest, and black lacquered chairs with gold chinoiserie.

Some of Bunny's furniture was in poor condition—chairs were scratched and upholstery was threadbare. That might have reflected neglect, but it was actually a studied way of life. Keen to avoid the bright, shiny, and new, Bunny liked things to look timeworn. Truman Capote quipped to *Time* magazine in 1978 that Bunny always carried a little scissors with her: "When things are looking a little too neat, she takes a little snip out of a chair or something so that it will have that lived in look."

She had saved everything. Tidying up in preparation for the sale, her staff at Oak Spring Farm had found boxes of her papers stuffed into closets and under beds: 1912 letters from her father, her Foxcroft report cards from 1926, old menus and seating charts, gardening award certificates from 1954, travel journals from trips with Givenchy, hundreds of pages of correspondence, marked-up appointment calendars, the detritus of daily life. A maid discovered a million-dollar necklace buried under a living-room cushion; Bunny had so many baubles that she had not realized one was missing.

Sotheby's scheduled five days for the sale: one night for her art collection, another evening for her jewelry, and three days for everything else. New Yorkers gossiped and gawked as they tried on Bunny's jewelry (ring size a tiny 4), sat on her dining room chairs, and imagined scenes from her privileged life. Yet there were clues signaling that Bunny's wealth could not protect her from heartache. The Foxcroft yearbooks of her childless daughter, Eliza Lloyd Moore, were shelved amid a display of books for sale. Eliza had died in 2008, and with Bunny gone, there was no one left to cherish these autographed volumes from her daughter's youth.

An intricate gold Verdura compact had been a gift to Bunny from her first husband, Stacy Lloyd, upon his return from serving in the

Office of Strategic Services (OSS) in London during World War II. Her monogram was spelled out by twenty-six rubies. Engraved with the dates he was off at war—September 18, 1942–January 27, 1945—he inscribed it "To Bun with all my love." But the marriage had ended less than two years later.

The sheer quantity of jewelry and precious objects was disquieting. When Bunny's grandson Thomas Lloyd and his wife, Rickie Niceta, arrived at Sotheby's sixth floor and saw the vast display cases filled with baubles, Rickie burst into tears. It wasn't grief that caused her reaction, but rather an insight into Bunny's psyche. "There was case after case, forty Rolex watches, bracelets, purses, rings," explains Rickie. "I felt like there had been a true hole in her heart, and she was desperate to fill it. She tried to fill the void by buying all that stuff. It made me so sad."

Indeed, those familiar with Bunny's shopping patterns acknowledge that there was a compulsive quality to her behavior. "I think Mrs. Mellon could not go to bed in the evening if she hadn't bought something during the day," says Akko van Acker, an antiques dealer based in Paris who was one of Bunny's confidants. Pierce MacGuire, the former director of Schlumberger sales at Tiffany's, says that Bunny wanted to possess virtually every design that the jeweler created but often did not bother to take her purchases home. "We kept them in a suitcase for her in the safe," he says. "She was a collector."

For Bunny's family members, friends, and former employees, the sale evoked a kaleidoscope of images. She could be down-to-earth and funny, regal and icy, extremely thoughtful and heroically stoic, breezily dismissive and willfully oblivious. She was elusive. Often people did not know quite where they stood, which version of Bunny might appear on any given day. Her ability to keep people off balance gave her power. She used her money as a reward and a weapon. Flipping the Oscar Wilde quip, she knew the value of everything and the price of nothing.

Legendary *Vogue* fashion editor Babs Simpson, one of Bunny's closest female friends dating back to the 1950s, admired her enormously. "I think that if Bunny had been born poor, she would have done something quite important, in decorating or designing, because she had innate talent and imagination. She was essentially creative," says Simpson, who at 101 had been following the sale from a Westchester assisted-living home. When Simpson was building an oceanside home in Amagansett, Bunny suggested installing a sunken garden. "Bunny scribbled it on a piece of paper and gave it to me, it looked like a Mondrian." The completed garden received accolades: Oscar de la Renta described it as "one of the most beautiful gardens I've ever seen."

Yet Bunny had a habit of dropping people without explanation, and after a half century of friendship, one day she dropped Babs. "I never felt badly about it, because that's the way she was," Simpson says philosophically. "I was sorry, but it wasn't upsetting."

Hairstylist Maury Hopson, famous for coifing celebrities including Elizabeth Taylor and Barbara Walters, viewed Bunny as an unusually refined and low-key client. "She put the *b* in *subtle*," says Hopson, a Texas native who got his start working at Kenneth Battelle's salon, which Bunny patronized. "She was so serene, she never raised her voice, she was very gracious. She didn't seem to have a big ego."

In her sumptuous apartment on a high floor at Manhattan's River House, overlooking the East River, Deeda Blair, the philanthropist and ageless style icon whose husband, William, had been an ambassador during the Kennedy administration, paged through the Sotheby's catalogues. Blair had shared an overlapping social life with Bunny and mutual friends such as Hubert de Givenchy and Perry Wheeler, the gardener who worked with Bunny on the White House Rose Garden. As Blair showed me the yellow Post-its that she had put on the catalogue flagging favorite items, she smiled in recalling the heiress's eccentricities.

"Bunny rang up and said she understood I was going to Paris for the collections," Blair recalled. "Would I take a very tiny package to Hubert? I said, 'Of course.' She said, 'I'll have my car meet you at the plane, he'll drive you into town and then take the package to Givenchy.' It was in my hand luggage. Mercifully, the French never open any bags. I had no idea what was in it." The package was beautifully wrapped and looked expensive, as if it might contain Schlumberger cuff links.

"I had lunch or dinner later that week with Hubert," she continued, "and I said, 'Did your package arrive safely?' He sort of found a way of telling me what it was. It was a stone with a cord tied around it." How absurd to go to so much trouble to hand-deliver a rock that Bunny found on a beach. Yet, as a taste arbiter, if Bunny liked even a humble object, her aesthetic approval had a transformational effect. As Deeda recalled, "It was special. He was thrilled."

Decorator and former antiques shop owner Howard Slatkin couldn't bring himself to attend the auction, saying, "It was too sad for me." He had seen those items at Bunny's homes. "She had the unique and rarest ability among the very rich, seriously rich, to put comfort as the first priority," he says. "Most of the super-rich want to let you know what they have and how grandly they live, she was the opposite."

Jackie Onassis introduced him to Bunny back in the 1980s, and he felt privileged to have spent time with the women. "They were so natural with each other, comfortable and relaxed. There was a lot of literature talk, they'd be reading the same books and discussing the same characters." Now hundreds of Bunny's books were on sale, including poetry by Emily Dickinson, Langston Hughes, and W. B. Yeats; novels by D. H. Lawrence and William Faulkner; and plays by William Shakespeare and George Bernard Shaw.

There were so many stories attached to Bunny's possessions, tales that reflected her sometimes rocky relationship with her second husband, Paul Mellon, and other family members. A silver tray played a starring role in an account by Bunny's longtime decorator, Paul Leonard. Shortly before he died of cancer in 2002, Leonard wrote an outline for an acid-tinged memoir with the title *Bunny Dearest*. He described joining Bunny and her husband for dinner and frequently seeing "Paul's verbal abuse, especially after he had a few Martinis."

Paul Mellon attacked Bunny's intellectual acuity on one especially memorable night. "It was quite a ping pong match and I could only be the silent observer," Leonard wrote. "Bunny's last resort was her female instinct to cry, or to try not to cry. I recall the door to the kitchen opening, with the butler David appearing holding a silver tray with a stack of Kleenex!"

Now four of these silver trays were for sale, with presale estimates of up to $10,000.

For Louise Whitney Mellon, who had been married to Paul Mellon's son, Timothy, the porcelain cabbages brought back memories of family tensions. Tim Mellon had been five years old when his widowed father married Bunny in 1948, and he did not always get along with his stepmother. Louise recalled that when she was dating Tim in 1983, visiting his waterfront Connecticut home, something sparked his anger toward Bunny. "Bunny had given Tim a version of the cabbage," Louise recalled. "We were at his house in Guilford, and he took it out and smashed it on the rocks. I think he felt better after that. I was surprised." Yet Bunny had managed to have the last word—she left Tim only one possession in her will, another porcelain cabbage.

Bunny's prized possessions, two Mark Rothko paintings, came with backstories, too. Bunny visited the artist's studio with Givenchy in the fall of 1970, several months after Rothko's suicide. Rothko's bold, oversized canvases stirred her deeply. Her husband was not a fan of abstract art, but she convinced Paul to purchase nine Rothko paintings.

An enormous, sunny orange-and-yellow canvas, painted in 1955, had shimmered on the wall of Bunny's Oak Spring Library; now it had a presale estimate at Sotheby's of $30 million. A second Rothko carried a $15 million estimate—a smaller, stark blue-and-purple canvas that had been painted by the artist in the torturous weeks just prior to his death.

During her lifetime, Bunny had taken advantage of the soaring value of her artworks. Bunny had received a $110 million bequest from Paul Mellon upon his death in February 1999, along with their properties and many valuables. But the cash flow necessary to maintain her standard of living was astronomical. "Her lifestyle cost her about $20 million a year," admitted Thomas Lloyd, her grandson. "She didn't want to pare down or fire any employees, a testament to how loyal she was." With a payroll of nearly two hundred people, including butlers, cooks, laundresses, maids, gardeners, mechanics, carpenters, two pilots on standby, a masseuse, a librarian, even a cheese maker for her own dairy, Bunny had lived in a way unimaginable even to today's hedge fund trophy wives.

In the years following Paul Mellon's death, she had rapidly gone through all the money that he left her. To raise cash, she sold the New York town house for $22.5 million, her Cape Cod estate to billionaire William Koch for $19.5 million, and her Paris apartment for an undisclosed sum. But those sums were not enough to keep her going. So Bunny had gone into debt, borrowing $250 million against her art and gambling—correctly—that the Rothkos would appreciate. Prior to the auction, Bunny's estate sold two of her Rothkos and a Richard Diebenkorn painting for an estimated $300 million. The proceeds from that private sale paid off her loans and fulfilled bequests to family members and friends.

With so much hype prior to the Sotheby's auction, it seemed impossible that the event could live up to expectations. But when Bunny's forty-three paintings went on sale on the chilly evening of November 9, the auction room was packed and the bidding was frantic. The rare blue Rothko beat the presale estimate, bringing in $39.9 million, while the orange Rothko canvas sold for $36.5 million to the Helly Nahmad Gallery. The designer Valentino lifted his paddle to win a Richard Diebenkorn *Ocean Park* painting for $9.7 million. The art sale brought in $158.7 million.

Bunny's jewelry received an equally enthusiastic reception at the November 21 evening auction. The diamond-and-ruby apple-tree brooch, estimated at $3,500, was bid up to $26,500; a bunny-shaped brooch of diamonds, with a presale estimate of $20,000, sold for $78,125. A whimsical charm bracelet with the fixings for Paul Mellon's drink of choice—a martini—went for $37,000, more than three times the expected price. The room turned silent as two out-of-town bidders, working through auctioneers by phone, kept raising their offers in $100,000 increments to buy Bunny's rare blue diamond. After twenty minutes, when the final buyer won with a record $32.6 million bid, the room erupted in applause.

Artworks and jewelry have an inherent resale value even if provenance adds to their luster. But the bidding was frenzied for virtually anything that had once belonged to Bunny Mellon. A piano stool, valued at $1,800, sold for $5,625; an antique maple child's chair, with a presale $200 estimate, sold for $2,375; a 1940s hooked rug of a jockey astride a horse, estimated at $300, went for $8,125. The paddles flew into the air.

Bryan Huffman, Bunny's confidant during the last decade of her life, had come from his home in Monroe, North Carolina, to bear witness and appeared mesmerized by the action during three long days. Every item jogged memories, and he free-associated for hours about their encounters. There was the time Bunny swooped in by private jet to visit his weekend mountain cottage, the late-night phone calls ("There was a thunderstorm at 4 a.m. and she was scared"), and her mischievous joy in supporting John Edwards's bid for the presidency. Colorfully dressed in a rust-and-orange tweed jacket with a silk pocket square, wearing Schlumberger cuff links that had been a gift from Bunny, he was surprised to see his inexpensive gifts to Bunny on sale, such as a blue basket that he had found for $18 at an antiques shop. In the catalogue, a bronze sculpture of a leaping rabbit was listed as "20th Century British School," but Huffman said that description was pretentious, explaining, "I got it at a decorator's showroom for $200."

After the basket sold for an astonishing $4,000, we began betting on the likely price of the sculpture. Neither of us guessed high enough. When the winning bid came in at $40,000, Bryan laughed so hard that he nearly fell off his chair. He found it bizarre that his tokens had morphed to gold by passing through Bunny's hands. I asked the winning couple, seated behind us, why they had spent so much. Looking at me as if I just didn't get it, the woman replied, "It was Bunny's bunny. We had to have it."

The sale of Bunny's possessions brought in $218 million, double the auction house's original estimate. Yet even as the stragglers left the building and employees prepared to ship her possessions to the far corners of the globe, there was a poignant undertone.

The auction house scene had resembled a real-life version of the last moments of the movie *Citizen Kane*, when a newsreel crew walks among the vast contents of his castle, Xanadu, marveling over the profusion of sculptures, paintings, and furniture collected by newspaper magnate Charles Foster Kane, a character based on William Randolph Hearst. The movie dialogue:

"How much do you think all of this is worth?"

"Millions, if anyone wants it."

"He sure liked to collect things, anything and everything."

"If you put all this stuff together, palaces, paintings, toys and everything, what would it spell?"

The auction had made Bunny Mellon famous again. But as with Charles Foster Kane, these possessions merely evoked tantalizing elements of her history, silent household props that had witnessed the drama of a remarkable twentieth-century life. There was so much more to tell.

Chapter Four

Childhood Treasures: A Bottle and a Book

Hidden in plain sight, unobtrusively tucked among her pricy treasures, were clues to Bunny Mellon's early life. Her Cape Cod staff had been warned not to throw out an old bottle of Listerine with a rusty cap, which she kept in her private getaway cottage, the Dune House. A worn 1913 children's book, *Flower Guide: Wild Flowers East of the Rockies,* was stored at her Virginia library along with rare fifteenth-century manuscripts worth millions of dollars.

These were cherished totems from her past, connections to the two dominant figures who shaped Bunny Mellon's life: her brilliant businessman father, Gerard Lambert, and her maternal grandfather, Arthur Lowe, a Massachusetts gingham manufacturer, politician, and outdoorsman.

From her self-confident and restless father, she learned resilience, good taste, and how to navigate the American aristocracy. Thanks to her grandfather, Bunny developed a sensitive connection to nature, paying close attention to plants and flowers, learning birdcalls and taking pleasure in the sounds of tree branches whooshing in the wind.

Her father was uninterested in religion; her grandfather pointed out the glories of God as seen through nature. Looking back on her life, Bunny wrote of her father and grandfather:

> They were great friends and each always spoke of the other with kindness and deep admiration. Being a child, the great compatibility between these two men I took for granted. Now I realize they created the structure, like the beams in a great barn, that are still there when life becomes too difficult, that keeps me going.

From the late 1880s into the mid-twentieth century in St. Louis, the Lambert family served as a cautionary tale to those who dreamed that money was the solution to all problems. The Lamberts were rich—wonderfully, fabulously rich—and spent their money ostentatiously on grand houses with large retinues of staff, and once automobiles and airplanes were invented, they snapped up the latest models equipped with every conceivable gadget. But despite their riches, for three generations the Lamberts careened from one tragedy to another.

The family fortune had been built on the unlikely success of an antiseptic liquid invented in 1879 by Dr. Joseph Lawrence of St. Louis. He was inspired by British physician Joseph Lister, who had pioneered antiseptic surgery by using carbolic acid on dressings to prevent infection. Dr. Lawrence created a gentler formula.

Jordan Wheat Lambert, the son of a Virginia banker, had been a chemistry major at Randolph-Macon College and moved with his wife, Eliza Winn, to St. Louis to join a wholesale drug company. Lambert licensed the right to manufacture and market Dr. Lawrence's new antiseptic and started his own firm to do so. To create instant credibility for the product, Lambert traveled to London and convinced Dr. Lister, who had been knighted by Queen Victoria, to permit the use of his name for the new liquid. The moniker: Listerine.

Sold to doctors and dentists, Listerine was an immediate success. Jordan Lambert built a large brick home with stained glass windows, an Oriental smoking room, and a playroom for his burgeoning family.

Gerard Lambert was born in 1886, the family's fifth child. Jordan Lambert, a civic booster, was active in the Knights Templar Conclave, the American Musical Association, and local Democratic politics. In 1887, he was among the local leaders who went to the White House to meet President Grover Cleveland and invite him to St. Louis. When the Democratic Convention was held in St. Louis in June 1888, Lambert helped organize the event.

But on December 31, 1888, the *St. Louis Republic* ran a story, "At Death's Door," reporting that Lambert was suffering from a bad cold, hallucinations, and nervous exhaustion from overwork. He died in January 1889 at the age of thirty-eight, likely of an infection. Weeks after his death, his grieving wife, Eliza, gave birth to her sixth child, a boy named Wooster. Two months later, the widow contracted pneumonia and died on March 30. The *St. Louis Republic*, trying to find a comforting coda to this tragic tale, wrote of the children, who ranged in age up to fourteen: "They will be well provided for financially as Mr. Lambert's estate is a large one."

But for the six rambunctious orphans—Albert, Jordan Jr., Marion, Lily (the lone girl), Gerard, and baby Wooster—their living situation was now tenuous. Their uncle John Winn and his wife, Clara, moved from Virginia to St. Louis to care for the Lambert siblings, taking them South each summer, where they experienced a different culture. "In the early Virginia days each of us had our own colored companion," Gerard wrote. "Mine was named George Washington."

After their uncle died and their aunt moved away, their grandmother took over the household, but then she passed away. The Lambert children subsequently raised one another. At age fifteen, a rebellious Gerard told his banker guardians that he would no longer follow their instructions and moved in with his twenty-one-year-old brother, Marion, who taught him to box, fish, and shoot. A skilled high school athlete, Gerard won the pole vault in the 1904 interscholastic Olympic, a statewide contest in conjunction with the St. Louis Olympic Games. One of his classmates was the poet T. S. Eliot. According to the biography *Young Eliot: From St. Louis to "The Waste Land"* by Robert Crawford, the future writer disliked and envied

Gerard Lambert, stating, "He was rich, he was good at mathematics (which I was not) and he was an athlete and won cups."

Smart, inquisitive, and spoiled, Gerard stood out from his classmates when he enrolled at Princeton by virtue of his excessive spending. He rented a five-room suite for himself on top of a bank building and installed a Pianola, bought a Peerless limousine, and hired a chauffeur. As he admitted in his autobiography, he liked to show off to his classmates by having his chauffeur drive him the few hundred feet from his home to the campus chapel. In 1907, at age twenty-one, he received a lump sum of $300,000 (the equivalent of more than $7 million today) and could count on an additional $50,000 per year in dividends. But after his tumultuous childhood, he yearned for stability.

During his senior year at Princeton, a pretty redheaded eighteen-year-old Briarcliff student, Rachel Lowe, nicknamed Ray, caught his eye at a party. Her father, Arthur, was a self-made success and an instant father figure for Gerard Lambert. Born in 1853, one of twelve children of a Scottish immigrant farmer, Arthur had been forced to drop out of school to help his father run a slaughterhouse. After marrying sweetheart Annie Parkhill, he launched a company with his father-in-law, a former factory worker, to manufacture gingham. A staunch Republican and history buff, Arthur was elected mayor of Fitchburg, Massachusetts, in 1893. As president of the National Cotton Manufacturers Association, he was an unofficial adviser on tariffs to President William McKinley.

His daughter Ray attended Miss Porter's School in Farmington, Connecticut, the premier finishing school of the era. A petite teenager at five foot two with a porcelain complexion, she had grown up in a Calvinist family with frugal New England values. The exuberant Gerard with his inherited wealth held out the promise of a more exciting life.

Wedding invitations went out in June 1908, and after Gerard's Princeton graduation, the couple tied the knot. After the de rigueur European honeymoon accompanied by a chauffeur and a valet, the couple rented an apartment in Manhattan at Sixty-Sixth Street and Madison Avenue, and Gerard began to cast around for a profession.

Back in St. Louis, Gerard's three older brothers—Albert, Jordan Jr., and Marion—had all gone to work for Lambert Pharmacal. Albert Bond Lambert ran the family company, but his true passion was flight. An amateur pilot and balloonist, he bought one of the early Wright Brothers flying machines, converted a hayfield into what would become the city's aviation center, Lambert Field, and helped the U.S. Postal Service develop the first airmail route.

The youngest family member, Wooster, was a playboy who sparked such entertaining headlines as: ANXIOUS MOTHERS SET SNARES FOR WOOSTER LAMBERT, RICHEST YOUNG BACHELOR IN ST. LOUIS to WOOSTER LAMBERT ARRESTED SIXTH TIME AS SPEEDER and ECCENTRIC WEALTHY YOUNG CLUBMAN OF ST. LOUIS PAYS $3000 FOR COLE LIMOUSINE TO SATISFY WHIM.

Sister Lily Lambert's life had been marked by heartbreak. A year after her marriage to millionaire James Theodore "Ted" Walker, Lily gave birth to a baby boy. A freak accident upended their privileged life in May 1906. Ted Walker noticed that the water pressure in their house was low. In the dark equipment shed, he struck a match to see the pump's gauge and gasoline fumes exploded. He died from the burns. The distraught Lily emerged from seclusion a few years later to marry her brother Albert's college classmate, physician Malvern Clopton.

Gerard had no desire to return to memory-laden St. Louis, and the burdens and expectations associated with being a Lambert. Remaining in Manhattan, he spent two years at Columbia's School of Architecture, tinkering in his spare time as an auto parts inventor. He patented several devices but could not make a financial go of it. However, his yearly Listerine income made it possible for him to rent summer homes in the Hamptons and buy his first yacht.

On August 9, 1910, at 2 a.m., Gerard and his wife welcomed their first child, Rachel Lowe Lambert, at their East Side apartment. The infant was never called by the name on her birth certificate. "From the moment of her birth Miss Fishback, Ray's trained nurse, called her Bunny and Bunny she has been to this day," her father wrote in his autobiography, recalling her as a "fat, chubby little girl."

But the joy of a firstborn in the house was tempered by another family crisis. Gerard's sister, Lily, contracted a tooth infection, which turned into septic poisoning. She died in November 1911, at age twenty-seven.

In mourning and unsure about his future, Gerard dropped out of architecture school and enrolled in New York Law School. His wife was as indecisive about where she wanted to live as her husband was about his career. At one point, Gerard was paying rent simultaneously on five different residences—a New York City apartment and Long Island homes in East Hampton, Westbury, Cedarhurst, and Roslyn—while the family was actually living at the Briarcliff Inn.

When Bunny was two years old, her mother gave birth in 1912 to a son, Gerard Jr. "Daddy is so glad to write you and tell you about your little Baby Brother," wrote Gerard to his daughter, in a note meant to be read out loud by Bunny's governess. "Brother came down from heaven early in the morning. Your Mama and Daddy were here when he came." He added that Bunny would have "such a good time" with her new playmate.

Gerard Jr., nicknamed Sonny, was a sickly infant who immediately endured an operation to fix a stomach problem. Ray Lambert was so distraught over the baby's condition that her husband consulted a doctor for guidance on how to calm her nerves. Bunny was no longer the center of attention.

Bunny's earliest formative memories were of flowers. "Life as I remember began for me in my godmother's garden behind the dunes in East Hampton," she wrote in an autobiographical essay. "I remember looking up and seeing large blossoms of white phlox not far above my head. I reached up to pick them and was told not to touch until I had permission. But the remembrance of the scent, the scene, the atmosphere is still clear. My mother said I was three years old then. This was the conscious beginning of life and my love of nature, outdoors and all its intricate meanings."

Bunny's parents were both preoccupied during her childhood. Her father was in mourning for his sister, and her mother was focused on the health of her infant son. Bunny's sense of alienation deepened when her younger sister was born in 1914, named Lily after her father's deceased sister. Ecstatic over the newborn, Gerard Lambert gushed that even as a baby, Lily was beautiful, a word that he did not use in referring to Bunny. She noticed, and it stung.

Bunny resented her sister and felt unattractive by comparison. She actively disliked her mother, who seemed uninterested in her oldest child. Nearly a century later, Bunny still recalled the pain of feeling like the odd one out in her family. Her confidant Bryan Huffman summarized the conversation: "Lily was the pretty one. Her father loved Lily, her mother loved little Gerard, it was important to her father that he had a son." Huffman, who has a photographic memory of some of their chats, adds that she told him, "I was left to be myself, and my grandfather Lowe loved me."

Indeed, he did. During the six weeks each summer that she spent with her maternal grandparents at their mansion in Fitchburg or their farm in the tiny town of Rindge, New Hampshire, Bunny received an ongoing tutorial on nature.

She recalled that her grandfather took her out for adventures, "leading me through woods and up mountains, and taking me on trips to Concord, Massachusetts, to learn and study the world of Thoreau, Emerson and Hawthorne." The two of them spent nights outdoors at the farm. "If the weather permitted, Grandpa and I slept in two hammocks strung on the screened porch," she wrote. "Grandpa would teach me about stars and the night sounds of animals." At home she was waited on by an army of servants, but her grandfather put her to work: When they were at his farm, Bunny would get up early to prime the pump and heat the water for her grandfather's shave. He set aside a small plot of land so she could create her first garden.

In his humorous and encouraging letters, Arthur Lowe paid attention to Bunny's girlish whims, teased her about her poor spelling, and encouraged "Dear Old Bun" to read about Abraham Lincoln, "one of the greatest men of our country."

Bunny loved fairy tales and concocted her own versions. In a letter to her grandfather, she wrote about the fate she imagined for good little girls and boys:

Dear Grandpa,

…As soon as they have gone to sleep lots of angels come down and take them up with them into heaven and there they have their little bed and the angels put them in it and put lovely sky covers over them.

While I was one of those tonight and when I awoke in the morning I woke before the angels had put me down in my little bed on earth and I saw the loveliest things, everything while I was in my little cloud bed and part of heaven had come down with me and someday I hope I can go to heaven and stay with you.

He replied, on stationery from Hotel Ormond, Ormond Beach, Florida:

My dear Bun,

…I am glad you have imagination. It will be splendid all your life to think out these lovely things. Do you know, when I go out in the early morning and hear the birds and the bugs and the crickets and the grass hoppers and the frogs and the flies and see the lovely butterflies and moths, I wonder if they don't belong to the fairy family.

Your little story about being taken up into the clouds and spending the night in cloud beds in the care of angels is really beautiful… God makes all these lovely beautiful things and gives us the minds and hearts to know about them and to love them.

Bunny would never become a regular churchgoer, but her grandfather's religious beliefs stayed with her. She would view the great outdoors as her personal sanctuary and conduct private conversations with God.

Gerard Lambert jettisoned law school without graduating but came up with new career options. Envisioning himself as a builder, he put his fortune into two simultaneous projects: constructing his dream estate in Princeton and embarking on a new business venture in Arkansas. Arthur Lowe owned cotton-growing operations in the state and Gerard Lambert aimed to replicate his father-in-law's success, albeit on a grander scale.

With typical bravado, he bought twenty-one thousand wooded acres near the city of Elaine, Arkansas, and threw himself into what the *Fort Wayne Sentinel* described in a headline as BUILDING A MINIATURE EMPIRE. As the newspaper gushed in a full-page feature about Gerard Lambert: "When he saw a rich wilderness and the soil that nourished its fertile growth, his big idealistic imagination set him to wanting a property of his very own—one which he could develop as he wished and work out the dreams that were stirring his brain." Gerard planned to make money by cutting down the trees and selling the oak and ash, and then planting cotton in the fields.

He built a lumber mill, a private railroad to haul the logs away, a cotton mill, shacks to house the workers, an electric light plant, waterworks, and a school. He planned to offer health care. Working with a partner, Henry Holbrook, the two men combined their names to call their new town Lambrook.

The population of Lambrook was largely African American; of Lambert's 650 employees, only fifty were white. In his 1956 memoir, *All Out of Step*, he revealed a casually racist attitude toward his employees. "It was the custom to give each colored family anywhere from twenty to forty acres and build them a house," he wrote. "They preferred small houses and I found they liked to line them inside with newspapers. These sharecroppers were not very intelligent about their economic affairs."

An uneducated workforce is easily exploited. If Gerard had built homes equipped with insulation, stuffing the walls with newspapers would not have been necessary. For the sharecroppers, it was impossible to get ahead, since almost every penny earned went back to their employer for rent and expenses.

Gerard Lambert may have been idealistic at the start of this venture, but he came to view his cotton plantation with the profit-at-all-costs eyes of a businessman.

Quiet and sensitive, self-described as "painfully shy," Bunny was attuned early to the frictions in her parents' marriage. One scene made
a lasting impression. "Daddy cut his foot with an ax and Mother told
him not to come in on the new floor," Bunny wrote decades later.
"She gave him a painter's rag to mind it and I stood by watching with
great fear."

Bunny took her father's side over her prim-and-proper mother,
who played the role of the disciplinarian. Her mother's stern reactions
stayed with Bunny. "One day I cut Lily's hair and was punished
for days by Mother," she wrote. Bryan Huffman recalls that Bunny
was critical of her mother: "Bunny said her mother was not very
nurturing. She said her mother was one of those phony religious
types—always had to have the bishop over for tea." Bunny's niece,
Lily Lambert Norton, says, "Neither girl got along with their mother.
She was too New England—strict, staid, rigid."

In the vast fifty-two-room Albemarle estate equipped with a ballroom and a library, the three children had the top floor to themselves.
Gerard and Rachel Lambert left the day-to-day upbringing to the
staff. Bunny recalled that her sister would "promenade through the
house with five or six bath towels pinned together as a train swaying
from her shoulder, a paper gold crown on her head." Their father
found Lily's antics adorable. "From her childhood she loved to dress
up like a queen," he wrote. "She liked to put on a beautiful costume
and pirouette and dance."

While her sister was twirling around the house, Bunny and her
brother were investigating the woods and stream on the property. She
was curious about the inner workings of the household, too, trying to
learn from the maids how to iron and burning her hands. Her father
had taken charge of the décor and upkeep. Bunny was intrigued by
his mixed message on appearances. As she recalled, the staff was constantly shining the brass and silver and polishing the floors, yet "chairs
and curtains were allowed to become shabby and 'sat in looking.'"
This was the epitome of WASP shabby chic, and Bunny would later
follow the same practices in her own homes.

Bunny was captivated by fairy tales and children's books, drawn to the nature-themed illustrations in works by Beatrix Potter and Kate Greenaway. These books inspired her own small-scale landscape creations. "Beginning in our garden sand-box, then later in flat wooden boxes like large seed trays, I built miniature gardens using blue paint, twigs and whatever helped to simulate these enchanted pictures." she later wrote. "Small plants lined my window sill and I gathered wild-flower seeds as if they were gold found in streams."

America entered World War I on April 6, 1917. Gerard Lambert's brothers were already involved in the war effort: Marion was working as a volunteer ambulance driver in France; Albert had organized the Aviation Reserve; and Wooster quickly trained as a surveillance photographer and joined an Army unit in France. Brother Jordan Lambert Jr., forty-three, was preoccupied with his own problems; he committed suicide in August 1917, said to be distraught over the disintegration of his second marriage.

The thirty-one-year-old Gerard Lambert could have avoided the conflict because of his age, but a month after his brother's death, on September 18, 1917, he enlisted in the Army's Air Service, the predecessor of the Air Force. Initially stationed in Princeton, he taught artillery observation and ran a gunnery school. In the summer of 1918, he was sent to London and attached to the Royal Air Force, where his assignment was to study night-bombing tactics. In his off hours, he played the man-about-town, including attending a week-end house party where he taught the fox-trot to Lady Randolph Churchill, Winston's mother. Gerard never saw combat.

Nonetheless, for Bunny and her two siblings, their father's absence was troubling. Arthur Lowe tried to boost Bunny's spirits. "Your Grand Pa is lonesome for his play mate," he wrote to her on September 21, 1918. "There is no one to go with him for the morning paper, no one to bring me the morning sunshine." When Bunny was operated on (for what was likely appendicitis), he complimented her bravery "to take the ether and let the doctor put a permanent mark on your little tummy. I envy you the joy you will have after it is all over and you join the society of those who have had an operation to brag and talk about."

When she visited her grandparents at their home in Fitchburg, Bunny witnessed the hum of activity at his fabric factory. "In the summer you could hear the sound of the looms clacking through the open windows and smell the dye of the cloth as it washed into the river," she later recalled. As much as she adored her grandfather, that was a sobering experience for a budding environmentalist.

Put to bed at 8:30 p.m., she stayed up to listen to the Friday night band concerts as the musicians played "The Star-Spangled Banner." "No one ever saw this scene of a little girl in a long night dress standing beside her bed, with a sense of pride in her heart...Grand pa was very patriotic and I was taught its importance."

Arthur Lowe encouraged her sense of independence, instructing his chauffeur to teach young Bunny to drive his Marmon touring car. As she later recalled, "At age seven or eight, as soon as my legs reached the pedal, I started."

Gerard Lambert was discharged from the Army on December 2, 1918. The following summer, he took Bunny with him to England to visit his childhood friend Lady Nancy Astor at Cliveden, the storied sixteenth-century estate just thirty miles from London. During the war, the stately home had been converted to a hospital for injured Canadians. Cabbages and potatoes had temporarily replaced flowers in the gardens, but the Astors were now restoring the place to its previous glory. This trip served as an early exposure for Bunny to the manners and mores of the British upper class, but it was the gardens that made a lifelong impression.

The triangular-shaped floral beds in the parterre—the French term for an ornamental garden—had been designed in 1855 by landscape architect John Fleming, who used dwarf foliage as distinctive accents and planted bluebells and spring flowers in the woods. An elaborate garden included topiary, yew hedges, a pagoda made for the 1867 Paris Exhibition, and a Roman balustrade from the Villa Borghese in Rome.

Bunny was fascinated by topiary, those ornamental plants pruned into shapes not seen in nature. She absorbed the sights, later recalling "seeing acres of yellow mustard and blue flax throughout Europe" and realizing that "flowers are the paint box of garden design."

Now back to civilian life, Gerard Lambert had to face the reality of his fractured finances. His Arkansas operation was running at a loss. But before he could address the problems, a vicious race riot erupted.

The black sharecroppers had become restive about their dismal pay. The *Chicago Defender*, a leading African American newspaper, reported that the market price of cotton was 45 cents per pound but the sharecroppers had been told they would receive only 24 cents per pound. An organizer for the Progressive Farmers and Household Union, Robert Hill, convened meetings of the sharecroppers to discuss pressing white plantation owners for better wages.

On the night of September 30, 1919, more than one hundred African Americans met at a church in Hoop Spur, hiring armed lookouts to keep away intruders. Several white deputies, seeking to arrest a man for an unrelated crime, blundered onto the scene. No one ever determined who fired the first shot, but after one deputy died and another was severely injured, the situation exploded.

White posses swept through the area, terrorizing the black population in murderous confrontations. The Arkansas governor sent in troops, who committed atrocities. As historian Grif Stockley wrote, "Although the exact number is unknown, estimates of the number of African Americans killed by whites range into the hundreds; five white people lost their lives."

When Gerard Lambert received a telegram about the riot he immediately headed for Arkansas. His company store had been turned into a jail and his black employees were being tortured. He recalled learning with horror that an overzealous trooper had doused a purported instigator with kerosene and set him on fire. While Lambert was on the premises, troopers shot a man who was trying to escape. The deputies threw his body out the window. "For the first time I felt sick," Lambert later wrote. "When I left the building, his body was still there, covered with flies."

Seven local white leaders, appointed by the governor to investigate, claimed that the black sharecroppers had planned to kill white plantation owners and produced a list of potential victims, which included Gerald Lambert. The prejudice of the era is exemplified by a *New York Times* article on October 7, 1919: SAYS NEGRO UNION PLOTTED UPRISING. The *Times* quoted the report of the "Committee of Seven," stating that organizer Robert Hill "played upon the ignorance and superstition of a race of children—most of whom neither could read or write."

No whites were ever arrested, but a grand jury charged 122 African Americans with crimes. Twelve black men were convicted of murder in the Arkansas riots and sentenced to the electric chair; many others were pressured into pleading guilty to lesser charges. The National Association for the Advancement of Colored People took up the defense of those who had received the death penalty, and won a series of court reversals. Ultimately, no one was executed.

Gerard Lambert was never accused of wrongdoing either in contemporaneous accounts or in historical chronicles of the bloody riot. But his employment and pay practices contributed to the unrest. In newspaper articles about the riot, the Gerard B. Lambert Lumber Company was identified as the town's major employer.

Unable to sell his now-notorious cotton and lumber business, Lambert hired a friend to run the faltering venture and withdrew from day-to-day operations. Although he tried to protect his family from learning about the debacle, the inquisitive young Bunny bumbled into disturbing facts.

Bunny liked to sneak into her father's home office. The door was locked except on the days when the cleaning lady came and left the door open during her lunch break. Bunny, who had just turned nine, slipped in and saw on her father's desk what she described as "horrible" photographs of his Arkansas employees' living conditions. "Daddy had a cotton plantation there and these pictures had been sent to him but were kept away from us, I suppose," she later wrote. "Later I heard there were race riots."

She had trouble reconciling the stark photos with her perception of her father as a good man. Could he really be responsible for people living in such misery? Her father never discussed "his difficulties," as she put it. When she wrote about her memories of Arkansas and her father in a never-published 2006 autobiographical essay, she was still trying to defend him by listing positive attributes.

"He was very kind about people who could not help themselves. He always tipped taxi drivers very well for he saw their home life in his imagination and felt a little extra might make a difference," she wrote. "When he went to see us in the hospital all his thoughts were for people who had to suffer the same thing but had no money to pay for a good doctor, extra medicine or help...Here thoughts were so painful to him and he was willing to empty his pockets without thought."

A mere child when the Arkansas riot occurred, even looking back decades later, Bunny found it hard to accept that her father had presided over such an exploitative and explosive company town.

Yet the experience changed her. Bunny grew up with a heightened sensitivity to the plight of others and a desire to help. "She was not the usual rich lady," says Vernon Jordan, the civil rights activist who headed the Urban League in the 1970s and met her during that era. "She cared about issues and she cared about people. But it was all, as I remember, quiet."

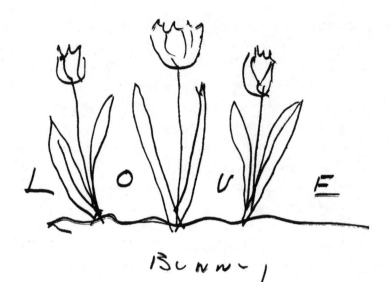

Chapter Five

The Making of a Young Gardener

For the first time in Gerard Lambert's life, money was a problem. The economic downturn after World War I had left the family firm, Lambert Pharmacal, struggling and he could no longer count on yearly dividends to fund his lifestyle. Albemarle was mortgaged to the hilt, and he was $700,000 in debt. The prospect of bankruptcy loomed.

Gerard had never worked for anyone before, and his disastrous Arkansas cotton operation was not a business experience to brag about. In desperation, at age thirty-five he took a fresh look at the obvious options that he had previously scorned. His three brothers were on the payroll of Lambert Pharmacal. In 1921, he took the train to St. Louis and asked his cousin Arthur Lambert, a company trustee, for a job. Ignoring his cousin's unenthusiastic response, Gerard uprooted his family from Princeton and rented out Albemarle. His return to his hometown merited an item on August 7, 1921, in the *St. Louis Post-Dispatch*: "Mr. and Mrs. Gerard Lambert...arrived some time ago and expect to remain here for two years."

At Lambert Pharmacal, Gerard concentrated on cost-cutting strategies, such as buying corks for Listerine bottles from a supplier to avoid a middleman, and finding a way to reduce taxes on the alcohol used in the product. But these gambits did not address the firm's long-term problems. Lambert Pharmacal had only one product, which it advertised in medical magazines. Drugstores categorized Listerine as a "disinfectant" or "toilet goods," which were uninviting product descriptions.

Gerard thought that better marketing might make a difference. Summoning the company's two Chicago ad makers to St. Louis for a strategy session in his brother Marion's office, he convened a discussion about new ways that Listerine could be used and advertised. Marion Lambert tossed out a notion, recalling, "Dad used to say it was good for bad breath." Gerard was appalled by the idea. As he later admitted in his autobiography, "I glared, reminding him that this was a respectable meeting."

Nonetheless, the company's elderly chemist, Arthur Deacon, was asked for his opinion and confirmed that Listerine would work for that purpose, mentioning in passing the word "halitosis." The *New Yorker* later described Gerard Lambert's reaction to that unusual word. "What's that?" Gerard asked. Arthur Deacon replied, "Latin for 'unpleasant breath.'" Gerard jumped on the idea, saying, "There's something we can hang our hat on."

On his way home that day, Gerard stopped at a photo agency, bought a stock portrait of a young woman, and that night sketched out an ad campaign about a girl who had all the advantages in the world but suffered from one humiliating handicap: halitosis. And even her best friends would not tell her.

In an early trial of market testing, he instructed the ad agency to run this new ad as well as a bland version showing a photo of a Listerine bottle with copy about how good it felt to gargle. Coupons for free samples were attached to the ads: The halitosis version brought in twice as many people eager to try the bad-breath solution.

Variations of this hall-of-shame ad ran in newspapers and magazines nationwide, resulting in a huge demand for Listerine. Gerard Lambert cowrote much of the ad copy with partners. These were catchy, clever, soap opera–style dramas: the woman who was "always a bridesmaid but never a bride"; "the secret the mirror won't tell you"; a newly married couple with the caption "till breath do us part."

This ad campaign was treated as déclassé by the world of high society—from then on, Gerard was sniffed at as a bad-breath emperor, the "father of halitosis"—but the money came rolling in. Gerard followed up that coup by launching Listerine toothpaste.

Homesick for Princeton, Bunny wrote a school essay with the title "Home Sweet Home," describing how much she missed the woods in New Jersey, where she recalled that "the birds are singing at all times of day." She faithfully wrote to her grandfather, drawing flowers, the sun, and the grass on her notepaper. For Bunny, it became a lifelong habit to add sketches of trees, plants, birds, and hearts to her correspondence. (Some of these images adorn this book.) Her grandfather replied on March 4, 1922, describing a recent trip to his farm:

> *The little trees were glad to see me, they miss bowing their little heads and holding out their little arms in welcome and acting as if they were saying, "Where is Bun?" They all waited to see her running around and hear her sing. I told everything about the place to put on their prettiest about June 5th because you were coming to have a picnic with them.*

A distinguished man with a white beard, unruly mustache, and thick white eyebrows, he looked as comfortable posing with a shotgun and a turkey in a photograph as he did wearing a suit and tie in his office. He told his granddaughter tales about growing up in the shadow of the Civil War, too young to enlist. "I remember clearly the April morning when we heard of the assassination of President Lincoln, the church bells rang out the sad news," he wrote in a family memoir.

When she visited her grandparents, Bunny resented the hours spent with her grandmother, who was determined to teach her the social niceties. "She had her social life with whist parties and household chores that she took seriously and ruled with an iron hand," Bunny wrote in a reminiscence. "On Thursdays, if luck failed and Grandpa went to Boston, I was dressed in my best clothes and went out with Grandma. We went calling in her fancy big car...I was always introduced as 'Rachel's child,' after shaking hands and making a curtsey.

In Grandma's mind I was always Rachel's child, in Grandpa's, I was Bun."

On Bunny's twelfth birthday, her grandfather wrote a note imagining her future: "Next birthday you will be in your 'teens.' Why when I am 100, you will be 43, old enough to be a grandmother. I am going to hang around until I am 100 if I can, just to see what kind of a grandmother you will make."

A bookish and introspective child, Bunny discovered the works of Thomas Hardy and devoured such morality tales as *Tess of the d'Urbervilles* and *Far from the Madding Crowd*, books that featured female protagonists grappling with society's expectations. "He influenced my life so much," she later recalled. "I read all his books. It taught me life was built on circumstance. Circumstance led you forward. Circumstance has always led me ahead."

After more than a year in St. Louis, Gerard informed his brothers that he was moving back to the East Coast to start an advertising agency in Manhattan, which would handle the Listerine account plus other clients. He resettled his family at Albemarle, in Princeton, and began putting in long hours establishing his agency. In his new office at 250 Park Avenue, he paneled the boardroom in walnut and installed a red leather sofa and matching chairs. A delicate antique French desk completed the wealthy-gentleman-at-work image.

In the summer of 1923, Bunny journeyed to Alaska with her grandfather and her cousin Nathalie Lowe, traveling by trains and a boat. En route, stopping overnight at the Hotel Vancouver, she wrote to her father:

Dear Daddy,

You better send a salesman to Vancove, BC and have him send some listerine. You can't get any here, at least where we have been... Grandpa told me to tell you to make some money because I was spending it very fast.

Bunny kept a twenty-nine-page handwritten journal, "A Visit to the Land of the Totem Poles." She described seeing glaciers ("a mass of blue...I thought I was dreaming when I saw it"), the excitement of close encounters with bears and buffalo, sharing a boat with "Indians who stared at you," and meeting with Alaska territorial governor Scott Bone ("very nice and somewhat jolly"). After touring an abandoned gold-mining camp, Bunny recorded her reaction to the living conditions: "No one unless they had seen the place will have known what they suffered."

For a girl about to turn thirteen, she paid unusual attention to the architecture and landscaping, recalling that in Vancouver, "one thing that stood out in my mind was a house of a good size covered with pink ramble roses and they were all in bloom."

En route home, the group stopped at Yellowstone Park, where she marveled at the geysers ("the main colors being a deep blue, pink, red and yellow"). In Salt Lake City, her grandfather took her to the Mormon Tabernacle; in Colorado Springs, the family toured the town in a new Pierce-Arrow and took a side trip to the rock formation the Garden of the Gods, which Bunny pronounced "perfectly beautiful." And in Denver, they went to see the grave of Buffalo Bill Cody.

Bunny brought back flower seeds from her travels. She liked to experiment in her greenhouse to learn about growing conditions. She wrote to tell her grandfather that she was testing out her Alaska finds, adding, "I hope that I will be able to put them in my garden in the spring."

———

Gerard Lambert was visiting St. Louis in 1924 when he learned that his older brother Marion had become critically ill while on vacation in Hot Springs, Arkansas. By the time Gerard arrived, Marion was delirious with double pneumonia and died a few days later at the age of forty-three.

Gerard had always been resilient, but his grief was a cloud felt by his wife and children. He immersed himself in work. Named as trustee of his brother's estate and responsible for the financial security of Marion's three children, Gerard agreed to take on the top post at Lambert Pharmacal. He became the long-distance president of the pharmaceutical company while continuing to run his New York advertising agency.

To boost sales of Listerine, he ran ad campaigns promising that the product was good for multiple uses, such as curing sore throats and halting dandruff, and even as an aftershave. The Federal Trade Commission, established in 1914, was not yet looking closely at truth-in-advertising campaigns. The unproven ad gimmicks reeled in the unsuspecting public, keeping the Listerine factory busy.

At home, Gerard turned his attention to improving the grounds of Albemarle. He had the lawn planted with special grass seed imported from Germany and became obsessed with maintaining the visual beauty. "After our grass had been well-established, if a single weed raised its ugly head, seven gardeners fell on it with a growl," Lambert recalled. "Our grass received more loving thought and attention than the inhabitants of the house."

When he decided to install a new garden, no local expert would do. Frederick Law Olmsted, the landscape architect who designed Central Park, the U.S. Capitol Grounds, and estates such as the Biltmore, died in 1903, but his two Boston-based sons, Frederick Jr. and John Charles Olmsted, had taken over the family business. Frederick Jr. had established a landscape architecture department at Harvard and designed the grounds for the National Mall and the Jefferson Memorial. Gerard hired the Olmsted brothers to work their magic on Albemarle, much to the delight of his eldest child.

"Every day after school I watched and looked at plans in a shed up by the greenhouse," Bunny wrote. She observed as a cornfield was transformed into a vegetable garden bordered with lilacs. She trailed after the gardeners and peppered them with questions. As an adult, she would make self-deprecating comments about having no real training in garden design, but she absorbed the principles of proportion, scale, and color in her own backyard. The Olmsted brothers moved apple trees to border the driveway, and then put in a six-foot-high hedge of English boxwood behind them to create a dramatic backdrop.

She would later write with Proustian longing about the grounds of Albemarle. "As a child, wild flowers were part of my feeling of freedom—hidden under larger plants or creating fields of lavender thistles that colored the landscape like a sea in the wind," she wrote. "The intense bright of the buttercups made me think that if ever I had to live alone in a cellar room, I would paint it yellow and never miss the sun." She was equally rapturous about the apple trees: "Children often find their symbols of stability and peace among the daily presence of things they love. For me, they were apple trees. The driveway to our house was lined with apple trees. Leaving early in the morning for school and returning in the afternoon, they were always there to welcome me. I knew their shapes by heart."

Bunny and her sister attended Miss Fine's School, a private day academy run by May Fine, whose brother Henry Fine was Princeton University's faculty dean. Woodrow Wilson's three daughters and Grover Cleveland's daughter had all attended Miss Fine's School. Rachel "Ray" Lambert made sure that her daughters wore fetching outfits, employing a live-in dressmaker who produced the latest styles. "As children we were beautifully dressed," wrote Bunny, remembering her embroidered petticoats and straw hats with black velvet ribbons. "Lily and I were dressed alike until I shot up like a pole bean."

At a time when petite femininity was the ideal, Bunny grew to be five foot nine, towering over her mother by seven inches and her sister by three inches. Self-conscious about her height, Bunny tried to hide it by slouching. Her grandfather exhorted Bunny, in letter after letter, to "Stand Up Straight." "Keep on at it and you will be as fine looking a girl and as healthy as any of them and the admiration of all," he wrote. Heeding his advice, she developed a distinctive posture, straight-backed even when seated.

Yet not even her grandfather's affection could mitigate Bunny's nagging sense of being unappreciated by her parents and unattractive compared to her sister. Those painful feelings shaped her in profound ways as she grew up. To hide her vulnerability, Bunny taught herself to appear self-sufficient to the point of being standoffish. Easily wounded and starving for love, she demanded unquestioning loyalty from those who became close to her. If she suspected that their attention was waning, Bunny preemptively dropped people without explanation, leaving hurt feelings in her wake.

What made her feel the safest were triangular relationships, where she could be the center of attention and play friends and suitors off against one another. In her journals, Bunny would later write about how she desperately wanted to let down her guard and open her heart but was terrified to do so. Alienated from her mother and her sister, she idolized her father. Although Bunny would develop a handful of female confidantes, she preferred the company of men.

As a teenager she rejoiced when two older cousins—the orphaned Ted Walker plus George Lambert, the son of aviator and businessman Albert Lambert—enrolled at Princeton University and became frequent visitors to Albemarle. George was a star athlete, a football player, and the captain of the varsity tennis team. The cousins played the piano and drums in the Lamberts' music room; Bunny's father joined in on the harmonica or ukulele. "Daddy used to clog-dance like crazy," she recalled. The two wealthy young men were both studying for their pilot's licenses, and they recruited the plucky Bunny as a passenger.

"One of my cousins had a plane," she reminisced. "He said, 'Hey, kid, do you want to fly to Lawrenceville?' He tied me in the plane with my sweater to the door handle. Started the propeller with his hand and jumped in." After the flight, he made Bunny promise not to tell her mother.

The cousins gave her advice on dating, such as how to play hard to get at dances. She counted on their muscle when she ambitiously embarked on building a small stone house and designing a formal garden on her parents' property. She mixed the concrete and put up the walls "with the help of cousins or anyone standing nearby," she recalled. She thatched the roof with bundles of straw and wire and painted the door blue. Her proud father gave her creation a favorable verdict. "There was a square walled garden in front with tiny boxwood bushes forming intricate patterns and rare shrubs and vines," he wrote. "From this first effort came many beautiful gardens, some done as professional jobs. She has the same talent in decorating and like her father, she loves to do things over. Nothing is ever finished."

The family spent summers in Southampton on Long Island, where Bunny and her siblings kept busy. As her grandfather wrote to Bunny one July, "Horse back riding, golf, tennis, swimming, music and I suppose the study of Italian and Spanish is quite a full program for vacation days."

Bunny loved horses and yearned for her own mount. On March 5, 1925, Arthur Lowe told Bunny that he had just seen a man "who says he has just the horse for you. He says it is the most lovable animal that ever was. He says if I get it, I will think more of it than I do of you. That would have to be some horse." Gerard Lambert built Bunny a stable with four stalls and a tack room complete with a fireplace.

Gerard Lambert could afford to keep his family in luxuries thanks to his dual income from Lambert Pharmacal and his ad agency, but he wanted long-term financial security. The go-go stock market offered tantalizing riches. In March 1926, he hired Goldman Sachs to take Lambert Pharmacal public at $41.75 per share. The deal was structured so that two classes of stock were issued and Gerard retained a controlling interest in the company. Gambling on the future, he became president of the newly organized firm with no salary, under the condition that he would receive 100,000 shares if he doubled earnings. He pulled it off in eighteen months.

For families of the Lamberts' social class, the children were expected to attend boarding school. Bunny's mother planned to send her daughter to her alma mater, Miss Porter's, but Bunny lobbied her parents to let her attend the horse-centric Foxcroft School in Virginia. "I was really scared of riding but I liked it, and collecting books about horses and the history of horses," Bunny recalled.

Her father was impressed by Bunny's poise in making her case. "Bunny, when she was in the pigtail stage, came to me one day. Bunny never raises a fuss, nor does she even raise her voice. She just quietly insists until she has her way," he wrote. "She thinks everything out in advance and then opens her campaign. In the firm way that she has always had, she announced that she wanted me to get her into the Foxcroft School. I told her I had never heard of it."

Based in rural Middleburg, Virginia, forty-six miles from Washington, D.C., Foxcroft was founded in 1914 by the unconventional Charlotte Haxall Noland, who still served as headmistress. Born into a pedigreed Virginia family whose prosperous family flour mill had gone under, she grew up in genteel poverty. A scholarship student at the Sargent School of Physical Education in Boston, Miss Charlotte, as she was known, returned to Virginia after graduation and ran a summer camp. The campers included Wallis Warfield, who would later scandalize English royalty when she became involved with King Edward VIII, who gave up his throne to marry her. (The Duchess of Windsor kept in touch with her former headmistress and brought her husband to Foxcroft for tea with Miss Charlotte.)

In an early catalogue promoting Foxcroft's virtues, Miss Charlotte promised to imbue in female pupils "the refined, cultivated minds and sympathetic personalities that have made the women of the South world-famous."

Foxcroft girls wore uniforms consisting of green jackets and fawn-colored corduroy skirts. They slept on an outdoor porch even during the winter, keeping out rain and snow by lowering canvas shades. As one early graduate recalled in a biography of Charlotte Noland, "On going to bed, we would undress and then dress again in flannel pajamas, wool socks, woolen gloves and on our heads Balaclava helmets. Arrayed like Polar explorers, we sallied forth, with the added comfort of hot water bottles. We then awkwardly climbed into our canvas sleeping bags."

But for young women who loved horses, this was *the* place that catered to their desire to canter, jump, and race. Riding was such an integral part of daily life that an Associated Press reporter described it as "one of the three R's" at the school. Foxcroft students participated in foxhunts and took two-day sixty-mile rides through the countryside. An education at Foxcroft was a status symbol in wedding announcements, but this finishing school was not considered academically rigorous.

Gerard Lambert took Bunny to Middleburg to meet Miss Charlotte. Shown into a drawing room, they were both tense as they awaited the arrival of the headmistress. "I sat on the edge of a stiff horsehair sofa with my knees knocking together," he wrote. "Bunny sat, very erect, on a rigid small chair." But Miss Charlotte interrupted Bunny's father mid-pitch to say, "Gerard Lambert, don't be a jackass. Your sister Lily was one of my best friends. Why, she used to give me the only decent clothes I ever owned. Of course any Lambert child can come to my school."

Grateful to her father for letting her have her way, Bunny still felt bruised by her mother's disapproval. "He was kind and sympathetic," she wrote. "He and my mother disagreed about the change in schools."

The Lambert family traveled to France in July, sailing back on the *Majestic* to New York. The two girls posed for a picture as they read side by side on the deck, bundled up in blankets and jackets during a chilly part of the voyage. Lily has elfin, delicate features and a bow of a smiling mouth, while Bunny, with angular features and the wind blowing back her hair, looks like a serious reader who is annoyed at being interrupted midsentence.

The family then headed to a rented Southampton ocean estate. For a charity benefit to raise funds for the Southampton Hospital, Bunny joined friends to perform in an amateur musical review. She played tennis at the Meadow Club. Her sixteenth birthday was celebrated in high style at her parents' home.

The *New York Evening Post* reported, "The Southampton younger set had one of the jolliest times of the season at the birthday dinner given by Miss Rachel 'Bunny' Lambert."

A fresh blossom from a prominent family, a quiet and thoughtful observer, a willowy tomboy transformed by lace and pearls, she was now coming of age and beginning her own march through the society pages.

Chapter Six

Tally-Ho in Virginia

When Bunny stepped off the train in The Plains, Virginia, to start her new life, she was met by a man driving a large open farm truck equipped with benches and horse blankets. He had been sent by Foxcroft to pick up students. Heading to the campus, the twisting and turning roads, passing through sloping meadows and forested woodlands, made the eight-mile drive seem much longer.

This was a rural world compared to the bustling college town of Princeton. Although she had studied at Miss Fine's School with the children of academics and gained social polish during her Southampton summers, Bunny felt like a naïf when she arrived at Foxcroft.

Thrust into the hothouse atmosphere of a boarding school with cliques, teenage backbiting, and minimal privacy, her new life was an adjustment. "Princeton was a town of learning...it was a country town that had a minimum amount of gossip," she wrote in reminiscence. "Learning seemed to be more of a world of discovery than of competition. It wasn't until later when I left and went away to boarding school that I discovered most other towns and our upbringing had different values."

The Foxcroft School had its own rituals. Charlotte Noland gave spirited Sunday sermons and led daily morning prayers but also encouraged a playful mystique. New students were warned that a ghost roamed the hallways, the spirit of a woman who had suffered a mental breakdown and was chained to a bed in the attic by her husband. At night, Miss Charlotte would tell her students ghost tales. Bunny was intrigued by the occult and by unworldly explanations.

The headmistress pushed her well-bred students to shed their ladylike impulses and climb rope, chin themselves on bars, and play to win on the softball field and the basketball court. But what really animated her was riding. "Miss Charlotte would come to morning prayers and announce, 'There's no school today, we're all going fox hunting,'" says one Foxcroft alumni.

Miss Charlotte did not want her charges to be squeamish, so in science class, she would dissect a dead squirrel with a penknife. Each October, she organized an evening hunt, as the girls stumbled through brambles and bushes following dogs attempting to tree a raccoon. On May 1, she would dress up as an elf and festoon the grounds with lollipop trees.

"Miss Charlotte was the most charming, understanding, whimsical, terrifying, honest, straight-to-the-point, optimistic, religious, worldly, far-sighted, courageous, persuasive, perceptive, ageless, superb-looking, regally dignified, absolutely unforgettable character I have ever known," gushed a Foxcroft graduate in a 1971 biography of the headmistress.

Bunny conscientiously did her homework at Foxcroft, but she was never a top student. According to her report card for her first semester, her highest score was in music (84), followed by English (82), French (80), mathematics (80), and Latin (65). "Bunny is working hard and I am pleased with her effort," wrote Charlotte Noland on November 6, 1926. At Foxcroft, Bunny consistently scored highest in deportment, receiving a perfect 100. Her grandmother and her mother had taught her well.

To help Bunny ingratiate herself at the school, Arthur Lowe sent her a box of clothing made by his company for Miss Charlotte. "Give my compliments to Miss Charlotte with the dresses," he wrote. "Bun, I think of you a lot. I hope you are the happiest sixteen year old in the world with a big desire to make others happy."

Dorothy Kinnicutt, a funny and outspoken girl whose father was a successful stockbroker, befriended Bunny. Her family had an apartment in Paris as well as a New Jersey estate, Mayfields. The two young women had been born just three weeks apart in 1910. Like Bunny, Dorothy went by a childhood nickname, which in her case had been bestowed by an older brother and stuck for life: Sister.

These sixteen-year-olds in dowdy school uniforms would become two of the most famous style icons of the second half of the twentieth century—Bunny Mellon and Sister Parish (her married name). They developed a similar understated aesthetic with an appreciation for Americana (hooked rugs, quilts, and folk art), painted floors, and painted furniture, and a knack for creating comfortable surroundings to showcase valuable artwork and high-end antiques. They would both play starring roles decorating the White House with Jackie Kennedy, who was a generation younger, born in 1929.

At Foxcroft, Bunny assumed the part of good girl while Sister rebelled. "By the time I turned 16, I'd hardly used my head at all, and I'd exhausted almost all of my parents' hopes for me," recalled Sister in a biography, *Sister Parish*, by her daughter Apple Parish Bartlett and granddaughter Susan Bartlett Crater. "My principal accomplishment at Foxcroft was the method I developed for avoiding exams. All I did was press a tender spot on my nose and I would get a nosebleed." The school was so concerned by Sister's poor grades that they insisted her mother take her to a psychiatrist.

Her classmates, who called her "Dot," thought she was a riot. "Whenever we want to be entertained and to hear the latest news and gossip, we fly to Dot and we always get it, if she is not at tea with some of the faculty," read Sister Parish's yearbook entry. "What will be our social world without her…"

Bunny's other friends at Foxcroft also came from wealthy East Coast families. Kitty Wickes had grown up shuttling among her parents' residences in Manhattan, Tuxedo Park, Paris, a Normandy chateau, and two adjoining Newport estates, Zee Rust and Starboard. Her lawyer father, Forsyth Wickes, collected eighteenth-century French art and porcelain. Bunny was a frequent visitor to the family's Newport home.

Her circle included Mary Augusta Field, a Vanderbilt descendant who grew up on Park Avenue and at High Lawn House, in Lenox, Massachusetts, where Edith Wharton was a neighbor. Bunny spent time with Mary King Wainwright of Philadelphia, whose father was the vice president of Penn Chemical Works and whose mother was a member of the Colonial Dames. Other noteworthy Foxcroft classmates included Grace Roosevelt, the granddaughter of President Theodore Roosevelt; Corinne Alsop, whose brothers Joseph and Stewart would become influential Washington columnists; and Beatrice Patton, whose military father, George S. Patton Jr., would make history as a brilliant and controversial World War II general.

Bunny was aware that her life was privileged, and when her parents gave her a new horse, she thanked them on March 14, 1927, promising to be more thoughtful instead of "acting like a spoiled brat":

Dearest Daddy,

I am sitting up in bed writing this in the early morning and that is why I am writing in pencil. There are thirty-five sleeping girls on all sides of me out on the porch so I am surrounded by great snores…

After getting that horse yesterday, I made a resolution never again to whine or be disagreeable. For why should anyone have any need to be unhappy when they have what I have. I am at the one school I have wanted to go to, where I am surrounded by people helping me get started in life…I have a wonderful home and have never known any unhappiness there. The only fault is that I have been thoroughly spoiled. A year ago, you gave me my stable, at Christmas a string of pearls and now a thoroughbred and most of all, you and mummy have given me love that I can never forget.

While Bunny was being showered with gifts, her brother, Sonny, was going through a tough time. His grades were so poor at the elite St. Paul's School in New Hampshire that he was quietly urged to withdraw. Gerard got his teenage son a job working in the carburetor department at a Chrysler plant, and arranged for him to live at a YMCA. Bunny wrote of her younger brother, "I felt sorry for him."

Sheltered as the girls were in rural Virginia, they kept informed about current events. In May 1927, when Charles Lindbergh made his historic transatlantic flight from New York to Paris, Bunny and her family had a special reason to cheer. Gerard Lambert's two brothers, Albert and Wooster, had been among Lindbergh's earliest financial backers, and the pilot had named his plane after his boosters, the *Spirit of St. Louis.*

When the school term ended, Bunny returned to Princeton. Her cousins Ted Walker, twenty-one, and George Lambert, twenty-two, were about to graduate. Ted had just come into a $5 million inheritance while George had treated himself to a bright yellow Pitcairn biplane. On June 24, George and Ted headed up in the plane toward Bellefonte, Pennsylvania, planning to land there to play a round of golf. As they flew across the coalfields, the motor sputtered and George Lambert lost control. The *St. Louis Post-Dispatch* reported, "As the plane swooped down upon a grain field, the tail struck a tree, turning the plane over."

The injured George crawled out of the wreckage, but Ted Walker was pinned down and died en route to the hospital. Searchers found a note that Ted had scribbled as the plane dived—"Good bye, Mal-Carol"—a farewell to his stepfather, Malvern Clopton, and his girlfriend, Carol.

Bunny was devastated by the death of her cousin. Arthur Lowe wrote to his daughter Rachel Lambert on July 2, "I am all broken up when I think of Mal and George Junior and Gerard and Bun, in fact it seems too dreadful to be true…What a sad, sad week you have had."

In an effort to comfort his distraught family, Gerard Lambert chartered a yacht, the *Sonica*, and headed up the coast to Maine. On that trip, Bunny fell in love with sailing—the rhythms of the ocean, the soaring seagulls, the sound of the flapping sails, the feeling of being away from day-to-day life. She was eager to try her hand on the tiller and learn to navigate the moods of the sea.

The family arrived in New London just as the fleet of the New York Yacht Club sailed into the harbor, led by a three-masted schooner, the

Atlantic, owned by Cornelius Vanderbilt. "As I saw her come around the point and headed into the anchorage, I was entranced," Gerard later wrote. The 185-foot yacht held a record for crossing the Atlantic Ocean in twelve days and four hours. The King of England and the former emperor of Germany had been guests on the vessel, which had six cabins and required a crew of thirty. Gerard impulsively decided to purchase the storied boat, paying $500,000 (6.8 million in current dollars).

The end of that year found Bunny recovering from a horse-riding mishap. "Now, Bun, I am sorry you slid off 'Hill Top' and broke your wrist. I'm sure Hill Top is sorry also," her grandfather wrote to her at Christmastime. "Give my affectionate regards to Uncle Mal if he is there and to all the family." Uncle Mal—Malvern Clopton—often spent vacations and holidays with the Lamberts. Now a wealthy man, he had inherited millions from his stepson Ted Walker's estate.

That winter, Bunny sang in the choir at Foxcroft and took classes in American history, modern art, and the works of Shakespeare. But she would later complain that her education had been "haphazard," a jumble of bits and pieces. The teachers rewarded Bunny's good behavior by putting her in charge of her classmates. Bunny served as cloakroom monitor, bed monitor, music monitor, and dining room monitor. Put in the position of keeping her contemporaries in line, she learned to impose order.

In May 1928, a famous visitor was spirited onto Gerard Lambert's Princeton estate: Charles Lindbergh arrived to spend the night. "Col. Charles A. Lindbergh kept his identity secret for fifteen hours while visiting Princeton last night and today," reported the *New York Sun*. Bunny later recalled the excitement of meeting the great man, although her sister, Lily, one-upped her by getting his autograph. Lindbergh was so impressed by Albemarle and his convivial host that two years later, he bought land nearby for his own mansion.

The newspapers gave Gerard Lambert full credit for luring this Midwesterner to the East Coast. COL. LINDBERGH BUYS SITE FOR HOME AT PRINCETON. AVIATOR TO HAVE G.M. LAMBERT, FLIGHT BACKER, AS NEIGHBOR, announced the *New York Herald Tribune*, erring on the initial of Gerard's middle name, *B.* for Barnes.

The booming sales of Listerine helped underwrite the Lambert family's extravagances, including the yacht, the Hamptons summer rentals, Bunny's Foxcroft tuition, and the Albemarle servants. The country was enjoying a stretch of prosperity, and the stock market was soaring. Gerard Lambert was an optimist by nature, but he had been sobered by his close brush with bankruptcy six years earlier. What if the good times did not last? Now forty-two years old, he had proved himself as the leader of his father's company. The company's profits were high and the stock had risen to $110 per share. He decided to cash in and retire.

In the fall of 1928, he sold his Lambert Pharmacal stock for $25 million, the equivalent of $340 million today. "Through sheer youthful recklessness and bad judgment, I had launched into two things that had driven me into debt, the Arkansas adventure and the building of the big place at Princeton. The debts these things created had been on my mind night and day," he later wrote. "When I found a way to pay them off I was content to quit, happy to be free again and with all the money I should ever need." He celebrated by buying another yacht, the *Vanitie*, from Harry Payne Whitney.

His sailing partner was the lawyer and historian Charles Francis Adams III, a direct descendant of President John Quincy Adams. Adams, who would go on to become secretary of the Navy, took a liking to the teenage Bunny, helping her improve her sailing skills. Years later, she remembered that he told her, "If you can learn to sail a boat, you will learn how to accept your life. You'll be calmed, you'll have too much wind, you'll be in a fog, you'll be in high waves."

She liked being part of this male world, later quipping, "I try to be a lady but I can swear like a sailor, thanks to Charles F. Adams."

Gerard Lambert and his wife had begun to lead separate lives. According to family lore, the churchgoing Ray suspected that her husband's late nights at the office and out-of-town trips masked affairs with other women. "They were never suited," recalled Bunny's sister, Lily, in an oral history. "Needless to say, in that era, you didn't divorce. You simply tolerated the situation. More and more he lived in New York City, he had an apartment there. In the summer, of course, he was on his yacht. Mother never took part in the sailing. Once she went on the J [a type of yacht] for about twenty minutes and put up a parasol. That was the end for her. She was taken ashore."

Dorothy "Sister" Kinnicutt, who had withdrawn from Foxcroft in June without graduating, was presented to society in November 1928 at a dinner dance at the restaurant Pierre's. The Park Avenue venue had been created by the Corsican restaurateur Charles Pierre Casalasco, who two years later built the Pierre Hotel. "My mother and her social secretary had planned the party for months," Sister recalled. Among the guests, bearing such distinguished names as Auchincloss, Belmont, Biddle, and Cushing, was a good-looking Princeton athlete, Stacy Lloyd Jr.

The son of a Princeton-educated Philadelphia banker, he had attended St. Paul's School, the same school that had ejected Bunny's younger brother. Samuel Drury, the headmaster of St. Paul's, wrote a glowing recommendation to Princeton for Stacy Lloyd Jr. "An excellent athlete and a thoroughly sound disposition," Drury wrote. "You can rely on him as far as he cares to go and will in addition find him an agreeable person to have around. His academic ability is about average, or perhaps better than average, but not extraordinary." Another faculty member added, "One of our best. Treasurer of the 6th form, beloved and trusted in all directions. Not a facile scholar, but persistent and ultimately successful. A young man who will do credit to Princeton."

Six feet tall with dark hair, a high forehead, and a winning smile, Stace (his nickname) had a distinguished pedigree. His great-great-grandfather Samuel Morris had been a commander and George Washington's bodyguard during the Revolutionary War. His mother, Eleanor, was featured in the Philadelphia society pages for her involvement in the Garden Club of America, the Colonial Dames, and horse-show charity benefits. The family summered at such aristocratic playgrounds as Watch Hill, Rhode Island; Saranac Lake in the Adirondacks; and the chilly shores of Northeast Harbor, Maine.

Thanks to his smoldering eyes and well-toned physique, people often commented on Stacy's appearance. "This is a very superior character, as good as he looks," wrote Samuel Drury. A classmate later wrote to the *Princeton Alumni News* that Stacy "had all the girls swooning over him. This is par for the course."

As a freshman at Princeton, he was chosen to row for the varsity crew team and later received a varsity letter for playing football against Yale. When his classmates chose accolades, Stacy Lloyd Jr. came in second for "most thorough gentleman." Reflecting his popularity, he was elected president of the Ivy Club, Princeton's oldest and most selective eating establishment, described by F. Scott Fitzgerald as "detached and breathlessly aristocratic." Gerard Lambert had been a member during his student days.

Bunny tiptoed into the social whirl with festivities of her own shortly after Sister Parish's splashy debut. In December, she gave a dinner for twenty people in the Oval Room at Manhattan's Ritz-Carlton Hotel. A few days later she was in bed with the flu. "Perhaps you took the high spots of city society in too large doses," her grandfather wrote in a teasing letter. "Well, you won't need to do that again."

She was due to finish boarding school in the spring of 1928. For Foxcroft students, there were two options at graduation: receiving a diploma if they were going to college or a certificate if they did not intend to continue their education. In Bunny's class of twenty-five students, thirteen young women received diplomas and twelve were handed certificates. Bunny was among those who received a certificate, while her closest friends headed off to Sarah Lawrence, Vassar, and the Sorbonne.

This became one of Bunny's great regrets, which she mentioned repeatedly even in her nineties, when she looked back on her life. "When she was graduating from Foxcroft, she wanted to go to college, but her father was adamant that what she would do was marry into an appropriate family and start producing children. That was the life he had brought her up for," says Bryan Huffman. "There was no reason for her to go out and do anything, since she was going to be a wife, mother, hostess. It grew to be a resentment for her, she felt badly that she had not gone to college."

Bunny would never have to support herself, but she had powerful creative impulses and would need to find a way to express them. "She told me in our first conversation that she always wanted to be a stage designer," Huffman says. "Everything about her was about establishing a scene or a stage."

At Bunny's commencement ceremony, the students sang "Go Forward, Christian Soldier" as they marched through the garden. Dr. Samuel Drury gave the commencement address. After a prayer and final words from Miss Noland, the students sang "Auld Lang Syne."

Bunny won an award for "Courtesy," and she was described as "calm and demure" in the Tally-Ho Yearbook. In a self-portrait for the yearbook, Bunny sketched herself sitting up in bed to greet the day, smiling at a bird, perched on the windowsill, with a flower in its beak.

Her grandfather had planned a celebratory graduation trip to a dude ranch in Sunlight Valley, Wyoming. On July 29, Bunny, Lily, and their grandfather boarded a train in Penn Station for Chicago. But en route, Arthur Lowe received a telegraph from Gerard Lambert with terrible news.

Bunny's cousin George Lambert, who had survived the earlier plane crash, was dead. Working as a flying instructor at Lambert–St. Louis Airport, George Lambert had been in the air with an eighteen-year-old student when his Eagle Rock training biplane slammed to the ground. Pilots who examined the wreckage believed that engine trouble forced George Lambert to try an emergency landing, but the plane went into a spin.

Dr. Malvern Clopton met Bunny's train in Chicago, and she accompanied him to St. Louis for the funeral. Then she and her uncle caught up with her grandfather and her sister in Wyoming. In a journal, Arthur Lowe noted Bunny's distress and his hope that the scenery would soothe her spirits. (In recognition of her status as a high school graduate, he called her by her given name, Rachel.)

He organized horseback riding and hiking and fishing jaunts; Bunny caught two trout. On August 14, he wrote, "Hard trip over top of the mountain. Some of the women were terrified at steep climb

and ride down over unknown trail and through burned over woods."
He noted a few days later, "Rachel has poor night...take 10 mile
ride." He could not alleviate her sorrow, but he could wear her out
with exercise. On August 19, he wrote with relief: "Rachel has good
day, goes to ride with Dr. C [Clopton] and I...Trails very dusty.
Moonlight party."

On that trip, Bunny learned that the sights and sounds of nature
could counter bouts of grief and despair.

Now that Gerard Lambert was no longer going to an office and
his daughter had time on her hands since she had finished at Foxcroft, the two of them became closer. Gerard took Bunny along
on sailing trips to the Bahamas with his yacht's previous owner,
Cornelius "Neilly" Vanderbilt. "We crossed the Gulf Stream in the
cool night air avoiding the glaring sun that baked down by day,"
she wrote in a reminiscence. "The sea was an unbelievable blue,
clear with white sand...I loved these voyages. The sea, the excitement of Nassau...with few cars and horse-drawn carriages with tall
canopies."

She became caught up in her father's interests and hobbies. An
orphan who had scarcely known his parents, the middle-aged Gerard
Lambert became interested in genealogy and traced the roots of his
Virginia ancestors. After tracking down Virginia cousins, he learned
that he was a direct descendant of Lewis Burwell, an Englishman
who had come to Virginia in 1640 and was considered one of the
First Families of the state. When Gerard heard that his newly discovered relative John Townsend Burwell was selling Carter Hall, an
estate built by Col. Nathaniel Burwell in 1792, Gerard jumped at
the chance to buy a piece of his family's heritage.

Set in the tiny town of Millwood, Virginia, on 580 unspoiled acres
with sweeping views of the Blue Ridge Mountains and the Shenandoah Mountains, the antebellum stone house featured eight immense
thirty-six-foot Doric columns. During the Civil War, Confederate
general Stonewall Jackson camped on the lawn. The wood-paneled

rooms boasted enormous fireplaces, and the curving staircase to the second floor was designed for making an entrance. It was just nineteen miles from Middleburg, and Bunny knew the area from her time at Foxcroft. With her mother firmly ensconced in New Jersey, Bunny was by her father's side as he embarked on a two-year renovation. He furnished Carter Hall with antiques and portraits by his grandfather, the painter John Wesley Jarvis.

"I was determined that, unlike some Yankees, I would not permit the Southern atmosphere to be destroyed," Lambert wrote. "We made it quite comfortable but outwardly nothing has changed." He encouraged Bunny to landscape the grounds and built a greenhouse for her use. "I'd get up early and work," she recalled. "I had pansies and forget-me-nots in the courtyard."

The Lamberts had congenial neighbors. The same year that Gerard bought his estate, John Hay Whitney purchased Llangollen, a home on one thousand acres in nearby Upperville. The twenty-five-year-old polo-playing Yale graduate, known as Jock, had inherited more than $30 million from his late father's estate. Engaged to Philadelphia debutante Mary Elizabeth "Liz" Altemus, a fearless rider who competed in shows, Jock Whitney installed new stables, a training track, a polo field, and a private airstrip.

Jock and Liz's wedding drew a glamorous crowd, including Fred and Adele Astaire along with Algonquin Round Table regulars Robert Benchley and Donald Ogden Stewart. Once these glittering figures departed, Liz Whitney was receptive to making new friends in rural Virginia and Bunny, four years her junior, fit the bill.

Bunny was honored to be taken up by this sophisticate. When Bunny sent Liz a $36 check from her Banker's Trust account, Liz endorsed it and added: "Your best friend. Hope everything alright with you & yours." Bunny was so touched that she saved the check among her favorite mementos.

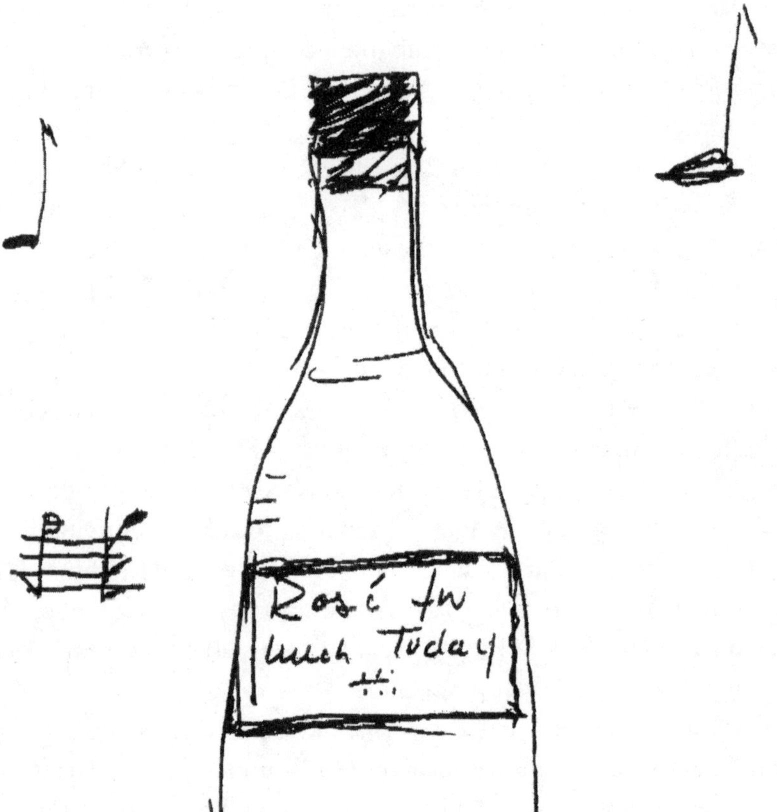
Rosé for
lunch today

The Debutante Dances Through the Depression

On August 9, 1929, Bunny turned nineteen, and her grandfather honored her entry into her twentieth year with an affectionate note: "You have fortunately escaped the dangers of the teens and have crossed the line into Ladyship [with] a great deal of wisdom and poise. It has been one of the joys of my life to see you mature. Keep up the pace, Bun."

The pace of her life was accelerating as Bunny prepared to make her debut. She was embarking on an endurance test that would require spending night after night on the town, clad in an ever-changing array of evening gowns. The marathon parties had become so stressful that in Manhattan, the Junior League and the Parents League established a pact, earlier in the year, to end the dancing by 3 a.m., although many families ignored the suggestion.

The orchid corsages, layers of chiffon, dueling orchestras, and groaning buffets all masked a seriousness of purpose. This was the American aristocracy's mating ritual, and the parents of the would-be brides were determined to put on a show, flaunting their connections and wealth. Bunny's Foxcroft friend Kitty Wickes made her debut in Newport on August 17 at the Clambake Club. Hailed as a "brilliant party" by the newspapers, the guests included Vincent Astor, former Rhode Island governor R. Livingston Beeckman, and Hugh D. Auchincloss Jr. (who would later become Jacqueline Kennedy's stepfather).

Bunny's own festivities began in early September with a small party given by her parents at Albemarle. In a debutante photograph featured on September 29 in the *New York Herald Tribune*, Bunny looks slender and elegant, standing tall in a flattering dark dress with a draped neckline over a white lace bodice. Her curly brown hair is coifed just below her ear, with a flattering wave. She gazes serenely at the camera, as if on the verge of a smile.

But during the week leading up to Bunny's celebration, the world began to tilt. On October 18, the stock market became untethered as prices plunged. By Black Thursday, October 24, panic had set in and a record 12 million shares were traded. The next day, President Herbert Hoover issued a reassuring statement insisting that "the fundamental business of the country... is on a sound and prosperous basis."

Albemarle was festooned with autumn leaves and chrysanthemums for Bunny's party on the evening of Saturday, October 26. The date coincided with the Princeton–Naval Academy football match, a plus for guests such as Gerard Lambert's sailing companion, Navy Secretary Charles Francis Adams. Reflecting the social standing of Gerard Lambert, the *New York Times* wrote about Bunny's party in its Sunday, October 27, edition, noting, "Among their guests were debutantes from New York, Baltimore and Philadelphia."

That same day on page one, a calming headline read: STOCKS HOLD FIRM IN NORMAL TRADING; POOL STILL ON GUARD. The article stated, "After one of the most disastrous weeks in its history, the stock market returned to normal yesterday."

It did not last. The market collapsed in the next week. By mid-November, an estimated $30 billion in stocks was gone, and investors and businesses nationwide were wiped out.

But Gerard Lambert did not have to worry about how to pay the orchestra for his daughter's party, thanks to his fortuitous decision to sell his Listerine stock a year earlier and put his money into conservative bonds. "When the depression struck, Lambert scarcely noticed it," wrote Jack Alexander in the *New Yorker*. "He spent money like a man who has twenty-five million dollars. Besides his fortune, he had determination and ingratiating charm."

Bunny and her friends continued to fox-trot the nights away, although many of their parents faced stupendous financial losses. Bunny's mother gave a formal tea at Albemarle for several hundred guests on November 20. Bunny's dance card was full: a ball at the Tuxedo Park Clubhouse, parties at Sherry's and the Delmonico, dances in the Ritz-Carlton's ballroom, an evening at an Upper East Side mansion, and a lavish Glen Cove, Long Island, party in an outdoor ballroom built just for the occasion. Cole Porter's new musical, *Fifty Million Frenchmen*, opened that November, adding such new romantic songs to the playlists as "You Do Something to Me" and "You've Got That Thing."

The young men on the debutante circuit included Laurance Rockefeller; C. Douglas Dillon, who would later become JFK's Treasury secretary; future syndicated columnist Joseph Alsop; Tracy Barnes, who would go on to join the fledgling CIA and help plot the Bay of Pigs invasion; and H. Page Cross, a Yale student whose architect father had designed such New York landmarks as the Tiffany & Co. building and the Art Deco RCA building. The younger Cross would become an architect himself and work on many projects for Bunny.

The female guests included famed beauty Betsey Cushing, who would become renowned with her sisters, Barbara ("Babe") and Mary ("Minnie"), for marrying well and often. (Betsey's first spouse was FDR's son James; Babe's first spouse was Standard Oil heir Stanley Mortimer Jr., followed by CBS founder William Paley; Minnie married and divorced Vincent Astor.) These society figures would make cameos in Bunny's life for decades to come.

Bunny began the New Year by sailing on the White Star Line's *Homeric* to England, joining her mother and sister, Lily. They cruised the Mediterranean and ports south, including Egypt. Bunny sailed from Southampton back to New York on the *Olympic*, arriving on April 15. Her next destination was Carter Hall, where her father had agreed to open the estate to visitors during Historic Garden Week. Bunny served as his hostess.

Tornados swept through Arkansas that May, touching down at Gerard Lambert's cotton and lumber plantation as if aiming directly for that cursed business venture. "Eleven Negroes were killed on the

Lambrook Plantation, on which virtually all buildings were demolished," reported the *Washington Post*. Floods washed out the roads, hampering rescue operations. Gerard finally sold the property within a year.

Stacy Lloyd Jr. graduated from Princeton in June. He had been admitted to his father's alma mater, the University of Pennsylvania's Law School. He stayed in New Jersey a few extra days after graduation to attend a debutante party for one of Bunny's Foxcroft classmates. Here was yet another enchanted evening, a glorious summer night where Stacy and Bunny were in the same room. Precisely when their romance began is uncertain, but Bunny was soon receiving bouquets from H.H. Battle's Flower Shop in Philadelphia, as Stacy became her serious gentleman caller.

They shared mutual interests—sailing, horseback riding, and golf—and similar backgrounds, with upper-class parents who were Episcopalian and Republican. Gerard approved of the Princeton athlete, while the status-sensitive Ray could appreciate the Lloyd family's pedigree. Bunny was overjoyed to be in love. When she later reminisced about her past, she made it clear to friends that this was one of the happiest times of her life.

Even as Stacy Lloyd headed off to law school, he was pursuing another dream. Hoping to row in the 1932 Olympics, he began the arduous training to compete in a one-man scull.

Bunny made the round of debutante parties in December 1930, attending the epic coming-out gala for Woolworth heiress Barbara Hutton at the Ritz-Carlton. Decorated to resemble a garden in moonlight, the ballroom was filled with silver birch trees and beds of roses and the ceiling was covered with blue gauze dotted with stars. Crooner Rudy Vallee and the Meyer Davis Orchestra entertained in the Palm Court, while a Russian ensemble and the Howard Lanin Orchestra appeared in the Crystal Room, performing until 4 a.m.

The chauffeured limousines en route to these Manhattan galas were now driving past destitute apple sellers on street corners and the breadlines of the starving poor. With banks folding and Congress and the White House dithering over what to do, tens of thousands had lost their homes. The opulence of these parties was so jarring that it caused a backlash. As David Patrick Columbia wrote in the book *Debutantes*, "The New York press had a field day covering Barbara Hutton's lavish debut... They called Barbara the 'Poor Little Rich Girl.' Fifty thousand bucks on flowers while ordinary Americans didn't have fifty cents a day to feed themselves? The publicity was so bad that she was sent to Europe to get away from the clawing press."

To escape the depressing northern climes, in January 1931 Gerard Lambert rented a mansion in the millionaire playground of Palm Beach, settling into the Villa Tranquilla, an Addison Mizner–designed nine-thousand-square-foot estate with eleven bedrooms on the ocean. Bunny and her father were joined by her Foxcroft friends Kitty Wickes and Mary Wainwright.

Bunny and her guests could dance at the Breakers, play golf at the Royal Poinciana Hotel, or watch a polo match at Phipps Field. The *Palm Beach Post* featured a photograph of Bunny in an article about well-dressed visitors. "Enough of the who's who have arrived that it's time to show the what's what in fashions," wrote Betty Schuyler. Bunny was pictured holding a tennis racket and a ball, wearing a pleated skirt, cardigan sweater, and scoop-neck blouse. She looked determined to win.

Bunny returned to Manhattan for Sister Kinnicutt's wedding on February 14, 1931, to St. Paul's and Harvard graduate Henry Parish, 2nd, the grandson of Henry Parish, the president of the Bank of New York. The *New York Herald Tribune* noted that Mr. Parish's "family long have been identified with the social and industrial life of New York." Unbeknownst to many of the guests, Sister's new in-laws, the Parishes, had suffered serious losses in the stock market.

The church was decorated to resemble a spring garden with tulips, freesias, snapdragons, daffodils, and blossoming cherry trees. Bridesmaid Bunny wore a pale pink chiffon sleeveless dress and a pink organdy picture hat. "Everything would have been perfect if I hadn't come down with a serious case of chicken pox on the day of my wedding," Sister Parish later recalled. "I broke out head to toe, developed a 102-degree fever, and as I walked down the aisle, my only thought was, Thank God for the veil."

That March, the sleepy horse country of Virginia made national headlines when Herbert Hoover's Treasury secretary, Andrew Mellon, purchased a four-hundred-acre farm. The austere workaholic Mellon, the son of a Pittsburgh judge, was one of the richest men in the world, with a banking, steel, gas, coal, and aluminum empire worth more than $500 million. An ardent art collector, he had recently acquired twenty-one paintings from the Hermitage in St. Petersburg, including five Rembrandts and two Raphaels.

Mellon, who had served as Treasury secretary under three presidents—Warren G. Harding, Calvin Coolidge, and Hoover—had become universally loathed for his restrictive fiscal policies and callously refusing to try to rescue the country from the Depression. With members of Congress threatening his impeachment, he would soon be eased out of the Treasury job and into a plum post as ambassador to Great Britain.

On his seventy-seventh birthday on March 24, Andrew Mellon announced that he had bought the Rokeby estate in Upperville. He let it be known that he was purchasing the property for his son, Paul, a Choate and Yale graduate now attending Clare College in Cambridge. But in truth, Mellon was buying the property for his former wife, Nora. Andrew Mellon and his tempestuous British ex-wife, the daughter of a brewery owner, had gone through a bitter divorce two decades earlier and he was eager to avoid speculation about reconciliation.

Married in 1900 when he was forty-five and she was a fetching twenty-year-old, Nora had given birth to a daughter, Ailsa, in 1901. Then she embarked on an affair with a British ne'er-do-well, Alfred Curphey, whose endearments were interspersed with schemes to acquire Andrew Mellon's money.

Nora asked her husband for a divorce but then abruptly changed her mind. Her second child, Paul, was born in 1907. Two years later, Nora demanded a divorce again, and this time the couple went to war. The public fight involved private detectives, security guards, a change in divorce law pushed through the Pennsylvania legislature at Andrew's behest, and headlines galore. After three years of wrangling, a settlement gave Andrew custody of the children eight months a year. A bewildered Paul was seen clutching his mother in a front-page photograph.

Riding had been a bright spot for Paul Mellon as a child. At Yale, he studied hard and played harder, enjoying New York speakeasies and flouting the laws of Prohibition enforced by his father's Treasury Department. His wake-up call came at 4 a.m. on Long Island, when the intoxicated Yale senior flipped his new LaSalle Phaeton. He saved his crushed gold cigarette case as a reminder. Now living in England, he had become serious about his studies but had also taken up riding again.

Paul got a firsthand description of his mother's new Virginia property in an April letter from David Finley, Andrew Mellon's top Treasury aide. "Your mother is perfectly delighted with the Virginia place," Finley wrote. "She was very enthusiastic about the beauty of the countryside, with the blue mountains rising almost at her door and peach trees and apple trees in bloom all over the place... There are four hunt clubs within a few miles, so that on your visits to her you should get plenty of that particular sport."

The Mellons' Virginia farm was just ten miles from Carter Hall. Gerard Lambert disapproved of the Treasury secretary, referring to him with disdain as a robber baron. That June, Paul appeared at the Upperville horse show with several of his mounts, but for the next several years he would be only an occasional weekend visitor.

After twenty-three years of marriage, Gerard and Rachel "Ray" Lambert decided to divorce. According to the stories passed down by family members, his wife had finally had enough of his wandering eye. "He was a bad boy," says Lily Lambert Norton, his granddaughter and Lily Lambert's daughter. "He was well known to have had a number of dalliances. Nobody ever felt it was a close marriage."

But Ray Lambert had her own secrets. Neglected by her husband, she had blossomed under the attentions of a man who had long been part of her life: Malvern Clopton, the St. Louis surgeon and widower who had been married to Gerard Lambert's sister. To Bunny and her siblings, "Uncle Mal" was a beloved and familiar figure. For Gerard Lambert, this romance represented a betrayal by a trusted in-law.

It was all a bit incestuous.

Rather than head to Reno for a speedy divorce—the Nevada legislature had cut the residency period for out-of-towners from three months to six weeks—the Lamberts opted to follow New Jersey law. If Gerard left New Jersey for two years, Ray could get a divorce on the grounds of desertion.

Although he had not planned to work again, a job offer in Boston presented a solution. The *Wall Street Journal* announced Gerard's new position as president of Gillette Safety Razor Co. on May 2, 1931. Turning around the flailing company presented an interesting challenge, but this was an unhappy period for Gerard. As he put it, he felt "exiled... filling in the time until Ray could get her divorce."

Even as Bunny was adjusting to her parents' breakup, her relationship with Stacy Lloyd was rocked when the Olympic prospect suddenly experienced a serious heart problem. Sentenced to bed rest, he dropped out of law school and moved to his grandfather's farm to recuperate. On June 5, St. Paul's headmaster Samuel Drury wrote to him, "You are the last person to suggest anything but health and wholesomeness and vitality, and therefore every indication ought to point to a sure return to the happy land of physical well-being. But thinking of you lying so quietly when people of far less physical competence keep jumping around the surface of the earth is one of life's anomalies!"

Stacy wanted to marry Bunny but worried that his health might give her father qualms. He wrote to express his concerns. Gerard replied on July 13, 1931:

Dear Stacy,

It was splendid of you to write to me in the spirit which your letter expressed so well. I do not imagine that it was easy. I can also imagine that the general problem has distressed you a great deal...

I want you both to know that I heartily approve of anything you may do, and would be only too happy to have everything work out for a happy marriage...

Bunny happens to be a very sensible and sane person...I believe she is thoroughly aware of the handicaps of the situation and that they do not disturb her in the least. I need not tell you of her loyalty and fairness, which can stand a test, such as you have been both through so well. Be a good fellow and take care of yourself and get well enough for me to see you and have a pleasant chat. Remember that you can always count on me.

Gerard then sent a supportive letter and a large check to Bunny when she turned twenty-one in August:

My precious Baby,

After Sunday, according to the law, you will no longer be a baby but I hope that day won't change you as far as I am concerned. No matter how many years go by I want you to feel that you can lean on me and your mother for the same sympathy and love which you have had since you were a little girl.

It hasn't been hard to love you and to be proud of you. Your character, and kindness and consideration of others have always made me very proud to have you as my daughter. I haven't a single complaint, my baby, except that time has gone so quickly.

This particular birthday is rather a turning point for you and so I thought I would give you a present of a little different sort this time. I am enclosing a cheque in your favor for ten thousand dollars, which you can put away for your very own, and to start a new cycle of independence in your life. I suggest that you put it in an entirely new bank and then do with it as you like.

I love you very much my Bunny girl, and I hope this birthday may be only one of many other happy ones for many years.

Your Daddy Dear.

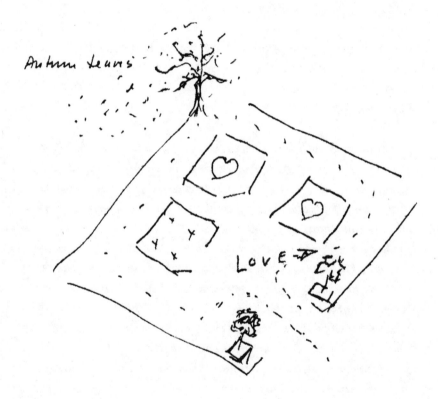

Chapter Eight

A Courteous Girl and
a Thorough Gentleman

At Carter Hall, Bunny was now the lady of the manor as the only Lambert in residence, and she channeled her energy into enhancing the property. Arthur Lowe shipped her more than two hundred trees, including pines, red pines, and hemlocks. He tried to comfort Bunny about her parents' divorce in a letter dated November 5, 1931.

"Now Bunny, you go on being Happy, I assume that you enjoy being Queen of Carter Hall, riding over the beautiful trails of Clarke County as I do tramping over my trails in Cheshire County...I hope you are well and happy," her grandfather wrote. "I hope Stacy is well and happy."

Arthur Lowe joined her at Carter Hall in time for the Piedmont Fox Hounds meet, the social event of the season held on Jock and Liz Whitney's estate. The couple had promised the winner a $5,000 prize, a phenomenal sum at the depth of the Depression when a new car cost roughly $640 and a starter house cost $7,000.

In the society magazine the *Spur*, writer Taylor Scott Hardin described the twenty thousand spectators who attended the November 17 event, a mass of shrieking bookies and "seething humanity." He wrote approvingly of the "magnificent informality" of the Whitneys' evening ball. "The dance floor was surrounded by a walk of sawdust, where there were tables with backgammon boards. Against the wall were bales of straw, serving as benches, and behind them were shocks of corn for decoration.

"The orchestra, Markel's, was superb...the guests were given an exhibition boxing-match and a concatenation of singing bouts by five or six Harlem niggers," he wrote, using an offensive slur common in the era. "What made the party unusual was its curious mixture of rusticity with sophistication...Mr. Whitney and most of the men were in formal scarlet, whereas Mrs. Whitney had on white duck trousers and a red sweater."

In the summer of 1932, Stacy and Bunny began to plan their nuptials. They joined Stacy's family to tour France, including a stop in Chartres, where the Gothic stone cathedral made a strong impression on Bunny. The couple sailed back on the *Europa* from Cherbourg on August 16 to New York, chaperoned by Bunny's uncle Wooster Lambert; Stacy's parents; and his siblings, Morris and Eleanor. On August 31, Stacy's father sent him a congratulatory letter: "I was delighted to hear from your mother that you have had a satisfactory talk with Mr. Lambert and that he was willing to have the engagement announced."

The stage had now been set. On September 3, 1932, the Associated Press ran the item: "Gerard B. Lambert, an official of the Gillette Safety Razor Co., and Mrs. Lambert today announced the engagement of their daughter Rachel L. to Stacy B. Lloyd, Junior of Ardmore, Penn." The *New York Evening Post* published an article highlighting their pedigrees:

There is interest here in the approaching marriage of Miss Rachel Lambert, daughter of Mr. and Mrs. Gerard Barnes Lambert of Albemarle, Princeton, N.J. and Carter Hall, Clarke County Va. to Mr. Stacy B. Lloyd Junior of Ardmore, Pa., which is to take place at the New Jersey home of the bride's parents on Saturday Nov. 26th...

Miss Lambert is a granddaughter of the late Mr. and Mrs. Jordan Lambert of Alexandria, Va. and is a direct descendant of Miles Cary and Lewis Burwell of Virginia...She is a member of the Junior League of New York. The Carter Hall estate in Clarke County, of which her father became owner some years ago, has been in the Burwell family for five generations.

Mr. Lloyd attended St. Paul's School in Concord, and was graduated from Princeton University in 1930, later taking a post-graduate course in law at the University of Pennsylvania. He was president of the Ivy Club at Princeton. His clubs are the Racquet Club, Whitemarsh Hunt and the Merion Cricket Club, all of Philadelphia. He is a member of the First City Troop, of which his great-great-grandfather Captain Samuel Morris was the commander under General Washington...He is a direct descendant of Governor Thomas Lloyd, deputy governor under William Penn.

Although Gerard and his wife Ray Lambert were separated, they nonetheless planned a large celebration for their eldest child. On October 25, Bunny announced the ten attendants for her wedding, including maid of honor Liz Whitney and bridesmaids Sister Parish and Leila Delano, the cousin of Democratic presidential contender Franklin Delano Roosevelt. Stacy's friend Nelson Rockefeller was listed as an usher. Bunny ordered an elaborate formal white satin wedding dress with a train as long as a Pullman car.

St. Paul's headmaster Rev. Samuel Drury agreed to officiate, writing to Stacy, "As you must know, you are one of my very dear boys and I wouldn't be away from you on your wedding for anything in the world." For Bunny, the true man of the hour would be her grandfather Arthur Lowe, that unconditional champion whose love and attention had given her stability within the rocky shoals of her family.

A month before the wedding, Arthur Lowe was en route home to New Hampshire when he suddenly became ill. Taken off the train in New Haven, he was transported to a hospital, but his wife sternly insisted that he come home immediately. Bunny's sister, Lily, later told an interviewer that when the medical staff called his wife, she said, "I expect Arthur home in my bed tonight." Lily added, "So he got back on the train and continued to Fitchburg, as requested by my grandmother, and died." He was seventy-nine years old.

This was a shattering blow. A decade earlier, Arthur Lowe had promised Bunny "to hang around until I am 100 if I can, just to see what kind of a grandmother you will make." Now, he would not even be present for her wedding.

The *New York Times* ran a solemn item about Bunny's wedding shower: "Mrs. Gerard Barnes Lambert has recalled her invitations for Friday, owing to the death of her father, Arthur H. Lowe."

Bunny and Stacy decided to go ahead with their Thanksgiving weekend wedding but to make it an intimate affair. "Owing to the recent death of the bride's maternal grandfather, Mr. A. H. Lowe, Miss Lambert has dispensed with all attendants, except a maid of honor and flower girl," noted the *New York Post*. Her attendants were still invited, including Leila Delano, whose cousin had just won the presidency in a landslide.

Gerard Lambert was legally required to stay away from Princeton for two years so his wife could get a divorce. He won special permission from the court to return to New Jersey to give his daughter away. "I crossed the state line, feeling like I should be under heavy guard, changed into my striped trousers at the Princeton Inn," Gerard wrote in his autobiography. He was able to walk Bunny down the aisle at Trinity Episcopal Church in Princeton, but he left immediately after the ceremony. Her mother hosted a small reception at Albemarle.

For Bunny, this was a subdued start to marriage, with her father fleeing, her grandfather newly buried, and only a small coterie of supportive friends as witnesses.

On January 12, Bunny and Stacy left for a honeymoon, taking the train to San Francisco and then sailing on the *Monterey* to Honolulu. In her ladylike way, Bunny would drop hints to her friends that married life was everything she hoped it would be. Many years later, she described her marriage to a friend, Dr. Bruce Horten, a Manhattan cancer specialist who became her confidant in the late 1980s. "She very much admired Stacy and thought he was elegant in his own way," says Dr. Horten. "I think she had a wonderful physical relationship with him." Sailing back from Hawaii to Los Angeles on the *Mariposa*, the newlyweds then returned to Carter Hall, which they planned to make their home.

Gerard Lambert was underwriting their living expenses at the Virginia estate, but Bunny was conscious of costs. During a Manhattan shopping trip, she stopped by Hattie Carnegie's shop. The four-foot-ten Hattie Carnegie, a Jewish refugee from Vienna, had been born Henrietta Kanengeiser but borrowed her patrician last name from financier Andrew Carnegie. Bunny's mother had often shopped at the store with her daughters.

Bunny and Hattie Carnegie had in the past discussed their mutual love of gardens. On this trip, Bunny saw two items that she wanted to buy—a silk flower-patterned dress and a navy coat with matching silk lining—but worried out loud that she couldn't afford them. According to Bunny, Carnegie told her, "We will make a bargain. You help me design my garden and I will give you a dress and a coat."

The canny Carnegie, who got her start as a Macy's messenger, must have been amused by this well-to-do young woman, so earnest and eager to show that she had talents of her own. Designing Hattie Carnegie's garden meant so much to Bunny that she would brag about it with pride seventy-one years later to the *New York Times.*

While Bunny was bartering for a dress, her classmate Sister Parish was facing a difficult financial situation. The plunge in the stock market had wiped out her in-laws and caused havoc for her parents, and now her husband had informed her that his salary at a brokerage firm had been slashed.

Sister had never finished her schooling at Foxcroft and had no training for a career. But she had received compliments on the décor of her New Jersey home. As a lark, she had taken on a few projects, such as redecorating the Essex Hunt Club and choosing the aqua color for a new restaurant called Howard Johnson's.

The twenty-three-year-old Sister opened a decorating shop in the exclusive borough of Far Hills, New Jersey, in 1933. Her new job was embarrassing to her status-conscious in-laws. "My husband's family felt very uncomfortable with my being in trade, as they called it," she admitted. "But it was the only thing I could do."

The two Foxcroft friends had been on similar paths. But now Sister had been forced to adapt to a new fiscal reality and test her talents while Bunny remained cocooned by her family's wealth. Bunny felt sorry for Sister and referred clients to her. But once Sister began to receive admiring attention for her good taste and style, Bunny experienced a touch of envy.

On December 30, 1933, Gerard Lambert gave a holiday ball for Bunny and Stacy at Carter Hall, a delayed celebration after their low-key wedding. The advertising showman got the attention and deferential press coverage he craved: The *Evening Star* of Washington called the party "one of the largest and most elaborate Christmas season entertainments to be given at a private home." The *Philadelphia Inquirer* ran a list of prominent locals attending the gala. Concerned that the house would not be large enough to accommodate the one thousand invited guests, Lambert built a temporary ballroom at the back of the house, constructed between two Colonial porches.

In a photo taken that evening, a smiling Stacy Lloyd and his new father-in-law, Gerard Lambert, both in black tie, are flanked by Bunny and her younger sister, Lily. Wearing a sleeveless white long gown with two layers of ruffles on the hem, holding a large corsage, her hair in a flattering bob, Bunny gives the photographer an earnest look. Lily, in a more daring, low-necked lace gown with cap sleeves, is trying to stifle a giggle.

Wedding bells rang—and rang again—for the Lambert family in 1934. After graduating from Foxcroft, Lily Lambert had convinced her parents to give her the money they would have spent on a debut so she could add to her collection of memorabilia related to British war hero Vice Admiral Horatio Nelson, a source of fascination since her childhood. With no suitors in sight, her mother set out to find Lily a husband, fixing her up with Princeton graduate William Wilson Fleming. "She felt it was time and I wanted to marry to be free," Lily later recalled. "I wanted out of the big house. I wanted to be on my own...A girl in those days, in my social standing, just couldn't go live in New York like they do today. Go take a job. That was unheard-of."

Like Stacy Lloyd, Ivy Club member William Fleming had attended St. Paul's School, and his father was a Princeton graduate and a lawyer.

Fleming was on track to graduate from Harvard Law School and join a Manhattan firm. The couple married in the spring, with Bunny as maid of honor, and eventually moved to a farm in Princeton. Lily grew disillusioned, recalling, "I didn't see much of him because they worked lawyers very hard in those days, unbelievable. He'd come home at two or three in the morning. We really had no life."

In July, Bunny and Lily's mother, Ray Lambert, married Dr. Malvern Clopton in her hometown of Rindge, New Hampshire. The president of the Washington University Corporation, a professor of clinical surgery and chief of staff at St. Luke's Hospital, Dr. Clopton's life centered around his hometown. Ray agreed to live in St. Louis as long as they spent summers at Cape Cod, where her parents used to rent a house. The *New York Times'* headline noted the complex familial relationship: ST. LOUIS SURGEON AND HIS LATE WIFE'S SISTER-IN-LAW MARRY IN NEW HAMPSHIRE. It was unusual for the *Times* to discuss marital assets, but the article noted that Clopton, fifty-eight, had inherited $3.75 million from his deceased stepson in 1927.

Gerard Lambert was now free to resume his life. As the president of Gillette Safety Razor Co., he had sparked innovations that would define the firm for the next three-quarters of a century. After installing new machinery to improve Gillette razors, he asked an engineer to color the blade a distinctive blue. Then he launched an ad campaign that was shocking in its time: full-page newspaper apologies labeled "A Frank Confession of the Gillette Safety Razor," which acknowledged that the product had been inferior and urged consumers to try the new Blue Blade. Not only did sales take off, but the company's brand still revolves around the iconic blue razor.

But the self-confident Lambert had taken a financial gamble. He told Gillette's directors that he did not want a salary but negotiated a huge stock bonus if he met certain financial targets. Although he improved the company's balance sheet, he did not make his numbers. He quit in 1935 with plans to devote more time to sailing.

On a yachting trip to the Bahamas, he met the divorcée who would become his next wife. Grace Lansing Mull, a native of upstate New York, was visiting her uncle and aunt in Nassau. Her childhood had been difficult—her alcoholic father abandoned the family and then died—and she had been raised in pinchpenny circumstances by her mother and grandmother. As a teenager, she fled into marriage with high school student John Mull. She described him as an alcoholic and a wife beater, but after their divorce she forgave him to the point that they were on friendly terms.

Gerard Lambert was enamored with Grace after their first meeting and began courting her. Flattered but wary, she wrote a letter to her ex-husband, confiding, "I have heard Jerry was a skirt-chaser" and his ex-wife was "very cold." Grace added that his children called and wired him every day. "Apparently ever since his divorce he's been terribly despondent but now he's a new man, they say...He's very generous too. No one can spend a cent when he's around."

He took her to see Carter Hall and meet Bunny. Grace was in awe of her surroundings and impressed by Gerard's wealth. "This place is beautiful," Grace wrote in another letter to her ex-husband. "The sort of house I've read about or thought about when I've thought about Virginia...Lots of portraits and Negroes everywhere and I have my own maid which delights me."

Grace reported that she and Bunny "got on famously right from the start. Jerry's daughter Bunny is really without a doubt the most amusing girl I've ever met anywhere. You'd be fascinated. She's so original. Her husband Stacy Lloyd—Philadelphian—is a nice sweet fellow."

Bunny and Stacy were building their own home on a thirty-acre plot of her father's property, on a winding road behind Carter Hall. The soaring ceilings and vast rooms of her childhood home, Albemarle, did not appeal to her; she wanted a cozier style, designing narrow rooms with low ceilings. Bunny and Stacy spent $125,000 (more than 2 million in current dollars) for their two-story, nine-bedroom white stone home, greenhouse, barns, and garage. They named it Apple Hill.

The front entrance was not prepossessing, but the back of the house had unobstructed views of the countryside and the mountains. The rooms meandered from one to another, often with one or two steps down to denote different areas. Fireplaces kept it warm in the winter, and decorative wooden shutters warded off the cold. The couple filled their new home with family hand-me-down antiques as well as their own finds.

After struggling to choose a profession, Stacy decided to go into journalism. He joined the *Winchester Star* as a reporter, working for editor Harry F. Byrd Jr., whose powerful reactionary senator father, Harry Byrd Sr., owned the newspaper. In the spring of 1935, Stacy bought the *Clarke Courier* in Berryville and began supervising editorial operations and hunting for advertisers.

When Bunny posed for a formal portrait by painter Francis L. Smith in 1935, she chose to be shown riding sidesaddle on her horse Buberry. Against the backdrop of fluffy white clouds and blue sky, fertile green grass and distant hills, she sits erect on her chestnut mount, ladylike and yet athletic, wearing a brown hat and well-cut brown jacket, the picture of the country gentlewoman.

Bunny and Stacy's weekends centered on sporting events—racing, foxhunting, horse exhibitions—organized by the Blue Ridge Hunt and the Piedmont Hunt Club. They attended hunt breakfasts with tables laden with country ham, sausage, and soda biscuits, and evening black-tie balls. Their friends included David Bruce, a Princeton graduate, lawyer, and World War I veteran who was married to Ailsa Mellon, the daughter of former Treasury secretary Andrew Mellon. After stints in the Foreign Service and as an investment banker, Bruce had repurchased his family's Virginia estate, Staunton Hill, and won election to the Virginia state legislature.

Bunny remained close to her maid of honor, Liz Whitney. When Liz went to the Madison Square Garden Horse Show in November 1935 to exhibit eight of her hunters, Bunny came along. Liz Whitney and Nina Carter Tabb, the *Washington Post* society columnist, organized a frontier covered-wagon show as part of the entertainment; Bunny donned a pioneer costume to ride in the wagon.

For Bunny, married life carried secret sorrows as she struggled to have children. She had no trouble becoming pregnant but suffered the heartbreak of three miscarriages. She envied her sister, Lily, who gave birth to a baby boy, David, in November 1935.

Instructed by her doctors to take to bed once she became pregnant again, Bunny was unable to attend her father's marriage to Grace Lansing in New York City in April 1936. "Bunny was pregnant and having a hard time of it," Grace later recalled. Bunny kept her spirits up by reading gardening books and designing a new garden. She commissioned a pergola and a trellis, and designed brick-lined flower beds shaped like hearts. She loved that romantic symbol, often sketching red hearts on correspondence to family and friends.

That fall, Gerard and Grace returned to Carter Hall for a visit. They were giving a party on September 23, with guests spilling out onto the porch, when Bunny went into labor in the upstairs bedroom. Stacy gave an exuberant shout out the window: "We have a boy!"

But the first few minutes of the baby's life were frightening. "I was a blue baby, umbilical cord wrapped around my neck," says Stacy Barcroft Lloyd III, repeating the oft-told family tale about his entry into the world. "That explains my nickname—my father called me Tough-ie." The nickname, which the family went on to spell as Tuffy, stuck, just as Rachel had become Bunny at birth.

In photographs with her baby, Bunny looks protective and maternal while Stacy grins with fatherly pride. Little Tuffy has a quizzical expression. Bunny's view of motherhood had been shaped by her own experience growing up with parents who employed a baby nurse, nannies, and governesses to care for their children. Bunny saw no need to strike out in a different direction.

She loved to cuddle and play with Tuffy, but Carter Hall was well staffed with servants who could change diapers and handle day-to-day chores. Tuffy was left craving attention from his elusive mother.

Chapter Nine

Paul Mellon's Rebellion

For Paul Mellon, the bleak, industrial landscape of his hometown, Pittsburgh, had come to symbolize all that was wrong with his life. He had been a dutiful son, sublimating his own desires to please his judgmental father. Pressured into joining his father's conglomerate as the heir apparent, after several years on the job Paul felt trapped in an unsatisfying career. Now twenty-nine years old and worth an estimated $50 million, he yearned for a different life.

Frail and gaunt at eighty-one, Andrew Mellon was counting on his son to take over the far-flung Mellon empire. The former Treasury secretary was consumed by fighting what historians would later describe as a politically motivated attack by President Franklin Roosevelt's IRS, which claimed that Mellon had committed income tax fraud (the charges would later be thrown out).

The industrialist was striving to secure his legacy as a patron of the arts by creating a National Gallery of Art in Washington. The owner of an extraordinary collection of paintings including masterpieces by Titian and Botticelli, he had pledged to give the federal government his $50 million art collection along with $15 million for land and construction.

His son, Paul, had never been interested in becoming a businessman. After writing for literary magazines at Yale and then at Clare College in Cambridge, he wanted to become a publisher, candidly telling a reporter, "I do not think I would be a great success as a banker or industrialist...I have ideas of my own about the business of book publishing." PAUL W. MELLON PLANS CAREER AS BOOK PUBLISHER, announced the *New York Herald Tribune* on July 8, 1930. The following day, the *Pittsburgh Post* reported, MELLON SCION GOES TO BANK JOB AFTER TALK WITH FATHER.

Andrew Mellon immediately installed his inexperienced son on corporate boards, including Pittsburgh Coal, Farmers National Bank, and Gulf Oil. Paul was mortified when newspapers mocked his rapid ascent. The *New York Herald*'s headline: MELLON SON RISES IN BANK TO DIRECTOR IN 43 DAYS.

His father meddled in all aspects of his life. When Paul became engaged, Andrew Mellon vehemently objected on the grounds that the woman was three years older, Catholic, and British. Andrew warned his son in a letter: "Women grow older faster than men, and differences of age which seem immaterial at thirty are accentuated after forty...If the girl is a devout Catholic, even if she should suggest her willingness to have her children not brought up in that Faith, she would be subjected to the most tremendous pressure by the Priesthood, especially in the view of the Mellon reputation for wealth."

In deference to his father's disapproval and anti-Catholic screed, Paul broke off his engagement. He did, however, turn his affections to a woman whom he knew his father would find equally inappropriate. Mary Conover Brown, a smart and striking Vassar graduate, was not only three years older but also a divorcée who suffered from asthma.

The daughter of a Kansas City doctor, she had been married to broker Karl Brown and now worked at a Manhattan art gallery. Paul's Yale classmate Lucius Beebe, a columnist for the *New York Herald Tribune*, introduced the two of them over cocktails at the Madison Hotel, and the tipsy threesome took a horse-drawn sleigh ride to the Casino nightclub in Central Park. The couple quickly became engaged. Mary was a cheerful extrovert who won over Paul's friends with her lively enthusiasm.

When Paul's sister, Ailsa, married David Bruce in 1926, President Coolidge and members of royalty attended the ceremony, and thousands stood on Washington street corners to watch the procession.

But only thirty people, including the divorced Andrew and Nora Mellon, witnessed Paul and Mary saying "I do" at his sister's New York town house on February 2, 1935, at 10 a.m. Mary wore a dark brown suit rather than a white wedding gown. An Associated Press story noted that the "swift-moving unobtrusive ceremony...took Mayfair residents by surprise." Following a leisurely honeymoon in Egypt, Paris, Holland, England, and Scotland, the couple returned to Pittsburgh, moving into his father's home.

Ever since Andrew Mellon had purchased Rokeby Farm in Virginia for his ex-wife, Paul had relished his weekends there. After breathing the fumes in Pittsburgh and descending into his father's coal mines, Paul was enthralled by Virginia's country life—the gorgeous vistas, the clean air, the small-town feel, and the farm folk. He renovated the stables at Rokeby and put them into full use, expanding his string of racehorses and buying mounts for foxhunting. He hired a trainer and developed relationships with jockeys. He was rewarded when three of his horses—Welbourne Jake, Drinmore Lad, and Chatterplay—went on winning streaks. He never tired of watching the horses fly around the track, their handsome bodies like living works of art. His father thought racing was a waste of time.

Paul made new friends in Virginia. The other Ivy Leaguers in the area included fellow Yalies Jock Whitney and Taylor Scott Hardin, the son of a prominent Washington physician, who had recently become a horse breeder, plus Princetonian Stacy Lloyd. Paul and Bunny's husband were among a small group who rode in the Saturday Piedmont Hunt in November 1936, chasing three foxes to ground.

Paul was now at a turning point. He desperately wanted to quit the world of business and move with Mary, who was pregnant with their first child, to Virginia. His mother was ready to sell Rokeby Farm; Paul agreed to buy it. He did not want to devote any more of his life to worrying about profits, dividends, balance sheets, and acquisitions.

While traveling with his father in a chauffeured limousine in Pittsburgh, Paul nervously mentioned his decision to acquire the Virginia farm. "Father replied in his quiet voice that he considered that sort of real estate purchase a poor investment in the current economic environment," Paul wrote in his autobiography, *Reflections in a Silver Spoon*, adding bitterly, "It might as well have been twenty years earlier, when I had asked him if I could have a dog, and the reply had been, 'Oh, you don't want a dog.'"

Paul was so upset that he went home and wrote an anguished memorandum about his father. "The years of habit have encased me in a lump of ice, like the people in my dreams, and when I get into any personal conversations with Father I become congealed and afraid to speak." Rather than be forever known as his father's son, Paul wanted to chart his own path. As he put it, "I have some very important things to do still in my life, although I am not sure what they are."

It troubled Paul that his father "ignores me, ignores my judgment or interest or actions. He had never encouraged me to do anything, never given me a word of advice or encouragement about business or my life." Paul was even suspicious of his father's motivations for creating the museum, writing, "The Gallery to him is just one more investment, one more tremendous Mellon interest...one more prop for the scaffolding which holds up his gigantic, intensive, mysterious ego." This document, which he quoted at length in his memoir, was a howl of pain.

Acting without his father's blessing, Paul not only bought his mother's four-hundred-acre estate but then purchased two adjoining farms, a 283-acre place owned by a New York couple, Mr. and Mrs. Gordon Grand, and a 181-acre parcel from Robert C. Fletcher.

On the same day that the *New York Times* got wind of Paul's land—November 28, 1936—and began preparing to publish a short item, Paul Mellon finally sat down with his father to discuss his future. Maybe the aging mogul was feeling intimations of mortality and realized that he could not rule from the grave. Andrew Mellon accepted with equanimity Paul's decision to quit the family business. "He was surprisingly receptive, much more than he had ever been before," Paul later wrote. "In fact, there was a reasonableness and a softness in him that took me back a little because I had always thought of him as being so different."

A month later, Mary Mellon gave birth to a daughter, Catherine

Conover Mellon. Articles noted that the infant was "heiress to one of America's greatest fortunes."

In the summer of 1937, Andrew Mellon was in Washington working on plans for the National Gallery—he had chosen architect John Russell Pope and ground had just been broken—when he was stricken with a bronchial ailment. He went to Southampton in July to recuperate at the three-story white frame house on the ocean that he had given to his daughter, Ailsa. He died on August 26, 1937, of pneumonia, with his son and daughter by his side. President and Mrs. Roosevelt were among the two thousand dignitaries who attended the funeral at East Liberty Presbyterian Church in Pittsburgh.

The bequests to his children were estimated to be worth hundreds of millions of dollars. The former Treasury secretary left the remainder of his fortune—publicly listed at more than $200 million but in reality much more—to the A. W. Mellon Educational and Charitable Trust. Andrew Mellon named his son, Paul; son-in-law, David Bruce; and attorney Donald Shepard as trustees. As philanthropists, they were instantly among the most powerful gift givers in America. The three men also became trustees of the National Gallery. Paul agreed to take over the presidency of the work-in-progress gallery to fill out his father's term.

Ailsa Mellon Bruce had been close to her father, but in keeping with the mores of the era, she was not given an official leadership role. Her marriage to David Bruce was strained and the couple, who had a four-year-old daughter, Audrey, led largely separate lives. To all appearances, Paul got along with his brother-in-law, although there were sibling-rivalry-style tensions, since Andrew Mellon had treated David Bruce with pointed approval, in contrast to his grudging behavior toward his son.

Paul, his wife, Mary, and their baby moved to Upperville, Virginia, even though this was not an ideal situation for Mary's health. As Lucius Beebe, the *New York Herald* columnist who introduced the couple, noted in a 1936 article about the horsey Virginia countryside: "Even Mrs. Paul Mellon, who gets asthma something terrible at the mere sight of a horse, has had to keep a stable." From now on, while the family would often head to Europe for lengthy stays, Rokeby Farm would be their home.

There was a disturbing postscript to Andrew Mellon's death. While packing up his father's possessions in Pittsburgh, Paul came across a cardboard box filled with old letters from his mother's older brothers. After skimming a few dull missives, he sent the box to his mother. His mother read the letters and panicked, insisting that Paul meet with her lawyer. In one letter—which Paul had not previously read—his maternal uncle John had provocatively suggested to Andrew Mellon that Paul might have been the product of an adulterous liaison instead of the Treasury secretary's son.

Paul found the insinuation unbearable. In this era before DNA testing, Paul scoured his father's divorce papers for evidence that his parents were together during the time when he was conceived. He convinced himself that Andrew was indeed his father. Paul was vehement on this topic in his autobiography, casting about for clues such as the resemblance between his own children and his father and noting that "I see in myself several characteristics that were also his: a habitual shyness and an almost obsessive attention to detail."

His mother insisted that the accusation was false and that Paul was Andrew's son. But the episode damaged Paul's relationship with his surviving parent. Paul wrote that "we were friends, with a certain amount of affection between us, although I would not have called it love."

Thanks to Jock Whitney, the hunt country was going Hollywood. Whitney, who was having much more fun with his inherited wealth than his Virginia neighbor Paul Mellon, invested in the movie *King Kong*, backed a new invention called Technicolor, and partnered with David Selznick to produce movies. Searching for film properties, Whitney acquired a soon-to-be-published manuscript by an unknown author: *Gone with the Wind* by Margaret Mitchell.

When Bunny and Stacy gave a dinner party in February 1939 to celebrate moving into their new home, Apple Hill, Liz Whitney brought her houseguests, Errol Flynn and his wife, actress Lili

Damita. Bruce Cabot, the star of *King Kong* and one of Flynn's close friends, visited the Whitneys and then returned to stay with Bunny and Stacy.

Bunny made the local newspapers when she drove Bruce Cabot to the Piedmont Hunt one afternoon, racing down the rural roads to catch up as Stacy, Paul Mellon, and Polish ambassador Jerzy Potocki chased the hounds. "Bruce Cabot was a friend of mine," Bunny later reminisced. "Bruce became sort of a houseguest in the attic. And Stacy used to say, 'When are you going to get that actor out of the attic?'"

Although her own life was comfortable, she became troubled by the inequities of Southern life. Virginia remained a segregated world, and Bunny was disturbed to learn that the area's elite whites-only public schools sent their "leftover" supplies to the woebegone, underfunded black schools. One night, she attended a meeting in Berryville of local black residents, where a speaker from Columbia University discussed the issue of fairness. "I was the only white face in the audience," Bunny later recalled. "I stood up in a timid way and said, 'I'm here because I want to help.'" In her autobiographical essays, she does not say what—if anything—she did at that time, but her interest in civil rights issues endured, and she would later use her clout to direct significant scholarship money to black students.

Stacy expanded his publishing operations by launching a weekly newspaper, initially called the *Middleburg Chronicle* and then renamed the *Chronicle of the Horse*. The paper covered steeplechasing, foxhunting, horse breeding, polo, fly-fishing, and even yachting— the leisure pursuits of the wealthy. To woo female readers, Stacy included a gossip column and a cooking column, and even ran personal ads for those searching for potential mates. (One hunt country denizen placed a hopeful ad stating that he was "not wealthy, of good social standing" and hoped to find a "young and charming wife...preferably in twenties, with income.")

Stacy and Bunny hosted the Blue Ridge Horse Show at Carter Hall each spring. "Everyone sat around on the ground under the widespreading old oak trees and had a gay, jolly, informal time, greeting old friends and watching the exciting events," wrote the *Washington Star*. "After the horse show Mr. and Mrs. Stacy Lloyd entertained at Carter Hall with an afternoon party. Members of society from all parts of the country were there, resting or walking through the many rooms of the famous Colonial mansion. Carter Hall is always at its best in the month of May, when the garden is in full bloom and the park so green."

Asked by an Associated Press sportswriter to explain the allure of the hunt, Stacy gave an eloquent description:

The bright earth, the curving hills, the tall trees, the green and living things, the forest with their scents and smells, the paths down which hounds gallop, the fences snaking over the hill, the cry of the pack floating back in the twilight or rising keenly out of the morning mist. These things are foxhunting: they are the pageant of the land, the land that nobody can take away from man. You live on it. You eat it, drink it. It is you and you are it.

He wanted to share his passion with his young son, who was afraid of horses. "I wasn't a horseback rider, much to my father's despair," recalls Tuffy Lloyd. "When I was quite young, we had a Shetland pony that I kept rolling off of the back end. I hated it. But he was determined that I would be a horse person."

In the summer, the family visited relatives, driving to Northeast Harbor, Maine, where Stacy's parents owned a home, and stopping off in Osterville on Cape Cod to see Bunny's mother and stepfather. Stacy would later fondly recall those Cape vacations, writing to Bunny, "We have had such funny times there with our motor trips, our golf and one or two disastrous sailing expeditions."

Retirement did not suit Gerard Lambert, who had returned to his New Jersey estate, Albemarle. Interested in public policy and real estate, he built an experimental low-income housing project in Princeton. Quite possibly, he was motivated by the desire to do penance for his squalid company town in Arkansas. Dreaming of uplifting the working class,

Gerard wanted to prove that attractive lodging could be created using private financing, which could then be converted to local city ownership through publicly issued bonds.

When Stewart McDonald, the head of Roosevelt's newly created Federal Housing Administration in Washington, D.C., learned about the innovative project, he offered Gerard a government job. Gerard and his second wife, Grace, rented a furnished home on Kalorama Road, the elegant Embassy Row area of the city. As the *New York Times* would later write of Gerard, "His stooped 6-foot figure, with an aristocratic bearing enhanced by a carefully kept gray mustache, was familiar in Washington where he was an adviser on federal housing."

The peripatetic and gifted millionaire also reinvented himself as a writer, penning a mystery, *Murder in Newport*, in which the murder victim and the investigator were both yachtsmen. "The plot is soundly constructed and the action is fast; the style is a trifle wooden but since that is true of nine out of ten detective stories, why quibble?" wrote a reviewer in the *Saratogian*. "Anyway, the yarn takes on a bit of added interest from the fact that Mr. Lambert is himself one of the most famous of American yachtsmen, who has taken up detective story writing as a hobby."

When Gerard Lambert met with President Roosevelt at Hyde Park to discuss his housing ideas, FDR brought up the mystery and suggested a sequel, *Murder at the White House*. The president followed with a note on August 19, 1938, writing, "Some day when we can have another family supper at the White House, I will tell you an amusing yarn about Newport in the middle of the night in the summer of 1902."

Gerard and Grace were invited to the White House for an informal lunch and a state dinner, but much to Gerard's frustration, his proposals to revamp the FHA did not go forward. He eventually resigned from his post to return to Princeton. His marriage was going through a rough patch. Grace Lambert had discovered that Gerard's domineering nature and extreme possessiveness were difficult to live with. "Jerry treated me like a child, almost," she later told her biographer, George Pitcher, for his book, *A Life of Grace*. "Even to cross the street or go downtown to the bank, I'd have to say where I was going. I didn't like that at all. He took away my freedom, which really frightened me...It was oppressive."

Gerard wanted to control what his three children could do with their inheritances. He set up $500,000 trusts (the equivalent of $8.5 million today) for each of his three children, structured so the assets could not be part of a divorce proceeding and the money could go only to his direct heirs. The children would receive regular disbursements (interest, dividends), but they would not be able to draw down the principal. This strategy assured that their children would inherit, too, and so on down the line. After his own divorce and his three brothers' expensive shenanigans (his younger brother, Wooster, shelled out $1.6 million in alimony), this represented an effort to protect the Listerine fortune.

His caution proved well founded given the divorce history of his children. Middle child Sonny, an airplane enthusiast working in the New York office of United Airlines, married a divorced blond model from Denmark, Elsa Cover. The groom was snidely described in the newspapers as the "heir to a mouthwash fortune." Grace Lambert felt sorry for her stepson. "He had a delightful personality; he was very handsome, charming, and had a delicious sense of humor," she later reminisced. "But he never accomplished anything, and was always in trouble of one kind or another. He could never do anything on his own. People gave him jobs because of his father." Sonny's wife divorced him, charging "extreme cruelty." His second marriage produced a son—Gerard Lambert III—but that union also ended in divorce.

Bunny's sister Lily's marriage to William Fleming was undone by the arrival of a last-minute guest at a dinner party in 1937. Lily had asked her husband to invite an extra man and he brought home Harvard law classmate John Gilman McCarthy, who worked for the New Jersey pharmaceutical firm Johnson & Johnson. "I will never forget it," Lily later recalled. "I was coming down the staircase in the hall and he was standing at the foot of the staircase...and that was it!"

She stayed married for several more years before eventually divorcing her husband to marry John McCarthy.

In October 1939, Bunny attended her ten-year Foxcroft reunion along with Mary Wainwright (now married to the wealthy Richard Auchincloss) and Corinne Alsop (now married to yachtsman and insurance executive Percy Chubb). In the alumnae bulletin *Gone Away*, classmate Eleanor Schley Todd wrote, "Shortly after arrival, we proceeded in a body to the costume closet and outfitted ourselves in middys and bloomers. With that all restraint fled and the Reunion was on in earnest." Bunny and her classmates challenged the current students to a basketball game and won. Miss Noland gave a dinner and the alumnae spent the night.

Left unmentioned in the cheery bulletin, however, was the topic that hung over the gathering. A few weeks earlier on September 1, Germany had invaded Poland, and on September 3 Britain and France had declared war against Germany. While the conflict was far from rural Virginia, it sent a shiver down the spines of these privileged young women, concerned for overseas friends and worried about what this war might mean for their own families. When the next issue of *Gone Away* was published a year later—printed by Stacy Lloyd on his newspaper press—the bulletin noted that many Foxcroft graduates were involved in war relief work.

Bunny and Stacy spent a memorable evening at the White House at the end of the year, attending a dinner given by President and Mrs. Roosevelt in honor of their son Franklin Jr. The entertainment: a preview of a new movie. "Mrs. Roosevelt invited all of Franklin's friends, about 25 of us, for Christmas dinner," Bunny later reminisced. "We saw the opening of 'Gone with the Wind' in one of the big rooms in the White House."

Eleanor Roosevelt described the night in her syndicated column: "Franklin Jr. and Ethel had a party for their young friends here last night, and I was interested to meet the children of some of our friends whom I had not seen in a long time. I find all these young people much better informed than I was at the same age."

The First Lady was impressed by the Clark Gable and Vivien Leigh epic, writing, "Though I could not believe beforehand that one would sit for three hours and forty-five minutes...I saw most of it and my mother-in-law sat through the whole performance, which began at 10 o'clock and did not end until 2 a.m."

Mary Mellon's transformation from divorced gallery shop girl to wife of a multimillionaire remained a source of gossip in Manhattan. The couple rented a house at 125 East Seventieth Street—which Paul would later buy—for use during trips to New York. Paul Mellon commissioned portrait painter Gerald Brockhurst to capture Mary's likeness. Wearing a dark cloak, her reddish-brown shoulder-length curls framing her prominent cheekbones, she smiled with warmth. When the portrait was displayed at the Knoedler Gallery in New York in October 1939, their friend *New York Herald Tribune* columnist Lucius Beebe teasingly wrote, "The portrait that got the most attention and some titters was of Mrs. Paul Mellon (you remember Mary Brown?)."

The Mellons were in Switzerland undergoing analysis with Dr. Carl Jung when war erupted in Europe. It was an odd juxtaposition, to be burrowing into their own psyches while the outside world was in crisis. "Jung urged me to record dreams, and I found, as the time passed, my dreams became more and more complicated and unfathomable and very long," Paul later recalled. Mellon respected Jung but was skeptical of analysis. "Mary's enthusiasm for Jung, meanwhile, seemed unbounded," Paul wrote. "She even went to his lectures in German." Mary hoped that analysis would cure her asthma but she appeared to be getting worse.

Paul was annoyed by her fragile health. "Within two years of our getting married, the little spray she used during attacks had to be replaced with a heavy oxygen cylinder, which we now carried about with us wherever we went," he later wrote in his autobiography. "Eventually that large cylinder became a growing irritation to me, it seemed as if it had become a rival for Mary's affections, a silent lover."

While Mary convalesced in Zurich from appendicitis in the spring of 1940, Paul left her to go on a two-week hiking trip in the mountains with Jung and the analyst's wife and daughter. That April, as Denmark surrendered to Germany and the Nazis invaded Norway, Paul and his family returned home to Upperville. The couple continued to correspond with Jung and, at Mary's initiative, founded the Bollingen Foundation to translate and print Jung's books in English.

Even as Paul was fleeing to Virginia, his brother-in-law, David Bruce, was heading into the fray. A few weeks after the Germans occupied Paris, Bruce landed in London in July as the special delegate of the American Red Cross. Soon he was dodging bombs during the London blitz and meeting with prominent government officials.

Despite his half-British heritage, Paul Mellon remained self-absorbed and diffident about the war. To distance himself from his father's world, he resigned from the presidency of the National Gallery and stepped down as a trustee. He decided to resume his education, enrolling at St. John's College in Annapolis as a freshman to study Greek and mathematics. Paul rented a house in Annapolis and commuted home to his wife and daughter on weekends. The couple bought a seven-hundred-acre property adjacent to Rokeby Farm and began to erect a stately Georgian mansion.

Inspired by the Colonial-era Hammond-Harwood House in Annapolis, Paul Mellon hired New York architect William Delano to partially copy the exterior and design a new twenty-five-thousand-square-foot house. The Yale-educated Delano had created palatial homes for Cornelius Vanderbilt, Harry Payne Whitney, and Vincent Astor, as well as restored a Virginia home for Ailsa and David Bruce. Paul and Mary Mellon's new mansion, which they dubbed "the Brick House," featured vast public living spaces with high ceilings, an industrial-sized kitchen, and two upstairs wings as living quarters. Meant to convey an Old World sensibility, the palatial house was fit for the son of a robber baron.

As the new occupants would soon discover, however, the house had a major flaw: The place was a cacophony of noise. Paul Mellon later published a monograph on the house describing the staircase as "a great open void from ground to roof through which voices and sounds, everything from running water to the operation of anything mechanical or electrical, reverberated. A bath being drawn on the second floor would simulate Niagara, and one expected to see water cascading down the stairway. It was an acoustical nightmare." This estate was the antithesis of the intimate home that Bunny had built just a short drive away.

Mary Mellon and Bunny Lloyd saw each other frequently, two women with an overlapping social circle and young children. They were friendly, although Bunny felt insecure that she was a high school graduate while Mary had attended Vassar and studied at Columbia and the Sorbonne. "She was a very enthusiastic person," Bunny would later say of Mary. "Very enthusiastic about a great many things. And Mary was older, of course. She'd been to school. Most of my knowledge came from having grown up in a house where girls didn't go to college. We got along surprisingly well—she with her formal education, I with my informal education."

That November, Mary Mellon chaired a charity dance for British War Relief while Bunny handled the decorations and gave a tea at Carter Hall for volunteers. Lord Lothian, the British ambassador to the United States, attended; Liz Whitney gave a dinner to fete the Mellons prior to the party. "The ball last night at the North Wales Club in Warrenton for the benefit of British war relief was one of the most brilliant and successful affairs ever given in the hunt country," wrote society columnist Nina Carter Tabb in the *Washington Post*, complimenting Bunny's handiwork. "Decorations for the club were the patriotic shades of red, white and blue and all the rooms were bright with flowers."

The two couples were constantly thrown together. William C. Bullitt, who had recently stepped down as the American ambassador to France after the Nazi invasion, came to Middleburg on Thanksgiving to see his daughter Anne at Foxcroft. The Lloyds and the Mellons were seated at his table during the school's hunt breakfast. Paul Mellon entered his horses in the Blue Ridge Hunt Horse Show at Carter Hall; Stacy rode his horse, Stormy Weather, in a race at Rokeby Farm.

There was a shake-up in the local social order in the spring of 1940 when Jock Whitney and his wife divorced. Charging her husband with desertion, the irrepressible Liz spent six weeks in Reno at a dude ranch, accompanied by several dogs and horses. Rather than lie low, she challenged a professional male jockey to a race, a spectacle attended by five hundred divorce seekers and sportsmen (she lost on her mount, named Enthusiasm). She rode a cow into the city to visit the nightclubs, quipping to the press, "The cow was a better companion than many people I've met in Reno."

Liz was granted $3 million, the Virginia estate, and her horses. Her friends were loyal: When Liz hosted race events at Llangollen, the Mellons and the Lloyds remained front and center.

Bunny had developed a taste for political activism, thanks to her father. Disillusioned after his brief experience with the Roosevelt administration, Gerard helped Manhattan district attorney Tom Dewey in his bid for the 1940 GOP presidential nomination.

Blazing his way into another field, Gerard partnered with his Princeton neighbor George Gallup to conduct polls. After Dewey fell short at the Philadelphia GOP nomination, Gerard recruited his family to help him work for GOP nominee Wendell Willkie, who lost to FDR in November. According to the Foxcroft alumnae newsletter, Bunny "was very active in the Willkie campaign."

Paul Mellon stepped into the spotlight in the winter of 1941 to honor his father's gift to the nation, the National Gallery of Art. The *New York Times* lauded the pink marble museum on Constitution Avenue, writing that "when the twelve-ton bronze doors swing open to the public the morning of March 18, they will reveal one of the most beautiful and enduring buildings ever erected."

Before a crowd of nearly eight thousand people at the opening ceremony, Paul gave brief remarks, insisting that the building "was the product of many minds, intent on giving America the best." He formally presented 126 paintings and twenty-six sculptures from his father's collection to the museum.

The attendees included diplomats from warring countries: the German chargé d'affaires, the Italian ambassador, and the minister from Vichy France. Using the occasion to send a message, President Roosevelt described the artworks as "symbols of the human spirit and of the world the freedom of the spirit has made—a world against which armies now are raised and countries overrun and men imprisoned and their work destroyed... To accept this work today is to assert the purposes of the people of America that the freedom of human spirit and human mind which has produced the world's great art and all its science—shall not utterly be destroyed."

At a time when some Americans—especially Lambert family friend Charles Lindbergh—were ardent isolationists and others were indifferent to the war in Europe, Bunny and her social set were ardently pro-British.

Bunny did her genteel bit for the British war effort by opening up Carter Hall in April 1941 for a week of garden tours, with proceeds going to Bundles for Britain, a group started by Manhattan socialite Natalie Latham that shipped much-needed medical supplies, clothing, and other useful items to the beleaguered Brits. Attracting buses of tourists from Washington, she served picnic lunches and showed off her spring blossoms. In June, Bunny, Mary Mellon, and Liz Whitney organized a charity ball at Buchanan Hall in Upperville with the proceeds going to British War Relief.

Bunny's father made a splashy sacrifice by giving up two yachts. He donated the *Atlantic* to the Coast Guard as a training ship and arranged to have the *Yankee* dismantled, with the $10,000 proceeds going to the Royal Thames Yacht Club, to be used toward building a fighting plane. He would later offer FDR the use of Carter Hall as a summer White House, but the president demurred.

That summer, Bunny and Stacy visited his parents at their Northeast Harbor, Maine, cottage, planning to celebrate his father's sixty-fifth birthday. The day before the festivities, Stacy Lloyd Sr. died of a heart attack. In an obituary, the *Philadelphia Inquirer* cited the accomplishments of the prominent financier, noting his heroism in World War I as a judge advocate who served in France and Italy.

Stacy Lloyd Jr. respected his father's war record. The Virginia newspaper publisher had begun to think about what role he might play in the current conflict.

Paul Mellon had made financial efforts to help the British—donating money to the Red Cross to pay for ten ambulances—but he finally felt compelled to become directly involved. After asking for advice from a family friend, Major General George Patton, Paul registered for the draft in the summer of 1941 and asked to join the Cavalry. The *Evening Star* pointed out that this was a purely patriotic act: "Had he not volunteered, Mr. Mellon would have been automatically deferred under recent rulings by the national headquarters of selective service. He not only is married and is the father of one child, but also, at 33, is above the age limit recommended as the new top for future inductees. Mr. Mellon said his wife is in thorough accord with his decision."

Sent in July to steamy Fort Riley, Kansas, to endure basic training, the American aristocrat who was now a lowly private was treated as a curiosity. Shortly after he arrived at the camp, a wire service reporter interviewed the multimillionaire about how he was adjusting. Mellon gamely replied that the first few days had left him "stiff and sore" but he was "getting tougher now."

His brother-in-law, David Bruce, had been hired by "Wild Bill" Donovan, the World War I hero who now headed the newly created Office of Coordination of Information. This agency would become the Office of Strategic Services (OSS), the precursor of the CIA. The clandestine agency hired so many Ivy Leaguers—lawyers, bankers, and academics—from the Social Register that the OSS was jokingly referred to as Oh-So-Social. The agency also sought other recruits with unconventional skills such as safecracking and forgery.

The OSS would soon become a full-fledged spying operation with agents stationed around the globe, fueled by secret slush funds and fake passports. David Bruce's diplomatic background and experience at the Red Cross in London made him the logical candidate to help Donovan run the new agency.

Although war news was now omnipresent, the gentry gamely carried on in the Virginia countryside. On November 16, 1941, the *New York Times* ran a feature: HORSE AND HOUNDS IN VIRGINIA: FOXHUNTING DAYS COME AGAIN TO THE PIEDMONT AND, WAR OR NO WAR, "TALLYHO!" RESOUNDS OVER FIELD AND ROLLING HILL.

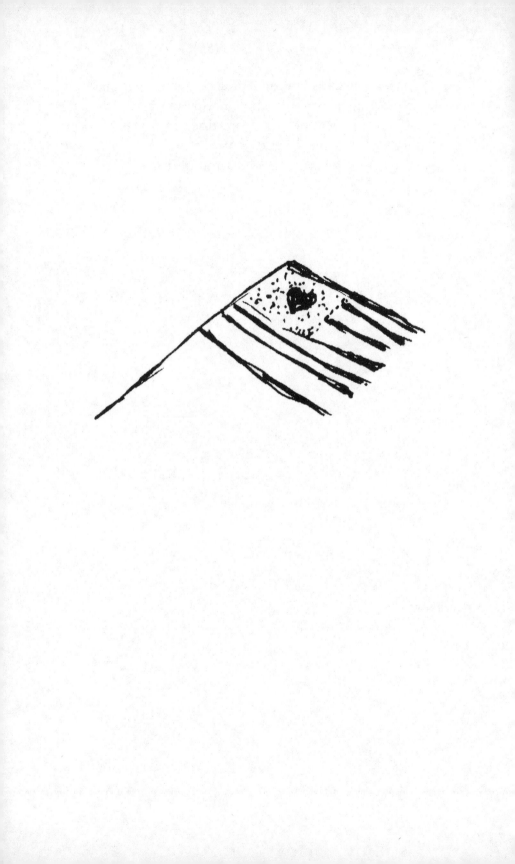

Chapter Ten

The War Years

Within days of the December 7, 1941, Japanese attack on Pearl Harbor, Stacy Lloyd's patriotism inspired him to join the war effort. As a thirty-three-year-old married man, he was unlikely to be drafted but did not want to sit on the sidelines. He called his friend David Bruce at the OSS and followed up with a letter on December 30, 1941: "I would like to do something useful... If Colonel Donovan does need some extra help in his office, I have 8 years running my own business."

Virginia senator Harry Byrd Sr. wrote a letter of recommendation: "I have never come in contact with a higher type man or more patriotic American than Mr. Lloyd. He is not only a man of the finest possible character but he is one of unusual capacity, of absolute conscientious devotion to any task he undertakes." Harold Dodds, the president of Princeton, described Stacy as "a man of good personality and character and all round capacity."

On February 1, 1942, Stacy went to work as David Bruce's assistant in Washington, with the understanding that he would eventually be sent overseas. Soon, there was other news in the Lloyd household: Bunny was pregnant again, due to give birth in late October.

Stacy was assigned to develop the OSS registry, a system to log, cross-reference, and track intelligence documents, classifying the material as Secret, Confidential, Restricted, or Free. On July 29, 1942, David Bruce wrote to an Army colonel that Colonel Donovan had requested that Capt. Stacy Lloyd (serial number 0911867) be sent to London to report to the OSS military intelligence unit.

Colonel Donovan made it explicit in a classified memo to Stacy that he would be working undercover: "Because of the special nature of your duties there, it no doubt will be advisable for you to conduct many of them out of uniform," he wrote. "You are hereby authorized by me to wear, or not to wear, a uniform, at your own discretion."

When Stacy informed his wife that he had been issued orders to head to the war zone, Bunny was so flustered that she blurted out, "You can't, we just got new lampshades." Stacy and a very pregnant Bunny spent a final weekend at the Waldorf Astoria in New York in mid-September before Stacy shipped out for London.

Gerard Lambert had joined the War Production Board and purchased a house on Kalorama Circle in Washington. Bunny moved in with her father and stepmother while she waited to give birth. On October 27, when Bunny headed for Garfield Hospital, she was so calm that she brought along her knitting socks for Stacy. Bunny gave birth to a daughter whom she named Eliza Winn, with "Winn" a tribute to her father's Virginia relatives. "I have never experienced the kind of joy I felt that night either before or after," she later recalled. "We had nothing but boys in the family with the exception of my sister. To have a little girl had been my greatest wish."

On Eliza's birthday many years later, Bunny reminisced in a note to her daughter: "The day you were born there was wind that swirled the dried leaves around with a crackle in the early morning, but by evening when we met it was calm and the sun was warm. I feel so close to that day and seeing a smiling baby wrapped in a warm blanket."

Stacy sent a telegram—"Delighted, wonderful news"—and followed up with a letter to "Dearest Hun Bun." "This damn war makes things an awful mess but it also makes very clear that you are the only thing in the world that stands out as being the best of everything and I love you very much. Take care of yourself Muffy and stay quiet." He helpfully advised her that if the milk from their Guernsey cows was too rich for the baby, she should buy a Holstein.

Gerard Lambert's job at the War Production Board was actually a cover for his true role. A believer in market research dating back to his days at Listerine, Gerard thought that gauging and shaping public opinion at home would be vital to winning the war. Rather than try to convince government officials that his idea had merit, he went ahead and spent his own money to create a national polling organization, the Research Council, to enable the White House to measure Americans' views on potential war strategies.

"Mr. Roosevelt always knew that I was a Republican and that I had made every effort to throw out the Democratic administration, but this didn't make a difference to him," Lambert wrote in his autobiography. "As this polling organization was financed by private funds, we were responsible to no one and our work could be kept confidential."

Hadley Cantril, the former chairman of Princeton's Department of Psychology, ran the secret polling operation out of Gerard's six-bedroom brick house just two miles from the White House. The two men became informal advisers to the president. "In March 1942, when FDR ordered General Douglas MacArthur, under intense Japanese assault, to withdraw from the Philippines to Australia, their polling confirmed the unpopularity of the move," wrote historian David Greenberg in his book *Republic of Spin*. He added that "Lambert drafted a statement, which FDR read out loud verbatim at his March 17 press conference," which framed the decision as a wartime necessity.

For the next few years, whenever the president and his Cabinet wanted to test ideas—would Catholics be upset if the United States bombed Rome, should the United States set up refugee camps for those persecuted by the Nazis—Lambert and his partner Cantril designed surveys and quietly reported their findings. Historians would later credit them as the first White House pollsters.

Stacy Lloyd's first job in London involved creating another information classification registry. He and Bunny wrote to each other constantly, but overseas mail delivery was sporadic and letters often took a month or longer to get through. Sometimes two or three would arrive in one day. The couple began to number their letters, so they could figure out what missives had not arrived.

Although Bunny had two young children to care for at home, she agreed to take in a war refugee. Eight-year-old David Brooke was the son of Charles Greville, the Earl of Warwick, one of the richest men in England, and his ex-wife, brunette beauty Rose Bingham, the great-granddaughter of Lord Lucan.

Rose was now volunteering in London at the Red Cross Washington Club, and she confided to Stacy that she was concerned about her son's safety. Stacy wrote to Bunny that he had warned Rose her son might find it difficult to adjust to the United States, since "all English children due to their accent and slightly different ways of doing things were apt to have a hard time with little American boys. To help the situation, I suggested she tell David not to talk about who he was in England and his Castles."

When Stacy contracted jaundice in January 1943, he recuperated at Rose's flat, fussed over by her personal physician, cook, and maid. During his convalescence, Stacy worried about Bunny, writing, "I do hope that you are not too lonely but if it is bad you should move to Washington with your father and Gracie or take a house there or in Philadelphia or Princeton. I don't want you to feel that you must keep the house open for me...I love to think of you being there as I can imagine what our life is like, what you are doing and what the children are up to but none of that is of the slightest importance in fact is extremely bad if you are lonely and unhappy by yourself."

At Stacy's request, Bunny sent him care packages: his favorite hair tonic, Kreml; Aunt Jemima pancake mix, maple syrup, Sportsman's chocolate bars, tins of butter, concentrated orange juice, ham, and sausages.

For a wealthy woman used to relying on her husband to run the farm, Bunny had her hands full managing the property with its horses, cows, and victory garden. She was also trying to keep an eye on her husband's struggling newspaper. Staff members had been drafted, advertising was sluggish, and horse shows had been banned. Stacy counseled his wife not to put too much of her own trust fund into supporting the newspaper.

Due to gasoline rationing, Bunny walked her young son to and from school and took the bus to get around. When her nanny was hospitalized for surgery, Bunny was on her own with baby Eliza. Her husband worried that she was unprepared to handle the primitive needs of an infant.

"You must have had quite a time taking care of Winn by yourself," Stacy wrote. "I was never too sure about your nursing qualifications unless you were really up against a tough spot and then you were fine, but in the shady places where it was not too hot work and your fears had time to function, you were a bit jittery."

David Bruce was transferred to London to direct the OSS's European operations. Stacy wrote to Bunny on February 9, 1943: "David arrived on Sunday night and he told me he had seen you the day before he left...I was so pleased to hear about you...He is going to be absolutely first class and it is a great relief to have him over here as he always makes a great deal of sense and does not get stampeded into things."

David Bruce and Stacy not only worked side by side but also spent free time together. David frequently invited Stacy to come along on wartime visits to his tailor or antiques shopping on Bond Street. "David seems to love company," Stacy wrote. "He hates doing things alone." When the impatient Stacy periodically found himself in hot water with other officers, he could count on David Bruce to rescue him from reprimand.

Stacy tried to downplay the dangers of London life and urged Bunny not to worry. At the same time, he was honest, writing, "We had the first air raid last night. The first alarm was during dinner and the second one was about 4:30 a.m. There was the most terrific AA [anti-aircraft] barrage it was like the loudest Fourth of July you ever heard...it was exciting but we could do without them."

Since he could not describe his classified work to Bunny, he emphasized his busy social life in his letters home. The popular Stacy attended lunches at Claridge's and dinners at Buck's Club, went hunting in Scotland and visited Ditchley Park, attended a dance in a garage where he met Clark Gable, Bob Hope, and Adolphe Menjou, and visited the estate of Ronald and Nancy Tree, where Winston Churchill often spent weekends. In a typical letter, he wrote to Bunny, "I went to a cocktail party given by Bill Astor. Adele Astaire was there and I asked her to have dinner with me next week. She seems to be a very amusing little woman who rattles along at a great rate and has a terrific tongue."

Adele Astaire, the dance partner and older sister of Fred Astaire, had retired from the stage in 1932 to marry Lord Charles Cavendish, the son of the Duke of Devonshire. She was now volunteering at the London Red Cross. Bill Astor was Viscount William Waldorf Astor, who was married to an American, Nancy Langhorne, the first woman elected to Parliament. Lady Astor had been one of Gerard Lambert's childhood Virginia friends. Stacy had no shortage of hosts and hostesses in England, mostly thanks to Bunny's family connections.

During his weekends at British country houses, Stacy paid attention to the landscaping and sent detailed descriptions to his wife. "In every garden I have seen over here the apple trees have been espaliered and replanted in straight lines looking like old gnarled men with their hands above their heads," he wrote, urging Bunny to try this at home, and complimenting her decision to plant English walnut trees.

Bunny missed her husband so much—and he sounded like he was having so much fun—that she suggested joining him in London, where she could volunteer at the Red Cross, too. She planned to leave their children in Virginia. Stacy adamantly rejected the ludicrous idea. London was a war zone, the Army discouraged wives from coming over, and the children needed their mother.

Stacy was assigned to help British officers debrief Polish prisoners of war who had been conscripted into the German Army. He received high praise for his work. "The British have shown him everything regarding their set-up and he is making a first-class job of it," reported a memo sent by Maj. Richard Heppner to the OSS Washington office. On April 23, 1943, Stacy detailed his interviews with seventeen

Polish POWs, recommending several men as potential OSS agents. He noted: "Korol reported the existence of a powder factory...in the Hamburg area which was so well concealed in the wood that it had never been bombed."

Stacy met with an Army general in London to discuss the possibility of dropping OSS agents forty miles behind enemy lines. He wrote to the recently promoted Brigadier General Donovan about this plan "to observe from concealment movements of enemy reinforcements during an allied invasion...I would like very much to take part in training these men and to form one of the parties during an invasion."

He assembled a team of men who spoke French, could handle radio communications, and had experience jumping out of planes. In an OSS memo, Stacy explained that the men "would be dropped along main highways in wooded areas, on high ground or near airfields occupied by the enemy to observe and report on enemy air movements of fighter and transport planes." He requested supplies for the "Proust Mission," including radios, counterfeit identity documents, ration cards, clothing, and disguises.

Paul Mellon turned up in England that spring after asking his father's longtime lawyer, Donald Shepard, to pull strings to get him a foreign assignment. He had been languishing at an Army base in Kansas, working as a riding instructor teaching military seat and elementary jumping. Mary Mellon, who had given birth to son Timothy on July 22, 1942, joined Paul in Kansas along with their daughter Cathy. This was a cushy post, but he felt irrelevant.

Once in England, Paul was given an equally safe and boring post in the countryside, working for a colonel in charge of victory gardens. He decided to use clout to improve his lot. "On getting to London, I had looked up my brother-in-law David Bruce," Paul later wrote. "I also went to see Stacy Lloyd, an old foxhunting friend whom Mary and I had known in Virginia."

Stacy welcomed his neighbor, writing to Bunny: "Paul has arrived and I have been busy showing him the ropes about wartime. He seemed somewhat at a loss." He added, "[David Bruce] thinks Paul has no gumption at all." In an act of friendship, Stacy said that he had "prodded" Bruce, who ran the London station of the OSS, to give Paul a chance. David Bruce had married into the Mellon family sixteen years earlier; it speaks volumes that he was reluctant to recommend his brother-in-law for a significant post.

Stacy took Paul out for dinner and gambling. "There was seldom less than several hundred dollars on the floor at a time," marveled Stacy at Paul's thick bankroll. "Fortunately having taken my life in my hands I came out twenty pounds to the good and at 12:30 I fled... they must have gone on until the wee hours but it was fun and I believe Paul enjoyed himself hugely... He tells me he saw you in New York and that you looked alright. I do hate to be away from you for so long."

Finally allowed to join the OSS Special Operations unit, Paul Mellon was given a paper-pushing job, assigned to set pay scales for French-speaking American soldiers who would be going behind enemy lines. Eager to prove that he did indeed have gumption, Mellon wangled a slot as the only American in a monthlong British combat training program in Hampshire to learn sabotage techniques such as silent killing, handling explosives, and breaking and entering.

He and Stacy decided to share London lodgings. "I am sure you will be amused to know that Paul and I have today taken a flat belonging to Rose's friend," wrote Stacy on July 14. "It is near Paddington Station in a place called Sussex Gardens." Stacy and Paul entertained frequently, although the culinary arts sometimes eluded them. On one memorable evening, after their guests had gobbled a casserole left in the oven, they belatedly realized that they had misunderstood the cook's instructions. "Paul said, 'My god, we ate the cat's breakfast for the first course.'" Stacy wrote to Bunny, adding, "I thought Paul would die laughing."

They also worked in the same building. "It is funny having Paul just across the hall from me," Stacy wrote. "He wanders in and makes his funny little remarks and wanders out again."

With bombs falling in London, the usual social restraints did not apply, and people scarcely bothered to hide their assignations. Stacy passed along the who's-sleeping-with-whom gossip to Bunny. David

Bruce had an assistant who became his girlfriend—Evangeline Bell, the Radcliffe-educated multilingual daughter of an American diplomat. The couple brought Stacy house hunting as they looked for a love nest together. With understatement, Stacy summarized in a letter to Bunny the wartime social mores: "It is funny the things that go on here."

He attended a "dreadful" dinner with financier Averell Harriman, his daughter Kathleen, and Pamela Churchill, Winston Churchill's daughter-in-law. Stacy wrote to Bunny: "Pamela Churchill is a girl of Mr. Harriman and also of Jock's, I think." (That is, Jock Whitney, another Virginia friend stationed in London.) Paul Mellon began to bring a friend, Molly Stansfeld, to evenings on the town. Stacy wrote, "She is a nice girl, not bad-looking but a friendly merry girl who does not seem to have a great many friends."

Bunny inevitably worried about what her own husband might be up to. After Stacy informed Bunny that he could not return on leave and could not explain why (he was working on top secret plans), she became furious.

"Muff, you did write and tell me once that if I did not come home you were going to get a new husband and the hell of it is, I cannot come home," he wrote to her on July 5, 1943. "Honest, Bun, I will get back as soon as I can. Now to the female question, there just is not anyone but you and hasn't been. I have had a careful look at all the girls in London just for the purpose of comparison and there isn't anyone to compare to you, I am absolutely convinced of it."

In late summer 1943, Allied troops began converging off the Southern coast of Italy, preparing to invade and fight their way north to retake the country. Stacy was initially sent to Algiers and then to Salerno, southeast of Naples, to secretly watch the harbor. On September 9, under rocket cover, fifty-five thousand Allied troops landed on the beach.

When Bill Donovan—now a general—arrived in Salerno in October, he was furious to discover that the OSS undercover operations were in disarray. He immediately demoted the local OSS station head,

Donald Downes, and gave Stacy a battlefield promotion to supervise the resistance fighters. In a letter to Bunny, Stacy proudly described the situation: "I was given by General D the most amazing bunch of scoundrels, prima donnas and odd fighters to organize. He fired the man that brought them together and put me in charge. The first week was a nightmare of banging people's heads together...I only hope that it is not too late and that the chaos or reorganization has not been so great as to get me fired too."

In two SECRET dispatches to the OSS Washington office, since declassified, Stacy described his work with colorful can-do candor. Stacy met with local fishermen, who agreed to smuggle an agent behind enemy lines. But to win their cooperation in the impoverished country, he had to help them buy and sell spaghetti on the black market.

He joined Army troops rolling in to take Naples, depicting the city as "bedlam" and the situation as "gloriously tarfu" (acronym for "things are really fucked up"). "We got instructions to round up the police force, which, in true Italian fashion was scattered to hell and bedlam and back...We packed the Police in trucks and then dropped them, like horse droppings, along the General's route...By four o' clock the General had marched in and had taken Naples, a deed which he could have done two weeks ago apparently. After requisitioning a house from the chief German collaborationist, a son of a bitch, I might say, who was rather ugly about being thrown out, but it is a nice villa, I toured back to Amalfi." As a gentleman at war, Stacy had high standards for what he deemed appropriate accommodations.

In another classified memo on October 19 from Naples, Stacy made a pragmatic plea for supplies: "The agents you recruit are invariably practically in rags and if you are sending them out to walk a hundred or so miles through enemy lines to their destination, their shoes will never make it." He begged for maps and jeeps: "Although we requisition civilian cars, they always break down and jeeps are the only things that can get you around once the bridges are blown up and you begin to get around to front lines with bodies."

He was sent back to London in November.

Bunny was developing a close bond with her British ward, David Robin Francis Guy Greville, who was just one year older than her son, Tuffy. Even by the standards of the wayward British aristocracy, young David came from a colorful family. His great-grandmother Daisy—said to have inspired the song "Daisy Bell (Bicycle Built for Two)"—had been the mistress of King Edward VII and had tried to sell his love letters. His father, Charles Greville, had acted in several Hollywood movies, including *Dawn Patrol* in 1938, under the stage name Michael Brooke. Born in 1935, David had adopted his father's stage name, calling himself David Brooke.

Gerard Lambert recalled David as "an absolutely charming boy," adding that Bunny "took care of him in Virginia, bringing him up as if she were his mother. But he often came to stay with us at Albemarle as he considered that place just another of his family estates."

Bunny took the children to visit her mother and stepfather on Cape Cod, and spent a summer at Watch Hill, Rhode Island, with her mother-in-law. David Brooke's mother, Rose, sent Bunny grateful notes, and commented after receiving a new batch of photographs, "He does look jolly sweet. I am proud of him thanks entirely to your care and good will."

But Bunny found that having two boisterous boys around the house plus toddler Eliza was too much. She sent her son and David off to the Stuyvesant School in nearby Warrenton in 1944. Her son, then eight years old, hated the boarding school and could not understand why his mother had made him leave home. Even now, more than seven decades later, Tuffy Lloyd recalls how homesick he felt, sadly recalling, "I was really young when I was sent to boarding school...I used to get into constant fights. I think it caused a lot of distance for me, kind of a gap, because I spent a lot of time alone."

Paul Mellon's wife, Mary, chose to have her daughter, Cathy, tutored at home rather than attend school. The two Mellon children apparently did not get along. "I am told that my older sister Cathy did not speak to me for the first five years of my life," Tim Mellon later wrote in his 2016 autobiography, *Tim's Story*, adding, "Now I think I should be thankful."

The Mellons' marriage was strained by the separation. Stacy informed Bunny on January 31, 1944, that Paul had a new girlfriend, Valerie Churchill Longman, who worked at the Red Cross. "I have not seen much of Paul lately as he will hustle himself off with this terrible girl Churchill Longman who is a terrible gold digger and will most certainly take him for plenty," wrote Stacy.

Paul fondly acknowledged that wartime romance in his 1992 autobiography. His friend and the book's coauthor, art curator John Baskett, says, "I always thought he should have married her. Valerie sounded absolutely enchanting."

Worried that Stacy had been unfaithful, Bunny was becoming increasingly jealous and suspicious. In his letters, Stacy constantly mentioned seeing Rose Greville but downplayed their friendship by passing along tales of her romances, such as her involvement with the American journalist turned Army public relations man Tex McCrary. (Their brief engagement made the newspapers.) Bunny's concerns were exacerbated when a friend in London passed on the gossip that Stacy and Rose had become an item.

Stacy denied repeatedly in his letters that he was seeing anyone and insisted that Rose "is devoted to you." He professed, "I have not been going about with the London girls... that kind of business is not worthwhile. I have got a very nice cat at home and there is not much point in trying to develop strange alliances over here."

A week later, he wrote, "There is a story going around at home that Paul and I are living here with Rose and Patsy Ward [a journalist]. Isn't it wonderful what can be dreamed up. Paul was furious when I told him... Rose is having her usual Sunday with McCrary and having Monday with Doug Gibson." Rose sent Bunny a telegram insisting that she had done nothing wrong.

Stacy was a handsome man, an ocean away in a war zone. Bunny brooded about his conduct. War is hell on the home front, too. Her late-in-life confidant, Dr. Bruce Horten, says, "She said it was such a tragedy that Stacy had such a wandering eye. All this talk came back to her from the time he was overseas and playing around with everyone."

In early January 1944, Stacy wrote a flurry of SECRET memos to Lt. Col. Francis Miller about the plan to insert OSS agents into France before and after D-Day. The American invasion of Normandy was on target for late spring. Stacy wrote a detailed schedule for agent field training including weapons practice, prisoner of war interrogation, defense against land mines and booby traps, camouflage, and concealment.

Stacy returned to the United States from March 22 to April 8, 1944, to brief his Washington superiors and see his family. "Major Stacy B. Lloyd of this city has joined Mrs. Lloyd at 'Apple Hill,' their home at Boyce, Va. after 18 months of duty overseas," reported the *Philadelphia Inquirer*. The visit felt all too short to Bunny and their children. "I didn't really know my own father because he was in Europe when I was growing up," says Tuffy. "He would send thin tissue letters back home. And a few little presents here and there." Some of the presents were wildly inappropriate, such as a bayonet that Stacy had taken off a dead German soldier.

Upon his return to London, Stacy wrote to Bunny, "I am so glad that we had our two weeks together and I had a chance to get a glimpse of everything. The children are such nice kids and you are doing so very well bringing them up." He had begun imagining their postwar lives, but his thoughts were disjointed. In his letters, he expressed concern about his need to make enough money to keep Bunny in the free-spending style that she was accustomed to, joking that keeping her happy was expensive.

He confided that General Donovan and David Bruce were discussing converting the OSS into a full-fledged government intelligence agency once the war ended and had asked him to join them. He was interested. But then he also thought that he might want to get a job at a big-city newspaper, hardly a moneymaking career.

"The more I stay over here, the more I feel that it is not going to be enough to sit quietly in Virginia all the rest of the time and run the two little papers. There is so much to do and so many interesting places to see," he wrote. "This is a bad time to talk or make decisions on future plans as everything is so upset and everyone so restless...All I know is that I love you very much and long to get back to you and join our lives together again."

Stacy fantasized about having a more intellectual life as a couple, proposing that they read books and discuss them. "I will never catch up to you and your gardening world, but you could brief me on a leading book or two and keep me up to date," he wrote, adding, "You will laugh but Shakespeare is a must, Gibbons too, and we ought to know more about Dickens, Kipling, Scott, Dumas, James Fenimore Cooper. We ought to have Walt Whitman, Wordsworth, Shelley, Keats, Milton in hand...

"I know you love to chatter along in the evening and so do I...and drop off to sleep at ten after a hard day's work, but there ought to be an hour of just plain reading and then we would have a bit more to chatter about in the evening."

In the wake of the D-Day invasion on June 6, 1944, the London office of the OSS juggled its staff. Paul Mellon finally got his wish to be closer to the action. Three weeks after D-Day, he was sent to Omaha Beach as part of a group of ten officers. He wrote in his autobiography that their mission was "to join up behind enemy lines with the French resistance...then harass the enemy by blowing up bridges and ambushing the Germans' armored divisions with mines and bazookas." En route in a jeep from Cherbourg to Normandy, he became delirious with pneumonia. He was sent to a field hospital and then flown to England to recuperate. He sent a telegraph to Valerie Churchill Longman, who visited him in the Shropshire hospital.

Stacy was also on the move. On July 7, 1944, David Bruce wrote in his wartime diary that he had received permission to "have Stacy Lloyd and a French liaison officer go to France immediately." Stacy was placed in command of the first Morale Operations unit in France, with the goal of spreading disinformation to the Germans.

A month later, David Bruce went to Saint-Pair-sur-Mer, a beach-side town in Normandy, where the OSS had taken over five villas. On August 18, Bruce wrote in his diary that Stacy had just returned safely from a dangerous near miss. Stacy had been accompanying three agents behind enemy lines, with sacks of propaganda leaflets stuffed into the spare tire. Sixty miles from Paris, the vehicle got a flat tire and they had to beat a hasty retreat.

David Bruce took Stacy with him to the Rambouillet hospital to see wounded French civilians. "It was a distressing sight, especially as a majority of them had been injured by American bombing or as a result of strafing on the roads by American planes," Bruce wrote in his journal. A doctor brought them to see his injured wife, who had been in a café when a U.S. plane machine-gunned German trucks. Hit by bullets, both of her feet had been amputated. Bruce ended that haunting scene by writing, "The Director of the hospital and his wife opened a bottle of port for us."

Bruce was a friend of Ernest Hemingway, the first American war correspondent to arrive in mid-August in Rambouillet, who contacted French resistance members. In the belief that the writer might have useful information, David Bruce put Stacy Lloyd in touch with Hemingway. When Army officers later investigated Hemingway's wartime activities to see if he had overstepped journalistic protocol and acted as a combat soldier, Stacy was interviewed and defended the writer's conduct.

"Colonel Bruce introduced me to him and said he might be able to help in the work I was doing, which was putting agents through the lines with propaganda directly to the Germans," Stacy told the investigators, according to a declassified transcript. "So I asked Mr. Hemingway whether he did know anybody who could help me and he said yes, he did, and he produced three people that he said from his talks with the French resistance would be helpful. I used all three of those people."

Asked if he could provide any other information about Hemingway's activities, Stacy replied, "No, sir, I cannot, except that he was working hard at the time interviewing as many people as he could on the situation and getting as much information as possible from as many people that either came to the hotel or heard that he was there and wanted to talk to him."

Bunny watched her friends suffer during the war. Her Foxcroft class-mate Beatrice Patton's husband, Lt. Col. John Waters, became a prisoner of war in Germany; classmate Mabel Bradley's husband was killed in action; and classmate Caroline Hazard Stout's brother died overseas. Each day brought Bunny fresh reminders that her husband and their friends were in peril.

On August 30 the *Washington Post* ran the headline: COL. JOCK WHITNEY, TURF FAMILY SCION, CAPTURED BY NAZIS. Whitney had joined the Army Air Corps Intelligence unit in 1942. Stationed in London where he often spent time with Stacy and Paul, Whitney was eager to see combat and received permission to go to France. In Aix-en-Provence, riding in a weapons carrier, he and his companions were ambushed by a German machine gunner. They dove into a ditch, but after grenades and bullets continued to fly, they surrendered.

Whitney was transported on a bus and then a series of trains that were strafed by American planes. Whitney and eleven other prisoners managed to unhook the lock on the train door and jumped off the moving train into a forest. With German troops just a half mile away, Whitney and his fellow prisoners were lucky to be found by a young boy, who introduced them to friendly French locals. Whitney told the press that being on the receiving end of Allied plane attacks was "the worst kind of hell."

That fall, Stacy, who had been promoted to lieutenant colonel, was sent to Luxembourg to run a Morale Operations unit. This was psychological warfare, distributing leaflets to the Nazis claiming that their women at home were cheating and fellow soldiers were defect-ing. His team included *New York Herald Tribune* theatre critic Walter Kerr and Howard Baldwin of the *New Yorker*.

"I think Italy was hard work but this really has been more of a grind," Stacy wrote to Bunny. He bought her tulip bulbs during a trip to Holland, noting, "They are not the mixed color kind as these are all up further north which is still in the hands of the Germans." Paul Mellon, now recovered from pneumonia, joined Stacy as his deputy but was unhappy about the new assignment.

"We got Paul all the way over here, he is a fantastic person," Stacy wrote in mid-October. "Really I do believe he is off his nut. He has some idea he does not want to work in this theatre because David is here and also that he ought to get out of oh so social [the OSS] and do something else."

Paul Mellon thought the new mission was ill conceived, writing in his autobiography that "at that stage things were moving so quickly that there was no time for ingenious moral-sapping schemes... It was difficult to persuade American combat officers and their men to risk their lives taking unknown civilians along with their patrols into enemy territory at night." Nonetheless, Stacy valued Paul's work and successfully recommended that he be promoted to major.

On October 24, 1944, OSS colonel K. D. Mann wrote to David Bruce and urged him to send Stacy home: "Am concerned about Stacy Lloyd in that he has had two years in pretty active service, has lost a lot of weight and is physically and mentally tired... We might offer him the job of deputy here in Washington, which type of desk work might not be attractive to him, but would give him a well-earned chance to come home and recuperate."

This was a classic example of the special treatment of the wellborn even during the rigors of wartime. A month later, Mann sent a follow-up note to David Bruce, explaining why he had requested the transfer in the first place.

"I can now disclose my real reason for suggesting that Stacy Lloyd might return to the United States," wrote Mann on November 25, referring back to information that he had received during an October trip to the capital. "Upon my arrival in Washington, I called Bunny and subsequently had dinner with her. It developed that she was in an extremely anemic condition, mentally upset, and that she would have to undergo a serious operation. The latter possibility soon developed into an actuality, but Bunny swore me to absolute secrecy in the matter, even though I requested that I at least be allowed to tell you and then you could use your own judgment about telling Stacy.

"I felt I was placed in a very difficult position since I am not an intimate friend of the family as you are. However, the operation took place three days ago, and her father told me last night that the operation was extremely successful and that Bunny should be home within a week."

Colonel Mann urged David Bruce to let Stacy know immediately that she was doing well. "As the situation now stands, there is certainly no reason to try to get Stacy back here, unless he himself so desires," wrote Mann. "Bunny is reconciled to him not returning for several months." Informed on December 6 of Bunny's illness, Stacy sent a telegram: "Just heard through Mann your operation hope you are better terribly worried can return if you are not better all my love."

The OSS allowed Stacy to come home. On January 16, 1945, he announced to Bunny that this was his last letter since they would soon be reunited: "Honestly Bun it will be so wonderful that I cannot possibly imagine it. The idea of being able to see you every day and to do what we like for a bit fills me with so much joy that I could not possibly tell you enough how happy I am."

He returned by military aircraft on January 25. Stacy was now on a sixty-day assignment to the OSS Washington office, but once that time passed, it was clear that the conflict was winding down, so he stayed in the capital.

Paul Mellon had taken over Stacy's position in Belgium. When the assignment ended in April, he volunteered to act as a conducting officer to parachute into France with five young women agents. He landed safely but then had to make his way out of the country.

Paul joined a group of Free French soldiers who were searching for foraging enemy soldiers in a booby-trapped vineyard. "We could hear bursts of machine-gun fire a mile or so away," he later recalled. A French soldier, who was walking right behind Mellon's group, accidentally tripped a wire and blew himself up. The horrific death was so meaningless and unnecessary that Paul questioned whether his entire wartime service had been worthwhile. He concluded, "I suddenly realized that our playing at war, playing at being propaganda artists, was thoughtless and foolish."

He received bronze stars for his service in the Rhineland and Ardennes campaigns. In his service discharge record, Paul was described as an "excellent all-around field officer. Calm, collected, possessed of good judgment and well-liked by those serving with him."

On May 22, he sailed home on the *Ile de France*. "I had to wait until August for my discharge from the Army," he later wrote, "but came home a very different man from the raw recruit who had left for Fort Riley four years earlier."

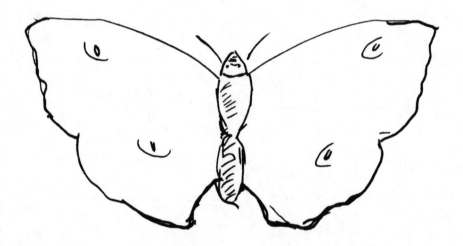

Chapter Eleven

Millions of Reasons to Remarry

For Paul Mellon, Stacy Lloyd, and their contemporaries, returning to their old lives was disorienting. This stoic generation of men was expected to block out the gruesome sights they had seen and ignore residual feelings about killing enemy combatants. If these former American military men experienced moments of sudden anger, depression, or jumpiness, they were encouraged to brush off those reactions rather than dwell on their feelings. Living in the present—with the jarring memories of the recent past—made for a rough adjustment.

Stacy was deactivated from the OSS in July 1945 and resumed his job as a newspaper publisher. As the government moved to establish the postwar intelligence-gathering version of the OSS—the Central Intelligence Agency—Bill Donovan was eased out by President Truman, so that job option for Stacy was no longer open.

Stacy gave Bunny a gold compact with her monogram, *BL*, spelled out in rubies, but the gift did not resolve the couple's problems. Instead of being overjoyed by her husband's return, Bunny remained wounded and suspicious. "I really only wanted one life," Bunny later told author Burton Hersh for his book *The Mellon Family*. "I was very happy with my first husband. It crumbled during the war. You know, there are a lot more casualties in war than death."

Tuffy Lloyd overheard his parents quarreling over money. Bunny wanted to renovate Apple Hill but Stacy was concerned about the cost. "My poor father came back after four years of war and looked at the house, said, 'Look, Bunny, we can't afford this roof.'" Bunny's husband complained that he had already borrowed $30,000 for home improvements and was worried about paying that sum back.

Money was not a problem for Paul Mellon, but returning home thrust him once again into the position of grappling with his father's legacy. Before joining the Army, he had resigned from the board of the National Gallery of Art. But now, there was a new vacancy. His sister, Ailsa, and brother-in-law, David Bruce, had embarked on divorce proceedings and Bruce stepped down as a museum trustee. Museum director David Finley, stressing that it was important that a Mellon family member remain involved, convinced Paul to rejoin the museum's board. Paul also returned to the helm of his father's multimillion-dollar charitable foundation.

The dinners and horse shows resumed in Virginia as if the war had never happened. Mary and Paul Mellon gave a dinner party in December 1945, including Bunny and Stacy, Liz Whitney, and Foxcroft headmistress Charlotte Noland. Paul and Mary then headed to their estate in Hobe Sound, Florida. "Everything is fine here," Paul wrote to Huntington Cairns, the secretary of the National Gallery. "The sun is wonderful and I am feeling much better." But in truth, Paul was miserable and felt emotionally estranged from his wife.

"I found myself restless and irritated," he later admitted in his autobiography. "We had been leading separate lives for the last four years, so it was hardly surprising that we had developed separately and had inevitably grown somewhat apart." As he explained in his memoir, he had grown critical of her personality flaws: "My life with Mary, interrupted as it was by my four years in the army, was a series of loving and friendly interludes punctuated by periods of misunderstanding and mutual aggravation. She had a very forceful, almost aggressive personality, but it was tempered with a sense of fairness and a mischievous sense of humor."

Upon his return to Virginia, Paul began giving his full attention to his racehorses. His horse Caddie won the Temple Gwathmey Steeplechase at the Belmont in what newspapers described as a "sizzling finish." On March 30, 1946, Paul and Mary welcomed the Piedmont Race, which had been suspended during the war, back to Rokeby Farm.

The Mellons and the Lloyds saw each other constantly. On April 13, both couples attended the twenty-fifth annual Middleburg Hunt Races. As columnist Nina Carter Tabb wrote in the *Washington Post*, "The turf course was in excellent condition for the six races and looked like a wide green ribbon as it stretched toward the Blue Ridge Mountains in the distance. Beds of yellow jonquils made a carpet at the foot of the grandstand and boxes which are built upon natural rock."

Mary Mellon resumed her participation on the racing and hunt circuit even though her allergies still acted up. That spring, she had an asthma attack that sent her to the hospital. A physician warned Paul Mellon that she needed to stay away from horses, saying, "You know, this thing can't go on much longer. It's a terrible strain on her heart."

But Mary continued to believe that the situation was manageable. To share Paul's life was to share his passion, and she was determined to remain by his side. Mary and Paul attended the Rolling Rock Horse Races in Pittsburgh in early October, where onlookers noted that she appeared to be in good health.

On October 11, Mary Mellon joined her husband on a morning hunt. She was cautious at these events, usually staying toward the back on her calm and well-trained horse. But as the couple began trotting home afterward, Mary began gasping for breath, a sign of an asthma attack. Paul galloped off to get help.

By the time he returned with a car, Mary just wanted to go home and go to bed. A few hours later, she became gravely ill. "While I was out of the room, our children's nurse rushed up to me, saying that she was alarmed by Mary's condition and urging me to come up at once," Paul Mellon recalled. "I went up to Mary's room and found her in a dreadful state. She died right there."

Mary Mellon was only forty-one years old. Her children, nine-year-old Catherine and four-year-old Timothy, scarcely knew their father since he had been overseas during their formative years. The family buried Mary in an old cemetery near their home. Paul was deluged with condolence notes, including a letter from his former analyst, Carl Jung, who wrote, "I share your grief and suffering."

Enveloped by a fog of guilt and sorrow, Paul found it hard to function. "I remained in a state of shock, drinking and smoking…more than was good for me and unable to concentrate," he later wrote in describing this period. He hired a friend to run his farm since he felt unable to handle the day-to-day operations.

Bunny and Stacy were solicitous, Bunny especially so. She had always liked Paul, appreciating his sly sense of humor and self-deprecating charm. She made herself available to him, a sympathetic presence who could offer advice on raising two motherless children. Now that Paul was a widower, she could imagine his future. Here was a man of enormous wealth at a vulnerable moment in his life. In his youth he had been one of the most eligible bachelors in the country. When he came out of his muddled state, women would besiege him. It was just a matter of time.

Bunny was thirty-six years old and she had never been a beauty. Her marriage was troubled; she worried that it would not last. This was her chance for a fresh start. And so, she made her move. "She pursued Paul at the outset," says Dr. Bruce Horten, recalling the version of the story that Bunny later told him. Paul Mellon leaned on Bunny for comfort and companionship until the end result was inevitable. Bunny told her husband that she wanted a divorce and planned to marry Paul Mellon.

Stacy was blindsided by this double betrayal by his wife and wartime friend, according to accounts from those who knew him. Anguished and angry, he found it hard to accept that Bunny no longer loved him. Stacy had informed Bunny during the war that Paul was cheating on his wife, but this information did not deter Bunny. She could not forgive her own husband for a suspected wartime fling, but she chose not to see Paul's philandering ways as a warning.

Paul and Bunny, both naturally reticent, never spoke about their relationship as if it had begun as a grand passion, a romantic love story for the ages. However, they enjoyed each other's company and believed they had enough interests in common to make a marriage, or more accurately a merger, work. "Paul and I married because I felt I could help him," Bunny later explained to Burton Hersh in a dispassionate account of the union. "We became partners to help one another and we remained that."

Paul presented an equally diplomatic and dry-eyed version of the courtship in his 1992 memoir. He sounded like a man relieved to have found a well-qualified replacement to fill an organizational vacancy in his life following his wife's death.

"Rachel Lloyd, or Bunny, as she is always called, my friend Stacy's wife, was very kind and understanding over my distress. The Lloyds both had long been intimate friends of Mary's and mine, and Mary had always admired Bunny, especially for her warmth and intelligence and for her expertise in gardening.

"The consequences of the war had left Bunny sad about her marriage. She was devoted to Stacy but bewildered, like so many other wartime wives, by the changes in his attitude toward her and toward their life in general, brought about by his long absence. It was clear that their marriage had effectively come to an end. Aware of this, and having known each other for so long, we decided to marry. It was hard for her to change a life of seventeen years, but circumstances being what they were, we saw it through."

People would inevitably gossip that it was all about the money for Bunny. The Mellon fortune, computed in dollar bills, could have carpeted Paul's fields, green as far as the eye could see. When *Fortune* magazine compiled its first list of America's richest citizens in 1957, Paul Mellon was number five, with an estimated net worth of $400 to $700 million (3.3 billion to 5.9 billion in today's dollars).

Bunny was a child of privilege, but this was castles-in-the-air money, guaranteeing a life of unimaginable luxury. After feeling strapped during her marriage to Stacy Lloyd and worrying about paying for a new roof, she could return to the carefree lifestyle of her youth made possible by her father's millions. But Paul was far wealthier than Gerard Lambert.

While Paul Mellon's bank balance was obviously a draw for Bunny, there was much more at stake. To be the wife of Paul Mellon meant ascending to a rarified and influential position. He was taking on the helm of a philanthropic empire. To be at his side would entail becoming a public figure, wining and dining presidents and princes, witnessing American history firsthand, helping put Andrew Mellon's fortune to good use.

The daughter of a man of consequence, until now the wife of a small-town publisher, Bunny was stepping up to a bigger life.

While Bunny was in the midst of untangling her marriage, she suffered two family losses. Her seventy-one-year-old stepfather, Malvern Clopton, who had been ailing for several years, died on April 22, 1947, at his home on Cape Cod. She had known him all her life, and her mother had forged a happy second marriage with the St. Louis surgeon.

Six months later, Bunny's brother, Sonny, was on a United Airlines flight from Los Angeles to New York on October 24 when a fire broke out in the luggage compartment. The pilot radioed the airport near Bryce Canyon, Utah, that he thought he could land safely—"May make it. Think we have a chance. Approaching the strip"—but minutes later the plane slammed into a hillside. Sonny, whose given name was Gerard Lambert Jr., was among the fifty-two who died. The Civil Aeronautics Administration determined that a design flaw caused gas to flow from fuel tanks into the cabin heating system.

Even though his marriage was dissolving, Stacy flew with his father-in-law to Denver but they were not allowed to go to the crash scene. The family gathered in Princeton for the funeral. This was the third plane crash to claim a member of the Lambert family.

Gerard Lambert had often acted impetuously, changing his life on a whim. Spurred by grief, he sold Carter Hall that December for more than $100,000. He was so eager to close the deal that he threw in a Gilbert Stuart portrait of George Washington. Carter Hall represented the past; the future was a new house that he and Grace had built on a sixteen-acre property in Manalapan, Florida, on the outskirts of Palm Beach.

Bunny was ready to make her break. That winter, she headed to her father's Florida estate and filed for divorce in Palm Beach, charging Stacy with mental cruelty. She hoped for privacy but her father's home—Gemini, an architectural curiosity—drew daily gawkers. Gerard had built two wings on either side of a road, with a connecting tunnel underneath the street. The family quarters faced the ocean, while guest quarters looked on Lake Worth. Strangers kept stopping by to stare and knock on the door, asking for tours. Gerard made an eccentric and segregated hiring decision: bringing in black staffers to tend the family quarters and a white staff for the guest wing.

Paul Mellon also went to Florida that winter, taking his children to his home in Hobe Sound, just forty-five miles away from the Lambert estate.

On March 9, 1948, the Associated Press ran a story announcing that Bunny had received her divorce and the settlement was secret. But the wire service got the real scoop: "Reports are current in Palm Beach social circles that Mrs. Lloyd will marry Paul Mellon, Pittsburgh financier and son of the late Andrew W. Mellon."

Rather than race directly to the altar, Bunny joined Sister Parish on a trip to London. Sister hoped to forge an alliance with Nancy Lancaster, one of the most revered decorators of the era and the owner of the London firm Colefax and Fowler. For Bunny, the trip was the equivalent of Old Home Week since Nancy, a Foxcroft graduate who was thirteen years her senior, had been a family friend of Gerard Lambert. In addition, Nancy and her previous husband, Ronald Tree, had entertained Stacy Lloyd during the war; she had since divorced and remarried.

Nancy, a wealthy Virginia expatriate, had become known for reinventing British country house style with the comfortable, romantic, and patrician décor of her forty-bedroom Palladium home, Ditchley Park. Nancy had hired the French decorator Stéphane Boudin to redo the house. She brought in landscape designers who installed cone-shaped yew topiaries along with pleached trees, a seventeenth-century technique in which trees were tied to bamboo or wires and then, as they grew, were bent to form a leafy canopy.

Bunny and Sister Parish were inspired by Nancy's innovations, and they would go on to replicate elements of her style. Nancy told her biographer, Robert Becker, that she did not like things to look "too perfect, too new or too stiff." She preferred flower beds spilling over rather than rigidly pruned, used aged chintz to recover furniture, and had workmen antique new leather to make it look old. She favored eighteenth-century-style beds "lit à la polonaise," four-poster beds draped with fabric, and slept between Porthault sheets. Lancaster collected vegetable-shaped china, an edible-looking medley of cauliflower and cabbages, as well as dozens of small gold and silver snuffboxes and cigarette cases.

Bunny fell in love with these objects, too. And with Paul Mellon's resources, she would soon be able to indulge in them.

On May 1, Bunny and Paul went to the Municipal Building in lower Manhattan for a marriage license. They were married the next day at the home of Sister Parish and her husband, Henry, at 24 East Eighty-Second Street. Rev. Dr. Edgar Franklin Romig of West End Collegiate Church presided over the small wedding. They did not bother with a maid of honor or best man.

Bunny's father disapproved of the match and declined to attend. Her widowed mother, Mrs. Malvern Clopton, announced the wedding in the *New York Herald Tribune*. Paul Mellon was described as "a financier and sportsman" and the member of such gentlemen's clubs as Scroll and Key at Yale, Racquet and Tennis, River and Links in New York, the Duquesne in Pittsburgh, and the Metropolitan Club in Washington.

Even after she put on her wedding ring, Bunny was unwilling to let go of one token of her old life. She continued to wear a horseshoe-shaped gold and sapphire pinkie ring that had been a gift from Stacy, a daily reminder of her first love. And a daily reminder to Paul of her conflicted loyalties.

She wrote to Stacy shortly after her marriage. Under the divorce settlement, he received Apple Hill. He replied on May 6 with a gracious and affectionate letter. He was indeed, as his Princeton class-mates had called him, a thorough gentleman.

My dearest Bun,

I cannot tell you what your note meant to me. You are such a wonderfully kind dear sweet girl. It seems very strange that we are apart but I shall think of you always and hope that you will be very happy.

Please don't let our paths go too far apart if we can possibly help it. I will always love you and wish that I had made you a better husband.

Take care of yourself and don't worry about too many things…I miss you and shall always miss you. Bless you my dearest Hun Bun—Stacy.

With its rolling meadows, forested nooks, meandering dirt roads, a tinkling brook that could turn into a raging river, and verdant acre upon acre set against the backdrop of the distant mountains, Rokeby Farm was breathtakingly beautiful. Paul and Bunny loved to walk the land. In the beginning, Paul simply enjoyed showing Bunny around, but these walks would become an integral part of their relationship.

Bunny had always paid great attention to her surroundings, to the trees and grass and sky. But she fell completely under the spell of Rokeby Farm. She loved the land in primordial fashion, seeing it as an endless source of wonder. She relished watching the seasons change, she liked to make daily visits to the trees and plants to see the buds unfolding, and she appreciated the noisy country sounds. Butterflies entranced her; she could watch them for hours. She often took a sketchpad with her on walks, a habit that her young daughter, Eliza, an aspiring artist, emulated.

Paul admired Bunny's single-minded devotion to the outdoors. "She had a garden when she was 5," he later told the *Washington Post*. "That led her into all kinds of other things—to trees, to landscape gardening. Everything she does in life—her reading, her architecture, her love of pictures—is related in one way or another to this main interest. To me, that is a very lucky thing for a person to have."

Bunny would never tire of Rokeby Farm. In letters to friends and family members, she described the day's sights and sounds with such comments as, "There are meadow larks singing in their flute-like voices" or "The apple trees are ringed with pink and yellow apples that the deer come feed on in late evening."

But she also looked at nature and its beautiful imperfections with a critical eye, envisioning ways to improve the vistas. Yes, that tree was magnificent, but wouldn't it be even more beautiful if the limbs were pruned to form a rounded shape? How about altering the view by thinning out a wooded area? Wouldn't it be fun to constantly change the flower beds and play with shapes and colors? Tulips and lilies of the valley in the spring could be replaced with towering sunflowers and delicate cosmos.

With Paul Mellon's vast property, encompassing nearly five thousand acres, she could experiment. The farm would become her canvas, where she could create an artistic landscape, a visual feast.

Paul and Bunny had been friends for a decade, but there were things they did not know about each other, personality traits and independent interests that would cause strains in the years ahead. He was punctual to the minute; she was usually late, annoyingly so. "Mother would run all over the farm with her pruning shears, her little jacket, her blue hat," recalls her son, Tuffy Lloyd. "Paul would say, 'Lunch has been announced, Bunny.' She'd say, 'Have another martini, I'll be right there.'"

Paul was an Anglophile—he loved British art and hunting and fishing in the English countryside—while she was a Francophile, enamored of Paris fashion, chic cafés, and historic gardens.

She was the ideal wife to preside over Paul's home—a stylish perfectionist with a flair for entertaining, a woman who knew how to hire, train, and supervise a staff, and who was constantly concerned with her husband's creature comforts. Paul was demanding with an idealized view of what was involved in a smoothly running household. He could be critical; Bunny bristled at his sarcastic comments.

Bunny was well-read and well versed in the art of making small talk. But she preferred small gatherings to large events and had mixed feelings about the public appearances required of her as Mrs. Paul Mellon, viewing them as a necessary chore.

Horse-mad as a teenager, Bunny had galloped through her first marriage but had lost her enthusiasm for the sport. After a bad fall, she had gotten back up on a horse to prove that she could, but riding was no longer a pleasure. The equestrian life was Paul Mellon's passion, and his schedule was built around riding, foxhunting, breeding horses, and traveling the world to watch his animals tear around the track winning trophies.

Bunny still liked the rituals. If a hunt started at their property, she would greet the riders and entertain them with refreshments either before or afterward. She loved the bracing sound of the horn. Early on in the marriage, she often joined Paul at equestrian events, but as time passed she came up with excuses and her husband chose not to press the issue, spending time instead with friends who shared his enthusiasm.

Merging two families in the wake of a death and a divorce was inevitably tricky. Mary Mellon had been dead for only nineteen months when Paul Mellon remarried, and the Mellon children were still in mourning, unwilling to readily accept a new stepmother.

Bunny and Paul were both children of divorce who had been brought up by servants, and neither had a template for creating a happy household. They were not, by either nature or ingrained experience, nurturing and involved parents. They tried to do what they thought was right but the children had grievances, which they would later recount to their own spouses.

"Tim greatly missed his mother," says Louise Whitney Mellon, an Upperville native who grew up with the Mellon children and later became Tim's second wife. "From Tim's residual feelings and memories, his mother really truly cared about him and was more hands-on. He was four when his mother died and to have another woman step in, who didn't have those feelings toward him and Cathy, I think that was a really unfortunate turning point for him."

Cathy Mellon told similar tales to her first husband, Virginia lawyer John Warner, who would later be elected to the Senate. Warner told me, "Either intentionally or unintentionally—I always give her the benefit of the doubt—Bunny showered Eliza and Tuffy with more attention than she did Catherine and Tim." When Bunny did try to advise or discipline her stepdaughter, Cathy resented it. Virginia Warner, the daughter of Cathy Mellon and John Warner, says, "Bun tried to be a stepmother but my mother wouldn't have it. The two of them were like oil and water. Mummy was untamable."

Bunny did not feel comfortable in the role of stepmother. "My greatest regret is that their mother didn't bring them up," she later admitted to Burton Hersh. "You're so much more strict with your own, you can't be strict with your stepchildren. A lot of things I would have liked to have seen done, Paul couldn't cope with."

When Bunny moved her own children into Paul's house in Upperville, her eleven-year-old son was caught off guard. "I was told by mother that she was going to get a divorce, but I never understood what in the world that meant to me," recalls Tuffy Lloyd. "I never in a million years thought I'd be going to visit the Mellons for more than a week or two at most. It really surprised me when I was helicoptered out of this world, the only world I knew, and was resettled in this place called Upperville." Apple Hill, his childhood home, would forever represent paradise lost.

"What it did to me psychologically—I don't trust my mother. I don't. She can send me one place one day, and then another day, somewhere else," he adds. "I didn't trust Paul. I didn't know him from Adam. I didn't even know that they were going to be married. It was a big shock, changed my outlook on my family."

Tim Mellon recounted in his memoir that the four children bonded over a dinnertime game that irritated Bunny. She had placed an expensive china cabbage on the table as the centerpiece. The children would hand platters of food to one another directly over it, risking disaster and eliciting a shriek from Bunny: "Don't pass that over the cabbage, it's a priceless antique." Tim added, "Of course, we learned to feint just such an action just to be treated with the response."

Bunny and Paul seemed to channel their unconditional affection toward their dogs. He liked terriers, she liked beagles, and their household, for decades, always included his-and-hers four-legged friends.

The parents were often out of town, leaving the children to be cared for by the household staff. The couple traveled in style on Paul's DC-3 private plane, which included sleeping berths and was decorated with French paintings of balloons and early aircraft, and the palette of his racing colors, gold and gray. Bunny, a nervous flier due to her family's mishaps in the air, was relieved that Paul had his own pilots as well as mechanics to ensure the craft was well maintained. She quickly came to take the convenience of the plane for granted. Neighbors and friends would marvel that she'd dispatch the craft to pick up an errant scarf.

The couple frequently spent time in Manhattan, where Paul owned a town house on the Upper East Side, at 125 East Seventieth Street. He indulged his new bride with trips to Paris and eventually rented a penthouse in the Hotel de Crillon for their use. On these jaunts, they began to build an art collection. "Shortly after we married in 1948, Bunny and I started visiting art dealers in New York and Paris," Paul wrote in his autobiography. "Bunny had always been interested in French history and in French nineteenth century paintings, partly inspired by her lifetime love of gardens and landscape gardens."

Andrew Mellon had never asked his children whether they were emotionally attached to any pieces in his art collection, donating the masterpieces to the National Gallery. Paul received only one painting from his father, a John Singer Sargent portrait of Miss Beatrice Townsend, painted in 1882. This was a sentimental gesture, since the pretty young girl, clad in a black dress adorned with a white lace collar and a red sash, clutched a terrier, Paul's favorite breed. He kept the Sargent in his Manhattan town house.

Paul purchased his first painting in 1936—British artist George Stubbs's depiction of a famous racehorse, *Pumpkin with a Stable-lad.*

His first wife, Mary Mellon, favored the folk-art simplicity of Grandma Moses. But only after Paul's marriage to Bunny did he become the darling of auctioneers and art dealers on both sides of the Atlantic.

National Gallery trustee Chester Dale, an ardent collector of Impressionist paintings, urged Paul to follow his lead. But it was Bunny's enthusiasm for those artists that carried the day. Art historian John Walker, Paul's Pittsburgh childhood friend who eventually became the National Gallery's director, wrote in his autobiography, *Self-Portrait with Donors*, "Bunny Mellon was soon far more influential than Chester. She is a very remarkable woman, a brilliant horticulturist and landscape gardener, the equal of any professional, and also an amateur architect...At the beginning, the pictures the Mellons acquired were only for the decoration of their houses. Their taste is very personal."

In 1950, the couple purchased a Berthe Morisot painting, *Hanging the Laundry out to Dry*, a bucolic country scene that resembled Rokeby Farm. A Claude Monet seascape caught their eye a few years later; *Cliffs at Pourville* showed a red-bonneted woman picnicking on a cliff above a harbor. They liked beach scenes, picking up Winslow Homer's *Dad's Coming!* featuring a woman and children on a beach, staring anxiously out to sea.

Aware that prices were likely to rise the moment an art dealer recognized that Paul Mellon was the client, Bunny liked to quietly materialize at galleries and gaze at her leisure, reporting back to Paul, who valued her judgment. "Usually Bunny and I have gone to look at pictures together, especially in New York," he wrote in his autobiography. "If, on the other hand, Bunny happened to be on her own in Paris and saw something she thought we should add to the collection, she had only to call me, and I invariably told her to go ahead."

An art dealer confided to the *New York Times*, "He never dickers. If he doesn't like the price, he won't say anything: he just won't buy." After all, a gentleman knows what things are worth, doesn't like to be taken advantage of, and never haggles.

Themes began to emerge in their collection. Paul was drawn to horses, as painted by Edgar Degas and Henri de Toulouse-Lautrec. Predictably, Bunny fell for art that showcased flowers, fruit, and outdoor nature scenes. In 1955, the couple purchased two spectacular Vincent van Gogh landscapes: *Flower Beds in Holland*, painted in 1883, featuring gorgeous blocks of red, yellow, blue, and white flowers; and *Green Wheat Fields, Auvers*, a mesmerizing artwork with undulating fields of green.

The Mellons eventually propped that painting on the mantel above their Virginia living room fireplace, where they lit toasty fires. Visitors would do a double take. But Bunny and Paul wanted to live with their art rather than worry about creating a climate-controlled sterile environment. Generations of their employees—gardeners, painters, handymen—would be called upon to move and hang the art, since Paul and Bunny did not think it was necessary to bring in professionals.

The paintings just kept coming. Bunny could not resist a Renoir featuring sprightly flowers in a vase, a Cézanne of three shapely green pears, a sumptuous Bonnard of purple plums in a straw basket, a Manet of a humble melon perched on an artist's wooden table spattered with paint, an early Picasso of a woman sitting in a lush garden, painted in 1901 when the prodigy was only twenty years old. She liked artwork that was sensual without being explicitly sexy. These paintings spoke to her, and thanks to Paul's inheritance, she did not have to pick out just one—she could have as many as she wanted.

Indeed, if the Mellons admired an artist's vision, they sought out multiple works, eventually acquiring thirty paintings by landscape painter Eugene Boudin. In 1955, the couple wandered into the Knoedler Gallery in Manhattan and saw on display seventy small wax sculptures by Degas of dancers and horses, made with beeswax, wood, rope, bits of tutu, and even human hair. There was a nude young dancer and a horse rearing into the air, ready to leap off the stand. "The collection haunted me for days," Paul Mellon later recalled. He bought all of them.

Drawn to paintings that told a personal story, the couple acquired Renoir's portrait of his son and a friend playing with toys; Paul Cézanne's sketch of his wife; self-portraits by Gauguin, Degas, and Matisse; a Monet called *The Cradle* of the artist's son; and Pierre Bonnard's evocative *The Artist's Studio*, showing an easel and a window with a view of a city, framed with blowing white curtains. These choices reflected a yearning for a deeper connection with the artists: It was as if the Mellons were inviting the artists' families to live in their home.

John Walker, the National Gallery director, was amused by the Mellons' idiosyncrasies. "Windmills, they can't abide and they are prejudiced against cows," he wrote in his autobiography. Walker believed that Paul and Bunny were drawn to paintings that evoked happy memories: "The Mellons...have the largest collection of beach scenes by Boudin I have seen anywhere. Sand, sea, sky, as he painted them, aren't these the elements of their childhood experiences...Or Degas horses and their jockeys pirouetting like ballerinas, how magically they evoke the excitement of the racetrack!"

Not every painting needed an aged patina; the couple appreciated contemporary work as well. Paul commissioned a portrait of Bunny by Charles Baskerville; Bunny loved the inexpensive folk art of Madeline Hewes, buying many of her paintings of fruit, flowers, and rural life. The couple hung their masterpieces side by side with humbler works, creating eye-pleasing juxtapositions.

They did not always agree on what they liked. Paul would later become absorbed with collecting British eighteenth-century art while Bunny favored contemporary American work. Although they did not buy with appreciation in mind, the value of their choices soared.

They enjoyed the hunt, the excitement of winning at auction, the pleasure of possession, being able to look at these works over morning coffee and late-afternoon drinks, watching the light change. Art was beauty; art was familiar; art was comfort; art was inspiration. The paintings on their walls served as the backdrop to the intimate moments of family life.

Bunny hired governesses to keep an eye on the four children. Rather than returning her son to the Rectory boarding school, Bunny enrolled him with Tim and Eliza at the Hill School, described by the *Washington Post* as the place "where sons and daughters of the MFH's

[Master of the Fox Hounds] and international polo players get elementary training before going on to Groton, St. Paul's, Foxcroft and so forth." (Cathy and Eliza both subsequently attended Bunny's alma mater, Foxcroft.)

At the Hill School, Bunny's son put on a good front about his changed circumstances. "I was Stacy Lloyd's best friend at the Hill School, we called him Tuffy in those days," recalls John Loring, who would grow up to become the design director at Tiffany's. "Tuffy was good-natured, outgoing, big smile, always in a good mood, never complained about anything. Mrs. Mellon would sometimes pick us up in her station wagon and drive us over to Winchester to go to the movie theatre to see a Buck Rogers film, we found them mesmerizing. Mrs. Mellon was terribly nice, down to earth."

Bunny's sophisticated taste received kudos when she arranged the items donated for the Hill School auction. The *Washington Star* wrote, "Mrs. Paul Mellon stayed until after lunch, it was her strategic placing of articles that turned the stage into an auction-goer's dream."

Bunny's daughter, Eliza, fared the best under the new regime, forging a loving relationship with her stepfather, whom she called "Da." Paul Mellon doted on the impish little girl and encouraged her to ride with him. He tried to build a relationship with Bunny's son by taking him on a fishing trip in 1951 to the rustic Camp Harmony Angling Club, located on the Restigouche River in New Brunswick. Bunny went to Cape Cod with Eliza.

Paul wrote to Bunny: "I love you and miss you and feel a thousand miles away, which indeed I am. It is impossible to phone...we are on the river most of the time...Tuffy is fine although we are both quite discouraged about the fishing...his spirits are good and he is being a very good sport." He thanked her for suggesting that they bring warm clothes, described the beauty of the river, and told her that he was taking lots of photographs to show her.

In his letter, Paul came across as unguarded and content. He was trying hard not to emulate his cold and distant father. He stressed his love for Bunny three times and apologized profusely for being apart from her on her upcoming birthday, August 9.

Paul remained interested in psychotherapy, and during a trip with Bunny to Europe, he reunited with Carl Jung. The eminent therapist's secretary, Marie-Jeanne Boller-Schmidt, in an interview for Jung's Archive, recalled that Jung could be "gruff" but made a real effort toward Bunny. "I shall never forget when Paul Mellon brought his second wife, Rachel Lambert, to introduce her to Jung...I suppose she is still called Bunny, and she was a very nice person. But to see C.G. [Carl Gustav] trying to charm her and succeeding very well was really a sight and quite amazing."

Bunny recalled going for a walk in the country with Jung and others. "He dropped back and said, 'You're the wise one. Keep picking flowers.' And he picked them with me."

———

Ten months after Bunny married Paul, Stacy Lloyd tied the knot with twenty-year-old Alice Woodward Babcock, a young woman from Woodbury, Long Island, who had graduated from the Brearley School in Manhattan in 1945 and studied at Bryn Mawr. Her father, Richard, was a Harvard graduate and Wall Street broker; her mother, Elizabeth, was an equestrian and artist who chronicled hunting events. According to family lore, Stacy and Alice met at the Madison Square Garden horse show in November 1947; he was a judge while she was competing in show jumping. Alice was described as an "accomplished horsewoman" in the *New York Times* December wedding announcement.

Stacy was starting fresh with a good-looking woman half his age. A photograph shows the newlyweds holding hands as they leave the church, with Stacy grinning while the slender, dark-haired Alice, in her white satin dress and heirloom lace veil, gazes down demurely. The reception was held at her family's thirty-four-acre Long Island estate, a Georgian Revival home built by architects William Delano and Chester Aldrich.

The couple returned to Apple Hill in Virginia to begin married life. Stacy had appeared regularly in local society columns during the previous decade, but now he and Alice faded from sight. The spotlight continued to shine brightly on Paul and Bunny.

Bunny disliked Paul Mellon's noisy Brick House, with its large echoing public rooms for entertaining. She thought the house was pretentious and poorly designed for a family of six. "Bunny told me that when she got married, no one could believe that she didn't want to live in the Brick House," recalls Bryan Huffman. Bunny was rebelling against what she perceived as a stuffy traditional style in favor of a modern and understated aesthetic.

Paul had acquired so many farms adjacent to his original land that his property now included twenty-four houses in various states of repair. An old nineteenth-century farmhouse known as Little Oak Spring struck Bunny's fancy. She hired workmen to renovate and enlarge the house. She sought decorating advice from the renowned British decorator Syrie Maugham, the ex-wife of the novelist Somerset Maugham; Bunny was the godmother to their daughter, Liza. Soon the Mellon-Lloyd clan moved down the road.

Inspired by the childhood memory of the fruit trees at Albemarle, she instructed the gardeners to plant apple and pear trees. She had more ambitious plans for a year-round growing season: vast flower beds and greenhouses. Once the greenhouses were operational, she began to enter her flowers in gardening contests. Her cyclamen won a first prize at the New York Garden Show.

Paul started a beef herd, which would eventually include 127 cows. His racing stable kept expanding: By 1954, he owned thirty-two horses, with such speedy winning mounts as County Delight, Benbow, and a gray gelding, Genancoke. Paul eventually bought his own racetrack in nearby Middleburg, fixing up the property and turning it into a training track for his horses and making it available to his horse-breeding neighbors.

Running a large estate in the middle of the Virginia countryside required a full-time staff of horse trainers, groomsmen, carpenters, machinists, painters, farmers, and gardeners, as well as a household of maids, housekeepers, laundresses, butlers, valets, and chauffeurs. The Mellons' payroll would grow to more than two hundred employees.

"We had what was like our own plantation in Upperville," recalls Tuffy Lloyd. "We had our own carpenters making furniture and tables.

I remember complaining to Eliza, 'I feel awful, I don't feel like I belong anywhere, there's the family and the world out there.' She said, 'Well, you might well ask, we're only one half of one percent of the rest of the country.'" This was a fiefdom with lifetime employment for the help—assuming they lived up to the Mellons' high standards—and jobs later on for their children. The Mellons were generous, providing health insurance and retirement benefits.

Paul gave Bunny leeway in running the family's domestic life. Bunny was uninterested in his Hobe Sound estate, Capricorn, where Paul had spent winters with Mary and the children. So he put it on the market for $150,000 and sold it in 1950. Bunny did not want to live with her predecessor's possessions. Parke-Bernet Galleries in New York advertised an auction in May 1950 of items belonging to Paul Mellon, including English and American furniture, Georgian silver, porcelain, and Oriental rugs. For Bunny, it was natural to want to put her imprint on her surroundings. But by doing so, she was erasing Cathy's and Tim's childhoods.

As much as Paul Mellon enjoyed whiling away the hours at racetracks and art galleries, he had a strong sense of civic responsibility. With hundreds of millions of dollars at his disposal, Paul Mellon began to embrace the pleasures and responsibilities of giving away Andrew Mellon's money.

He knew that he could make others happy with the flick of a pen. Faced with so many worthy causes and entreaties, Paul initially put money into areas that were personally relevant. The psychic damage inflicted by his battling parents had made Paul sympathetic to troubled adolescents, and he was grateful for the healing effects of psychotherapy. In 1949 he gave $2 million each to Yale and to Vassar, Mary Mellon's alma mater, to improve their psychiatric and counseling services.

He sought ways to support innovative scholarship. Paul, a former *Yale Daily News* editor, later explained to *Boston Globe* reporter Thomas Winship, "I guess my interest in education began at Choate and carried over to college. You know these college newspaper editors; we always want to change things and campaign for something different. When I got out of college and the question of giving money arose, my thoughts turned to education."

He gave $4.5 million to Stringfellow Barr, the president of St. John's College, where Paul had studied, to help launch a new independent university; $800,000 to fund Trinity College's new library to preserve rare books; $300,000 to St. John's for general expenses; $3,000 to the local Clarke County high school for books; and $5 million to Yale to restore Constitution Hall. He also joined the board of the Ford Foundation's new education initiative.

Once he had dreamed of being a book publisher; now Paul sought to encourage literary endeavors. His Bollingen Foundation, underwritten with $20 million, not only published books but gave out prestigious poetry awards. The independent foundation embraced controversy, giving the 1949 prize to Ezra Pound, who, despite his literary reputation, had been indicted for treason for his pro-Mussolini propaganda broadcasts during World War II and was in a mental hospital.

Paul and his sister, Ailsa, who had grown up vacationing in the unspoiled playgrounds of the rich, had a mutual interest in conservation and historic preservation. "I heard from friends in the National Park Service that there had been a move to buy up a lot of Cape Hatteras for a national park, but it had bogged down and there was a road planned that would have brought hot dog stands and that sort of thing," Paul told the *Wall Street Journal*. "We got interested, flew over it, and made up our minds in a few months." In 1952, he and Ailsa donated $618,000 to save North Carolina's Outer Banks from development, turning the land into the Cape Hatteras National Seashore.

As word spread about his generosity, Paul was assiduously courted as a man who could make wishes come true. That power flowed to Bunny, too, with the presumption that she had her husband's ear. She occasionally wrote her own checks, giving money to Foxcroft and to the *New York Herald Tribune*'s Fresh Air Fund to allow inner-city children to attend camp. Like Paul, she, too, was a committed environmentalist. In the years ahead, the couple would give millions to the National Park Service, the Audubon Society, the Wildlife Fund, and the Nature Conservancy.

The Mellons were much in demand, and the invitations piled up. It was a coup when they agreed to appear at such events as a charity ball on George Washington's birthday to raise money for the Mount Vernon Citizens Association. Bunny soon needed to hire a social secretary.

Although neither Paul nor Bunny was especially devout, they were Episcopalians who believed in being involved in their community. In 1949, Bunny joined the Mary Neville Guild of Upperville's Trinity Episcopal Church, working on a fashion show to raise money for the congregation.

But the church, built in 1895, required more than the proceeds from a charity lunch to fix the substantial deterioration. "It was badly in need of repairs," Bunny later wrote in an autobiographical essay. "It did not have a proper foundation and was infested with termites." Paul had been thinking of memorializing his first wife by installing stained glass windows at the church, but he now agreed to fund a bolder plan: building an entirely new church.

The couple brought in architect H. Page Cross, a Yale graduate whom Bunny had known during her debutante years. At Bunny's behest, he designed a Medieval Norman French church. "I have been greatly influenced by the simple stone churches of France and Sweden," Bunny wrote in reminiscence. "Although the churches were small, they were landmarks in rural communities surrounded by wheat fields, flax and forests. They were used daily as havens of rest and peace for all who lived nearby."

She wanted to create a similar ambience, as well as add a new Parish Hall for church suppers and community activities, plus a walled garden for quiet contemplation. Land was set aside for a small private graveyard for the Mellon family. Work on the $2.5 million project began in 1951 but took nine years to complete, largely because Bunny

was determined to find the best materials and most talented craftsmen.

The exquisite stained glass windows were made in Holland from
glass fragments salvaged from European bombed churches and greenhouses. A window was dedicated to Mary Mellon. A storied British
firm cast the Westminster bells, and a medieval door was imported
from France. The blue stones for the walls were cut from boulders
in the nearby Blue Ridge Mountains; the roof trusses were made of
Douglas fir, which were dry-aired in a shed for three years. A master
woodworker carved Virginia native plants on the pews, including ivy,
dogwood, lupine, and thistle. Animals and birds and bees were carved
onto the stone columns.

Bunny's fingerprints were all over the design, including the church
landscaping. "Locust tree to be planted in fall to give more shade in
court—exact location selected by Mrs. Mellon," wrote one of her gardeners. "Take out stones next to wall along walk for vine planting and
for one bush."

When the church doors opened to the public, Bunny was lauded
for creating this unexpected gem in the countryside. "The present
Mrs. Mellon is responsible for much of the perfectionism in the
building," wrote the *New York Times*. The *Washington Star* had a
similar reaction: "It is all quite perfect, amazing to find in a sleepy
Southern village, and is the gift of Mr. and Mrs. Paul Mellon to the
Upperville Community."

This would be Bunny's lasting local legacy. She constantly tinkered
with the landscaping. She did not go to church services often, but she
liked to visit when the place was empty, to breathe in the ambience
and commune with God.

"I'm a different sort of Christian," Bunny informed a new church
rector, Robert Banse Jr., many years later. "I don't really come by to
pray. I come in to talk with God because he's a dear, dear friend of
mine."

Chapter Twelve

The Best-Dressed List

Bunny had always been fashionably attired, but the world had not noticed. But now that she was Mrs. Paul Mellon, the wife of an American plutocrat, her appearance was of interest to the arbiters of good taste. In 1949, the year after she married Paul, Bunny made the best-dressed list for the first time, knocking off her sister-in-law, Ailsa Mellon Bruce. In the results of the annual poll of American fashion designers, Bunny was listed as residing in Pittsburgh, the home base of the Mellon fortune, where she rarely spent time. But the *Pittsburgh Press*, pleased by the local honor, put Bunny's picture on page one of the feature section.

For the women on the best-dressed list, no outfit was complete without the sparkle of a diamond bracelet or a necklace dripping with emeralds. Those who wanted something more exotic than the offerings of Tiffany's and Harry Winston patronized Fulco di Verdura. The Sicilian Duke had established his Manhattan store in 1939 with backing from Cole Porter and Vincent Astor. The Duchess of Windsor was a client, and Katharine Hepburn wore his jewelry in *The Philadelphia Story*.

His floral-themed pieces—a sapphire-and-emerald flower with a canary diamond center or a bouquet with cabochon sapphires and emeralds—sold for as much as $15,000. He created whimsical brooches from shells and pebbles, encrusted with precious stones. "What I get a kick out of is to buy a shell for five dollars, use half of it, and sell it for twenty-five hundred," Verdura told the *New Yorker*. The adventurous Duke collaborated with Salvador Dali to create surrealist jewelry.

Paul Mellon commissioned the jeweler to make customized fruit-and-vegetable-themed jewelry for Bunny. In 1950, Paul gave Bunny a delicate brooch of a gold espalier apple tree, adorned with twenty-six ruby apples and diamond leaves. Other Verdura gifts would include a pineapple-shaped pin; a rooster brooch made of gold, diamonds, pearls, and rubies; a gold-and-diamond box featuring oak leaves; and a spray of purple amethyst flowers with diamond centers and gold leaves.

For dinners at their homes in Manhattan and Virginia, the Mellons dazzled their guests with such table decorations as a luscious Verdura pomegranate with ruby and citrine seeds and a blue rock crystal rhinoceros. Paul was such a keen admirer that he became Fulco di Verdura's biggest customer.

As much as Bunny appreciated the inventive Verdura offerings, she became even more enamored of the intricate concoctions of Jean "Johnny" Schlumberger, a Frenchman who made jewelry in the shape of fantastical seashells, starfish, leaves, and stars. "His ornaments are too wonderful," wrote Diana Vreeland in *Harper's Bazaar*. "With Johnny, there's always perfect color. His blue is the azure of a harem sky, his yellow has the clarity of the sun, his pink is the color of a perfect rose, his green is the color of a fern unfurling...A Schlumberger lights up the whole room."

The jeweler's career had begun by serendipity after he purchased china flowers at the Paris Flea Market and mounted them on clips as gifts. After the grande dame of fashion, Madame Schiaparelli, commissioned him to make clips and elegant buttons for her customers, he incorporated precious stones. Schlumberger came to New York at the end of 1940 to design clothes for Chez Ninon, a boutique financed by Ailsa Mellon Bruce. Eager to strike out on his own, he opened a jewelry store. "I try to make everything look as if it were growing, uneven, random, organic, in motion," he told the *New York Times*, describing his design philosophy.

Bunny met Schlumberger when she began to shop in his store, but she did not pay attention to the jeweler until they ran into each other at the bedside of a mutual friend, British decorator Syrie Maugham, who was critically ill. After that sobering visit, Schlumberger took Bunny to lunch, beginning an enduring friendship.

Paul indulged Bunny's enthusiasm for Schlumberger as she began to collaborate with the jeweler on designs. Her Schlumberger treasures included a dancing starfish clip of rubies and diamonds, and two gold bracelets patterned with diamond butterflies and incorporating turquoise, sapphires, and amethysts. For a table decoration, Schlumberger crafted a golden sunflower with stems of diamonds and emerald-studded leaves. Bunny would eventually own more than 140 pieces of jewelry and table decorations made by Schlumberger, and she regularly gave his bracelets, necklaces, and cuff links to friends and family members as gifts. The jeweler wrote a grateful note to Paul Mellon, who was paying the bills, stating that "the confidence and faith you have put in me" had spurred his creativity.

A handsome man who shared his white clapboard Upper East Side home with a longtime male companion, Johnny Schlumberger invited Bunny to join him on a trip to Paris. Even though she had already made the best-dressed list, he thought she could do better. He wanted to introduce her to Cristóbal Balenciaga, the Spanish designer who had opened up a Paris couture salon in 1937. Fashion reporters described Balenciaga's creations as "subtle" but "sumptuous," "spectacular" and "colorful," and "comfortable" and "flattering."

"It was not until 1954 when I met J.S. [Johnny Schlumberger] and he could not tolerate my clothes and suggested we go to Paris and Balenciaga," Bunny later wrote in a reminiscence. Bunny took one look at Balenciaga's designs and decided she wanted him to create everything she wore, from her lingerie to her day dresses to her ball gowns. She even convinced Balenciaga to design her gardening clothes.

Yes, her gardening clothes. If Bunny had wanted to send a message to the world about her new wealth and social standing, this was a brilliant move. She would forever be known as the woman who wore couture while weeding her flower beds.

To get to know his new free-spending client, Balenciaga invited Bunny and Johnny for a weekend at his country house in Orleans. The son of a Spanish fisherman, Balenciaga had apprenticed himself at the age of twelve to a tailor and opened his first salon six years later in San Sebastian. Bunny was impressed by the self-made Balenciaga's background and his exquisite taste, describing his garden as "a wonderful mixture of roses and wildflowers." In a reminiscence, she wrote, "Johnny and I left for Paris that afternoon but I was aware of a new and charming friendship. That summer I went to visit him [Balenciaga] in Spain at his house by the sea...Our friendship lasted for many years."

The young woman who had once traded a garden design for a Hattie Carnegie dress was now a trendsetter. *Women's Wear Daily* mentioned her frequently with such descriptions as: "Mrs. Paul (Bunny) Mellon at the St. Regis was wearing one of Jean Schlumberger's lovely pearl and diamond flowers pinned to her brown and white Balenciaga suit."

Bunny was developing a New York life. She had her hair coiffed by Kenneth Battelle, the discreet and erudite hairdresser who dressed in pin-striped suits and white shirts and catered to the Social Register. Kenneth became a close friend. Babs Simpson, the legendary *Vogue* fashion editor, three years Bunny's junior, joined her social circle. "We all knew the same people," recalls the tart-tongued fashion insider. "She was very bright, she had that extraordinary eye, she had extraordinary curiosity, she wasn't superficial. I admired her in a serious way...She was charming looking but she wasn't a beauty. She had a good figure and good posture and she dressed well, she always looked attractive."

Simpson, who became Bunny's confidante, adds with a smile, "She would always get crushes on people who were talented. Talent attracted her tremendously." The magazine editor noticed that Bunny appeared oblivious to the fact that many of these talented men were gay. "I think very often, she didn't realize it. There was a certain naïveté there," Simpson says. "She was also a very romantic person. I don't think she really grasped what homosexuality was about, in terms of men and women. She enjoyed the companionship of homosexual men because their interests were often the same."

Many wealthy women of Bunny's era had discovered the advantages of spending time with accomplished gay men, who were happy to accompany them to the ballet, the opera, and other events that left their husbands cold. The husbands were not threatened by these relationships. Babe Paley and her friends, such as Marella Agnelli, Gloria Guinness, and Slim Keith, enjoyed the company of Truman Capote, and the writer took up Bunny, too.

Bunny surrounded herself with an ever-changing array of good-looking, charming, and talented gay men—designers, artisans, florists, and decorators—who were pleased to keep her company and enjoy her patronage. Johnny Schlumberger, one of her closest friends, sent Bunny frequent notes from his overseas travels, saying he thought of her often, signing off with "so much love my darling."

The nation's capital had long been perceived as a dowdy fashion wasteland, but one bright spot emerged in Georgetown: a dress shop run by Dorcas Hardin, mother of three and the wife of a respected physician, B. Lauriston Hardin. Dorcas was described as "one of the most attractive and beautiful women of the Capital's Younger Set" in a *Washington Star* society column. The Hardins were social acquaintances of Paul and Bunny. Lauriston's twin brother, Taylor Hardin, ran a horse-breeding farm near Rokeby Farm; the Hardins' daughter, Diana, attended Foxcroft with Cathy Mellon.

"Bunny and Dorcas were friends, very good friends," recalls Martha Bartlett, a Washington resident now in her nineties, whose husband was Pulitzer Prize–winning *Chattanooga Times* journalist Charles Bartlett. "Bunny gave Dorcas' daughter a beautiful coming out present, a gold bracelet."

The stylish and effervescent Dorcas began selling clothes from her Georgetown row house in the late 1940s and then opened a shop in the neighborhood. "She knows the ins and outs of the Washington social whirl and the type of clothes necessary to make a good appearance in it," gushed *Women's Wear Daily* in a May 9, 1955, feature. "She is fortunate in her appearance. A honey blonde, with clear skin, blue eyes and a slender figure, she wears clothes well."

Dorcas, who suffered from premature hearing loss and relied partially on lipreading, sold handmade French lingerie as well as cocktail dresses. She invited designers to give fashion shows and personally advised her customers on flattering styles. Her shop had become an informal clubhouse for Washington society.

Marion "Oatsie" Leiter Charles, one of the city's legendary grande dames, was a regular at Dorcas's store. "It was a meeting place for Georgetown," she recalls, sitting in her Newport, Rhode Island, carriage house, which once belonged to Edith Wharton. "If you didn't have plans for lunch, you just stopped by Dorcas's, everything worked out. She was a marvelous woman...Every man was in love with her. She had enormous charm, she was good-looking but she wasn't a beauty."

Mrs. Hugh Auchincloss shopped at the store with her two daughters, Jacqueline and Lee Bouvier, who would grow up to become Jackie Kennedy and Lee Radziwill. What Lee recalls is Dorcas's warmth and enthusiasm. "She was such an up[person], so cheerful," recalls Lee. "What were we going to buy—some little dress?—but she made you feel so welcome. I'm sure I got a few things there, I know my mother did." Bunny bought her clothing in Paris, but when she and Dorcas each gave large parties, they often included each other on the guest lists.

Stacy Lloyd and his new bride celebrated the arrival of a baby boy, Robin, on October 4, 1950. But their joy was short-lived. The polio epidemic was sweeping the country and Stacy's wife, Alice, contracted the terrifying disease. She was left crippled, unable to use her arms and vulnerable to periodic problems with her lungs. Stacy Lloyd received an outpouring of advice, including the suggestion that his wife might fare better in a warmer climate. They chose to move to St. Croix, in the Virgin Islands.

In October 1952, Stacy sold the *Chronicle of the Horse* to Russell Arundel, the master of the Warrenton foxhunt. The *Washington Star* noted that the newspaper, "under Stacy Lloyd's leadership, grew into the backbone of all thoroughbred reporting over the entire country."

In a parting editorial, Stacy wrote about the joy of small-town reporting: "Many men in newspaper work in great daily papers often have an ambition someday to own a country newspaper. In it lies an absorbing interest, the entire life of a community which passes in and out through its doors and the story of which rolls each week off its presses."

In St. Croix, he began an unlikely career as a dairy farmer. Stacy leased land, bought fifty milking cows, and sold the milk out of his jeep. He joined with other farmers on the island to create a collective, and he built a dairy plant to bottle the milk. Despite her disabilities, Alice handled the bookkeeping.

Stacy wrote to Bunny often to inquire about their two children and provide updates on his new life. "It is nice here and you would like this part of the coast," Stacy wrote. "The beach stretches along for miles and while there are a lot of little houses there is nothing pretentious. It is all quite simple and informal...Our house is as big as a minute but we are squashed in pretty well by now." He apologized for not writing more often, explaining that he had minimal privacy at home.

Stacy purchased a vintage 1934 clipper bow yacht, named the *Bounty*, and took Alice and Robin out sailing. "The Bounty was their sanctuary, a refuge from the unending demands of running a milk plant and a farm," wrote Robin Lloyd in a feature for *Classic Boat* magazine. "For my father, sailing the boat was a way to replenish his soul." With money tight, Stacy rented out the boat to bring in cash.

Alice's health remained precarious, and even a minor cold could turn into a major problem. "It is rather frightening as she cannot get her breath and she starts coughing, tears stream down her face and she just gasps for breath," Stacy wrote to Bunny. "She is completely over it now, Thank Goodness. I am thankful we are in a warm climate where the chances of another cold are slim."

By leaving Virginia, he had become an absentee father to the two children from his first marriage. Tuffy and Eliza visited their father in St. Croix during school breaks and summer vacations. The distance made Bunny look back on her first marriage with increasing affection and regret. She sent her ex-husband and his family Christmas gifts every year, such as a Madeline Hewes painting, sweaters and shirts for Stacy, new clothes for Alice, and toys for Robin.

As much as the peripatetic Gerard Lambert frequently insisted that he was happy to sail his boats and stay out of the public eye, he could not turn down another opportunity to shape history. In early 1952, he was roped in by the leaders of the committee to draft World War II hero Dwight Eisenhower as the Republican presidential nominee. Gerard and a friend paid for pollster Arch Crossley to survey voters in New Hampshire, the first primary state. Their poll accurately forecast that Ike, even without campaigning, would defeat conservative favorite Ohio senator Robert Taft.

Asked by the victorious Eisenhower forces to oversee polling for the fall presidential race, Gerard, who paid for the surveys himself, ran his operations from a suite above the Nassau Tavern in Princeton. Not only did his polls help guide Ike in his campaign travels, but they also helped save Richard Nixon's place as the vice presidential nominee on the Republican ticket.

In September 1952, Nixon, then a young California senator, was accused of operating a slush fund to pay for his political travels. Amid a chorus of demands that Ike drop "Tricky Dick" from the ticket, Gerard's polls found that voters were unmoved by the scandal.

As former Eisenhower chief of staff Sherman Adams recounted in his autobiography, *Firsthand Report*, "The Lambert reports...proved to be more reliable than any of several private polls being conducted at the time...The Lambert polls showed that less than 20 percent of the people interviewed saw anything wrong with the Nixon fund."

These surveys, combined with Nixon's successful televised Checkers Speech—he denied accepting gifts, other than his dog Checkers—

ensured that Eisenhower continued to support his embattled running mate.

Ike's victory spurred Gerard Lambert to move to Washington in 1953. "New in Washington and they are bound to add much to the social scene are the Jerry Lamberts of the Listerine fortune. They have not only rented one house for a year but have bought another," wrote Betty Beale in her column, Exclusively Yours, in the *Washington Star*. She described Grace Lambert as "petite and dainty; her husband attractive and good looking." The article mentioned that Jerry's daughter was married to Paul Mellon.

The Lamberts purchased a ten-bedroom, eleven-thousand-square-foot brick home at 3041 Whitehaven Street with a garden overlooking the lawn of the British Embassy. Gerard began writing his memoir, *All Out of Step*, to be published by Doubleday. He was rewarded for his campaign service with a lunch at the White House with President Eisenhower and presidential adviser Arthur Burns. Secretary of State John Foster Dulles, who had been Gerard's classmate at Princeton, invited the couple to a dinner for the Shah of Iran, Reza Pahlavi, and Empress Soraya.

But the allure of Washington faded quickly. Lambert found the city uncongenial, and he was struggling with marital problems. He and his second wife had always enjoyed drinking, but now they were reaching for the bottle too often. Grace would eventually enter rehabilitation facilities on several occasions to dry out.

Three years after Gerard Lambert came to Washington, the couple returned to Princeton. Although they had sold Albemarle a few years earlier, they had retained one hundred acres and built an English-style brick cottage called the Pink House. The couple moved into the Pink House, where Grace could resume breeding champion Labradors. Gerard's autobiography won praise from the *New York Times*, which described his "rambunctious career" and "successful buccaneering" and concluded: "If Gerard B. Lambert had never existed, it would probably be necessary for John O'Hara to invent him."

Bunny and Paul had admired Gerard's Washington home; Paul bought it from his father-in-law. The Whitehaven mansion would serve as a convenient home away from home for Paul for the next forty years, a place where he could spend the night when he was in the city for National Gallery business, or have privacy away from Bunny and the children. When another house on Whitehaven Street came up for sale, he bought that one, too, and used it as gallery space for his art collection.

For Bunny, the Whitehaven house served as a useful staging area when she was in the city and needed to change for evenings on the town. But she rarely spent nights there, preferring to be chauffeured back to her beloved Virginia.

Five years into their marriage, the frictions between Bunny and Paul had become increasingly evident. Paul's desires had been catered to all of his life, and he was used to the world revolving around him. In public life, he was gracious albeit reserved, never known to utter an unkind word, but at home, he could be acerbic and mercurial. "Paul had these kinds of changeable moods," says Bunny's son, Tuffy. "He could be happy then very upset, and he'd get moody and mad, he couldn't stand any criticism of something he liked."

Paul had his own complaints. He and Bunny did not always agree on what was best for their four children in their household. Taking for granted Paul's seemingly unlimited resources, she ran up enormous bills. Paul's advisers thought that Bunny's spending was out of control and tried to rein her in, a battle that would continue for decades.

And then there was the issue of another woman. Paul had been unfaithful to his first wife during the war. Tim Mellon came to believe that his father had rekindled his affair with his British paramour, Valerie Churchill Longman. As Tim wrote in his 2016 autobiography, he was only ten years old when he was sent to boarding school. "My father took me to look at Eaglebrook in Western Massachusetts and the Fenn School in Concord, outside Boston," Tim wrote. "He settled on Fenn. I suspect now that the reason was to provide himself cover so as to be able to visit Valerie Churchill when he came up from Virginia occasionally to take me out for the weekend...She moved to Boston after the war and lived in an apartment overlooking the Charles River basin."

Bunny turned to a surprising confidant to express her concerns about her troubled marriage—her ex-husband. It must have been ironic for Stacy to hear about his ex-wife's woes, since she had left him for Paul Mellon. Stacy urged caution, writing, "It is a much better idea not to do anything drastic as I believe you would be very lonely and perhaps regret it after you had made the move."

With the marriage at a breaking point in the mid-1950s, Bunny suggested that they separate. As her son later recalled, Bunny said, "Paul, look, if you don't want me around here, I'll take Eliza and Tuffy and we'll move away." She had called Paul's bluff; he wanted to work things out.

They both went into psychoanalysis. "Bunny and I had been married for about five years, and we both [history repeats itself] needed psychological help or at least support and counsel," Paul wrote in his autobiography. Paul underwent Freudian analysis with Dr. Jenny Waelder Hall, a native of Austria who had trained in Vienna with Sigmund Freud and his daughter, Anna. Bunny was referred to another Freudian analyst but became frustrated by the impersonal boundaries. As Paul put it, "It was a hopeless project from the beginning."

For her second session, Bunny brought a Christmas gift of flowers from her greenhouse to the therapist. "The psychiatrist refused to accept them but immediately began questioning her motives," Paul continued. "Well, if you knew Bunny, you would realize why this was the end of the session and the end of the treatment and I thoroughly sympathized. Bunny went elsewhere for counseling and eventually was helped greatly by one or two psychiatrists of a more human and understanding type."

The crisis passed, but the marriage continued to have its ups and downs. During troubled periods, it was easy for the couple to find excuses to be apart. Paul had business in Pittsburgh, New York, and Washington, and spent at least one month per year in England. He took frequent hunting and fishing trips. His horses were always racing somewhere around the country. Bunny could escape to the Hotel de Crillon in Paris or to Manhattan. Away from each other, Paul and Bunny wrote each other loving letters, professing devotion, keeping it light.

But the experience may have left Bunny feeling that she could now allow herself the freedom to look elsewhere for attention and affection. She had been close to Johnny Schlumberger for several years, but at some point their relationship became a romance.

When scenic painter Paul Leonard went to work for Bunny several years later, he quickly picked up on her involvement with the jewelry designer. "I soon discovered that he was her lover but theirs was a strange relationship," Leonard wrote in a reminiscence. "Johnny was French and not easily controlled. He was clever as a scheming child and very attractive—one felt that in his presence you were walking on the edge. He was dangerous and magnetic. His objects and jewelry of gold and enamel were encrusted with thorns and spikes: they seemed to say, 'I am beautiful but don't come near me!' Johnny was the perfect foil for Bunny but her ultimate control was money, and she would dole out commissions when the whim suited her."

Rumors spread about Bunny's relationship with Schlumberger. "I always thought it was just known, that it was not a secret that they had a romance," says Pierce MacGuire, a Tiffany executive who had the office next to the jeweler and would become director of the store's Schlumberger sales. "He had a male companion for life but he had other relationships."

Later in life, Bunny gave an expurgated account to her confidant Bryan Huffman. "She talked about making secret plans with Schlumberger, meeting at JFK Airport, and running off to Paris together," Huffman says. "I think she had emotional affairs but I don't think they were physical ones. She did say that she wasn't sitting home knitting while Paul had affairs."

Although Bunny had put tremendous effort into fixing up a house at Rokeby Farm as the family's main residence, she disliked the final result. She wanted to start over elsewhere on the property. She hired her childhood friend, architect H. Page Cross, to fulfill her vision. They decided to move part of the farmhouse to serve as the bones of the new house and expand around it.

Bunny liked the white stone that she had used at Apple Hill, and she worked with Cross to design a simple two-story home with a country-cottage feel. The house included a ground-floor office for Paul with Gothic-style built-in bookcases, a game room, a room for cutting and arranging flowers, a large kitchen for staff-cooked meals, and an intimate eat-in blue-tiled space for Sunday night family dinners.

Since Paul was an insomniac, often rising at 4 a.m. to read, the couple opted for separate bedrooms. On the second floor, Bunny and Paul had back-to-back rooms and private bathrooms. Bunny's large and airy bedroom was decorated with a four-poster bed and a blue cushioned window seat where she could gaze out at a meadow. A corridor off her room led directly to Eliza's bedroom. Paul's small bedroom with its built-in bookcase was designed as a monastic and shipshape space for a man who liked simplicity and order.

Per Bunny's instructions, the wood floors were painted in geometric patterns, Scandinavian style, and then sanded so the workmanship would not look new. She chose subdued shades of paint for the walls and instructed the craftsmen to distress finishings. She stockpiled bolts of the fabric used to upholster furniture, in case she needed to redo her favorites in the future.

Bunny loved the country air so much that she declined to install air-conditioning, a decision that would dismay guests during periods of humid hundred-degree Virginia heat. She designed a terraced walled garden behind the house, with flower beds shaped like butterflies. Paul's office faced directly on the garden, and in good weather he could often see Bunny planting and weeding alongside the gardeners. She set aside an area in the garden where the family could play croquet. She would later add a large room dedicated solely to storing her collection of garden baskets, furnished with a "lit à la polonaise" metal daybed. Near the main house, carpenters built a miniature theatre, complete with a ticket booth, where Eliza and her friends could perform plays.

The family moved into the new house, dubbed Oak Spring, in

1955. Bunny's son was then attending the Middlesex School in Massachusetts. Tuffy was stunned to see his new quarters at home. In designing the house, Bunny did not create a room for her son, putting him instead on the second floor of an adjoining building. Perhaps she thought a teenage boy might relish the ability to come and go at will, but he felt exiled. "I was put on the top floor of the chauffeur's garage, I could hear the chauffeur sloshing around underneath," Tuffy recalls. "Eliza and Cathy and Tim had rooms in the house. I felt left out."

The modern stone structure was considered unusual in an area renowned for grand country estates and for a man of Paul Mellon's stature. Rather than an ostentatious or showy statement, the house seemed designed with a reverse-snobbery aesthetic. Bunny's neighbors looked askance, but this home would later be celebrated as a triumphant display of Bunny's muted taste.

Paul was happy with the new residence. After growing up within a dark, depressing home in Pittsburgh and roaming the cavernous Brick House, he was pleased that Bunny had brought sunlight and ease to his daily life. Paul trusted her eye enough to give her carte blanche, from now on, in planning far-flung vacation homes.

"Bunny's quest for comfort and informality has been nurtured with care; a little natural shabbiness in an old chair cover is sometimes purposely overlooked," Paul wrote in his autobiography. "The result, I think is that the houses feel lived in and loved. More important to me than anything else, they feel cheerful."

The walls were covered with museum-quality masterpieces, but the children took the art for granted. Paul loved telling a story about an afternoon when Eliza brought her classmates home. One of the girls looked around and asked, "Who paints?" Eliza replied, "No one here. Da buys them in the store."

The empty Brick House was turned into a storage area for paintings as well as the couple's growing collection of rare books and manuscripts. Paul collected first editions, including hand-painted manuscripts by the British poet and artist William Blake. Aware of Bunny's love for childhood classics, Paul bought her a set of mint-condition first editions from the estate of the distinguished British illustrator

Arthur Rackham, who drew watercolors for J. M. Barrie's *Peter Pan in Kensington Gardens, Fairy Tales of the Brothers Grimm,* and Hans Christian Andersen's story *The Emperor's New Clothes.*

With encouragement and funds from her husband, Bunny began to acquire antiquarian botanical and nature-themed volumes, with hand-painted illustrations that qualified as works of art on their own. Religious artwork with floral illustrations caught her fancy: She purchased several versions of the Book of Hours, including a 1486 volume by Parisian miniaturist and calligrapher Antoine Vérard. She bought items of historical relevance, including a letter by Thomas Jefferson about his garden.

Other prized acquisitions included Maria Sibylla Merian's 1789 illustrations, with notes written in German, about the transformation of caterpillars into butterflies; and British botanist James Bateman's 1837 dainty and colorful lithographs of orchids.

The flowers bloomed on the pages of Bunny's books: lush, erotic, symbolic, and mysterious, capturing her imagination.

The spring and summer of 1955 tested Bunny's organizational skills as she juggled multiple trips plus entertaining responsibilities. In March, she and Paul welcomed the Piedmont Point-to-Point races to Rokeby Farm with a lunch for Treasury Secretary George Humphrey, followed by an evening party for hundreds of horse owners, trainers, and riders. Paul and the Treasury secretary were both on the board of the National Gallery of Art, along with Secretary of State John Foster Dulles and Supreme Court Justice Earl Warren.

In May, Bunny flew to England to celebrate the twenty-first birthday of her wartime ward, David Brooke, at his family's estate, Warwick Castle. "Bunny and David's mother were in tears most of the time," wrote her proud father, Gerard Lambert. "There was a dinner where Bunny sat on the present Earl's left, with Princess Margaret on his right. The castle was illuminated with floodlights and after dinner all the tenants and townspeople gathered in the courtyard and cheered...David took Bunny into an enormous room and rehearsed his speech to her just like a little boy, then he went out and spoke to the people in the court."

Upon returning to Virginia, she finalized plans for her stepdaughter Cathy's debutante party at the Brick House. The pretty blonde Cathy Mellon was now attending Mount Vernon Junior College. Rather than pose for a studio portrait, Cathy was photographed perched on an old wooden fence on the farm, wearing a strapless long white dress with a bouffant skirt, the personification of country elegance.

Bunny finally had the chance to realize her fantasies about becoming a set designer as she transformed the farm for Cathy's party. The horses were moved out of the broodmare barn so the space could become a food fair, with box stalls offering seafood, hamburgers, petits fours, and bacon and eggs. A large dance floor was installed inside a tent on the lawn. A Philadelphia caterer handled the food, and an orchestra came from Florida to play at the all-night event. Early Sunday morning, firecrackers were launched, "which sounded like any number of battles of Manassas," the *Washington Star* wrote.

This was not simply a dance for Cathy and her friends; it was a coming-out party for the host and hostess. Paul's Washington connections were triumphantly on display. The guests included Treasury Secretary Humphrey, Air Force Secretary Harold Talbott, Secretary of Defense Charlie Wilson, Mrs. John Foster Dulles, White House chief of staff Sherman Adams, Army General John Hull, South Carolina senator Strom Thurmond, Missouri congressman Bill Hull, Virginia senator Willis Robertson, Postmaster General Arthur Summerfield, and the Dutch and Finnish ambassadors. Foxcroft headmistress Charlotte Noland witnessed firsthand the transformation of her shy pupil into a hostess extraordinaire.

Cathy Mellon was formally introduced to society that evening but soon began dating a man who was not at her party—John Warner, a Korean War and World War II veteran. Ten years older than Cathy, he had graduated from the University of Virginia Law School and was now an assistant U.S. attorney. The couple met at a dance at the Chevy Chase Club.

"A lot of hostesses in town in the old days had lists of young men who would come to a party well-dressed, didn't drink too much or cause a problem," Warner recalls. "I was fortunate enough to be in that group." He couldn't afford a new tuxedo on his government salary. "Some of the guys said, 'Don't go to Brooks [Brothers] and buy all that stuff. When all the rich guys die, they give their clothes to this church.' So I went there and bought a beautiful tuxedo." He was courting the trust-fund daughter of a multimillionaire in secondhand clothes.

Paul and Bunny made him feel welcome at their first meeting on the farm. As he recalls, "Bunny took me by the hand and said, 'Hopefully, you'll become one of the family, make yourself at home.'" Early on, she explained her eccentric décor.

"There was one chair and you could see it was badly worn, slightly tattered. Bunny saw me eyeing the chair and she said, 'John, that chair is an old one. It's not a rare antique; it's from this century. It clearly has material that ordinarily would be changed.'" But she added, "Some people come to visit us and are ill at ease and a bit overwhelmed. If they see that chair, and it's kind of comfortable and reminds them of chairs in their own homes, it puts them at ease."

Paul Mellon appreciated the convenience of owning a DC-3 private plane, but he was annoyed by the time it took to get to a commercial airport. The drive from his Upperville farm to National Airport in Washington, D.C., took nearly ninety minutes. He sought to install a private airstrip at his Middleburg Race Track, just eight miles from his home. But the neighbors were concerned about noise and rallied to block it, signing a petition that convinced the Loudon County zoning board to turn him down.

Undeterred, Paul wangled a permit instead to put in the airstrip on his Upperville farm, even though doing so required tearing up acreage that he had used to host the Piedmont races. Once the strip was operational, he and Bunny could leave for a trip with just five minutes' notice. One of their favorite destinations was Cape Cod, where they often rented summer cottages.

Bunny had grown up visiting her grandparents on the Cape and her widowed mother still owned a house in the quaint town of Osterville, near Hyannis. Ready to build a home of their own, Paul purchased more than twenty-six waterfront acres in the wealthy enclave of Oyster Harbors, a private island connected by a small bridge to the mainland, considered part of Osterville.

Working again with architect H. Page Cross, Bunny created a sprawling seven-thousand-square-foot house on a bluff overlooking the water. Made of concrete to withstand the salt air and storms, the U-shaped structure was covered in wood shingles, which were painted to look weathered. The spacious living room and dining room faced the ocean. Once again, Bunny and Paul had adjoining second-floor bedrooms.

Bunny's decorating choices reminded her son of his maternal grandmother, Rachel Lowe Lambert Clopton. "For someone who could not stand her mother, her bedrooms in both Virginia and Cape Cod were a lot like her mother's—a chintz ottoman chair, same kind of sheets, curtains were blue and yellow and white," says Tuffy Lloyd. "It's always been ironic in my mind that she was so close and yet so far."

This time around, Bunny gave her son the best quarters in the house, a two-story suite of rooms that included a ground-floor living room and a large bedroom above, facing the water. "I was fortunate," he says. "It was very nice and had a magnificent view." Tim Mellon's bedroom was tucked in the back by the kitchen.

Impressionist paintings and seascape-themed works graced the walls. In time, the couple added round-the-clock security guards to protect their possessions. Land was cleared so that Bunny could put in a tennis court and plant flower and vegetable gardens and fruit trees. She added a greenhouse and a pergola. She kept her gardeners busy, instructing them to plant thousands of annuals each year.

The newspapers had a field day describing the Mellons' extravagance. NO SAND DUNES? HE MAKES HIS OWN was the headline accompanying an Associated Press article. "There were no sand dunes on Paul Mellon's summer estate—an unthinkable situation on sandy Cape Cod...Mellon trucked in more than 2,000 tons of soft white sand ten miles from Sandy Neck, in Barnstable and constructed a 20 foot high dune between his house and Nantucket Sound."

That October, Paul honored Bunny's efforts with a humorous typed two-page document, "CERTIFICATE OF GENERAL MERIT & GOOD STANDING." He stated that she had conducted herself exceptionally well during the previous six months, with "calm, sensible behavior, and general cheerfulness and good humor...Under various stresses and strains of moving houses and chattels, children, china, chintz, cherished chests etc., she has exhibited unusual cheerfulness."

He wrote that "the aforesaid Bunny Mellon of Buntown" had his permission to spend at least six weeks in Virginia—avoiding all stressful travel to New York—and could "chop, prune, dig, plant espalier and arrange flowers in any order that she deems most fitting." He signed it with his "best love," "a big kiss," and "a gigantic hug."

Chapter Thirteen

A Constant Gardener

At the Mellons' properties in Virginia and Cape Cod, the gardeners who maintained the grounds frequently discovered little piles of trimmings beneath the trees and bushes. The twigs and branches had been left by Bunny, who liked to walk the land using her pruning shears in the way an artist wields a paintbrush, improvising to change shapes and the play of light.

For Bunny, her landscape and gardens provided daily creative challenges. She looked forward to the seasonal cycle: perusing seed catalogues and ordering brightly colored packets, watching as the first buds pierced the soil. She was constantly scribbling notes, such as "make garden of iris and poppies" or "flowers for Sept. in Va—linnaea, white cosmos, large sunflowers, nigella, Persian jewels."

Bunny worked side by side with her gardeners, a give-and-take relationship in which they showed one another techniques. "She taught you," says Bob Childs, a tree pruner who worked on Bunny's Cape Cod property for nearly fifty years. "It wasn't just about the trees and planting, it was about the sea and the sky. She'd take a tree down so she could see the sky."

Bunny did not mourn when Mother Nature ruined her painstaking efforts. After a hurricane hit the Cape, destroying her vegetable garden and knocking down tree limbs, Childs recalls that Bunny told him, "This is a chance to change it all." Fulfilling Bunny's exacting vision required a lot of effort by her staff. "She liked her gardens to look natural but manicured," explains Bob Hoxie, who worked as a Cape Cod gardener for Bunny for seventeen years. "Everything was managed."

She credited her staff with inspiring her efforts. "The creation of a garden is the work and thoughts of many minds," Bunny wrote in an autobiographical essay. "Like a piece of cloth, it is woven of numerous threads. When I think of gardens, of planting and growing plants, the first thought is of space and light...Like music and poetry, there is a different rhythm to every design."

Whether planning her own gardens or designing versions for friends, she considered everything including the shadows cast by nearby trees or buildings, the likely direction of the wind, the quality of the soil, the required upkeep, and visitors' likely response to the sight of the colors and shapes. "I feel public gardens as well as private should have an atmosphere that inspires and one can relate to," she wrote. "There must be a feeling they can take home." She was patient. If it took five years or more for a tree to flourish, she was willing to wait for the eventual reward.

As a girl, she had brought seeds back from Alaska to her New Jersey garden, and she continued to collect finds on her travels. "Sometimes the Mellons would fly in and if she had special cuttings and plants, she'd come from the plane straight here to the greenhouse while Mr. would sit in the car and wait for her," says gardener George Shaffer, who began working for the couple at their Virginia farm in 1965 and stayed in the job for nearly fifty years. He was responsible for nurturing her purple-hued black parrot carnations, red-edged white pheasant eye narcissus, and hummingbird tulips. An entire greenhouse room was devoted to citrus trees, which produced oranges, grapefruits, and limes.

Bunny liked to experiment. Growing miniature topiaries became her passion, planting rosemary, thyme, myrtle, and santolina, and pruning the plants as they grew to resemble small bay trees. "When we began, as far as I knew, they were unique in America although I have read references to such trees in my old gardening books," Bunny wrote. These miniature plants became her trendsetting signature, adorning her rooms as decorative objects and serving as gifts for friends. She would bring small forests of topiaries to the National Gallery as centerpieces for galas. "These trees, after many years, are still an astonishment and a joy," she wrote, "each beginning so improbably with a frail thread of plant lashed to a sliver of bamboo."

In the garden directly behind her Virginia home, Bunny created a visually appealing border for her fruit and vegetable beds: Apple trees were allowed to grow just a few inches above the ground and then twined along posts. Her large vegetable gardens, located by the greenhouses, produced cauliflower, tomatoes, onions, broccoli, beets, and squash. Even in winter, she could indulge in greenhouse-grown cherry tomatoes, sautéed for breakfast.

Spending time in her gardens sent Bunny into reveries. "It is very beautiful here," she wrote in a note in the 1950s from her Virginia home to Huntington Cairns, the secretary of the National Gallery. "The flowers, bees and new greens everywhere turn one into a useless dreamer when there are so many things to be done."

In the summer of 1957, John Warner followed tradition by asking Paul Mellon for his daughter's hand and received his blessing. Bunny still looked up to her father for approval and asked Warner to take the extra step of meeting with Gerard Lambert, even though Gerard was not directly related to the bride-to-be, Cathy Mellon.

The federal prosecutor joined Gerard for lunch. "He greeted me very formally," Warner recalls. "He said, 'Bunny is a favorite of mine, I want her to be happy. You'll be occupying an important role in this family. Tell me about yourself.'" Warner adds, "He really cross-examined me. It wasn't what I was expecting but it was memorable."

The wedding ceremony took place at 4:30 p.m. on August 8 at St. Peter's Episcopal Church in Osterville, Cape Cod. The bride wore pearls and a short white organdy dress with a high neckline and a shoulder-length veil. In her white gloves, she carried a bouquet of white daisies. The reception was held at the Mellons' home on the island of Oyster Harbors. The large dining room and living room opened out to a terrace where thick grass grew between stones set in a diamond pattern. The view was of a salt river with small boats floating by; on the other side of the river was the uninhabited Dead Neck Island.

The groom was in the middle of trying a legal case, so there was no time for a honeymoon, much to the annoyance of his bride and her family. "Paul lent us his plane so Catherine and I could fly back, so I could be in the courtroom Monday afternoon," Warner recalls. "That didn't sit well with anyone." The newlyweds moved to a house in Georgetown, a gift from Paul Mellon, along with a Virginia farm plus a plot of land in Oyster Harbors for their own home.

In the fall of 1957, Bunny and Paul scored a social coup. Queen Elizabeth, crowned in 1953, was planning her first official visit to the United States, including several days in Washington, D.C. The twenty-eight-year-old monarch, who owned a large stable of horses with a winning track record, wanted to take a look at America's top racing stock.

Paul Mellon's Middleburg horse training track featured seven stables housing 130 horses owned by the region's best breeders. Paul's father had been the ambassador to Great Britain in 1932, Paul's mother was British, and Paul had attended Clare College. Paul and Bunny invited the Queen and Prince Philip to visit the track and come to tea at their farm; the royal couple accepted.

Democrats in Washington attacked this scheduled royal pilgrimage to visit Upperville's wealthiest citizens. Walter Louchheim, whose wife, Katie, was the vice chairman of the Democratic National Committee, complained to *Washington Star* columnist Betty Beale: "What goodwill will Elizabeth foster by choosing this as the only private home she will visit?"

London's *Daily Herald* described the jousting among American hostesses for the honor of entertaining Her Majesty, pointing out that the royals were breaking with British protocol by visiting the home of a divorced woman. "The battle is over now," the newspaper announced. "Victory has gone to a woman who could never have won had she lived in Britain—Mrs. Rachel Mellon, who will entertain the Queen and Prince Philip in her home, is a divorcee. Before her marriage to forty-eight-year-old multimillionaire race horse owner Paul Mellon in 1948, she was the wife of Stacy B. Lloyd," the British newspaper continued. "Dozens of America's top hostesses would give their minks and jewels to change places with Mrs. Mellon."

That sentiment became the theme of the news coverage, with syndicated society columnist Cholly Knickerbocker opining: "Naturally, Washington hostesses are green with envy."

Every minute had been scheduled during the Queen's Washington visit: three state dinners hosted by President and Mamie Eisenhower, a college football game between Maryland and North Carolina, a visit to Congress, lunch with Vice President Richard Nixon, and a garden party at the British Embassy for twenty-four hundred guests.

Bunny and Paul usually shied away from publicity, but both of them granted interviews. Bunny gave a house tour to the *Washington Post*'s Muriel Bowen for a feature that carried the gratifying headline: MOST ENVIED HOSTESS IN THE COUNTRY TODAY. Bunny was described in the article as "tall, slim, vivacious."

Trying to downplay the Mellon wealth, the empress of Upperville played the naïf. "We are tremendously honored and thrilled that the Queen and Prince Philip should visit us," Bunny said. "But why in the world are so many people interested in knowing about us? We live a plain ordinary sort of country life down here."

The shrill ring of the telephone interrupted the interview as the butler informed Bunny that the *Sunday Times* of London wanted to know if she would be using déclassé teabags for the Queen. A tea drinker herself, she explained that she would be relying on loose Chinese tea leaves. (This detail was picked up by dozens of newspapers; the *Montana Standard*, in Butte, wrote a tongue-in-cheek item praising Bunny for avoiding a diplomatic incident.)

The Mellon home was described by the *Washington Post* as "a very cozy sort of place—oft-cushioned settees, warm color schemes and lots of flowers arranged in brass-girthed mahogany wine coolers. It is an unpretentious house, mostly one-story with several luxurious touches—the racks of exquisite glass and china, and handsome paintings by van Gogh, Forain and Munnings."

Bunny pointed out the new primrose yellow curtains in the drawing room. Sounding like an ordinary housewife who had been nagging her spouse about improvements, she said, "I've been telling Paul for ages how much we wanted new curtains. The Queen's coming has been a wonderful excuse for getting them."

Bunny planned to wear a tweed dress, although she explained apologetically that it was "made in France but very English." She presented herself as a homebody who reluctantly spent time in Washington, New York, and Pittsburgh but was always eager to return to Upperville, stressing, "Gardens have always been my life."

Worried that frost might endanger her gardens before the Queen's visit, Bunny made special precautions: Her flowers were tucked in at night. Timber cradles had been erected around the flower beds, holding up yards of white cotton. Showing the reporter the garden with its night covers, Bunny announced with a laugh, "The garden looks as if we have hung up the wash."

On the much-awaited sunny Sunday, the Queen and Prince attended church twice with President and Mamie Eisenhower—going from the Episcopal Washington National Cathedral to the president's church, National Presbyterian—followed by lunch at the British Embassy. At 1:30 p.m., the Queen, in a blue-green tweed suit, matching hat with a feather, and beaver coat, was driven to Middleburg in a gray Rolls-Royce, while her husband followed in the president's bubbletop car, with the Secret Service and motorcycle policemen accompanying the motorcade.

Families lined the roads, waving British flags. At Paul Mellon's horse-training facility, the Queen inspected eighteen yearlings and saw Elkridge, the leading American steeplechase winner. Paul and his trainer stayed by her side to answer questions. Bunny's friend Liz Whitney met the Queen and gave her a framed picture of her prized horse, Mr. Gus.

Foxcroft students watched the motorcade head toward Rokeby Farm. "It was a big deal when Queen Elizabeth came to Upperville," recalls Sydney Roberts Rockefeller, then a Foxcroft student. "We all lined up along the long road and along came the Queen. We all had Brownie cameras."

Bunny's well-tended garden was a riot of color: orange and yellow dahlias, pink-and-blue Michaelmas daisies, and other fall blooms. The small family gathering included three of Bunny's and Paul's children— her son, Tuffy, who was home for the weekend from Middlebury; Eliza, now at Foxcroft; and newlywed Cathy and her husband, John Warner. Tim Mellon had the flu and was confined to the Milton Academy infirmary. The only outsider was Foxcroft headmistress Charlotte Noland. Paul later explained that she was invited "because my wife and daughter attended Foxcroft, because Miss Noland knew the royal family and because she is so representative of the community here."

Bunny lectured the group beforehand about how to behave. As John Warner recalls, she announced, "The protocol is that you do not speak to the Queen until she has spoken to you and more or less asked you a question."

Soon there was a knock on the door, and a Secret Service agent announced that the royal party was heading up the driveway. "The rest of us stayed in the living room while Bunny and Paul went out to escort them in," Warner says. "The Queen walked around, Mrs. Mellon introduced her. They made the full circle of the room and the last person was Miss Charlotte. Miss Charlotte curtsied, and then she bluntly said to the Queen, 'Look here, young lady, I want you to sit right here next to me and we'll have the nicest of talks.'" John Warner laughed at the memory of the headmistress's forthright approach. "I sat there and I thought, wow!!!"

Paul and Bunny took the Queen and the Prince on a tour of the farm and stables, wheeling around on a farm vehicle. When Eliza returned to Foxcroft, she couldn't resist telling friends about the lunch. "Eliza had an incredible sense of humor," recalls Sydney Rockefeller. "As the Prince was leaving, she sidled up to him and said, 'See you later, alligator.' And he said, 'After a while, crocodile.'"

Several days after the Queen's visit, Paul gave an interview to *Boston Globe* reporter Thomas Winship. "Nothing was terribly different," he insisted. "Of course we wanted everything shined up at home and at the stable for her visit. That doesn't mean we don't always keep our stable shined up."

The mogul made a favorable impression on the reporter. "The queen's sole citizen host is a Mellon and a multimillionaire all right, but the public is badly mixed up if it thinks Paul Mellon is a hard-boiled financier of the old school," wrote Winship. "He is more at home discussing modern poetry (which he writes himself), experimental education, psychiatric medication or Sudbury's Wayside Inn than he is talking business or politics...

"Paul Mellon apparently took the entertaining of Queen Elizabeth and Prince Philip at his Upperville, Va. estate with about as much fuss and feathers as most folks work up when they have the next-door neighbor in for Saturday night baked beans and brown bread."

That fall, America's own royal couple continued to ascend. Massachusetts senator John F. Kennedy drew enthusiastic crowds as he traveled the country. At the 1956 Democratic Convention, Kennedy had sought—and nearly won—the chance to run as Adlai Stevenson's vice president, losing by only thirty-eight votes on the second ballot to Tennessee senator Estes Kefauver.

The charismatic forty-year-old, widely considered the Democratic front-runner for the 1960 nomination, was trying to appear nonchalant about his future as he campaigned for a lopsided reelection. In a November 1957 interview with the Associated Press, he insisted, "I'm not interested in 1960. I'm tremendously interested in my Senate job and want to stay there."

The story ran in the *Washington Post* under the headline: DOTH PROTEST TOO MUCH? NOT TOO RELUCTANT IS THE COY KENNEDY.

Paul and Bunny were aware of Jack Kennedy—everyone in Washington was aware of Jack Kennedy—but it would take the intervention of mutual friends to eventually make a connection.

The war hero from Massachusetts had been elected to Congress in 1946 and the Senate in 1952, becoming known on Capitol Hill for his pursuit of the ladies. "I'm the only person I know who wasn't propositioned by him," Marie Wasserman Ridder told me, only half joking. She met Kennedy when she was a war widow working for the *Philadelphia Bulletin* and living in Georgetown. "I was a young reporter on the Hill in 1946, he lived two houses down," she explained.

They occasionally dated and he took her to a dance, but quickly spotted someone more to his liking. "Across the hall was a beautiful blonde girl. He said, 'Kiddo, do you know her?' I said, 'She is known as the Mata Hari of the Defense Department. She is so important because of her excellent knowledge of Russia and Russian.' He said, 'She's dancing with an old friend of mine, shall we double-cut?'" Ridder did not mind, and she would marry the friend, newspaper chain owner Walter Ridder.

She worked side by side on Capitol Hill with Jacqueline Bouvier, the stylish photographer for the *Washington Times-Herald*. "I met Jackie on the job, as a reporter," Ridder recalls. She was puzzled by Jackie's elusive persona, adding, "She was outgoing and not outgoing, both. You never knew if she was going to greet you as her long-lost sister, or not."

John Warner had dated Jackie Bouvier before he became engaged to Cathy Mellon. "She was a little shy, a little withdrawn but very lovely and gracious and fun, she had a good quick wit," he recalls. "I escorted her to a very proper house party on one of those islands in Maryland. I remember sitting on a dock with her and the moon was up. Jackie was an intriguing woman. She said, 'Oh, I look at that moon, I see great white horses galloping over the moon.' Sort of surreal kinds of stuff. I'm a hard-boiled prosecutor, I wasn't able to take all that in."

Jackie often struck people as guarded. The divorce of her socially prominent Catholic parents had played out in the New York tabloids. Her mother, Janet, the daughter of a well-to-do Manhattan developer, separated after eight years of marriage from her husband, stockbroker and horse fancier "Black Jack" Bouvier, weary of his womanizing and alcoholism. Jackie was seven and her younger sister, Lee, was three when their parents split up in 1936.

Following her 1940 divorce, Janet Bouvier married the wealthy divorcé Hugh Auchincloss. Their main residence was Merrywood, a twenty-six-room Georgian mansion on forty-six acres, overlooking the Potomac River in McLean, Virginia. Auchincloss had inherited his parents' retreat, Hammersmith Farm in Newport, an even more glorious Victorian waterfront estate.

The couple needed ample bedrooms. From his previous marriages, Hugh Auchincloss was the father of three children and had a stepson, Gore Vidal. Hugh and Janet would go on to have two more children, Janet Jr. and Jamie. Jackie, who adored her ne'er-do-well father, had a tense relationship with her critical mother. Her younger sister, Lee, was also unhappy at home. Many years later, Lee told the *New York Times*, "My mother simply had me, sticking me with a series of horrible governesses."

Jackie was educated at Miss Porter's School, followed by stints at Vassar and the Sorbonne, graduating from George Washington University in 1951. "I always wanted a job on a newspaper," she later explained. "When I walked into the offices of a Washington paper and asked for a job, they gave me the 'inquiring photographer' column. They had been sending two people out on it, but they taught me how to use a Speed Graphic and I asked the questions, took the pictures and wrote the column."

She was assigned to cover President Eisenhower's inauguration (interviewing Vice President Richard Nixon and his wife, Pat) and was sent to England for the coronation of Queen Elizabeth. (She asked bystanders, "What is your greatest thrill?" and "Do you think Elizabeth will be England's last Queen?")

Jackie was friendly with another New York transplant to Washington, Martha Bartlett. "I've known Jackie since she was twelve years old," she told me. Martha and her husband, Charlie, a well-connected reporter, fixed up the senator with Jackie at a dinner party at their home in 1951, and two years later the couple became engaged. HEIRESS PHOTOGRAPHER CLICKS WITH KENNEDY, CAPITAL'S "MOST ELIGIBLE," heralded *Newsday*.

"The wedding was marvelous," recalls Oatsie Leiter Charles, who attended the couple's September 1953 nuptials in Newport, along with twelve hundred guests. "A lot of people from the Kennedy side were from New York and all dressed up for a proper wedding. On the Newport and Bouvier side, they came neatly dressed but not with proper clothes."

Jack and Jackie purchased a white brick Revolutionary War Virginia mansion, Hickory Hill, in McLean, converting the top floor into a nursery in anticipation of their first child. But after Jackie gave birth to a stillborn premature baby girl in August 1956, she recuperated in Newport and refused to return to Hickory Hill.

The marriage was in trouble. JFK's infidelities, even then, were flagrant. Jack had been sailing in the Mediterranean when Jackie gave birth and took his time getting home. But the couple patched things up and Jackie became pregnant again. Jack Kennedy sold the estate to his brother Robert and bought a three-story redbrick federal house at 3307 N Street in Georgetown.

Kennedy had insisted to the Associated Press that despite his family money—his father was reported to be worth north of $200 million—he was frugal. "He seldom carries more than a couple of dollars in his pockets, often has to borrow cab fare and insists that his wife run their Washington home in suburban Georgetown strictly within the limit of his $22,500 Senate salary," the AP wrote. That was a public relations concoction, since the couple lived well beyond his government paycheck. That December, Jackie gave birth to a healthy baby girl, Caroline.

Jackie liked to get away from life as a senator's wife to go foxhunting. Her Virginia friends included the widowed and remarried Adele Astaire, who lived on a 180-acre farm in Middleburg with her second husband, Kingman Douglass, the former assistant director of the CIA. Adele thought her two friends might like each other and brought Jackie to Bunny's home for tea.

As Bunny recalled, "That evening Dellie called and said, 'Young Mrs. Kennedy wants to call you, but feels I should ask you first if she should.'"

The next day, Jackie made the call and told Bunny, "I loved your house but I don't like mine." Bunny was flattered, later recalling, "She had noticed every detail with enthusiasm, but it was not until she said, 'I even loved the stale candy in the antique jars,' that she won me over. I agreed to go to Washington and see if I could help."

When Bunny arrived at Jackie's Georgetown home, she found Jackie sitting on the floor, looking at books. Jackie greeted her by saying, "I don't know how to do a darn thing in this house. Wait until you see Jack's room, it's full of pictures he bought at the drug store." (A Cape Cod general store featured work by local artists.) A nanny wheeled in Caroline's pram, and Jackie showed off her baby.

Bunny was charmed by Jackie's high-spirited enthusiasm and curiosity. Bunny usually preferred the company of men, but elements of Jackie's life—a father she adored, a strained relationship with her mother, and the difficulty of coping with an adulterous husband—struck a chord. The women became so close that Bunny would later write, "As friends, Jackie and my conversations were continuous, as if time and place never broke the atmosphere that surrounded the subject at hand—relating our immediate thoughts without introduction."

The Kennedy compound in Hyannis Port was just a short boat ride away from Bunny and Paul's Osterville home and the couples began to socialize together. Paul Mellon was ten years older than John Kennedy but they knew each other's worlds: Both had attended Choate, their multimillionaire fathers had both served as the American ambassador to Great Britain, and they both traced their ancestry back to Ireland.

Some friendships burn bright but then fade over time. Bunny and Jackie would endure, turning to each other for comfort in terrible times, celebrating joyful landmarks together. The friendship was a constant in their lives. Many decades later, Jackie would put those feelings in writing, telling Bunny: "You have meant as much to me as any person in my life."

———————

Paul and Bunny had been looking for an unspoiled winter getaway, hoping to find a more scenic and relaxing spot than very social

Palm Beach. The couple fell in love with Antigua, the former British colony in the Caribbean, with white sand beaches, groves of mangoes and figs, and such a primitive infrastructure that telephones were a scarce novelty. Paul acquired twenty-seven pristine waterfront acres in the private Mill Reef Club in Antigua. The two-thousand-acre compound, established in 1946 by Connecticut architect Robertson Ward, included a clubhouse, a golf course, and tennis courts.

This luxurious spot stood out amid the neighboring poverty. In a 1956 travel feature in the *New York Herald Tribune*, writer W. Storrs Lee noted, "Visitors to the island will find the living standards of the natives incredibly low, and pathos as well as picturesqueness in the crowded Negro settlement."

Bunny once again worked with architect H. Page Cross to design and build a spacious pastel-colored home that resembled an old West Indian plantation. Construction dragged on for several years. The Mellons hired and trained local workmen and employed a large local household staff.

The three-bedroom main house included a vast living room, a library, and a wine cellar. Foot-thick walls kept the home cool—as always, Bunny refused to install air conditioners—and the wooden floors were painted. The large terrace overlooked Half Moon Bay, and a guesthouse was built nearby. Bunny planted a citrus orchard, built an orchid nursery, put in vegetable and flower gardens, and added two greenhouses.

"Mrs. Mellon was very anxious to make this island paradise home totally self-sufficient," wrote Paul Leonard in his autobiographical essay. "She had gardeners trained, set up care and maintenance schedules and imported all sorts of tools and equipment. We set up a laundry. Washing machines were unheard of but we had some imported."

Once again, Paul Mellon was pleased with his wife's creation. "It has an open plan of rooms and courtyards, so that wherever you are standing you enjoy a view into a brick-paved courtyard, filled with lime trees, breadfruit and olives, or out over the bay towards the coral reef, or into another white-walled sparsely finished room," Paul wrote in his autobiography. "There is an indescribable feeling of peace, with the warm air softly cooled by the trade winds."

The warm climate allowed Bunny to grow exotic edibles. She brought fifty-eight different types of seeds down one year, including five varieties of watermelon (Congo, Dixie Queen, New Hampshire Midget, You Sweet Thing, and Sugar Baby); seven kinds of lettuce (Bibb, Matchless, May King, Great Lakes, Butter King, Oakleaf, and White Boston); three types of squash (Early Prolific Straightneck, Chefini, and Black Beauty); and Red Boy and Early Scarlet Globe radishes. The names conjured up a garden of earthly delights.

By private plane, Antigua was a quick hop to Guadeloupe, where Johnny Schlumberger had a home. Bunny was a frequent visitor; he would whisk her off to nearby rustic islands, Les Saintes. "But it was a test of survival," Paul Leonard wrote. "No maids, no butlers, no chefs. It opened up a romantic new world."

Bunny also dropped by St. Croix to see her ex-husband, Stacy. Her son found it disturbing, fretting that his parents were rekindling their love affair. "I couldn't believe this, my father was living in St. Croix at that time," Tuffy said. "He used to say, 'Bunny, I'd love to see you for lunch, can you fly over to St. Croix and we'll have lunch and you can fly back.' She said, 'That's fine, let's do that. Where shall we meet?' 'The Comanche Inn is always good, we could meet there.' So they did that a few times, to my complete dismay."

When two of the wealthiest men in the world battle over a painting, the world takes notice. Paul Mellon made headlines in 1958 when he outbid Greek shipping tycoon Stavros Niarchos in a London auction for a Cézanne painting, *Boy in a Red Waistcoat*, paying a record $616,000.

"I had a top price but my wife and I wanted this painting very much, so it was a high one," Paul told the *New York Times*. "I wish we had gotten it for less but we are happy to have it." At the London sale, he paid an additional $565,000 for two Manets.

Whether bidding high at an auction or pushing himself physically,

Paul was going through a period of proving himself. In 1959, he signed up for a hundred-mile endurance ride in Virginia, a three-day gauntlet through mountainous trails and forests. The fifty-two-year-old won the heavyweight class and the championship on his silver gray gelding Silversmith.

"The horse in best condition at ride's end was the winner," proclaimed Aubrey Graves in the *Washington Post*, adding wryly, "The condition of the rider was of no official interest to the judges. Thirty horses competed in the three-day ride marathon, which took them over five mountain tops... By ride's end, one-third of the starters had been disqualified for fatigue, lameness or overtime."

Paul was jubilant about the win. "I have always been very competitive," he wrote in his autobiography, noting proudly that he subsequently competed seventeen more times in the April race during the next twenty years, and won five times. "I have ridden through driving snowstorms and pouring rain, or, worse, on sweltering hot days with temperatures over eighty degrees." What mattered to Paul was that he had won by virtue of skill, in a situation where his inheritance was irrelevant.

The Mellon farm remained the destination of choice for visiting royalty. When Japanese Crown Prince Akihito and his wife, Michiko, came to Washington, they requested a tour of the National Gallery followed by a trip to Rokeby Farm. Of course the Mellons said yes.

Bunny had added a greenhouse, known as an orangerie, behind her walled garden. She hired French artist Fernand Renard to paint a trompe l'oeil mural in the orangerie, featuring straw baskets and personalized objects from her gardening hat to a wedding ring hanging on a hook. Johnny Schlumberger designed the finial, a lead urn filled with flowers. A canopy of latticed metal struts, with crab apple trees twined up the sides and overhead, created a leafy walkway from the walled garden to the orangerie. Paul was amused by Bunny's spare-no-expense creation, quipping to guests, "I call that the Bunny Mahal."

Bunny usually relied on local gardeners, but with the Washington society columns heralding the talents of landscape architect Perry

Wheeler, she sought him out to rework the garden at the Whitehaven Street house that had once belonged to her father.

Wheeler, a Georgia native, had served in the OSS and earned a graduate degree in landscaping from Harvard. Post cereal heiress Marjorie Merriweather Post hired him to design the French gardens at her Washington mansion, Hillwood. His garden for hostess-with-the-mostest Perle Mesta was described by the *Washington Post* as a "dream spot" with "blue and white magic."

His clients treated him as a friend rather than the help. Wheeler and his companion, Jim Snitzler, who shared a Georgetown home, were in demand on the evening society circuit. Often quoted about trends, Wheeler quipped to the *Post*, "In Georgetown you keep changing your garden just like ladies change their hats."

In 1959, he began working for Bunny. Cost was never mentioned in their initial conversation, so he wrote Bunny a note explaining that he charged $12 an hour, the equivalent of roughly $100 today. In the backyard of the Whitehaven Street house, he put in climbing roses, Chinese tree lilies, and espaliered hyslop crab apple trees.

Bunny asked him to update the landscaping at Trinity Church in Upperville and refine the gardens at Rokeby Farm. She had developed a fascination with gray leaf plants. Perry Wheeler researched the types available from Kingsville Nursery, writing her a memo recommending the *Elaeagnus angustifolia* ("lovely willow-leaf form with gray leaves"); the *Amelanchier asiatica* ("even the bark is striped gray, flowers are gray-white"); and the tamarix summer glow ("gray foliage, very fine thread-like; flowers pale pink").

Their rapport soon transcended a working relationship. "Perry was a very, very close friend of hers for many years," says Deeda Blair, a philanthropist whose husband served as ambassador to Denmark and the Philippines. "He worked a lot with Mrs. Mellon. They had a total meeting of the minds. I knew him very well, he had a wicked sense of humor, very amusing, very intelligent."

Bunny liked him so much that she invited Perry and his partner to build a weekend house on a plot of land at Rokeby Farm. If Bunny was lonely late at night or couldn't sleep, she would sometimes call Perry for a soothing conversation.

Her past caught up with her at times, with a bittersweet poignancy. She did not regret her marriage to Paul Mellon, but there were might-have-been moments when she wondered what her life would have been like if she had stayed with her first husband. So it was a symbolic blow in 1959 when Stacy told Bunny that he had decided to sell the home that they had built together, Apple Hill.

He could no longer afford the upkeep, and since he was living in St. Croix full-time, he thought it was time to face facts. "It is silly to keep the house for years for Tuffy and Eliza when the chances are they will marry and want something different," he wrote. "What I am planning to do is list the house for sale with brokers for $200,000. If it can be sold at that price it could be money that could eventually go to our children."

Stacy eventually reduced the price to $125,000 to find a buyer, selling it to his friend William Tupper. Bunny had never gotten around to taking her possessions. Stacy invited her to pick out what she wanted. He asked to keep gifts that Bunny had given him in happier times.

"In my dressing room I have always liked very much the little mahogany bookcase you gave and the bureau is a nice one. The sets of books you gave me I would want: Dickens, Surtees, Conrad." He added, "I wish we did not have to do all of this but a house that none of us can use seems to be wasting away."

As she reflected on her old life with Stacy and contemplated her future, Bunny had begun to search for ways to understand the various forces converging on her world. In 1960, she became fascinated by astrology, commissioning horoscopes from Ferdinand Ostertag, a German Holocaust survivor who wrote a column for *Harper's Bazaar*. Describing the character traits of Leos—Bunny's sign—he wrote in one column: "Like kings, they regard themselves as the center of their 'realm,' expecting loyalty and tribute from their 'subjects'... This tendency to be self-centered might be interpreted as selfishness; however contrasted with it is magnanimity of the heart." A man with artistic interests, Ostertag had helped translate Wassily Kandinsky's book, *On the Spiritual in Art*.

In a series of 1960 horoscopes for Bunny, which she saved, Ostertag speculated on her likely moods on specific days, from depression to frustration with family members to joie de vivre. He advised her to "lay low" at times to avoid "friction" with a partner.

But in early June, Ostertag gave her an upbeat prediction, saying that she was entering a period that would be "very harmonious and revitalizing" and that she would feel "unusually energetic and enterprising and 'full of pep.'"

The Mellon and Lloyd children were now reaching milestones of their own. In her appointment calendar for June 1960, Bunny noted that three of the children were graduating within one week. The athletic and artistic Eliza, who finished Foxcroft on June 8, had been nicknamed "Dizzy Lizzy" by her classmates. The headmaster noted on one report card that Eliza was a "scatterbrain" but is "always pleasant, a good sport," and seemed "happy as a lark." Recognizing that academics were not Eliza's forte, Bunny arranged for Eliza to go to Paris and live with a family, ostensibly to improve her French and paint, rather than attend college.

Tim Mellon, who graduated from Milton Academy on June 11, had been accepted at his father's alma mater, Yale. Tuffy Lloyd graduated from Middlebury two days later. Fluent in French, he had signed up to take special courses after a CIA recruiter came to campus. But his father, recalling his own experiences in the OSS, was opposed to Tuffy's plan to join the agency, warning that it was a stressful life and that he would never be able to tell anyone what he did for a living. But Tuffy had a sense of wanderlust and he had no desire to return to Virginia and the often tense atmosphere at home. "I wanted to get as far away as I could from my family," he recalls. Tuffy went to work for Project HOPE, a humanitarian aid ship that traveled to war-torn countries. He would soon be heading to Saigon.

The 1960 presidential race was now dominating the headlines. Paul and Bunny attended a dinner at the F Street Club for Vice President Richard Nixon, an evening designed to woo big-money donors to support the GOP presidential candidate. The forty-eight guests included Henry Ford, IBM president Thomas Watson, and Undersecretary of State C. Douglas Dillon. Bunny, who was placed two seats away from Nixon, took an immediate dislike to the man.

"I thought he was just awful," she later said. "I watched him all through dinner. I called up a few friends like Joe Alsop…I even prayed and asked God. I became a Democrat, it was as simple as that."

Her husband, a lifelong Republican, wrote $2,500 checks to both the GOP House and Senate campaign committees and $5,000 to the Virginia Republican Party. Paul's son-in-law, John Warner, had joined the Nixon campaign as an advance man. Aware of Bunny's feelings, Paul would later tease her in a note about "your Prince Charming—Nixon."

Bunny's new friend Jackie Kennedy was discovering the perils of life in the spotlight. Everything she said or did—or didn't do—was news. The *Boston Globe* ran an article headlined MILLINERY EXECUTIVES RAISE THE QUESTION: WHY DOESN'T SHE WEAR A HAT? The *Washington Post* devoted an entire feature to her hair: JACKIE'S HAIR-DO IS "LE CYGNE" (French for "swan"). The *Chicago Tribune* gushed about her skills as a political asset: THE EXTRAORDINARY MRS. KENNEDY: JACKIE'S SHY FRIENDLINESS, HER LACK OF AGGRESSIVENESS, ARE BIG VOTE GETTERS FOR HUSBAND.

Washington Star columnist Betty Beale speculated about what tone she would establish as First Lady, writing, "Jackie has been so enormously successful in shunning public appearances that even her good friends don't dare predict her interpretation of the role as White House hostess."

Now four and a half months pregnant, Jackie skipped the Los Angeles Democratic Convention in July, where her husband won the presidential nomination on the first ballot, beating rivals Lyndon Johnson, Adlai Stevenson, and Stuart Symington. The next day Jackie spoke to reporters at the Kennedy compound in Hyannis Port. Asked how she thought it would feel to live in the White House, she laughed and replied, "I don't know. You tell me."

In mid-August, when Bunny returned from a trip to Europe, she found several messages from Jackie Kennedy. The presidential hopeful's wife wanted to see Bunny immediately. Jackie showed up at the farm several hours later, confessing that she was overwhelmed by the prospect of becoming First Lady. After entertaining royalty and Cabinet secretaries, Bunny understood what it was like to stand by a powerful man and handle a public life.

As Bunny later recalled their conversation, Jackie was anxious about what her own responsibilities would be if they moved into the White House, saying, "Jack may be president…what will I do? That big house and all those curtains."

On November 8, 1960, Paul and Bunny went to the post office in Upperville to cast their votes for president. As Tim Mellon wrote in his autobiography, Paul recounted the husband-wife dialogue that ensued:

"Paul, may I please borrow your pencil to complete my ballot?" Bunny asked.

He replied, "You're going to vote for Nixon, aren't you?"

"No, I'm going to vote for Kennedy," she said.

Paul's response: "Then no, you can't borrow my pencil."

Chapter Fourteen

The Best Friends

POVE

LIZONCL

Time seemed to be moving at warp speed. Bunny had led a leisurely existence but after Inauguration Day, she was at Jackie Kennedy's beck and call, commuting to the White House as an informal adviser. The First Lady wanted to quickly make her mark with a stylish new way of entertaining, even as she tackled the job of redecorating the dowdy mansion.

Bunny was honored to be involved. "Jackie became as loyal as she could be," she later told author and TV host Chris Matthews. "She asked me, 'Will you come now and help me fix up this house? It's terrible. And don't ever call me First Lady, ever, because I'm just at work here. This is a job, I've got to do it for Jack.'"

Bunny knew that greenery could enhance a drab room in far less time than it took for a paint job. At her request, the dreary potted palms at the White House were replaced with pretty fig trees. She filled her chauffeured car with blossoms from her greenhouses and brought them to 1600 Pennsylvania Avenue, where she showed the government staff how to make elegant floral arrangements. "Mrs.

Mellon had exquisite taste and that's what Jackie admired most of all," says Letitia Baldrige, who was then Jackie's White House social secretary. "I saw Mrs. Mellon when she'd come to the White House to do little or big jobs. She taught other people. She helped out so much."

Bunny searched the White House for distinctive props that could be deployed with flowers. White House historian William Seale later described Bunny's behind-the-scenes endeavors: "She drew from basement cupboards long unused porcelain containers, vases, and soup tureens and made other containers out of old china tableware, terracotta flowerpots, and other unlikely storage artifacts."

President Kennedy would occasionally seek Bunny out for brief chats. "The president would just come and go," she recalled to Matthews. "He was friendly and wonderful. That atmosphere of that was very warm." Bunny's efforts brought glory to Jackie Kennedy. In April 1961, the *Boston Globe* noted that in the past, "floral decorations were arranged with all the magnificence of a gangster's wake" at the White House, but now the flowers "have the controlled beauty of a Flemish painting."

The First Lady "pours flowers into deep straw baskets or enormous copper containers or silver mugs," reported the *Globe*. "She likes to put them on tables at the eye-level of chairs sitting in deep armchairs...Wild flowers like Queen Anne's lace are combined with anemones and garden flowers such as tulips, lilacs and roses." These were all Bunny's signature touches.

Diana Vreeland, who had become the editor of *Vogue*, sent Bunny a newspaper clipping stating that the new White House style was influencing florists, adding: "Your floral ideas are really 'Getting Around.'"

Changing the floral arrangements was easy compared to the daunting task of making over the entire White House. Occupied since 1800, the 132-room building was badly in need of refurbishing. Presidents had been allowed to take favorite pieces of furniture when they left, leaving little of historic value. Harry Truman renovated the deteriorating building in the late 1940s, but after the project went over the $6.5 million budget, reproductions were ordered in bulk from the New York department store B. Altman & Company. Mamie Eisenhower's penchant for pink had so dominated the family quarters that the press had nicknamed the White House the "Pink Palace."

Sister Parish, Bunny's Foxcroft roommate, completed a rush job redecorating the family quarters but there was much more to do. "Jackie and I painted the ballrooms at the White House," Bunny recalled. "It was very dark and she and I painted it white with gold trim." Jackie went on a treasure hunt through White House storage areas, unearthing antiques. "Jackie and I were like two kids rummaging around in the attic," Bunny told a companion, Nancy Collins, many years later. "We found Lincoln's desk." But with only $75,000 in federal funds for improvement, the First Lady would need donated antiques and cash gifts to make her new home into a national showplace.

At Sister Parish's suggestion, Jackie created a Fine Arts Commission for the White House to acquire English, French, and American antiques, dating back to the early 1800s. Bunny and Sister were among the dozen wealthy and well-connected members, including two National Gallery of Art directors (the retired David Finley and current head John Walker); Henry du Pont, the multimillionaire chemical heir and creator of the Winterthur Museum; and socially prominent New York philanthropists Jane Englehard and Jayne Wrightsman. The group vetted the objects offered by the public as well as donated money and gifts.

Bunny also served as a conduit. Her decorator friend Nancy Lancaster, based in London, alerted Bunny that she had discovered antique French wallpaper, dating back to the 1830s, which showed patriotic American scenes. Wallpaper of that description soon materialized in the White House Diplomatic Reception area.

Bunny often saw Jackie on weekends, since the Kennedys rented a weekend retreat, Glen Ora, in Middleburg. The First Family's six-bedroom mansion included stables, a tennis court, a playhouse, a swimming pool, and a lawn large enough to land the presidential helicopter. Most weekends, Jackie took her children to the house, which was just a short drive from Rokeby Farm. Paul Mellon quipped that Bunny and Jackie had become "the mutual admiration society."

The First Lady felt safe confiding in Bunny, admitting that her sloppy husband had cleaned up his act. "She told me that Jack used to throw his bath towels all around the bathroom," Bunny told Chris Matthews. "Ever since he's been president, he folds his up."

―――――――――

With her best friend in the White House and her daughter, Eliza, entering her debutante season, Bunny decided to give the ultimate coming-out party. Her idea was to transform Rokeby Farm into an homage to France, inspired by the acclaimed 1913 French novel, *The Wanderer*, by Alain-Fournier. The protagonist in that evocative book wanders into the forest and discovers a mysterious lost chateau where revelers are dressed in 1830s costumes.

Bunny wanted to create a dreamscape: a temporary ballroom that would evoke Versailles, along with Paris sidewalk cafés, an omelet booth, an astrologer's shop, a bistro with a honky-tonk piano, and a tent city to house the male college guests.

The planning for the June 16, 1961, party began months in advance. The Dowager Duchess of Devonshire, Mary Cavendish, wrote to Bunny in March, thanking her for the invitation and an offer to provide air tickets. "The party would be such fun and then to see your house about which Delly [Adele Astaire] has told me so much," the Duchess wrote.

Bunny's ex-husband, Stacy Lloyd, assured her that he would do his best to come. "Many thanks for your invitation to Eliza's coming out party," he wrote to Bunny on April 26. "Alice has written to her Mother to see if she will come out here to take care of her while I am away."

The *Washington Star*'s Betty Beale wrote that the Mellons' upcoming event "has started a rash of intriguing rumors because this couple, who shy from all publicity, gave such a superb party" for Paul's daughter, Cathy.

French party planner Jacques Frank, known for staging extravagant events for wealthy Europeans and Americans, including debut parties for Henry Ford's two daughters, was Bunny's first choice. But she disliked his designs and replaced him with architect H. Page Cross and two young stage designers, partners William Strom and Paul Leonard.

Bunny hoped to create a visual surprise. Guests would arrive at the formal Brick House, which showcased Paul's art collection, and then exit outdoors into an artificially created canopy of trees, made from real saplings twined around arched chicken wire and stuffed with lemon leaves. The temporary ballroom and fanciful shops would be constructed nearby. Folk artist Madeline Hewes was commissioned to paint murals to hang in the shops.

In June, the president and the First Lady headed to Paris for a summit meeting with President Charles de Gaulle. Jackie's chic style and command of the French language brought her so many accolades that the president quipped, "I am the man who accompanied Jacqueline Kennedy to Paris and I have enjoyed it."

But that visit was followed by a two-day grim trip to Vienna, where the president held tense meetings with Soviet leader Nikita Khrushchev. Kennedy had hoped for a thaw to move forward on a nuclear arms treaty but instead was angrily lectured by Khrushchev on the merits of Communism and America's mistake with the failed Bay of Pigs invasion in Cuba that April.

Even more worrisome, Khrushchev threatened to consolidate the Soviet hold on East Berlin. Berlin had been a Cold War flashpoint since the end of World War II, when the city was divided into two sectors. In 1948, Soviets blocked the Allies' access by rail and road to sectors of West Berlin; the Allies organized the Berlin airlift to drop food and supplies. The Soviets lifted the blockade in 1949. Well-educated East Germans had been fleeing to West Berlin.

A somber President Kennedy and his wife stopped off in London, where he discussed the frustrating Khrushchev meetings with Prime Minister Harold Macmillan, and the couple attended a dinner given by the Queen at Buckingham Palace.

The European trip would have multiple repercussions for the beleaguered new president, but one offbeat observation stayed with him. He had been entertained at superb gardens: the ornate swirling concoctions designed for King Louis XIV by André Le Nôtre at Versailles, the Baroque flower beds and maze at Vienna's eighteenth-century Schönbrunn Palace, and the elaborate grounds of Buckingham Palace. The president was aware that the White House had nothing that could match these glories or serve as a backdrop for ceremonial occasions.

The countryside of Virginia was abuzz with hammers and saws as more than two hundred workmen spent a month at Bunny's farm toiling to create her faux French village. She hovered, checking daily on the progress. "I felt like an artisan in the seventeenth century at the service to the Queen," recalled Paul Leonard, a graduate of the Art Institute of Chicago and Yale Drama School, in an unpublished essay. "I remember, one day she found me painting some theatrical stonework, and asked if we could paint some moss on the stones to make it look older."

Over afternoon tea in her living room, Bunny explained to Leonard and his partner, Bill Strom, that she was willing to move heaven and earth—well, at least earth—to achieve the best visual effect. "Oh, the room didn't used to be as nice as this until I removed that hill over there," she told them. "I just hated the way it reflected light." The handsome twenty-nine-year-old Leonard would soon join Bunny's permanent payroll, working on her homes and parties for more than fifteen years.

When Eliza Lloyd returned from Europe, she appeared to be startled by her mother's efforts on her behalf. "Eliza arrived from Paris not having a clue as to the magnitude of this party in her honor," wrote Leonard. "I remember this young 18-year-old completely in awe...her jaw dropped when she walked through the Brick House into this fantasy world." He sensed mother-daughter tension, or, as he put it, "psychological problems."

The weather turned cool the day of the party, so Bunny installed heaters in the ballroom. Peter Duchin, the piano player son of society bandleader Eddy Duchin, had been hired to perform. The musician had grown up on the Social Register circuit and attended his share of deb parties, but Bunny's elaborate efforts stood out.

"It was pretty over-the-top, lots of things you weren't used to," recalls Duchin, who was only twenty-three years old at the time and grateful for the opportunity to play. "This was among the first jobs I had—her party and Truman Capote's Black and White Ball." Bunny befriended Duchin; he would play at her parties and lunch with her and Jackie in the years to come. As he says, "Bunny was kind of droll, classy, fun to be around, not intimidating in any way."

The night of the party, Bunny's friends, including Katharine Graham, the wife of *Washington Post* publisher Philip Graham, and Adele Astaire, gave dinners at their homes for the guests. Late in the evening, the revelers made their way to Rokeby Farm. The narrow country roads became snarled with traffic on that chilly night. According to an account in the *Washington Star*, Bobby Kennedy saw a young man in a beat-up convertible put on a bathrobe over his evening clothes to warm up. Concerned that security guards might turn the youth away, the attorney general hopped out of his warm car and rode with the stranger to the farm.

Bunny, wearing a gown of draped orchid chiffon, and Eliza, in a white satin dress embroidered with green leaves and red and white flowers, stood in the Brick House in front of an Henri Rousseau jungle scene painting, receiving guests as Paul Mellon mingled with the crowd.

Jackie Kennedy, who had attended Adele Astaire's dinner, arrived at the party at 12:30 a.m., wearing a gown with a white satin top and a skirt made of tiers of black lace, with a single red rose tucked at her waist. The president had begged off, sidelined at home with a painful back, so the First Lady was escorted by artist William Walton. Jackie stayed for ninety minutes, spending most of her time admiring the art collection.

For many of the seven hundred guests, the evening was a welcome respite from the drama of recent months. One appreciative guest quipped to the *Washington Star* about the Mellons' attention to detail: "Except for the traffic jam, if we had planned the Cuban invasion that way, we would be in Cuba now."

The attendees included CIA director Allen Dulles; assistant defense secretary Paul Nitze; presidential advisers McGeorge Bundy, John Kenneth Galbraith, and Arthur Schlesinger Jr.; and *New York Times* Washington bureau chief Arthur Krock. Georgetown dress shop owner Dorcas Hardin and Oatsie Leiter Charles represented Washington society. The New York contingent included CBS chairman William Paley and his best-dressed wife, Babe; writer Anita Loos, the author of *Gentlemen Prefer Blondes*; decorator Billy Baldwin; and Pulitzer Prize–winning Broadway and film director Josh Logan.

"That was the most spectacular party I went to," recalls William Brooks, one of the eligible young men on the debutante circuit that season. Brooks, now the director of Vermont's Henry Sheldon Museum, was a guest of Katharine Graham's daughter Lally. "I had a dance with Eliza that night and at the brunch the next day we got to talk and that led to a friendship. She was a very charming person, a great smile."

Fireworks erupted in the sky over the lake, then the revelers returned to the ballroom, lingering until 5 a.m. "I've never in my life seen a thing so well done—so easy, so gay, so marvelously pretty, so enchanting in every way without being pretentious or pompous," wrote columnist Joe Alsop in a thank-you note to Bunny.

Several guests jotted down recollections. Arthur Schlesinger noted in his journal that "everything was done with great style," he had "a particularly nice time with Babe Paley," and he "had a splendid time helping spend the ill-gotten gains of Andrew Mellon." Katharine Graham wrote in her autobiography, "The dancing carried on until the early hours of the morning. Someone said an entire vintage year of Dom Perignon was consumed that night."

The lavish event impressed society writers. "The Mellon affair was the first debutante party in the United States to top the million dollar mark," wrote Dorothy McCardle in the *Baltimore Sun*. In current dollars, the sum was equivalent to 8 million. The *Washington Post* headlined the event: IT'S PARIS IN VIRGINIA FOR THE FIRST LADY, hailing Bunny's "creative genius" in designing a French pavilion and called the party "one of the most glamorous debutante parties ever given in the Washington area."

For all of her excess, Bunny punctuated her entertaining with warm gestures toward the staff. Before taking down the decorations, she gave a party for the children of the workmen who had created the magical scene.

The party was a triumph for Bunny, but her artistic and spirited daughter, who was more comfortable in paint-splattered jeans than couture, appeared to be uncomfortable. As Paul Leonard wrote, "Eliza hated the party." Bunny was strong-willed and believed that she knew what was best for her children and stepchildren. They often profoundly disagreed.

Bunny's relationship with her stepson, Timothy Mellon, was going through a difficult phase. During his senior year at Milton Academy, Tim had fallen in love with Bryn Mawr student Susan Tracy, the daughter of Osgood Tracy, the president of Esso Standard Oil Co. Shortly after he arrived at Yale for his freshman year, Tim proposed and Susan accepted. When Tim broke the news to his father on an overseas trip together, Paul Mellon gave his son the impression that he was pleased. As Tim wrote in his 2016 autobiography: "He seemed to have no particular objection and expressed happiness that I had found someone special. But upon our return to the U.S., after he had talked with my stepmother, the {you-know-what} hit the fan. In no uncertain terms, I should not get married until having graduated from Yale."

Paul and Bunny took Susan Tracy's parents to dinner in New York to convince them to cancel the engagement. Tim belatedly learned many decades later, from Susan's sister, "that my stepmother went so far as to tell the Tracys, 'This girl simply will not do.'" The incident happened more than fifty years ago, but it was so telling and troubling that Tim Mellon chose to include it in his book.

———————

That July, Bunny offered a helping hand when Jackie Kennedy planned a state dinner at Mt. Vernon in honor of Pakistan president Mohammad Ayub Khan. Bunny provided the flowers and loaned tables, iron chairs, and yellow tablecloths. "I went early to watch the setting up," says Marie Ridder, who covered the event for *Glamour* magazine. "Bunny was doing the flowers and she did it herself. She worked hard, she wasn't fancy."

The 135 guests traveled on four yachts down the Potomac River to George Washington's home for an evening featuring French cuisine and performances by the National Symphony and the Lester Lanin orchestra. But the dinner caused an uproar when reporters learned that private companies had underwritten the expensive gala. Tiffany's lent its decorator, a Philadelphia tentmaker (who had done the honors for Eliza's debutante party) provided a pavilion and utility tents, and bandleader Lester Lanin donated his time. FREE SERVICES TO PRESIDENT TARNISH "MORAL LEADERSHIP" headlined a column by J. A. Livingston in the *Abilene Reporter-News*.

"The cost was so outrageous that Congress reared up and screamed and yelled about it," recalls Letitia Baldrige. "To simply erase the criticism, Mrs. Mellon quietly paid for the new tent. She did things that would be considered extravagant, but it was out of kindness."

Philadelphia Inquirer columnist John M. Cummings came to the administration's defense: "President Kennedy has enough on his mind to induce sleepless nights without the carping criticism of narrow-minded pipsqueaks who object to the cost of a dinner...the White House felt impelled to explain that many of the trappings that gave the party an extra flair were donated." He noted, as did other journalists, that Mrs. Paul Mellon was a close friend of the Kennedys and there was nothing wrong with helping a friend.

The once-publicity-shy Bunny had gone from being written about as "wife of" to being identified as "friend of."

Jackie Kennedy escaped to the Kennedy compound in Hyannis Port that summer with her two children while the president joined her for weekends. Nine-month-old baby John Jr. was crawling, and three-year-old Caroline liked to swim. Weather permitting, the family's weekends included cruises on the president's father's boat on Nantucket Sound as well as Sunday Mass at St. Francis Xavier Church in Hyannis.

But these Cape Cod respites were hardly relaxing for the president as he juggled multiple domestic and foreign crises. With Soviet threats in Berlin heating up, presidential weekends involved in-person briefings by Adlai Stevenson, then the American ambassador to the United Nations, Secretary of State Dean Rusk, Defense Secretary Robert McNamara, and General Maxwell Taylor.

Katharine "Kay" Graham and her publisher husband, Philip, who was struggling with severe depression, had rented a Cape Cod house that summer. Bunny called to invite them to come to lunch with the Kennedys. "I'm sure she didn't need us, but I was excited," Graham wrote in her autobiography. "I pleaded with Phil to go and he hesitantly accepted."

On the morning of Sunday, August 14, President Kennedy received word that the Soviets had begun to lay wires and barriers along the twenty-seven-mile border separating East Berlin from West Berlin. Nonetheless, he continued with his plans to go to the Mellons', bringing along Jackie and Caroline, his sister Eunice Shriver, and artist William Walton.

"We were all waiting on the Mellons' beach in Osterville when we saw the president's boat approach, with the press boat following," recalled Kay Graham. "Jack and Jackie jumped off and came into the beach." Kay brought a camera to capture the occasion.

Jackie had called Bunny that morning to alert her that the president was going to ask her to design the Rose Garden. At the Mellons' beach house by the water, Kay Graham took a photograph of the president and Bunny deep in conversation, sitting at a small table covered with a checked tablecloth.

Many years later, Bunny still recalled the president's words: "Come and do the Rose Garden. It's a mess. It's got about four little baby roses in it, and what I want is something different." She replied, "Oh, Mr. President, I'm a gardener but I don't know if I can do something as big as this." He said, "Yes, you can."

A few days later, Jackie joined Bunny, Paul, and magazine editor Horace "Ho" Kelland on a trip to Boston, flying on the Mellons' plane. After dinner at the Ritz-Carlton Hotel, they headed with a police escort to the Colonial Hotel to see Noël Coward's musical *Sail Away*, starring Elaine Stritch. Coward recalled in his diary that "the theatre was a howling inferno of Press Photographers and reporters." An iconic photo captured Jackie, in a sleeveless dress with a white top and black skirt and white gloves, smiling gamely while Bunny, in a patterned dress and white gloves, looks protectively at her friend. After the show, they greeted the cast backstage before flying back to the Cape.

Bunny stopped by the Cape Playhouse in Dennis that week to bring a picnic lunch to Eliza, who was working there for the summer. Outside the theatre, a six-foot-three young man was painting a canvas backdrop for the show. As Frank Langella, then twenty-three, recalled his first sight of Bunny: "She was dressed in a dark blue heavy linen skirt, a boat neck pullover, a floppy hat, espadrilles and carrying a picnic basket... Soft, unfussy hair. Suddenly, she plopped down next to me with her picnic basket and examined my stencil work as if it were the new Mark Rothko. She asked me so many questions, 'Where was I born, where did I go to school, what were my plans, did I have a girlfriend?' I had her total focus. Eliza appeared, 'Oh, I see you've met my friend Frank.' [Bunny replied,] 'He's a painter.' Eliza said, 'Sure he is and I'm the queen of Romania.'"

Langella had been cast in the summer-stock theatre's production of *Under the Yum Yum Tree*. Several days later, Eliza told him that her mother wanted him to join the family and some friends for Sunday lunch. "And since actors will go anywhere for free food," he recalled, "I cleaned myself up Sunday and I drove to the Cape House in my broken down station wagon." The Bayonne, New Jersey, native was astonished to meet the distinguished guests. "We were eight for lunch. Eliza, myself, Bunny Mellon, Paul Mellon, Adele Astaire, Noël Coward, and President and Mrs. John F. Kennedy."

Noël Coward was pleased to spend the afternoon in such august company. "Mrs. Mellon is a dear woman with perfect taste and perfect manners," he wrote in his diary. "The Kennedys left at about four o'clock and we waved them away from the jetty. It was curiously moving to see that attractive young couple wearing gay colours, shooting off among the grey-green 'Boudin' sea followed and preceded by armored coastguard cutters. Altogether a day to remember."

Chapter Fifteen

A Rose by Any Other Name

Outside the Oval Office in the White House, a venerable magnolia tree still produces shimmering pink and white spring flowers. Andrew Jackson planted the magnolia tree in 1829, in memory of his late wife, Rachel, as a living tribute to love and grief. The rest of the landscaping at 1600 Pennsylvania Avenue has changed significantly through the years, reflecting the trends and tastes of the inhabitants.

In 1903, President Teddy Roosevelt's wife, Edith, installed a nostalgic Colonial garden with paisley-shaped beds of sweet peas, jasmine, wildflowers, and daisies. After Woodrow Wilson took office, his wife, Ellen, had those beds demolished. But she died in 1914 before her ambitious new design could be installed. Wilson's second wife, Edith, oversaw the plot's transformation into a sophisticated rose garden with clipped privet hedges.

But by 1961, the media-savvy President Kennedy believed the garden looked forlorn and outdated. He wanted to apply his campaign slogan—"We Can Do Better"—to the White House grounds. Under the existing design, long rows of hedges broke up the 90-by-125-foot West Garden, limiting the number of people who could stand during ceremonial functions or be seated at outdoor dinners. Kennedy wanted to be able to use the space, rather than just gaze at it from his office.

Bunny was initially baffled by the prospect of creating a visually elegant stage set, using trees, flowers, and hedges to serve as a backdrop for state occasions. She brought Perry Wheeler along on her first visit to the garden, and the two of them sat on a white bench under Andrew Jackson's magnolia tree.

As they mulled the possibilities, the president stepped out of the Oval Office. "What do you think can be done? Have you any ideas?" he asked, as Bunny later recalled. Put on the spot, Bunny was vague, saying that she would have to think about it. To convey that she was serious about the project, she sent the president a copy of Thomas Jefferson's gardening notes.

A few weeks later on a chilly October night, Bunny strolled by Manhattan's Frick Museum on Fifth Avenue, just a few blocks from her East Seventieth Street town house. Industrialist Andrew Frick—Andrew Mellon's business partner—built the mansion in 1913, with a spacious garden including three large magnolia trees. That evening as Bunny walked by, she noticed that the autumn weather had stripped the trees bare of leaves, but the stark branches reaching toward the sky retained a sculptural appeal.

"I had often admired these trees before, but this evening they had a special importance to me," Bunny later wrote in an essay for White House History, a journal. "Their pale silvery branches with heavy twigs seemed to retain the light of summer. I knew the pattern of growth would continue to give form in winter and would catch raindrops as well as tufts of falling snow."

She could suddenly envision how the White House garden might look if all four corners were planted with magnolia trees, which would unify the space and soften the edges. "On either side of the large lawn there could be a border twelve feet wide in which to plant smaller trees, roses and other flowers," she wrote. Even though she could now imagine the possibilities, the prospect of moving forward was daunting. Perry Wheeler agreed to help, but this was a project that would involve working with the National Park Service and the federal bureaucracy.

———

That fall, Bunny and Jackie put their combined clout behind a charity event: an exhibit of Johnny Schlumberger's jewels at the Wildenstein

Gallery to raise money to preserve Newport's deteriorating mansions. This event burnished the reputation of Bunny's friend Johnny by treating his creations as museum-worthy art. Jackie's mother, Janet Auchincloss, who spent summers in Newport, joined the gala's committee.

Bunny agreed to loan her jewel-encrusted Schlumberger pieces and let her name be used to publicize the exhibit. Her most noteworthy possessions included a large cross, of emeralds, sapphires, and aquamarines, originally commissioned by the French government; a gold cigarette box; and six jewel-turbaned blackamoors from her twenty-two-piece collection of these small, exotic statues of African men. Johnny Schlumberger remained an ongoing presence in Bunny's life; she noted their dinner dates in New York, Antigua, and Paris in her appointment calendars. According to Paul Leonard, Jackie was wary of Schlumberger because of what she perceived as the jeweler's "control over Bunny."

Jackie and Bunny attended a dinner on October 31 at Schlumberger's Upper East Side home, then the designer escorted them to the opening. In an article headlined THE ART OF JEAN SCHLUMBERGER, the *New York Herald Tribune* praised his "craftsmanship and genius" as well as his "wit and off-hand glamour."

Two weeks after the Schlumberger opening, Jackie placed Bunny in a prime seat at the president's table at a White House state dinner honoring Puerto Rico's governor, Luis Muñoz Marín. Pablo Casals, the eighty-four-year-old cellist, gave an after-dinner recital that lasted until 11:30 p.m.

As Bunny recalled, President Kennedy used their proximity to inquire, "Bunny, where is my garden plan?" She replied, "I'm afraid it is still in my head, Mr. President, not yet on paper, but I will finish it soon and send it to you soon." The impatient president smiled and responded, "That's the story of my administration."

As the year wound down, news accounts highlighted the friendship between the Kennedys and the Mellons. On November 18, Jackie joined Paul Mellon for the Piedmont Fox Hunt, a sporting event that began at 11 a.m. in Westview, Virginia. Forty minutes into the chase, Paul and his horse successfully leapt over a split-rail fence but Jackie's horse, Bit of Irish, balked.

Photographer Marshall Hawkins told reporters: "The horse stopped but she didn't." Jackie went flying over the horse's head and landed across the fence on the grass. The photographer said the fall "knocked the wind out of her a little bit." But the First Lady brushed herself off and got back on her horse a few minutes later to rejoin the hunt. The fox got away.

Bunny helped Jackie prepare for the traditional White House Christmas receptions by recommending the services of set designers Paul Leonard and Bill Strom. "Mrs. Mellon introduced me to Jackie Kennedy, who was at the debutante party, and the next thing I knew I was decorating the Christmas tree at the White House," Paul Leonard later told the *New York Times*. "It was fun being around the White House in those days. It was so relaxed. I used to drive in there with my station wagon loaded with Christmas decorations, and nobody would even check."

The two designers decorated the eighteen-foot balsam tree in the Blue Room with the theme of Tchaikovsky's *Nutcracker* ballet, using blue velvet ribbon, musical instruments, tiny imitation mice, a stage-coach, birds, and even the seven dwarfs. The tree won plaudits when the Kennedys held a reception for twelve hundred people. Four-year-old Caroline was seen by the press tugging her father's hand to try to waylay him into the room for yet another sighting of the tree.

Jackie loved the decorations, gushing in a letter to Bunny on December 13 that she was "bewitched" by the sight and visited the tree twice a day. She wrote that Caroline and her friend Mary Warner—the daughter of Cathy Mellon and John Warner—had mischievously tried to pull off the ornaments. Jackie was full of compliments. "What will I say when you do the rose garden?" Jackie wrote, joking that she was running out of superlatives and would have to compliment Bunny in Japanese from now on "as I have no words left."

Christmas was merry in the Mellon household: Paul wrote Bunny a rhyming note saying that she would find "a small Utrillo" beneath her pillow.

On January 24, 1962, Bunny sent watercolor sketches of her design for the Rose Garden, along with detailed renderings, to the president. She signed her name "Rachel Lambert Mellon," as if to underline her professional commitment. Her streamlined design eliminated the existing hedges and opened up the space to allow for as many as one thousand people to use the garden. With magnolia trees anchoring the corners, the lawn would be framed—as if it were a picture—with borders of trees and flowers.

Two sides of the White House garden would feature crab apple trees in diamond-shaped beds, surrounded by roses and perennials, with a boxwood border. Within two days, President Kennedy approved the proposal but requested one change.

Since he planned to speak to large groups with cameras recording the scene, the president wanted to alter the steps that led from the White House down into the garden to create better sightlines. As Bunny recalled, he told her, "They're too low and they're not adequate. When I'm giving someone an honor, I want them to be one step above me and I want a platform. In other words, two regular steps then a platform about this wide and then two rows."

The president asked Bunny to complete the garden in four months and to keep costs down, although the National Park Service would cover the expense.

Bunny's first task was to find a government gardener to execute her design. She began visiting Park Service gardens, even venturing to Anacostia, one of Washington's most impoverished and crime-ridden neighborhoods, to see the Kenilworth Aquatic Gardens.

Irvin Williams, the head gardener who had worked at this rarely visited outpost for more than eight years, proved knowledgeable about the eighty varieties of water lilies and nine lotuses in his care, including such exotic specimens as the tropical Royal Platter, a lotus with six-foot, saucer-shaped leaves. The thirty-six-year-old West Virginian had previously worked briefly on the White House grounds in 1949, pruning and spraying the trees.

Bunny instinctively felt that she "had a meeting of minds" with the lanky and unflappable Williams, a married man with five children who tended his own home vegetable and flower gardens. She asked Jackie to arrange for Williams to be transferred to the White House as chief gardener, impulsively whisking him from obscurity into a prestigious job that he would hold for nearly fifty years.

On Valentine's Day, Jackie Kennedy gave an unprecedented televised tour of the newly redecorated White House, accompanied by CBS correspondent Charles Collingwood. A record eighty million people tuned in to watch the First Lady, who was wearing a sheath dress, triple strand of pearls, and stylish bouffant hairdo as she strolled through the building. In her distinctive, whispery voice, she offered up snippets of history as she showed off the paintings and antiques acquired by her Fine Arts committee and credited donors by name.

There were revealing moments in this soft-focus hour. Allowing the TV crew to film in the Lincoln bedroom, she pointed out a series of paintings of Abraham Lincoln that graphically illustrated how he had aged in the job. "Here is what the White House did to President Lincoln and here is how he changed," she said, highlighting a gaunt portrait that she noted was "made one week before his assassination."

She gestured admiringly at Lincoln's ornate carved wooden bed, which had been purchased by Mary Lincoln. "She bought a lot of furniture for this house which made her husband cross," Jackie said. "He thought she spent too much money." That was a not-so-subtle jab at her own husband, who had repeatedly complained about her own copious expenditures.

The president appeared toward the end of the tour to praise his wife and describe how reassuring it was to live among these historic treasures. "I think that the great effort that she has made has put us more intimately in contact with the men who lived here," he said. "This country has passed through difficult days, but it has passed through them."

Work was scheduled to start soon on the new Rose Garden, a major construction job that entailed tearing out the existing greenery and excavating four feet down. Bunny headed to her Antigua home to relax in anticipation of the grueling task ahead. In her absence, Perry Wheeler handled the liaison with federal employees, who were now balking at fulfilling her design. "How I wish you could have been at the Interior Building yesterday when I went down to meet with the Park Department boys about the garden," Perry wrote to Bunny on March 8. The government workers objected to Bunny's plan to install the large magnolia trees because they were concerned that digging next to the White House might disrupt underground electronic cables.

"Their only solution seemed to be to abandon the idea of any trees," wrote Perry, adding that he warned them that if that happened, Bunny would want to redesign the entire garden. "This threw them into the state of shock that I expected because they right away mentioned that everything was ordered, scheduled." He won that argument.

Once the president approved the $23,458 estimated cost, work began on March 19. Bunny supervised the archaeological dig. "The garden was filled with rubble and relics and yielded many curiosities, such as Civil War Horseshoes and bits of pots from the old greenhouses," Bunny later wrote. The president and his confidants frequently walked out of the Oval Office to check on the progress. Attorney General Robert Kennedy recalled, "Often, during Cabinet meetings, we would see her out there in the rose garden—a little figure with a bandana around her head."

On March 31, a workman poked a shovel deep into the earth and suddenly alarms went off and security guards materialized. The Park Department's fears had proved prescient. The workman had cut the cord connecting the president's office to the Strategic Arms Command, vital communications that would allow him to launch a nuclear attack. America was at the height of the Cold War, with relations with the Soviet Union on the brink of erupting, and this little mishap could have had catastrophic repercussions.

"This startling experience was handled with calmness; not even the president reprimanded us for the deep digging," Bunny later wrote.

"However, months later he asked me if I had found any other interesting objects in my gardening pursuits!"

Bunny had been searching Washington for mature magnolia trees: She finally found the perfect specimens by the Tidal Basin, one of the most scenic spots in Washington overlooking the Jefferson Memorial. The Parks Department turned down her request for those trees. Perry Wheeler informed Bunny in a letter that he had been told that "those trees would be too costly to move and that they can buy trees in a nursery cheaper." He and Bunny made their case to head gardener Irvin Williams, who overrode the objections and arranged to dig up the trees and transplant them.

The White House lawn was planted with bluegrass and the flower beds were filled with blue and white pansies, the first batch in what would be a constantly changing array of seasonal flowers. Since the president had asked for plants that had been popular in Thomas Jefferson's day, the gardeners planted primroses, periwinkle, delphinium, shasta daisies, columbine, and anemones, followed by fall chrysanthemums.

With a nod to politics, the president accepted a gift of pink-tinged yellow rosebushes from Texas, the Speaker Sam variety named after late Speaker of the House Sam Rayburn, the mentor of Vice President Lyndon Johnson. The other newly planted rosebushes included the bright red World's Fair variety along with white Frau Karl Druschki and pink Doctor roses.

The garden was unveiled on April 24, 1962, although it would remain a cultivated work in progress. "The president loved the garden and got a lot of pleasure from walking around it," Lee Radziwill told me. "He liked and respected Bunny enormously, also Paul." Radziwill described her own reaction upon seeing the garden: "It's so peaceful. It's a place of peace in the White House."

William Walton, the artist who was close to Jack Kennedy, later wrote, "His pleasure in that garden was infinite. He loved to show the garden to visitors and it got to be a joke among the staff and Secret Service that none dared walk on the President's grass. He was likely to poke his head out of the French door and holler 'get off the grass!'"

Bunny was quoted in newspaper articles describing the design as "traditional American...straightforward...with nothing tricky." *Los Angeles Times* columnist Bill Henry wrote: "Formerly a maze of hedges and thorny bushes which forced the Chief Executive and his guests to run a kind of obstacle course, it is now an orderly design surrounding a neat square of lawn."

Tom Wicker of the *New York Times* was equally enthusiastic, writing, "Nobody knows whether it's the Old Rose Garden or the New Flower Garden but whatever it is, it's beautiful and it's right outside the President's office." The president and First Lady were so pleased that they asked Bunny to tackle a second project, redesigning the White House East Garden.

Paul Mellon had heard about his wife's work on the Rose Garden but had not seen the final creation. On June 5, Paul gave Jackie Kennedy an after-hours preview at the National Gallery of Impressionist paintings on loan from André Meyer, the Frenchman who headed the investment-banking firm Lazard Frères. A photographer captured Jackie's delight as she gazed at a Degas portrait of Mary Cassatt. The First Lady had recently managed a coup: convincing French cultural minister André Malraux to loan the *Mona Lisa* to the National Gallery for an upcoming exhibit.

Once Paul and Jackie finished their tour, she invited him to the White House to see the Rose Garden. He hopped into her chauffeured black limousine, while Jackie instructed a Secret Service agent to drive Paul's gray Mercedes-Benz to the White House. The press reported with great amusement on what happened next: The agent couldn't figure out how to start the foreign car. The problem was finally solved when Gallery director John Walker found the instruction manual in the glove compartment.

As soon as the new Rose Garden was completed, the president began using it for ceremonial occasions. In August 1962, he swore in Anthony Celebrezze, the former mayor of Cleveland, as the new Health and Education secretary. The garden was the backdrop when JFK gave a distinguished service medal to an FDA official for keeping the harmful drug thalidomide off the American market. In September, Kennedy invited the award-winning University of Arkansas choir to join him there. In early October, he welcomed Algerian premier Ahmed Ben Bella to the garden with a twenty-one-gun salute, which prompted Jackie to crouch behind a rosebush holding on to young John-John, so the toddler wouldn't be frightened by the smoke and noise.

In mid-October, for a terrifying thirteen days, the Cuban missile crisis roiled the White House. During the greatest foreign policy crisis of the postwar era, when the United States and the Soviets went eyeball to eyeball over Russian nuclear missile sites in Cuba, the Rose Garden served as a dramatic backdrop as President Kennedy agonized with advisers to come up with a strategy to avoid a nuclear war with Russia. Particularly haunting is a photo of Jack and Bobby Kennedy conferring—with the future of the world in the balance—in the garden that Bunny designed.

On October 30, two days after the crisis ended and the Russians had backed down, the president wrote to Bunny, "I need not tell you that your garden has been our brightest spot in the somber surroundings of the last few days."

Bunny's relationship with Jackie Kennedy just kept getting stronger. After Bunny arranged baskets of flowers for a White House luncheon for the president of Chile, Jackie wrote to her, "Now even de Gaulle would think Versailles a bit tacky if he came for dinner here." Jackie added that Bunny was the "adored patron saint" of everyone at the White House from the "lowliest groundsman" to the president.

The First Lady was now seeking painted-from-life portraits of the six presidents who had followed George Washington. Thomas Jefferson had posed for artist Rembrandt Peale in Philadelphia in 1805, but the whereabouts of the painting had been unknown for decades.

Princeton professor Alfred Bush, a Jefferson scholar, discovered it in 1959, tucked into a closet at the Peabody Institute in Baltimore, mistakenly labeled as a reproduction. This was treated as big news in Bunny's hometown, Princeton, where her parents still lived; it's likely that they told her about the discovery. Paul and Bunny bought the Jefferson portrait and donated it to the White House.

Jackie wrote to Bunny in a December 1962 note that the painting and Jefferson's "terrible sadness" mesmerized her. She could see the weight of the presidency in his face. But what she really wanted to stress in her letter was her appreciation for having such a loyal and selfless friend in Bunny.

"Everyone else comes heralded by trumpets through the front door—and there you are in working gloves fixing all the flowers." Jackie added that she felt "badly" that Bunny, who disliked publicity, was subjected to "that terrible spotlight that is the onus of our friendship."

Jackie sadly acknowledged that many people wanted to be her friend to stand in the reflected glow of that spotlight, whereas Bunny was her friend despite the unwanted attention. In a poignant note, Jackie added, "If you ever just fade away into the mist, I will understand."

In January 1963, the most famous painting in the world—the mysterious *Mona Lisa*—arrived at the National Gallery. The Leonardo da Vinci masterpiece, stolen in 1911 from the Louvre and recovered two years later, received the kind of rousing welcome (and security) granted to a visiting head of state. Bunny and Paul attended a dinner at the French Embassy with the Kennedys and other dignitaries, followed by a viewing at the museum.

By now, Bunny had established rituals to prepare for such events. She imported her favorite Manhattan hairdresser, Kenneth Battelle, who also made house calls at the White House to style Jackie's bouffant. Bunny and Kenneth had become "soul mates," says Amy Greene, beauty editor and wife of photographer Milton Greene. "And Mr. Mellon liked him. He would invite Kenneth as an extra man, they would talk about art. Mr. and Mrs. Mellon started Kenneth's art collection."

Bunny still bought her clothes from Balenciaga, going to Paris for fittings and spending tens of thousands of dollars a year on his creations. Now that she was attending so many high-profile events, she needed a fresh infusion of ball gowns. With her closets overflowing, she decided to make room for the new by getting rid of the old. Bunny found the perfect charitable recipient: the Duchess of Devonshire. Deborah, known as Debo, the youngest of the six famous Mitford sisters, gratefully accepted Bunny's hand-me-downs.

"You can't imagine what a time we had opening them and pulling out the things one by one, each more exciting than the next," Debo wrote to Bunny in 1963, on behalf of herself, her sisters, and her mother-in-law, the Dowager Duchess. "There will be some fierce fights before they are properly sorted out."

Debo did not want her social circle to know that she was wearing Bunny's castoffs. She cheerfully admitted to Bunny that she had just had a close call during a shooting weekend with their mutual friend, decorator Nancy Lancaster. Nancy had admired Debo's red Balenciaga gown and inquired about which Balenciaga vendeuse had arranged to make the dress. "I swallowed, went pink," wrote the Duchess, and "luckily everyone started talking at that moment."

Bunny loved to shop. Actor Frank Langella recalled seeing Bunny at the Carlyle Hotel in 1963, laden with shopping bags. He teased her, saying, "You look just like a New York secretary who won the lottery. I'm going to call you Myrtle." She replied, "I'm going to call you Harry." They used those nicknames with each other for half a century. "Every note she sent to me was signed Mertz," he recalled. "Everything I've sent back was 'Love, Harry.' This woman had an enormous gift for personal relationships."

The Mellons collected witty and entertaining companions. Gerard Lambert introduced Princeton professor Charles Ryskamp, who taught eighteenth-century literature, to Paul and Bunny. A Yale graduate who had studied in Cambridge, he collected Old Masters prints and could knowledgeably discuss art with Paul. Princeton professor Alfred Bush recalls, "Charles's summer routine soon included spending much of August with Mr. and Mrs. Mellon at their compound in Osterville at Cape Cod." Bunny was fond of him and designed a garden for Ryskamp's Princeton home. At the professor's request, Paul made grants to the Princeton University Library to purchase rare books.

In April 1963, Paul and Bunny were named "Collectors of the Year" by the Virginia Museum of Fine Arts, an occasion marked by an exhibit of their British paintings at the Richmond museum. Paul had been on a buying binge, snatching up hundreds of undervalued artworks. He had imported a British curator, John Baskett, who spent two years living on the Mellons' farm, cataloguing the works.

"Paintings were arriving in large numbers every week," recalled Baskett, who became one of Paul's closest friends. "In the Brick House, we had racks put up on the top floor. I created rotating exhibitions so Paul could see his recent purchases."

The curator saw a more relaxed side of the formidable couple. "On Sunday nights, the staff had evenings off and we had dinner in Bunny's kitchen," he recalled. "They always had caviar from Maison Blanche and vodka, which I always drank but they said they didn't want, and soup, and cold meats. It was amusing on one occasion because I wanted to help with the washing up and they said, 'No, we've got it organized.' I've got this view of them with aprons on and a dish-cloth as I left the room."

The Virginia exhibit, organized by Baskett, was a tribute to Paul's astute eye and busy checkbook. There were 324 paintings and 127 watercolors, featuring sporting paintings, landscapes and seascapes, works by J. M. W. Turner, William Hogarth, John Constable, Thomas Gainsborough, and the poet William Blake. In his remarks at the gala dinner, Paul made a point of praising his wife, calling her "a brilliant artist in her own right in the fields of gardening and architecture."

Now in their fifties, they were both flourishing. Elected in January to the presidency of the National Gallery, Paul was relishing his role as a patron of the arts. But he was traveling so much that he told the *New Yorker*, "I find it's a little confusing when people ask where I live." He explained that he considered the Upperville farm to be his home, but he spent four days a month in Pittsburgh, another five days or so in New York and, most weekdays in Washington; plus, he periodically visited his racing stables in England. Meanwhile, Bunny had received national acclaim for her rejuvenation of the Rose Garden. Their children were adults, with lives of their own.

Tim Mellon, a junior at Yale, married Susan Tracy that June, unwilling to wait until graduation. "My parents finally relented to the accelerated schedule, but only with extreme grudge," he wrote in his autobiography. His sister, Cathy Mellon Warner, and stepbrother, Tuffy Lloyd, were among the attendants at the June wedding. Bunny's son was now working at the U.S. Information Agency, soon to be stationed in Laos, a posting he insists to this day was not associated with the CIA.

The week after the festivities, Bunny went for a walk with Jackie Kennedy, who was pregnant again, due in late August. The Kennedys had nearly finished building a seven-bedroom weekend house, with a swimming pool and horse stables, at Rattlesnake Mountain in Atoka, Virginia, less than five miles from Bunny and Paul's home. Bunny was now working with Jackie on the design for the White House East Wing Garden.

The First Lady envisioned this as a private family spot, with a croquet or badminton court, a splashing pool, and an herb garden for the White House chef. As Bunny later wrote in *House & Garden*, Jackie "could see an old-fashioned grape arbor with hanging baskets of scented geraniums, and tubs of lemon verbena, heliotrope, and mignonette. Here one could read, have tea and entertain. An arbor would be in the tradition of this large, but nevertheless Southern country house." Jackie's idea for the croquet court reminded Bunny of a scene from *Alice in Wonderland*. She had recently seen holly topiaries shaped like chess pieces at a nursery and thought they would give the garden a whimsical feeling.

Once again, Perry Wheeler played intermediary, sending memos detailing Bunny's wishes to White House gardener Irvin Williams. The notes include such suggestions as "Use big Cherry laurels in northeast and northwest corners of East Garden, next to building (instead of Yellow woods)." Concerned that Perry was hurting financially because of this unpaid help, Bunny sent him a check "for the work, inspiration and heart you put into the gardens at the White House...without your support and understanding I could not do it and you cannot go on helping and living on air."

Bunny left for Paris in July. She spent a weekend at Balenciaga's country house and then headed to England to see the gardens at Sissinghurst Castle, the former home of Vita Sackville-West and Harold Nicolson.

She returned to Virginia just as back-to-back tragedies were befalling her friends. Katharine Graham's husband, Philip, the president of the *Washington Post*, committed suicide, killing himself with a shotgun at the family's weekend Virginia home. Bunny attended the August 8 funeral.

The following day, Jackie Kennedy was at the stables on Cape Cod, taking Caroline and John riding, when she felt labor pains. She wasn't due for three weeks. Flown by helicopter to the Otis Air Force Base hospital, she gave birth to a four-pound, ten-and-a-half-ounce baby, Patrick. The premature baby suffered from a lung complication, hyaline membrane disease. He died two days later. Bunny, who had suffered through three miscarriages, sent flowers and a note:

Dearest Jackie,

There are no words to tell you how deeply my thoughts and feelings go out to you this morning.

Knowing your great sensitivity and courage it is heartbreaking that you should have such sadness.

Day and night please call if there is anything I can do for you.

Paul joins me in our thoughts of you and the President today.

Much love, dearest Jackie.
Bunny

After recuperating for several weeks, Jackie still could not face returning to the White House. She accepted her sister Lee's offer to join her on a two-week October vacation in Greece, sailing on the yacht of Greek ship owner Aristotle Onassis. The president urged his wife not to go, but she was determined to make the trip. On October 1, the sisters joined Onassis on his yacht.

Bunny left the country as well. She and Paul flew to Paris on October 4 to watch his horses race at Longchamps. After he left for London, she kept busy, spending time with Evangeline Bruce, the second wife of David Bruce; lunching with Johnny Schlumberger; shopping with her daughter, Eliza; and then heading to the country to stay with Balenciaga. ("Lovely weekend, one of the happiest ones," she noted in her appointment calendar.) After returning home, she went to the White House on October 29 for discussions about the gardens.

Some two weeks later, as Bunny was packing to leave for a trip to Antigua, she called Jackie to see how she was doing. In Bunny's memory of that conversation, Jackie replied that she was feeling much better, so much so that she had decided to accompany Jack on a campaign trip.

On November 18, Bunny left for Antigua. Two days later, Jackie joined her husband on a reelection swing to Texas, with scheduled stops in San Antonio, Houston, Fort Worth, and Dallas.

Chapter Sixteen

November 22, 1963

The island of Antigua was a sleepy, remote paradise, famous for its laid-back lifestyle where visitors could truly get away from it all. "There is no television. There is an Antiguan radio station that broadcasts music all day," wrote *New York Times* reporter Nan Robertson in January 1961. "When news of the outside world comes on, the static makes it seem as if the announcer is speaking Urdu through a mouthful of sardines." The *Times* described Antigua as "romantic, idyllic and slightly wacky."

Bunny and Paul's Antigua home remained a work in progress, with two hundred island craftsmen still toiling on the estate. On this trip she had brought along architect H. Page Cross and scenic painter Paul Leonard. At 4 p.m. on a sunny November Friday afternoon, the laborers finished for the day and gathered near the Mellons' home, awaiting buses. The crowd suddenly grew hushed.

Paul Leonard was standing on a ladder inside the house, a paintbrush in his hand, when one of the local workmen found him and blurted out the news. President Kennedy had been shot and killed in Dallas. As Leonard recalled, "My first reaction was to find Mrs. Mellon."

She was outside talking to H. Page Cross, discussing plans for the driveway. "I ran down to her and reached for her hand and said, 'You must come with me,'" Leonard wrote, in an account of the day. "She must have sensed the desperation and the look on my face because her first reaction was, 'It's not Eliza, is it?' I assured her no, but hand in hand, we went back to the monkey room to try to digest this shocking news."

They turned on the radio but all they could get was a French station, relayed through Martinique from Paris, and the station signal was dim. Bunny kept repeating, "I must get home for Jackie."

Torrential rain prevented her from leaving that night; the airport was closed. Bunny huddled in her bedroom with the only working radio. She sent a Western Union telegram at dawn to Perry Wheeler: LEAVING ON FIRST PLANE TODAY PLEASE GIVE MY LOVE AND THOUGHTS TO ALL WE WORK WITH MUCH LOVE BUNNY.

She finally caught a Saturday afternoon flight to New York City, where her husband met her at the airport. Paul told Bunny that James Bernard West, the White House usher known by his initials J.B., was trying to reach her. After a trip to her Manhattan apartment for a change of clothes, Bunny returned to the airport at 11 p.m., where the Mellons' private plane and pilot were waiting to take her to Washington.

"Lightning was flashing and the storm was like the horribleness of the occasion," Bunny later told historian William Manchester in an emotionally raw interview on June 19, 1964, for his book, *The Death of a President*. (Manchester used some of these quotes, but many have not previously been published.) "Fortunately we have our own pilots for our private plane and they are courageous . . . we landed a little after midnight and I went straight to the White House."

Bunny had been steeling herself for this moment, but what she saw took her breath away:

I walked up to the front door of the White House through lines of soldiers and there was dead silence. I saw the black crepe over the doorway as I walked between the soldiers and the only sound there was the clicking of their heels as I passed and they came to attention. I went in the front door and standing inside was Mr.

West. There was not a soul there but him, he seemed to be all alone in the White House, and he put his arms around me and I gave him a big kiss. We went to the Blue Room and sat down.

For a few moments, they let grief overtake them. "I was all choked up but Mr. West, with tears streaming down his face, said, 'It's too awful and Mrs. Kennedy is the most remarkable woman and she has never lost her head and has directed everything. If you should see her and she wants to talk, you must let her talk.'

"He told me that she had fallen asleep. I brought a thing of flowers and told him to put them by her bed and that I would stay. He told me that I could not wait all night because 'you have a job to do tomorrow. Mrs. Kennedy wants you to arrange the flowers at the [Capitol], at the church, and at Arlington.'"

The last time the country had mourned a president who died in office was 1945, and the ailing FDR had been felled by a cerebral hemorrhage. But an assassination had entirely different overtones. For Bunny Mellon, who was not a government employee, to be assigned to create these floral arrangements—which would set the mood for all three events—was unprecedented.

"I was exhausted but I was not daunted or even tired because I knew what I must do," Bunny explained. Grateful to be of use, she scribbled a note to the widowed First Lady: "With my deepest love Dearest Jackie. Sorry to take so long to get back—Bunny." The usher took Bunny to see the president's coffin in the East Room, allowing her to say a private good-bye.

"I went in alone and there were the four soldiers there and the coffin covered with the flag. It was like the fall of all the hope of youth—as though youth had tried and had been thwarted...I saw the crepe around the East Room. It was not sentimental tragedy—it was most dignified. All this went back to the simplicity and youth and dignity of President Kennedy. It was a terrible thing and it seemed as though this country had symbolically killed something."

The next morning at 9 a.m. Bunny and her chauffeur stopped by the White House to pick up Jackie's aides, Nancy Tuckerman and

Pamela Turnure, then headed to the Capitol. They met with an Army chaplain to discuss the flowers for the rotunda, where the president's casket would lie in state. "He told me the army were to be my assistants," Bunny wrote. That was a startling turn of events. "He showed me where they would bring the coffin." Since she had not spoken to Jackie yet, Bunny had to intuit the First Lady's wishes.

"I knew Jackie would not want flowers to look like a funeral," she told William Manchester. Floral tributes were being delivered from foreign leaders as well as ordinary grief-stricken Americans. Bunny realized that her job would require diplomacy as well as artistic vision: "When I saw the flowers arriving I knew that it was important that they be displayed in some way because of the countries which were sending them, and that they must be recognized for the feeling they were displaying."

The president of the Allied Florist Association of Greater Washington warned her that local florists had decided to stay open on Sunday to fill orders. The blossoms would just keep coming, fragrant masses symbolizing the nation's loss.

Making a quick decision, she issued orders: The floral tributes from heads of state should be placed in the entrance hall. The only flowers permitted near the casket in the rotunda would be a bouquet from Jackie and a red, white, and blue wreath from the newly sworn-in president, Lyndon Johnson. Bunny asked for greenery, such as palms, to soften the look of the space.

When she left the Capitol, she could not find her car and driver in the crush of vehicles. Time was of the essence. The Army chaplain commandeered an Army car and two soldiers, who drove her down Pennsylvania Avenue toward the White House. They got stuck in traffic three blocks away. Bunny got out and ran to the entrance. But since she had not brought any identification, the guard would not let her into the White House.

Frantic, she ran to another gate, where she was recognized and allowed to enter the building. She headed to the basement. "There I saw Mr. West standing with his hands to his head in a look of desperation on his face. He was out of his mind because he couldn't find a black veil [for Jackie]. He asked me what to do, and I racked my brain and had no idea." (A White House maid ultimately made the veil.)

The funeral cortege was about to leave, but Bunny chose not to watch. She did not want this sight imprinted on her memory and feared falling apart at a moment when it was imperative to function. "I had no time, neither could I bear it. Really my heart was breaking, and for lots of reasons, because of my country and because I knew what this woman was bearing. The world was watching her, I couldn't."

Accompanied by White House floral arranger Elmer Young, Bunny went to see the Cathedral of St. Matthew the Apostle, where the president's funeral service would be held. The gargantuan redbrick church, completed in 1895, seated twelve hundred people. "It was such an enormous church that I didn't know how it could be decorated. I decided the best thing would be to have two simple urn-like things. Rented urns appeared but they were so terrible, in such terrible taste that they would not do."

After conferring with Pamela Turnure, Bunny chose two blue vases from the White House that had been gifts from France. She chose a mixture of white flowers—daisies, white chrysanthemums, and stephanotises, a fragrant white version of jasmine—for the solemn church setting.

Her next stop was Arlington National Cemetery, accompanied by Elmer Young along with Perry Wheeler. They decided to decorate the hillside by the grave with the flowers arriving at the Capitol. The plan: The next day, after President Kennedy's casket was taken to the church, the flowers would be transported to the cemetery. Bunny wanted the hillside to resemble "an enormous blanket" of flowers.

Returning to the White House around 6 p.m., Bunny was informed that Jackie wanted to see her. This was the first time the friends had spoken since the world shattered. "We sat down facing each other in the West Sitting Hall," Bunny told William Manchester. "She had far more dignity than I did. Bobby and Lee were there and Bobby was awfully sweet. Jackie said, 'You know Bobby.' We shook hands. He said, 'Thank you for all the pleasure [of] the garden you gave the President.'"

Jackie appeared composed. But she needed to talk about what happened in Dallas, describing to Bunny what it was like to be by her husband's side when shots exploded and he was hit in the head, blood and tissue splattering everywhere. Jackie said her instinctive reaction was to want to "put it back"—to put her husband's brains into his skull.

As Bunny recalled, Jackie told her: "It was horrifying and not disgusting. I wanted so much to hide, protect, take care of him." As a devout Catholic, Jackie's faith had been tested; she could not understand why God had allowed the murder to happen. "She said, 'I really believe in God, I believe in Heaven, but where has God gone?'"

Bunny recalled thinking at the time that Jackie's idea of heaven was "a child's conception"—that she spoke of "clouds and green fields and warm sunlight." Jackie told Bunny that "Jack will be with Patrick and the other baby," referring to their stillborn child.

They finally talked about the flower arrangements. Bunny was relieved to hear that she had guessed correctly about her friend's wishes. Jackie told her, "I don't want the church to look like a funeral—I want it to look like spring. I want it not sad because Jack was not a sad man, he was a simple man and the one thing he hated most was anything that looked like a funeral. He hated the funeral look of the flowers that were sent to Patrick. He didn't want a funeral look because he loved flowers."

Jackie had one more request: She asked Bunny to put together a simple basket of flowers, similar to what Bunny had sent her four months earlier after Patrick died. Jackie planned to leave the basket at the cemetery. Even though it was late in the season, Jackie wanted to use flowers from the Rose Garden. She urged Bunny to write her own note to the president and put it "scrunched down" in the basket.

Bunny made a twilight visit to this now-haunted landscape. "I went out in the rose garden with a basket and some scissors. It was really remarkable...dozens of white roses in bloom in November. It was almost pitch dark, and the only light I had was the lights from the house. I picked all I could get and took berries off the hawthorne and crab apple tree...The flowers still in bloom in the garden were blue salvia, a few chrysanthemums, and the roses and berries. From my own greenhouse I took nicotiana, red geranium, blue cornflowers and several colored carnations—all flowers that I knew had been blooming in the rose garden."

She created the arrangement at her home on Whitehaven Street. And early Monday morning, she wrote a brief personal farewell: "Thank you, Mr. President, for your confidence and inspiration. Love, Bunny."

That morning, her chauffeur drove her to Arlington National Cemetery as Bunny held the basket in her lap. But Army officers would not let the car near the gravesite. "I got out and walked and the horror of the grave thing hit me—all those apparatuses and all that equipment," she recalled. "I was stopped by the Army and they said I would have to leave the basket."

Worried that it would disappear in the chaos, Bunny explained that this was Mrs. Kennedy's basket and urged the guards to call the White House, to no avail. Finally, a Secret Service agent recognized her and agreed to help. "They assigned a Secret Service man to the basket, and I know that it was there because Jackie told me she saw it. They gave me an escort, a police car, and I had to pick up my husband and we arrived at the church and were the last ones in."

Bunny spent the service second-guessing herself, wishing she had done a better job. Perhaps she could have brought in magnolia trees or done something else to make the church springlike? It was easier to think about the flowers than to confront the loss. After the service, Bunny and Paul chatted on the steps of the church with Prince Philip, who had been a guest at their farm six years earlier. Happier times.

As the long rows of cars headed to Arlington Cemetery, Bunny decided not to follow suit. She would later say that she and Paul were in a rush to get back to Manhattan to see an unidentified friend in the hospital. But it's likely that she could not face bearing witness as the president's coffin was lowered into the ground. Instead, at the private Butler Aviation terminal, just four miles from Arlington, the couple lingered by the television, watching the burial from an emotionally safe distance.

"We could hear the cannon and the trumpet from Arlington and see the planes go over and see everything at the gravesite on television. We were much closer to the ceremony, in other words, than if we had been in a car in the line."

Now alone with Paul, she could take a deep breath and allow herself to grieve.

Chapter Seventeen

Carrying On

When Jackie Kennedy moved out of the White House two weeks after the assassination, Bunny arranged for decorator Billy Baldwin to help Jackie get settled in a temporary Georgetown home. Bunny assumed that her labors in the presidential gardens were now over. But then she got a phone call from the new First Lady.

"Two weeks after Mrs. Johnson moved into the White House, she invited me to come to see her," Bunny later wrote in an article for *House & Garden*. "It was a hard decision to return to the White House so soon after Mrs. Kennedy had left and I still can't remember in which room we met."

Lady Bird Johnson asked Bunny to complete the second garden and consult on plantings for the Rose Garden. Although Bunny knew it would be painful to visit this setting that had once given her so much pleasure, she agreed to carry on. Bunny made one request: She wanted the East Garden to be named "the Jacqueline Kennedy Garden." The name change required an act of Congress, but Lady Bird shepherded the paperwork through.

Hoping that a sunny climate might soothe Jackie's spirits, Bunny invited her to visit Antigua in late March 1964. Along with her Secret Service detail, Jackie brought her sister, Lee; Lee's husband, Stas Radziwill; Bobby Kennedy (whose wife, Ethel, declined to make the trip); and Chuck Spalding, a friend of both Kennedy brothers.

"It was wonderful," Lee Radziwill says. The ocean waves, the sunsets, and the ability to go for a private walk on the beach—all of it was healing. "We had a totally carefree time," Lee adds. Even five decades later, she can recall the peaceful atmosphere and Bunny's understated taste. "It was very simple and all the colors of the rooms were difficult to figure out because they were so subtle. All the maids were dressed in a particular pink uniform and they looked wonderfully Caribbean. All the furniture was very simple, very comfortable."

But just four months after the assassination, the guests remained overwhelmed by grief. Bunny brought in set designers Paul Leonard and Bill Strom as staff, since Jackie felt at ease with the duo who had decorated the White House Christmas tree. "Jackie was like a walking Zombie, there was no doubt she was still in a state of shock and Bobby was doing all he could to keep her head above water," wrote Paul Leonard in an unpublished reminiscence. "Bobby was very instrumental in helping her through these days. It was difficult to keep the press away, and all the members of the Mill Reef Club."

Bunny attended church in Antigua with Jackie and Bobby on April 5. Jackie had brought along a book that resonated—*The Greek Way*, by classics scholar Edith Hamilton, with essays about history, literature, and civilization. She gave it to Bobby, who spent time reading it in his room and underlining passages.

The book suggested that arrogance and hubris doomed the leaders of fifth-century Greece. This volume became his constant companion, which he quoted in speeches. As his biographer, Evan Thomas, wrote, "RFK went on to buy all of Hamilton's books... The saving grace for Kennedy was the exaltation Greeks found in suffering... The Greeks understood that 'injustice was the nature of things,' but that the awfulness of fate could be borne and redeemed through pain."

On April 28, Bobby Kennedy sent Bunny a belated but heartfelt thank-you note, which included a joking reference to the Bay of Pigs invasion:

Dear Mrs. Mellon,

I have not written earlier because quite frankly I was trying to arrange a coup to take over your house on Antigua. Not being able

to round up the necessary forces on the island I thought of organiz-
ing a group of volunteers in the United States and capturing your
house and beach with them. I also had to abandon that idea because
I couldn't obtain landing craft from the Navy.

You can gather from all this how much we enjoyed our stay. You
were really so thoughtful. It meant a great deal in Jackie's life as I
know it did in mine. Without your wonderful kindness I am not
certain Jackie could have borne the pain.

So my thanks to you for all you did that week for us and my
thanks for what you did for the President and Jackie and really for
all the rest of us these past three years.

With great affection, Bobby

The attorney general was now contemplating his own political future. Pressure was mounting to force Lyndon Johnson to name him
as the vice president on the 1964 ticket. Bobby's name had also been
tossed out as a potential contender for a Senate seat from New York,
although he had no particular ties to the state.

Bunny, who supported Bobby's political ambitions, wrote to him
on what would have been John F. Kennedy's forty-seventh birthday,
May 29:

Dear Bobby,

It is impossible to let this day go by without sending you my love.
All thinking people are filled with sadness.
Loving Jackie and knowing you even a little I have faith that one
day there will be a light in all this darkness.

With love, Bunny

Bunny had always prided herself on her ability to keep going. Being
busy kept dark thoughts temporarily at bay. At Jackie's request,

she agreed to design the landscaping for President Kennedy's grave. Fulfilling her commitment to Lady Bird Johnson, Bunny began making regular treks to Washington to consult with Perry Wheeler and White House gardener Irvin Williams on the second garden.

But that wasn't enough activity to satisfy her restless energy. She wanted a new forward-looking project. "My wife is fond of building things," Paul Mellon told the *Wall Street Journal* in a 1964 feature about his philanthropy (THE MELLON MILLIONS: HOW A WEALTHY FAMILY PUTS FORTUNE TO WORK FOR BENEFIT OF PUBLIC). "So I'm building her a new house in New York on East 70th Street."

What a complicated, expensive, and time-consuming endeavor this would turn out to be. Paul had owned a brownstone on the street since the 1940s, but Bunny wanted a bigger home. So the couple bought the adjacent house, demolished both properties, and began work on a new four-story house designed by their favorite architect, H. Page Cross.

Even though the Mellons only sporadically spent time in Manhattan, they wanted a place to stay during the two years of construction. So they rented two adjoining apartments at the nearby Carlyle Hotel. For a woman of Bunny's rarified sensibilities, the prospect of living with standard hotel décor—even as a temporary measure—was unacceptable.

Bunny insisted on renovating the Carlyle rentals before moving in, commissioning Paul Leonard to paint trompe l'oeil murals on the walls and making other alterations. "She was an eccentric," recalls Lee Radziwill with a laugh. "She had the ceilings lowered in the Carlyle Hotel, while she was building her house. She was a very tall woman so that seemed ironic."

In their peripatetic travels, the Mellons were here, there, and everywhere. To help Paul in his role as the president of the National Gallery, Bunny had taken on corporate-wife entertaining responsibilities. In June, she arranged a dinner at the Sulgrave Club for the Shah of Iran and his wife, Empress Farah, to celebrate the opening of an exhibit of Persian art at the National Gallery. In photographs of that evening, the Empress of Iran and the Empress of Upperville look equally dazzling in their prominent jewelry.

The next day, June 6, Paul flew to New York to see his horse Quadrangle compete in the Belmont Stakes. The horse was a 13–2 long shot, since rival Northern Dancer had won both the Kentucky Derby and the Preakness. But Paul's bay swept away the doubters, winning the $110,850 purse by two lengths. "My wife will be awfully mad at me for making her miss this race," Paul told the *New York Times*, explaining that she was resting after the gallery gala.

In truth, Bunny had other plans for that afternoon, noting in her appointment calendar that Jackie and Bobby Kennedy were coming for tea. A few days earlier, Lyndon Johnson had said at a press conference that he would not try to block his attorney general from running for the Senate from New York.

Later in June, the Mellons flew to England to watch Paul's two-year-old horse Silly Season compete in the opening day of the Ascot races. While the Queen of England looked on, Silly Season triumphed, beating the British contenders. Bunny joined her husband in the winner's circle, and the couple celebrated afterward at dinner with David Bruce, now the American ambassador to England, and his wife, Evangeline.

Bunny's jet-setting was a source of amusement to her ex-husband, Stacy Lloyd. "Eliza wrote to me that you were off to Europe for a week... You were such a little home body at one stage in our lives and I used to move around for the newspaper while you kept the home fires going," Stacy wrote to her on July 23, 1964, from his home in St. Croix. "Now you are the real globe trotter, moving around like an express train while I stay home and very seldom budge."

He was in a nostalgic mood, thinking about bygone days and their children. "What a way life has of evening everyone out, tossing us around like ships on a sea, throwing us up on a beach, pulling us back into the water all for some grand scheme that no one has caught on to just yet," he wrote. "I think often of Tuffy living in Luang Probang, a little town in Laos... We certainly never thought that the little boy Francis Smith painted on the donkey under the apple tree would be one of the comparatively few Americans sitting out a nasty communist war in one of the quaintest of Far Eastern towns on the other side of the world."

Bunny's ex-husband complimented her for the way she was bringing up their daughter. "Eliza is so enthusiastic about her painting, it
is grand you have gotten her started on another artistic angle," Stacy
wrote, adding, "I catch so many glimpses of you in her as she gaily
moves in and out of my life."

Paul Mellon, aware that Bunny had a limited tolerance for a day at
the races, often went to the track with friends. In November 1964, the
Washington Star noted that at a race in Laurel, Maryland: "Paul Mellon, squire of Rokeby Farm near Upperville, was in his front row box
chatting with Dorcas Hardin of Georgetown." The philanthropist and
the attractive dress shop owner had overlapping interests; she, too, appreciated art and was a regular at National Gallery events. Dorcas's
star was rising in the nation's capital and her appealing personality
often received favorable mentions. *Star* columnist Betty Beale noted
that many women wished "to be as bright and gay come what may as
flame-haired Dorcas Hardin."

When Katharine Graham's mother, Agnes Meyer, gave a lavish party
that December in Washington, D.C., Bunny stole the show. Syndicated columnist Eugenia Sheppard gushed that Bunny "was dressed
from head to foot by Balenciaga" in a high-necked black mohair gown
with an embroidered cape and matching black mohair pumps. She
wore Schlumberger diamond butterfly bracelets on her wrists.

Bunny's mantra—"Nothing should be noticed"—did not apply to
the way she dressed. She put great time and effort into her appearance, aware that she would be singled out for attention. Bunny would
never be the best-looking or most sexually alluring woman at any
party, but she could comfort herself by being the best clotheshorse,
the epitome of style.

After being hounded by the press and curious bystanders at her
Georgetown home, Jackie Kennedy decided to move to Manhattan

with her children. While her new apartment at doorman-secure 1040 Fifth Avenue was being renovated, she moved into the Carlyle Hotel. Now Jackie and Bunny were just an elevator ride away from each other when Bunny was in town.

In January 1965, the friends made the International Best-Dressed List; Jackie won the number one slot, and Bunny was lower on the list. Paul Mellon was on a hunting trip when the list was announced, and he sent his wife a congratulatory note, using their nickname for each other: "You are a beautiful and well-accoutred and very well appointed Éléphante and we are all (that is, all the animals) very proud."

Bunny had yet another chance to put on her best jewels and a Balenciaga gown that spring when Lee Radziwill gave a party at her Fifth Avenue duplex for her sister. The Lester Lanin band played for the one hundred guests, who included the newly elected New York senator Bobby Kennedy. "Mrs. Kennedy is still depressed over her great loss, particularly when she goes home at night, Lee said," wrote columnist Betty Beale in the *Washington Star*. "Jackie had such a gay laughing whirl she stayed as long as the orchestra played which was until 5 o'clock in the morning. She even took part in a Russian dance and did it better than most of the guests who tried it."

The gossip columns charted Jackie's every move, noting that she and Bunny were often out and about together. A typical item in *WWD* described the women lunching at La Cote Basque: "Both looked radiant in sleeveless whites as they compared notes on shopping discoveries, fashion and books."

Unlike her famous friend, Bunny was not always recognized in Manhattan, and one day when she arrived at a posh New York restaurant for lunch, the maître d' seated her at a bad table by the kitchen. When Jackie arrived, the staff went into conniptions. "Jackie wouldn't put up with snobbery for one minute," Bunny recalled. Jackie declined the groveling offer to move them to a more prominent place, insisting, "If my friend is there, so am I."

Bunny was an inveterate gift giver, but she truly fussed over the presentation when bestowing tokens on Jackie. "We spent hours walking on the beach at Bunny's Cape Cod home in Osterville, searching for the perfect open clamshell to present Jackie with pearl earrings," recalled Paul Leonard. "It was endless, searching for the right color, the right shape, still attached and could open and close with ease. Finally, perfection. When tied together with sea grass, it was a work of art in itself."

Jackie gave her first dinner party in New York in September for John Kenneth Galbraith, the former American ambassador to India, preceding the opening of an Asia House exhibit of Indian art. Wearing a black sleeveless ruffled Balenciaga gown and white gloves, Bunny arrived at the dinner at the same time as Truman Capote and Lee Radziwill, a sight captured by photographers. The *New Yorker* had just published an excerpt from Capote's upcoming book *In Cold Blood*, a true-life crime thriller that would turn the already renowned author into a best-selling sensation. Later that night at Asia House, Bunny and Truman wandered the galleries together. The evening took a lively turn when Jackie and her guests, who included Andy Warhol, headed to the restaurant-turned-discotheque Sign of the Dove, where they were taught to do the frug by society dance instructor Killer Joe Piro. Jackie left at 2:30 a.m. and the partygoers finally cleared out at 4 a.m. The widowed First Lady was officially back in the social swing.

Jackie's children remained close to Bunny and looked forward to spending time with her. "For John and me, a visit to Bunny's house represented the biggest treat we could imagine," recalled Caroline Kennedy in a written reminiscence. "Mostly because she was someone who loved and understood us, and took care of our mother. Bunny taught me to knit and to needlepoint, to paint and to plant, and to want piles of blue handkerchiefs stacked in my closet. Walking down our hallway, I could always tell when Mummy was talking to Bunny on the phone because her voice sounded so happy."

Despite Bunny's best-dressed status and the admiring comments in the society pages, her childhood sense of inferiority about her appearance had never left her. She had grown up hearing from her parents that her younger sister, Lily, was the pretty one. Bunny disliked photographs of herself, judging the results harshly. She had a poignant reaction to a photo shoot with fashion and celebrity photographer Milton Greene, who had become renowned for his friendship and candid shots of Marilyn Monroe. Hairstylist Kenneth Battelle was the intermediary who arranged for Bunny's pictures.

"Kenneth said that Bunny Mellon needs a publicity picture and of course she doesn't have one, so can you photograph her at four o'clock at the Carlyle," recalls Amy Greene, the photographer's widow. "They worked until eight o'clock and had the best time. She had a very long strand of pearls and she was dangling and playing with it—it was heaven. When she saw the prints of the first sitting, she looked up at Milton and said, 'You made me pretty.'"

During Jackie Kennedy's short tenure as First Lady, she had managed to save from the wrecking ball the early nineteenth-century historic houses on Lafayette Park, directly in front of the White House. Seized by the federal government under the Eisenhower administration, the town houses had been scheduled for demolition, to be replaced by new government offices. After Jackie convinced her husband to intervene, JFK hired architect John Warnecke to come up with a new design that preserved the homes and moved the footprint of the government building.

Paul Mellon had a special interest in the project, since he had owned one of the houses on the square and used it as his office until the government took his property under eminent domain. In a tribute to the Kennedys and a reflection of their own interest in historic preservation, in 1965, Paul and Bunny donated $409,000 from his Old Dominion Foundation to restore the seven-acre park and add two fountains.

Just across the street, the new Jacqueline Kennedy Garden was completed in April 1965. Bunny had bowed out of the work a few months earlier. The reason: She could not tolerate President Johnson's vulgar vocabulary. LBJ left his windows open and when she worked in the garden, she was subjected to a stream of expletives as he cursed on the phone or at people in his office.

As Bunny's late-in-life confidant Bryan Huffman recalls, "Bunny told me that one afternoon, she just simply put her things back in her basket, had them call for her car, and went home and sent Lady Bird a note, saying how much she had appreciated the opportunity but that under the circumstances she did not think she could continue. She loved Lady Bird but she found him offensive."

Nonetheless, Bunny agreed to return for the garden's dedication. Jackie declined to attend, sending word that it would be unbearable for her to return to the White House. Her mother, Janet Auchincloss, spoke at the ceremony, choking up as she uttered, "I know you will understand if I cannot express how I feel about this tribute to my daughter...I cannot think of a more fitting memento of the years she shared with him than to have this lovely garden." Bunny had followed Jackie's original request and included a croquet court and planted crab apples, hollies, and magnolias.

Now that she was the country's most famous amateur gardener, Bunny was asked by *Vogue* to write an article about her favorite plants. Bunny often jotted down her thoughts on scraps of paper, appointment calendars, notebooks, or whatever was at hand. Her letters to friends and family members included vivid descriptions of flowers, plants, and the view outside her windows. She read poetry and liked to play with language. But to write for a national magazine was a professional leap. In December 1965, *Vogue* published Bunny's essay on her love for green flowers and her signature topiary herb trees.

"Green flowers are enchanted flowers, magic flowers, the witches of the garden," she wrote. "They give an impression of reflected sunlight, the light of a Bonnard painting. Truly green, these flowers range from the colour of emeralds to the colour of moonlight on white flowers." She praised the beauty of green zinnias, Green Dragon and Green Magic lilies, nicotiana, auriculas, and green tulips.

Her myrtle topiaries came from a clipping from George Washington's estate, Mt. Vernon, she explained. To Bunny, these tiny plants "recall[ed] the pure quality of a mellow monastery garden."

Bunny's article sent hostesses and nurseries nationwide scurrying to follow her lead. Miniature topiaries were featured in all the best households, a trend that would last for a half century.

Bunny enjoyed teaching novices to create artful displays. She gave her Virginia gardener, George Shaffer, the responsibility of creating daily flower arrangements for the house. "There are colors that I would never have put together, but she had an eye to see it," he recalled. "When I started doing the flowers, she would work with me. She'd say, 'See that little streak, the little bit of red down in the throat of the orchid, that goes perfect with this.'" If an especially pretty flower drooped, she showed him how to put a Band-Aid around the stem to save it for one more day.

The Rokeby Farm gardens and greenhouse grew an abundance of vegetables, fruits, and flowers, far more than Bunny and Paul could use. Bunny dispatched their private plane to deliver boxes of the excess to friends in New York, Washington, and elsewhere. Each blossom and cauliflower cost a small fortune, considering the staff salaries, plane landing fees, and fuel. But the couple's friends felt honored to receive these artistically arranged and deluxe care packages.

Kenneth thanked her for "those incredible fantastic, extraordinary flowers. Really in a lifetime no one could ever know such flowers unless they were lucky enough to know you." Princeton professor Charles Ryskamp, who also had a Manhattan apartment, wrote that he was delighted to receive "a bunch of early summer flowers from you. They cheered my apartment and I carried them to Princeton and they've been on my desk all weekend."

Bunny was honored three times in 1966 for her gardening design talents, but she was put in the awkward position of having to prove her bona fides. The Horticultural Society of New York gave her an award for designing the two White House gardens along with the Middleburg, Virginia, community garden. The Massachusetts Horticultural Society voted to give her a gold medal for excellence in landscaping. The Interior Department honored her for the Rose Garden and the East Garden.

But due to her amateur status, one finicky official questioned whether she had actually done the work. Perry Wheeler asked her to speak with Mr. Zack, the head of the American Landscape Association.

"We agreed to meet in the Rose Garden where he could question me as they felt there must have been a ghost designer," she wrote in her journal. "He was a nice man and expected sort of a pompous blue-haired garden club woman who did not really plant on hands and knees... He asked where I studied and I said, 'Never.'"

Instead, Bunny explained that while growing up in her father's house in Princeton, she had tagged along with the Olmsted brothers when they installed the gardens. As she recalled with evident delight, her answer ended the interrogation, since the official replied, "I was an apprentice on that job."

At the Interior Department ceremony, Bunny downplayed her accomplishment, wistfully saying, "Really this whole award should go to President Kennedy and not to me."

For the auction houses and art dealers who specialized in Impressionist paintings, the name Mellon had a magical connotation. Sibling rivalry played out in gallery showrooms as Paul and his sister, Ailsa, vied over paintings. "Sometimes I might find myself looking at a picture with Jay Rousack of Wildenstein, and he'd say that he had just shown it to Ailsa," Paul wrote in his autobiography. "My reaction was always to insist that he not tell her that I was interested in it since that would goad her to make up her mind and she would snap it up!" Visitors to Paul and Bunny's homes were aware of the couple's staggering art collection, but Ailsa led a quieter life, so few people had seen her acquisitions.

She owned a vast Manhattan apartment and an even larger Long Island estate, Woodlands, a sprawling mansion on 120 acres that had been a wedding gift from her father. The divorced Ailsa had a longtime beau, G. Lauder Greenway, a well-to-do Yale graduate who served as chairman of the Metropolitan Opera, director of the Philharmonic Symphony Society, and vice chair of New York University's

Institute of Fine Arts. Ailsa named Greenway as the president of her own charitable entity, the Avalon Foundation, which made yearly grants of more than $4 million to museums, universities, and medical institutions.

She occasionally appeared at museum openings but shied away from a visible social life. As her concerned brother, Paul, put it, "After her disturbed childhood she had gone on to lead a rather sad life. Following marriage and divorce she became somewhat withdrawn and indecisive."

For the twenty-fifth anniversary of the National Gallery, Ailsa and Paul agreed to loan their favorite Impressionist possessions, an astonishing 246 paintings. The exhibit included fifteen Degas, a dozen Monets, a dozen Renoirs, six Gauguins, and four Cézannes. Paul had recently spent $800,000 for Cézanne's *Houses in Provence* at Parke-Bernet Galleries.

Bunny and Paul gave a dinner at the Sulgrave Club, which was attended by Lady Bird Johnson. Afterward, the guests headed to the museum for a private tour. In the *New York Times*, society writer Charlotte Curtis decided to take Bunny down a notch with a catty comment, pointing out that she was "wearing a shimmering turquoise and white Balenciaga dress that wouldn't stay snapped in back, diamond and pearl jewelry and false eyelashes."

Paul had become a more confident public speaker and he told the guests that his home now looked denuded—"the walls are bare and grimy"—and quipped, "It is very embarrassing for a collector to be caught with his paintings down." Continuing in this vein, he said, "We parted with them, more in sorrow than in anger. Or again, more in Seurat than in Ingres."

Paul remained determined to create his own legacy rather than simply be the caretaker of his father's monument. Ignoring the entreaties of the National Gallery's curators, he announced later that year that he was donating his $50 million collection of British art to Yale, along with $12 million for the construction of a museum.

"It would have pleased me to give them to the National Gallery," he explained. "The trouble was, it could never have hung more than an infinitesimal part of this very comprehensive collection, so the vast majority would have been in storage. I didn't like the idea of that."

In the spring of 1966, Bunny and Paul moved into their new eight-bedroom Manhattan mansion. Meant to evoke the French country-side, the airy rooms flowed into one another and the house included Bunny's favorite elements: painted wooden floors in geometric patterns, handsome ceiling moldings to add old-fashioned grandeur, louvered window shutters, and fireplaces with marble mantelpieces. The French doors in the first-floor library opened onto a backyard garden with a reflecting pool and gazebo. With eleven thousand square feet of space in one of Manhattan's most desirable neighbor-hoods, the house was forty feet wide, more than double the usual eighteen-foot-wide city town house.

Bunny had hired her friend Nancy Lancaster's London-based firm, Colefax and Fowler, to decorate the house. John Fowler, a principal in the firm, directed the work but did not want to leave London, instead sending his sketches and fabrics to Bunny's New York employees, Paul Leonard and Bill Strom.

Bunny was always searching for unique gifts for Caroline and John Kennedy, and her new house provided inspiration. "Bunny decided to do a dollhouse for Caroline Kennedy, a copy of her living room on Seventieth Street," recalls Henry Heymann, a retired University of Pittsburgh theatre professor who had been Leonard's Yale classmate. "It was a three-foot-by-three-foot box. Bill and Paul were making Louis XVI–looking chairs, and a copy of the Cézanne painting *Boy in a Red Waistcoat*. It was absolutely ravishing. The walls were wonderful coral-colored, striated. There was an extension like a country kitchen with a wood stove and country-style furniture."

En route to New York on his plane, Paul sent a note to Bunny stressing how much he loved her and appreciated this "beautiful and comfortable and brilliantly done" home. "Don't think I take it for granted because I don't," he wrote, urging her to "rest awhile and enjoy it."

Although always portrayed as press shy, in truth Bunny hungered for the right kind of attention. A year earlier, the *New York Times* had featured her Foxcroft classmate (SISTER PARISH CREATES DISTINCTIVE INTERIORS BY INSTINCT), describing Sister as one of interior design's "most charming, talented and successful practitioners."

Perhaps Bunny was not consciously competing with her boarding school classmate, but she craved recognition on her own terms. So she gave a tour of her Manhattan house in April to society columnist Eugenia Sheppard. The writer rhapsodized over "the floor painted in a diamond pattern to look like an old Italian villa. The silk sofa pillows painted with her favorite herb trees..." She described Bunny's home as "a little piece of beauty and perfection, far away from the rest of the world, behind a dark green gate."

For the Mellons, enough was never enough. They wanted living quarters for their staff and a place to park their own cars. Paul bought a carriage house just down the block at 165 East Seventieth Street, a thirty-three-foot-wide Neo-Italianate structure that had been built as a stable in 1902 but converted to a home in 1929. The ten-thousand-foot space included a twelve-car garage, which took up the entire first floor. The couple allowed employees Paul Leonard and Bill Strom to live rent-free in an apartment in the building.

Dating back to her childhood, Bunny had watched her father's restless and relentless quest for real estate. He had built Albemarle in Princeton, renovated Carter Hall in Virginia, created his Florida getaway on an impossible plot straddling a highway, renovated a Washington home, and then built the Pink House in Princeton. In recent years, Gerard Lambert had continued to buy and sell, acquiring a house in Nassau, a home in Miami, an eighty-five-acre farm outside Stowe, Vermont, and a larger 450-acre farm nearby. As his wife, Grace, later told the *New York Times*, "At one point, we had so many houses that if I wakened in the middle of the night, I had to think twice about where I was."

Bunny and Paul owned homes in Virginia, Washington, Antigua, Cape Cod, and Manhattan. Now she wanted to look overseas. That June, decorator John Fowler wrote to Paul Leonard: "The next thing we (you and me) are to do, so Bunny says, is to find an enchantingly small apartment for her in Paris and you and I will do it up. That does sound fun, I must say, don't you think."

Birthdays can be precarious occasions, a time to either hide from the world or celebrate in public. As Jackie prepared to turn thirty-nine, she agreed to let Bunny give a party at Cape Cod. Bunny hired former White House chef Rene Verdon to create a feast of Jackie's favorite dishes, including rock bass, rack of lamb, shoestring potatoes with truffles, string beans with almonds, Bibb salad, and Brie, ending with fresh peaches poached in syrup and covered with raspberry sauce.

The guests came from Washington and New York, a mixture of politics, society, and the arts: former defense secretary Robert McNamara, David Bruce, Billy Baldwin, Bill and Babe Paley, Mike Nichols, Leonard Bernstein, Averell and Marie Harriman, Jock and Betsey Whitney, Kenneth Battelle, author William Styron, and playwright Lillian Hellman. Jackie wore a sleeveless pink Grès dress.

Paul Mellon wrote a toast to the former First Lady for the August 5 party:

> Bunny said, "In the middle of this bash
> Just get to your feet and make like Ogden Nash,
> And with your usual savoir faire and dumb serenity
> Offer a birthday toast to Jackie Kennedy."

Highlighting her riding skills, he added:

> I've seen her flying across the hills of Virginia
> With a verve and dash that would throw the fear of God in 'ya.

Bunny wanted to surprise Jackie. Only at the end of the dinner did former White House chef Rene Verdon come out to take a bow. As he later recalled, Jackie exclaimed with pleasure, "Oh, Rene, it's not true!

I knew there was something familiar about the dinner but I didn't know why."

Bandleader Bill Harrington played Broadway show tunes for the guests, until Bunny's daughter, Eliza, and Mike Nichols convinced him to switch to rock 'n' roll. Afterward, Kenneth wrote to Bunny: "Really, what a glorious party. Don't you ever do anything just a little bit wrong. And even better the sweet dear reaction of Mrs. K. made all your efforts probably seem more than worthwhile."

That fall, the two women were inseparable in Manhattan: attending the opening of the new Whitney Museum and the wedding of Jackie's former aide Pamela Turnure, and commuting to Brooklyn for painting lessons with stage designer Oliver Smith (*Camelot, My Fair Lady*) at his brownstone on Willow Street.

The friends occasionally spent weekends in New Jersey. Jackie rented a retreat in horsey Bernardsville. Bunny periodically stopped by Jackie's home, since she could combine the trip with a visit to her divorced parents, both living in Princeton. Bunny preferred the company of her father and stepmother, Grace, whose home was just a short drive away. As David Fleming, Bunny's nephew, recalled, "Bunny spent a lot of time with Gracie, more than she did with her own mother."

Jackie and her two children often vacationed with Bunny on Cape Cod and Antigua. Caroline Kennedy recalled, "A picnic on the Cape meant kites flying, a daring swim across the river, a sail in her little black boat, flags snapping in the wind on the top of the picnic house. An afternoon visit to the studio to paint special shells and feathers, drink ice tea and listen to the grown-ups whisper was the highlight of summer.

"And in the winter, Antigua was our idea of heaven—we got to pick the menu for dinner, John got unlimited Coca-Cola and pretty much everything else from Cora [the cook] and I would sit on Bunny's bed in the morning and listen to her plan the day's activities. Then I would go back to my room and copy her—making lists with a Schlumberger ivory and turquoise pen on the blue and green stationery of all the things my imaginary household would be doing that day."

In the fall of 1966, the social echelons of New York and Washington were abuzz with anticipation over Truman Capote's upcoming Black and White masked ball at the Plaza Hotel in honor of Katharine Graham. The widow had taken over her husband's job as publisher of her family's newspaper, the *Washington Post*. Capote spent months choosing the guest list, and gleefully announced that he had made five hundred friends—and fifteen thousand enemies—when the invitations went out.

Paul Mellon declined the coveted invite, but Bunny attended the gala along with Babe Paley, Frank Sinatra, Lee Radziwill, Rose Kennedy, presidential daughter Lynda Baines Johnson, Norman Mailer, and Arthur Schlesinger. The true proof of Bunny's status came the next day. Recovering from the party's aftermath, Truman Capote lunched with Bunny and Italian aristocrat Marella Agnelli and an unidentified man at Lafayette restaurant. *WWD* featured a caricature by artist Kenneth Paul Block, describing the foursome as looking "fresh as daisies." Truman could have selected any of his five hundred guests to dish with that day, but he was making a statement by dining with these high-society companions.

Paul Mellon was keenly aware of his sister Ailsa's neuroses and felt sorry for her daughter, Audrey Bruce. A quiet and anxious child, she was so embarrassed by her family money that she hid on the floor of the chauffeured limousine that took her to private school in Manhattan. "Audrey was extremely shy and introspective—a true introvert," Paul wrote of his niece. "Publicity frightened her, public occasions repelled her, renown would have meant nothing to her."

Yet as an adult, Audrey had carved out a satisfying life. After eloping as a Radcliffe student in 1955 with Stephen Currier, a Harvard graduate, the couple became left-wing trust-fund social activists. Audrey volunteered as a nurse's aide at New York Hospital, where the staff was unaware of her monied background. The couple used

Audrey's fortune to found the Taconic Foundation, directing more than $1 million to such civil rights groups as the NAACP and the National Urban League. The *New York Times* credited the couple with "playing a quiet but powerful role in the national fight for Negro civil rights." Stephen joined the board of Lady Bird Johnson's beautification project. The couple, who had three children, lived in Manhattan but owned a two-thousand-acre Virginia horse farm, less than twenty miles from Bunny and Paul's home.

Heading off on vacation, the Curriers were on a chartered plane on January 17, 1967, from San Juan to St. Thomas in the Virgin Islands, when the pilot radioed a request to change his route. The Piper Apache plane suddenly vanished. Lady Bird Johnson set in motion a vast federal search for the plane, but it was never found. After two weeks, the Curriers were declared legally dead. The mourners at the Manhattan funeral included Bobby Kennedy, New York governor Nelson Rockefeller, New York mayor John Lindsay, and Lady Bird Johnson.

The Curriers' orphaned young children—Andrea, ten; Lavinia, nine; and Michael, six—inherited a multimillion-dollar fortune. The Mellons were not a close-knit family, and no blood relative stepped up to take care of the children. Their grandparents both declined the responsibility. Ailsa Mellon Bruce was in poor health; her ex-husband, David Bruce, and his second wife, Evangeline, were busy with their own children and his career as a diplomat. A Yale professor and his wife raised the children instead.

The three Currier children longed for a close relationship with Paul and Bunny, but their contact was mostly limited to Easter visits and the occasional afternoon tea. As Lavinia Currier recalls, Paul made it clear that he did not want to be involved.

"We had an overwhelming situation after our parents died," she recalled. As a teenager, Lavinia and her siblings made an appointment to meet with Paul to ask for his guidance on running their Virginia farm. He said, "'I'm going to give you the name of my banker in Pittsburgh.' I remember thinking, what am I supposed to do with this?"

When her brother, Michael, asked Paul to mentor him in collecting art, Paul rebuffed him, too. As Lavinia recalls, "Michael at one point wrote a 'you're not a good uncle' letter, Uncle Paul wrote back and said, 'You're right. It doesn't interest me particularly.'"

She blames his attitude on the ingrained Mellon heritage. "Every family has a culture, and our family's culture is everybody has their own domain and people value their privacy and don't get involved," Lavinia Currier says. "You don't roll your sleeves up and come to the fore when something happens. I remember as a child, it was surprising to us."

Bunny deferred to Paul's wishes—these were his relatives—but tried to compensate with thoughtful gifts and by conveying her interest. "She wasn't warm and fuzzy, she didn't give you a big hug but was always attentive and deeply intuitive," Currier says. "I liked Bunny very much."

Paul and Bunny scarcely saw each other during this period. He traveled constantly, attending to Mellon family and charitable business or watching his horses race. Bunny spent long stretches in Paris and at their other homes. En route from Virginia to St. Louis, Paul ruefully wrote to Bunny, who was in New York, "We are ships that pass in our own ships."

Old age had not mellowed Gerard Lambert. "He was a charismatic genius but somewhat introverted," recalls his grandson John McCarthy Jr., the son of Bunny's sister, Lily. "He liked having us grandchildren around and he was amused, but he was in his own world. The dinners at the Pink House were always formal—Granddaddy and Gracie at each end of the table, candlelight, filet mignon, chateau Latour, desserts made by their own pastry chef, a butler serving. He'd get up three-quarters through the main course and say good-bye and leave. He went to bed early, around 9 p.m. He had an eccentric side to him."

The Listerine heir's millions had always served as insulation, allowing him to distance himself from other people, who often bored him. Brilliant and impatient, he had a magnetic personality but he made split-second decisions. If he tired of one of his many residences, he would often just walk away, letting others remove the contents and handle a sale. As David Fleming, John McCarthy Jr.'s half brother, put it, "Granddaddy Lambert was a character. He did what he wanted."

In the mid-1960s, Gerard Lambert's health began to fail. "Jerry began not being very well," his wife, Grace, later recalled. "He'd have spells of feeling agitated and panicky...He had arteriosclerosis. He began to get very weak, and finally we had to have a nurse for him all the time. I didn't see any diminishing of his mental capacities—just a loss of energy and a loss of interest in things. His world got smaller and smaller."

By 1966, he was turning away visitors. "He wasn't particularly fond of seeing his own two daughters during his last months," Grace stated in her memoir. "It was too much of an effort for him to see them, and he didn't want them to see him in his weakened condition."

Nonetheless, Bunny made the pilgrimage to be with her father in his final days, bringing her daughter, Eliza, along. On the evening of February 25, 1967, Gerard Lambert told his wife, "Gracie, I'm tired, I want to die, I'm so tired." He closed his eyes and fell asleep. He never woke up, dying at age eighty.

"I was in the guest room when Gracie knocked on my door," Bunny wrote in a reminiscence. Naturally, she took over the floral arrangements. "For a few hours they took him away and then returned him to the library. We put a blue cover over the coffin and flowers from the greenhouse. I made him a wreath of magnolia branches with blue cornflowers and paper white narcissus...As I wove the wreath (it took a long time—the branches were stiff and needed careful bending), Eliza and my brother Gerard's son sat on the floor with me...There was no horror of death. But they never left my side."

Gerard Lambert was hailed by the *New York Times* as the man who "built a fortune from Listerine mouthwash by making the word 'halitosis' nationally infamous." He was lionized as an international yachtsman who competed in the America's Cup, and as the savvy businessman who "helped develop Gillette's razor into very nearly its present successful form." Even his hobbies—as a mystery novelist, an amateur magician who extracted coins from children's ears, a harmonica player who carried the instrument in his pocket at all times—were given their due.

Foxcroft headmistress Charlotte Noland sent Bunny a condolence note: "I have known him since he was a little boy and always been so fond of him. I never forget his bringing you down to Foxcroft when you were a little thing only thirteen years old, and how funny and shy you were, but what a big place you filled in Foxcroft; and I never forget your lovely sewing."

The funeral was held in Princeton. Now it was Jackie Kennedy's turn to don black in recognition of her friend's loss, and to be by Bunny's side during the church services. But Jackie's presence attracted press attention, leading to a row between Bunny and her sister, Lily. Many years later, Bunny told her friend Bryan Huffman what happened. "Bunny's sister was upset that Jackie came to the funeral and upstaged everything," he says. "Lily was furious that Bunny had pulled Jackie up to sit with the family. Bunny and Lily had a falling out, they were already on tenuous terms." The sisters, stubborn women with a lifetime of rivalry and grievances, were estranged for several years.

A few months later, Bunny and Jackie were seen touring beaches in Nantucket, sparking rumors that Jackie was looking for a seaside escape. But once again, Bunny was the one on a real estate hunt. Her father had left her $200,000 in addition to a life trust, and she decided to use the money in a way that he would appreciate.

She bought two hundred acres of windswept beachfront property, a gorgeous swath of land. Although she and Paul already owned a vast Cape Cod estate, this purchase was meaningful to Bunny because she had used her own money. It was hers.

"Wildflowers grew and birds found a haven under skies that nearly touched the ground," she wrote in a journal. "No large trees interrupted the closeness to earth. Lawyers [and] family members shook their heads but it was my investment in freedom. Migratory birds stopped by, even an albatross flew barely touching the ground on its way north.

"Little by little with the help of new friends found on the island, a small part of the land was cleared. A picnic home 12 × 12 replaced a rug on the grass where Jackie K and I could go for a day without the unexpected hazards of weather or winds. This was followed by a so-called 'Maintenance House' for small equipment + to help clear the land. The attic above was too attractive to leave empty." Bunny furnished it and added plumbing so she could spend the night. She left the remainder of the land alone, but planned to eventually build a house there.

After nineteen years of marriage, Bunny felt that she and Paul had become closer and had found a good balance in their relationship. "My Darling Élephant," she wrote to him on May 1, 1967, using their nickname for each other, "this is the happiest anniversary I can remember." She wanted him to know that she appreciated their "shared interests" and tolerance of each other's "strength and weakness."

A few months later, there was sad news in their social circle: In early November Dorcas Hardin's husband, Lauriston, died from what was described as a shooting accident. According to the *New York Times*, the sixty-four-year-old doctor died "of a gunshot wound from his own gun while hunting at his farm, Eagle Point, near Chesterton, Md."

Family friends say that he had been diagnosed with a fatal illness and decided to choose his own exit. As Oatsie Leiter Charles recalls, "Laurent had cancer. He called up Dorcas and said, 'I'm going.' He drove to the farm and shot himself. She knew." Friends and neighbors rallied around the pretty and popular Dorcas, trying to comfort the bereaved widow.

As the president of the National Gallery, Paul Mellon felt obligated to make long-term plans for the museum's future. When his father, Andrew Mellon, originally bought land for the museum, he presciently purchased an adjacent nine-acre parcel and donated it to the government for a possible expansion. Now that several decades had passed, current gallery director John Walker warned Paul that if they didn't take action, the government might use the land for a different purpose.

Paul and his sister, Ailsa, announced in November 1967 that they were donating $20 million to add a new wing. The next step was choosing an architect who could come up with a design for the triangular-shaped property that would not clash with the Beaux Arts–style National Gallery.

The modernist man of the moment was I. M. Pei, the Chinese-born, Harvard- and MIT-educated architect who had changed the skyline of Denver with the Mile-High Center and worked on urban renewal projects in Washington. Jackie Kennedy had chosen Pei in 1964 to design the John F. Kennedy Library in Boston; Bunny was familiar with his work. Pei won the commission to design the new National Gallery wing. As plans for the museum moved forward, Pei became a frequent visitor to Rokeby Farm.

Paul turned sixty that June, a time to reflect on his life to date. In a commencement address at the Carnegie Institute of Technology, he referred to the many "dreadful crises" of the era, from the threat of nuclear war and "giant mushroom clouds," to the war in Vietnam, race riots at home, poverty, and environmental desecration. He sounded like an old fogey as he lamented the assaults of modern life: "There is the diminishment of personal privacy everywhere—unasked-for music and airport squawk boxes—jets roaring—horns blowing—sirens wailing."

Yet he ended on an upbeat note, urging the graduates to explore the beauty of the world: "There is no substitute for the world of direct sensual experience: the red and gold of October leaves, a shiny black grackle among the white blossoms of a honey-locust, a scarlet cardinal framed in the black branches of a December tree against the cold, blue sky, the brilliance of the summer stars, a child's smile."

This taciturn man closed by citing yet another emotion that he hoped they would experience: "And though I have left it to the end of my catalogue—perhaps most important—the thrill and mystery of love between a man and a woman: sensual, emotional and spiritual."

Bunny and Paul were frequently apart, but this was testimony guaranteed to warm a woman's heart.

Chapter Eighteen

1968

At Cristóbal Balenciaga's salon in Paris, the designer had established a special workroom devoted solely to creating Bunny's wardrobe. More than fifty employees worked on her evening gowns, dresses, suits, lingerie, and denim gardening skirts. Fashion writers estimated that Bunny, who bought multiples of outfits to stock her many homes, spent $150,000 per year at Balenciaga, the equivalent of $1 million today.

But at the age of seventy-three, Balenciaga decided to retire. When Bunny went to see him in March 1968, he gave her advance warning prior to the official announcement. To soften the blow, Balenciaga nominated a successor, graciously introducing her to Hubert de Givenchy, who had apprenticed in Balenciaga's salon before opening his own business in 1952. As Givenchy recalled to me in his lilting, French-accented English, "I was introduced to Mrs. Mellon by Mr. Balenciaga. When he had to close his own house, he take Mrs. Mellon by the hand, and cross the street, George V, and show Mrs. Mellon my studio. [He said,] 'Now Bunny this a place you must be dressed because I cannot dress you anymore.'"

The son of a French marquis, Givenchy was known in Hollywood as Audrey Hepburn's favorite designer, the man who created her exquisite outfits for the movie *Breakfast at Tiffany's*. He was drop-dead good-looking, a towering six foot six with a thick mop of hair and a charming demeanor. Givenchy concocted formfitting jersey sheaths, flowing Baby Doll dresses, daring gowns with nude midriffs, or hems that hit knee-high in front and trailed floor-length in back, belted coats with rolled collars, raglan sleeves and flared skirts, and an ever-evolving sculptural array of flattering outfits. Jackie Kennedy and her sister, Lee Radziwill, wore his clothes. He was considered a magician whose clothes could make slender women look curvy and slenderize plump physiques.

He already had many glamorous clients, yet Givenchy insists that he was worried about making a good impression on the famous Mrs. Mellon. "She's very shy, timid. I'm thinking certainly Mrs. Mellon will never come and ask me to dress her," Givenchy says. "She's sad."

Bunny was indeed saddened by Balenciaga's finale. "The night before he closed his shop in Paris, I sat with him in the late afternoon in his third floor atelier," she wrote in reminiscence. "Always aware of the details, he said, 'the shoulders of the dress you are wearing need adjustment. Leave it to me tonight and I will send it to you tomorrow.'"

He sent her out the door wearing an Air France stewardess white blouse and a blue skirt. "Leaving his shop on the Avenue George V, I heard the iron shutters go down. He was leaving his work in Paris and going back to Spain. We saw each other many times after he closed his shop."

Givenchy sent Bunny sketches of his next collection. "Mrs. Mellon, to my great surprise, order a large quantity of clothes from the first choice, my house," he recalled. "I am surprised, I think this is incredible, Mrs. Mellon does not know so much my work but she gives me so much confidence."

The spring of 1968 would always be etched in Bunny's memory as a time of public suffering on par with the death of a president. A few weeks after she returned from Paris to Virginia, the nation was engulfed in a shocking wave of violence.

On April 4, civil rights leader Martin Luther King Jr. was assassinated in Memphis, shot by ex-convict James Earl Ray. Riots exploded across the nation, with some of the worst looting and fires in Washington, Chicago, Baltimore, Detroit, and Harlem. Blocks of stores were turned into charred wreckage and jails overflowed, with more than forty-two hundred arrests in Washington alone. The Associated Press estimated that more than thirty people died nationwide in the riots, twenty-five hundred people were injured, and property damage reached more than $26.5 million.

Bunny's home in Virginia was forty-five miles away from the flames of downtown Washington, but she decided to flee to the Upper East Side of Manhattan for a three-day trip. Paul headed to rural Virginia for his annual hundred-mile race. Jackie Kennedy remained in New York City, where columnist Earl Wilson spotted her having lunch at Restaurant Orsini with Aristotle Onassis.

On April 8, Bunny went to Kenneth's hair salon for an appointment. Billy Baldwin had decorated the cheerful five-year-old society clubhouse with antiques and a wild array of wallpaper and carpets with clashing stripes, flowers, and paisley patterns.

Jackie was sitting in the lobby, hanging up the house phone, when Bunny arrived. Without preamble, Jackie turned to Bunny and announced, "I have to go to Martin Luther King's funeral tomorrow... Nelson Rockefeller has offered to take some friends down and kindly asked me. I can't do that. It makes me nervous—so many people." (Rockefeller was to be accompanied by sixty-two mourners, including Mayor John Lindsay, Archbishop Terrence J. Cooke, Rabbi Harold Gordon, and philanthropist Brooke Astor.)

As Bunny later recalled in an unpublished reminiscence, she immediately offered up her private plane and pilot, Walt Helmer, plus volunteered to accompany Jackie to the services at Ebenezer Baptist Church in Atlanta, where King's father was the pastor. The two women left early the next morning in a plane stocked with picnic baskets of food packed by Bunny's butler.

"Arriving in Atlanta at 8:00, we drove to Mrs. King's house," Bunny wrote. "Jackie wanted to pay her respects to Mrs. King and her family. The door was opened by Harry Belafonte holding the hand of a little girl dressed in a very frilly pink dress. Overjoyed to see Jackie, they led us to Mrs. King's bedroom where the child jumped on a huge red-and-gold bed. Mrs. King, who was dressing for the funeral, was delighted to see Jackie, who with her quite strong presence comforted her with understanding and warmth."

En route to the church in a chauffeured car, the two women were accompanied by Bunny's pilot and a member of the White House security staff. "It was not long after leaving the house that the crowd grew and we were grateful for these two men," Bunny wrote. "The driver, feeling important, started a constant blowing of the horn to separate the crowd. Jackie jumped forward and with strong words, tapping him on the shoulder, said, 'Stop blowing that horn! This is their town.'" Bystanders noticed the famous passenger and began to surround the vehicle.

Their predicament appeared frightening to reporters. The *New York Times'* Homer Bigart wrote that "the figure that evoked the sharpest pang of sentiment was Mrs. John F. Kennedy, widowed— like Coretta King—by an assassin. Recognized by surging crowds as she was led toward the church, Mrs. Kennedy was suddenly caught up in such a pressure of people that she had to be pulled and pushed through the narrow door. For a moment, her face appeared strained and frightened."

Jackie and Bunny were seated to the left near the wall, about ten rows back in the immense church, which seated more than twelve hundred mourners. This was the designated VIP section. "We started sitting alone, then slowly people began arriving," Bunny wrote. "People of political importance started settling around us (like flocks of migrating birds). Bobby Kennedy arrived on my right and with his help, we could put names to faces." Teddy Kennedy, now a Massachusetts senator, was seated next to Jackie. The foursome soon found themselves in close quarters with the man who had been JFK's biggest political rival.

"Richard Nixon sat behind us. He tapped Jackie on the shoulder, leaned forward, and said, 'I know how many memories this must bring to you.' She stared straight ahead. After his second attempt she whispered to me, 'Tell him that's enough.'"

More than 120 million people viewed the funeral, which was

carried live on television. What stayed with Bunny was the music. "Few instruments, just voices numbering a hundred or more. The voices sounded to come from distant lands, from seas, deserts, plains, lakes and mountains. It overwhelmed the emotions of the congregation, and when the last voice was heard and prayers read, people began to move toward the doors."

To avoid the crowds, Jackie and Bunny were spirited out a side door. "We went into the church cellar, through a long corridor or tunnel and were picked up by a waiting car on a quiet street," Bunny wrote. "Bobby Kennedy had left us to walk in the famous march behind the mule team to the cemetery. The plane took off and we untied our big basket put together by Peter with a sense of relief and safety."

She added, "That evening Paul called from the mountains of West Virginia far from the awareness of one day's events. He listened patiently, then said, 'You two girls had a busy day.'"

For Jackie, the experience was an excruciating reminder of all she had lost, mixed with grief for the King family and the country. Back home in New York that night, she wrote to Bunny, expressing gratitude for her "healing love" during these difficult times. "I couldn't have done it," Jackie wrote, without Bunny's comforting presence. She added, poignantly, that Bobby Kennedy wanted Bunny to know that he felt the same way.

A few days later, a reporter from WWD witnessed Jackie and Bunny lunching together at Lafayette, and he commented favorably about their trip to the funeral: "Mrs. Kennedy can be a great moral force in this country. Senator Kennedy is surely aware of her strength and her appeal... The social butterfly has come down to earth."

The death of Martin Luther King and the riots jolted Paul Mellon out of genteel complacency. As a philanthropist, he believed in the power of education to lift people out of poverty, and he began directing hundreds of thousands of dollars from the Andrew Mellon Fund to traditionally black schools such as Spelman College in Atlanta, Tuskegee University in Alabama, and Howard University in Washington. He contributed to the United Negro College Fund and the National Fund for Minority Engineering Students.

Bunny had her husband's ear, and it is likely that she encouraged his efforts. She had been concerned about racial inequality ever since her childhood, when she saw the distressing photos of the workers' living conditions at her father's cotton mill.

Paul would ultimately pour more than $300 million into scholarships for minorities and programs to increase minority attendance at a variety of colleges ranging from Northwestern to North Carolina Central University.

His father had made his fortune in coal mines and factories from the work of uneducated and often ill-treated laborers. Now the Mellon name was becoming synonymous with good works.

Bunny's two children had been living overseas, but in 1968 both came home. As a public affairs officer for the United States Information Agency in Laos, Tuffy Lloyd had just won the newly created Averell Harriman Award honoring junior foreign service officers for outstanding creativity, originality, and moral courage.

The *Washington Post*'s Chalmers Roberts had interviewed him in Laos a year earlier for an article describing the American aid effort to help 250,000 refugees forced to move because of the war. Many had been maimed by mines or suffered from malnutrition and malaria. The reporter wrote that Lloyd "had learned enough Lao to carry on a conversation with dictionary in hand" and was helping out at a mud-floored fourteen-room school for four hundred children. An article in the *Foreign Service Association Journal* stated that Stacy Lloyd (referred to by his full name) "threw away the handbook" and took an imaginative approach to trying to broach peace between rival tribal leaders.

Bunny and her ex-husband both attended their son's award ceremony. As Tuffy's half brother, Robin Lloyd, recalls, "Our father wore that with pride; he felt his son had done something important." Tuffy decided to leave the USIA and return to America, where he would soon go to work for pollster and family friend George Gallup.

Eliza Lloyd had come back from Europe with her very own

trophy—a viscount. She was engaged to marry British aristocrat Henry Dermot Ponsonby Moore, known as Derry, the son of the eleventh Earl and Countess of Drogheda. His father was the managing director of the *Financial Times* and the chairman of London's Royal Opera House. Derry had graduated from Eton and Trinity College in Cambridge, served as a second lieutenant in the Life Guards, and studied painting in Salzburg.

Four years Eliza's senior, Derry had established a Manhattan-based travel agency, Ports of Call, with a well-connected friend, Susan Stein (whose father, talent agent Jules Stein, founded the Music Corporation of America). With offices at Saks Fifth Avenue, Ports of Call handled bookings for celebrity clients such as actor George Hamilton and singer Bobby Darin. Susan Stein told the *Washington Post* that when the dashing Derry's engagement was announced, their female staff did not handle the news well: "The girls were in a state of shock. They wore black all week as a symbol of mourning."

Thrilled that her daughter would possess a title—Eliza would become Lady Moore—Bunny enthusiastically threw herself into wedding planning. The mother of the bride planned to wear a green-and-white silk-print Balenciaga for the May afternoon Virginia wedding, but Eliza asked Yves Saint Laurent to design her wedding gown, a white empire-waist dress with a Delft blue sash and a scalloped embroidered hem with a long train. Kenneth Battelle blocked out the weekend so he could style the hair of mother and daughter.

Jackie Kennedy agreed to attend the wedding—a true measure of friendship, since she still did not want to be anywhere near Washington, D.C. "She was tense about it," her mother, Janet Auchincloss, later told the press. Caroline Kennedy was scheduled to be a flower girl, along with Paul Mellon's granddaughters, Virginia and Mary Warner, while young John Kennedy Jr. would serve as a page with Miles Gilbert, Sister Parish's grandson. "I had a perfect dress from Givenchy with a blue satin sash," recalls Virginia Warner, adding that she approved of the groom. "I thought Derry was kind of a cool cat, he was cute, he was classy in that English way."

The ceremony was to take place at Trinity Episcopal Church, the stone sanctuary that Bunny and Paul had built in Upperville. But the couple had to import a minister. Their congregation was up in arms over an antebellum sermon that Trinity's Reverend Francis Rhein had given in the wake of Martin Luther King's assassination. According to an article in the *Washington Post*, Rhein described Negroes as "really children, in their capacity for understanding...They do not have the mind, the intellect, the ability, or the position we have." Paul and Bunny were appalled and quietly arranged for Reverend Dr. Seymour St. John, the headmaster of the Choate School, Paul's alma mater, to perform the marriage ceremony instead.

The Mellons planned to hold the reception at their home in a tent with a painted dance floor. Bunny ordered Porthault linen for the tables and brought in her favorite Manhattan florist, Robert Perkins of the Greenery. Paul chartered a plane to bring ninety of the three hundred guests from New York to Dulles Airport and hired buses to transport the group to Upperville. The RSVPs included columnist Joseph Alsop; Jackie's mother and stepfather, Mrs. and Mr. Hugh Auchincloss; Evangeline Bruce; *Vogue* fashion editor Carrie Donovan; Fred Astaire's daughter Ava Astaire Bostelmann; Lord and Lady Glendevon; and Lord David Brooke, Bunny's childhood ward.

Stacy Lloyd flew up to give away his daughter. He and Paul Mellon both gave eloquent toasts at a dinner the night before the wedding. Paul included such lines as:

> We mourn the exit of this wild
> Alarming, charming, madcap child.

The arrangements were perfect. With Bunny, every party was always seamlessly organized. But as morning dawned on the wedding day, May 14, a last-minute and very unexpected problem developed.

Eliza did not want to go ahead with the ceremony.

She told her mother that she was having second thoughts. As the sky clouded over and a rainstorm swept in, Eliza voiced her doubts. A young woman who loved her mother deeply but rebelled at Bunny's controlling persona, Eliza yearned for a way out of what she believed would be a mistake. She begged her mother to call it off.

Bunny did not want to hear these words. She was convinced that Eliza was just having the jitters. Later in life, Bunny told her friend Bryan Huffman that she deeply regretted insisting that Eliza go ahead with the ceremony. "She'd get this faraway look in her eye and say, 'Really, it was a mistake. But there were all those people out there, hundreds of guests.'" Huffman added, "Bunny wasn't coaxing Eliza, it was, 'You will go through it, there's no backing out.'"

The bride arrived ten minutes late to her own 4 p.m. wedding, and twelve minutes later, the deed was done. Newspapers carried glowing accounts of the fairy-tale wedding. CEREMONY IS LIKE A GAINSBOROUGH PORTRAIT, gushed the *Washington Post*, noting that Paul Mellon was rumored to have given the bride a $2 million wedding gift.

"Millionaire sportsman Paul Mellon, who possesses one of the finest collections of British art in this country, added a new British portrait to his family gallery when he married his step-daughter, Eliza Lloyd, to Henry Dermot, Viscount Moore," the *Post* reported, noting that young John Kennedy Jr. was clad in white knickers, white shoes and stockings, and a bolero jacket for the ceremony.

Eliza gave her marriage a try. She and Derry spent time in Paris and then Los Angeles, but called it quits after three years. Paul Mellon's lawyers handled the financial negotiations. Once the divorce came through, Paul wrote an epitaph to his earlier wedding eve poem, lamenting the expense incurred by the breakup. He wrote that the British viscount had seemed "nice," but that his love had come at a "fancy price."

Bunny continued to address her letters to "Lady Moore" as if she could not get over the loss of the title, much to Eliza's chagrin.

For Eliza, the divorce represented freedom from the life that had been expected of her and that she had discovered she didn't want. Her desires went in a different direction. She was gay. Now she could pursue romantic relationships with women. But it would be a long time before she was ready to introduce a female companion to her mother.

On Bunny and Paul's anniversary that May, he had sent her a poem—"three cheers, we've bumbled through these twenty years..." He always thoughtfully celebrated the major occasions in their lives. The national attention given to Eliza's wedding put the couple front and center in the gossip columns. They had often been depicted as globetrotters, embarking on separate travels. But the first hint of trouble came in a Walter Winchell column, which suggested that the Mellons' marriage was on the rocks.

The gossip columnist wrote, in a syndicated column published June 3: "Financier Paul Mellon denied a *Washington Post* query that he and his wife plan divorce. Intimates say that if they change their minds the $ettlement will be between $15 and 20 million."

That was quickly followed by a competing story by society columnist Aileen Mehle, who wrote under the pen name Suzy. The syndicated columnist was friendly with Bunny, and the two women attended the ballet in New York, often along with Jackie. As Aileen Mehle told me, "I met her in the early 1960s. We traveled in the same circles."

RUMORS OF MELLONS RIFE BUT HAPPILY ALL WRONG was the headline on Suzy's syndicated column in the *Palm Beach Post*. "Ladies and gentlemen. The Paul Mellon marriage is as solid as a rock. Maybe even more so. Therefore, let's have done with the persistent and foundless rumor that Paul Mellon, one of the world's richest men and his tall attractive wife, Bunny, noted for her exquisite taste and her green green thumb, are splitting.

"You will find them together at their New York town house, then Washington, D.C. town house, then Virginia country house and the place at Antigua in the West Indies, I thank you."

The item quieted the chattering classes. At least for the time being.

Again. Oh dear Lord, not again. On June 5, Bobby Kennedy had just finished speaking at the Ambassador Hotel in Los Angeles, celebrating his victory in the California presidential primary. He was being taken out through the kitchen when gunfire rang out—Sirhan Sirhan shot him four times at point-blank range.

Bunny was at home in Virginia when she learned of the assassination. Once again, the Kennedy family asked her to help with the funeral arrangements. She accompanied Robert McNamara to Arlington National Cemetery to pick out a gravesite for Bobby. They settled on a spot just sixty feet from his brother's final resting place.

On June 9, Bunny was photographed wearing a black sleeveless sheath dress and straw hat, directing the placement of flowers at Arlington, readying the spot. But services were first held that day at St. Patrick's Cathedral in New York. The coffin was borne through the streets and taken on a train to Washington and then to the cemetery. Kennedy was buried in moonlight, as mourners stood by with lighted tapers.

Bobby had been Bunny's houseguest in Antigua, she had just seen him at Martin Luther King's funeral, and he was her friend. Bunny was distraught but tried to comfort Jackie. As the coffin was lowered into the ground, the *Los Angeles Times* noted that it bore a few mementos: "a single red poppy, a single sprig of evergreen, a small American flag, and a bouquet of yellow roses tied with a yellow ribbon and carrying a single blue political campaign button reading 'Kennedy.'"

A week later, Bunny returned to the cemetery. The Kennedy family and cemetery workers wanted her advice on arranging the large floral tributes that kept arriving. According to the *Washington Post*'s Maxine Cheshire, Bunny suggested that large wreaths be placed in a horseshoe arch nearby, with just small bouquets from family and friends left on the grave.

Jackie wrote an emotional letter to Bunny on June 21, and included a few snapshots that she had taken of her children getting ready for Eliza's wedding along with news clippings. She was grateful for Bunny's involvement in the season's back-to-back funerals.

"If only Jack could come back + give you the Medal of Freedom...I can see the amused look there would be in his eyes + hear that wicked chuckle he had when he was really enjoying himself—because of course it would happen in the Rose Garden—and as much as he loved you— he would have picked a day when it couldn't hurt the grass!"

Paul and Bunny decamped for Cape Cod to recover. Their life there had a comforting rhythm: Bunny went sailing in the morning with local boatbuilder Chester Crosby, who took Paul out on the water in the afternoons. Despite the spring tragedies, Paul and Bunny went ahead with a birthday dinner for Jackie on July 28. Paul wrote a poem to toast Jackie as well as his wife and Eliza. He quipped that they basked "in reverse notoriety" and liked to paint and "palaver."

That August, Jackie wrote a lengthy letter to Johnny Schlumberger, asking him to make a wreath-like plaque for JFK's grave, a project that had been on hold. Jackie asked the jeweler to add a cornflower to the design in honor of Bunny, who at the president's behest had planted the blossoms on the roof of the White House.

"He liked to wear one as a boutonniere—he always did—my children remember that so well and it is her favorite flower," Jackie wrote.

She apologized that it had taken so long to request the plaque: "For me, it was Bobby who had to make any decision that had to do with his brother. When Bunny went to him—he was so harassed—with more burdens than any man should bear. He was just starting to speak out against the war in Vietnam...and wondered if it might be wrong to have anything military there—when peace was what his brother died for...

"If at any time you or Bunny had brought it up again—we were too wounded." Now that the Kennedy family was working on creating a memorial for Bobby, Jackie thought it was time to finish her husband's grave.

Jackie had been romantically linked to such eligible bachelors as architect John Carl Warnecke, Tony Award–winning director Mike Nichols, and British aristocrat and widower David Ormsby-Gore, also known as Lord Harlech. *Washington Post* syndicated humor columnist Art Buchwald devoted an entire column in March 1968 to "the Jackie watchers," a group he estimated at more than five thousand people. He joked that he had tracked down the "Jackie room" of a newspaper wire service, which was staffed with journalists tracking her every move, and he spoofed their travails. "The joint chief was nervously smoking his cigar. 'How many photographers do we have in the Yucatan?' 'One hundred and fifty,' an aide said. 'We'd better send in another 75, to be on the safe side.'"

In recent months, Jackie had been seen frequently in the company of Aristotle Onassis. In the spring, Jackie joined Ari on his yacht the *Christina*, cruising in Nassau with her two children. He gave her a ride on his private plane to Palm Beach when she spent the weekend there with friends. In August, she sailed with him on his yacht in Greece, chaperoned by brother-in-law Teddy Kennedy.

When Frank Langella visited Bunny at Cape Cod in the summer of 1968, he spotted Jackie sitting on the floor, trying on jewelry that had been given to her by Onassis. When he and Bunny later reminisced about that day, she told him, "Jackie was trying to decide whether or not to marry Ari."

After Labor Day had come and gone, Jackie and Bunny lingered on the Cape as the former First Lady pondered her next move. Rather than spend time at Bunny's sprawling residence, they switched to a neighboring two-bedroom cottage on the water called the Dune House, which Bunny had built for her own use to get away from the staff and her family. On September 13, Bunny wrote to her daughter, "Last night Jackie + I lit the fire in the Dune House and sat until darkness watching the light disappear and the stars come out."

That peaceful moment was followed a few weeks later by a mob scene in front of Jackie's Manhattan apartment, as reporters and photographers impatiently waited for Jackie to emerge. She had let word out earlier in the day that she was engaged to Onassis. Twenty-three years her senior, the billionaire had been carrying on a long public affair with Italian opera star Maria Callas.

Art Buchwald quipped, "The Jackie watchers had been so keen on keeping tabs on Lord Harlech that only a skeletal force had been watching the Greek coast. And apparently these watchers had gotten fat and lazy after listening to Maria Callas sing for the last 15 years. There is going to be a definite shakeup in the Jackie Kennedy Intelligence Agency."

As the reporters hovered outside, Bunny kept Jackie company inside, bracing for the public attention. The two women finally emerged onto Fifth Avenue and the cameramen swung into action. *WWD* featured a photograph of Jackie with Bunny by her side, with a headline that read: SHE'S OFF, SHE'S LOVELY, SHE'S ENGAGED . . . SHE'S ALL SMILES.

Bunny believed that Jackie needed a strong, wealthy protector and encouraged her to marry Onassis. "She said she talked to Rose Kennedy about the marriage because Rose was upset," says Bryan Huffman. "Bunny told her that it would be a good thing for Jackie. Just like Bunny marrying Paul Mellon, I think she thought this was a way for Jackie to get a leg up financially." Jackie would no longer need to ask Bunny for the use of her private plane; Onassis had an entire fleet.

Bunny had often been portrayed in the press as Jackie's Svengali. "Mrs. Mellon has had more influence in shaping Mrs. Kennedy's taste than anyone else in her life," Maxine Cheshire declared in the *Washington Post* earlier in the year.

In an homage to Bunny, Jackie brought in stage designer Paul Leonard to update Onassis's home. As Leonard later put it, "I went out to Skorpios after she married Aristotle Onassis to help her 'fluff up' the island."

Chapter Nineteen

Paul and Bunny in Love

—with Others

When Paul Mellon traveled to London, he usually spent time with John Baskett, his former art curator. Baskett had launched his own business as an art dealer with Paul's financial backing, and he scouted paintings and rare books for both Paul and Bunny. The two men were close, sharing details of their personal lives, including Baskett's divorce and bachelor status.

So when Baskett fell in love again, he was eager to introduce his new romantic interest to his benefactor. "Paul was in London, staying at the Barclay. I rang him," recalled Baskett. "I told him, I've got a girlfriend. And he said, 'So do I.'"

That may have been the first time that Paul Mellon confided to a friend about his romance with Dorcas Hardin, the widowed Georgetown dress shop owner who had been seen with him at the races several years earlier. Paul and John and their girlfriends went out to dinner in London, the first of many merry evenings. "She had a very good sense of humor, we had a lot of fun," Baskett recalls. "Dorcas was a very nice woman."

Dorcas was just a year younger than Bunny, and for decades the women had been guests at each other's homes. Baskett believes that Paul and Dorcas began seeing each other around 1966, although some in Georgetown suspect the romance started earlier. Paul's heartfelt 1967 commencement speech, mentioning the life-transforming and sensual pleasures of love, was likely inspired by his relationship with Dorcas. Gossip about the affair may have sparked the Are-the-Mellons-Splitting item in Walter Winchell's 1968 column, although Dorcas's name was not mentioned in the press.

The lovers were discreet, but word inevitably spread. "I was talking to David Bruce one night at a dinner at a club in Georgetown," recalls Oatsie Leiter Charles. "Somehow, David said something about Paul and Dorcas. I nearly broke my neck rushing downstairs to tell Lily Guest and Hallie Covington." As Marie Ridder adds, "Everyone knew about the affair. How could you not? Dorcas would wear this green stone—not an emerald but enormous—and she'd say, 'You know who gave it to me.'"

This relationship was not just a midlife crisis fling. Paul Mellon was in love.

It is unclear how and when Bunny learned about the romance. But once Paul admitted his feelings for Dorcas, Bunny took it hard. She left for Princeton to confide her woes to her stepmother, Grace Lambert. Grace subsequently discussed the vexing situation with a trusted family friend, Princeton professor Alfred Bush. "Grace told me that Bunny came to her in tears after Paul had asked for a divorce," says Bush, who had met Bunny and Paul on many occasions. "I recall Grace saying that Bunny came to her in great distress."

Bunny had gone into the marriage with her eyes wide open. She had grown up with a charismatic father who was a philanderer. From an impressionable age, she had come to believe that this was what powerful men did—they took mistresses. During World War II, her first husband, Stacy Lloyd, had regaled her in his letters with the stories of the married Paul Mellon's London romances. For a man of Paul's wealth and status, the only surprising element was that Dorcas was age-appropriate, rather than a twenty-four-year-old chorus girl. Yet in its own way, that was even more painful for Bunny to accept.

Her own relationship with Johnny Schlumberger had taken place out of the public eye and had never appeared to be a threat to her marriage. But Paul's strong feelings for Dorcas had the potential to upend Bunny's entire life.

Bunny was determined to hold on to the title of "Mrs. Paul Mellon." Hurt and angry, she did not want a divorce and made it clear that she would tolerate her husband's desires. "It was a rather eighteenth-century arrangement," says Baskett. "It was accepted by Bunny, obviously, otherwise they would have gotten divorced." The Mellons decided to stay married to each other but lead separate lives.

"My take on it—but with no evidence—is that it would have been Bunny who responded to Paul that the marriage should continue since she would allow him any freedom he wished," says Alfred Bush. "He knew that she would continue to create a world at the various Mellon properties that no one else could match and that Paul certainly appreciated. Dorcas was no competition as chatelaine."

Paul's relationship with Dorcas became the equivalent of a second marriage. They saw each other in Washington—at his house or hers—and at hotels in New York and London. Dorcas attended National Gallery parties but kept a diplomatic distance from the Mellons at public events. Paul and John Baskett occasionally had dinner with Dorcas and members of her family.

The affair became an open secret in Washington, yet the press never covered it. "It was clear something was going on and it was big. It was known in upper-class circles," recalls Vernon Jordan, the Washington power broker, who knew the cast of characters and thought Dorcas was "very nice and classy."

But there were awkward encounters. Bunny's sister, Lily McCarthy, was dining with her husband at the private Wianno Club in Cape Cod one evening when Paul arrived with Dorcas. Even Bunny's son, Tuffy, became aware of the distinct rhythms of the relationship, recalling, "He had this thing with Dorcas every Tuesday. Every Tuesday he'd go to Washington and have supper with her."

For Bunny, it was emotionally complicated to put on a public face and her reactions varied. At times, she made denigrating remarks about Paul's sexual prowess, which were promptly passed along as prurient gossip. "Bunny did not think Mr. Mellon was very good in bed," recalls Marie Ridder, who often went riding with Paul as part of a group. "How do I know that? She made a remark about Dorcas— wished her luck in that department. Bunny said it to Charlie White-house, who repeated it with glee." (Whitehouse, a Yale graduate and former CIA operative, was a State Department diplomat and friend of the Mellons and the Kennedys.)

Bunny periodically told intimates that she was the one who offered Paul a divorce, and that he had insisted on staying married. Her explanation was that he liked how well she ran their homes. Bunny did not want people to feel sorry for her, so she insisted that she was aware of the situation. Dorcas had lost partial hearing; people often raised their voices to communicate with her. Bunny repeatedly told friends that when Paul came home—and she suspected that he'd been with his lover—she would tell him, "Paul, you don't have to yell. You're home now."

And so, they carried on. Paul sent Bunny loving letters when they were apart as if nothing were amiss, with comments such as, "I miss you and our little house very much." He wrote rhyming doggerel for her birthdays and made a point of giving her romantic Valentine's cards. Bunny continued to help Paul entertain at National Gallery functions; he underwrote her spending sprees and gave her extravagant gifts of jewelry and art.

On holiday together in Antigua or Cape Cod, they brought house-guests as buffers, such as John Baskett or Princeton professor Charles Ryskamp. But despite her public pronouncements, the affair wounded Bunny, and she was wary of acquaintances who appeared to be close to her rival. "Bunny was a great nice friend, she'd been to my house, I'd been to her house, we'd talk on the phone, nice friendly re-lationship," said one Georgetown hostess, now in her nineties. "Then, one day I went to the Golden Door in California for a week, at the same time—but not with me—that Dorcas Hardin was out there. Bunny dropped me like a hot potato."

Bunny could commiserate with Jackie Kennedy. "Bunny told me," says Bryan Huffman, "that she and Jackie had both had painful experiences with their husbands and they shared these confidences with each other." Martha Bartlett, who had introduced Jackie Bouvier to Jack Kennedy, says that the former First Lady stood by her best friend. "Jackie would ridicule Dorcas, so I had the feeling Bunny ridiculed her, too," Martha says. "They thought she was a horse's ass." Martha defended the Georgetown dress shop owner, saying, "Dorcas was lovely, warm, fun, divine, good company, everything was warm and cozy. I'm sure Paul Mellon found it an enormous relief after Bunny."

That was a common view. First as Gerard Lambert's daughter and then as Paul Mellon's wife, Bunny had become used to people fawning over her, and she had never bothered to ingratiate herself with Washington society. While always polite, she was not especially outgoing or warm or interested in expanding her small circle of friends. She had dealt with her childhood insecurities and innate shyness by assuming, in public, a regal above-it-all persona.

So there was a certain amount of schadenfreude when people learned that the aloof Mrs. Mellon had received her comeuppance at the hands of a well-liked shop owner. The wives of senators, congressmen, and Cabinet members shopped at Dorcas Hardin's store. When *Vogue* published a ranking of Washington power players, Dorcas ranked higher than restaurant and hotel chain founder J. Wilard Marriott.

"Dorcas was a lady," says Kenneth Jay Lane, the costume jewelry designer. "Dorcas sold my jewelry, that's how I knew her. She was part of nonpolitical Georgetown society. She was hardly anyone you would think of as anyone's heartthrob. I didn't know she was Paul Mellon's mistress until later. She was a nice breezy lady, could have been played by Billie Burke on the screen." (The dulcet-toned actress portrayed Glinda the Good Witch in *The Wizard of Oz*.)

Paul and Bunny's household staff inevitably became aware of the delicate situation. Oliver Murray, the butler at the couple's Washington residence, helped facilitate Paul's rendezvous with Dorcas. "At dinner they would talk and laugh," Murray later told journalist Sally

Bedell Smith. "She was cheerful and fun. Bunny was not bubbly like Dorcas."

Family members tried to ignore the elephant in the room. "I knew enough to know," says John Warner, then Paul's son-in-law. "I just turned a deaf ear to the whole thing." Warner did his best to remain on good terms with both of his in-laws. "They treated me kindly. I heard a little bit about spatting. Bunny would sometimes come to me and lament about things. I just listened."

Bunny's friends tiptoed around the situation. "Everyone knew about Dorcas but nobody talked about it," recalls Amy Greene, who, with her husband, photographer Milton Greene, had been befriended by Bunny, vacationing with her in Antigua. In this inbred world, Dorcas's son Teddy worked as Milton Greene's assistant. "I saw Dorcas all the time," Amy Greene adds. "She'd come up to New York to take her son to Brooks Brothers. She was quietly elegant, you'd say she was a great, commanding woman—it was old-time religion, like a great French courtesan. She knew her role and played it to the hilt and kept him happy. Bunny didn't mind. She could go play."

For a gentleman regarded as kind and thoughtful, Paul behaved in one way that was uncharacteristically cruel. When he wanted to talk to Dorcas on the phone, he could have easily made the three-minute drive from the couple's Upperville residence to the nearby Brick House.

Instead, he remained at home, sitting in his ground-floor office and—because of his lover's hearing problems—talking at top volume. Anyone in the vicinity could hear his side of the conversation. Perhaps he was willfully oblivious; at least that was how Bunny chose to play it. Her in-house decorator, Paul Leonard, recounted to friends that one day he and Bunny happened to be near Paul Mellon's office when the art collector was speaking to Dorcas. "We heard every word and were sitting there in hysterics like little children."

Knowing laughter was preferable to tears.

In the summer of 1969, Bunny embarked on a two-pronged strategy to quiet the rumors about her marriage. Despite her limited interest in racing, she appeared by Paul's side that spring at the Kentucky Derby and then the Preakness to watch his Thoroughbred Arts and Letters. The horse came in second both times.

Then Bunny did something that, for her, was quite extraordinary: She gave an interview to the *New York Times*. Although the subject was ostensibly her enviable lifestyle, in truth, she was publicly claiming her position as Mrs. Paul Mellon.

Writer Sarah Booth Conroy began her article by describing Bunny standing outside her Virginia home and repeating the phrase: "Nothing should be noticed. Nothing should be noticed."

Bunny explained that this was her decorating philosophy: "Nothing should stand out. It all should give the feeling of calm. When you go away, you should remember only the peace."

In case readers wondered why Mrs. Mellon was deigning to speak to the press, the next paragraph contained quotes that, to the initiated, spoke volumes.

"I've never given an interview before," Mrs. Mellon said. (Actually, she had spoken to the *Washington Post* about Queen Elizabeth's visit back in 1957, and allowed Eugenia Sheppard to write about her Manhattan home.) She claimed to dislike seeing herself in the society pages. "When I am photographed even, I sort of squint up my eyes so it all goes away. But my husband and I talked it over the other day, and we said we were tired of reading in the press all sorts of wrong things about the way we live. A woman reporter calls my husband periodically to ask when we are getting divorced.

"My husband said, 'Perhaps it's because they really haven't ever seen the way we live.'"

Bunny gave the writer and a photographer a tour of her sun-splashed home with its Degas, Corots, and Pissarros, and her rare book collection. Her guests toured the garden bursting with red poppies and green flowers, and her conservatory with its trompe l'oeil mural. She invited the journalists for an impromptu lunch of fettuccini, tiny asparagus, cottage cheese, homemade bread, and wine.

In talking about her marriage, Bunny referred to her husband in formal fashion, as if she were using the *Times'* honorific. "Mr. Mellon and I meet on art and books. He has such a wonderful light sense of humor. He's really such fun to be with. He writes clever bits of poetry and teases me all the time. I like it."

Buying art remained a joint pleasure, and Bunny mentioned that she had recently become interested in abstract paintings. "This summer, I called my husband from Europe and I said, 'Don't be mad but I'm bringing home two abstractions.' Mr. Mellon said, 'Don't be crazy, I'd like to see them.'" One of the new acquisitions was a Mondrian.

Bunny added that she, too, enjoyed artistic pursuits. "I keep a sketch pad with me at all times at airports and train stations," she said. "I'm never lonely when I have my sketch pad."

She evoked her Camelot experience by allowing the journalists to see a cherished gift from Jackie, the oversized scrapbook featuring Bunny's design of the Rose Garden. "Of course, Jacqueline was a true and loyal friend of mine a long time before she went into the White House," Bunny said. "I can't say anything but good about her. People see only the clothes and they don't see her. Her marriage? Just right for her, I'm sure. Aristotle Onassis is a wonderful man. So intelligent. And so charming."

Bunny made kind remarks about Lady Bird—"I don't think Mrs. Johnson was ever properly appreciated. I really liked her"—and dropped a hint about her desire to remain involved with the White House garden. "Of course, I would be happy to help Mrs. Nixon, but she hasn't asked me. I am a Democrat. My husband teases me about it all the time. But gardens aren't political. I tell my husband, 'Trees have to be watered no matter whether the Administration is Republican or Democratic.'"

Surrounded by her beautiful possessions, demonstrating her good taste and powerful connections, Bunny conveyed that she was a woman to be envied, not pitied. It was a masterful performance. The article was a public relations triumph even if the *New York Times* writer could not resist one reference to "Marie Antoinette who played milkmaid in the country."

There would be no more nosy gossip columns questioning the Mellon marriage.

Nothing should be noticed. Especially not her husband's affair.

The day after the article appeared, Bunny joined her husband at the Belmont Stakes, where Paul's horse Arts and Letters finally soared past the competition. The champion was named the Horse of the Year, leading to a complimentary profile of Paul in *Sports Illustrated*.

Paul was often in the public eye but his sister, Ailsa, avoided publicity. Still considered a beautiful woman, she had recently dithered on yet another marriage proposal from her beau, G. Lauder Greenway. She was preoccupied with decorating her new apartment at 960 Fifth Avenue. Paintings, chandeliers, carpets, nothing but the best would do. National Gallery director John Walker recalled, "She wanted the apartment to be unparalleled among her friends." But Ailsa never got to live in it.

"When she was at last ready to move in, after four years of preparation, she was told she ought to go to the hospital for a minor operation," Walker wrote in his autobiography. "She never left her hospital bed, never slept in her new apartment." At age sixty-eight, on August 25, Ailsa died at Roosevelt Hospital, of what was said to be cancer.

The *Washington Post* described her as a "shy woman" who "managed to live a life of privacy and quiet." Ailsa left her beloved Impressionist paintings to the National Gallery, including seven Renoirs, four Pissarros, three Monets, and works by Matisse, Van Gogh, Seurat, and Cézanne. The bulk of her wealth, which *Fortune* magazine had estimated a year earlier at up to $1 billion, was left to the Andrew W. Mellon Foundation, where Paul remained a trustee. He sadly described his sister as an unhappy woman who never got over her daughter's death.

He remained determined, in contrast, to live, live, live. Ratcheting up his real estate acquisitions, he bought a town house in New York at 713 Park Avenue, a rare private home amid the grand co-ops on the leafy street. The twenty-foot-wide, five-story limestone building, with eighty-five hundred square feet of space, included a backyard garden. Paul set up his office in that building, just a block away from the Mellons' residence at 125 East Seventieth Street.

That fall, Bunny headed for Paris to try on the new wardrobe that she had commissioned from Hubert de Givenchy. To their mutual delight, Bunny and the designer hit it off as their small talk headed in surprising directions. "Mrs. Mellon came to Paris for a fitting, and we start to work together," recalls Givenchy. "I am so happy to work with her. Not only does she have great taste but she knows perfectly what she wants for her. Extremely simple."

He was intrigued by his new client's knowledge of art, design, and gardening. "This is very different from other customers who are only interested in clothes," he said. Seventeen years her junior, he thought he could learn from her. "She has an extraordinary imagination," he said. "She is so creative, what is marvelous is that she always, always has ideas. Of course, we have a great rapport."

Bunny was not only grateful for the seamless transition but was in awe of the charming couturier. Following up on their meeting, Givenchy sent her a sweet, tentative note on October 17, expressing his pleasure that she had called him a new friend and adding, "I am sure you understand that I had the same feelings for you."

Bunny confided to her journal on November 5: "Hubert called. I know I miss some of his thoughts and sentences and he probably does not understand my French. He said my French was better. I can't imagine why except I speak to myself in French when I am alone. I hope my enthusiasm will not damage this new and heavenly relationship."

Bunny turned up in Manhattan that fall for a small party in honor of Jackie and Ari's first wedding anniversary, held at Jackie's Fifth Avenue apartment. The columnist Suzy covered the party, writing that the two inseparable friends were both wearing black pants ("which could be a fashion first" for Mrs. Mellon) and noting that not only did Jackie appear "happy," but her former mother-in-law, Rose Kennedy, had joined the celebration.

A few weeks later, Paul and Bunny hosted a party at the Sulgrave Club for an exhibit of Old Masters drawings on loan from the Devonshire family, Bunny's British friends. "Mrs. Mellon was aristocratic in a black high-necked, long-sleeved, easy-skirted dress by Givenchy," said the *New York Times*. Worried about running into Dorcas, Bunny had dressed defensively, determined to look her best.

"Wore lovely black dress that Hubert designed," Bunny wrote in her journal. "Felt very protected and pretty and able to view other women from inside its little fortress."

Right after that party, Bunny called astrologer Jeane Dixon, known as "the Seeress of Washington" and the author of a syndicated horoscope column, and asked for an "urgent" appointment. With her world reeling out of control, and with few people other than Jackie whom she could confide in, Bunny wanted insight about her life and future. Rather than consult a therapist, she turned again to astrology and also threw herself into reading about the occult.

"Bunny always had stacks of books on her bedside," recalled Lavinia Currier, Paul Mellon's great-niece. "We'd pick one up, we'd discuss Madame Blavatsky [a famous Russian spiritualist] or séances." Bunny's interests eventually became public. "Mrs. Paul Mellon, married to one of the world's richest men, doesn't need a fortune-teller to tell her that her future is secure," wrote Maxine Cheshire in the *Washington Post*. "But nevertheless, her personal maid is well known among Washington's servants community as a reader of cards and palms and she tells her friends she reads for 'madam' all the time." Bunny's address books during the next forty years would include listings for astrologers, psychics, and self-proclaimed witches.

On New Year's Eve, as the calendar changed from 1969 to 1970, Bunny and Paul spent the holiday at their Antigua estate with her daughter, Eliza, and actor Frank Langella. In his book, *Dropped Names*, Langella recounted a late-night mishap that occurred when Bunny began to dance by herself that night in the garden, tripped over a plant, and broke her ankle:

I was summoned to her room at 3 a.m. to find her lying on her bed, leg up on a pillow, and her ankle bound tightly with a Balenciaga scarf. Paul was sitting on a chair beside the bed looking enormously relieved to see me come in. He instantly got up and said:

"Bun, I'm going to bed. Frank will keep you company."

"Gosh Paul, it hurts very badly."

"Well, you brought it on yourself, dear."

Paul Mellon does not come across as a sympathetic spouse. The actor sat with Bunny through the night and joined her the next day on the plane back to New York, where she was treated at the Hospital for Special Surgery.

Bunny had never lacked for male companionship, and with Paul preoccupied with Dorcas, she had even more freedom to issue invitations and make her own plans. A constant stream of men, almost all of them gay, were pleased to be asked to accompany her to the ballet in Manhattan, vacation with her at Antigua and Cape Cod, or spend time with her in Paris. "She was very happy with homosexuals, walkers, they adored her," says Amy Greene. "There was this nicety inside this lady, you're thrilled with being with her because she's nice."

Paul Leonard, her handsome employee, looked great in a tuxedo and could do double duty as her escort. Perry Wheeler, the landscape architect who had worked with her on the Rose Garden, remained a cherished companion. The others who received frequent dinner and weekend invitations included Horace "Ho" Kelland, a New York writer and best-dressed man-about-town; hairdresser Kenneth Battelle; decorator Billy Baldwin; and Andy Oates, a weaver on Nantucket with a fabric business and a shop selling handmade sweaters and baskets.

Bunny was sympathetic when her gay friends experienced prejudice. Oates and his partner, Bill Euler, wanted to buy a Main Street building in Nantucket but ran into trouble getting a loan. Liz Winship, who worked for the men and now owns their store, Nantucket Looms, recalls, "The bank denied them the money. Back then, they were two gay guys... Bunny, who had been a great patron of the loom from when they first started in 1968, talked to Paul Mellon, and he held the mortgage on the property for twenty-five years. That's how wonderful and generous she was."

Bunny appreciated the company of her male companions, although it appeared that most of these relationships ended at the bedroom door. If the men kissed they did not tell, although a few, like Paul Leonard, hinted that more was at stake. Leonard's Yale classmate and lover during their graduate school years, Henry Heymann, recalled, "He would look arch. It was clear something was going on but he didn't brag. He was such a spectacular looking guy and so sweet. I don't think he was in love with her, but he loved her. He was overwhelmed by her." Bunny wrote in her journal about Paul Leonard: "I love it when he is around. He is fast becoming a unique and marvelous friend."

But now Bunny had a new man in her life: Hubert de Givenchy. "I never feel alone since Hubert has become my friend," she wrote in her journal. "A call from the Prado on my breakfast tray. A few words written bring with them a closeness and a warmth. He makes me feel like a woman loved and I can dare to unfold petals of feeling that mostly stay closed."

For Givenchy, Bunny was a muse, an inspiration, a dear friend who expanded his worldview. From the way he described his relationship with Bunny to me, he cared about her deeply and loved spending time with her, but this was not a romantic liaison. Givenchy was touched by Bunny's girlish charm.

"She's amusing because she tell me, 'I love fairy tales.' She's always tells me about when she was young she dreamed of fairy tales and she has books of fairy tales," he told me. "It's so amusing to see someone, like a grande dame, she dreamed like a little girl. She dream about love, about beauty, about plants, about painting, about color, she had no limits."

That March, he visited Bunny in Antigua, after requesting—and receiving—permission to bring along his friend and frequent traveling companion, Philippe Venet, who had been a tailor at Givenchy's atelier before opening his own salon. The three of them went to Tunis that summer with an entourage. "It seems impossible that I shall ever see H alone," Bunny wrote in her journal on August 23. "It is frustrating... One longs to discuss ideas. Aldous Huxley once said to me, at a large luncheon of people interested in the arts, if one could only capture the thoughts that are being mixed together of all the subconscious minds in the room: 'We all say such small things while we think more interesting ones.'"

She was besotted with Givenchy, writing, "How can I ever tell this man that his thoughts and way of doing things literally makes me helpless and weak with joy."

In September, Givenchy spent the weekend with Paul and Bunny at their farm, as part of a Washington trip to showcase his latest collection. He told me that he enjoyed his time with them as a couple, explaining, "Paul was very English in a way, very strict, very nice, very good sense of humor, very amusing. Paul and Bunny are charming together, sometimes they don't have the same point of view, but always nice to each other."

A *New York Times* photographer captured Givenchy fondly gazing at Bunny at the fall fashion preview at the Shoreham Hotel, a benefit for the Washington Symphony Orchestra. The designer praised Bunny to the *Times*, saying, "She is, how do I say it, the most refined woman, not in America but in the world. Everything she does with such simplicity, such taste, such color sense. Even the flowers she plants in her garden are so perfect."

Washington Star columnist Eleni wrote: "He's considered the best-looking Paris designer... Mrs. Paul Mellon, who flew Givenchy to Washington in her plane, was planning to take the famed fashion visitor and personal friend to Cape Cod for the weekend following the show."

Bunny had been collecting Impressionist art for two decades, specializing in landscapes and still lifes, but her new French friend introduced her to the colorful abstract canvases of American painter

Mark Rothko. "She was very avant garde. Mr. Mellon was more for Cézanne, for Renoir, for Degas, Mrs. Mellon is more adventurous," Givenchy told me. "When I said Bunny, you must buy Rothko for the National Gallery, she said, 'Paul doesn't like Rothko.' But this is not the question. I said, 'He is an important painter, you must have him in the National Gallery.' She agreed."

Rothko committed suicide in February 1970. Givenchy and Bunny visited the artist's studio in Manhattan that November, and she was immediately captivated by the undulating colors and the emotion in the works. This was such a memorable moment that Bunny could still recall her reaction, more than forty years later. "I walked in and saw them for the first time and there they were, dozens of them, and I thought, 'Oh, boy,'" Bunny told me in the summer of 2011. "Paul thought I was crazy but he helped me pay for them. I started out with the Impressionists and after that I just went wild with the Modern."

Bunny purchased five paintings, with prices ranging from $55,000 to $180,000, for an estimated $475,000. She could not get enough of the artist, and on March 2, 1971, she purchased two more Rothkos for an additional $420,000. She chose selections that conveyed the arc of the artist's work and moods: a massive 1955 canvas, five feet by nearly seven feet, featured cheerful blocks of yellow and orange, while a more somber but gorgeous purple and dark indigo had been painted shortly before the artist's death.

Bunny bought her paintings through the Marlborough Gallery, unaware that she was stepping into a legal morass. In 1971, Mark Rothko's twenty-year-old daughter, Kate, sued her father's executors and the Marlborough Gallery's owners, charging them with double-dealing and flipping one hundred paintings that the gallery had valued at $18,000 each, and then selling the art for hundreds of thousands of dollars to collectors. At the trial, Bunny's purchases were cited as a prime exhibit of the gallery's bad behavior. As Lee Seldes put it in his book, *The Legacy of Mark Rothko*, "Kate Rothko won." Rothko's executors were ousted, the gallery was fined, and a sweetheart sales contract was canceled. Bunny did not have to testify at the trial or return the artwork, although she hired lawyer Alex Forger, the chairman of Milbank, Tweed, Hadley & McCloy, to look out for her interests. He would end up representing her for four decades.

For Bunny, nonchalantly dropping six-figure sums on artwork was part of her normal yearly spending. She loved to shop and was generous to her friends. At Tiffany's, the sales staff eagerly looked forward to fulfilling Bunny's Christmas gift list. "What she would buy from us was extraordinary," says Pierce MacGuire, of Tiffany's. "She would buy twenty-five to thirty-five things from us. She'd even buy gifts for the manicurist at the St. Regis Hotel. She gave everybody Schlumberger. On her mother, she'd spend $100,000, for the manicurist $2,000 or $3,000. She'd buy something for herself, or Mr. Mellon would buy something for her for several hundred thousand dollars."

The distinctive Tiffany blue box was considered a status symbol in most circles, but Bunny thought it was déclassé. "I told her once about a new way of packaging that I'd seen at a shop called Azuma on Madison Avenue," recalled Paul Leonard. "They would vacuum seal anything in an ordinary can. You had to use a can opener to open it. Bunny thought it was a grand idea, but we must create a wonderful label on the can too!! So Jackie received a tin can with Schlumberger earrings."

The discreet sales staff at Tiffany's was aware that Paul Mellon was also purchasing gifts in the store for the other woman in his life. Pierce MacGuire adds, "Paul was buying jewels for Bunny from Schlumberger and jewels from Verdura for Dorcas. Everyone knew."

———

That May, Bunny joined Givenchy, Philippe Venet, and their friend Hélène Bouilloux-Lafont on a cruise in Greece. She wrote in her journal of Hubert, "His thoughts are so like the ones I have had all my life but never found anyone who shared in this way…I never wanted to distrust and held on to the belief one could trust but like animals we know when there is danger. With Hubert, I begin to feel no danger, just respect."

On the trip, she found herself appreciating the simplest sights— a small Greek church, a large fig tree, a hill covered with yellow daisies—and sketching them in order to remember the trip. In a postcard to Paul Leonard, she wrote, "The boat is so attractive and as 4 people go we are doing very well. Hubert is so attractive to everyone. And runs it all like a ballet...I have so much to tell you and have missed you so much. Hugs + love."

Bunny's friendship with Givenchy was of interest to gossip columnists. On July 26, 1971, *WWD* noted that she was purchasing a home in Paris: "Some say it's to be near her favorite store—Givenchy couture, which turns out everything from her bed sheets to Bunny's Sunday best." Syndicated columnist Jack O'Brian wrote a few months later: "Mrs. Bunny Mellon of the of course Mellon millions has been constant hostess for the visiting Hubert Givenchy, with whose Paris dress salon she spent a tight little clothes budget last year of $170,000—in that one atelier alone."

Paul Mellon made a rare appearance in Paris, which was Bunny's territory. His three-year-old horse, Mill Reef, named after their Antigua home, became the first American Thoroughbred to win the Grand Prix, setting a new record. But Paul was not interested in spending time at his wife's new Paris residence. As Givenchy recalls, "Paul don't like France, he liked England where he had his horses. Bunny made a beautiful room for him in her apartment, but Paul come one or two times in Paris for the Grand Prix, or something for horses."

As a World War II veteran, Paul was uncomfortable with Bunny's choice of Parisian real estate. The house had belonged to Baroness Maggie van Zuylen but was commandeered by the Nazis and used as Gestapo headquarters. Described in newspapers as the "notorious" 84 Avenue Foch, the premises served as a location where the Nazis interrogated captured Allied prisoners.

The ghosts did not deter Bunny. Not only did she love the appearance of the house, but the location happened to be convenient: Aristotle Onassis owned a fifteen-room apartment on the same block, at 88 Avenue Foch, so Jackie and Bunny could easily pop into each other's homes.

To furnish Bunny's new Paris home, Givenchy arranged for her to meet Diego Giacometti. The brother of sculptor Alberto Giacometti, he created fanciful, rustic-style bronze furniture, often adorned with tiny animals. "I just loved him," Bunny later recalled. "We met in his studio, which was very small. We spoke French to each other. He's Italian and could not speak English and I spoke English and not Italian. I asked him to design a chandelier." She commissioned numerous tables and chairs for her homes.

In the City of Light, Bunny felt freer, away from prying eyes, able to move around the city unrecognized. "I love shopping late in the evening in Paris," she wrote in a journal entry. "We sort of move through the streets lit by lamps in another century."

Yet she remained firmly rooted in the here and now, and American politics remained a subject of intense interest. Bunny loathed Richard Nixon. In September 1972, when Bunny and Paul were asked at a Washington party who they planned to vote for in the coming presidential election, she announced that she was supporting George McGovern, at a time when he had been abandoned by many establishment Democrats.

"I'm going to vote for him," Bunny said. "It's so sad the way things are in the country right now. We need a change." Her husband gently disagreed, saying, "Unfortunately, I've always been a Republican and I'm not going to change now." Once again, their votes canceled each other out, although this time Paul's candidate won.

Chapter Twenty

The Spending of a Robber Baron Fortune

Tuffy Lloyd had decided to become a journalist. In February 1972, he wrote a lengthy opinion article for the *Washington Post* about Laos, weighing in on the embattled country's precarious state, torn between North Vietnam and China. In March 1973, he went to work as a researcher for Washington muckraking columnist Jack Anderson, the Pulitzer Prize winner whose work appeared in more than one thousand newspapers. Tuffy's father had been a gentleman newspaper publisher, but this was scruffier work. Anderson's staffers were known to dig through garbage to ferret out classified documents.

An item in the *Washington Post* announcing Tuffy's new job described the thirty-five-year-old, who had inherited his father's good looks, as a man with "a cleft chin like Cary Grant" and "the stepson of one of the richest men in the U.S., Paul Mellon."

The Mellon connection was a blessing and a burden for Bunny's children as they sought to carve out their own careers. It was hard for them to escape the omnipresent shadow, although at least they did not bear their stepfather's moniker. "I'm ever so glad my name is

Lloyd rather than Mellon," Tuffy Lloyd told me. "To have to explain Mellon would have been catastrophic."

When his sister, Eliza, began to show her paintings at New York galleries, she told friends that she wondered whether her talent carried the day or whether her stepfather's and mother's reputations as wealthy collectors opened doors.

The siblings had very different and very complicated relationships with their mother and stepfather. Tuffy felt like the odd man out in his own family. "Mother was kind of aloof," he says. "She was a bit of an enigma." He was eager to please and appease her, but his preoccupied mother took him for granted. He did not perceive Paul Mellon as a supportive figure, either, admitting, "I didn't particularly like him. But he was of the generation where his father was very cold, he grew up with a tough mother. Paul wasn't a warm person."

Eliza and "Da," as she called Paul, had a teasing and easygoing relationship. But there was nothing easygoing between Bunny and Eliza. Bunny had always been protective of Eliza, and it was hard for her to let go. Eliza was attached to her mother but felt smothered. Their friction reflected the tenor of the times and the generation gap. Bunny, who had a formal upbringing, still wore white gloves. The free-spirited Eliza was influenced by the emerging force of feminism plus the 1960s antimaterialistic ethos of flower children. Bunny gave orders to her staff; Eliza would skip into the kitchen and offer to cook eggs for the housekeeper.

"Eliza didn't dress like her mother, she didn't think like her mother," recalls Amy Greene, the *Glamour* editor. "Every daughter rebels against her mother." She adds that Eliza was trying to find her creative niche. "Eliza was very pretty, and she was a good, small painter, miniatures, very talented."

Eliza split her time between Paris and New York City. She lived for a time in an apartment in Paul and Bunny's East Seventieth Street carriage house. Bunny yearned to be involved in her daughter's life. When Eliza bought a summer home in Little Compton, on the coast of Rhode Island, Bunny surprised her by purchasing an adjoining property as a gift. Eliza was enraged at her mother for interfering.

"Eliza was a rebel but kept within the bounds where respectability was needed," says her brother, Tuffy. "She would think nothing of sailing to Cape Cod with only ten gallons of gasoline for the motor if something happened. She was just bold. She took a race-car driving course outside of Paris and got very good at that." Eliza's fearlessness worried her mother. Virginia Warner, Paul's granddaughter, recalls hearing Bunny fret when Eliza took off on her boat. "Bun would say, 'How can she go like that? Shouldn't someone go with her?' Eliza would say, 'Mummy, I'm okay, I'm my own person.'"

Outsiders found the family dynamics perplexing. At a cocktail party in Washington in 1973, Tuffy met Anne Emmet, who had been Eliza's Foxcroft schoolmate. Newly divorced with three young children, and an attractive and engaging Briarcliff graduate, Anne had just moved back to the city from Dayton, Ohio. Her family was Washington royalty: She was a descendant of William Corcoran, creator of the Corcoran Gallery, and Levi Morton, vice president under President Benjamin Harrison. Her uncle David Finley had worked for Andrew Mellon at the Treasury Department, served as the first president of the National Gallery, and had been a father figure to Paul Mellon. Anne grew up visiting her family's storied estate, Oatlands, built in 1800 on 261 acres in Leesburg, Virginia. In Social Register terms, Anne and Stacy Lloyd III were a suitable match.

As the romance progressed, he brought Anne to Cape Cod, along with her children, to meet his mother and stepfather. The visit left Anne baffled. Paul made disparaging comments to his stepson. Bunny vehemently disapproved when Anne's son wanted to play with the children of Cathy Mellon and John Warner, who had a home nearby. There was tension on all sides. Anne later learned that Eliza was not currently on speaking terms with her mother.

Anne's introduction to the Mellon family came during a fraught time. Bunny was pretending that all was well in her marriage, but it was a struggle to ignore the obvious. Paul was in mourning for his mother, Nora, who had died in June at age ninety-four. A veteran of decades of analysis, he had never forgiven his mother for her adulterous behavior that led to his parents' vicious divorce.

Despite the awkward timing of Anne's visit to the Cape, she made a good impression on Bunny, who conveyed her reaction to her ex-husband, Stacy Lloyd. "Thanks so much for your letter about Anne and it is so helpful to hear your first hand observations and to be sure that he had made a good choice," replied Stacy. "She sounds like a grand girl and I am just as pleased as punch that he seems to have found what he has been looking for. It seems we are all connected in one way or another as her father Grenville Emmet was at school with me."

In October, Stacy "Tuffy" Lloyd III and Anne Emmet announced their engagement and set a wedding date for November. The bride-to-be, whose parents had divorced when she was young, sought guidance on planning the ceremony. "My mother had been ill, she was an invalid," recalls Anne. So she turned to her mother's dearest friend for advice.

The friend was Dorcas Hardin.

Dorcas had recently been lauded in *WWD* for giving "the prettiest dinner parties" that mixed senators, congressmen, and "just plain folks" and featured Dom Pérignon, Limoges china, Vermeil candelabras, Rigaud candles, and a touch of the fragrance Floris on her lightbulbs.

"When I told Dorcas that I was getting married," says Anne, "she said, 'That's wonderful. Why don't I dress you—get you your wedding dress and your trousseau?' I said, 'This is fabulous.'" Since Anne had been living in Ohio until recently, the bride-to-be was unaware of the relationship between Dorcas and Paul Mellon. As she recalls, shaking her head in wonderment, "No one said anything to me."

Only after Anne and Dorcas had gone to New York to commission a designer to make the gown did Anne learn just what she had blundered into. "Two weeks before the wedding, Bunny called up and said in a quiet voice, 'I believe Dorcas is making your dress. Don't invite her to the wedding.' By then I knew what it was about, people were starting to whisper. I was wooing my new mother-in-law. So I told Dorcas that she couldn't come and she said, 'I know.'"

The *Washington Post*'s account of the couple's November wedding portrayed Stacy "Tuffy" Lloyd III as marrying up. "Members of Washington's old-line white society, whose families came here no later than the 1800's, have sometimes been referred to by those outside their ranks as cavedwellers," the *Post* noted. "Saturday, it was relaxed enough for Mrs. Anne Emmet Pepper, a cavedweller, to marry Stacy B. Lloyd, a relative newcomer by comparison."

Jackie Kennedy Onassis did not attend the wedding but her mother and stepfather, Janet and Hugh Auchincloss, came to the ceremony at St. John's Church at Lafayette Square, along with former ambassador Henry Cabot Lodge, Alice Roosevelt Longworth (the daughter of President Teddy Roosevelt), and columnist Joseph Alsop. Bunny's first husband, who came up from the Virgin Islands to be his son's best man, wrote to Bunny afterward: "The nicest part of it all was finding myself next to you at dinner. It brought a chapter of Tuffy Tales to a very happy ending. They seem to be off to a good start. Anne is very sensible. I believe Tuffy has very much in mind that consideration of her happiness."

Pleased that her son had found a life partner, Bunny was kind and helpful to her new daughter-in-law. "She was wonderful to me from Day One," Anne recalls. "She encouraged me. I felt like a flower opening up under her tutelage."

Tuffy left his job working for Jack Anderson to pursue a more suitable profession, opening a travel and antiquarian shop, Lloyd Books, on Connecticut Avenue, that catered to the city's social elite, politicians, and historians. He later moved it to Georgetown. Happy in his new work, he created a friendly and welcoming environment. "We had regulars who came in every day to sit and chat," says Marci Nadler, who worked in the store. "It was like the TV show *Cheers* but there wasn't a bar." Tuffy created travel quizzes for customers, who received discounts if they knew the answers, and celebrated the mailman's birthday. As Anne says, "Everyone went."

Even as Tuffy was settling down, his stepsister Cathy Mellon's marriage was ending. Cathy and her husband of sixteen years, John

Warner, now the secretary of the Navy, decided to divorce. In recent years, Cathy had been spending time in California, leaving her husband at home with their three children.

Looking back now, Warner blames his marital woes on the wrenching divide in the country over the Vietnam War. "The affection Catherine and I had for each other was real and deep. But then I went to work for Richard Nixon," Warner explained to me in the summer of 2016, sitting in his downtown Washington, D.C., law office, where he was still practicing law at age eighty-nine.

Under the Nixon administration, Warner was part of the Pentagon team orchestrating American tactics in the Vietnam War, while Cathy opposed the conflict. "I went there regularly. It put terrible stress on the family. Catherine became involved—I don't say this with anger, sadness but not anger—with some of the groups who were peace people," Warner said. "That lured her to California. I was sitting here trying to be secretary of Navy and trying to raise three children. Paul and Bunny were wonderful."

Warner says that Paul Mellon's lawyers arranged for a "very generous" settlement; newspapers put the figure at $10 million along with real estate holdings. "I wanted joint custody with Catherine, I hoped she'd reappear, which she eventually did," Warner said. He and his ex-wife both remarried two years later. Cathy Mellon tied the knot with Ashley Carrithers, a divorced Ohio man who was a decade her junior. According to the *Washington Star*, Carrithers ran a commune in Northern California called None of the Above, devoted to "simple living, to raising your own food and building your own houses...It was a far cry from the unlimited wealth and service that had always surrounded Cathy."

John Warner married the actress Elizabeth Taylor. Even the *New York Times* found it noteworthy when the Social Register dropped John Warner but Cathy Mellon retained her blue-blood status.

Unimpressed by celebrity, Paul and Bunny disapproved of the much married and flamboyant Liz Taylor, and their lunch and dinner invitations to Warner dwindled. As Warner recalls, "Paul said to me, 'This Elizabeth Taylor thing, how's that going to work out?' I said,

'Paul, I'm not sure.' He was very polite, saying, 'I somehow think, John, that won't fit.'"

The job was unofficial and unpaid but it suited Bunny's creative urges. The National Gallery frequently held opening galas to celebrate new exhibits; Bunny took charge of the party décor. This gave her a public opportunity to demonstrate her skill with flowers, trees, and other objects against the backdrop of art and culture. Just as her unusual flower arrangements at the White House—using bowls, baskets, and unexpected containers—had enhanced Jackie Kennedy's state dinners, Bunny sought to replace generic museum entertaining with fresh, stylish touches.

For a groundbreaking exhibition of Soviet-owned Impressionist paintings in 1973, Bunny filled wicker baskets at the National Gallery with sheaves of wheat, tulips, peach blossoms, poppies, sunflowers, and anemones, meant to evoke the Russia spring. "I'll never forget, Bunny did the most amazing flowers for the table," recalls Deeda Blair, a philanthropist and gardener whose husband, William, was a diplomat. "A beautiful basket, quite large, sheaves of wheat and poppies. Some of them may have been real and some may have been silk. It had not been done before, great originality to what she did. We went to one or two other dinners, that's how I got to know her...She set trends."

When the National Gallery staged an exhibit of modern art, Bunny lent six of her Rothkos, joining works by Robert Motherwell, Jackson Pollock, and Louise Nevelson assembled by the gallery. Bunny asked the renowned New York gallery owner and sculptor Betty Parsons to make fourteen painted wood sculptures as table centerpieces. Parsons had launched the careers of many of the artists whose works were being shown, and Bunny was one of her clients.

The seventy-three-year-old Parsons was ecstatic when she received this commission. "The most amazing and terrific thing," Parsons blurted out to her staff, according to a biography of the gallery owner by Lee Hall. "Mrs. Mellon. Bunny. A great gardener. You should see what she has done with her house in Virginia. And a great, great patron of the arts. She knows everything. She has everything. All the best artists. She bought from me for years. And she's married to this perfect genius who is also very, very rich." Parsons worried that her sculptures would not be well received, brooding—"They'll hate my work"—but her table sculptures for the National Gallery sold out. Parsons would subsequently show Eliza's work at her gallery.

Bunny had fully embraced abstract art and her new favorite was Californian Richard Diebenkorn, whose blue, yellow, and peach Ocean Park series of paintings received rapturous reviews. "Diebenkorn's art is about sensuous pleasure," wrote *Time* magazine critic Robert Hughes, who described the artist's work as "one of the most exhilarating meditations on structure." Bunny purchased an Ocean Park painting in 1974; she would go on to own nine of the artist's celebrated canvases.

Paul Mellon did not share his wife's enthusiasm for modern work, but in his role as the president of the National Gallery, he understood its importance. His father, Andrew Mellon, had envisioned a museum that would feature time-tested Old Masters, and in keeping with his wishes, the gallery's initial bylaws prohibited the acquisition of works by living artists. That policy lasted from 1941 until 1962, when National Gallery president Chester Dale forced a change by donating works by the still-breathing Pablo Picasso and Georges Braque.

Two decades later, the museum was still trying to play catch-up. At the gala for the modern art exhibit, Paul announced that he hoped this display would help change the National Gallery's image from "a stuffy maiden aunt who lives only in the past and won't change the furniture in the parlor and won't raise the blinds unless company is coming on Sunday."

As much as Bunny relished working on these events with the gallery staff and her own florists and gardeners, she dreaded attending them. Hugh Jacobsen, a Washington architect who worked on many of Bunny's homes, says, "She hated being 'Mrs. Mellon,' because she was on the spot and the press was always there. She had to be center stage all the time. She did not like being a public person. She was happiest in her garden, at her country home."

Nonetheless, Bunny and Paul worked the receiving lines together, starring in photographs with presidents and members of the Washington establishment. If a reporter wandered up to chat, they were pleasant, offering up a few bons mots.

But Bunny was always relieved to be home again. "The sun is just up," she wrote to Eliza, in one of a series of letters filled with nature imagery designed to bridge the gap with her daughter. "I am alone making breakfast in the kitchen. The silence, the softness of the dew covers the plants and the strawberries. It is cool. I have a fire going in the small stove. There are small white roses and green apples. I have made coffee + a boiled egg with herbs just picked. Robinson [the dog] is enchanted and waits for his share of breakfast. But it is really the shadows I want to send you. The shadows and a white stone wall. Much love, Mums."

Bunny's mother, Rachel Clopton, died in December 1974 in Princeton, New Jersey. David Fleming, Bunny's nephew, called to break the news. "Bunny arrived and took charge and planned everything," he recalled. "She did a beautiful job, even my mother stepped back." Bunny and her sister, Lily, were now the last direct connection left in their family.

The sisters rarely saw each other and had carved out different lives. Lily Lambert Fleming McCarthy, fascinated since childhood by British admiral Horatio Nelson, had built a collection of memorabilia that became the centerpiece of the Nelson Museum in Norfolk, England. Her husband John McCarthy's career as a television industry executive had taken the family to Paris and then Greenwich, Connecticut, and the couple planned to retire in England. Bunny sent her sister expensive gifts of Verdura and Schlumberger jewelry, generous gestures that also represented one-upsmanship.

Their charismatic and confident father had molded the sisters, and in one key way they replicated his behavior. Like Gerard Lambert, his daughters could be capricious in relationships, cutting people off without explanation. "The girls just had this funny thing," recalls Lily

Lambert Norton, Lily Lambert's daughter. "When it's over, it's over, and don't push and come back because you're not going to win. You probably never knew the reason it ended."

The purges of old friends within Bunny's social circle became increasingly noticeable by the mid-1970s. No one knew what to make of her dismissals. Maybe she worried that people were taking advantage of her generosity, since so many of her intimates benefited from the Mellon largesse. Maybe she felt diminished by Paul's affair and thus was quick to take umbrage if her male friends did not appear totally devoted. Whatever the reason, Bunny developed a reputation for being mercurial and sometimes cruel.

"She got tired of people," says Babs Simpson, the *Vogue* editor who was Bunny's friend for a half century. "She never said anything nasty about anybody, she just used them up." John Baskett, the art curator who worked for Paul for decades, recalls, "Bunny sometimes had friendships that suddenly evaporated. Paul said to me, 'Funny it hasn't happened to you, but of course it wouldn't, Bunny is very fond of you.'"

It was tricky being Bunny's friend. The hairstylist Kenneth Battelle once sent her a note stressing that he worried about displeasing her and asked for forgiveness in advance. "I do feel as I told you the other a.m. that there is a danger of hurting you. I cannot worry about that and I cannot let it happen," he wrote, adding, "You must have had so many disappointments. I am frightened to think of how vulnerable you really are. I do not under any circumstances or for any reason want to hurt you. Don't let me."

Kenneth survived within the golden circle; Sister Parish did not. Friends since their teenage years, they had once been so close that Bunny married Paul at Sister's New York apartment. Jackie Kennedy dropped Sister during the White House years; Sister claimed that the rift had been due to Jackie's belief that Sister had kicked the young Caroline Kennedy. After that ruckus, Bunny let her relationship with Sister lapse. The women nonetheless remained connected since Sister Parish's daughter, D. B. Gilbert, worked as Bunny's social secretary for fifteen years. After D.B. and her husband, Riley, decided to leave Virginia and move to Maine for a fresh start. Sister Parish wrote to thank Bunny for helping the couple.

At the end of her note, Sister acknowledged the rift in their friendship, wistfully writing, "No use saying 'Call me' but I would love it."

Perry Wheeler, who had helped Bunny design the Rose Garden, found himself persona non grata for no discernible reason. This was particularly awkward, since he and his partner had built a home on a plot of land on Bunny's farm, at her behest. Perry confided in his friend Deeda Blair as he tried to figure out what had gone wrong. "They used to talk constantly, but then he was kind of dropped," recalls Blair. Several years went by and then Bunny, feeling lonely, picked up the phone again. "She went back to Perry because she needed someone to talk to and she would call late, late, late at night, twelve or one o'clock in the morning," says Blair. "She'd talk for an hour or so. Go over her problems."

Johnny Schlumberger had a serious stroke in 1974 and moved from Manhattan to Paris. "It was kept very quiet, he went back to Paris to die, and then the most miraculous recovery ensued," says Pierce MacGuire of Tiffany's. "He could travel and do anything a normal person could do, but he could no longer draw; he lost control of the small muscles in his hand. His career as a jeweler was virtually over. Bunny stopped communicating with him." Schlumberger confided to friends that Bunny had dropped him. Oscar de la Renta, who had known the jeweler for decades, says sadly, "He was really hurt." Johnny and Bunny did eventually have a rapprochement; five years later, he sent her a thank-you note for flowers and for thinking of him.

Bunny often treated the employees and artisans who worked for her as friends, blurring the social class lines. Her unconventional approach could be confusing to the staff, leading to misperceptions and then abrupt reminders of who truly held the power in these relationships.

Ever since the Yale-trained stage designer Paul Leonard had gone to work for Bunny in 1961, it had been an exhilarating ride as he jetted around the world in the Mellons' private plane. Playing a dual role as decorator and scenic painter, he worked on Bunny's properties and helped stage the National Gallery galas. "He was the magic painter. I met him a couple of times, he was terribly nice," says Deeda Blair. "He was painting in the house in Washington, which they didn't use very often. Bunny wanted a mysterious color, she wanted shadows in it, shadows caused by sunlight. He was an absolute genius."

Bunny lent the outgoing and talented Paul Leonard to such friends as Jackie, Kenneth, and Hubert de Givenchy so that he could paint their floors and spruce up their homes. He became such a close friend to Eliza that she left him a note one day that read, "I am here and you are here and that is all that matters." Bunny also sent Paul Leonard doting letters, calling him "Dearest Dear Honey Bunch" and mentioning her dreams about him.

"Paul Leonard was just wonderful," recalls Susan Cabral, the Mellons' Cape Cod housekeeper. "From the time he would step in the front door, he'd make everything fun. The sandwiches we'd make, we had to cut the crust off the bread. He'd say, 'Who goes through all that, Susan?' I said, 'My sentiments exactly, but we have to.' He'd say, 'No, no, no.' He'd slap together sandwiches. He'd get away with it, for her it was fun."

Yet by the mid-1970s, Paul Leonard was miserable, conflicted about his sexual identity. His primary romantic relationships had been with men, but he now felt unsettled about his future. At this vulnerable moment, a friend suggested that Leonard attend a Manhattan spiritual gathering run by Italian mystic Oric Bovar, a former opera coach who now specialized in astrology.

Bovar had attracted an artistic following; comedienne Carol Burnett and actress Bernadette Peters would later confirm to the *New York Times* that they knew him. The charming but domineering Italian was known to chart horoscopes, assign meditations, and lecture at group meetings. Newcomers either put their faith in his autocratic instructions or fled. When the actress Marsha Mason accompanied her husband, playwright Neil Simon, to meet Bovar, she recoiled, later writing in her autobiography, "I met the devil…As we ate and listened to his catty and unkind remarks—everything he said sounded negative—all I kept thinking was, 'What on earth must Neil be think-ing?'" Others left as well. Burnett and Peters both insisted to the *Times* that they cut off contact with the self-styled mystic.

Bovar had begun to marry his followers off to one another, a tactic that would later be followed by Korean religious leader Rev. Sun Myung Moon. When Paul Leonard attended his first meeting of Bo-var's group, he was introduced to Valerie Pedlar, a British graphic designer who made lithographs for Frank Stella and Jim Dine. As she recalls, "Who should walk in but the most handsome man I'd ever seen in my life." Two weeks later, at their guru's urging, Paul and Va-lerie eloped. As she acknowledges, "I really didn't know the person I was marrying but I knew I loved him."

Bunny thought she did know Paul Leonard, and she was shocked that he had joined a cult and married a stranger. Adding insult to injury, Valerie promptly moved into Paul Leonard's Mellon-owned carriage house. "I discovered from Peter, the butler, that Madame had taken to bed for six weeks when she heard about our marriage. I thought, this is silly, if we could just meet," says Valerie. She called Bunny and introduced herself; Bunny hung up. Valerie tried again, walking to Bunny's New York residence at 125 East Seventieth Street. The guard let her through the front gate, but the butler delivered the curt message: "Madame says she's not at home."

Furious at what she perceived as a betrayal, Bunny excised Paul Leonard from her life. She fired him and evicted the newlyweds.

Rather than leave in a huff, he trained his replacement, Nedra Parry, a theatre arts major who until recently had been working in Paul Mellon's tax office. She became Bunny's personal shopper, help-ing with decorating. Leonard had been in the midst of working with Bunny on the décor for the upcoming King Tut exhibit at the Na-tional Gallery. "Paul Leonard was very kind to me, telling me, 'Don't do this, do that,'" Nedra recalled. "He tried to make things easy for me." He cautioned Nedra that despite Bunny's egalitarian manner, Nedra should know her place. As she says, "That was the best advice Paul Leonard gave me: 'Just remember, you're an employee.'"

Paul Leonard tried to establish his own business as a decorator but received the cold shoulder from Bunny's friends. "To all the people he had worked for in the past—including Jackie, who was amazingly influenced by Bunny—he was persona non grata," Valerie lamented. Paul Leonard had known the former First Lady and her children for more than a decade. When he decorated a room at the prestigious Kips Bay Decorator Show House, he was thrilled when Jackie came to see his work, but disappointed by her remarks. As Henry Heymann, Leonard's Yale classmate, recalls, "Jackie went to see Paul to apologize and say, 'Bunny's my best friend, I can't do this.'"

Paul Leonard never stopped trying to return to Bunny's good graces. He wrote to her in May 1977, "You have given a treasure, your friendship, which I hold very dear to me and carry with me always, much love, Paul."

Even though Oric Bovar had brought Paul and Valerie together, they quit the cult before everything unraveled. The messianic guru had begun telling people that he was the reincarnation of Jesus Christ. He was arrested on December 8, 1976, after he was found trying to revive a man who had been dead for two months. Instead of informing the authorities, Bovar and his followers had kept watch on the corpse for signs of a miracle. On the eve of his trial in April 1977, Bovar leapt to his death.

Jackie Kennedy had married Ari Onassis in the hope of finding emotional security and financial stability after the horrors of the assassinations of her husband and her brother-in-law. But shortly after the couple wed, the indiscreet Greek tycoon resumed his affair with opera star Maria Callas. Although he felt free to pursue his mistress, he was ferociously jealous of Jackie, monitoring her comings and goings and expressing annoyance that she was spending too much time in Manhattan. Their spats became public.

Jackie and Ari were living apart but had not yet divorced when Onassis died in March 1975 in Paris. Jackie hired Alex Forger, chairman of the law firm Milbank, Tweed, Hadley & McCloy, to negotiate a settlement with Onassis's estate. He won her an estimated $20 million. A tall and patrician Yale law graduate and Democrat who looked like he came straight out of central casting, Forger had previously worked for Bunny, when her Rothko purchases were cited in the legal wrangle involving the painter's heirs.

After a phone conversation with Jackie on April 10, 1976, Bunny jotted down in her journal extracts from Jackie's emotional remarks, in which the former First Lady stressed just how much their friendship meant and how eager she was to spend more time together, even fantasizing about anchoring a boat near Bunny's Cape Cod house.

That fall, Jackie took a job as an editor with Viking Books. She didn't need to work for a living but wanted to carve out her own identity. Jackie began to spend time with a new suitor, international diamond merchant Maurice Tempelsman, the head of a large mineral consortium. He was born into an Orthodox Jewish family in Antwerp, Belgium, and his family had fled the Nazis in 1940 and made their way to the United States. An early supporter of JFK, long involved with Democratic politics, he was Jackie's age, five foot seven, and portly, the antithesis of her glamorous image. First publicly linked to Jackie as a "business friend" in 1975, he became a constant in her life, and the new couple quietly spent time with Bunny. According to newspaper accounts, Tempelsman, who was married with three children, separated from his wife in 1984, but the couple never divorced.

Jackie continued to call on Bunny for landscaping advice. The John F. Kennedy Library in Boston was rising from a landfill at the Columbia Point Peninsula. I. M. Pei had designed the building overlooking the harbor, and landscape architect Daniel Urban Kiley was brought in to design the grounds.

As Pei would later admiringly tell *Vanity Fair*, "Bunny was asked by Jackie to come and look at it and said, 'Jack loved the dunes. We've *got* to bring some of the dunes here.' And we said, 'How can you bring the dunes there?' It was all muck, no sand, nothing there... We were building on man-made land and it's very difficult to make it look natural... Bunny said, 'Never mind. We'll try.'

"And she brought her own men, and I tell you, in a matter of months it became a dune. But at what effort, my gosh! We had to plant the seedlings of the dune just like the way people transplant hair. That's the perfectionist in her."

––––––––––

Paul Mellon had been famous from birth, and Bunny had been featured in her share of headlines, but there came a moment in the mid-1970s when the Mellons went from flesh-and-blood human beings to metaphoric symbols. They represented the American aristocracy—the well-bred superrich in contrast to gauche Texas oil money. In an era defined by high inflation, economic stagnation, and gas lines, the Mellons floated above it all in a bubble of privilege and inherited wealth.

Their luxurious lifestyle made for irresistible copy. A two-part July 1976 feature in the *Washington Post* about the Virginia horse country began with an anecdote about Paul and Bunny's farm, describing how the thirty-five stable hands spent every Thursday polishing the brass fixtures, including light switches, door handles, latches, hinges, and horse stall nameplates. Talk about indulgent: It took thirty-five people an entire day just to shine the brass.

According to the *Post*, "About 200 persons work full time at Rokeby Farms, chipping old paint and applying new coats, tending gardens, combing lush green fields for thistle plants so prize cattle, broodmares and foals don't eat them by mistake." Writer Donnel Nunes added, "A private security company regularly patrols his acreage—a new development in the wake of political terrorism and kidnappings beginning in the late 1960s, according to farmhands."

Paul and Bunny had become caricatures, fantasy figures who existed in a rarified private world. Bunny's perfectionism had reached an absurd level, and people could not stop talking about it. She instructed her kitchen staff that when they opened a bag of Lay's potato chips, they were to take out the broken pieces before serving the snack to company.

After workers dug a hole for a pool at her Cape Cod home and poured the concrete, Bunny impulsively decided that the deep end needed to be where the shallow end was, and had them dig out the concrete and start again. Bunny dispatched the Mellons' private plane on absurd errands: from Antigua to Martinique to pick up a pound of butter, and from Virginia to Nantucket for a purse containing a lipstick and suntan lotion. Even Jackie Kennedy Onassis marveled to a friend, "Bunny will send the plane to pick up a hat."

Assuming that Paul would always take care of her, Bunny did not press her husband for financial details. In 1977, Bunny had lunch at her Manhattan town house with her lawyer Alex Forger, who urged her to write a will. When he asked Bunny what her assets were, he was startled by her response.

"I don't think I have any," she told him. "I don't think I own anything." The Verdura and Schlumberger jewelry, the Rothkos, the Mellons' homes, even the Meissen plates—as far as Bunny knew, she was not legally entitled to any of it. As Forger recalls, "She had no idea what she was going to get."

After he followed up with a request to Paul Mellon for information about Bunny's assets, Forger received a five-page listing of Bunny's jewelry. As the legal discussions over Bunny's future inheritance began, Bunny raised a long-simmering frustration. When she wanted to make a philanthropic donation, she had to ask Paul for money and his permission. She found this process to be humiliating.

Paul was mystified to hear that this dependence bothered Bunny— "All she has to do is ask me," he told Forger—but nonetheless agreed to put $500,000 per year into a charitable fund so that Bunny could make independent gifts.

In early 1978, Bunny became ill with a serious ailment. (Family members say she was treated for cancer but could not recall the precise year.) She wrote in her journal in January 1978, "In a way, being knocked down by this illness was a good thing. It kept me in one place although in the early days, I felt so badly that I think my soul left my body for higher ground, like a flood where waters envelop the house."

As always, she drew sustenance from nature, writing about "the blue, blue hills beyond the snow covered fields. The detail of the pansies beside my bed." She wrote down admonitions: "Bring beauty +

calm back, don't give it away. Think, meditate + pray whether needed or not. Do not dwell on negative thoughts for a second. See love in its proper light. Read."

The world at large might focus on the thousands of dollars she spent on clothes or her jet-setting itinerary, but Bunny's interior landscape revolved around the sights and sounds of the outdoors. In letters to friends and family members, she always described a moment in each day that had given her joy, and sketched a flower or a tree as an illustration. Her images conveyed a playful worldview; the notes were treasured as collectibles. (Hundreds of Bunny's letters were shown to me by her intimates, dating back forty years or more, in the course of reporting this book.)

"A very small dove is wandering in + out of the rosemary plants," she wrote to Eliza from Antigua in 1978. "Birds and white butterflies. Beyond the sea reaches across the world + the sky circles the world. A yellow green finch hangs upside down on the orange tree. I see all this from my bed, no screens, no doors."

Bunny was emotionally attached to her trees and plants, as her gardener George Shaffer learned when he suggested replacing a citrus tree near the Virginia dining room. "I thought it was looking bad, we could do better," he says. "I wanted to take it back, repot it, put something better in. She said yes, and then called me back to say, 'That's my friend, I like to keep my friends around.'"

Yet few people saw that side of Bunny. In December 1978, Bunny was the subject of a nasty profile in *WWD*, the fashion publication owned and run by the mischievous John Fairchild, who delighted in tweaking the wealthy. Described as an "Ivy League Eccentric," Bunny was portrayed as a modern-day empress who kept apples "boiling on the stoves to fill the house with the smell of the farm" and amused herself when ill with the flu by having her "carloads of evening jewels" brought to her in bed so she could admire her riches.

Adding a frisson of naughtiness, the story stated, "Safe Ivy League pleasures aside, Bunny did venture out dancing with Givenchy one night late last spring. And to Infinity—the Manhattan bastion of gay, bisexual and third-sex chic—of all places."

Ignoring the rumors about her relationship with the designer, Bunny was photographed two months later in the front row of Givenchy's next fashion show in Paris.

She remained a frequent visitor to Givenchy's country home, Le Jonchet, a seventeenth-century chateau surrounded by a moat in the Touraine region.

At that chateau one day, looking out a second-floor window, she spied a large oak tree and had a sudden inspiration. As Givenchy recalls, Bunny told him, "'You see, the shadow of the tree? Tomorrow, if we have the same day with the same sun, let's try to take the design, the proportion of the shadow.'" The next day, they took chalk and outlined the ground in the shape of the shadow. Givenchy adds, "Now Bunny says, 'We're planting, as soon as possible, that big shadow with a little flower, scilla, very beautiful blue.'" He followed her advice, and was pleased by the result, adding, "It was a wonderful idea. This is all Bunny's imagination."

As he approached seventy, Paul Mellon was presiding over the creation of two magnificent cultural institutions: the Yale Center for British Art, a three-story modernist glass, concrete, and steel building designed by architect Louis Kahn; and the innovative new East Wing at the National Gallery by I. M. Pei.

The British artworks that Paul had been amassing for decades—including 1,800 paintings, 7,000 drawings, 5,000 prints, and 16,000 rare books—would be housed at Yale. There were portraits by John Singer Sargent, landscapes by J. M. W. Turner, and sporting paintings by George Stubbs. The opening exhibit was suitably called, "The Pursuit of Happiness."

Paul's achievement in Washington was even grander, a six-hundred-thousand-square-foot new structure. I. M. Pei had designed an exuberant and unusual soaring triangle-shaped museum featuring a central court with an eighty-foot-high skylight, which was welcomed as an off-kilter architectural triumph. Even as the cost soared beyond the original $20 million estimate to more than $100 million, Paul continued to fund the gift by tapping various family foundations. He traveled the country with Pei, presided over construction meetings, and remained deeply invested in the outcome.

Bunny befriended the architect. "People are so different," she wrote in her journal. "I guess it's chemistry but when someone comes along and you click with them, it is like taking off on a rocket. That's how I. M. Pei affects me. He's got it all not an ounce of pompousness. He's real full of joy and he is honest so is his work."

In the months leading up to the openings of these two museums—Yale in April 1977, the East Wing in May 1978—Paul and Bunny acceded to the hunger for information about their lives and roles as benefactors. They granted interviews to select newspaper and magazine writers and spoke to author Burton Hersh for his book about the extended Mellon family. The couple was surprisingly honest about the frictions in their marriage.

Burton's book, *The Mellon Family*, published in early May 1978, was a dishy generational tale. Bunny's grievances were front and center. "Paul's very paradoxical," she told Hersh. "A writer, a scholar, very sensitive and gentle, kind to his friends, to me, certainly. Then, on the other hand, he's got the robber baron. It's going to be done like that and you just duck, boom! And you say, but have some consideration. But there is no consideration. His mother pointed it out to me, she put her hand on me and said, 'My dear, I understand. His father was like that.'"

For his part, Paul conveyed that he was not enamored of Bunny's friends, making a sarcastic remark about a photo of Bunny with one of her decorators. Reflecting the prejudices of the era against homosexuals, Paul's cousin Matthew Mellon was quoted as saying, "Bunny has this place over in Paris with a whole [bunch] of fairies running around in it. She keeps these fairies building things."

Bunny's children were not quoted in the book, but Tim and Cathy Mellon spoke to the author, making comments about their stepmother. "Bunny made things just difficult enough so that my father would give in," Cathy told the author. When asked about Bunny, Tim replied, "I hope you don't want to open that can of worms."

Hersh never mentioned Dorcas Hardin but slyly noted that the financier J. P. Morgan "reserved the tenderest of devotion for Old Masters and old mistresses. Paul Mellon is sentimental, and nobody would expect less fidelity from him."

Paul and Bunny spoke to journalists from *Time* magazine, which ran two articles. Art critic Robert Hughes wrote an appreciation of the new National Gallery building and praised Paul's use of his patrimony, stating that "no other living American has committed himself to art patronage on this scale." In a profile, *Time* writer Gerald Clarke portrayed Paul as an aloof man who conveyed an "imperial remoteness," while Bunny was described as a woman of "great, if somewhat eccentric style."

The writer captured the marital tensions: "Like many other couples of unlimited means, the Mellons are apart as often as they are together. Bunny spends much of her time in Paris. When Paul inexplicably refused to buy her an apartment there, she bought it herself. When he goes to Paris, he stays at a hotel. There are other hints that the Mellon marriage falls short of the middle class ideal of togetherness."

Once again, Bunny let her resentments about her husband show: "If I were describing him in a nutshell, I would say that he is very sensitive and extraordinarily insensitive...He stays very remote." She called Paul a "Jekyll and Hyde." Bunny lashed out at Paul's eighty-eight-year-old lawyer and financial adviser, who tried to rein in her spending: "Stoddard Stevens took away a good deal of the poetry from my husband's life. He came along when my husband needed a father figure, and that's what he got."

Nonetheless, the *Time* writer concluded: "Outspoken as Bunny is, there is no indication that their marriage, on its own terms, is anything less than happy." On its own terms? What a convoluted sentence: The writer simply did not know what to make of their lives.

If Bunny was particularly upset during this period, it might have been due to her realization that Paul's wandering eye had continued to wander. While Dorcas remained the central other woman in his life, family members say that he had a series of other brief flings through the years. This situation left Bunny feeling constantly unsettled and casting a gimlet eye on other females in the vicinity.

Bunny regretted granting the interviews to *Time* and biographer Burton Hersh. "I feel like a train or truck has hit me," she wrote in a journal entry that spring. "All this personal publicity, unnecessary cheap. Why didn't someone warn me? I feel sick day + night. Why can't it rest with the Gallery…Paul is very sweet, not nagging or grumbling. It helps so so much."

For the opening-night gala for the East Wing, Bunny sought to outdo herself with decorations that would complement the building, with its giant red, blue, and black Calder mobile hanging over the central court. Alexander Calder had recently died of a heart attack, but Bunny convinced his family and estate to loan small Calder stabiles as table centerpieces. She fussed over the lighting, bringing in soft-toned hurricane lamps.

The gallery's event planner, Carol Fox, was impressed by Bunny's unusual ideas. "She had trapezoidal tables made, I'm sure no one had been seated at a trapezoidal table before," recalls Fox. "She had specially woven tablecloths. She thought all that through, they were white but had blue thin stripes. It looked like an architectural drawing, she was saluting I. M. Pei." Bunny commissioned Nantucket weaver Andy Oates to make the fabric. She brought in topiary trees to block the sight of the caterers at work.

As Bunny and Carol were walking through the space, a caterer dropped a bottle of champagne, which shattered on the marble floor. Bunny smiled and quipped, "That's the way this building's floors should be washed—with champagne."

A *Time* magazine photographer captured Bunny and Paul heading into the museum. Wearing a red-and-white long gown with short sleeves and pearls, Bunny gave a gracious half smile as she turned her face away. Paul grinned with delight and affection as he looked directly at the lens woman, Diana Walker, the daughter of Dorcas Hardin.

The artists Willem de Kooning and Helen Frankenthaler attended the gala along with Mark Rothko's daughter, Kate; Henri Matisse's grandson Paul Matisse; Barnett Newman's widow, Annalee; and top officials in the Jimmy Carter administration. (The president got his own special tour with Paul and Bunny a few days later.) Bunny arranged for a last-minute surprise that night.

"Just as the last speech ended, this incredible sound filled the East Building, and the spotlight came on," recalls Carol Fox. "There, on the stage—and *nobody* knew about it—was Benny Goodman! He was Mr. Mellon's favorite musician, and he was playing this wonderful swing music. The place just went wild. Then we danced until two o'clock in the morning."

Bunny had done her husband proud. Now they could set off on their independent paths yet again, Paul to the Grand Tetons in Wyoming for several weeks, Bunny heading home to Virginia. "I think Bunny was lonely sometimes, I think she was lonely for Paul," says her friend Amy Greene. "He had his separate interests."

On July 10, Paul wrote to Bunny from Wyoming to say, "Hope you and the doggies are well and that it's sunny." Whatever the outside world thought of their lives, they conducted a civilized correspondence.

Chapter Twenty-One

The Book Stops Here

The books were piled on shelves, stacked topsy-turvy on the floor, and stored away in handmade boxes tucked in closets. Bunny's burgeoning collection included a 1585 treatise on medicinal herbs and an 1839 catalogue by the Duke of Bedford's gardener featuring sprightly illustrations of willows. The history of the natural and commercial world could be found in first editions about the tulip mania in Holland in 1637 and Charles Darwin's volume on his 1831 great voyage of discovery.

Bunny was spending a fortune to acquire rare books and folios; her collection would eventually be valued at $70 million. London bookseller John Saumarez Smith, of the Heywood Hill bookshop, recalls that unlike many of his aristocratic clients who bought volumes to grace a guest bedroom or a leather-bound library, "Bunny read a lot of the books I sent. She would send me notes, 'How did you know I would enjoy this as much as I have?'"

She began running out of storage space, explaining, "By the 1970's, a lifetime of collecting fine books and botanical art by a practical gardener finally forced the question of where to put it all—especially where it could be easily retrieved and used, when needed."

Paul encouraged her to build a library. What Bunny had in mind was a separate building on her Virginia farm that would not jar with the whitewashed stone residence. H. Page Cross, the architect who had designed her Virginia and Antigua homes, had recently died, so she selected Harvard-educated Modernist architect Edward Larrabee Barnes, who had made a name for himself with the soaring Walker Art Center in Minneapolis. Barnes simultaneously accepted commissions to build two prestigious Manhattan projects—new headquarters for IBM and the Asia Society—so Bunny's library was not his priority. He broke ground in 1976 for her building, but it took five years to complete.

During construction, Bunny visited the site daily when she was in Virginia, evaluating the progress and making suggestions. "She had the entire building made in plywood, full-scale, and she'd walk around and look out the windows," says Sam Kasten, a weaver with Nantucket Looms, whose firm had been commissioned to make fabrics for the library's window treatments, couches, and chairs. "Now you'd have computer-generated models. She'd do a mock-up, move the windows, make them bigger, change the cant of the building so you could see certain trees a mile away."

To turn her personal library into a professional collection, Bunny hired a staff to catalogue her volumes. "She had books scattered everywhere," recalls Dita Amory, who was finishing her master's degree in art history at the Institute of Fine Arts when she went to work for Bunny in 1978. A descendant of the wealthy horse-breeding Phipps family, Dita deliberately did not refer to her pedigree during the job interview. Dita, now a curator at the Metropolitan Museum, recalls, "She laughed for years that I did not mention my family and wanted to get the job on my own merit."

Bunny already owned more than one thousand volumes, but she hungered for more. "She was constantly acquiring," Dita says. "People sent her offers all the time, and I managed that process. When books came, I laid out all the new offerings. She'd peruse them and we'd return what she did not like. It was her reference library, her study collection as a horticulturist. She knew every book in that library."

As the library neared completion, Bunny hired a new decorative painter. Malcolm Robson, a British painter whose clients included members of the royal family, specialized in distinctive striating and marbling. His first meeting with Bunny diverged from the usual client conversation. "She said, 'Let's walk around the garden, let's pick out some herbs and colors and I'll show you what I like,'" he says. "That's how she used to work, picking out nature's colors."

Bunny, a debutante during the Depression, was born into a wealthy family and would later marry the fifth-richest man in America. *(Collection of David Fleming)*

Born in 1910, the oldest of three children, Bunny was a quiet, observant child who fell in love with flowers and trees as a three-year-old.
(Permission of the Gerard B. Lambert Foundation)

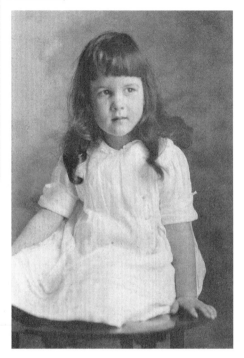

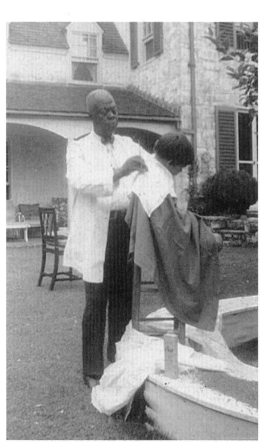

Bunny's father employed a large retinue of servants. Here she is, getting a home haircut.
(Collection of David Fleming)

Arthur Lowe, Bunny's maternal grandfather, was a gingham manufacturer, politician, and nature lover. Bunny adored him but thought his wife, Annie, was too strict. *(Collection of David Fleming)*

The garden at Albemarle, the sprawling estate that Bunny's father, Gerard Lambert, built in Princeton, New Jersey. *(Collection of David Fleming)*

Bunny loved to sail with her father, the brilliant advertising man and yachtsman Gerard Lambert, who raced in the America's Cup. *(Permission of the Gerard B. Lambert Foundation)*

Lily Lambert, Bunny's younger sister and rival, skipped a debut so she could use the allotted money to add to her collection of Admiral Horatio Nelson memorabilia. *(Collection of David Fleming)*

Bunny, right, and her sister, Lily, on the deck of the *Majestic*. Bunny felt insecure about her looks in comparison to her pretty sibling. *(Collection of David Fleming)*

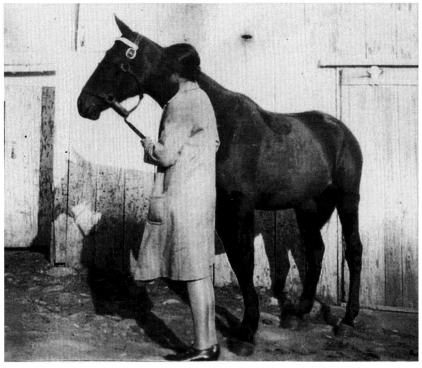

Bunny lobbied her parents to send her to Foxcroft, where riding was one of the three Rs. *(Collection of David Fleming)*

Portrait of Bunny riding sidesaddle on her horse Buberry, by Francis L. Smith, 1935. *(Permission of the Gerard B. Lambert Foundation)*

Paul Mellon received his graduate degree at Cambridge. He wanted to go into publishing but his intimidating father, Andrew Mellon, insisted that Paul join the family conglomerate. *(Bettmann/Getty Images)*

Paul Mellon with his first wife, Mary, on their honeymoon in Naples, February 10, 1935. *(AP Images)*

Bunny's wedding to Stacy Lloyd Jr. was a subdued affair, since her grandfather had just died. *(Ira L. Hill Collection, Archives Center, National Museum of American History, Smithsonian Institution/Permission of the Gerard B. Lambert Foundation)*

Her grandfather's advice—to try to help her country—remained a guiding principle. *(Collection of David Fleming)*

Stacy Lloyd Jr. with son Tuffy, born in 1937. *(Permission of the Gerard B. Lambert Foundation)*

Paul and Bunny Mellon head for Antigua on their private plane. The couple owned multiple homes in seven locations, including Paris and Nantucket. *(Joshua Greene. © 2017 Joshua Greene, www .archiveimages.com)*

Bunny Mellon found it difficult to be a stepmother. From left, Cathy Mellon, Tuffy Lloyd, Bunny Mellon, Tim Mellon, and Eliza Lloyd. *(Permission of the Gerard B. Lambert Foundation)*

Bunny began building a new home on the island of Antigua in the 1950s. *(Joshua Greene. © 2017 Joshua Greene, www .archiveimages.com)*

President John F. Kennedy asked Bunny Mellon to design the White House Rose Garden during a visit to her Cape Cod home on August 14, 1961. *(Photograph by Katharine Graham/Zuma Press)*

Jackie Kennedy and Bunny Mellon attend a performance of Noel Coward's musical *Sail Away* in Boston on August 17, 1961. *(AP Images)*

Bunny directs the placement of flowers at Robert Kennedy's gravesite at Arlington National Cemetery in June 1968. *(AP Images)*

Jean Schlumberger, the jeweler who was one of Bunny's close friends, created this necklace for her in 1956; the flowerpot of amethysts, emeralds, and diamonds in 1960; the bird brooch in 1965. She bought more than 140 pieces of his work.
(Photograph of flowerpot by Katherine Wetzel; photographs of necklace and brooch by Travis Fullerton. Virginia Museum of Fine Arts, Collection of Mrs. Paul Mellon)

This dramatic pleached arbor of crab apple trees at the Mellons' Virginia farm led from the garden to an orangerie with a trompe l'oeil mural. *(Photographs by Fred Conrad/New York Times/Redux)*

Bunny cultivated miniature topiaries, grown from rosemary, myrtle, thyme, and santolina, setting off a national trend, May 1982. *(Photographs by Fred Conrad/New York Times/Redux)*

Bunny's private library, which housed rare books on horticulture and children's fairy-tale classics, would eventually hold ten thousand volumes. *(Photographs by Fred Conrad/New York Times/Redux)*

Bunny and Hubert de Givenchy at a Paris fashion show on April 28, 1976. Givenchy made all of her clothes, including her gardening outfits.
(Milton Greene. © 2017 Joshua Greene, www.archiveimages.com)

The vivacious Dorcas Hardin, Paul Mellon's companion, in her popular Georgetown dress shop in 1977. *(Photograph by Gerald Martineau/*Washington Post/*Getty Images)*

Bunny adored her airy island home in Antigua, which guests described as "paradise."
(Joshua Greene. © 2017 Joshua Greene, www.archiveimages.com)

Bunny's son, Tuffy Lloyd, center, with his two sons, Thomas (left) and Stacy IV (right). Bunny played favorites, but toward the end of her life, she became closer to her family. *(Permission of the Gerard B. Lambert Foundation)*

Bunny with her artist daughter, Eliza Lloyd Moore, shortly before the accident that left Eliza paralyzed. *(Permission of the Gerard B. Lambert Foundation)*

Thomas Lloyd, Bunny Mellon's grandson, and his wife, Rickie Niceta, on their March 2006 honeymoon. *(Collection of Thomas Lloyd and Rickie Niceta)*

Former senator John Edwards, awaiting the verdict on charges of accepting illegal campaign contributions. The jury acquitted him on one charge and deadlocked on the others; prosecutors dropped the case. *(Shawn Rocco/*Raleigh News & Observer*/Zuma Press)*

Bunny with her dear friend Robert Isabell at the Chicago Flower and Garden Show, where they collaborated on an exhibit, March 2002. *(Permission of the Gerard B. Lambert Foundation)*

Bunny on her 101st birthday with North Carolina decorator Bryan Huffman, August 2011. *(Collection of Bryan Huffman)*

Jacqueline Kennedy Onassis with Bunny at the Mellons' Upperville, Virginia, farm. Caroline Kennedy recalls, "They were like a pair of twins with their own special language, their own love of mischief..." *(Photograph by George Shaffer)*

Paul and Bunny Mellon loved to go for walks on their nearly five-thousand-acre farm. Despite their differences, at the end of his life, Paul said, "I'm glad I stayed married to Bunny." *(Photograph by George Shaffer)*

During lunch together that day, Bunny abruptly left the table. As he recalls, she got up, she said, 'Excuse me, there's a plane taking off on the runway.' She went outside and looked up. 'I just want to check where my husband is going. It looks like he's going to New York.'" The Mellons were so disengaged that Paul had not informed his wife of his plans.

She remained fixated on improving the landscape at Rokeby Farm. One day she was looking out a library window when she announced to Robson: "Look, that's all wrong. The hill is in the wrong place. I'm going to move it." Robson laughed and added, "Next time I went back three months later, she'd moved the hill to make the view better."

Workmen created a road so that Bunny could drive the short distance from her home to the library, but she declined to pave it— guaranteeing a muddy mess in bad weather—and insisted that the grass look overgrown as if the path had always been there.

The completed white stone library included a sunny seventy-five-foot-long main room with recessed wooden cabinets to house more than three thousand volumes and manuscripts. A small two-story tower included a second-floor office for Bunny. The cozy kitchen sported hand-painted blue tiles, and underground stacks supplied storage space. A large sundial was installed on the front of the building.

In Bunny's office, a beat-up wooden trestle table served as a desk, and a blue country hutch was used to store her original Rose Garden renderings and other garden designs. Sitting at her desk, she could look out the left window at the canopied trellis of crab apple trees leading to her orangerie, or look right to a vista of trees and rolling meadows. A fireplace warmed the room in winters. Bunny hung photographs of her father playing the ukulele at Carter Hall; her friend Liz Whitney with her dogs; Paul Mellon with a horse; her daughter, Eliza, on a pony; and her son, Tuffy, at the beach. Eliza's whimsical watercolor sketch of flowers, on a brown paper bag, was framed and hung behind Bunny's desk.

Bunny's aesthetic vision was so understated—nothing should be noticed—that most people simply noted how comfortable and pretty everything was, without understanding how much work had gone into it.

After a three-day stay at the farm, Nantucket weaver Sam Kasten sent her a note saying that he had learned a lifetime of design during his visit. "I was just so awestruck and illuminated by what I saw," he says. "I wrote to say that she changed my life, thank you. She called me. She was in tears, saying how appreciative she was that I appreciated it. She said, 'Nobody really notices what I do.'"

Now that the library was a permanent fixture, Bunny increased the staff. Dita Amory hired nineteen-year-old Tony Willis, whose father was the Mellons' paint shop foreman and whose mother cleaned the Brick House. Tony had started doing odd jobs for the Mellons as a ten-year-old helping his parents, but he had no relevant library experience. "I had known Mrs. Mellon, but I wasn't close to her," he says. "When Dita introduced me to Mrs. Mellon, we just clicked. She was always so good to the young."

After Dita Amory returned to Manhattan in 1982, Bunny trained Tony Willis to become the new librarian. Bunny and Paul paid for his community college classes and sent him to a rare books summer program at the University of Virginia. Quiet and observant with an easygoing sense of humor, Tony became her trusted lieutenant, traveling with Bunny, sitting in on meetings, working with her on acquisitions, and strolling with her on the property. She was constantly trying to teach Tony about flowers and plants. As he recalls, "I'd walk with her in the garden, she'd always stop to say, 'You have to see this.' She'd bring in a flower."

She encouraged him to plant his own home garden, conveying her life philosophy. "A garden is always evolving and changing, a place to work when there's a sad moment in your life, or there's a happy moment," says Tony. "At the end of the day when you look at what you've done, it's very satisfying. It gives you the extra push to go on or mend your broken whatever. I think Mrs. Mellon used that at many moments in her life. The garden was always her place. It was like therapy."

As Bunny neared her seventies, she was aging gracefully, subtly dying her hair. She always wore a blue hat to protect her face from the sun.

Her physically energetic work in the garden, plus exercising with a Pilates instructor, kept Bunny in good shape. But she was becoming self-conscious about her appearance.

When John Loring was named the design director of Tiffany's in 1979, he mentioned to the company's vice president, Van Day Truex, that he had been a childhood friend of Bunny's son, Tuffy, and had known her many years ago. Truex promptly arranged a lunch date with Bunny, one of the jewelry company's best clients.

"I arrived to go to lunch and Van was looking perplexed," Loring says. "He said, 'It's the strangest thing. Bunny Mellon telephoned me about an hour ago and said, "I'm going to have to decline the lunch. I was enthusiastic about it but I've thought about it and I can't bear to have him see me as an old lady. He knew me as a young woman and a very attractive young woman, and I can't have him sitting at a table looking at me as I am today. I can't have it."'"

The elite move in small circles in Manhattan. Loring would go on to write six Tiffany's entertaining and decorating books that were edited by Jackie Kennedy Onassis. "I found myself seated at big dinners with Mrs. Mellon—not at the same table but maybe three feet away. Out of respect for Mrs. Mellon, I never did say, 'Mrs. Mellon, I'm Tuffy's old friend Jack.'" Sometimes Loring spoke at these events, so she knew who he was. "Occasionally we'd have to cross paths, I'd nod and smile and say good evening and keep going. I tried not to acknowledge any official meeting since it might make her uncomfortable."

There was still a shadow on Bunny's life—the presence, just offstage, of Dorcas Hardin and the other women in her husband's world. Sometimes Paul's affairs were too painful to ignore. Bunny's steely self-control would slip, revealing just how wounded she felt. Her step-granddaughter Virginia Warner, the daughter of Cathy Mellon and John Warner, witnessed Bunny's pain.

When Virginia left Bennington College in 1980, Bunny invited her to move into one of the Mellons' New York homes while Virginia tried to decide on a career, ultimately getting her real estate license and taking courses in gemology. "She was so sweet to me," Virginia recalls. "She just wanted me to figure out what I wanted. I went everywhere with her, traveled everywhere." Virginia became aware that Bunny was suffering. "Once we flew up to the Cape and she was crying, and trying to hide the fact that it hurt her—it hurt her that Granddaddy was with another."

To help Virginia deal with her own life struggles, Bunny encouraged her to see Bunny's New York psychiatrist, accompanying her on an appointment. "When I did go with Bun, the topic was insecurity," Virginia says. "And she confessed, 'We're all insecure, we just have to make do with what it means and how to take care of ourselves best when it occurs.' I thought, wow, how can someone be so insightful about herself and what she was struggling with too? It helped me."

Bunny believed in the virtues of psychiatry, but she remained intrigued by the spirit world and the occult. At the recommendation of a friend, in the early 1980s she made an appointment to have her fortune read by Beverly Newton, a psychic in Fredericksburg who had consulted with police departments about missing persons cases. Bunny appreciated Newton's insight, and was drawn to the psychic's warmth and comforting demeanor. "We became friends and we talked every single day out of friendship," recalls Newton, describing a relationship that continued for nearly thirty years. "After that first visit, I did not charge her."

Bunny would describe her dreams or talk about politics or the weather or the people in her life. She was finding it increasingly difficult to trust others. "She thought most people were there because of the influence she wielded or what they could get from her," says Newton. "She enjoyed special friendships, but I would say that she was a lonely person, some of it self-inflicted. She chose to be a loner."

Bunny had developed a love/hate attitude toward the press. She sought recognition for her talent but wanted to draw a curtain around her private life. To celebrate her achievement with the library, she gave an exclusive interview to *New York Times* writer Paula Deitz in June 1982. An oversized photo on the front page of the Home section showed Bunny, in her Givenchy gardening hat and clothes, gazing reverentially at a tiny topiary plant. A terrifyingly large pair of pruning shears is tucked under her arm, a jarring juxtaposition.

The article described Bunny as an "inherently talented" woman and quoted I. M. Pei as saying, "Mrs. Mellon has the combination of sensitivity and imagery with technical knowledge that you only find among the best professionals." Bunny stressed her pride in the library's construction, explaining, "All the materials relate to the earth: clay tiles, hand-woven linen and the wood is from our own trees." The headline was all that she could have hoped for: THE PRIVATE WORLD OF A GREAT GARDENER.

This was such a positive experience that Bunny decided to write an article of her own about her experiences creating the Rose Garden, which was published by the White House Historical Society's 1983 journal, and then reprinted in *House & Garden*. Bunny subsequently wrote a story for the magazine about her work on the Jacqueline Kennedy Garden at the White House.

Bunny praised the gardener whom she had discovered toiling away in obscurity at the Park Service so many decades ago. "Still under the loyal and watchful eye of its first and only gardener, Irv Williams, the crab-apple trees have been extensively pruned, allowing more sunlight to fall on the plants growing beneath," Bunny wrote of the Rose Garden. "The osmanthus holly hedges have been clipped back creating more light and air... The magnolias have reached a greater height, their strong gray branches filling the empty corners of long ago."

Jackie had been a frequent houseguest at Bunny's homes but now she wanted her own summer retreat. She purchased 375 acres of beachfront property in the tiny town of Gay Head on Martha's Vineyard, paying $1.15 million, and turned to her best friend for advice. "Jackie once described Bunny to me as a visual genius," recalls Jane Stanton Hitchcock, a novelist who had been married to Paul Mellon's cousin William Hitchcock and was friendly with both women. "Jackie went to Bunny to design her house in the Vineyard and Bunny plotted out the land and situated her house. They trusted each other, visually. Bunny had the greatest understated taste of almost anybody."

Bunny recommended that Jackie use Georgetown architect Hugh Jacobsen, who had done work on her properties in Paris, Antigua, and Virginia. "She was indeed a perfectionist," says Jacobsen of Bunny. "She believed in me and the funny stuff I was doing." Unlike most clients, he learned that neither Jackie nor Bunny worried about the cost of their projects or going over budget. "That's what was marvelous," he says. "They had so much money. But you were never allowed to be quoted in the press about their money. Then they were no longer your friend, you were encroaching."

At the tiny Martha's Vineyard Airport, the Mellons' Gulfstream II became a familiar sight. Bunny's staff ordered fabric and wallpaper on Jackie's behalf to decorate the beachfront getaway. Invisible from the road, Jackie's three-story cedar-shingled house included three bedrooms and a barn-style guesthouse with two additional bedrooms. Jackie decorated one room especially for Bunny.

Bunny designed the landscaping for Jackie's property. "There's no place like it," Martha's Vineyard building inspector Zachary Zandler told United Press International in 1981. "The vegetation and the mixture of plants—it's all small scale, like bonzai. It has incredible rocks, wild life and fresh water ponds."

In autumn and spring, Jackie returned to Upperville to go foxhunting. She initially stayed in a renovated log cabin guesthouse on Bunny and Paul's farm, and eventually rented her own house nearby. Bunny often sent the plane for her. Jackie wrote to Bunny and Paul on March 30, 1981, "There is such a thing as making your guests too happy...you might have a definite problem with that."

Jackie got to know Bunny's staff. "Whenever Jackie was coming up, Bunny would send her flowers and brownies or chocolate chip cookies," recalls George Shaffer, Bunny's gardener. "I knocked on the door, Jackie opened it. She said, 'George, come on in and eat a brownie with me.' She was such a down-to-earth person."

On November 22, the anniversary of her husband's assassination, Jackie usually arranged to spend the day in Virginia. "She wanted to be unnoticed. She'd slip down there in November," says Joe Armstrong, a Manhattan magazine publisher who had become a friend to the former First Lady. "She'd go out riding. She'd make a fire and sit in the fireplace and read. She said, 'I'm not going to be photographed coming out of church. I want to be alone and be quiet.'"

He called to check on her one year on November 22, asking what she was doing. She replied, "I've just been out riding, seeing hawks making lazy circles in the sky"—a reference to the song "Oklahoma," from the musical of the same name. Jackie often mentioned her friendship with Bunny. "It was 'Bunny this, Bunny that,'" he recalls. "Obviously she gave Jackie a lot of support."

Bunny had remained in close touch with her ex-husband, Stacy Lloyd, and described one of their visits in a letter to Eliza. "Daddy + I had a wonderful day together in St. Croix," Bunny wrote. "He looked marvelous and was in calm happy spirits. He has a wonderful farm—300 cows. Acres of land has been cleared and sowed in grass. A new milking machine from New Zealand and a man to help him from Kansas. We lunched in a little restaurant by the water."

A year later in 1979, Stacy's wife, Alice, died, succumbing nearly thirty years after she had contracted polio. After spending decades in St. Croix due to his wife's health, Stacy was now free to travel. He kept his island home but began to visit Virginia to see friends and spent time at his family's estate in Northeast Harbor, Maine, which he had inherited.

Eliza showed her paintings at the Parsons Gallery in the fall of 1980. *New York Times* art critic John Russell took notice, writing, "Eliza Moore in this early stage of her career has by no means got her act together, but there are things—notably the large 'Orange Pastel' in the big room and the motorized 'FDR Drive' in the little one—that suggests that she will be well worth watching."

Stacy Lloyd sent his daughter a supportive note: "I do hope your show is going well and that you are blessed with what you have put into it. What work it must be!" Bunny encouraged her daughter as well, writing to Eliza, "I hope you will ask me if I can help with your projects. (I know that it helps if you are not finished just to get a reaction. Because anything we do, we do alone. And for me I get scared.)"

Bunny's tempestuous relationship with her daughter had improved. Eliza tested the waters by introducing to her family a serious girlfriend, Doris Sanders, a divorced writer nineteen years her senior. An Illinois native who graduated from Columbia Journalism School, Doris had previously lived with the novelist Patricia Highsmith, and in 1958 the two of them published a children's book, *Miranda the Panda Is on the Veranda*. For many years, Doris split her time between Paris and Manhattan, and as a freelancer, she had written cultural features for *Newsday*. Like Eliza, she, too, had been divorced after a brief marriage.

"Doris loved Eliza, she doted on her," recalls Virginia Warner. "It was a little too intense for me, but they were very nice." The couple bought a town house at 97 Barrow Street, a redbrick neo-Greek home built in 1847, and spent summers at Eliza's home in Little Compton, Rhode Island.

Eliza's relatives had mixed feelings about the romance. "We went to see Eliza and Doris in Rhode Island," recalls Anne Emmet, Tuffy's wife. "Doris was middle-aged, sour, complaining." Louise Whitney, who later married Tim Mellon, got the impression that the family endured Doris in tight-lipped fashion, saying, "I don't think Bunny and Paul liked Eliza's girlfriend very much. They were mannerly about it."

Bunny tried to make her daughter's lover feel welcome when Doris joined Eliza at Cape Cod for Bunny's August birthday celebration. "Eliza was a free spirit," recalls Susan Cabral, the Mellons' Cape Cod housekeeper. "Mrs. Mellon was always a lady, no matter what she felt about you. She tried to accept Doris. When Eliza would come in the summer, Mrs. Mellon would have little packages wrapped up for her, seashells and bath soaps. She'd go down to Doris's room and do the same." Sleeping in the same room apparently wasn't an option.

Bunny was thrilled when Eliza invited her to visit Little Compton, writing to her daughter afterward: "It has wrapped me in a mist of gentle thoughts so that the outside world does not exist...It touched me so much, your warmth and sweetness and caring." Bunny wrote a separate thank-you note to Doris as well.

Although Doris had introduced Patricia Highsmith to her family, she was secretive about the relationship with Eliza, according to her niece and goddaughter Kathryn Myers. "Doris wouldn't give us her telephone number. If I wanted to talk to her, I'd have to wait for her to call," Myers said. But Doris did let slip that she enjoyed visiting the Mellons at their homes. "She said they were important people and they were involved with an art museum."

Eliza brought Doris to St. Croix to meet her father, who accepted the romance with equanimity, happy that his daughter had found love. As Robin Lloyd, Eliza's half brother, recalls, "My father told me that he liked Doris. She was accepted." After the visit Stacy wrote to Bunny, "They seem quite inseparable."

In 1981, Stacy Lloyd took wedding vows for the third time, marrying Virginia Ida (known as Vieta or Vidy) Boy-Ed, a Virginia acquaintance of many years and a fellow horse enthusiast. He sold his St. Croix dairy, but kept his house on the island, and bought a farm in Berryville, Virginia, where he began raising cattle.

During the course of his marriage prior to Alice, Stacy had tried to hide his contacts with Bunny. He often sent Bunny apologetic notes for being monosyllabic with her on the phone because Alice was in the vicinity. But his new wife was not threatened by Bunny. Stacy's letters now included invitations to Bunny to visit.

Bunny wrote to Eliza and Doris after a trip to see the newlyweds in St. Croix. "Pool looks like part of the sea. House is all fresh and painted. Daddy v. happy. Vieta v. kind." When Stacy and his new wife began to pursue the hobby of driving horse-drawn carriages, Bunny sent thoughtful gifts. Stacy was touched, writing to her, "I just cannot thank you enough for the beautiful carriage lamp you found and sent for my birthday."

Bunny and Hubert de Givenchy remained so close that he created a special bedroom sanctuary in his chateau, Le Jonchet, for Bunny's use on her visits, decorated with her favorite shade of blue. "I make a room for her here," he recalled, speaking to me by phone from that estate. "Completely in her spirit, with the color she like, she has her own clothes, crayon and pencil, and colors. She liked to work. She would sketch."

Bunny was so touched that she wrote down Givenchy's remarks in her journal in October 1980. "This room waits for you and the whole house is different when you are in it. It is a pretty room, almost floating in space with the open corridor below. You can look so far away and the top of the trees blow in the wind." She added, "There were tears in his eyes."

Deeda Blair, also the couturier's client and friend, recalled, "I once stayed at Givenchy's, in Bunny's room. It was fantastic. A very large room. She and Hubert had sketched a blue-and-white print, there was an unusual raffia rug, all painted furniture, all of it covered with this blue-and-white print... It was the most deliciously comfortable room I've ever been in, everything was thought of. It was really her room, I don't think he used it as a guest room very often."

Givenchy says he had never had a friendship like this before, a true meeting of the minds. "We travel, we enjoy, we go to see exhibitions, we have a marvelous life together. For me, I learn a lot, of course," he says. Bunny introduced him to new worlds. "When we are in Antigua, she loved gospel, we go to the church for the black people, she adored to be there. She said, 'I think black is really beautiful.'

"She had no limits. People say to me, 'Mrs. Mellon is strange, she's not like the others.' I think she's really normal." He adds, "Bunny always wants to create something, she never stopped. She have an interest in so many things, which is why it was exhilarating to have a friend like her."

Bunny had her special friend; Paul had his love affairs. He enjoyed splurging on jewelry for Dorcas Hardin. His favorite jeweler, Fulco di Verdura, had sold his New York business and retired to London in 1973, but Paul still frequented the Manhattan store, now run by Joseph Alfano. "Paul Mellon was our best client, he would shop like no one else," says Ward Landrigan, the former director of Sotheby's jewelry, who bought the Verdura business in 1985 from Alfano. Paul encouraged Dorcas to let him know what jewelry she fancied.

"Mr. Alfano told me that Mrs. Hardin will come in and look around, sometime later, Mr. Mellon will come in," Landrigan recalls. Dorcas's choices were to be passed on to Paul via the phrase, "It has been admired."

Landrigan was amused by the game and enjoyed his dealings with the couple, who stopped by the store, separately, four to five times a year. "He would never talk about her. He was so discreet," Landrigan says, adding, "I became very fond of Dorcas. She was unpretentious, smart, beautiful. They never came in together. Dorcas would come in for her famous half cup of coffee. Two and a half hours later, she'd be rearranging my furniture." Paul, who had a penchant for colored stones such as topaz and tourmaline, had the jewelry shipped to his Washington house.

Bunny had never allowed professional photographers to shoot the interiors of her homes, concerned about her privacy. Hubert de Givenchy told Bunny that she ought to have a record made for herself, and recommended photographer Joshua Greene, who had been on assignment in Paris shooting the fashion shows. Bunny knew Joshua's parents—legendary photographer Milton Greene and his wife, Amy—and hired him to document her homes in Paris, Manhattan, and Antigua. "Her sense of style and taste was top-notch extraordinary," Greene recalls. "I loved getting on her private plane. She had white boxed lunches with real linen, real silverware, sandwiches amazingly presented, elegant and simple. Martha Stewart, eat your heart out."

During a trip to Antigua in 1980, traveling with Bunny, Paul Mellon, and Hubert de Givenchy, Greene appreciated the leisurely lifestyle—breakfast brought in on a tray, walks into town, afternoons at the beach, hours perusing the books in the library, convivial evenings. "She was always soft-spoken, the conversations were about art, fashion, and people who did extraordinary things," he recalls. "She liked to listen and when she would tell a story, it always had a moral compass or a lesson." His radiant photographs capture a carefree moment in time, Bunny looking happy and relaxed at her island home.

Two weeks after Ronald Reagan was elected in November 1980, a reporter buttonholed Bunny at a National Gallery party and asked for her verdict on the election. *WWD* reported that Bunny observed, "The American people made their choice and I think that's marvelous...If the whole country wanted this, then that's what's really important because it speaks for the nation." Art collector Paul Mellon was more reticent about the Reagan victory: "I haven't the slightest idea what he'll do."

Shortly after the inauguration, Nancy Reagan, an avid reader of the fashion press, called Bunny and asked her to return to the White House to consult on the Rose Garden. "Bunny thought Nancy was a little socially supercilious but she loved Ronald Reagan, she thought he was so dashing," says Bunny's friend Bryan Huffman, who spoke with her about the era.

Bunny and Nancy had just begun working together when the president, leaving the Washington Hilton on March 30, 1981, was shot by John Hinckley. Once the president was released from the hospital and returned to convalesce at the White House, Nancy Reagan began to slowly resume life as usual.

"Bunny was in the White House a few weeks after he'd been shot. She and Nancy were looking at plans involving the Rose Garden, and the president came in wearing some sort of beautiful dressing gown," says Huffman, repeating Bunny's recollections. "He was so tall and attractive and said, 'Uh-oh, it looks like you girls are up to a lot of trouble here.' Bunny thought he was so charming."

Once again, Bunny and Paul found their names on the guest lists for White House galas. That May, Paul and Bunny were invited to the White House for a dinner in honor of the soon-to-be-married Prince Charles. The group included Cary Grant; Audrey Hepburn, Givenchy's muse; and *Vogue* editor Diana Vreeland.

Paul then headed off to England in July for the races. He sent Bunny postcards from his journeys, addressed to "Dear, dear Éléphante," their mutual nickname, and signed, "All my love, dearest E." He almost always mentioned how much he missed her.

When Tuffy Lloyd and his wife, Anne, welcomed their first child in May 22, 1976, a boy named Thomas, Bunny did not go to the hospital to see the baby. Maybe at age sixty-five she wasn't emotionally ready to become a grandmother. The new parents chose Bunny and Paul's friend Charles Ryskamp, now the director of the Morgan Library, as the infant's godfather.

By the time the couple's second child, Stacy Lloyd IV, arrived on October 28, 1977, Bunny's priorities had changed. At the hospital, she was besotted by the infant. "From that day on, she loved that little boy," says his mother, Anne Emmet. Anne was initially pleased but soon became concerned when Bunny began to give preferential treatment to young Stacy in relation to his brother, Thomas.

The Lloyd brothers were both good-looking and athletic, but otherwise they could have come from different gene pools. Thomas did well at school while Stacy was a free spirit with different interests. Bunny became Stacy's champion.

"I remember, early on, always going to my grandmother, she was always there for me," Stacy IV recalls. "From my earliest memories, she was a second mother to me. She was a great friend and a companion. I never ever felt awkward around her. That uncomfortable silence you can have with people, I never did." He pauses and smiles at a memory. "Going out to the farm, the rosemary smell and the lavender smell, I'd never smell them anywhere else, only on the places she lived," he adds. "I began to identify those smells with happiness."

Bunny's special feelings toward Stacy IV came at his brother's expense. At Cape Cod, one of the housekeepers recalled, "Stacy was the one that got the attention. Stacy was invited here without Thomas." Thomas Lloyd admits that it was painful to be treated like a less important member of the family. "My grandmother did a lot of things when

I was little that clearly conveyed her preference for Stacy," Thomas says in a matter-of-fact tone of voice. "It created a lot of friction."

To keep her grandsons occupied during their trips to Cape Cod and Antigua, Bunny hired Timothy Patterson, a graduate of Sandhurst and a member of the Queen's Highlanders, a Scottish regiment of the British Army. His brother Neal was Bunny's Nantucket caretaker. During a five-year period, Tim took the boys out sailing and hiking. "I'm into the hands-on, old school thing, have focus on what you're doing, get lots of exercise, stimulate your brain," recalls Patterson, who later became a landscape gardener thanks in part to Bunny's encouragement. "I think it gave Mr. and Mrs. Mellon pleasure to see them happy and active."

Thomas viewed Tim Patterson as an ally in fraught situations. During one emblematic Cape Cod visit, Thomas spied his father and brother getting into a car one morning and driving away. They were headed for the airport and Bunny's private plane. "Tim walked up to me and said, 'Thomas, I'm really sorry. But it looks like your grandmother is going to take Stacy and your father to New York City for the day for shopping but you can't go. I'm so sorry you're in this position.'"

Stacy IV recalls happily returning from a Manhattan trip with his grandmother, laden with toys from F.A.O. Schwarz, and then feeling guilty when he realized that Bunny had not bought anything for Thomas. "I was oblivious to it until my teen years," he says. "I thought whatever these adults are doing, it's right. Thomas would never say anything, how would I know it hurt him?" Stacy IV finally began to worry that his brother resented him for being the principal recipient of GranBunny's affection. "I try to put myself in Thomas's shoes and understand what it was like not to have that," he says. "It's hard for me to grasp."

Bunny's behavior had repercussions within the family. Her son and his wife argued over what to do. Every now and then, Bunny would make an effort toward Thomas, and he could see what he had been missing. As he recalls, "When my grandmother opens up to you, you feel privileged, you feel like you've won the lottery."

Gifts and money were among Bunny's weapons in her efforts to control her relationships with her children. Now that Tuffy had two young sons plus his wife's three older children from her first marriage, the family's Cape Cod visits wreaked havoc with the serenity of the Mellon household.

Bunny and Paul had previously purchased an adjoining waterfront property, which included an eighteenth-century house. Bunny renovated the Putnam House and added a guest cottage and flower and vegetable gardens. But even though Bunny told her son and daughter-in-law that this was their house, she never put the home in their name, retaining ownership. She gave her two children hefty checks each year, creating an ongoing dependence.

Marriages end for many reasons, but Anne believes that Bunny's manipulative behavior toward her son and grandsons was one of the factors leading to Anne's divorce from Tuffy in 1987.

For divorce lawyers, the Mellon family was the gift that kept on giving. Timothy Mellon, who had been quietly living in Guilford, Connecticut, and using his inheritance to buy railroads, broke up with his wife, Susan. Cathy Mellon's second marriage to Ashley Carrithers hit the skids. (Her first ex-husband, Virginia senator John Warner, also parted ways with Liz Taylor.)

Even in aristocratic America, where finances allowed for mistresses and sequential marriages, this family's failure to form lasting relationships was striking. Both Bunny's parents and Paul's parents divorced; Bunny and her two siblings all divorced; and now all four of the Mellon and Lloyd children had torn up wedding certificates.

Cathy appeared distracted and upset about her second divorce when she attended a National Gallery gala, confiding her troubles to her seatmate, museum special events staffer Carol Fox. "I knew the agony she was going through," says Fox. A few days later, a troubled Paul Mellon called Carol into his office to say that his daughter had informed him that she was dropping the last name Mellon in favor of her mother's maiden name, Conover. "He was hurt. He could not understand why she would cast off his name," Fox recalls. "I said, 'Mr. Mellon, Mellon is such a well-known name and respected and it's hard to live up to. I think she never knows whether people like her for her name or for herself. She wants to find a way to be herself, and I don't think it implies any kind of rejection of you or the family or the name. So give her a pass.'"

In early 1984, Tim Mellon married a childhood friend, divorced artist Louise Whitney. "He's very smart, I always liked him," she says. Louise was impressed that Tim, who flew his own plane, had a strong work ethic, saying, "Tim has worked hard to make his own way, he's not one to just sit back and be a playboy." Paul and Bunny attended the wedding at Tim's second home in New Hampshire.

Marrying into the family of a billionaire had its amusing moments. Although the Mellons had owned their Washington house for decades, Louise discovered that Paul had never explored it. "We went to some National Gallery thing, we went back to the house. We were hungry. We didn't want to get Murray the butler up. Tim and I said to his father, 'Let's go to the kitchen to get a snack.' Paul said, 'I think the kitchen is over here.' I said, 'Paul, you've got to be kidding. You don't know where your own kitchen is?' He said, 'Well, I've only been in there twice.'"

Bunny gave her new daughter-in-law some blunt advice at the Virginia farm, after the two of them had walked past Paul's office and overheard him on the phone loudly talking to Dorcas.

"Bunny told me, 'He thinks that no one else can hear, but they're both deaf. I can hear everything.'

"I said, 'Bunny, that's got to be so hard.'

"She said, 'Louise, you have to make your own life. Have your own joy, your own projects, the things that give you purpose. Don't make a man your only focus.'"

For trendsetters such as Jackie and Bunny, it was fun to shop together and seek out new discoveries. When twenty-three-year-old Howard Slatkin opened a tiny store selling artisan-style housewares in Far Hills, New Jersey, he was stunned on Day One when Jackie came in. "I thought it was an amazing talisman," he recalls. When he dropped off packages at Jackie's New Jersey home, she introduced him to the visiting Bunny, who then came into his store.

Bunny encouraged Slatkin to open a shop near her Manhattan town house. "I did open a shop there and I got to know her better, since when she was in town, she'd have me over," says Slatkin, now an interior decorator whose work is featured in shelter magazines like *Architectural Digest*. Slatkin, who toured Bunny's homes in Virginia, Antigua, and Paris, was struck by her willingness to befriend people whose families had never been in the Social Register. "The only criteria for entering her world was who she wanted to be with," he said, "not what family they came from or whether they went to Foxcroft or did our grandparents know each other."

When Jackie and Bunny were in Virginia, they went antiquing, often visiting a country store with rusty chairs piled up on the front porch in Millwood, Virginia, near Carter Hall. Malcolm Magruder, a Columbia University graduate, launched the shop in 1982 after returning to Virginia to take care of his grandmother.

Magruder had family ties to both Bunny and Jackie. "Jackie's mother and my grandmother were bridge partners," he says. As a young woman, his mother, Georgene, had worked for Stacy Lloyd at the *Chronicle of the Horse*, and after Stacy's wife, Alice, contracted polio, Georgene accompanied the couple to St. Croix for a few months to care for Alice.

Bunny and Jackie would take Malcolm to lunch after shopping in his store. "People like to say Bunny was like the mother Jackie never had, but I saw them as partners in crime," he says. "They were like sisters. Bunny was great fun, but she wasn't as much fun as Jackie."

The women bought gifts for each other. "Bunny was always getting things for Jackie for her place on Martha's Vineyard," he recalled, such as a sailboat-themed chandelier. He sold them weather vanes, child's chairs, and antique gardening books. Jackie bought a folk-art watercolor of tulips and a tree branch full of carved birds and leaves. "If I knew they were coming, I would arrange a section of the shop they would respond to," he says. "If you made something look important, that would kill it."

Jackie kept Paul Mellon company at the Virginia races that Bunny shunned. In March 1984, the *Washington Post* reported, "A reticent Jackie Kennedy Onassis was out in the Northern Virginia hunt country this weekend standing in the back of a light blue pickup truck watching the Rokeby Challenge Bowl races in Upperville. She was there Saturday as a guest of Paul Mellon, whose farm, Rokeby Stables, has sponsored the 3 1/2 mile Challenge Bowl since its inception in 1939...After the races, staying close to Mellon, she mingled a bit with the Middleburg crowd but spoke to only a few people."

That year, Bunny came up with yet another way to make the meals at her home more luxurious. She built a dairy to produce fresh milk, butter, and cheese. Allen Bassler, who was hired to run the dairy, made more than two tons of cheese a year, including such varieties as Parmesan, Dutch Gouda, Swiss, Derby Cheddar, and Colby. Bunny and Paul gave the excess to their friends.

Paul Mellon had begun to experience health problems. After an operation at the Mayo Clinic for a polyp, he developed an infection and an ongoing case of diverticulitis. Bunny was not with him for the operation, but once it became clear that he would be there for a few weeks, she flew out to see him. Since he had complained about the dreary hospital room, she brought along a few of his favorite paintings.

His next medical ordeal was serious. As John Baskett recalls, "He rang me up in 1983 to say that he'd been diagnosed with prostate cancer, but that it was very slow and not to worry too much. He did have one or two operations and radiotherapy."

Paul Mellon accelerated his plans to give a substantial part of his art collection to the National Gallery, handing over ninety-three paintings, including six Monets and two Gauguins. He explained his timing to the *Washington Post* by saying, "I'm getting older." He announced that he wanted to honor Bunny's influence by listing the paintings as donations from the collection of "Mr. and Mrs. Paul Mellon."

Using the honorific "Mrs." rather than her given name, Rachel, or nickname, Bunny, did not appear, in the feminist 1980s, to be much of a tribute, but Paul was a traditionalist. He stressed to the *Post* that "Bunny has had an enormous impact on the collection," stating that she was responsible for choosing 20 percent of the artworks, he had chosen another 20 percent, and "picking the other 60 percent was really a joint endeavor."

Paul, the once spry athlete who had competed vigorously in yearly hundred-mile rides, now had difficulty climbing the stairs in his Washington residence. But he did not want to admit to physical ailments. His butler, Oliver Murray, sought a face-saving solution. As Malcolm Robson, the painter, recalls, "The butler told him one day, 'I'm really having a struggle with the stairs, do you think we could put in an elevator?' Mr. Mellon replied, 'Yes, I think I could do that.'" He adds, "It was done for Mr. Mellon, the butler was fine."

In 1985, on the eve of his seventy-eighth birthday, Paul made the momentous decision to retire as chairman from the National Gallery, which had been the center of his life for four decades. Paul had been a powerful force, choosing directors, arguing over conservation techniques, financing the East Wing, and donating tens of millions of dollars' worth of art. That spring, President Reagan awarded Paul one of the first presidential National Medals of Arts.

To mark his farewell, Paul granted a lengthy interview to Paul Richard of the *Washington Post*. Impressed by the philanthropist, the reporter wrote:

> He is a trim, attractive man, soft-voiced and attentive. He writes poems for his friends, and sometimes, on the spot, produces little well made drawings . . . He strikes those who encounter him as self-deprecating, mild and impeccably polite. It is hard to speak of Mellon without making him appear too good to be true . . .
>
> He is pouring drinks for guests, Mellonian Martinis, one-third gin ("I like the taste") and two-thirds Russian vodka ("They say vodka's better for you") pre-mixed and then nearly frozen.

Bunny and Paul spoke affectionately to the reporter about each other, a striking change from the scalding comments they had given to journalists seven years earlier. "I wouldn't have married Paul if he wasn't a poet," Bunny said while giving Paul Richard a tour of her library.

Bunny stood next to Vice President George H. W. Bush in the receiving line at the National Gallery's Andrew W. Mellon dinner on May 3, greeting Supreme Court Justices Warren Burger and Sandra Day O'Connor, and Defense Secretary Caspar Weinberger. When Paul took the microphone to give his swan song dinner speech, his prepared remarks followed an unconventional path. Before these distinguished VIPs, he spoke about his difficult relationship with his judgmental parent.

"Thoughts of my father always bring me mixed emotions," Paul told the group. "He had a very contradictory nature. On the one hand, there was his autocratic and single-minded view of the world as a financial and industrial chessboard. On the other hand, although much less often, one glimpsed a softer side, as he might praise you for some, probably rare, good marks in school."

He stressed that his sister, Ailsa, who had died in 1969, "suffered greatly" from their parents' divorce, which had crippled her relationships. It pained Paul to think of the life that she could have led. Collecting art was one of her few pleasures; her paintings and sculptures remained on view at the National Gallery. As Paul put it, "It is as though each painting represents some small, unrealized happiness, like an unfolding flower in the sun whose roots were never very far below the surface soil of her sadness."

Now that he was leaving his post, he felt free to use his retirement speech to offer a rare glimpse of the turmoil beneath his calm demeanor.

Paul closed by saying that he was proud of his family's legacy as patrons of the arts. The Mellons had mattered. In an effort to leave the audience with a smile, Paul promised that this is "not a personal good-bye because you may count on me haunting these marble halls and treasure chambers of beauty for as many more years as fate will allow me—and who knows, perhaps after that!"

Chapter Twenty-Two

Entertaining the Royals (Again)

It had been four years since Prince Charles married the demure Diana Spencer, and since then she had become the most photographed and sought-after young woman in the world. But the Princess had never set foot on American soil. In 1985, the couple agreed to attend the Treasure Houses of Britain exhibit at the National Gallery in November. As the *Washington Post* reported, "Hostesses have been clawing for weeks for invitations to the social whirl."

The royals' four-day schedule included a White House dinner with the president and Nancy Reagan; a British Embassy gala; a National Gallery party for high rollers who had given at least $250,000; a tour for Diana of a drug rehab facility; and meetings for Charles about community architecture. One private home was included on the royal itinerary: Paul and Bunny, who had entertained the Queen and Prince Philip nearly thirty years earlier, were giving a lunch for Charles and Di at their farm. The Queen had bestowed knighthood on Paul back in 1974 and the family ties remained strong.

But when the British Embassy sent over the list of guests who would be accompanying the Prince and the Princess, Bunny faced a dilemma. Even she didn't have enough space in her dining room to accommodate the entire party.

Unfazed, Bunny took inspiration from her father's ingenuity back in 1932, when he built a temporary pavilion at Carter Hall to give her a belated wedding party. She decided to tear out a wall of her home and move an outdoor stone wall to build a temporary addition. Her in-house carpenters, handymen, and machinists could handle the construction, but Bunny wanted reinforcements.

Decorator Alison Martin was summoned on short notice to meet with Bunny at the farm. Bunny came out of the house to greet her, trailed by her terrier, Patrick, and asked one question, "Are you discreet?" As Alison recalls, "I got the message loud and clear. I eventually learned it was the Chuck and Di show."

Bunny was so concerned about creating the perfect ambience that she swallowed her pride and asked Paul Leonard to work on the project. Fired by Bunny several years earlier for the sin of getting married without her approval, he was pleased to be reinstated. In October, Leonard gave an interview to the *New York Times* about Bunny's preparations for the royal visit, explaining, "We're building a pavilion, a latticework gazebo that connects the dining room to the living room. With the excitement of doing something like this, it got a little out of hand." Leonard waxed fondly about his relationship with Bunny as if they had never had a falling-out, saying, "She did sort of change my life, that's for sure."

The octagonal addition measured sixteen by fifteen feet and included French doors. House painter Malcolm Robson recalls that when he asked Bunny to choose a color for the walls, "she came out with a painting. I think it was a Renoir, and she said, 'You see the background color, that's what I want. I'll leave it on the mantel for you to keep an eye on.' I said, 'No, I've got the color, you will take it away from here.' I didn't want any paint getting on it. This was a world-class painting!"

As the date of the luncheon approached, Dita Amory, Bunny's former librarian, received a call from her. "She said, 'Eliza doesn't really want to come for lunch, will you come?' It was a big honor for me." But what a painful turn of events for Bunny. The entire world was panting for a seat at her table, yet her own daughter rebuffed the invitation, reinforcing the message that she did not want to be part of her mother's world. "I think Eliza was shy," Dita Amory says, protective of both women. "Mrs. Mellon adored her daughter, but there were periods when they were distant."

Although the lunch was scheduled for November, Bunny decided to create a false summer. The gardeners put in roses, azaleas, cosmos, and sunflowers. Just as she had done when Prince Charles's parents visited, she arranged for sheets to cover and protect the blossoms from cold weather.

On the day of the lunch, Bunny asked gardener George Shaffer to wait in the orangerie behind her home to be available to answer questions. "Princess Diana and Caroline Kennedy were running around the garden like schoolgirls," Shaffer recalls. In this democratic environment, he was honored to shake hands with Prince Charles.

Louise and Tim Mellon joined the lunch, but Louise felt uncomfortable when she saw the seating chart. "Bunny relegated Cathy Mellon's children to the hinterlands. I was a tag-along family member with Tim. I felt terrible that some of the family members were pushed out. I was at Diana's table. She was lovely. She was so self-deprecating and gracious." Virginia Warner, the daughter of Cathy Mellon and John Warner, says that she had no qualms about her place since she was seated with childhood playmate John Kennedy Jr.

Princess Diana, John Kennedy Jr., and Virginia Warner went outside together at one point to look at the horses. Warner recalls with amusement watching Kennedy try to teach the Princess how to whistle with a blade of grass.

Bunny sent Polaroids to her daughter afterward to show Eliza what she had missed. A few weeks later, the addition was torn down, the wall was replaced, and the outdoor stone wall was rebuilt. Months had been spent constructing a handsome space that had been used for roughly three hours. Now only the photographs remained of the octagonal pavilion, and the house bore no traces of the royal visit.

A few months later, Bunny found herself in the midst of planning yet another exclusive event: the wedding of Caroline Kennedy, now a student at Columbia Law School, to Edward Schlossberg, who headed his own museum interior design firm.

Jackie Kennedy Onassis, who now had a full-time job as an editor at Doubleday, hired a trio of society event experts: party planner George Trescher, Upper East Side caterer Sean Driscoll of Glorious Foods, and the reigning floral genius Robert Isabell. The dark-haired, handsome Isabell, who had opened his own firm in 1983, was known for his creative arrangements and chaotic working style. As society bandleader Peter Duchin recalls, "I've done a lot of jobs together with him, he was very difficult and demanding. Treated me one way, and my trumpet player another way."

A small-town boy from Duluth, Isabell had moved to Manhattan at age twenty-six and immediately landed a job at the nightclub Studio 54, arranging flowers and demonstrating his theatrical skill amid the decadent bedlam. "He was soft-spoken and shy," says Ian Schrager, the co-owner of the nightclub. "Robert had this exceptional eye, impeccable taste. He fabricated props. He made these discs, they looked like flying saucers with flowers." The floral designer brought in four tons of glitter for New Year's Eve, covering the floor as if it were snow. Studio 54 event producer Michael Overington adds, "He had fearless ideas of what to do, the bigger the better. We did a party where there were piano players, we were going to have one or two. Robert said, 'You need a dozen, like Busby Berkeley.'"

Bunny was not initially impressed by Isabell when they met to discuss Caroline and Ed's wedding. The floral designer and George Trescher suggested using cellophane ribbons to decorate the ceiling of the tent; she was appalled. "I interrupted and said, 'You can't have that, she has to have real silk ribbons,'" Bunny later wrote in describing the scene. "As the discussion went on the next question was tablecloths. They suggested rather garish colors. Again, I interrupted and said, 'No. She has to have well designed cotton or linen cloths in pastel colors that could be made by Tilletts.'" (Fabric designers D. D. and Leslie Tillett, friends of Jackie, received the commission to create the wedding tablecloths.)

Out of Bunny's earshot, Isabell turned to George Trescher and asked incredulously, "Who is this woman telling Mrs. Kennedy what to do?"

Six weeks before Caroline's wedding, Jackie and Bunny flew to

Hyannis Port with the rest of the team to see the church and the Kennedy compound, where the reception for four hundred people would be held. What stayed with Sean Driscoll is how the usually imperious Isabell was "entranced" with Bunny, deferring to her with awe.

Crowds lined the streets near Our Lady of Victory Church in Cape Cod on July 19, hoping to glimpse the bride and groom. Jackie relented and posed for the cameras. Maurice Tempelsman, who had moved into Jackie's Fifth Avenue apartment several years earlier, was as usual unobtrusive. Security guards kept away interlopers, so they were not able to see Senator Ted Kennedy give away his niece.

Bunny and Robert Isabell decorated the church porch with barrels of purple and white cosmos, and tied honeysuckle and white roses to the pews. By the end of the event, Bunny's opinion of the florist had changed. As magazine editor Babs Simpson remembers, "She told me that she was very enthused about him."

The day after the wedding, Bunny met with Dr. Bruce Horten, a Manhattan cancer pathologist, and a colleague of his at her Cape Cod home to discuss her desire to underwrite and build a medical lab in Antigua to improve the island's substandard health care. "She was in ecstasy because the wedding had gone so well, she had been so concerned about the weather," Horten recalls. "She was so engaging, so sparkling, she put me completely at ease. I thought, 'How can someone in her capacity be so open to a perfect stranger?' "

Now that Bunny was well into her seventies, her social circle was getting smaller as old friends drifted away. Bunny was in the market for new companionship. An accomplished man with an array of cultural interests, Dr. Bruce Horten fit the bill. He felt honored to be on the receiving end of Bunny's invitations, frequently joining her and Paul as a houseguest while he worked on a new lab.

"They had these very rigid evenings in Antigua," he recalls. "You always turned up for cocktails at 7:30, never 7:25 p.m. At 8:15 was dinner. They would serve the most awful wines. Bunny would talk about the bargains she would get."

After dinner, Paul would play Scrabble with another guest, and

Bunny would adjourn with Horten for private conversations. She would often complain: "Paul has been very difficult." As Horten recalls, "He'd ignore her or laugh at her interests, since his interests were not her own. But he had that very patrician way of being amused, a beatific smile. He was very, very polite...She spoke to me about the early years with Paul and how wonderful they were."

He was surprised to discover that Bunny's friendship with Jackie Kennedy Onassis was a point of contention with Paul. "Mr. Mellon never really liked the way Bunny did things for Jackie," Horten added. "He got very annoyed. I was down in Antigua with them when Bunny told Paul that Jackie wanted her to be a sponsor of the American Ballet Theatre again. I remember Mr. Mellon looking quite disgruntled. He didn't say, 'You can't do it' but shared his feelings." For Bunny to serve as a sponsor meant that she would be responsible for buying a table.

For those who made it into the Mellons' inner circle, the next step was meeting the extended family. At a dinner party at her Manhattan town house, Bunny introduced her daughter, Eliza, to Dr. Horten, who soon found himself drawn into a mother-daughter conflict.

"Eliza was living with Doris, who was older and very school-marmy," Horten says. "They had a beautiful home, and I was invited to dine there. It was as if Eliza had found another mother. Eliza was so girlish and had a fantastic sense of humor, she was fun, had her mother's sparkle."

She also had her mother's sense of pride. For a family with all the money in the world, disputes periodically erupted over relatively minor issues. Paul Mellon had given Eliza a four-hundred-acre Virginia farm but insisted on putting in easements so that riders and hikers could have access to the land. Worried that the restrictions would lower the property's value, Eliza adamantly opposed her stepfather's proposal. Paul was annoyed and offered to buy the land back from her. Eliza stubbornly argued over the price.

Her father, Stacy Lloyd, was drawn into the fight, writing to Bunny, "I am wondering if Eliza could have given the property in Virginia to Doris in a will, and having told Doris, she was faced with the problem of making a change that would suit Doris. This might explain, although poorly, her insistence on more money than the farm is worth."

Eliza was so angry that she ceased contact with her mother. "Eliza quit corresponding with Bunny, there was no exchange at first," Horten recalls. "Much of her private life was excluded from Bunny, made Bunny very unhappy. Doris told Eliza, 'Don't speak to your mother, you will ruin our relationship if you do.' Doris was a very strong woman."

Adding to Bunny's sense of isolation, Johnny Schlumberger died in Paris in late August 1987, at the age of eighty-seven. Their unconventional relationship had been a source of great joy to Bunny through the years. Even though their connection had periodically waxed and waned, she still wore Schlumberger's enamel bangle bracelets daily, keeping him by her side even in absentia.

All the various stresses were just too much for Bunny, sending her into an emotional tailspin. A houseguest in Antigua was startled to be woken in the middle of the night by the sound of Bunny's voice. "I spied Bunny on the lawn at three in the morning, saying to the sky, 'I'm so depressed.' I wondered if I should go out to comfort her but I thought, probably not, it's a private matter. I didn't do anything at all, but I did feel very very sorry for her. She was looking so upset."

The family's longtime housekeeper at Cape Cod, Susan Cabral, sensed Bunny's turmoil. "When you think about it, even though she was Mrs. Paul Mellon, she was a lonely little girl. She was always looking for a true friend, a confidante. You can have all the jewelry and the clothes, fly here, fly there. Mrs. Onassis, too. Those two clicked together. They were lonely."

Bunny felt so insecure that she lashed out at close friend Charles Ryskamp, who vacationed each year with Paul and Bunny in Cape Cod and Antigua. One morning on the Caribbean island, he was reading a newspaper by the pool when Bunny turned up for a swim. She wished him good morning; he did not respond. She tried again. Still no response. Perhaps he was preoccupied or did not hear her. "She was livid," says Bruce Horten, who witnessed the incident. Bunny swam

her laps and left. She then had an employee give Ryskamp a note, saying that he was no longer welcome, and the plane was waiting to take
him off the island. He left.

To deal with her depression, Bunny began seeing a psychologist,
who arranged to get her a prescription for Prozac. Her spirits improved. John Baskett recalls, "We were having our drinks before
dinner and she said to Paul, 'I feel much better, I'm taking my
Prozac.'" She repeated that thought to Bruce Horten. "She was ecstatic, she felt so good," he says. "She called me up, 'This is a miracle,
I feel so much better, I can get back to the garden library. I feel like
my old self.'"

Traveling to Paris allowed Bunny to escape to another world. She
spent an October afternoon with I. M. Pei at the Louvre, where he
showed her the dramatic glass-and-metal Pyramid that he was building to replace the old entryway. Trying to reconnect with Eliza, Bunny
wrote to her about that afternoon: "It was an extraordinary experience. It will be the most marvelous museum—his concept of light and
space. I was overexcited and lucky to see all this."

Her trips to France were still voyages of discovery. During a weekend with Hubert de Givenchy at his country house, the couturier
took her for a jaunt. Without explanation, he parked the car and
beckoned her to follow. He strode into a courtyard, opened a door,
walked down an empty corridor, and opened yet another door, which
led to a vast outdoor space. This was the back route into Versailles,
and they were now standing at the entryway to the king's kitchen garden, the Potager du Roi.

"Turning into this gray mist and down a pebbled ramp covered
with moss and dried leaves, we came to a forest of espaliered fruit
trees, towering high on the surrounding walls," Bunny later wrote.
"Trellises outlined beds of vegetables—row upon row of red and green
cabbages, artichokes, blue green leeks, beets, and the feathered tops of
carrots. Pears hung from the small twigs that climbed the wall or covered the trellises." The garden dated back to 1678. Jean-Baptiste de La

Quintinye had spent five years transforming this swampy landscape into a geometrically designed vegetable garden for King Louis XIV.

Bunny returned to the garden again and again and wrote about it for the June 1988 issue of *House & Garden*. But a dispute over the photos to accompany the article damaged her friendship with Nantucket weaver Andy Oates, a talented amateur photographer. He not only wove fabrics for her many homes—Bunny was one of his firm's biggest clients—but also accompanied her on trips to Antigua and Paris. She asked him to take the photographs to go with her magazine story, and brought him with her to Versailles. "So excited about our article," Oates wrote to her right before the trip.

When she subsequently informed him that the magazine had decided to go with another photographer, he became upset and told her so. Bunny cut him off. After he called repeatedly and her staff kept saying that she was unavailable, he wrote an anguished note lamenting "how things have deteriorated in our friendship."

His Nantucket Looms colleague, Sam Kasten, says, "She had her cycles with people. She'd spend time with people and then she wouldn't. It was very upsetting to Andy because he loved her." Liz Winship, who worked at Nantucket Looms and now owns the store, agrees, saying, "Andy was such a kind, soulful man. He didn't know what happened. She just used him and abused him. She stopped coming into the store."

Disagreeing with Bunny was not a good career move, as decorator Alison Martin learned as well. She spent six years on retainer working for the Mellons and recalls the experience fondly, saying, "Once you were on their side of the rope, you were regular people. I always went through the front door, never the trade entrance."

The problem occurred when she was hired by Bunny's son, Tuffy, to decorate his new home after his divorce. Alison and Bunny went together to see the house but disagreed about where to put a doorway to the living room. "I remember thinking, I can advise Stacy to do what his mother wants, or advise Stacy to do what I think he should do for the house as an architectural question," she says. "Stacy was paying for it." Martin gave her honest opinion, in front of Bunny, and then paid the price.

"The lawyers called and basically fired me," she says. "I got a letter that said the Mellons would not be needing my services. It was a great experience and we got along really well, but Mrs. Mellon didn't want anyone contradicting her."

Employees sometimes got caught in the crossfire between Bunny and Paul. When Bunny was annoyed at her husband, she would ask her Virginia maid to tell Paul that she was not feeling well and would not be joining him for lunch. "He knew I was lying, and he knew it was my job to lie," says the woman, who added that Paul used to smile at these excuses and began to call her "Doctor." But one afternoon, right after the couple had left Virginia for Antigua, the woman was fired without explanation, after a dozen years on the job. It had apparently become too awkward for the couple to retain this witness to their manipulative behavior.

The staff could not help but take sides. "It wasn't easy to be Mrs. Paul Mellon," says Susan Cabral, who was the couple's Cape Cod housekeeper for fifteen years. "It took a lot of strength, perseverance, and abuse. He was a sweet man, but his temper was instantaneous."

On May 16, 1990, a third-floor fire swept through Kenneth Battelle's salon, leaving the building in ruins. Bunny tracked Kenneth down to offer condolences and help. "Thank you for your most lovely, loyal and caring support during this horror I am experiencing," he wrote to her. "I do not yet know how it will all resolve itself or I will work it out, but I can only say your expressions of caring have helped save my sanity."

His records had been destroyed. Bunny provided free office space for Kenneth's secretary in the carriage house that she and Paul owned on East Seventieth Street. Although he had twenty years left on his town house lease, his landlord evicted him, citing a clause in the lease about fires. When Kenneth finally reopened at the Waldorf Astoria two years later, Bunny commissioned florist Robert Isabell to decorate the salon with vast quantities of flowers.

Bunny and Paul were generous to their friends: offering up their

Antigua home for vacations, underwriting medical bills, arranging for cars and drivers, or quietly paying tuition for children. Clare Balding, the daughter of Paul's British horse trainer Ian Balding, credited Paul with underwriting her Cambridge education. Bunny's former British ward, David Brooke, the Earl of Warwick, did not lack for material wealth, but Bunny still enjoyed making arrangements to give him Savile Row suits. Brita Bonechi, whose parents owned a pioneering Manhattan craft and design store that Bunny patronized, recalls, "I called her my fairy grandmother because she sent me these totally amazing Christmas presents each year. She sent me an entire art box because I was a painter, a chair, quite a lot of Schlumberger jewelry. I got gifts for pretty much sixty years."

Bunny surprised people with unexpected thoughtful gestures. Tim Patterson, the Scottish Highlander who looked after Bunny's grandsons during vacations, was stationed in Kenya on an Army exercise. He mentioned in a note to his brother, who was Bunny's Nantucket caretaker, that the mosquitoes were fierce.

"The only way we could get mail was delivered by helicopter, lowered by a winch," he recalls. "Someone came up to my camp [and said], 'You've got a package from New York.' It was mosquito cream from Mrs. Mellon with a beautiful handwritten note. She had a gentle kindness about her."

Bunny and her ex-husband, Stacy Lloyd, had begun sneaking off to lunch together. They would meet in the tiny town of Millwood, within walking distance of their former marital home at Apple Hill, at the antiques shop owned by Malcolm Magruder. Then they would go to lunch at a converted train station nearby.

"Stacy was one of the most superior people I've known on the face of this earth," Malcolm Magruder says. "That man was just extraordinarily charismatic, one of those people who just had understated charm and elegance, nothing pretentious about him at all. Bunny knew I was friends with Stacy and very loyal to him. They used to come and meet at my shop. It was a little awkward, because Stacy had married a woman who we all loved and thought was wonderful, Vidy."

Nonetheless, Malcolm found it touching to see the septuagenarian ex-spouses together. "Stacy never came out and said, 'Keep this between you and me.' It was always understood, 'This is my children's mother, and we're going out for a nice lunch.' But at the same time, he would roam around the shop. 'Do you have a nice antique basket? Do you have a red ribbon we can put around it? Can you find a few little pretty things to put in it?' By the time it was done, it was clear there was affection."

Stacy would usually arrive first, but one time Bunny turned up before him. Making conversation, Malcolm said, "You and Stacy are wonderful friends." He didn't ask why they had divorced, but the question was implicit. Bunny replied in shorthand, saying, "It was a war marriage."

Yet decades after their divorce, she still wore Stacy's sapphire pinkie ring.

In her own way, Bunny was competitive with her husband. Paul had launched the Yale Center for British Art and a sister facility in London, the Paul Mellon Centre for Studies in British Art; both underwrote scholarly research. Bunny's Oak Spring Library was modest by comparison, but she was interested in sparking serious intellectual consideration of her interests—plants, flowers, and natural history.

Bunny commissioned British author Sandra Raphael to write two books about her collection of botanical manuscripts and rare books. Distributed by Yale University Press, the books received glowing reviews. In the *New York Times Book Review*, on March 25, 1990, gardening writer Paula Deitz praised *An Oak Spring Sylva* as a "vivid social history tracing the importance of trees both ornamentally and economically over a 300 year period."

The *Washington Post* was equally enthusiastic about the second volume, *An Oak Spring Pomona*, which focused on fruit cultivation. "The whole exercise might appear exceedingly dry and esoteric, but it is quite the reverse," wrote reviewer Adrian Higgins. "You cannot peruse the chapters in 'Pomona,' for example, without realizing how much the world has changed since the 17th Century. While we blithely drop by the supermarket to pick up oranges and grapes, these same fruits were once accessible only to kings and noblemen who had the power and wealth to build walled gardens and greenhouses and staff them with skilled gardeners, or commanded great fleets to bring fruit back from the colonies."

Sandra Raphael was supposed to write two more volumes but was dismissed after displaying tin-eared insensitivity. As London book-seller John Saumarez Smith heard the tale: "Paul took Sandra to one of those grand dinners at the National Gallery. 'The Stars and Stripes' were played and everyone stood up. Sandra stayed seated—this wasn't her country and she thought, 'I don't need to stand.' But she had insulted her hosts." Soon afterward, she received a letter saying her services were no longer needed.

In 1989, Bunny commissioned Italian botanical scholar Lucia Tongiorgi Tomasi, a professor at the University of Pisa, to write the next two volumes of the series, which took two decades to complete. "I began to frequent the library every three or four months," Tomasi recalls. "Every morning she was coming to the library, we are choosing the books and we are talking and we became friends. Bunny had an incredible eye, she understood immediately the beauty of the objects and manuscripts. She wasn't always aware of the historic importance of the objects. I wrote the books, but it was a collaboration. It felt like a team between us."

Tomasi's *An Oak Spring Flora*, published in 1997, was a well-written exploration into how flowers were portrayed in artworks from the fifteenth century onward. The lushly illustrated *An Oak Spring Herbaria*, published in 2009, traced the history of medicinal herbs. Reviewing those two volumes in *House Beautiful*, Martin Filler wrote that "this series promises to become an indispensable part of the ever-broadening culture of gardens...visitors to Bunny Mellon's garden of knowledge can harvest the fruits of her lifetime labors."

Feeling a twinge of her mortality, Bunny was concerned about the future of her library, operating under a foundation named after her father, Gerard B. Lambert. In the fall of 1990, Bunny and Paul began talks with the Smithsonian to see if the federal government might be interested in taking over the library. Bunny wrote to her former British childhood ward, David Brooke, to say that she was pleased that the library would "be enjoyed long after I move on."

But the Smithsonian had already discovered that such gifts can come with expensive strings. Post cereal heiress Marjorie Merriweather Post had left her Washington, D.C., estate Hillwood, thirty-six rooms filled with Fabergé eggs and Russian art, to the Smithsonian along with a $10 million endowment. But the museum returned the gift to her estate in 1976 after discovering that it cost too much to maintain. The patriotic Post also gave the government her 128-room Palm Beach mansion, Mar-a-Lago, to be used as a presidential retreat, but the government returned that property, too, citing the million-dollar yearly maintenance. (Eventually purchased by Donald Trump and turned into a private club, Mar-a-Lago has now become his presidential getaway.)

Paul Mellon offered a $30 million endowment to the Smithsonian to support Bunny's library. But that sizable sum was not enough to convince the government to take on this inconveniently located building, which had not been designed for the use of scholars.

In 1991, Madeleine Jacobs, a spokeswoman for the Smithsonian, told the *Washington Post*, "It actually would have required us to raise a great deal of money ... This did not seem like a project that should be on the list." Mellon's lawyer Carroll Cavanagh insisted that his client accepted the decision with equanimity, saying, "Mr. Mellon is never distressed about anything."

Fifty years had passed since Paul Mellon formally presented his father's art collection to the nation at the opening of the National Gallery. Now with the half-century anniversary approaching, the museum asked prominent collectors to donate works in celebration.

Paul and Bunny studied the walls in their homes. He picked out the Cézanne that had once broken auction records, *Boy in a Red Waistcoat*, and agreed to eventually give the museum a Winslow Homer, *Dad's Coming!*, one of the first paintings the couple had purchased together in 1954. He gave Bunny a life interest in the artwork. The couple jointly agreed to donate their Degas wax sculptures.

Bunny was credited with giving the museum two untitled 1955 Rothko works (a somber oversized red, black, and white canvas; and a cheerful painting with orange and white blocks); and a 1622 Balthasar van der Ast painting, *Basket of Flowers*; as well as ten whimsical Alexander Calder bent-metal sculptures, including a black camel with a blue head and a red tongue.

Paul was always happy to donate art to the gallery, but Bunny put on the brakes. Hubert de Givenchy recalls that she confided in him about an argument with her husband over a Picasso. "They had a charming portrait of a boy by Picasso," he says. The painting had been a birthday gift from Paul to Bunny and she'd hung it in her Virginia bedroom, but now he wanted to give it to the gallery.

"Paul insisted and Bunny insisted," Givenchy said. "She wanted to be protected." To the best of his recollection, Givenchy believes that Bunny asked her lawyer for help and won that round.

Paul had been profiled by dozens of newspapers and magazines over the years, but now that he had retired from the National Gallery, he wanted to put his own recollections on the record and write his autobiography. He discussed the potential project with his analyst, Dr. Jenny Waelder Hall, later telling *Vanity Fair*'s Martin Filler: "I remember talking to her about it in analysis and saying that I found it hard because I'd get bogged down in the details. And she always said, 'Well, don't do it that way. Do it just with vignettes, because those are the interesting things anyhow.'" Paul tapped his friend John Baskett as his amanuensis. Baskett, based in London, flew in regularly to interview and tape Paul and write the book.

Until now, Paul had not talked publicly about his parents' rancorous parting and his discovery of the letter claiming that Andrew Mellon might not be his father. "We were down in Antigua and he said, 'Let's get started,'" Baskett recalls. "He told me about his parents' divorce. I had known him for thirty years and he'd never uttered a word about it before. In the office, in Washington, people said there's a great secret and he never speaks about it. Suddenly out it all came. We walked back to lunch and he looked as if he was walking two feet off the ground."

Baskett was especially careful about the passages that mentioned Bunny and the couple's marriage. "I knew them so well I didn't need to talk to them about it. I'm quite sure she did read it. I said, if there's anything you think I got wrong or you don't like, let me know, I'm just the scribe." The couple did not ask for changes.

Paul Mellon's memoir, *Reflections in a Silver Spoon*, was published in the spring of 1992. Dedicated to Bunny, the book received mostly favorable reviews. The British *Spectator* called the autobiography "as likeable as its subject." Harvard child psychiatrist Robert Coles, in his *New York Times* review, lingered on Paul's account of how analysis had helped him recover from his bruising childhood. Coles concluded that "he appears a thoughtful person, humbled in certain ways by his enormous fortune and the power connected to it."

But a few reviewers quibbled. In the *Washington Post*, social historian Stephen Birmingham faulted Paul for his unwillingness to reveal much about his personal life. "In the area of romance he is decidedly reticent. His love life is described in a kind of shorthand and it is here that the tone of the book becomes edgy, guarded, defensive." He writes of Paul's description of his first marriage—"Where was love in any of this? Where—dare we ask—was sex?" Birmingham added, "But though Mellon can vividly describe an autumn sunset on his Virginia farm or a herd of prize cattle or a filly's flank, he does not tell us whether he ever found Bunny pretty."

WWD writer Susan Watters seized on Paul's statement that he and Bunny "have been careful to allow each other to develop our own interests." Watters suggestively added, "The names of those interests are discreetly missing from the text." Despite the central role that Dorcas

Hardin continued to play in Paul's life, she had been airbrushed out of the picture.

While Paul had been working on his book, Bunny turned her attention to her favorite pastime: real estate. Her two latest ventures were situated an ocean apart: a house on Nantucket and a new apartment in Paris. "She built the Nantucket house to fly over for the day or two or three days with Jackie," says Givenchy. "She designed the house with great style and proportion. It's absolutely ravishing."

Bunny preferred constructing homes with multiple outbuildings, rather than one megamansion. Working with Virginia architect Thomas Beach, Bunny put up a 5,200-square-foot shingled house on her two-hundred-acre plot in Nantucket along with several guest cottages. "She wanted the house to be as close to the ocean as possible, she wanted to hear it at night," says Janine La Farge, the widow of Bam La Farge, the Harvard-educated master carpenter who worked on the project. Worried about erosion, he urged Bunny to site the home farther from the beach, but she ignored his concerns.

Handy with drafting tools, Bunny created her own architectural renderings while spending time in her small Nantucket apartment over a shed. "She'd have breakfast in bed and then draw. She'd bring Bam these designs she had drawn about where the fireplace should be and where the bricks would go and how it would all work visually," says La Farge. "She was so visual, every day was a work of art. It wasn't just what she could afford to acquire, it was incredible, what she made."

The location of the Nantucket house, so close to the ocean, made it impossible for trees to thrive nearby due to the salt air, winds, and sandy soil. So Bunny devised an alternative: She had carpenters create life-size wooden models of trees and installed them on the property to create visual interest.

On the other side of the Atlantic, Bunny decided to sell her Paris apartment at 84 Avenue Foch. "There began to be break-ins along Avenue Foch," explained Dr. Bruce Horten. "Women of ill repute, plying their trade in the Bois de Boulogne, began just walking up the street." She bought a smaller apartment on the Left Bank a few blocks from the Louvre, at 15 Rue de l'Universite. That meant another round of renovation and decorating.

Malcolm Robson was painting the wooden floors in the Paris apartment when Bunny showed up with Givenchy. "He was about to walk all over our floors, which hadn't been protected yet," Robson says. "I said, 'You can walk on it but we can't have any shoes on it.' So he took off his shoes but he had the biggest hole in his sock. Everyone just cracked up laughing."

Bunny favored high-low touches at her homes: placing Madeline Hewes folk-art paintings next to million-dollar masterpieces, rag rugs with eighteenth-century silver dinnerware, antique asparagus- and cabbage-shaped tureens with inexpensive woven baskets. She put together a mélange of furniture that looked old but often wasn't. "She'd come up with pieces of furniture and ask us to make them look like they were eighteenth century," recalls Malcolm Robson. "We would make antiques." Her signature color was blue, and there were touches of blue in every room, from the fabric draped on her French polonaise-style beds to the cushions on a window seat.

These two new homes fulfilled different elements of Bunny's personality: the nature lover and the urban sophisticate. The Nantucket property was stark with a wildness that contrasted with her manicured Cape Cod estate. In Paris, her new home was on a meandering side street, near chic shops and Michelin-starred restaurants.

In quest of finishing touches for the Paris apartment, Bunny visited an antiques store that was run by Givenchy's friend Akko van Acker, a native of Holland. She stayed for three hours—"We talked as if we knew each other for twenty years, she was so warm and sympathetic," van Acker recalls—and soon he became her newest confidant and traveling companion, spending time with her in Paris and visiting her homes in Virginia, Cape Cod, and Antigua. "She loved to go to museums and to the tea shop with the lovely little cakes," van Acker adds. "I walked with her to antique shops."

He enjoyed being swept up in her world, amused by Bunny's subtle humor and how much she valued her anonymity. "One day, she was paying for something with a credit card," he recalls. "The sales clerk saw her last name and said, 'I bet you wish you were one of the people from the Mellon bank.' Bunny said, 'Oh, I would like that.'"

When she brought van Acker to the National Gallery in Washington, a security guard chastised Bunny when she pushed the button for the executive elevator to her husband's office, insisting that she was not allowed to use it. As Akko recalls, "She could have said, 'This whole museum belonged to my father-in-law.' Instead, she said, 'I'm so sorry' and went to the other elevator for the public. She would never say who she was."

Aware that Akko lived with a male partner, Bunny nonetheless chose not to acknowledge his committed relationship. "I'm 100 percent gay," he says. "Bunny knew of my friend Ricardo. But when she wanted me to come over, she never invited him to come."

What stayed with van Acker was Bunny's emotional neediness at that point in her life. "She called me every day, whether I was in Paris or St. Tropez, and spoke to me for an hour and a half," he recalls. "When Bunny liked someone, she would want them around night and day, available all the time." It was flattering, but it was also too much.

Eliza Lloyd and her girlfriend, Doris Sanders, broke up in 1992. Eliza turned to her mother for comfort, pouring out her feelings in an emotional conversation. She was eager to mend the wounds in their relationship. On October 11, 1992, Bunny wrote to Eliza that she had prayed to God for guidance after hearing "your heartfelt tears of distress" and wanted to underline "the great, great happiness you are in my life. I wish always that I could do more to show it. You mentioned giving me grandchildren. Don't you think your work as an artist that are on my walls and elsewhere are more than grandchildren?"

Bunny conveyed her acceptance of Eliza's sexuality, writing, "If a daughter has been from birth the Joy of my life, you don't expect or want her to be anything that God has not planned." This was the opening that Bunny had been longing for. Her daughter needed her.

That December, she wrote to Eliza every day, describing life on the farm with such observations as, "The sun is shining bright. 28 degrees cold. Last night the stars were out in the light of a December sky. The maple has come down outside my window...The wind is blowing in wild ways across the mountain...the sycamore is crayon white against the dark grey sky...Today I go to Washington to see the Secretary of the P of Wales for tea...Snowstorm on its way here tonight."

She regaled Eliza with tales from a day trip to Nantucket: "We lost our beach in the storm but the little house was a fortress...Nantucket yesterday was a world apart, the East Coast covered in clouds, the tiny island sparkled in warm sunlight, the ocean was calm with the air. Christmas lunch a delight, seven of us with fresh scallops. Your mother was in heaven!"

Most of all, Bunny rejoiced in her newly regained closeness with her daughter: "Your voice has given me joy and energy to live out the many activities of today. The sun is also working its way through the grey sky...Today you will be arriving, the great joy for me. All night the wind has been cleaning the sky and fields, birds and leaves fly together. Tonight we will all share Christmas Eve. So much love, Mums."

For Paul and Bunny, who had chosen to maintain their marriage despite their difficulties, it was dispiriting to watch their children struggle with relationships. After Tim Mellon asked his second wife, Louise, for a divorce, Bunny and Paul were solicitous toward their distraught daughter-in-law. "Bunny called all the time," says Louise Whitney Mellon. "Paul was very supportive. Paul asked me not to take back my maiden name. I was flabbergasted."

Prior to the breakup, Paul Mellon had proposed Louise for a seat on the board of the National Gallery, and he insisted that she still had his support. She got the prestigious appointment. Tim went on to marry a woman whom he had known for many years, Patricia Freeman, the former wife of diplomat Charles W. Freeman Jr., who had been Tim's close friend dating back to their time at Milton Academy and Yale. Tim and Patricia would later divorce, too, and then remarry again.

For Paul, breeding horses had been one of the great joys of his life. He and his trainers would carefully plot the matchmaking process, buying stallions with impressive pedigrees. He liked naming the new-borns with monikers such as Arts and Letters and Key to the Mint. The stable boys were used to his impromptu visits.

But feeling his age, Paul decided to close down his horse-breeding operation and sell many of his yearlings. "I intend to keep racing and steeple chasing for the rest of my lifetime, although on a reduced scale both in the United States and in England," he wrote in a memo to his employees in July 1992. "The reasons for these difficult decisions may not be pleasant to talk about, but are nevertheless very real. At eighty-five, I cannot know how much longer I will live. I want to concentrate on winning races."

He had done well at the racetrack over the years, but his Thorough-breds had failed three times to capture the Kentucky Derby. It was a source of yearly frustration that he could not break into the winning circle.

Now the clock was ticking. Paul thought he finally had a serious contender for the 1998 Derby: Sea Hero, sired by Polish Navy to the mare Glowing Tribute, born in March 1990. But after a promis-ing start, the horse slumped into a losing streak. Nonetheless, when the field looked relatively weak, Paul's veteran trainer, Mack Miller, decided to enter Sea Hero in the May 1, 1993, Kentucky Derby. Dur-ing past races, the horse had been equipped with blinders, but jockey Jerry Bailey opted to remove them for the Derby. The odds for the horse started at 30–1, then narrowed to 13–1.

Bunny rarely attended the races with Paul, and he had arranged to be accompanied to the Derby by his granddaughter, Virginia Warner. But he had just recovered from pneumonia, and Bunny was con-cerned about his health. As Paul headed out the door of their Virginia home, dressed formally in a gray suit with a brown fedora and a walking stick, she asked him to wait a minute while she got her straw hat and joined him. After all, it was their forty-fifth anniver-sary. When the plane touched down and they arrived at the track, she later confessed to *Sports Illustrated* writer William Nack that she found it disorienting to go from "a quiet country life into the wild excitement."

As Sea Hero made his move toward the front of the crowded pack, a photographer captured Bunny's animated expression as she looked up at the heavens seeking divine help. "Bunny was a fantastic cheerleader," recalls Virginia Warner. Paul gazed with disbelief as the race headed to the finish line, later telling the *Washington Post*, "Actually, I couldn't see him coming around the turn. I didn't really see him until about a sixteenth of a mile from the finish."

Surging down the track, Sea Hero came in first, paying $27.80 for a $2 bet, and winning a $735,900 purse. "You can't put into words what this means," Paul told reporters. "It's very exciting, something you never believe is going to happen until it does." He plucked a red rose from the garland draped on Sea Hero and presented it to Bunny as an anniversary gift.

I. M. Pei invited Paul and Bunny to join him in Paris that October for the opening of his Pyramid entrance to the Louvre, but they declined the invitation. Paul was not feeling well and he was reluctant to travel.

Bunny sent her regrets to Pei in a heartfelt note, conveying how much they longed to celebrate with him: "I spoke with Paul. He was pleased with the idea and expressed how much he would love to go...but it is unwise for him to fly right now. And I could tell by his expression that he was suggesting I go but also stay here...

"I really want to come, dear I.M., but there is no one at the moment to stay with him. I try to make life as easy as possible for him right now. He is doing very well and his racehorses are co-operating. Paris & the Louvre are especially marvelous in the autumn light all dressed up—Bravo!!"

The Mellons were practical and believed in planning ahead. In this crisp autumn weather, with intimations of winter, came thoughts of their mortality. Bunny and Paul remained attached to the stone Gothic house of worship that they had built, the Trinity Episcopal

Church in Upperville. Each year, the Mellons donated odds and ends—furniture, fragile porcelain, books—to the Trinity Church auction, and locals bid a premium for Mellon-related items.

Tucked behind the church, to the left, was the small private Mellon burial area with the graves of Paul's parents, Andrew Mellon and Nora McMullen Mellon, and his sister, Ailsa Mellon Bruce. Bunny and Paul planned to be buried there, too. Rather than leave the decisions about their headstones to their heirs, the couple made an appointment with a stonemason.

"It is hard to explain that ordering one's gravestone is interesting + creative," Bunny wrote on November 14, 1993, in a follow-up note to the mason, adding that they felt "happy and inspired" by the outing. "Paul is so happy with the same marble as the National Gallery that all seems well." His gravestone would include lines from a Robert Louis Stevenson poem: "Home is the sailor—home from the sea, And the hunter, home from the hill."

Bunny wanted a carving of a leafy tree with curving branches and the words, "The Lord is My Shepherd." On the back of her tombstone, she wanted engraved a verse from St. John, words that appealed to her love of nature.

"The wind bloweth where it listeth, and thou hearest the sound thereof but canst not tell whence it cometh, and whither it goeth: so is every one that is born of the Spirit."

She stressed to the stonemason that she was in no rush to meet her maker, writing, "Hope I can live long enough to finish the many things already started."

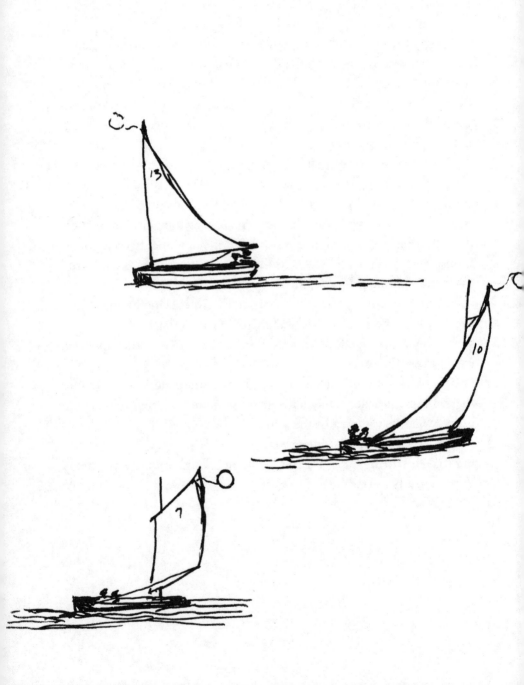

Chapter Twenty-Three

Exits and Entrances

Jackie Kennedy Onassis was a familiar figure in Middleburg, Virginia, recognized but not unduly fussed over in the quaint Main Street shops. When Louise Whitney Mellon spotted Jackie at the hairdresser's on a wintry day, she was surprised by the former First Lady's fragile appearance. "She looked so wan and pale," Louise recalled. "I thought, that's not good."

A few weeks later, the *New York Times* broke the story in February 1994 that Jackie was being treated for non-Hodgkin's lymphoma and had been undergoing chemotherapy for a month. Nancy Tuckerman, Jackie's spokeswoman, put a positive spin on the situation, saying, "There is an excellent prognosis. You can never be absolutely sure, but the doctors are very, very optimistic."

Jackie was still going into her office at Doubleday three days a week, Tuckerman added, and working the other two days at home. The disease had been diagnosed after Jackie complained to her doctor of flu-like symptoms.

In March, Jackie agreed to chair the American Ballet Theatre's May 9 spring gala, a tribute to the late Oliver Smith, the theatre and ballet stage designer who had given Jackie and Bunny art lessons. "We are thrilled," said Blaine Trump, the honorary cochairwoman. "You don't take on a chairmanship unless you plan to be there." This news was greeted with the upbeat *Times* headline: JACQUELINE ONASSIS TO RETURN TO THE SOCIAL SCENE.

But Jackie was concerned enough about her health to update her will on March 22. In April, she was hospitalized at New York Hospital–Cornell Medical Clinic for surgery, reportedly for a bleeding ulcer. Nancy Tuckerman insisted to the press, "She's doing well. She's snapped back."

On April 24, a photographer caught Jackie in a rare outdoors appearance, sitting on a Central Park bench with Maurice Tempelsman. Wearing a raincoat with a blue scarf covering her hair, she looked frail. Bunny arranged to spend more time in New York to be available. As Jackie's sister, Lee, recalls, "When Jackie was very ill, Bunny would come over to have lunch with her at the apartment."

Jackie entered the hospital on May 16 and was discharged two days later. Only then did a hospital spokesman confirm to the *New York Times* that her condition was dire and that she was experiencing "serious complications of her malignant lymphoma." The cancer had spread to her brain and lymph nodes. Jackie's family had brought her home to die.

Hundreds of reporters and photographers took up a deathwatch vigil outside of her Fifth Avenue home. Senator Ted Kennedy came out to speak to the crowd. "I think all the members of the family are distressed by the medical reports," he said. "All the members of the family love her very deeply. We wanted to be here this evening. She's resting comfortably. I had a good chance to talk to John and Caroline."

Inside the apartment, Bunny sat by the unconscious Jackie. The singer and songwriter Carly Simon, who had been close to the former First Lady for many years, recalls, "When Jackie was dying, I was allowed to go over to be with her at her bedside. When I got to her apartment, Bunny was seated at her bedside and praying. Jackie was in a coma. Bunny said, 'Do you want to sit by her bed?'"

A recording of monks chanting was playing in the background. Jackie was flanked by her son and her longtime companion. "John was standing on one side of the bed, Maurice was standing on the other side, both in their impeccable suits," Simon adds. "Bunny went over to sit on the couch. I was whispering, 'Jackie, I love you.'" The former First Lady never regained consciousness, dying at 10:15 p.m. on May 19, at the age of sixty-four.

The floral deliveries began arriving immediately. This was Bunny's arena, and she took charge as she had done after John F. Kennedy was assassinated, this time arranging the flowers for Jackie's bier. Two dozen roses sent by Frank Sinatra did not meet her artistic standards. "I'm not using these," Bunny told a friend, tossing the garish bouquet aside.

Lee Radziwill rode with Bunny in the limousine to Jackie's funeral. The pairing was a reflection of Jackie's attitude: one sister by blood and one sister by choice.

"No one else looked like her, spoke like her, wrote like her or was so original in the way she did things," said Ted Kennedy in his eulogy, adding, "She graced our history. And for those of us who knew and loved her, she graced our lives." Maurice Tempelsman read the poem "Ithaka," by the Greek poet C. P. Cavafy, and closed by saying, "And now the journey is over. Too short, alas, too short. It was filled with adventure and wisdom, laughter and love, gallantry and grace. So farewell, farewell."

Bunny had arranged for Paul's private plane to bring the casket of Jacqueline Bouvier Kennedy Onassis to Washington so she could be buried beside her first husband in Arlington National Cemetery. As Lee and Bunny rode together to the airport, the tension of the day finally got to Bunny. Making conversation, Lee told a story about her daughter's cat, and Bunny burst out laughing. "It was completely out of context," Lee recalls. "But for some reason she thought it was funny." Bunny had held herself together all day; her emotions had to come out somehow.

Florist Robert Isabell joined them on the plane, keeping an eye on the flowers on the casket. Bunny found his presence calming, writing later to thank him. "You sat with me in Arlington while the grave was being dug in the most simple way, it could have been a country church yard...I hope we meet again, with flowers or without."

At the Arlington cemetery, a brief eleven-minute service was held before Jackie was interred. "God gave her very great gifts and imposed upon her great burdens," President Bill Clinton said. "She bore them all with dignity and uncommon common sense…We say good-bye to Jackie, May the flame she lit so long ago burn ever here and always brighter in our hearts."

Millions around the world mourned Jackie; magazines put out special editions to commemorate her life. The images were indelible: the glamorous First Lady, the blood-spattered widow, the dressed-down editor looking content with her later-in-life companion.

For Bunny, it was excruciating to lose her best friend, who should have outlived her. Summing up their friendship, Jackie had thanked Bunny several years earlier in a letter for "the love and care, the strong and wise support, the laughter, the adventures we have had, all you have meant to the children." In her will, Jackie left Bunny two miniature Indian paintings.

"She was your soul mate," wrote Paul Leonard in a condolence note to Bunny. Frank Langella recalled the women's "secret rapport" and the "rare and precious" nature of their friendship. In the aftermath of Jackie's death, Bunny would page through the scrapbook that Jackie had given her in 1966 to commemorate her work on the Rose Garden.

The Rose Garden shimmered in Bunny's memory as her most important lasting contribution to the nation. That fall, Bunny went to the White House with her longtime lawyer, Alex Forger, now the president of the Legal Services Corporation, the federally funded nonprofit that provides civil legal services to the poor. At this White House celebration of the twentieth anniversary of the agency, Forger proudly introduced First Lady Hillary Clinton to Bunny, explaining that Bunny had designed the Rose Garden.

Bunny was used to receiving accolades and deference, but she thought that Hillary appeared completely uninterested, saying, "How very nice," and then walking away. As Forger recalls, "Bunny was steamed."

Stacy Lloyd had been an avid foxhunter as a young man, but now he preferred the sedate pleasures of carriage driving. At his summer home in Northeast Harbor, Maine, he and Vidy would often take their horses and carriage and travel the paths at the Acadia National Park. At age eighty-six, he was proud of his robust health. His grandson Thomas Lloyd recalls, "He was a vegetarian, very healthy, very fit."

He was in better physical shape than his World War II roommate Paul Mellon, who continued to battle prostate cancer. Stacy often wrote Bunny solicitous notes about Paul's health. "Tuffy told me that you and Paul were not getting off to Antigua as planned," Stacy wrote to Bunny on January 3, 1994. "I am so sorry that he is not well and hope things are better and you will get away soon."

Late that year on a wintry afternoon, Stacy hitched up a new horse to his carriage on his Berryville farm. Training a new horse was a physically challenging task for an octogenarian, but Stacy had the confidence of a man who had been around horses for his whole life. But today, things went disastrously wrong.

"He got in the cart alone with this horse that he was breaking," says Robin Lloyd, Stacy's son from his second marriage. "The horse took off and he wasn't strong enough to pull the horse in. The horse went plowing into a fence. The cart turned over. His lung, his rib cage gave way. The foreman got there while my father was still alive and asked, 'Are you okay?' The last thing my father did was shake his head, no." Stacy Lloyd died on December 6, 1994.

Bunny was distraught. With Jackie, she had been able to bid a loving farewell, but Stacy's death was a thunderbolt. There would be no more affectionate lunches, no more reminiscing about their early years together, no one left to care as much as she did about their two children.

Even though she had divorced Stacy more than forty years earlier, Bunny believed she was entitled to equal respect at the funeral as Vidy, Stacy's widow. An hour before the service was scheduled to begin, Bunny arrived at the empty church and sat down in the front row. Vidy did not want her there but chose not to make a scene. As Thomas Lloyd says, "This poor woman, Vidy, who has lost her husband, is the bigger, better person." Bunny was gently encouraged by another mourner to move to the second row and reluctantly complied.

But then Bunny ignored a request that she refrain from attending the reception after the funeral. "Vidy said to Eliza, 'Please do not have your mother come back to my house after the funeral,'" recalled Anne Emmet. "Eliza said okay. And then Bunny came back to the house."

Bunny had now lost the two people who had been the anchors of her life. On December 26, she acknowledged to Eliza in a letter that she had been "shaken and rattled" by the deaths. "You have helped us all when we lost your father, but he is _not_ gone," Bunny wrote. "He never will leave us. He will always drive horses + sail boats and send us flowers."

Eliza had become much closer to her mother, but she still kept secrets. Diagnosed with breast cancer, Eliza went through treatment and surgery but never told Bunny. She could not bear to give her grieving mother something else to worry about.

Paul Mellon's ongoing medical issues had begun to take a toll. Nearly a decade earlier, a nurse from the Winchester Medical Center, Nancy Collins, had taken care of him at home during a short illness. The cheerful six-foot-two West Virginia native fit in well with the household. Bunny tracked Collins down—the nurse was now living in Oklahoma—and hired her full-time to take care of Paul, giving the nurse, her husband, and her two children a rent-free house on Rokeby Farm, right near the greenhouses and plane runway.

————

That June, Hubert de Givenchy announced that he was retiring at the age of sixty-eight. He had built his couture salon, launched in 1952, into such a monolithic success that the company was worth $45 million when he sold it to Louis Vuitton in 1988, staying on to run it.

But the world of high fashion had peaked, and there were fewer grande dames like Bunny who were willing to pay six-figure sums for yearly couture wardrobes. Givenchy's parting with the new owners of his company was wrenching. The designer was given no say in the selection of his successor—Vuitton chose bad-boy British designer John Galliano—and Givenchy was informed by press release.

Givenchy used his farewell interview with *WWD* to salute his two favorite clients: "I've met the most extraordinary people, like Audrey Hepburn and Mrs. Mellon. But now that's changing and it's time to go."

The designer, who had been named president of the World Monuments Fund France, announced that he would devote his time to restoring the twenty-two-acre king's kitchen garden, the Potager du Roi, at Versailles. He asked Bunny to help. "She is fascinated by this enormous potager," he told me. "Paul and Bunny are very generous to give a lot of money to restore the Potager and restore Versailles." Bunny met with the Versailles gardeners as they began to replant the beds, and she convinced Paul to underwrite the cost of fixing the central water basin and fountain.

At the gala for the garden's reopening, she was honored with La Croix d'Officier de l'Ordre des Arts et des Lettres by Jean-Pierre Babelon, director-general of Versailles. All the workers stood up and clapped when she received the award.

Bunny was in a mischievous mood that night. Even in her eighties, she still liked to play games with the men in her life, trying to stir up rivalries. At the dinner, Bunny was seated next to Hubert de Givenchy at the head table, but shortly after the event began, she got up and moved to another table to join her friend, antiques dealer Akko van Acker. As he recalls with a laugh, "Hubert was furious that she sat with me."

One of the great sadnesses of old age is witnessing the mounting toll of loved ones in the obituary columns. Bunny's friend Evangeline Bruce, the wife of David Bruce, died in December 1995. A month later, Bunny's British ward, David Brooke, the Earl of Warwick, died at age sixty-one. Aware of his impending death, he sent her a note: "I look with great affection on the American part of my life & my time with you. You could not have been sweeter & I must have been a trial when you had to look after me yourself."

Weary and depressed, Bunny confided to Hubert de Givenchy that she was feeling her age. He tried to cheer her up in a phone call. "You said the most attractive thing yesterday," she wrote to him later in a fax. "When I said 'I was like an old ice box with broken wires,' you said, 'No, like a music box who has lost some notes.' That was charming and adorable of you—made me very happy."

She scribbled down his words of wisdom on a notepad. "Hubert's thoughts: 'It's never too late to be chic and pick yourself up.'"

Her spirits improved during her summers on Cape Cod with Paul. The couple seemed to get along better there, or at least that was the staff's impression. Bunny and Paul usually arrived in July, and the Cape served as a base until mid-September, although Paul might jet off to the racetrack in Saratoga or to New York for a business meeting, and Bunny might spend a day in Nantucket or visit Eliza at Little Compton. They almost always had houseguests; John Baskett and Akko van Acker were among the regulars. Chef Rudolph Stanish, who first began working for the couple in the 1960s and had become known as "the omelet king" for the rich and famous, usually joined the household staff for a few weeks.

Paul was an early riser, and he faxed his breakfast order to the kitchen; Bunny used the bell to let the staff know that she was awake. She liked to read the papers and lounge in bed; Paul would sometimes pop in to show her transparencies of artwork. Even though they were donating and selling some paintings, they were also still collecting.

They both liked to sail, but they never headed out on the water together. They did not want to spend twenty-four hours side by side. Chester Crosby, a local boatbuilder, had accompanied them for many years, but in 1982 he had passed the job to his thirteen-year-old grandson, Ned Crosby.

Ned had become a fixture in the Mellons' summer life. Several times a week, depending on the weather, Ned would take Bunny out around 9:15 a.m., waiting for her at the dock. "It was so peaceful, all you'd hear were the terns. I'd see her blue hat walking along the path and she'd slowly come into view. I can hear her high-pitched voice: 'Neddy, good morning, how are you?' We had a routine of how we left the dock that my grandfather had shown me. She would tack down the river, which is pretty narrow."

In the afternoon, he would take Paul Mellon out on a different boat. Crosby noticed that the couple kept an eye out for each other. "If we sailed by the house in the morning, Mrs. would look and say, 'Oh, there's Paul,' he'd open the windows and wave to her. Every time we sailed past the house in the afternoon, Mr. Mellon would get the air horn in the hope of seeing Mrs. Mellon. There wasn't a time when we sailed past the house that they weren't looking to see if the other happened to be looking out."

When Eliza sailed over from Little Compton, Bunny would ask Crosby to go back with her on the forty-mile trip to make sure she was safe. "I'd see them together a lot," Crosby recalls. "Or Mrs. Mellon would say, 'Eliza and I are thinking...' I remember thinking they had turned into best friends." Tuffy Lloyd would come to the Cape for a few weeks, usually with his two sons. "I'd always go see her in the morning," recalls her grandson Stacy Lloyd IV. "She'd have all this stuff on the bed, books, newspaper articles, she might as well have been sleeping in a single bed."

Bunny took daily walks in her garden with its towers of sweet peas, cosmos, dark blue Sea Breeze salvia, zinnias, pots of delphinium and nasturtium. She liked lima bean sandwiches, fresh from the vegetable garden. If chief gardener Lisa Rockwell was on her hands and knees weeding, she could nonetheless sense Bunny's presence, recalling, "You could smell her because she wore Givenchy perfume—she's around."

Bunny had very strong feelings about the look of her gardens. "We did 'phlox of sheep' one year," Lisa says. "She walked into the garden and I asked, 'What do you think?' She said, 'It looks like old ladies' underwear.' She hadn't taken two steps out of the garden before we began tearing it out of the ground and putting something else in."

For the staff, it was challenging to work on the Mellons' gardens and lawns because Bunny had unconventional demands. "When we cut the grass, she'd want it raked into piles because it looked kind of farm-y," says Chris Harvie, a caretaker. "We had to leave the apples under the trees. It's a real pain when you're mowing and attracting bees but she liked a natural look."

Housepainter Ronald Brumsfield says that Bunny did not want ordinary paint colors. "She'd point to a house where the paint job was probably fifty years old and say she wanted it to look like that," he recalls. "We'd paint it white and then gray and yellow, with each one showing through. I was up at their garage one day, scraping off the loose paint. I got a call saying, don't repaint it, she liked the way it looked."

In September 1996, as Hurricane Edouard approached Cape Cod, Bunny refused to let her staff board up the house. John Kennedy Jr. was en route with his fiancée, Carolyn Bessette. "Trees were bending over, we were racing the clock," recalls Chris Harvie. "Mrs. Mellon said, 'I don't care if there's a hurricane.'"

Bunny had a special affinity for the handsome young man, so reminiscent of his father, and he treated her like a family member. "John loved Bun but he talked back to her," recalls Virginia Warner. "He'd say things like, 'Oh, come on Bun, what do you mean by that?' He teased her. He appreciated her." As Susan Cabral, the Cape Cod housekeeper, recalls, "They were like mother and son. She thought the world of him."

Driving over from Hyannis, John arrived in time for a brief visit. His wedding was coming up in a few weeks, and he wanted to introduce his bride-to-be to Bunny. Once the couple left, the staff was allowed to ready the house for the gale winds.

Bunny loved storms. She and Paul would send their private plane away to avoid potential damage, but they would stay put with their generators and their staff, listening to the howls of nature.

Four days after Hurricane Edouard, Bunny accompanied Eliza to the Virginia Lynch Gallery in Tiverton, Rhode Island, to see a show of Eliza's work. Despite the small-town venue, this was a prestigious gallery that showcased works by artist Chuck Close and glassblower Dale Chihuly.

Virginia Lynch was impressed by Eliza's paintings. "I looked at her slides and liked them very much," she later wrote. "They told me that here was an artist who was extremely sensitive and unusual in her approach to expressing her feelings about beauty, about form, and their relationship to the world around us."

Bunny was proud of her daughter, sending a note to Virginia Lynch thanking her for a wonderful afternoon at the gallery. "Never has Eliza's work been so carefully hung," Bunny wrote. "She cares and tries with such faith and courage that it is rare to see her understood with sensitivity and respect."

Tuffy Lloyd had watched the evolving relationship between his mother and his sister. "I think Eliza was very close to Mother in terms of temperament. I don't think she was the perfectionist that Mother was. Her paintings reflect an abstract quality that goes more into the essence of things—like wind and light. It wasn't an attempt to capture the detail that Mother had in her consciousness."

Paul Mellon was winding down parts of his life. He sold his thirty-thousand-square-foot Washington house at 3041 Whitehaven Street. National Gallery director Earl Powell received an invitation to lunch there with Paul, prior to the moving-out date. "He had a famous butler, Oliver Murray, he was there and handed me a big martini and a list of paintings and works of art in the house," Powell told me. He recalled that the butler stated: "Mr. Mellon would like you to look at this, anything you see on the walls that is not on the list that you want, let me know." The National Gallery received a total of eighty-five artworks from Paul's collection.

When Paul and Bunny went to Cape Cod for a week in April 1997, the staff noted that he spent most of the time in his room, eating meals from a tray. While looking after her husband, she was simultaneously trying to cheer up her dearest friend. "Hubert, you are not an 'Old man', don't say this," she wrote to Givenchy in Paris. "It upsets me to hear you say it. Your kind of glamour never dies."

Paul turned ninety years old on June 11, and Bunny gave him a birthday lunch on their Virginia farm at the Brick House, the large Georgian mansion that he had built for his first wife and converted into a private art gallery. Bunny's son, Tuffy, says, "She decorated the Brick House and it was just splendid, with simple but pretty wild-flowers, nice silverware, linen tables, good wine." Family members were amused that Bunny graciously included one of Paul's "special friends." As Lavinia Currier recalls, "Even at Paul's ninetieth birthday, there was a young woman there that he was obviously affectionate with."

Paul had frequently missed celebrating Bunny's August 9 birthday, but this year he was with her in Cape Cod along with Bunny's two children for a picnic at the beach house, the same beach house where, so many years ago, JFK had asked her to design the Rose Garden.

For decades, Bunny and Paul had independently circled the globe, sending each other letters professing their love. Now that Paul was ill, he was dependent on his wife, and she devoted herself to his care. The staff noticed a renewed sweetness and affection between them.

Aware that his time was running out, Paul was nonetheless still revising his will, advised by attorneys at Sullivan & Cromwell. Alex Forger, who had returned to private practice after serving as president of the Legal Services Corporation, agreed to represent Bunny in the negotiations as well as establish a law office to handle her needs. As the negotiations dragged on, Bunny fretted about how much money she would receive from Paul.

As a welcome distraction from Paul's illness, Bunny embraced opportunities for recognition. She allowed the British magazine *Country Life* to photograph her library and her garden for two glowing features that ran in December 1997 and January 1998. She was not quoted directly in the articles, but the writer, Christopher Ridgway, used such phrases as "Mrs. Mellon believes," conveying that they had spent time together.

Ridgway was charmed by the seemingly artless but rigorously orchestrated elements of her garden, writing, "The tapestry of this area lends itself to a sense of a formal garden gone wild: plants are allowed to grow between the cracks in the brick terrace, but the shrubs and trees, including the holly are clipped."

Concerned about her library's future, Bunny invited the National Gallery director Earl Powell and executive librarian Neal Turtell to lunch at the farm to see if they might be interested in taking over the library. "Paul was ill at that point," Turtell told me. At Bunny's invitation, he began visiting the library once a month to learn about the collection.

"Bunny would either join us for lunch or at least come by and say a few words to me. She wanted to make sure I understood it wasn't simply a botanical or horticulture collection but a collection of imagination and exploration." He asked why she had first editions of Mark Twain's work, and she replied, "Remember Neal, this is a library of exploration and these are young people, Tom Sawyer and Huckleberry Finn, who are exploring their lives."

Bunny was still collecting. "I was there one day and there was an auction in London," Turtell says. "She said to me, 'I may have to interrupt you because I'm waiting for the results in London.' She's on the phone. Her eyes started widening, she got this great big smile on her face. 'Yes, I got it!' "

Despite the National Gallery's long history with the Mellon family, museum officials turned down the offer for Bunny's library. As National Gallery director Earl Powell says, "The idea just ran its course. It didn't make a lot of sense."

Paul's health was now seriously deteriorating. During a rare trip to Manhattan, he stopped at Verdura to buy one last present for Dorcas. "He was quite ill," Verdura owner Ward Landrigan recalls. "He didn't want to sit down, he'd lean on the back of a sofa."

Yet Paul valued his enduring relationship with Bunny. They celebrated their fiftieth wedding anniversary on May 1, 1998, over lunch at the farm, joined by Paul's son, Tim, and Bunny's daughter, Eliza. Eliza created a fanciful Maypole with garlands of ribbons and flowers. At the end of the festivities, Paul Mellon confided to his nurse, Nancy Collins, "I'm so glad I stayed married to Bunny."

Bunny charted Paul's decline in her journal with entries such as "Paul down and not well. Wish I could cope better" and "Hubert called, gave me a lift." She arranged for a ramp and stairwell chairlift to be installed at their Cape Cod home. "She was just very thoughtful, so caring," says John Baskett. "Admittedly, she had a lot of staff, but she made sure everything was done correctly."

During Baskett's annual visit to the couple in Antigua, Paul made an unusual request. "He wanted me to give him his injections of morphine. I said, 'I'll kill you if I do it wrong.' He said the nurse can teach you to do it. Bunny said she didn't like sticking needles in people's arms. Some people are like that but it didn't bother me. So I was allowed to perform these kinds of roles."

Paul tried to be stoic, but the pain and the illness wore him down. In her journal, Bunny described a frightening trip to the hospital during a snowstorm in Virginia. "Paul was too weak to care about life. We drove him through a blizzard making new tracks in the snow...the driver barely out of his teens. His youthful outlook gave me confidence that we would see beyond the blinding snow hurled by winds to reach the hospital." At the medical facility, Paul's doctors warned Bunny about the "frightening possibilities." She resorted to prayer: "Searched for a glimmer of hope with the power and belief in God."

Thirty-six hours later, Paul had revived. Bunny decided to go ahead with plans for a trip to Antigua to meet Hubert de Givenchy, his friend Philippe Venet, and a Frenchwoman, Helene. Bunny had been looking forward to the break from Paul's sickbed: "Fear + aloneness had been a frightening cloud for days," she wrote in her journal. "Now H would be here, his warmth and affection."

But once she arrived in Antigua, Bunny felt guilty, writing, "One part of me was still in the hospital, the other searching for strength, all the while working on being friend, hostess + fighting tiredness."

John Baskett accompanied Paul to the Winchester Hospital in June 1998 for his checkup. "He finally had a really delightful and very good surgeon," Baskett recalls. "Paul said, 'I want to know how long I am going to live, for the dispensation of my will.' The doctor said, 'You'll be fine, Mr. Mellon, until Christmas. Just after Christmas you won't feel well and six weeks later you'll be dead.' Paul didn't turn a hair."

That summer on Cape Cod, Paul was too weak to go out on the

boat, so instead he sat and talked with Ned Crosby, his sailing companion. Tired of the harsh medical regimen, he said that he was now taking only palliative drugs. "Mr. Mellon told me he had stopped taking his medication, he couldn't live with the pain and the uncertainty, he said the heck with it." Crosby recalls, pausing to wipe away a tear. "He was going to live the rest of his life and be comfortable."

For the wealthy, death and money are inevitably intertwined. Paul Mellon still had not signed off on a new will. Bunny was infuriated by his lawyers' proposals, writing in her journal in October 1998 that they were "really nasty about Paul helping me. Can't believe how awful...v. deceitful to me. Cried my heart out."

Paul eventually agreed to give Bunny virtually all of their real estate and many cherished paintings, including seven canvases by Mark Rothko, five paintings and three gouaches by Richard Diebenkorn, two paintings by Georges Braque, and works by Henri Rousseau, Nicolas de Staël, Claude Monet, and Joan Miró. Paul gave her a life interest in dozens of other artworks—including twelve paintings and sketches by Winslow Homer, ten sumptuous paintings by Pierre Bonnard, thirteen artworks by Georges Seurat, and works by Cézanne, Degas, and Sargent—that would go to the National Gallery after her death. But she still did not know how much money she would receive.

Bunny tried to make note of anything positive. "Beautiful Day," she wrote in her journal on October 25. "Tired but rested, went to Library. Eliza called. V. proud of her and all she does." Two days later, she added, "Eliza's Birthday. In Paris, she sounds v. happy."

In November, Bunny called John Baskett in London and urged him to come to Virginia to see Paul. "She knew it was coming. She was upset, obviously, and she was in tears when she spoke to me on the phone about it," Baskett says. He flew over for a final visit and was impressed by Paul's lack of self-pity. "He kept a rather jolly attitude even though he was weak. The butler later told me, 'You might like to know Mr. Mellon wept after you departed.'"

Paul had been thinking for several years about what would happen at the end of his life, telling an interviewer at one point that he did not fear dying. "I would like to believe in life after death but I don't,"

Paul said. "I've had so much pleasure in my life that it doesn't bother me that I'm not going to exist afterwards. Anyway, I feel like when I'm in the country in Virginia and sometimes when I'm in England that I'm in heaven. I have had heaven already."

Paul was bedridden at the couple's Virginia home when the lawyers convened to discuss the remaining items in his will. Paul had ordered a new plane several years ago that had not yet been delivered, and his attorneys were insisting that Bunny should pay for it. Alex Forger, Bunny's lawyer, pressed Paul and he conceded, "That's not right, she should get the plane." Bunny was due to inherit the couple's Manhattan residence at 125 East Seventieth Street but not the nearby ten-thousand-square-foot carriage house; Paul agreed to leave her that property, too.

The issue of money came up again: Paul planned to give Bunny $85 million. That was a significant sum, but Bunny's lawyer pointed out that it was not enough to underwrite the lifestyle that Bunny was used to. "I should raise it," Paul acknowledged. As Forger recalled, "I asked for another $25 million. I didn't want to push my luck." Paul agreed to the sum, and signed his final will on November 19.

Bunny was so involved with her husband's care that Paul's doctor finally told her that she needed a break. She flew to Cape Cod but returned to Virginia within twenty-four hours, writing in her journal, "felt I should come home to Paul." Bunny noted in her journal that she was very calm and so depressed that she "could not move." But she tried to put up a good front. During the Christmas season, she put on a red dressing gown to greet Paul in festive fashion and sat by his bedside, showing him the holiday cards they had received. New Year's came and went, and as nurse Nancy Collins recalls, "Mr. Mellon hung on."

In late January, Eliza flew in to be at her stepfather's bedside and comfort her mother. The two women were in and out of Paul's room during the final hours. At around 11 a.m., on February 1, 1999, he died almost exactly to the date that his doctor had prophesied.

The encomiums poured in. A PATRON SAINT WHO GAVE AS GOOD AS HE GOT was the headline in the *Wall Street Journal*, as writer Eric Gibson praised Paul's "inherited sense of noblesse oblige." The *Wash-*

ington Post was equally reverential: PAUL MELLON'S GREATEST GIFT: THE PHILANTHROPIST LEFT BEHIND A FINE EXAMPLE OF THE ART OF LIVING. The *New York Times* saluted him in an editorial for his gifts to the National Gallery and Yale, and for saving the shoreline of Cape Hatteras. "He loved horses, he loved art, he loved books. He would have been the first to say that life does not offer riches greater than such things." *Newsweek* opined that "he embodied an entrepreneurial philanthropy that is peculiarly American and he leaves a land dotted with the monuments to the use of private means for public good."

The funeral was held at Trinity Episcopal Church in Upperville. Putting together the guest list, Bunny deferred to what she believed were her husband's wishes. As John Baskett recalls, "Bunny generously invited Dorcas to the funeral, and Dorcas, equally correctly, thanked her and declined. Which I thought was admirable behavior on both of their parts." Bunny then went one step further. "Do you know about the gracious thing that Bunny did?" asks Marie Ridder, one of Paul's riding companions who attended the funeral. "She invited Dorcas's children to Paul Mellon's funeral and put them right up front."

That frigid February, Bunny left for Cape Cod, a place where she could be left alone to grieve. "We had a huge snowstorm, and she seemed good," recalls Chris Harvie, a caretaker. "She came within a week of his passing. She seemed like herself." Even though Bunny was in good health, she asked Nancy Collins to stay on, aware that she might need her services someday. "I was really a companion," Collins says, "but also a nurse."

Paul Mellon's bequests sent joy through the philanthropic world. The National Gallery and Yale each received $75 million, with 230 paintings divided between the two institutions; the Virginia Museum of Art received $10 million and a Van Gogh. Paul left $20 million to Carnegie Mellon University; $10 million to his alma mater, Choate Rosemary Hall; $8 million to Cambridge University; and $5 million to St. John's College. He gave Dead Neck Island in Osterville, across from his Cape Cod home, to the Massachusetts Audubon Society along with $500,000. He left two paintings to his former daughter-in-law Louise Whitney Mellon.

But while these recipients of Paul's largesse were celebrating, Bunny immediately began worrying about whether she would have enough money. She began pinching pennies in ludicrous ways. She demanded that the staff turn off the lights to save on electricity whenever she left a room. She cut back on the outlay for her gardens.

As Virginia gardener George Shaffer recalls, "Mrs. Mellon called me, after things had settled, and asked her [me to help her] save money. She didn't have the money Mr. Mellon had. I had a list of what we were growing, I met with her, we went through the list." She trimmed her gardening budget by 10 percent. Yet she thought nothing of dispatching her private plane on minor errands or keeping all of her properties fully staffed although she rarely spent time in them.

At nearly ninety years old, Bunny was now in charge as Paul's lawyers disengaged from decision-making responsibilities. On February 26, she sent a letter to the staff, saying that she was changing the name of the property from Rokeby Farm to Oak Spring Farm, and she would be making decisions about which properties to keep.

Comfortable with her Manhattan-based attorney, Alex Forger, now seventy-six years old, she asked him to supervise her far-flung properties and handle her legal affairs; he brought in additional staff. To accommodate the legal team, Bunny purchased office space on a high floor in the Essex House, a Central Park South hotel with sweeping views of the park.

Paul and Bunny had relied for many years on New York accountant Kenneth Starr to handle their taxes, pay their bills, and even invest some of their money. The Bronx-born, Queens College–educated accountant, the son of a high school principal, was an unlikely choice for this aristocratic family, but Paul had admired Starr's hardworking and eager-to-please persona. Bunny was fond of him, and her son used Starr's services as well. Given his name, people sometimes mistakenly believed that he was the other Kenneth Starr—the Washington, D.C., independent counsel whose zealous pursuit of Bill Clinton's sex life triggered the impeachment drama.

The ability to drop the Mellon name had helped the accountant Kenneth Starr build a prosperous business with such clients as Mike

Nichols; author Kati Marton and her diplomat husband, Richard Holbrooke; and actors Sylvester Stallone, Al Pacino, and Joan Stanton, who had played Lois Lane in the radio show *The Adventures of Superman* and whose daughter, Jane Stanton Hitchcock, had been married to Paul Mellon's cousin. Paul Mellon had believed that Kenneth Starr was reliable and trustworthy and that was all many people felt they needed to know.

Starr had begun raising large pools of money from clients and making what he promised would be gold-plated investments. Bunny had counted on Starr before her husband's death but now she relied on him even more, giving him power of attorney to manage her millions and pay her bills.

Eliza began to spend more time on the Virginia farm and immersed herself in learning the day-to-day minutiae, eager to help her widowed mother. "Eliza would be here, with her pencil and pen, asking questions, looking to see what was going on, how things were done," Shaffer says. "She was going through a learning process."

Eliza took Nancy Collins aside one day, urging her to take good care of Bunny, and passing along a phone number. "She's all I've got," Eliza told the nurse. "If something happens, I want you to call me."

Making a break with her own past, in 1998, Eliza sold the Barrow Street house that she had shared with Doris Sanders and then purchased the entire top twelfth floor of a Greenwich Village coop. The 1909 limestone building at 30 Tenth Street featured sunny loft-like spaces with soaring ceilings. With more than three thousand square feet at her disposal, Eliza had ample room for her painting studio as well as living space.

When Bunny was awarded an honorary degree from the Rhode Island School of Design that June, Eliza accompanied her to the ceremony along with Alex Forger. Deprived by her father of the opportunity to attend college, Bunny looked jubilant in a photograph as she stood onstage in her black cap and gown. She was so pleased by the honor that she eventually gave $1 million to the school for scholarships to be named in honor of art gallery owner Virginia Lynch.

After the ceremony, Bunny joined her daughter for a few days at

Eliza's vacation home at Little Compton. But the respite was marred when Bunny fell and broke her wrist. Hard as it was for her to accept, her age was showing.

She was no longer surprised when contemporaries died, but she was rocked that summer by the death by a beloved and much younger friend. John Kennedy Jr., piloting a plane from New Jersey to Martha's Vineyard, became disoriented and crashed into the ocean. Kennedy, his wife, Carolyn Bessette, and her sister Lauren perished. "Bun was inconsolable," recalls Virginia Warner. "I called and she could barely speak. She loved him so much."

That fall, Bunny and Eliza went to Paris together. After years of strife, they were enjoying each other's company. Eliza felt that she was making a breakthrough as an artist. She had been painting abstracts for decades, but now she had switched to taking photographs. Ashton Hawkins, the executive vice president of the Metropolitan Museum, wrote to Bunny to say that he had visited Eliza at her loft and found her current work to be "interesting + beautiful. I am proud of her."

As Eliza's half brother Robin Lloyd recalls, "She began to photograph patterns, such as a grate in a storm gutter. I think she felt she was on to something. There was a certain mystical, supernatural, otherworldly aspect of what she photographed. She called them clouds or angels. Maybe she felt she was looking into another way of seeing the world, what she was representing in her photographs. Some people in the art world thought she was on to a new direction and was finding her voice as an artist."

Eliza reconnected after nearly thirty years with a friend from youth who had attended her debutante party—William Brooks, who was working at the Virginia Lynch Gallery. "I have a self-portrait that she took, in the mirror. Her art was very abstract," says Brooks, now the director of the Sheldon Museum in Vermont. Brooks spent a day in New York with Eliza that fall, attending the Outsider Art Exhibit. "We had a great time, we went to the show, walked around New York, she bought a piece of art. We went back to the apartment and she cooked me dinner. It was a wonderful New York day. Obviously Eliza had all sorts of advantages, but she wasn't ostentatious, she was simple in the way she approached life, a very genuine person."

Bunny spent her first Christmas without Paul, with Eliza. On Christmas Eve, her daughter brought in a large box that had been left out front addressed to Bunny. Inside were dozens of lilies of the valley and violets—spring flowers, a hopeful reminder of the season ahead—from Robert Isabell.

The floral designer was coming off another triumph, decorating the White House for President Bill and Hillary Clinton. The previous year, Isabell had put up a six-hundred-pound, twenty-four-foot fir wreath with blue hand-dipped bulbs for the White House South Portico. This year, he had created eight towering cone-shaped wire topiary trees for the Grand Foyer.

Bunny invited him to her Upper East Side house for a drink. Charming and shy, he was almost as knowledgeable about flowers as she was. As Bunny later recalled, Isabell asked her, "Can I be your special friend?" Suddenly, the New Year seemed full of possibilities.

Black Willow

Chapter Twenty-Four

Enduring the Unendurable

Manhattan's flower district in the West Twenties radiates an old-fashioned feeling. In the morning, vendors place the latest blossoms in buckets outside their shops as trucks roll by, making cacophonous sounds. Robert Isabell walked through the area en route to work, usually pausing to pick out flowers to send to Bunny via Federal Express. As his staffer Joe Heffernan recalls, "We all memorized her address since he sent her a few stems every day."

Their friendship, nearly fifteen years in the making, had come alive. "Robert started talking about Bunny Mellon, and then it really blossomed to a real relationship," says Ian Schrager, the hotelier and former Studio 54 owner. Illustrator Cathy Barancik Graham, one of Isabell's closest friends, recalls, "He was completely enamored with her. He knew so many people, but this was a connection aesthetically. She had an extraordinary eye, as did Robert, and a great love of nature and beauty. That's what I think they connected so deeply on."

Bunny marveled that Robert had gotten past her defenses, telling him in a note, "The gardeners must have planted me too deep! But light is creeping in!" Bunny described a flower that he had sent her as looking "like a wide-awake smile."

They spoke by phone twice a day, morning and evening. She sent him wooden crates filled with flowers and vegetables from her greenhouses and gardens, along with notes like: "So many things are 'better' + know it's your magic thinking + flowers, will try my witchcraft for you."

They were an unlikely pair: the pillar of WASP society and the boy from Duluth who frequented New York's notorious gay nightclub, the Mineshaft, an anything-goes, heavy-leather emporium.

Robert Isabell had become famous for creating extravagant events, such as the lavish fiftieth birthday party for Wall Street buccaneer Saul Steinberg, who had been buying up Old Masters by the truckload. Isabell transformed a party tent at Steinberg's Hamptons beach home into a scene resembling a seventeenth-century Flemish eating house with nude models posing in tableaus of famous paintings by Vermeer and Rembrandt.

"He was the first one that all of New York society went to, for a wedding, a gala, a private party," *Vogue* editor Anna Wintour told the *New York Times.* "If you could afford him, he was a great magician. All the great society hostesses—Pat Buckley, Annette de la Renta—used him, and because they used him, all the others wanted to use him." Yet, like Bunny, Isabell could be elusive, enjoying the advance work for his events but preferring to watch from the sidelines rather than mingle with the guests.

Bunny was turning ninety on August 9, 2000. Eliza asked Robert Isabell to plan a surprise party on Cape Cod. Friends noticed that Eliza had begun to reflect elements of her mother's style. Excited about her new work, she was eager to land another show. "I went to look at her photographs with my husband, who runs an art gallery," says Dita Amory, Bunny's former librarian turned curator at the Metropolitan Museum, recalling an April visit to Eliza's loft. "We had a wonderful time. She served us radishes. There was a table full of fruits and vases and plants, it was perfection. It was Mrs. Mellon revisited."

Eliza was developing a new philanthropic art project with Diane Brown, a former art gallery owner. Friends since 1992, they met when Eliza took a tour that Diane was leading of the Venice Biennale. "My marriage was ending, her relationship was ending, we'd talk and commiserate," says Diane. Their new venture began after Diane confided to Eliza about her moment of terror while going through a CAT scan. "I was really afraid, and the only way I could get out is I imagined a painting going across the ceiling, and I felt like I wasn't even there,"

Brown says. She suggested to Eliza that they create a foundation to install art in hospitals. Eliza enthusiastically agreed to come up with seed money for what would become RxArt.

On Thursday, May 4, 2000, the two women celebrated signing the incorporation paperwork, going to dinner at the FireBird, a festive Russian restaurant on West Forty-Sixth Street. "Eliza loved Cole Porter music and somebody was singing it that night, and she was superexcited and it was super fun." Eliza mentioned how pleased she was about her mother's new friendship. "She talked about Robert, how he and her mother were kindred spirits."

That weekend, Bunny flew to Chicago for her grandson Stacy IV's graduation from Lake Forest College. She had invited Eliza to join them, but her daughter begged off. That Saturday, Diane Brown called Eliza to invite her to watch the Kentucky Derby together. Eliza's answering machine picked up with the cheerful message: "Hi! I'm gone but I'll be back." When Brown did not get a return call, she says, "I thought, she's got something else."

No one could reach Eliza that day or evening. She was not at home or picking up messages. It took more than twenty-four hours before her family and friends were able to piece together where she was and what had happened.

At 11 a.m. that Saturday morning, Eliza had left her home on foot and headed ten blocks south to Houston Street. Obeying the traffic signal, she began to cross the street when suddenly a truck barreled into her. "From what I was told, she was crossing the road and the truck didn't see her," says Robin Lloyd, her half brother. "It turned right and going at sufficient speed, hit her. She was thrown back against something hard and metallic, I think her head hit a bench."

An ambulance brought her to nearby St. Vincent's Hospital, where the unconscious Eliza was given a CAT scan. At 2:30 p.m. the chief resident on duty, Dr. Kraig Moore, looked at the results, examined Eliza, and came to the determination that she was brain-dead, according to subsequent trial testimony. He claimed that he passed on his diagnosis by phone to the attending physician on call, Dr. Ahmed Rawanduzy, and they decided it was pointless to do surgery.

Eliza's driver's license listed her former Barrow Street address; she had not gotten around to updating her license to reflect her new home on Tenth Street. The authorities reportedly tried the Barrow Street address and were unable to track down a family contact. Thus there was no relative on hand to demand a second opinion.

It was Sunday around lunchtime when Eliza's New York housekeeper was informed about the accident and called Bunny's Virginia home. Nancy Collins came up to Bunny's bedroom to break the news. Collins was so distraught that before she could say anything, Bunny knew something was wrong, asking whether something had happened to Nancy's husband. "No," the nurse replied, "it's Eliza. There's been an accident."

"How bad?" Bunny asked. "Critical," Collins replied. Bunny told the nurse to go home, pack a bag, and return as soon as possible so they could leave for New York. Her private plane was being serviced, so she had to go to Dulles Airport, accompanied by the nurse, to fly commercial.

By the time Bunny got to Manhattan, Robert Isabell had located a prominent neurosurgeon, Dr. Jamshid Ghajar of the Cornell Medical Clinic, who had been profiled in the *New Yorker* for his innovative techniques. He examined Eliza early Sunday evening and immediately recommended surgery to remove a hematoma pressing on her brain. She was transferred to another hospital and he operated that night. "Everyone was in shock," says Diane Brown, who saw Bunny at the hospital. "Everyone was hopeful."

Eliza came out of her unconscious state and was able to open her eyes. But she had suffered severe brain damage. She would never speak or walk or use her arms again. Unable to communicate by any means, she would need twenty-four-hour care for the rest of her life.

A jury would later rule that St. Vincent's Hospital and the two doctors who saw Eliza there had committed medical malpractice. Dr. Ghajar testified that if the doctors had intervened immediately, the outcome might have been different.

"Her injuries were on her right side, language and comprehension on the left side. No evidence of severe damage on the left side," he told the jury. "What really did her in was having this big clot, blood clot sitting and pushing her brain over and squashing her brain over this period of time. The earlier it's taken out the better chance of a good outcome."

This once-vibrant woman would now be fed through a feeding tube. Just how much brain function she retained was unknowable, but Bunny seized on any reaction by her daughter as a sign that Eliza was fighting to break through. Bunny needed to believe that with enough prayer and the right treatment, her daughter would recover.

At the hospital, Bunny got an additional sad surprise, discovering that Eliza had been treated for breast cancer. It pained Bunny that her daughter had kept the news from her and that she had been unable to help at that time.

Bunny's friends rallied around. "The great love of her life for Bunny was her daughter Eliza," says Hubert de Givenchy. "It was a terrible thing when Eliza had her accident in New York. Bunny suffered so much for all those years…she thought Eliza would one day recover and be better. It was a terrible thing." Akko van Acker joined Bunny in New York, sitting with her in the hospital by Eliza's side during several visits. "Bunny was a very strong woman," he says. "I never saw her crying although she was very sad. She didn't show her emotions."

There were difficult decisions to be made. Eliza was transferred to a rehabilitation facility in Alexandria, Virginia. Bunny visited daily, but the lengthy round-trip on traffic-clogged roads was exhausting. She did not want to leave Eliza in an institutional setting, so she renovated the sunny house, Spring Hill, on her property, which had been built by landscape architect Perry Wheeler. "We made it really pretty," recalls painter Malcolm Robson. "We striated walls and painted the floors. Mrs. Mellon wanted to make it as pretty as possible, because she was certain that even though Eliza couldn't communicate, it would be nice for her."

Bunny spent her ninetieth birthday, August 9, on Cape Cod. Robert Isabell had gone ahead with the surprise party that he and Eliza had planned. He welded a cast-iron canopy bed and set it in the middle of a field of wildflowers. A pale "Bunny blue" coverlet completed the romantic picture, with floating white curtains that fell onto the grass like wedding trains.

Bunny lounged on the bed that afternoon, greeting her son, Tuffy, along with Caroline Kennedy and her children, Tatiana and Jack; Mike Nichols and Diane Sawyer; playwright Wendy Wasserstein; lawyers Alex Forger and Jane MacLennan; Ken Starr, her financial adviser, and his third wife, Marisa.

Bunny tried to put aside her sorrows. As Diane Brown says, "A surprise party in a field of wildflowers, people who came from all over— you have to enjoy the moment."

Bunny jotted down highlights in her journal: "Children with Cokes in bathing suits...Kenneth wandering around with basket...Stacy and 'power hug,' Jack holding parasol over his mother's head, Tatiana playing the harpsichord...Alex giving me a daisy to count the petals, Robert in his blue shirt + jeans, Mike passing food with elegance...Moon coming up. Ospreys fishing, sail boat going by, bed curtains blowing in the wind like a sail boat."

Her old life was over. Her elegant Paris apartment would remain vacant. Now Bunny stayed close to home. Each afternoon she would drive her BMW over to see Eliza, sit in the room, and knit quilts and sweaters as classical music played in the background. Concerned that Eliza might feel claustrophobic, Bunny had aides put her in a converted van and drive her around the countryside. Bunny hired every type of medical provider—physical therapist, music therapist, speech therapist, other specialists—to see if Eliza could communicate with the blink of an eye or the tap of a toe. She even brought in a psychic. "Bunny became very spiritual," says Lavinia Currier, Paul Mellon's grand-niece. "She was trying to feel what was going on in the other world." But nothing tangible improved.

Bunny encouraged visitors. Paul Leonard sat by Eliza's bed, talking softly of happier times. Robin Lloyd, Eliza's half brother, called frequently, since the nurses thought Eliza might recognize his voice. Eliza's brother, Tuffy, visited along with his sons. Diane Brown brought her daughter Sarah Brown, *Vogue*'s beauty editor. William Brooks, who had known Eliza since her debutante party, made the trip, recalling, "I was shocked because she couldn't talk, she couldn't move very much. I just said hello and talked, carried on a soliloquy about how we met and how much I loved her."

Frank Langella recalled that Bunny refused to give up, telling him, "Frank, I know it. I just know it. She is coming back to us." Bunny's nephew and niece, Peter Fleming and Lily Lambert Norton, made the pilgrimage. "To me, it was heartbreaking," says Lily. "When you were around Bunny with Eliza, she was, 'Come on, you can do it, you can come out of it.' They tried everything you could even think of, hoping there would be some magic." Eliza appeared to perk up for a moment when Peter spoke to her in French, but no one could tell whether anything got through.

John Baskett flew in from England. "Bunny said, 'You must go see her,'" he says. "I walked into the room and she looked terrible, pipes everywhere, head back, one eye looking this way and one eye the other. I was so shattered that I burst into tears, unfortunately. I was ushered out of the room."

How do you endure the unendurable? For Bunny, every day was a profile in courage as she confronted her inability to bring her daughter back from the abyss. "I had war, and war changed my life," she told Nancy Collins. "Eliza being hit is no different than war. You have no choice." Bunny befriended Dr. Jamshid Ghajar, donating roughly a million dollars to his medical research into brain injuries. The physician visited to monitor Eliza's care, and Bunny offered him the use of her Nantucket home.

"Bunny was my muse," Dr. Ghajar later recalled. "She sent me to Nantucket to think about the brain and how to help those with brain injuries." Bunny occasionally accompanied him. "In Nantucket we walked together through wildflowers to the cliff overlooking the ocean, and she spoke about the wind that comes over the ocean and blows all the world's worries away."

Bunny reminisced with him about Eliza's childhood. As he recalled, "I remember her telling me that when Eliza was a baby, she used to pat Bunny on the back, as if to say, 'Don't worry Bunny, everything will be all right.'"

Bunny turned to her usual sources of comfort, nature and books. She was still purchasing rare garden manuscripts, filling up an addition that she had put on her library, which now held nearly ten thousand volumes. A large orange-and-yellow Rothko dominated the main room, which was a peaceful place to read, daydream, and chat with librarian Tony Willis. She could sit in her second-floor office, with photograph scrapbooks and blueprints of the gardens that she had designed, and gaze out at the countryside.

Bunny occasionally spent a few days at Cape Cod. The solicitous staff worried about the stubbornly independent nonagenarian. "She didn't want anyone to go to the beach with her, she wanted to go off by herself," says Linda Evora, a housekeeper hired in 1999. "She didn't want anyone to watch her swim." So employees would hide along the shoreline nearby, ready to come to the rescue if need be.

At an age when most people are de-acquisitioning, she instructed her chauffeur to take her on jaunts to local Cape Cod antiques stores, often stopping en route at the occult shop Lavender Moon to have her fortune told. She looked for hopeful signs everywhere. "Swimming early this morning an 'angry tern' not wanting me in the river dove at my head," she wrote to Robert Isabell. "Out of the sky came a Big Sea gull + scared him."

She treated the florist as her confidant. "Good morning darling," she wrote to him. "Things are a bit better. Eliza's nurse just said when I asked how she was, 'Good.' First time we heard that word. Your flowers are everywhere." After a trip to her other Massachusetts home, she informed Robert that "yesterday in Nantucket was so peaceful + calm that a big rabbit sleeping on the lawn never moved except to look up + see who it was. He eats my flowers etc. but feels no guilt. It was a marvelous day."

She tried to distract herself with projects. The Metropolitan Museum's Costume Institute was planning an exhibit of Jackie Kennedy's clothing from her White House years, with Caroline Kennedy and her husband, Ed Schlossberg, as chairs of the opening-night gala.

Bunny wrote an essay for the catalogue, describing her first encounter with Jackie in 1957 and the evolution of the "friendship that brought us both continuous joy."

Bunny brought Robert Isabell as her date to the Metropolitan Museum gala for the Jackie Kennedy Onassis exhibit. "Robert was so proud to have Bunny on his arm," says James Reginato, a magazine writer and Isabell's friend. "The irony is that she had been discreet for so long, a lot of people did not know who she was. The more sophisticated people in the room knew, but others were too young to know who she was. I was struck by how charming she was, how sweet. She wasn't grand in the sense of being off-putting. She had a kind of girlish charm. Robert was introducing her to people he knew. They were having a great time."

The night's guests included two First Ladies (then White House resident Laura Bush came for cocktails, and Hillary Clinton came for dinner), Senator Ted Kennedy, Lee Radziwill, Mayor Michael Bloomberg, and the movie stars of the moment, Gwyneth Paltrow and Renee Zellweger. On display were eighty-eight outfits that Jackie had worn as First Lady. Bunny had seen those gowns and hats in real time.

Bunny's relationship with Robert Isabell was the human connection that kept her going. She sketched flowers and the sights at her farm and faxed them to him. The intensity of her feelings was evident in the daily notes that she sent him from December 30, 2001, to January 6, 2002, writing first from New York and then Virginia.

"Like an old fashioned blizzard the snow was falling when I woke up. It cast a peaceful silence over the city that lasted all day. After calling Eliza, I did nothing. Lay in bed with the feeling of floating." A few days later, still in Manhattan, she included colorful sketches: "Drawing the orchids before taking them to Virginia. They are very complicated + very sensual. Most flowers like this are. The tangerines are innocent by comparison."

Once back at her farm, she wrote, "The air today seems like snow will come over the mountain. Dear Robert, you have fallen on a hopeless Romantic…Playing the piano in the library this morning, I looked out and watched the sun falling on the Red Barn. I wish you were here. You just called from Miami. My heart said, 'He's back.' I like independence but I'm not independent anymore."

———————

Bunny spent that winter arranging for an exhibit of Eliza's photographs and paintings at the Virginia Lynch Gallery in Tiverton, "Angels of Light, Portraits of Shadows." A handsome catalogue was commissioned for the opening on June 23, 2002. It began with a now poignant 1998 quotation from Eliza:

> The more I pursue
> The more I see—or discover
> It is more than fascinating
> And through these spirits
> Whether in field or studio
> I am always seeing
> And never alone.

She was never physically alone now, yet Eliza was truly alone in her inability to communicate. In keeping with Bunny's wishes, the catalogue burnished Eliza's credentials as an artist.

"What inspired Moore was a matter of light and shadow, a chiaroscuro of hours, an impressionism of weather, fugitive juxtapositions," wrote Lilly Wei in this history of Eliza's work. "Into her studio's windows with their high, many-splendored views of Manhattan, the light pours in shifting as if on a dimmer, now blinding, a constant inundation not unlike the ebb and flow of water, which is another medium important to Moore."

The essay was written as if Eliza still occupied the studio and was busily working away, stating that "this recent body of work indicates that she has found a new and vital direction for her art as it quietly, wittily muses on the pleasures and conundrums of perception."

This was Bunny's wish fulfillment: She did not want her daughter to be forgotten.

That summer, Bunny invited her sailing companion, Ned Crosby, to join her for lunch at her Cape Cod home. Paul and Bunny had treated Ned like a family member: Paul took Ned along on his private plane to the races in Saratoga, and the couple allowed Ned to dock his wooden boat, *Defiance*, in a protected harbor on their property.

Bunny was in an upbeat mood at lunch. "She was almost giddy," he recalls. She handed Ned an envelope containing the deed to the harborfront land that he had been using. Bunny told him, "With the relationship I had with your grandfather and all he's done for us, with your family having sold the boatyard, I think a Crosby ought to have a place on the water." The land was worth roughly $500,000. "It was a crazy amount for me," he says. "I was shocked."

For Bunny, this ocean coastline brought back a lifetime of memories. Ever since her late husband had published his autobiography, *Reflections in a Silver Spoon*, Bunny had been contemplating writing a memoir of her own. She had held conversations about a potential book project with several writers including novelist Jane Stanton Hitchcock and gardening writers Martin Filler and Mac Griswold. Now, in her house overlooking the blue-green waters, she decided to tackle the project on her own. She began at the beginning:

August 9, 2002. Today is my birthday. I was born 92 years ago in NYC at the corner of 66th Street and Madison Avenue...The nurse in charge presented me to father and mother saying, "The baby looks like a 'little Bunny.'" Since then I have been called Bunny...Today I am in Cape Cod...The household consists of dear and loyal people who have been with Paul + Me, some as long as 35 years. The wind is blowing from the North, a relief after two weeks of heat...

Across the sound, my new house on Nantucket has been lifted up on giant steel beams in preparation to move it away from the sea that is rapidly eating away at the land. All the millions of daisies of last year are under the waves. I am trying to be brave.

She wrote essays about her childhood and the two men who had influenced her outlook on life: her grandfather Arthur Lowe, and her father, Gerard Lambert. She jotted down memories of such searing events as attending Martin Luther King's funeral with Jackie. She sketched her ideas for garden design. She scribbled on scraps of paper, sometimes just a few paragraphs here and there. She dictated free-associated thoughts to Nancy Collins, listing topics that she planned to revisit.

"There are advantages in writing the story of your life at such a late age," she wrote. "First, you know the thoughts and interests that guided you up and down the road traveled, like Pilgrim's Progress that I read early in life."

Thinking back on her marriage to Stacy Lloyd, Bunny concluded that their union had been doomed by their repressed upbringing. "Stacy + I grew up in the same environment + the war took Stacy away for 3 years," she told Collins. "War created the difficulties that we were brought up unable to deal with."

She planned to call her book *Encounters*, focusing on her relationships with other people. But Bunny never pulled these essays and fragments into a coherent manuscript. She was insecure about whether anyone would even care about her life, and anxious about her spelling, making notes about it in the margins. Yet she retained amazing recall about places and moments and feelings, and in expressive prose, left a trove of insightful material for future biographers.

Now that her friendship with Robert Isabell had become all-consuming, other relationships dropped away. "Robert became the friend that I used to be," says Akko van Acker. "I felt the big flame had gone down a bit. He went with her all the places that I went before. She didn't call me every day, after that." But at least van Acker remained in touch with Bunny and saw her sporadically. Magazine editor Babs Simpson noticed with sadness that her half-century friendship with Bunny was over. "I realized the phone wasn't ringing anymore and I knew it would happen sometime because it happened to everybody," Babs said. "I was sorry but it wasn't upsetting."

Since Bunny was no longer traveling to France, and the retired Hubert de Givenchy no longer visited couture clients and stores in the United States, they did not see each other often. Still, he called every week and they faxed each other notes. "After Bunny met Robert Isabell I am not frequently in New York," Givenchy says, adding that Bunny did introduce him to the florist on one occasion. "I know they have this great friendship. Bunny was very attached with Robert and did wonderful things for him. I understand he's a nice man."

When Bunny was asked by Chicago photographer Victor Skrepneski to create an exhibit for the Chicago Flower and Garden Show in March 2002, she brought Isabell in as her collaborator. Working on the sketches together, they used many of Bunny's favorite elements, including espalier trees, an herb garden, and beds of freesia, primroses, forget-me-nots, tulips, and blue hyacinth. Bunny purchased a nineteenth-century American eagle weather vane from Christie's for the exhibit, to be donated afterward to the city of Chicago.

Seven tractor-trailers transported the soil, wood, and other materials from the East Coast to the exhibition hall. Bunny came to watch as Robert and his team installed flower beds and built a wooden slat house, filled with eighteen-foot camellia trees, a moss-covered metal urn stuffed with flowering spring branches, and a metal canopy daybed of Robert's design. Bunny and Robert were photographed together sitting on the daybed as Bunny held Robert's hand; the caption could have read: "Best Friends."

Bunny's son, Tuffy, and grandson Stacy IV joined them for the opening party. After three days in Chicago, Bunny wrote to Mayor Richard M. Daley to tell him how much she enjoyed meeting him and seeing the parks in his city.

"It is very inspiring to know that in this country of turmoil and disillusion, there is a corner working to improve the life and spirit of all those living there. Being a gardener with a wonderful public spirited grandfather from New England, my appreciation was extra special."

At the Chicago airport, as Bunny was preparing to take off in her private plane, the Windy City lived up to its reputation, tipping the aircraft to the ground and damaging the wing. Bunny returned to her hotel. Although her brother, two of her cousins, and Paul's niece and nephew had been killed in airplane crashes, she had trained herself to assume the best. As she told her nurse Nancy Collins, "When you fly, you just have to pretend you're a kite."

Paul Leonard continued to make trips to Virginia to visit Eliza, and Bunny sent him grateful thank-you notes. But then he experienced his own health crisis, diagnosed with renal cancer. "I am not scared," he wrote to Bunny in May 2002, but added, "It's been a tough year in every way, emotionally and financially...Hope all is as well as it can be for you and dear Eliza."

His optimism waned as his prognosis quickly grew dire. "He didn't tell Bunny he was dying, but he knew. They were in touch quite a lot," recalls his wife, Valerie. Worried that his wife and daughter would be left destitute since he had not put much money aside, Paul Leonard wrote to Bunny to ask if she would help him financially. She did not reply.

During the final weeks of his illness in the fall of 2002, he read through Bunny's letters and burned many of them in the fireplace, the words vanishing in puffs of smoke. He did not want his family to see the intimate correspondence. "Has Bunny called?" he asked his wife repeatedly. He couldn't believe that Bunny would not respond to his request or try to say good-bye. As Valerie says, "The day he died, he had been saying it for the last week, he asked again, 'Did Bunny call?'"

The *New York Times*, in a November 3 obituary, noted that Paul Leonard's "graphically patterned, subtly tinted floors were trod on by jet-set aesthetes from Jacqueline Kennedy Onassis to Ralph Lauren." Bunny was described as his "reclusive" patron, the woman who helped him discover "his true metier, interior decoration."

She was lonely in Virginia, eager for distraction and human company. Internationally acclaimed architect Errol Adels had built a Palladian mansion for himself in Upperville, and his friend Hubert de Givenchy urged him to call Bunny. But Adels did not want to intrude. "One day my phone rang," he recalls, and the woman on the other end introduced herself as Bunny Mellon. "I've been waiting for my phone to ring for three years," she told him. "Don't you think we've waited long enough?" She invited him to come for lunch that afternoon.

"She answered the front door herself. She said, 'Dear boy, do me a big favor and why don't you mix us a drink, I'll have a Bloody Mary but be gentle with me.'" The architect was impressed by her resilience. "Bunny's life was not a happy one, she had just endured Paul's death and Eliza's accident and Mrs. Kennedy had passed away, but she smiled and she was full of an energy that you don't attribute to a woman that age. Instead of reminiscing, every comment was looking forward, there was a project, something to be done, a wall to be built, a tree to be pruned. She had so much energy and charm."

After that first lunch, he would occasionally take Bunny for country drives or they would walk her property. One moment stayed with him. "I was walking across her terrace," he recalls. "There were little tiny flowers growing up beneath the cracks in the pavement. She said, 'Oh, Errol, please don't step on that flower.'"

Bunny sold her New York town house to Irish businessman Tony White and his wife, Clare. Bunny wrote to Givenchy to express her relief: "It is so exhausting all these responsibilities that taking N.Y. house away is wonderful."

But she still wanted a Manhattan base and rented a three-room apartment at the Mark Hotel. "The 'Mark' has allowed me to change the baths, put in shutters and paint the walls, new carpets and our own furniture, like doing a dollhouse." She remained in denial about Eliza's prognosis five years after the accident, writing to Givenchy, "Eliza is coming along—I am sitting with her as I write this letter. When she can speak it will help her + us to know what she needs. Dr. Ghajar is a wonderful brain doctor + says she will speak soon."

In acknowledgment of Eliza's changed circumstances, Bunny had begun revising her will but found the process to be morbid. Bunny wrote to her lawyer, Alex Forger, to complain that she found it difficult to listen to the frequent comment—"after she's dead"—by the surveyors and others who were spending time on the farm to work on the legal niceties.

In her new will, signed on October 9, 2003, she left $20 million each to her daughter, Eliza, and to her son, Tuffy, who also received a Monet painting. Her executors, Alex Forger and investment adviser Ken Starr, were authorized to manage Eliza's affairs. Bunny gave a mere $200,000 each to her grandsons, Thomas Lloyd and Stacy Lloyd IV, but made them the beneficiaries of the 1939 trust left by her father, Gerard Lambert.

The will contained symbolic gestures: Caroline Kennedy was set to receive a long gold chain with pearls and a Schlumberger antelope pin. Bunny made philanthropic donations as well, leaving the bulk of her Schlumberger jewelry and boxes to the Virginia Museum of Fine Arts and a portion of her Nantucket land to the Nantucket Conservation Society.

Thanks to the appreciation of her art and real estate, she had assets worth more than $500 million. Bunny wanted to do something meaningful with her money and create a lasting legacy. She requested that her art and property be auctioned off, with the bulk of the proceeds going to fund her Oak Spring Garden Library, to be run by the entity that she had created, the Gerard B. Lambert Foundation.

Both the National Gallery and the Smithsonian had turned down the opportunity to take over this remote outpost, located in the middle of the Mellons' farm. Designed to meet Bunny's aesthetic vision, the library had not been set up to accommodate researchers and there wasn't even a parking lot; the small staff parked on a hillside with their emergency brakes on. But Bunny wanted what she wanted. It would be up to her executors to find a way to turn the library into an education and training facility for horticulture, botany, and landscape design.

Bunny did not leave anything in her will to Robert Isabell. How-

ever, when Isabell wrote his own will a short time later, he took the
surprising step of making a generous gift to Bunny's pet cause. A millionaire who owned Manhattan real estate and a thriving business,
he gave $400,000 to his family members but then granted artwork
(a Richard Diebenkorn drawing, a Fabergé flower, an Irving Penn
self-portrait) plus the bulk of his estate to Bunny's Oak Spring Garden Library. He named as coexecutors his friend Cathy Graham and
Bunny's lawyer Alex Forger.

The floral designer was well liked by Bunny's family, who could
see how much the relationship mattered to her. As her grandson
Thomas Lloyd says, "Robert Isabell and my grandmother, they were
like brother and sister. They laughed, they fought, Robert was head-
strong. He genuinely adored my grandmother."

Since Robert Isabell was forty-two years younger than Bunny, the
actuarial tables made it unlikely that she would see his bequest come
to fruition. But for Bunny, this represented a tangible demonstration
of his love. She asked Robert to consider moving to Upperville to run
the Oak Spring Garden Library, and he told friends that he might actually do so, someday. She soon added Isabell as an executor.

Bunny had always spent money without thinking about tomorrow,
and now this practice was catching up to her. Maintaining her properties cost a fortune, plus Eliza's twenty-four-hour care was expensive.
Bunny still employed more than two hundred people, and even if she
no longer needed six laundresses or a dairy, she didn't want to fire anyone. She was still buying art and giving expensive presents. Her pilots
and her jet were ready to take off at a moment's notice, although she
scarcely traveled. The millions from the sale of her New York property
would only temporarily relieve the problem.

The easiest solution would have been to sell assets that had soared
in value, such as her art collection. But she loved the paintings, and
Robert Isabell convinced her to take advantage of the appreciation instead. Her lawyers arranged for the Bank of America to loan money to
Bunny, with the art as collateral. That loan would ultimately balloon
to $250 million.

At age ninety-three, Bunny's life revolved around daily rituals. As a teenager she had sketched a picture of herself sitting in bed, looking at a bird perched on her windowsill. Now she left slices of apple on the windowsill directly facing the four-poster in her second-floor bedroom so she could see the birds nibbling and hear their chirping.

She spent time with Eliza each day, although sometimes her daughter was driven over to Bunny's residence for a change of pace. Bunny often whiled away the time at her library and took short walks around the farm. With her strong grip, she was still pruning trees, much to the amazement of the gardeners.

But her eyesight was becoming blurry, a troubling development. The medical diagnosis was macular degeneration, a disease that is incurable and progressive and can lead to blindness. Bunny could still see enough to read and get around on her own. She turned to a 1942 book by her friend Aldous Huxley, *The Art of Seeing*, about his own experiences dealing with faltering vision. She still drove around the farm, but returning to her home one day, she misjudged and smacked the BMW into a stone wall, leaving a dent in the side. She reluctantly gave up her keys.

Like clockwork, at 6:30 p.m. Bunny watched ABC's *World News Tonight*, committed to remaining up-to-date. She had been following presidential elections since childhood but had not been directly involved since Bobby Kennedy's assassination in 1968.

As the race for the Democratic nomination began to heat up in 2003, Bunny became fascinated by John Edwards, the boyish North Carolina senator who was jousting for the Democratic nomination against Massachusetts senator John Kerry, former Vermont governor Howard Dean, Congressman Dick Gephardt, and others.

The son of a mill worker, as he constantly reminded voters, Edwards had made a fortune as a personal injury lawyer. Edwards and his wife, Elizabeth, a bankruptcy lawyer, had their lives shattered by tragedy in a way that Bunny could understand. Their sixteen-year-old son, Wade, died in an auto accident in 1996, a loss that helped propel Edwards into a 1998 Senate race in an effort to do something meaningful with his life.

As a freshman senator, Edwards's jury-charming manner and astute networking helped catapult him into the limelight. By 2000, Edwards was on Democratic presidential nominee Al Gore's short list for vice president, although Gore ended up choosing Connecticut senator Joe Lieberman.

Although Edwards had a North Carolina twang—in contrast to JFK's Boston brogue—Bunny saw similarities between these two young men in a hurry. John Edwards had unveiled a compelling and prescient stump speech that highlighted what he called "the Two Americas," the gulf between the rich and the poor. These themes, which had been part of Bunny's life ever since her childhood discovery of the sorry living conditions of her father's Arkansas employees, still resonated with the richest woman in Upperville.

On the eve of Virginia's February primary, Bunny wrote and paid for a political ad supporting Edwards that ran in the *Middleburg Life*, her local newspaper: "Blowing from the Mountains of the Carolinas and Virginia. A New South Wind. Clear and Fair. Vote for John Edwards. Bringing Hope, Peace & Strength." Edwards failed to make the breakthrough that Bunny had hoped for in the Virginia primary, but the North Carolina senator ran strongly enough in the primaries that the victorious John Kerry chose him as his vice presidential running mate.

A few weeks after the November election, which the Kerry-Edwards ticket lost narrowly to George W. Bush and Dick Cheney, North Carolina decorator Bryan Huffman spent Saturday night at the Red Fox Inn in Middleburg after visiting relatives in Virginia. That Sunday morning, he woke up with an urge to attend church. There was a church nearby, but he opted to drive the eight miles to Upperville's Trinity Episcopal Church, the Gothic stone masterpiece that Bunny and Paul had built. "I loved every aspect of that church," Huffman recalled. In the parking lot, he jotted a note to Bunny thanking her for this wonderful place of worship and dropped it off at the nearby post office.

He did not include a phone number but his father, an attorney, had the same name. Bunny tracked down Huffman a few days later at his parents' home in the small town of Monroe, North Carolina. "We just fell into the conversation," he recalls, as she talked about being inspired by the cathedral at Chartres and her desire to create something majestic in Upperville. After talking for ninety minutes on the phone, Bunny invited him to lunch.

The forty-year-old decorator, a history major at the University of North Carolina at Chapel Hill, was aware of Bunny's work on the Rose Garden and her reputation as a decorating genius. "I was nervous just driving up," Bryan recalls of their first meeting in February 2005. "It was fun to talk on the telephone, but to actually meet this woman, who the design community puts up on a pedestal, she's a legendary figure."

He still savors the details of the visit: "You expect this grand stiff person and then she just pops in and hugs you and welcomes you into the living room. She grabs your hand and she has a tremendous grip because she does pruning. The Van Gogh is over the fireplace, the fire is blazing. We just laughed and talked. I didn't know then that her nurse, Nancy, was hiding behind the drapery panel, to make sure she didn't need to hurry through lunch. Bunny, unbeknownst to me, gave her the thumbs-up."

Since Bryan was from North Carolina, Bunny made a point of showing him a framed copy of her political ad for John Edwards, which was hanging on a wall next to a Renoir. "I love your senator," she announced, adding that Edwards reminded her of John Kennedy. Edwards was taking time off from politics to care for his wife, Elizabeth, who had breast cancer, but there was talk that he would run for president again.

After the meal, Bunny took Bryan to meet Eliza. Perhaps because Bryan had not known Eliza before the accident, he did not blanch at the sight of Bunny's daughter in her wheelchair with a feeding tube. "She smiled at me," he recalls. "Bunny said, 'She likes you.'" He had passed an unwritten test.

At the end of the visit, Bunny gave Bryan packages of her dairy's cheese, and once he got home, he sent her flowers. "It was lovely to meet you and find we have so many ideas in common," Bunny wrote in a thank-you note. "Please stop by again—for a Happy Welcome!"

They began to talk frequently by phone. After Bunny ran out of day-to-day events to discuss, she kept Bryan on the phone by telling captivating stories about her past. "I thought their friendship was crazy on one hand and perfect and predestined on the other," says Carol Kendrick, Bryan's married younger sister. "When Bryan was in high school and did service projects, he was always spending time with these older women who had wonderful stories and huge personalities. He has always found older people interesting."

When Bunny turned ninety-six in August, Bryan was invited to her birthday party, a small lunch with her son, Tuffy; her grandson Stacy IV; and her librarian, Tony Willis. During Bryan's visits to Bunny, Eliza was often wheeled in to join them at meals. "She would bring Eliza to the table. A nurse would hover," Bryan says. "We would just talk about regular things. Bunny was very tender and loving towards her, would include her in the conversation—'Mommy loves you.'"

Now with Bryan Huffman and Robert Isabell, Bunny had two good-looking acolytes, both more than forty years her junior, phoning and sending her flowers. Robert brought a touch of New York sophisticated glamour to her life, introducing her to his friends such as singer Bette Midler and designer Norma Kamali. Bryan, a Southern gentleman, was a patient and curious listener who could make her laugh. He sensed her sadness and wanted to help.

"Bunny needed a diversion from Eliza, something to spark her interest," Bryan recalls. She often brought up John Edwards in their conversations. "She was so smitten with the idea of him," recalls Huffman. He had a pipeline to the senator: His sister Carol had gone to law school with Edwards's top aide, Andrew Young. Bryan Huffman asked her to arrange a meeting between the politician and the heiress.

Andrew Young had never heard of Bunny, and he was initially dubious about the prospect of introducing his boss to an elderly woman in the Virginia horse country. "I tried to explain to him who Bunny Mellon was," recalls Kendrick. "He got off the phone. Relatively quickly, I got a call back. He said, 'We would like to meet her.'" Kendrick speculates: "Someone had Googled Bunny Mellon and realized that would be a good connection to make."

Bunny was thrilled when Bryan informed her that he was making arrangements for the senator to come to the farm to see her. On Thanksgiving Day, 2005, she wrote to Bryan:

Thank you so much for a very special surprise! It is an unbelievable joy to look forward to!

It brings back the excitement of the day John Kennedy walked into the house, before he was elected president.

To meet Sen. John Edwards is history repeating itself—again.

Thank you with much affection. Bunny.

Chapter Twenty-Five

A Perilous Political Affair

John Edwards was running late. The tousle-haired ex-senator had been expected at Bunny's farm by 4:30 p.m., but as the sky darkened, the ninety-five-year-old heiress began to worry. "She was so nervous," recalls Bryan Huffman, who had driven up from North Carolina for the December 1, 2005, introduction. "She kept asking, 'Is he coming?'" The anxious Bunny finally decided to go to her room and rest.

The meeting had been on and off all week. An Edwards aide had called Huffman the day before to complain of a sudden schedule conflict—and suggest a bold solution. Edwards would be willing to come to Bunny's farm if her pilot would fly him to Raleigh that evening. "I was irritated," Huffman says, but Bunny immediately agreed to the request.

As Edwards and his aide Josh Brumberger drove from Washington, D.C., to the farm, they discussed their expectations. As Brumberger recalls, Edwards found it hard to believe that a wealthy woman in rural Virginia with the last name of Mellon had taken an interest in his candidacy. "We thought, 'Is she real?'"

After arriving at 6 p.m., ninety minutes late, the ex-senator excused himself to use the restroom while his youthful aide was ushered into Bunny's living room, with its gold-and-white butterfly-patterned sofas and Impressionist artwork. When Bunny came downstairs, wearing a cashmere twin set, wool pants, pearls, and Schlumberger bangles, she mistakenly began speaking to Brumberger as if he were Edwards, a reflection of her deteriorating eyesight.

Edwards, who had been briefed, began the conversation by asking, "How did you meet Jackie Kennedy?" With pride, Bunny regaled him with the tale of her first meeting with Jackie—in that very room— and her work on the Rose Garden. Flashing the smile that jurors had found so compelling, the former trial lawyer did not have to sell himself to this rapt audience of one. It was evident to both observers— Huffman and Tony Willis—that she was smitten.

After accompanying Edwards to her private airstrip to bid him farewell, once the plane took off Bunny turned to Bryan Huffman and announced, "I can just feel it. That's the next president of the United States."

Up in the air in Bunny's plane, Edwards was mulling over the meeting as well. "We were both pretty impressed," says Brumberger. "We met with lots of people worth hundreds of millions of dollars, so you got jaded. But this was unique. There was a sense, we were just with someone from an American dynasty and royalty. John held her in a different regard from the donor base, she was a historic figure."

A few weeks later, Bunny received her first written request from Edwards for money. As he prepped to run for president again in 2008, the former senator was setting up an antipoverty think tank at his alma mater, the University of North Carolina Law School. While ostensibly a goodwill gesture, the poverty center was meant to serve as the launchpad for his political ambitions. Since campaign law did not apply to this supposedly altruistic venture, Edwards aimed high, asking for $1 million.

Prior to Paul Mellon's death, Bunny had been unable to make large contributions without her Republican husband's permission. Now she could do what she wanted with her money. Pleased to be involved, she noted in her journal that she celebrated receiving the December 21 solicitation from Edwards by having a second daiquiri.

Bunny spent a quiet New Year's Eve sipping Veuve Clicquot while she sat with Eliza. She still believed that the mute Eliza had some comprehension of the world and was using facial expressions to send messages to her mother. Bunny wrote to Bryan Huffman, who had sent the champagne, that Eliza "gave me a big understanding smile. Such a joy for me, Bryan, that she is able to do this after 6 years."

John Edwards called Bunny twice in January, eager to forge a personal bond and, more likely, close the deal. Bunny was so enthusiastic about his prospects that she ultimately gave $3 million to two of Edwards's entities, the poverty center and the One America Committee, his political action committee. Edwards began to phone Bunny every few weeks.

His aide Andrew Young, who had brokered their first meeting, made sure that her name was on the politician's call list and would often update Bunny himself. Known for his fierce loyalty to John Edwards, Young was willing to take on the lowliest of tasks, from picking up his boss's Thanksgiving turkey to helping Edwards and his wife move into their new Chapel Hill mansion.

Edwards's staff faxed Bunny copies of his speeches and newspaper stories charting his travels as he railed against the Bush administration and talked about remedies to cure poverty. This armchair political activity was a welcome distraction from the sorrows in Bunny's life. Her sister, Lily, now a ninety-one-year-old widow living in a Pennsylvania nursing home, was dying of cancer. They had been rivals for most of their lives, but Bunny now realized how much she would miss her younger sister. As the clock wound down, she sent flowers, signing her notes with their mutual childhood nickname, "Tush," and called Lily frequently, trying to catch up on a lifetime of memories.

"The nurse had to hold up the phone to my mother's ear," says Lily Lambert Norton, Bunny's niece. "I thought it was so tragic that the sisters only became close at the end." Bunny reminded her sister how as children they kept their "good luck" slippers tucked under their beds to ward away nighttime fears. When Bunny learned that her sister had died on February 4, she wrote in her diary, "I prayed and I cried. I prayed she was alright."

Yet she decided to skip her sister's funeral. Rather than mourn the past, she cheered herself up by calling Bryan Huffman to announce that she wanted to see his family's mountain retreat in Jefferson, North Carolina, and would be flying in on her plane within twenty-four hours. "I had no time to prepare," says Bryan, whose weekend cottage is a three-hour drive from his home in Monroe. His mother, Billie Huffman, accompanied him and made cheese soufflés for lunch.

In a thank-you note to Billie Huffman, Bunny wrote, "Bryan is a most unusual young man. Bright + great fun. In the middle of our happy relationship, he suddenly brings in Senator Edwards—the last thing I expected. Now we are all working together to adjust the mess Pres. Bush has put us in."

———————————

The Regency Hotel on Park Avenue serves as an unofficial political clubhouse, with a ground-floor restaurant where prominent New Yorkers and visiting politicians go to see and be seen. On February 21, 2006, the room buzzed with the kind of electricity that accompanies the presence of a potential presidential candidate: John Edwards was meeting with a donor.

A slender blonde, sitting nearby, could not take her eyes off Edwards and thought that he was gazing her way too. Rielle Hunter, a divorced forty-one-year-old former actress, had long ago developed a reputation as a party girl. Her cocaine-fueled antics had inspired a character in a 1988 novel, *The Story of My Life*, by her former boyfriend, Jay McInerney. But Rielle, born Lisa Jo Druck, was now financially tapped out, staying at a friend's home in South Orange, New Jersey, and trying to reinvent herself as a New Age spiritual healer.

After John Edwards left to go out to dinner, Rielle, wearing jeans and a black turtleneck, walked over and introduced herself to Josh Brumberger. "I can't believe it, he is so amazing," she told Brumberger. "I've seen him on TV. I know I can help him."

Timing is everything. When John Edwards returned to the hotel, he ran into Rielle and her two friends on the sidewalk. She blurted out, "You are so hot!" Flattered, he stopped to chat. Women often flirted with Edwards, and his staff tried to deflect the advances. Observing the scene from the hotel lobby, Brumberger rushed outside to break it up, saying, "Busy day tomorrow." Walking into the hotel, Edwards turned to his aide and said, "Thanks, I didn't know how I was going to get away from all three."

But in the privacy of his room, the ex-senator, who had Rielle's business card, called and invited her to join him. Rielle later acknowledged that they spent the night together. And so began John Edwards's dual life on the campaign trail.

After a trip to Antigua, Bunny returned for the March 25 wedding of her grandson Thomas Lloyd. A graduate of Dickinson College, he was working as a producer for a movie-and-television company in Washington. His bride-to-be, Anna Cristina Niceta, known as "Rickie," was a Hollins College graduate and account executive for the high-end catering firm Design Cuisine. The couple had been dating for six months before Thomas told Rickie that his grandmother was the famous Bunny Mellon.

Rickie, a pretty and high-spirited woman from a close-knit Catholic family, was baffled when Thomas described his strained relationship with GranBunny. As Rickie recalls, "I remember him saying, 'I have no idea what I've done, she really doesn't care for me.' You could tell he felt tremendous pain, embarrassment, and sorrow. He couldn't even look me in the face."

When Thomas called to tell his grandmother that he was engaged, Bunny asked to meet Rickie. "You will," he replied, but left things vague. He never knew how his grandmother would behave toward him, and he did not want to subject Rickie to GranBunny's unpredictable moods. Family members subsequently alerted him that Bunny was considering skipping the wedding. He steeled himself for the outcome, recalling that his thought was: "If she wants to come, great, if she's not going to come, it's not going to define who I am as a person. I didn't feel GranBunny had to be part of my life for Rickie to be part of it."

On the day of the ceremony, the family got together at the groom's father's house in Washington. Bunny not only attended but made a real effort to be warm and sociable. "It was so poignant," recalls Anne Emmet, Thomas's mother. "We were all at Stacy's house and Bunny was fussing over Thomas. He was so pleased to finally have the attention of his grandmother." Bunny brought Robert Isabell—referred to by her family as "her boyfriend"—as her date. She wrote in her journal that the wedding, which included an hour-and-fifteen-minute Mass, was "tiring" but that "Robert was a great help."

Bunny's other grandson, Stacy IV, was working in Chicago at a sales job that he detested, selling ATM machines. As he recalls, "I had lunch with my grandmother when I felt the most desperate and said, 'Can you give me inspiration? Can I do anything for you?'" Bunny hired him to work in her library. Stacy IV moved to a house on her farm, taking on projects such as cataloguing and digitizing books and articles. He says, "It was such an opportunity to give me a job to get on my feet."

When John Edwards and Andrew Young came to the farm for lunch, Bunny invited her grandson to join them. Stacy IV had an instinctive sense of what was happening—he believed that the ex-senator was exploiting his grandmother—and he was offended. "I was so turned off by him," Stacy IV says. He came away from the lunch with a poor impression of the politician: "He was just happy to have Andrew there to keep me occupied while he spoke to her. Edwards could not have sounded more uninterested in me. It was like, 'I can't charm Bunny if this guy is here.' I didn't trust him."

But Bunny defiantly believed that John Edwards could do no wrong. Imbued by a sense of patriotism and a desire to be relevant, she saw this campaign as a chance to elect a liberal Democrat to the White House. "This wasn't a shallow thing with a handsome man," stresses Tony Willis, her librarian. "She really took it seriously and wanted to help the country."

Bunny welcomed the opportunity to express her views to the candidate. She favored woman's rights, she believed in universal health care, and she wanted to protect the environment. She was forward-thinking, supporting gay rights at a time when it was not a priority for Edwards or his rivals. "She felt that whoever you loved, you should have a choice," Willis said. "Mr. and Mrs. Mellon wanted to make sure their employees had health benefits, why not let all Americans have that opportunity? On the issues that were important to her, she felt that John Edwards would be the good Southern gentleman to put it together."

In a normal campaign cycle, Edwards would have been the Democratic front-runner, since he had been his party's 2004 vice presidential nominee. But he was running against two superstars: the eloquent newcomer, first-term Illinois senator Barack Obama, and the glass ceiling–shattering senator from New York, Hillary Clinton.

Bunny disliked Hillary, dating back to their 1994 encounter at the White House. Bunny thought the former First Lady had not been suitably appreciative of Bunny's creation, the Rose Garden. In Bunny's notes to Bryan Huffman, she referred to Hillary in derogatory fashion as "the old rag" and "the elf."

Nights were the loneliest times for Bunny. During the days, her household of cooks, laundresses, butlers, maids, and housekeepers was bustling with activity. She could always find something to do. Bunny hired a favorite masseuse, Marie Colandrea, to be her companion, and either Marie or nurse Nancy Collins was available to chat or take her for a drive to look for wildflowers.

"We knew when the violets came out, and where they were—the spring beauties, the dog tree violets, the wild daisies," recalls Nancy Collins. "We would drive around and she'd have me pull over on the road and start picking. If I said, 'I can't pull over there, it's a bad spot,' she'd say, 'Oh, come on.'"

Bunny paged through *The Witches' Almanac*, with its myths and incantations. She still followed astrology, paying attention to the times of year when Mercury was in retrograde and trying to avoid making major decisions or commitments during those periods. Every afternoon she spoke to psychic Beverly Newton, discussing her dreams and her life on the farm. "Bunny called me her witch, but I'm not one, we laughed about that," says Newton. For one of Bunny's birthdays, Newton bought a certificate to name a star in her honor, telling her friend, "Bunny, when you die, you can look down on all of us and wish us well." Newton adds, "She loved that."

Bunny had dinner on a tray in her room and then most of the staff went home, although there were always a few employees around for the overnight shift. In the quiet of the countryside, with scarcely a neighboring light to be seen from her window, everything hit her. It was excruciating for Bunny to sit in bed and think about the suffering of her daughter.

Bunny called Bryan Huffman one night around 11 p.m., apologizing that it was so late. He told her that she could call whenever she wanted. On June 9, 2006, she sent him a grateful note: "Your words, 'call me anytime,' have not been part of my life for a long time." In another note to him, she added, "It was very kind + understanding of God to send you down the road. I really needed your unique friendship and aid to keep me going."

She asked him to call her each night around 9 p.m. From then on, he kept an eye on the clock and ducked out of evenings with friends at the appointed hour to make the call. "Some nights we would talk for five minutes," he said. "Sometimes it would last for an hour. Her mind was engaged in what was happening in the world, she still got the news from newspapers and television." During virtually every phone call, she wanted to discuss the fate of John Edwards, or as she called him, "our candidate."

At Bunny's request, her lawyer Alex Forger held a political fundraiser for John Edwards on December 14 at Bunny's family legal office in Manhattan's Essex House, with its grand vista of Central Park. Bunny did not attend, but the Mellon name had clout and Edwards received a favorable reaction as he worked the crowd. Three of Bunny's lawyers—Forger, Jane MacLennan, and Samuel Polk—had already given $2,300 each to Edwards's campaign. As permitted by law, Bunny gave $2,300 to his campaign to win the Democratic nomination plus another $2,300, reserved for the general election in the fall if he became his party's nominee.

At Bunny's request, her attorneys gave Edwards two more Manhattan fund-raisers. The candidate's wife, Elizabeth, was the featured attraction at one gathering. After writing a best-selling book about her battle with breast cancer, Elizabeth had become a beloved figure in her own right. Her seesaw difficulties with her weight had made her an even more sympathetic figure. Ever since *People* magazine in 2000 had labeled her husband "The Sexiest Politician Alive" for his "clean-cut boyish charm" and family-man values, John's popularity was tied to his devotion to Elizabeth. They sold themselves to the public as a loving unbreakable team.

Elizabeth wanted to meet her husband's benefactor but Bunny turned down the request. As Forger candidly puts it, "She didn't like wives."

On December 28, 2006, John Edwards made it official. He flew to New Orleans, which had been devastated by Hurricane Katrina, for a photo opportunity to announce that he was running for the presidency. Dressed in jeans and a khaki shirt as he cleared debris from a home in an impoverished black neighborhood, he declared to reporters, "Instead of being tangled up in a lot of the squabbling that goes on in Washington, I've been out doing stuff."

Bunny was excited that it was becoming real. "I watched our candidate and he is the best," Bunny wrote to Bryan on December 31. "But I must try and not be broken hearted if he doesn't win."

Indeed, behind the scenes, the fledgling campaign was already troubled. John Edwards had hired Rielle Hunter back in July to produce campaign videos called webisodes, which allowed her to travel around the country and overseas with him. Rielle later claimed that she and Edwards even made a sex tape. The campaign staff gossiped that the couple scarcely bothered to hide their affection for each other.

When Josh Brumberger spotted Rielle leaving the ex-senator's hotel room, the episode confirmed his concerns about an affair. He tried to broach the topic with Edwards. "I tap-danced around it, telling him that people are starting to snicker about how you're having a different relationship with her than you have with other staffers," Brumberger told me. That October, he confided his fears to two of Edwards's top aides. When one of them, Peter Scher, brought the subject up with Edwards, the infuriated candidate denied the story. In a widely reported incident, Edwards blew up at Brumberger. Shortly afterward, Brumberger left the campaign.

Now, just three days after John Edwards had officially announced his presidential candidacy, his suspicious wife, Elizabeth, learned about the self-destructive affair. Sensing that something was amiss, on

New Year's Eve she found her husband's special cell phone and hit redial, reaching Rielle, who answered, "Hey, baby."

After days of screaming fights, Edwards reportedly insisted to his wife that this fling was over. Rielle lost her campaign job but continued to fly around the country to secretly join Edwards. Her airfare and hotel bills were expensive. Andrew Young would later claim that he used his own credit cards to book her travel, at Edwards's request, because the wealthy politician believed that his wife, Elizabeth, was monitoring his spending.

Life unraveled for John Edwards in March. He cut short a campaign trip in Iowa to fly back to North Carolina. In a heartbreaking news conference in Chapel Hill, with his wife by his side, he announced that Elizabeth's breast cancer had recurred with a vengeance and was incurable.

Never before in modern politics had a candidate's wife announced that she was dying from Stage Four cancer. Almost everyone in politics assumed that Edwards would withdraw from the race to be with Elizabeth and their children at home. In addition, both Edwards and his wife knew that if he became the Democratic nominee, his affair with Rielle Hunter could explode in lurid headlines at any moment. Elizabeth's cancer gave her husband the opportunity to withdraw from the race without damaging his reputation or jeopardizing his party's chances to regain the White House.

Nonetheless, in a breathtaking display of narcissism, Edwards announced that with his wife's support, he was continuing his campaign. "We have no intention of cowering in a corner," he vowed. Elizabeth Edwards gave heroic interviews, telling Katie Couric: "Either you push forward with the things that you were doing yesterday or you start dying."

A few days later, according to Rielle, Edwards joined her for a tryst in Washington, D.C., followed by meetings in Seattle and New York City. During a night at the Regency Hotel, where it all began, she became pregnant.

Unaware of John Edwards's affair, Bunny remained eager to assist his efforts to win the White House. She saw her moment when the press revealed that Edwards had charged his campaign for two $400 haircuts by a Beverly Hills stylist, as detailed in a Federal Election Commission spending report. For a multimillionaire whose campaign theme revolved around alleviating poverty, the haircuts made him a target as a blow-dried phony.

Andrew Young called Bunny to shore up her support. "The timing of your telephone call on Friday was 'witchy,'" Bunny wrote to him on April 21, 2007. "I was sitting alone in a grim mood—furious that the press attacked Senator Edwards on the price of a haircut. But it inspired me—from now on, all haircuts, etc. that are necessary and important for his campaign—please send the bills to me...It is a way to help our friend without government restriction."

She contacted her lawyer, asking him to make the arrangements. Alex Forger reminded her of the federal limits on campaign contributions and told her that she could not underwrite Edwards's personal expenses. "I had a conversation with Bunny about what she could and could not do," Forger told me. On April 24, Forger e-mailed Andrew Young to rescind Bunny's offer, politely stating that she was unable to take on more financial projects, but "she continues to be one of the senator's most ardent supporters."

Things should have ended here. But the possibility of more Bunny money proved too tantalizing to ignore. That summer Andrew Young called Bryan Huffman to ask him to pass on a request to Bunny. "Andrew said they needed money for a special project, that we would help the senator go to the White House," Huffman recalled. "They needed a half million dollars but it could be spread out, they needed a commitment from several people." However, according to Huffman, Young did not explain how the money would be used.

The "special project" was unorthodox: paying the living expenses of Rielle Hunter, who was due to give birth in February, just after the Iowa caucuses and the New Hampshire primary. Rielle had informed the candidate of his impending fatherhood on July 11, but the prospective parents wanted to keep it a secret to protect his candidacy and—as far as Edwards was concerned—his marriage.

Bunny didn't inquire what the money was for: All she cared about was helping her candidate. But Bunny needed a secret way to funnel cash to Edwards that would outwit her own cautious advisers.

Feeling like the Mata Hari of Upperville, Bunny called Bryan Huffman with a madcap plan. Her lawyer and financial manager never questioned her expenditures for redecorating and buying furniture. Since Huffman was a decorator, she would send checks to him under the pretext that she was on an antiques-buying spree, and he could then pass the money to the Edwards campaign.

Huffman thought this plan was ludicrously eccentric but willingly played along since she was so delighted by the notion. When Bunny's first $25,000 check arrived, she made it out to him with a note dated June 13, joking about her gambling debts.

Dear Kissin Cousin,

Thank you so much for lending me strength to pay my bets. Horse racing is sometimes productive like Paul winning the Derby otherwise I have to borrow.

Concerned about the tax repercussions and worried that someone might think he was taking Bunny's money for himself or doing anything improper, Huffman did not deposit the check in his own bank account. Instead, he endorsed the check and sent it via Federal Express to Andrew Young. Unbeknownst to Huffman, the Edwards loyalist then decided that his wife, Cheri, would deposit the check in her account, using her maiden name, Pfister. That became the convoluted pattern.

In the following months, the checks for "furniture" kept coming. Bunny made an event out of it, tucking the checks into boxes of La Maison du Chocolat, wrapping packages with ribbons, including little drawings with her notes. On June 16, she wrote to Huffman, "Thank you for arranging for me to purchase the lovely simple dining room chairs for $65,000." Of course, there were no actual chairs involved, simple or otherwise.

During the summer of 2007, six months before the Iowa caucuses, Bunny remained single-minded in her efforts to boost her candidate. After Lady Bird Johnson died on July 11, Caroline Kennedy attended the funeral and called Bunny to fill her in. Bunny used the conversation to lobby for John Edwards. Describing her conversation with Caroline, Bunny wrote to Huffman: "I told her she should vote for Edwards but she was busy with other thoughts." Caroline Kennedy and her uncle, Senator Ted Kennedy, would jointly endorse Barack Obama.

Bunny's enduring friends did not share her newfound enthusiasm. "The last time I spoke to Bunny was on the telephone," recalls Amy Greene. "She was working hard with that dreadful senator. She giggled. I thought she was getting old and they were ripping her off." Bunny asked Bryan to drop off a batch of Edwards for President buttons at the Manhattan salon of Kenneth Battelle; the hairdresser looked askance at the offering.

Bunny's homes were decorated with a staggering array of world-class paintings. But now she viewed her collection in a new light. She informed Huffman on July 29 that she was taking out a loan against her art so that she could contribute money to John Edwards. Her notecard featured the Monet painting *Woman with a Parasol*, which she and Paul had donated to the National Gallery.

Dearest Bryan,

I bought this painting years ago when I was Romantic.
*   Now I have Rothko. I don't know how I picked them, but interesting we are borrowing on their success so I can help Senator Edwards. Isn't it strange, a modern painting may get a Pres. of the U.S.*

On August 22, Bunny sent another check with a note thanking Bryan for "negotiating for the antique table in Charleston." No such table existed.

Bunny was writing these checks from her personal account, but the sums were larger than her usual outlays. In October, Chase Bank alerted her financial manager that Bunny did not have enough money in the account to cover a $150,000 check to Bryan Huffman. The sum was transferred so the check would not bounce, but since this was out of the ordinary, a bookkeeper in Kenneth Starr's office alerted Bunny's lawyer Alex Forger. "I asked Bunny, 'What is it for?'" Forger recalls. "She told me, 'Buying furniture from Bryan.'"

It was heady for Bunny to watch the Democratic presidential campaign unfold, relishing her secret role. "Our friend spoke very well and clear this morning on 'Meet the Press,'" Bunny wrote to Huffman on October 7, adding, "Some 'spirit' from nowhere said, 'Bunny, don't waste any time on anyone else. Just go ahead and do what you need to do!' If our country lets him slip away then we will see, what next?" Bunny remained opposed to Hillary Clinton, adding, "The Old Rag won't get it."

Three days later, the *National Enquirer* published a bombshell story: PRESIDENTIAL CHEATING SCANDAL! ALLEGED AFFAIR COULD WRECK JOHN EDWARDS' CAMPAIGN BID. The newspaper reported that a former Edwards campaign staffer had confessed to friends about the romance. Edwards convincingly denied the allegation, insisting to reporters, "The story is false. It's completely untrue, ridiculous... I've been in love with the same woman for thirty-plus years, and as anybody who's been around us knows, she's an extraordinary human being; warm, loving, beautiful, sexy, and as good a person as I have ever known."

The candidate was concerned that the damning article in the supermarket tabloid might sway his wealthy donors. Bryan Huffman got a reassuring call from Andrew Young. "We were told that the *National Enquirer* was making things up, Andrew told us not to pay attention. 'Can you believe that rag of a newspaper?'" He ruefully adds, "So Bunny and Bryan, these innocent dupes at the center of these things, knew nothing."

The story of the alleged affair did not have traction, and the mainstream media did not pursue the claim. But the *Enquirer* kept digging, and on December 19 produced another scorching headline—JOHN EDWARDS LOVE CHILD SCANDAL—showing a photograph of the seven-months-pregnant Rielle.

The weekly tabloid revealed that "in a bizarre twist," Andrew Young, who was married with three children of his own, claimed to be the father. Rielle backed him up with a statement: "The fact I am expecting a child is my personal and private business. This has no relationship to nor does it involve John Edwards in any way. Andrew Young is the father of my unborn child."

Hounded by the press, the purported lovers—along with Andrew Young's long-suffering wife, Cheri, and their children—fled to California. The out-of-work Young worried about making payments to complete a large mansion that he was building for his family in Raleigh.

This odd group needed money to live on. Texas attorney Fred Baron, who had made a fortune suing the tobacco companies, was Edwards's campaign-finance chairman and often lent his plane to ferry Edwards around the country. The lawyer stepped up to help his friend John Edwards, giving Andrew and Rielle $15,000 per month for expenses. At least Baron was aware of the situation and knew where his money was going.

All the warning signs were there, but the national press still did not pick up the story of John Edwards's affair. The tale seemed implausible against the backdrop of the heartwarming tale of marital devotion that John Edwards and his cancer-stricken wife sold to the press. On the eve of the Iowa caucus, Edwards, in the eyes of the media, still had a plausible, if long-shot, chance of winning.

Unaware of the campaign drama, Bunny remained determined to aid her candidate. That December, she called Alex Forger, asking for help. She was now ninety-seven, her eyesight was dimming, and she was having trouble writing checks. How should she make out a check for $175,000? This was a worrisome phone call for Forger, but Bunny blithely insisted to her lawyer that the money was for furniture. Canny and mischievous, she was having a marvelous time.

On January 3, 2008, Barack Obama swept to victory in the Iowa caucus with 32 percent of the vote, but John Edwards came in second, narrowly edging out Hillary Clinton. Five days later, New Hampshire voters went to the polls, and this time around Hillary was the victor, with Obama in second place and Edwards limping home a distant third. A disappointed Bunny wrote to Bryan to complain about the former First Lady's win: "The Old Rag is awful."

Loyal to her fast-fading candidate, Bunny sent another check for $200,000 to Bryan, which he dutifully forwarded on to Andrew Young.

Edwards staked his hopes on making a comeback in the South Carolina primary, but as Obama soared, the 2004 vice presidential nominee ended up in a weak third place. He dropped out of the presidential race on January 30, facing the press with his wife and three children by his side in New Orleans. A sadder but wiser Bunny wrote to Bryan Huffman: "My heart tells me our Senator made the elegant move to leave the Old Rag + Obama alone in their own world... Thank you for sharing our ups and downs."

Bunny's final foray into presidential politics was over. But she was still the matriarch of her family and capable of asserting her whims. On February 7, 2008, her grandson Thomas's wife, Rickie, gave birth to a premature baby girl, who was placed in the intensive care unit. Her parents named her Fiona. Since the couple's first child, a boy, had been stillborn eleven months earlier, the arrival of the baby girl was a special cause for celebration. Fiona was Bunny's first great-grandchild.

But after the infant came home from the hospital, Thomas got a call from his father, who was with Bunny in Antigua. Tuffy sounded distressed as he passed along the message that GranBunny disliked the name Fiona and was planning to call the baby Lucy.

Bunny had ignored Thomas for much of his life, and now she was trying to force a name change on him. Bunny's obtuseness is hard to fathom. Maybe she presumed that her grandson's concerns over his future inheritance would sway his judgment. Thomas politely told his father that Fiona would remain his daughter's name.

A few months later, the couple brought Fiona to see Thomas's father, who used a weekend house on Bunny's farm. When she heard that they were visiting, Bunny summoned them to lunch along with her other grandson, Stacy IV. Making small talk, Thomas asked his grandmother what she had been up to lately. Bunny explained that she had been organizing possessions stored in the nearby Brick House, the Georgian mansion that Paul Mellon had built for his first wife. Then Bunny dropped a backhanded bombshell, mentioning that Thomas's brother, Stacy IV, had visited during the week, adding, "He did very well, he left with a Picasso."

Here was yet another glaring example of her favoritism. As Rickie recalls, "I looked at Thomas, and he looked at me, and we both started howling with laughter. Stacy thought we were laughing at him and said, 'Don't be mad.'" Under her breath, Rickie whispered that it was better the painting went to him than a stranger.

As it turned out, there was no reason for sibling jealousy—the Picasso was a reproduction. Rickie was astonished by Bunny's cruelty toward both her grandsons, saying, "She wanted Thomas to feel badly. And she led Stacy to believe it really was a Picasso."

Bunny remained incorrigible. Her grandsons lived near each other in Virginia but upon learning that Thomas and Rickie planned to drive to Cape Cod, a nearly eight-hour trip, Bunny offered her plane to transport Stacy IV. The brothers only discovered what had happened when they both arrived separately at the Osterville house.

Bunny's divisive antics eventually led Thomas and Rickie to seek couples therapy for guidance on how to cope. As Rickie recalls, the therapist lectured both of them. "I was sitting there crying and he said to me, 'Don't you dare think you can marry into a family and make them what your family is.'" And then he turned to Thomas and stated, "How dare you not protect your wife from the craziness that is your family."

That April, Kenneth Starr, Bunny's accountant and money manager, was sued by ninety-year-old Joan Stanton, the retired actress and mother of three who had inherited more than $70 million from her deceased husband, Arthur Stanton, a Volkswagen distributor.

She charged that Starr had mismanaged her finances and cost her millions by inveigling her into signing over power of attorney and then putting her money into "illiquid, speculative and inappropriate investments." The lawsuit created ripples in New York circles thanks to Joan Stanton's well-connected daughter, novelist Jane Stanton Hitchcock.

Jane and her former husband, Paul Mellon's cousin William Hitchcock, had given an anniversary party for Bunny and Paul in the 1980s. Jane had been close to Jackie Kennedy and, at Jackie's advice, had used Alex Forger as her divorce lawyer. Bunny and Jane had worked side by side arranging flowers for Jackie's funeral. When Bunny initially contemplated writing an autobiography, Jane was one of the writers she approached, but the novelist demurred.

After Jane Stanton Hitchcock discovered documents that she believed revealed disarray in her mother's finances—from a $4.5 million loss on Planet Hollywood stock to a $5 million line of credit taken out on her East Hampton estate—she tried to interest the Manhattan district attorney's office in investigating Kenneth Starr. When prosecutors declined to pursue her allegations, she encouraged her mother to file a civil suit.

Starr's new lifestyle had already turned off some clients. The balding accountant had divorced his third wife, who had been stricken with multiple sclerosis, to marry Diane Passage, a statuesque pole dancer at the New York strip club Scores. According to an article in *Vanity Fair* by Michael Shnayerson, Starr was so preoccupied with his new wife that clients complained that basic paperwork was languishing and left the firm. New York's tabloids wrote about the Joan Stanton lawsuit, causing other Starr clients to pull out their funds.

Bunny had the opposite reaction. She found it impossible to believe that Ken Starr would behave unethically toward his clients. The trusted money manager insisted to Bunny's attorney Alex Forger that this lawsuit was just a family fight over money and Jane Stanton Hitchcock's concern about her inheritance. "Ken was dead-set against Jane," Forger recalls. "He said that Jane created the whole issue, that she was jealous. He insisted there was nothing to it."

For Jane Hitchcock, who saw herself as a whistle-blower, the social repercussions hurt. "I heard that Ken and Robert Isabell and Bunny were all talking about me and impugning my reputation," she told me. "It was very painful." Convinced that there would be other victims—"I knew that what Ken had done to one person, he would do to others"—she contemplated trying to warn Bunny. But mutual friends told her that Bunny disapproved of the lawsuit and would be unlikely to take the call.

The Edwards campaign was over but there were lingering aftereffects. Bunny had written a $200,000 "furniture check" in January, but it was not cashed until March. Puzzled by the oddity of the delayed check, endorsed by a third party that no one had heard of—Andrew Young's wife, Cheri Pfister—a bookkeeper in Kenneth Starr's office asked the bank for copies of Mrs. Mellon's checks for the past year and forwarded the packet to Bunny's lawyer.

Forger decided to dig deeper for an explanation. "Later in life, Bunny loved to play games, she loved fairy tales and horoscopes and wishes," Forger says. "Games appealed to her. There was this intrigue. She didn't want me to know she was giving to John Edwards, maybe I would disapprove. I kept asking, 'Where is the money going?'"

When his staff called Bunny's farm in April to ask about the furniture that she had supposedly purchased, they learned that the chairs and table listed on her checks did not exist.

In the eight years since Eliza Lloyd's accident, she had often been plagued by infections and health scares but always managed to recover. Even with the diminished quality of her existence, there was something heroic about Eliza's will to live.

"Bunny spent time with her every single day and that was hard," says Beverly Newton, Bunny's friend and psychic. Bunny lamented, in her phone calls to Newton, "With everything I have, I can't save her."

In early 2008, Beverly Newton had a powerful dream about Eliza—"I saw her in a field of daisies"—and called Bunny to relay the image from her subconscious. The two women concluded that this dream was a sign. "I believe it means that she's going to die," Bunny told Newton, who replied, "I believe she is, that she doesn't have much longer."

Eliza's health deteriorated that spring until it became clear that there would be no more reprieves. On May 7, sensing the end was near, Bunny asked librarian Tony Willis to stay with her until Eliza died. "Mrs. Mellon told me, 'It's not going to be easy but we can do it,'" Willis recalls. During the final hours in Eliza's ground-floor bedroom in her mother's home, at one point Eliza appeared to be alert, her eyes focusing, looking around as if seeking something. Bunny urged her daughter on: "You see that angel? You go to that angel and everything is going to be okay." Willis tears up as he describes the scene. "I saw this loving mother help her daughter, who was so ill, transition." Bunny wrote in her journal: "Lost my dear Eliza at 10:30. She looked like an angel."

Robert Isabell flew in to comfort Bunny and make the funeral arrangements, organizing the flowers for the church funeral. Bunny asked Rickie, her grandson's wife, to assist by bringing in her employer, Design Cuisine, to cater the reception. Bunny appeared calm and composed as she ushered Robert and Rickie to her storage area to choose the china from her vast collection. They settled on the eighteenth-century blue-and-white porcelain that had graced the tables at Eliza's 1968 wedding.

Bunny invited John Edwards to the funeral, but the task of actually getting him there was left to Bryan Huffman. "I kept calling his office to make these entreaties," Huffman recalls. "Bunny wanted John Edwards on one side of her and Caroline Kennedy on the other. The senator finally did call her and said he didn't want to share that day, and he would come privately to commiserate with her about their children." (Edwards was referring to the 1996 death of his son Wade in a car accident.)

Assigned to escort Bunny to the funeral, Huffman came to Bunny's house that morning and was summoned to her bedroom. Wearing a blue-gray boucle suit, she completed her outfit by putting on a beret, to which she pinned a John Edwards button. After Huffman gently convinced her that the campaign button was inappropriate, Bunny reached under her bed and pulled out cases of valuable jewelry, replacing the button with a diamond brooch.

The May 13 service at the Upperville Trinity Episcopal Church was led by Rev. Robert Banse Jr. Lilies of the valley were placed on Eliza's casket. Eliza's brother, Tuffy; half brother, Robin Lloyd; and stepbrother, Tim Mellon, delivered eulogies, along with actor Frank Langella, who had once dated Eliza and then became her mother's dear friend, and Eliza's Foxcroft classmate, gardening writer Mac Griswold. Caroline Kennedy was by Bunny's side. The service ended with the hymn "Go Forward, Christian Soldier."

The mourners made their way back to Bunny's farm. "I think people were relieved," says David Fleming, the son of Bunny's sister, Lily. "It was very sad, the accident was such a terrible thing." His wife, Kathy, recalls, "When we went back to the house for the luncheon, it was beautifully set up, a huge buffet, beautiful linen napkins, just perfect."

Alex Forger sought out Bryan Huffman at the lunch. The six-foot-three lawyer has a jocular manner, but he can be an intimidating and imposing figure. Forger cut to the chase and asked, "Tell me about the furniture that we've been buying."

"That's when the whole bottom dropped out from under me," Huffman recalled. He blurted out the entire tale—there had never been any furniture; all of Bunny's money had been meant to help John Edwards.

After the conversation ended, Huffman went to find Bunny. "Mr. Forger has just asked me about the furniture," he told her. "The jig is up."

Chapter Twenty-Six

The FBI Makes House Calls

Hot coffee

Even though John Edwards's presidential campaign had ended in January, he remained a potent political force. The desperate cover story—that Andrew Young was the father of Rielle Hunter's baby—had held. With the *National Enquirer* marginalized, both Hillary Clinton and Barack Obama vied for Edwards's endorsement.

On May 14, Edwards strode onstage to join Barack Obama at a campaign rally in Grand Rapids, Michigan, to give the Illinois senator his blessing. After Obama clinched the Democratic nomination, the former North Carolina senator was mentioned as a potential running mate. By July 8, NPR host Guy Raz told Edwards on air, "It's an open secret that you are on the short list" to be vice president. Edwards replied, "I will do anything that Senator Obama asks me to do, including this."

Hedging his bets, Edwards went to see Bunny in July with an audacious proposal. He wanted to start an antipoverty foundation as a launchpad for yet another political comeback. Afterward, Edwards described to Andrew Young a "long and wonderful" conversation with Bunny, adding, "She's a terrific person...and I think we can completely count on her." In the belief that a lucrative position would be waiting for him at the antipoverty organization, Young followed up with Bunny's money manager, Ken Starr. Sums ranging from $3 million to $50 million were discussed.

Edwards continued to live a charmed life but nonetheless insisted on taking self-destructive risks. On July 22, the *National Enquirer*, tipped off that Edwards would be meeting Rielle and her baby daughter, Quinn, staked out the Beverly Hills Hotel in Los Angeles. The newspaper's reporters caught the former senator trying to sneak out of a basement entrance at 2:40 a.m. A photo of Edwards holding the baby ran in the tabloid. That image finally destroyed his reputation.

In an attempt to control the damage, Edwards agreed to give a late-night interview to ABC anchor Bob Woodruff. Bunny, who received advance warning that Edwards planned to admit to the affair, was untroubled by his extramarital romance. Her father had affairs, politicians had affairs, and while her husband Paul Mellon's affairs had pained her, she had come to believe that these escapades were the prerogative of men of the world. "Bunny said that she didn't know why people made such a fuss over girlfriends," recalls Bryan Huffman. "All powerful people had girlfriends, what did that have to do with anything?"

During the Woodruff interview Edwards tried to make himself appear less like a cad by maladroitly claiming that he had begun the affair while his wife was in remission from cancer. Asked whether he was the father of Rielle's daughter, Edwards insisted, "That is absolutely not true" and added that he would "be happy to take a paternity test." Repudiating the photograph of himself with the infant, he said, "I don't know who that baby is. I don't know if the picture has been altered, manufactured..."

Woodruff stated that the network's investigative team had learned that Edwards's former campaign-finance chairman, Fred Baron, had given Rielle $15,000 per month to pay her bills and keep her quiet. Edwards insisted that this was news to him. "Is it possible that he was worried that in fact something had happened with me and he wanted to help?" Edwards said. "Of course that's possible." Edwards said that his wife had forgiven him, stating, "Elizabeth knows absolutely everything."

The former senator apparently believed he could talk his way out of this mess, but the public recoiled at his revelations. Rather than tamp down the scandal, he gave it new life.

FBI agent Chuck Stuber, who worked in the agency's Raleigh office, was on vacation in Alaska when he watched the embarrassing TV episode. "I thought, there you go, another politician having an extramarital affair, this time it's our senator in North Carolina."

But when Stuber returned to work, his boss asked him to open an investigation into Edwards to determine whether campaign money had been illegally used to finance the mistress. Stuber earned graduate degrees in law and accounting, and his specialty was investigating public officials for corruption. (He spent twenty-nine years with the FBI, retiring in 2014.) In the fall of 2008, Stuber contacted the U.S. attorney's office to discuss a potential Edwards investigation. He was urged to hold off making calls until after the November presidential election, for fear of being perceived as playing politics. He got started on document research instead.

Bunny invited John Edwards to visit her after the ABC interview to recover from the stress. He brought his friend John Moylan, a South Carolina lawyer and adviser. "Elizabeth Edwards asked me to go along because John had just had such a hard public fall," Moylan recalls. The two men arrived on August 14 and spent the night. "All went well," Bunny wrote in her journal. "Had a wonderful talk before dinner with John." As Moylan recalls, "John wanted to talk to her about what he might do next. She kept saying that he reminded her of John Kennedy. I didn't see any expression of condemnation from her. She had such high hopes for him."

But a collision between Bunny's protectors and the Edwards camp had been set in motion. Alerted by the ABC interview to Fred Baron's involvement in the emerging scandal, Bunny's lawyer Alex Forger called Baron to inform him about Bunny's secret "furniture" checks. Baron, then seriously ill with multiple myeloma (he would die in October), said he knew nothing about Bunny's money and speculated that this sounded like an Andrew Young "scam."

Fred Baron hung up the phone and immediately called John Edwards to fill him in on the conversation. Edwards then called Forger and vehemently denied any knowledge of $725,000 sent by Bunny for his benefit. "Edwards said that he was not aware of the checks and upset that Andrew had gone after Bunny for money," Forger recalls. His phone just kept ringing. Bryan Huffman was the next on the line. He had just heard from Andrew Young, who was panicked that Edwards was denying responsibility and throwing him under the bus.

Young consistently insisted—at the time and for years to come—that he and Edwards had discussed asking Bunny for money and that all of his actions had been done at the former senator's behest and with his full knowledge.

Bunny wrote in her journal on August 31, "Worried about John Edwards." But after she spoke to him by phone, she felt reassured. She discussed the situation with Bryan Huffman. "John Edwards called her up and smoothed it all over, all of the blame went on Andrew Young," Bryan says. "He denied any knowledge. Andrew Young became public enemy number one."

John Edwards continued to call Bunny on a regular basis and she marked down the dates: September 15; October 10 ("talked to John Edwards, not happy"); a cryptic note on October 12 ("talked to John Edwards. Trying to help him with friend"); and October 18 ("John Edwards and Caroline called").

As much as she hated to turn down any request from John Edwards, she declined to contribute to his new antipoverty foundation. Her lawyer and money manager opposed the grandiose notion. Her handwriting had become nearly illegible, so she dictated a letter on October 20 to her librarian, Tony Willis, for John Edwards, expressing regret that she could not provide the money.

———

Within days after Barack Obama won his historic victory, the FBI in Raleigh stepped up their investigation of John Edwards for possible campaign-finance-law violations. Chuck Stuber and another agent knocked on the door of Andrew Young's new mansion. Bitter and angry at Edwards, Young hired a lawyer to negotiate with the prosecutors and received immunity to testify.

Bryan Huffman was interviewed by the FBI at his mother's home in Monroe, North Carolina, with his sister Carol Kendrick, an attorney, sitting in. "As we talked and my mother brought out ginger cookies, they began to understand that my brother was not a sophisticated criminal," Kendrick recalls. "My brother is a very, very smart person but in this case, he was pretty naïve about the implications." The FBI agents told Huffman that he had been fortunate to use Federal Express when he sent Bunny's checks to Andrew Young, since if he had put a stamp on an envelope, he could have been prosecuted for mail fraud.

Alex Forger was concerned that Bunny had not paid taxes on the hundreds of thousands that she had given, in convoluted fashion, to help John Edwards. Forger filed a belated gift tax return on Bunny's behalf, paying a large sum including late penalties to square things with the IRS.

On March 20, 2009, by prearrangement, Chuck Stuber, along with an IRS agent and an assistant U.S. attorney, drove from Raleigh to Upperville to interview Bunny at her home. Most people quake at the thought of meeting with the FBI but Bunny, at nearly ninety-nine years old, was looking forward to it.

She greeted the delegation at the door and cheerfully announced: "I'm here to defend John Edwards." While Forger sat by protectively, Bunny charmed the agents with her stories about designing the Rose Garden. "It didn't seem like she was worried or scared," recalled Stuber. "She was amused by the whole process, that she was in the midst of something of such magnitude that the FBI was interested in her." She told Stuber to call her Bunny, but the agent decided it was more respectful to call her "Miz Bunny," in his Southern drawl.

Stuber insists that Bunny was never in legal jeopardy, despite her financial subterfuge. "I don't think it crossed anyone's mind," he says. "I thought she had been taken advantage of. She was an almost innocent bystander who was swept up in this corrupt effort by other people. With Miz Bunny, she didn't have any agenda at all, she wasn't trying to gain any influence in the White House." Bunny took such a liking to the FBI agent that she added him to her list of male telephone buddies, chatting periodically about their disparate lives.

Robert Isabell's phone calls, faxes, and visits to Upperville remained the high point of Bunny's days. She was knitting squares for an afghan as a gift for him. The florist party planner extraordinaire was proud of his relationship with Bunny. During his visits to her farm, when she napped, he would occasionally ask his friend Cathy Graham, who had a weekend house nearby, to come over. "When he took me through the greenhouse, I thought I would faint, I'd never seen anything so beautiful," she recalls. "You'd go into one room and it was all nasturtiums, straight out of an Art Nouveau painting."

Bunny had tried to spark a rivalry between her gentleman callers—Isabell and Bryan Huffman—but the two men declined to take the bait. Isabell felt sufficiently secure in his position as Number One Friend that he was not threatened by the small-town North Carolina decorator. When the two men overlapped at Bunny's farm on occasions such as her birthday and Eliza's funeral, they were cordial. Bryan Huffman listened with patient amusement as Bunny confided to him in their nightly calls about the latest thing that Robert Isabell had said or done.

After conquering New York society with his imaginative party décor, Isabell had become tired of working for demanding divas. "Robert grew bored with his business," says hotelier Ian Schrager. "Because he became a little difficult as he got older, he started to lose some clients." Isabell had regularly handled the flower arrangements for the Metropolitan Museum's Costume Institute Ball, but that prestigious annual job ended as *Vogue* editor Anna Wintour sought new talent.

Hoping for a new career as a real estate developer, Isabell purchased two properties in the up-and-coming Meatpacking District, near the soon-to-be-renovated High Line railroad tracks, and then made his big move, paying $45 million for a building at 837 Washington Street. His market timing was terrible, since he took that gamble right before the market crash of 2008. "He paid too much and didn't have financing," says Schrager. "He was starting to do desperate things to get it financed."

By the summer of 2009, close friends noticed that the fifty-seven-year-old Isabell was wilting under the pressure. He laid off most of his full-time employees and hired them as freelancers to handle party bookings. He sounded morbid as he contemplated the future. "He was in the midst of writing a new will," recalls Liz Garvin, a lighting designer who had worked for Isabell since 1991. "He was talking about it, he had this phobia about being buried."

Over the July 4 weekend, Isabell went to the Hamptons to arrange two parties: a lunch for Jane Wenner, the divorced wife of *Rolling Stone* publisher Jann Wenner; and a party for writer Lally Weymouth, the daughter of *Washington Post* publisher Katharine Graham. When he called Bunny en route—she was in Nantucket—she happily reminisced about her childhood visits to Southampton.

He seemed detached that weekend. "Robert wasn't feeling well," recalls Garvin, who was working at both events. "He went for a walk on the beach and tuned us all out." That evening he had a relaxed dinner with Ian Schrager and fashion designer Norma Kamali before going to Weymouth's home to supervise the party details. "Very late Saturday night he called on his way back to New York," Bunny later recalled in a written reminiscence. "He was very tired and always needed to get back to his own bed in New York."

Isabell was scheduled to fly to France to consult on a party for newspaper heiress Anne Cox Chambers, so Bunny did not worry when she didn't hear from him the next day. But when several days passed without a call, she panicked and began phoning Isabell's friends. Nobody knew where he was.

Two of Isabell's employees finally went to his house that Wednesday along with a security consultant who worked on the floral designer's parties. The door was locked from the inside and the police were called to open it. When they gained entrance, an awful smell pervaded the air in the July heat. Isabell was found dead in his bed, believed to have suffered a heart attack. His body was transported to Virginia, where Bunny commissioned an aboveground mausoleum in an old cemetery on her property.

"I think she was really in love with Robert," says Ian Schrager, who accepted Bunny's offer to visit the farm, along with Norma Kamali, to see Isabell's final resting place. "She started to tell us—she didn't know whether Robert thought about her the same way she thought about him."

Her friendship with Isabell was so well known that she received interview requests. Bunny wanted to honor and claim her friend, so she broke her usual silence and sang Isabell's praises to *New York* magazine: "His way of looking at everything was completely unique. He would come down here to the country, two or three times a month, with armloads of flowers. He was elusive and very, very attractive." At the request of Isabell's friend, writer James Reginato, Bunny wrote a wistful reminiscence for *W Magazine*, referring to her discussions with Isabell about the future of her Oak Spring Garden Library. "Each day we shared thoughts and happenings," she wrote. "As I grew into my late 90's, we planned what he would do to carry on."

Reginato visited Bunny's farm at her invitation. "She was ninety-nine. I was amazed by how strong she was and lively, very warm and animated," Reginato recalls. "She walked me around the garden and then went to see Robert's grave. She talked to him. 'Hi Robert.' It wasn't sad, she spoke to him in a sweet way."

The losses, oh, the relentless pace of the losses. Jackie and Stacy and Paul and her sister, Lily, and Eliza and now Robert, too. Teddy Kennedy had personally called to tell her that he had an inoperable brain tumor and his days were numbered. Bunny could not understand why she had outlived so many people she loved, most of them many years her junior. Even Dorcas Hardin had passed away. Baffled by God's plan for her, Bunny wondered what she was meant to do with whatever time she had left.

Bunny had suffered from depression before, and this latest loss could have sent her into a dark spiral. Instead, she figured out what she needed to do. "I stayed with her after Robert's death, I thought it would take her out," recalls Bryan Huffman. "But she moved on to another project." Nancy Collins, Bunny's nurse, concurs, saying, "Bunny never looked back, she dwelt on what she was given. She looked forward."

Building things had always given her pleasure. Inspired to honor her daughter, Bunny embarked on constructing a "Memory House" to feature Eliza's paintings and photographs. She sketched out her wishes and brought in a contractor. The spacious art-gallery-style building, adjacent to Bunny's library, was designed to include four large ground-floor rooms and a basement with ample storage space.

Bunny eerily re-created Eliza's studio in one room, with an easel, paintbrushes, and squeezed tubes of paint, as if the artist had just stepped out for a moment. A Diego Giacometti chandelier and tables decorated the building. Photographs of a laughing, happy Eliza looked out at the rooms, along with a photo of the teenage Bunny on a sailboat with her father, Gerard Lambert. The shrine included other cherished artwork, such as a cheerful Picasso painting of flowers.

Hungry for companionship, Bunny turned to her son, Tuffy, now in his seventies and living in Washington. She asked him to move to the farm, and she promised to renovate a house for him on her property, called the Hunter Barn, and build a separate library to accommodate the collection of this former bookstore owner. Standing for long periods had become difficult at her advanced age, so Bunny had Nancy Collins place a chair out in a field where she could contemplate the best angle to construct her son's library. Even with her deteriorating vision, Bunny had strong feelings about every aesthetic choice. After a mason put up a stone wall along the driveway to her specifications, she decided that she didn't like the angle and made him take down the wall and redo it.

Tuffy remained on good terms with his ex-wife, Anne Emmet, and happily informed her that he would be selling his Washington home and moving to Upperville, since his mother needed him. Aware of how long he had waited for recognition from his mother, aware that because it now suited Bunny, she would be taking her son away from his friends and his own life to live in isolation on the farm, Anne recalls that her thought was "It's too little, too late."

––––––––––––––––––––

A grand jury in Raleigh was impaneled to hear from the key figures involved in the John Edwards fund-raising scandal. Rielle Hunter testified on August 6. The FBI asked to interview Bunny again in November, this time without her lawyer present, and she agreed. Chuck Stuber wanted to know whether Bunny would have written the checks if she had known the money was meant to go to Rielle Hunter.

"Miz Bunny had an interesting take on mistresses," he recalls. "It was like—'Everybody does this.'" But she also told him that if a man wanted to keep a mistress, he should pay the cost himself, rather than rely on someone else's largesse. Stuber adds, "She didn't want her money going to support John Edwards's mistress."

Stuber came away with one assertion that he deemed valuable to the prosecution's case. John Edwards had publicly insisted that he was unaware of Bunny's checks on his behalf and that it was all a con by Andrew Young. But Bunny claimed that Edwards thanked her for the cash. That comment convinced Stuber: "Edwards knew about the money."

Bunny remained so committed to John Edwards that in a follow-up phone call with Stuber, she naively asked if he would intervene in the case. "She told me that John Edwards is kind of down right now, he could really use a pick-me-up. Can you do anything to help him out?"

That January, an ABC News helicopter hovered over Bunny's farm to shoot footage for an upcoming segment on Andrew Young, who had written a tell-all book, *The Politician*, about his tangled experiences with John Edwards. "We were up in her bedroom and there's a helicopter trying to take pictures," recalls nurse Nancy Collins. "She didn't like that. She thought it was silly."

On the eve of the book's publication, John Edwards finally admitted to fathering Rielle's daughter. "It was wrong for me ever to deny my daughter and hopefully one day, when she understands, she will forgive me," he said in a statement. Elizabeth Edwards responded by separating from her husband.

Life on the farm for Bunny resumed its peaceful routine. An employee would often fish in her bass-stocked pond early in the morning so that she could have fresh catch for breakfast. Using a camera that her first husband, Stacy Lloyd, had given her, Bunny took pictures of the budding and blossoming flowers in her garden. She stopped by her library most days to sip a Coke while gazing at her favorite bright-yellow Rothko. She liked to get out in the countryside.

"We'd get in the car sometimes and just ride," says Nancy Collins. A favorite destination was Carter Hall, Bunny's father's former estate, now run by the aid organization Project HOPE. "She would walk in like she still lived there," Collins recalled. "We went straight up the steps to the second floor. She'd say, 'This is where my room was, this is where Tuffy was born, Daddy's room was around the corner.'"

For years, Bunny had shunned interview requests related to her friendship with President Kennedy and his wife, Jackie, but she relented when former White House speechwriter and MSNBC host Chris Matthews asked to speak with her for his book *Jack Kennedy: Elusive Hero*. During their taped meeting, she apologized for her diminishing vision. "I have hardly any eyesight. I see your shape. And I see your hair...All of a sudden in the last six months, it makes me so sad, it's very hard for me to talk to you and tell you all I know when I just can't see."

But Bunny rolled back through the years to share her favorite stories. In a mostly unpublished thirty-one-page transcript of the interview, graciously given to me by Chris Matthews, Bunny animatedly discussed the day that JFK asked her to work on the Rose Garden, the aftermath of the Cuban missile crisis ("He was upset about Cuba...I heard him talk so much about it that I sort of felt with him"), and Jackie Kennedy's awareness of her husband's infidelities ("She saw his faults").

Bunny explained that after the president's death, Jackie became adept at hiding her feelings. As Bunny put it, "She had a wonderful way of pulling the curtain down, like boom. She hid herself behind this curtain. I've never seen anyone who could be so well mannered and calm but if she didn't want to say or do anything, she didn't."

As the conversation rambled and Bunny discussed her childhood and life with Paul Mellon, Matthews mentioned that he knew and liked Senator John Warner, who had been married to Bunny's step-daughter, Cathy Mellon. Bunny launched into an angry late-in-life diatribe about her stepdaughter, saying, "Cathy had an idea that she was something great and it just irritated the heck out of me. I couldn't teach her anything."

She then pulled herself back to explain how she handled disappointing relationships. "If I don't like somebody, I just say goodbye dear and goodbye. I've met a lot of interesting people, and some of them are good and nice and some of them are just shams. They think they're something, they're not."

The author could not resist bringing up John Edwards. "He's a very, very nice guy," Bunny replied. "What went wrong with him? I mean, I just sort of feel someone came and put an injection in him and made him a little naughty. Even now, I'm for John Edwards."

For a woman nearing her one hundredth birthday, a change of heart seemed unlikely, and yet Bunny had finally warmed up to her grandson Thomas Lloyd and his wife, Rickie. Thomas had left his job in TV production to become an insurance agent, working with small businesses. When the couple's Alexandria, Virginia, home, which Bunny had never visited, became uninhabitable due to a roof leak, Bunny invited them to stay at her farm while repairs were made. Rickie was then pregnant with her second child and the nanny had just quit; Bunny suggested importing a Swiss nanny. When Rickie informed her that they did not have a spare bedroom, Bunny responded with shock: "You don't have staff quarters?"

Thomas received a phone call from Alex Forger, who reported with dry humor that Bunny was gravely concerned about the living conditions of her great-grandchildren. Bunny helped the couple buy a new house, contributing $1 million.

When the couple's baby boy, Teddy, was born in April, she was eager to see him. His older sister, Fiona, an adorable sprite who made her great-grandmother laugh, had worn down Bunny's resistance. A video shot by Thomas one morning shows Bunny in her four-poster bed with Fiona snuggled up next to her, as the two of them happily play with a stuffed animal. Bunny coos with delight, "He's a dear doggie. Shake hands with him." Bunny had never been interested in children, but now she had been given a second chance.

Yet for a widow worth an estimated half-billion dollars, she remained parsimonious toward her family. She had revised her will to leave her two grandsons $2 million each, up from the initial $200,000, plus the remainder of the Gerard Lambert trust. She made no provisions for her great-grandchildren, not even an educational trust.

Her grandsons had grown up flying on her private plane, vacationing at her Antigua estate, dining with seventeenth-century silver utensils off antique Meissen plates, cosseted by her well-trained staff while surrounded by artworks by Renoir, Degas, and Rothko. As specified in her will, they would be able to pick out a few modest items, but if they wanted other possessions that belonged to GranBunny, they could bid at auction beside total strangers.

Even though Bunny had convinced her son, Tuffy, to move to the farm, she did not give him the house that she had renovated for his use. Instead, she left him a "life estate"—he could live there until he died, paying taxes and maintenance, but he could not sell it or bequeath it to his two sons.

Bunny rarely discussed her plans with her relatives and they typically discovered her decisions as a fait accompli. Her son was hurt and angry when informed that not a single acre of the Virginia farm, which he had moved to as a child in 1948, would remain in his family. He and his children were emotionally attached to the land, but she had decided to sever the connection.

"My grandmother was the puppet master, things were done behind closed doors," says Thomas Lloyd, who broke the news to his father and urged him, albeit unsuccessfully, to make his feelings known to Bunny. "My father's fear of her was so great that he didn't want to have a conversation with his own mother."

Bunny had been born into wealth and married the inheritor of a robber baron fortune, but she decided that her descendants would not share her lifestyle. Her priority was now philanthropy, heeding her grandfather's call to do good for her country. She put her son and two grandsons on the board of the Gerard B. Lambert Foundation so that after her death they could decide how her millions were spent. But she would be the last empress of Upperville.

———

In his sunny Manhattan office on a high floor overlooking Central Park, Alex Forger, now eighty-seven, still presided over Bunny's legal affairs, although he employed two seasoned attorneys to handle day-to-day matters. Forger kept an eye on Bunny's finances, and he became concerned when he noticed that Ken Starr had transferred $5.75 million of Bunny's money into an escrow account. The men met for lunch to discuss the matter.

"He told me that he was bundling her money with other investors to make a major investment," Forger says. "I told him I would prefer you put it back in Treasuries. A week later, he said there were some complications with the paperwork. He outright lied. When the money didn't come back, I called the D.A.'s office, since what he said didn't ring true to me."

The authorities were already investigating Starr after receiving complaints from other clients. On the morning of May 27, 2010, federal agents arrived at Starr's Upper East Side home, a triplex condominium with a thirty-two-foot pool and a garden. According to a *Vanity Fair* article by Michael Shnayerson, Starr's wife, exotic dancer Diane Passage, told the agents her husband was not there. But when they showed her a warrant and told her that they were giving her one last chance to answer, she admitted that her husband was hiding in a bedroom closet.

Charged with defrauding clients in an estimated $30 million Ponzi scheme, Starr was denied bail and jailed, with his assets frozen. His frantic clients were initially unable to get any information on what had happened to their accounts. Starr had held power of attorney for Bunny and Tuffy and managed money for her two grandsons. When the family met with Forger in Upperville over Memorial Day weekend, Bunny was frightened, asking, "Is it very bad? Do I have to sell the plane? Do I have to let people go?"

It was bad. Court filings would subsequently list Bunny as a creditor who had lost $12 million; the true number was closer to $18 million. Her son, Tuffy, lost $10.375 million including college funds set aside for his grandchildren. The money that vanished included a multimillion-dollar settlement that he had just received from the malpractice lawsuit against St. Vincent's Hospital over his sister Eliza's care.

"It was a jaw-dropping experience," says Thomas Lloyd. "Ken was someone my grandmother trusted for years and years. The same thing with my father, who is open-minded and trusting." (This was such a wake-up call that Thomas Lloyd changed careers and became a certified financial planner, joining a wealth management firm with the hope of helping others avoid similar disasters.)

Bunny had previously invited writer James Reginato to bring a photographer to the farm over Memorial Day weekend for a *Vanity Fair* article on her gardens and her legacy. They happened to turn up on the same day as Alex Forger. Bunny was so rattled that she declined to have her portrait taken. "This Ken Starr thing so took the wind out of her sails," Reginato recalls. "She looked so much more frail than she'd been. She was so diminished."

Starr eventually pleaded guilty and was sentenced to seven and a half years in prison. (He would serve less than six years.) Ordered to make restitution to his clients, he filed for bankruptcy. Jane Stanton Hitchcock was pleased to receive a call from Bunny, who told her, "Jane, I am so, so sorry. You were right all along."

Bunny had been planning to give herself an elaborate one hundredth birthday party, summoning her grandson's wife, Rickie, to the farm to discuss the catering arrangements. Rickie had become an observant student of Bunny's style. (Her entertaining and organizational skills would lead to a White House job as First Lady Melania Trump's social secretary.) At lunch with Rickie, Bunny announced that she had decided to cancel her party on the advice of her doctor, who thought she was too weak for an elaborate celebration.

In honor of the August 9 centennial, Caroline Kennedy flew in, and Bryan Huffman and librarian Tony Willis joined the family for the low-key celebration. Caroline brought an elaborate cake shaped like the historic Nantucket Lightship, which Bunny had helped save with a financial contribution. Bunny loved the cake so much that she had her carpenters make a wooden replica.

"I would phone her on big events like her birthday," said Dr. Bruce Horten, a confidant from her earlier years. "She told me, 'When I hit one hundred, I will begin subtracting.'" She actually did it, telling friends and family that she was now only ninety-nine.

The grand jury in Raleigh was still investigating John Edwards, and on December 3, 2010, Bunny's family members—her son, two grandsons, and Rickie—were called to testify. Only Stacy IV had ever met John Edwards, so there were no questions about the legal issues. Prosecutors were trying to ascertain whether Bunny was compos mentis and able to make her own decisions.

This line of questioning had evolved out of the well-publicized Brooke Astor case. The wealthy Social Register centenarian, suffering from Alzheimer's, had been victimized by her son and his attorney, who were convicted of conspiring to steal her money. The Raleigh grand jury wanted to ensure that no one had twisted Bunny's arm when she signed the so-called furniture checks.

"I explained to them, there's nobody telling my grandmother what to do," recalls Thomas Lloyd. "You can't tell my grandmother what to do, she's going to do what she wants."

Bunny had been sitting by the phone all that day, waiting to hear about the Raleigh grand jury, so she was pleased when Rickie called that evening to fill her in. Rickie explained that she had been asked "the weirdest questions": Was I ever alone with you? If you wanted to talk to me, could you reach me? Was Bryan asking you to give the money? Was it Alex Forger? Do you have free will?

Bunny was fascinated by every detail, including Rickie's description of what the jurors were wearing. "She loved being the center of attention," Rickie recalls. "She was laughing." After hearing about the jurors' questions, Bunny remarked, "I think these are just country folks who have no idea how normal we are." The comment made Rickie smile, since "here I was unpacking from her private plane."

Elizabeth Edwards, the wife of John Edwards, died of breast cancer in December 2010, at the age of sixty-one. The obituaries mentioned her husband's infidelity and the tortured nature of their marriage. A POLITICAL LIFE FILLED WITH CRUEL REVERSALS was the headline on the *New York Times* story.

It took another six months, but the grand jury finally acted. John Edwards was indicted on June 3, 2011, for violating campaign-finance laws by "secretly obtaining" money from Bunny and the deceased Fred Baron to conceal his mistress and their baby. "I will regret for the rest of my life the pain and harm that I've caused others," he told reporters. "But I did not break the law. And I never, ever thought that I was breaking the law."

Edwards turned himself in at the Greensboro, North Carolina, courthouse for fingerprinting and a DNA swab. "Even that day, he was a politician," recalls FBI agent Chuck Stuber. "I remember shaking his hand, he gave me a big smile: 'Great to meet you.' He kept asking questions about my family, my wife, and my kids. Most people you're arresting aren't this cordial."

Worth an estimated $30 million, Edwards did not want to pay for a costly trial on the six-count indictment, which carried a maximum penalty of thirty years in prison. So he reportedly asked Bunny for the money. She turned him down. Enough was finally enough.

When I spoke to Bunny on the phone a few weeks later for an

article for *Newsweek*, she remained loyal to the former presidential candidate. "John Edwards, I've been sticking up for him because I've known him from way, way back," she told me. "I've always been behind him and I thought he'd be a good president."

She said that it was odd, at this point in her life, to be in the headlines. "I just want to live quietly and garden, that's all." Bunny was still brooding over the Ken Starr debacle. "I felt it was just terrible because I trusted him and we're in sort of a hole because of that. I don't know what made him go berserk like that." She felt especially guilty about encouraging friends to rely on Starr, saying, "The worst thing is the people he stole money from. It's terrible to have people not loyal to you. I try to forget him, there's nothing I can do."

She was feeling her age. In her whispery voice, she said, "I had a very serious operation a little while ago and ever since then I've been very very weak. I was on death's door but the man operated. I'm going along on very weak wheels." She put off my request to meet in person, explaining, "I went to the hospital in Winchester yesterday and the doctor said to take it easy, don't try to see people. The best way is to lay low for a while. But here I'm talking to you, as friendly as anybody. I'm so glad to talk to you."

Chapter Twenty-Seven

Everything Should Be Noticed

In the spring of 2012, as John Edwards's trial grew near, Bunny was virtually alone in her continuing devotion to the disgraced politician whose framed picture retained a place of pride on her bedside table. A CBS News / *New York Times* poll found that Edwards was viewed favorably by only 3 percent of Americans.

With Edwards barred by court authorities from speaking with her, with so many of her intimates now deceased, Bunny felt claustrophobic on her farm. Even though her long-distance vision had deteriorated so that she could scarcely see more than shapes, one sparkling day she impulsively asked that her Falcon Jet be brought down from Dulles Airport to her airstrip. Her plan, which she carried out with brio, was to fly over the Blue Ridge Mountains to better commune with nature.

In her nightly phone calls with Bryan Huffman, who was scheduled to testify at the trial, she raised the fanciful possibility that they were both in legal jeopardy. As Huffman recalls, one night she gushed on the phone: "Bryan, just imagine, if we go to jail for this we could get cells next to each other and do them so attractively. Very spare, attractive, and warm, we could talk through the bars."

During opening arguments on Monday, April 23, prosecutor David Harbach portrayed the ex-senator as an amoral and ambitious schemer willing to do anything to salvage his presidential ambitions and desperate for money to hide his pregnant mistress. "This was dangerous," said Harbach. "The mistress was a loose cannon, unemployed and needing money—and he [Edwards] knew it. He made the choice to accept hundreds of thousands of dollars so that he could become president."

The Edwards defense team offered a set of motives that had little to do with politics. Allison Van Laningham, one of Edwards's defense lawyers, wrote the word "HUMILIATION" on a white tablet, insisting that Edwards's conduct was driven by his efforts to prevent his wife from finding out about Rielle Hunter and the baby. Van Laningham wrote down the words, "FOLLOW THE MONEY," stressing that "not one penny went to the John Edwards for President campaign or to John Edwards...John Edwards is a man who has committed many sins but no crimes."

There were two central issues in the case: Did Edwards knowingly solicit the money in violation of campaign laws? Did Bunny and Fred Baron intend to make personal gifts to Edwards, or were the checks designed as political contributions to elect him to the presidency?

In deference to her advanced age, Bunny was not asked to testify, but her name was invoked in court almost every day. She avidly followed each development. "She read everything," says her nurse, Nancy Collins. With the courtroom packed with out-of-town reporters, Bunny's conservative Republican stepson Timothy Mellon flew in from his Connecticut home to watch a few days of testimony.

The trial lasted nearly six weeks, featuring twenty-four government witnesses and a paper trail of 488 exhibits. The government's central witness was Andrew Young. The former Edwards loyalist painted John Edwards as a mastermind who urged him to ask Bunny and Fred Baron for money.

But Young's credibility was undermined when he sheepishly admitted that he had siphoned off hundreds of thousands of dollars of Bunny's money to pay for his new $1.5 million house in Raleigh. Even prosecutor Harbach acknowledged, "Andrew Young's hands are not exactly clean either."

Bryan Huffman won kudos for his aplomb on the stand. "After two weeks of somber testimony from witnesses in dark suits, the interior decorator breezed into the windowless courtroom in yellow checked blazer, matching yellow tie and pocket square," wrote Michael Biesecker in the *Spartanburg Herald-Journal*. "His mouth perpetually poised in a smile, he spoke in a drawl suited for the sitting parlor of an antebellum mansion."

Huffman told the jury that Bunny had a huge crush on Edwards and that she reveled in their secret method of sending money to the ex-senator. But he stressed that Bunny was disturbed when Edwards asked for $50 million to fund his would-be foundation. "She was rather apoplectic at the size of the request," Huffman testified. Mimicking her whispery voice, he repeated her words at the time: "I cannot believe that the senator wanted me for my money all along."

After the government rested its case, the defense presented a mere handful of witnesses, choosing not to put John Edwards on the stand. In closing arguments, the prosecution and the defense argued over the fundamental question: Who do you believe? A former Democratic vice presidential nominee and ex-senator who claims he knew nothing about the money, or his aide whose wife deposited the cash and who spent most of it on himself? Abbe Lowell, one of Edwards's defense lawyers, declared that Andrew Young and his wife, Cheri, "could shame Bonnie and Clyde."

For nine days, the jury deliberated, finally announcing on May 31 that they had acquitted John Edwards of one count, finding that it was not illegal for him to take $200,000 from Bunny in 2008, after his presidential candidacy had ended. But the jury deadlocked on the remaining five counts. After the judge declared a mistrial, the government chose to drop the case rather than try it again.

"Mrs. Mellon was very relieved that he didn't have to serve jail time," says Tony Willis. "She was just tired of it, all the fuss." John Edwards called her as soon as Abbe Lowell gave him permission to do so. "I have no doubt that John Edwards liked Bunny," Lowell later told me. "He admired her intelligence, her life, her adventures. There was a mutual affection between them." But in the public eye, the relationship appeared tarnished: Edwards was perceived as having exploited

Bunny, taking advantage of the financial generosity of a besotted, if knowing, elderly woman and treating her as his personal ATM.

Bunny had no regrets. She had tried to heed her grandfather's advice to help her country, and the experience had given her a late-in-life sense of purpose. On those nights when John Edwards called her right before striding onstage for presidential primary debates, she had felt connected to something momentous.

When she talked it over from time to time with Bryan Huffman, she would often end with the same wistful line: "Didn't we have fun?"

Asset-rich but now cash-poor due to the millions of dollars stolen from her by Ken Starr, Bunny put several of her homes on the market. She sold her Paris apartment to her friend Akko van Acker for an undisclosed sum. (Subsequently unable to find a buyer for his own Paris residence, van Acker then sold Bunny's place to one of his former employees.) Conservative billionaire William Koch, who owned a Cape Cod property that adjoined Bunny's Osterville estate, bought her property there for a reputed $19.5 million in 2013. In order to create a private compound, Koch then paid $7 million to Ned Crosby, Bunny's former sailing companion, for the modest acre and a quarter of adjoining land that she had given him.

Bunny owned two other Cape Cod properties. She planned to leave the eighteenth-century Putnam House to her son, but tentatively agreed to sell to William Koch the Dune House, the cozy, two-bedroom, waterside Cape Cod cottage with a pool that had been her favorite getaway. At the last minute, her son, Tuffy, learned—via word passed on by a Cape Cod gardener—about the potential sale of the Dune House and asked his mother to give him the property instead. This would eventually allow him to give each of his sons a Cape Cod home. Bunny transferred the title to her son as a birthday gift.

Bunny fantasized about continuing to visit the Dune House but knew that the one-story property did not have rooms to house her staff. So the centenarian designed a guest cottage for the property. Her grandson Thomas Lloyd took on the task of carrying out her wishes, working with a builder to turn GranBunny's sketches into reality.

Even after her Cape Cod and Paris staffers were laid off, Bunny retained 130 employees at her remaining homes in Upperville, Antigua, and Nantucket. The butlers, cooks, and housekeepers were comically underemployed. She had quirky requests that her employees were reluctant to fulfill: The nature lover wanted her staff to dispense with mousetraps and leave cheese out to feed the hungry creatures in winter.

Hubert de Givenchy still checked in weekly. "Sometimes she's tired, sometimes she sleeps, sometimes Nancy or Tony Willis said she's not available," Givenchy recalls. But when they did chat, they reminisced about old times. "We talk and we laugh. Sometime Bunny would say, 'Oh, you know I am very very old.' I said, 'You are not old at all, you stay with your spirit.'"

He recounts his memory of a typical conversation:

I tease her—"Do you think you have an evening dress you prefer for tonight?"

"I have a lot of evening dresses but I am not going out anymore."

"But Bunny, tonight I am coming to take you and we are going to dance together at Studio 54."

"Hubert, you never change, what I like with you is that you are always happy."

"Bunny, I am happy because I speak with you."

Bunny no longer walked the short distance between her home and the library. Driven past the building by car, she was often too weary to get out of the automobile. Tony Willis would stick his head out the window to wave or run out to chat. Likening the librarian to the yearly harbinger of spring popping out of the ground, she started calling Tony "the Groundhog" and joked about "the Bunny" and "the Groundhog."

Her diminishing eyesight was debilitating. Her grandson Stacy IV, who had left his job at Bunny's library to work on a start-up, came back frequently to visit. He was saddened to see her struggle. "We were eating lunch and she was having a hard time picking up the food," he recalls. "The next day, she said, 'I feel so embarrassed, I don't want to ask for help.'"

At Bunny's request, Bryan Huffman moved up his calls, reaching her at 4 p.m. rather than 9 p.m. "I still talked to her every day, but she sounded weak," he says. Bunny could read, but she had to hold up publications to her nose to make out the words. The obituaries brought daily jolts of sadness as younger friends passed away. Hairdresser Kenneth Battelle and Nantucket weaver Andy Oates both died at the age of eighty-six. She had been planning her own funeral for years and was still envisioning her send-off. It would be the final perfect Bunny Mellon production.

Bette Midler had agreed to sing and Frank Langella had promised to deliver a eulogy. Bunny chose the hymns: "O God, Our Help in Ages Past," "In the Bleak Midwinter," and "Go Forward, Christian Soldier." The American Boychoir, a touring teenage ensemble that until recently had occupied her father's former home, Albemarle in Princeton, New Jersey, agreed to perform per her wishes.

Even though her closets contained racks of magnificent Givenchy and Balenciaga couture, she wanted to be buried wearing the simple college graduation gown that she had worn to receive an honorary degree from the Rhode Island School of Design. Her father did not believe that a young woman of her generation was worth sending to college; she would spend eternity proving him wrong. Bunny chose her honorary pallbearers as well as the favored farm employees who would actually be responsible for moving her coffin.

All was in readiness. And yet every morning, she woke up once more to the sound of birdcalls in Upperville and carried on. John Edwards called occasionally. For Bunny, these conversations served as validation that he genuinely cared and that their relationship had not been solely about her money.

She was winding down emotionally. "Sometimes Bunny would call me and tell me, 'Beverly, I'm so tired, can I go now?'" Beverly Newton recalls. "I would say, 'I'm sorry, it's not your time yet. Let me rephrase that, I'm not sorry you're going to live, I'm very happy, but I do know it's not your time yet.'"

Bunny made regular trips to Trinity Church in Upperville, choosing quiet times so she could have the place to herself. "She always lit the cross on the altar. She would sit in the same pew towards the back, she'd kneel," recalls Nancy Collins. In good weather, Bunny would perch on a bench outdoors in the Mellon private cemetery and talk to deceased members of her family, telling "Éléphant," her nickname for Paul Mellon, about farm life and reassuring Eliza, "I'm going to be with you soon."

In conversations with Reverend Robert Banse Jr., the church rector, Bunny raised questions about what would happen after she died.

"Mrs. Mellon believed there was life to come," he later recalled. "We would talk about it and she looked forward to being with Eliza and Mr. Mellon again and the other people she had loved in her lifetime. She'd say, 'Reverend Banse, do you think I'll make it to heaven? You know, I have made mistakes along the way.' I would always respond, 'Welcome to the club.' I did everything in my power to assure her over and over that she would be very much in the presence of a living, loving God."

Christmas had always been Bunny's favorite holiday, and she relished shopping for gifts. In December 2013, she asked Nancy Collins to drive her to Middleburg. When they reached the holiday-festooned shops on Main Street, Bunny waited in the car while Nancy obeyed her instructions to go into a store and bring out a stack of cashmere scarves for her approval. Bunny looked at the colors and asked, "Which one do you want?" The trip had been all about buying her nurse a Christmas present.

Each year, Bunny gave a Christmas lunch for her employees, held in a farm garage that had been cleaned, painted, and decorated with a holiday tree. "Mrs. Mellon would always go to each table and talk to every person," recalls gardener George Shaffer. This year, she did not have the stamina to table-hop. "She came to the Christmas lunch but Nancy helped her, she had a nice comfy chair for Mrs. Mellon to sit in," he says. "People came to her, rather than her coming to each table. She seemed really happy."

By March Bunny was exhausted, sleeping way beyond her normal hours. Her nurses believed that she would not last much longer. Bunny had an intuitive feeling about her own body clock. On Friday, March 14, when Nancy Collins asked if she should call the rector for last rites, Bunny replied, "In three days."

That afternoon, she asked to see Tony Willis. She wanted to thank him for his work on the library. Instead of saying good-bye, she discussed the cold weather and the upcoming storm predicted by meteorologists. "Tony, it's going to snow," she told him. Bunny took a childish pleasure in snowstorms, and she was looking forward to the transformation of the farm into an old-fashioned postcard.

Bunny called Hubert de Givenchy that weekend, and they had a lighthearted chat about cruises they had taken to Venice and Greece. After four decades of conversations, she still welcomed the sound of his melodious voice. Bunny also spoke to Frank Langella and John Edwards. She wanted to wring pleasure from every last moment, to bask in the affection of these men who had mattered.

Friends and family members were summoned as Bunny weakened. Her son, Tuffy, now living roughly a quarter of a mile away on his mother's property, was in poor health but came to her bedside. Alex Forger flew in from New York, Bryan Huffman drove up from North Carolina, and Bunny's grandsons, Thomas and Stacy IV, arrived to bear witness.

When Bryan went up to Bunny's bedroom, he took her hand and was surprised that her handshake remained so strong, a legacy of all those years of pruning trees. "She was on morphine, so she was kind of out of it, but she still had that grip," he recalls. "She kept hold of my hand."

The scene was leavened by Bunny's great-grandchildren, Fiona and Teddy, who kept playfully dashing in and out of the room. As Bryan recalls, "Little Fiona was grabbing crocuses, and saying, 'GranBunny, you've got to feel better, we've got to go outside.'"

At the end of the afternoon, Thomas Lloyd's wife, Rickie, and their two children headed back home to Arlington, but he stayed on to spend the night at his father's home. His grandmother had been a powerful force, and he had worked hard to build a loving bond with her in these final years. He wanted to be nearby if needed. His brother, Stacy IV, who as a child had energetically jumped into Bunny's bed in the morning, carefully lay down beside GranBunny to hold her in his arms one last time. He finally left for his home, a short drive away. Bunny appeared to be unconscious by the time the Episcopal priest came to give her last rites.

The fluffy snow came down steadily that night. The window in Bunny's room had been left open, as she had requested, so that she could be as close to nature as possible. Around 2 a.m., she slipped away. The nurses would later say that it felt as if Bunny's spirit sailed out the window into the snowstorm.

Caroline Kennedy, who had been named the American ambassador to Japan in 2013, was halfway around the world when she learned of Bunny's death. So many memories came back to her of all the time they had spent together. Caroline sent a eulogy to Bunny's family that stressed just how much Bunny had meant to her and how much she would miss this lifelong family friend:

Her world was beautiful, well-built and infinitely interesting— she had the best books, the best food, the prettiest house with painted floors, a garden like George Washington, plates with camels on them, paintings that made you re-examine the world around you, and stories of sailing huge J-boats, sitting on Calvin Coolidge's lap, glamorous debutante parties, the war, Balenciaga himself, digging up the Rose Garden hot line to Moscow, saving the Nantucket Light Ship, discovering Mark Rothko, and sitting next to the Chief Justice.

Those are the parts that don't include her commitment to fairness and justice, her lifelong interest in politics that she pretended not to have, and her intense and steadfast love of the people she cared about. She brought American history to life with a heart and soul devoted to her country, to the power of the natural world, and to God.

When I was packing for Japan, I came across half a sixpence wrapped in West Indian cloth that was our special symbol. When I was ten, I asked her to be my other godmother and, as usual, she came up with a better idea. I would be her Sixpence Child. If I ever needed her, I was to send the sixpence and she would come to help me.

Bunny has already helped me more than I can say—but I keep it with me all the time.

Thank you, Bunny and God Bless you always.

On the morning of March 28, a steady line of cars headed toward Trinity Episcopal Church in Upperville. The few shops were closed and the town seemed deserted, as if everyone was going to Bunny Mellon's funeral.

A sign outside the chapel welcomed Bunny's "farm family" and directed the overflow to a tent set up behind the church. My husband and I slipped into a back row next to John Baskett, the art curator and Paul Mellon's biographer, who had flown in from London.

Moments before the service began, John Edwards and his daughter Cate, arrived at the chapel. This was a sticky etiquette situation. Bunny had wanted Edwards to be an honorary pallbearer, and the loyal Nancy Collins had argued with Bunny's family that her wishes should be upheld. But Thomas Lloyd was adamantly opposed. Alex Forger called Edwards to explain the situation but encouraged the former senator to attend even without the honorary position, since Bunny wanted him there. Then the night prior to the funeral, Timothy Mellon, Bunny's stepson, over dinner with Rickie Niceta and Thomas Lloyd, told them that he would walk out if John Edwards even entered the church.

Now, just outside the doorway, an usher who was unaware of the controversy recognized Edwards and welcomed him, saying, "We've got seats up front." But event planner Roger Whyte, hired by the family, blocked entry. "I'm so sorry but the church is full," Whyte announced. Convinced that this must be an issue of mistaken identity, the former senator introduced himself, saying, "I'm John Edwards." As Whyte recalls, he replied, "I'm aware, sir, and I do apologize, but there's still no space in the church." Whyte says that he had to repeat himself several times before the ex-senator and his daughter finally retreated to the overflow tent, joining the latecomers and those who had been on the periphery of Bunny's life.

For a long-planned funeral marking the passing of a legendary 103-year-old grande dame with a Social Register pedigree, the two-and-a-half-hour service offered up surprising moments of raw emotion. Bunny's genial son, Tuffy, shuffled unsteadily to the front. Perhaps because he had been ill recently his remarks were unfiltered, offering a free-associated tour of family life. He harked back to his childhood and brought up the event that ruptured his life—his mother's divorce from his father, Stacy Lloyd. "As bad luck would have it," he told the mourners, "she got married again to a man named Paul Mellon."

The audience stirred nervously as he discussed Bunny and Paul's "fight over money and building these houses" and the time that he thought they might divorce, too. He also recalled his furious reaction upon learning that his divorced parents, Bunny and Stacy, were meeting frequently at the Comanche Inn in St. Croix, recalling, "I had never seen such blatant blasphemy in my life."

His voice cracked as he ended on a poignant note. "I miss Mummy, we got along pretty well. I will miss you truly. Be safe and take care of God."

His son Stacy Lloyd IV gave a heartfelt speech about what "GranBunny" had taught him. "I will always think of her when I look at Cape Cod dune grass as it blows in the breeze, or when I'm on the farm and see a flower." He recalled her patience when she took him out on her boat. "She said, 'Stacy, one of things I just love about sailing, I love the flapping sound of the water as it hits wood. I love the creaking sounds of the planks and the hull, the silence that pierces through.'"

His older brother, Thomas Lloyd, candidly admitted that as a child he found his grandmother to be "intimidating" and they "were not particularly close." Once he became an adult, he said, "God blessed me with the connection of my own two children, Fiona and Teddy, and their collective fearlessness, which I lacked as a child, brought joy and laughter to my grandmother. The children would come into her living room shouting her name. Fiona took her first steps in that living room and her first steps were not to me, she took them to her great-grandmother."

He started to cry as he talked about how grateful he was for GranBunny's long life. "Her extended time with us gave me the chance to have a relationship the shy little boy always longed for."

In his booming voice, the actor Frank Langella entertained the crowd with anecdotes dating back to the summer of 1961. At age twenty-three, as Eliza's date, he was invited to a luncheon given by Bunny at her Cape Cod estate, where he was stunned to discover the other guests were President Kennedy and his wife, Jackie, along with Noël Coward and Adele Astaire.

"Like the flowers in all the gardens she loved to tend, she brought me into bloom," he said, describing his long friendship with Bunny and dwelling on their nicknames for each other, Harry and Mertz. "She taught me how to listen. She taught me how to keep my mouth shut when I was uncertain. She taught me how to dress, never to be vulgar...Never boast. Keep your victories and your grief private. Be curious, above all. Be loyal."

He mused about the life that Bunny could have had. "Think of all the red carpets that she never stepped on, the self-promoting interviews she never gave, the plastic surgeon's knife avoided, the honors rejected, the galas never attended. Can you think of anyone, anyone at all in her position whose face has appeared so rarely in newspapers?"

During their conversations in recent months as her health declined, he said, "She never once complained to me. She would say things like, 'Oh, I've been such a slowpoke lately. I have so much more to do, I've got to get started.'" Their final conversation had occurred at 5:46 p.m. on Saturday, March 15. "The last clear sentence she said to me on the telephone, before she hung up and died several hours later: 'Harry,' she said. 'Call me soon.'"

The weather had been dark and gloomy that morning with drizzling rain. But then Bette Midler, in a black dress and a "Bunny blue" scarf, walked up to the podium and smiled at the congregation. The sun suddenly burst through the clouds and the stained glass windows shimmered with colored light as the singer performed an a cappella version of "The Rose."

Bunny's coffin was carried outside to be interred in the Mellon family graveyard. A tenor sang "Shenandoah," and then came the startling sound of a hunter's bugle, a tribute by the local hunt club to send Bunny off with the favorite sound of her youth. Milling around afterward, the mourners murmured about how the change in the weather—blue skies and now beautiful springlike day—felt like a parting gift from Bunny.

At Bunny's farm, a large tent had been set up in a field for the reception. Rickie Niceta had decorated it with Bunny's signature touches: The tables were covered with bolts of chintz and miniature topiaries from the greenhouse; a buffet featured ham and biscuits and crab sandwiches.

Many of Bunny's employees had come from Cape Cod and Nantucket to join the throng. Bunny had thought of everything: She wanted her butlers, maids, housekeepers, and gardeners to be guests at the reception, so outside help had been hired to check coats and circulate with trays of Bunny's favorite drinks, Bloody Marys and daiquiris.

The Memory House, a tribute to Eliza, was open and a steady stream of people wandered in. Their voices grew somber at the sight of the photographs of Eliza as a carefree young woman, and the haunting re-creation of her art studio. The rooms were a heartrending reminder of life's random tragedies, and the mutual suffering of Eliza and her mother.

But outside in the tent, this was a day for memories and laughter as people affectionately recalled Bunny's perfectionist ways. She had insisted that her Cape Cod gardeners rake up the fall leaves before her visits and then just prior to her arrival, artfully put the prettiest versions back on the lawn. Even toward the end of her life, she still instructed her staff to take out broken potato chips before serving them to company. Of course, perfectly shaped Lay's potato chips were served.

People lingered for several hours, unwilling to break the spell. For this final afternoon, everything looked the same, as if Bunny might appear at any moment with a pair of pruning shears in hand.

The moving vans arrived within days to transport to the National Gallery the many paintings that Paul Mellon had left for Bunny's lifetime use, which would now become government property. Ten months later, Bunny's possessions were sold at Sotheby's, including fabulous concoctions of rubies, emeralds, and diamonds.

Missing from the auction lot was a modest item, a gold and sapphire pinkie ring, shaped like a good-luck horseshoe. It had been a wedding present to Bunny from her first husband, Stacy Lloyd, more than eighty years earlier. Paul Mellon had adorned Bunny with the finest creations from Verdura, Cartier, and Van Cleef & Arpels. But at the end of her life, when she drew up her final instructions, this token of young and hopeful love was part of what she chose to take to her grave.

Acknowledgments

As I recently drove down the country roads to Bunny Mellon's library in Upperville, Virginia, past the rolling meadows and mountains in the distance, approaching her sprawling farm with its artistically pruned trees, once again I found myself thinking about what an extraordinary experience this has been for me as a biographer.

Not only have I received full cooperation from her family and estate, but I have been able to spend ample time at Bunny Mellon's glorious homes, walking in her lush gardens, witnessing firsthand her design and décor achievements, immersing myself in the ambience that she created. I now see the world a little differently after spending three years trying to view it through Bunny's eyes.

This book would not have been possible without the help and guidance of many people, but a few have been standouts.

My energetic agent, Gail Hochman, and my accomplished editor, Gretchen Young of Grand Central Publishing, were both so enthusiastic about this book idea that they made a handshake deal at the May 2014 party in celebration of my last book, *The Phantom of Fifth Avenue*. Gail has been a terrific partner on my three book projects, jumping in when I need her. Gretchen has an astute eye for what works and what doesn't, and her editing suggestions improved the manuscript.

This book project was set in motion in the summer of 2011 when I interviewed Bunny Mellon for *Newsweek*, in the middle of the John Edwards scandal. Bunny told her family that she liked the article, and after her death in March 2014, her opinion carried weight.

Bunny's grandson Thomas Lloyd and his wife, Rickie Niceta, invited me to Bunny's funeral and, at the reception afterward at her farm—aware that her story would attract other writers—urged me to take on this biography. Helpful at every step of the way, they encouraged "GranBunny's" employees and family members to speak with me and shared family correspondence.

Let me stress that this is not an authorized biography. There were no strings attached to my research or writing. I am very grateful that so many key figures trusted me.

In August 2015, my husband, Walter Shapiro, and I joined Thomas and Rickie and their two young children, Fiona and Teddy, for a long weekend at Cape Cod, where they put us up at Bunny's beloved waterfront cottage, the Dune House. Her desk was still decorated as she left it, with dried flowers that she plucked from her garden. For three days, I got to wake up in her world and live with her possessions.

Bryan Huffman, who spoke to Bunny Mellon virtually every night for a decade, provided the initial entrée to her world, convincing Bunny to speak with me for my *Newsweek* article. Bryan provided a wealth of entertaining anecdotes, shared Bunny's letters to him, joined us for the Cape weekend, and has constantly cheered me on.

The two lawyers for Bunny's estate—Alex Forger, who represented Bunny Mellon for forty years; and Jane MacLennan, who joined him in doing so for the last fifteen years—were a joy to deal with on this project. Trust and estate lawyers have a reputation for saying no, but Alex and Jane just kept saying yes and then thinking of further ways to enhance my research. They patiently met with me more than a half-dozen times to answer questions, and they graciously allowed me to use Bunny's sketches to illustrate the book. At their direction, the staff at the Oak Spring Garden Library assisted with my work.

Stacy Lloyd IV was very close to his GranBunny and passed along heartfelt memories, arranging for an interview to take place in the living room of Bunny's Virginia home, where so much of her family life occurred. Anne Emmet, the mother of Thomas and Stacy Lloyd IV, provided smart observations about family dynamics.

I am grateful to Bunny's son, Stacy "Tuffy" Lloyd III, a good-natured and kind man who spoke with me on several occasions. He died on March 16, 2017, at the age of eighty, almost three years to the date of his mother's death, a sad and untimely loss.

At Oak Spring Garden Library, librarian Tony Willis, who worked for Bunny for more than thirty years, and Nancy Collins, the former private nurse for Paul and Bunny Mellon who now works at the library, spent weeks good-naturedly sharing recollections and helping me go through more than forty boxes of Bunny's correspondence, journals, and memorabilia.

I benefited from the guidance of Kimberley Fisher, a veteran library employee knowledgeable about Bunny's rare books and artworks; the help of Jim Morris, who digitized Bunny's photos; and jack-of-all trades Ronnie Willis. Gardener George Shaffer, who worked for Bunny for fifty years, showed me around her three greenhouses and allowed me to use his photographs.

Bunny Mellon's extended family went out of their way on my behalf. Senator John Warner and his daughter Virginia Warner (Paul Mellon's granddaughter) provided invaluable insights. Robin Lloyd, the son of Stacy B. Lloyd Jr., shared his father's declassified OSS files from the National Archives and filled in gaps in the narrative. Bunny's niece and nephews—Lily Lambert Norton, John McCarthy Jr., David Fleming, and Peter Fleming—spoke at length about their grandparents, Gerard and Rachel Lambert, and the rivalry between Bunny and her younger sister, Lily. David Fleming also provided me with wonderful family photos. Louise Whitney Mellon, now divorced from Paul Mellon's son Timothy, and Lavinia Currier, Paul Mellon's great-niece, both discussed Mellon family dynamics.

Early supporters make all the difference at the beginning of a book project, when you feel like you are floundering. Sally Bedell Smith, the author of the 2004 best seller *Grace and Power: The Private World of the Kennedy White House*, provided a list of sources from her research. Chris Matthews, a friend since he and my husband both worked as speechwriters for Jimmy Carter, sent over, unbidden, a transcript of an interview that he conducted with Bunny Mellon for his own book *Jack Kennedy: Elusive Hero*, which included significant unpublished material.

Oscar de la Renta and his wife, Annette, whom I got to know while writing my first book about their close friend Brooke Astor, made crucial early contributions. Oscar called Hubert de Givenchy and retired *Vogue* editor Babs Simpson and convinced them to speak with me. Oscar was ill and died several months later; this was an extraordinary parting gift. Givenchy, one of Bunny's dearest friends, shared poignant stories in two lengthy phone interviews from France. Simpson, then 102 with a sharp-witted memory, met with me at her Westchester assisted-living home.

Valerie Leonard, the widow of Bunny's longtime decorator Paul Leonard, and her friend Henry Heymann shared stories and shipped me a large box of Bunny-related correspondence and material, including Paul Leonard's essay, "Bunny Dearest." Valerie died in 2015; I miss her laugh and resilient spirit. I am grateful to Valerie and Paul's daughter Samantha Leonard for allowing me to use the essay.

John Baskett, who worked as a curator for the Mellons and cowrote Paul Mellon's biography, spent many hours with me on the phone and over lunch at his home in London, describing his friendship with the couple. Antiques dealer Malcolm Magruder, who knew Bunny and her first husband, Stacy Lloyd Jr., drove me around Carter Hall, the antebellum mansion owned by Bunny's father, where she spent her formative years.

At the National Gallery, Anabeth Guthrie helpfully arranged interviews with director Earl Powell, executive assistant Angela LoRe, librarian Neal Turtell, and curators Kim Jones and Mary Morton. Archivist Maygene Daniels provided guidance on the extensive Mellon-related files.

Thank heavens for long memories: Four well-connected Washington, D.C., women who are now in their nineties—Martha Bartlett, Marie Ridder, Marion "Oatsie" Leiter Charles, and Nancy Pyne—summoned up tales of years gone by. Deeda Blair, who had an overlapping social circle with Bunny, shared her thoughts on Bunny's taste and gardening prowess. Aileen Mehle, whose pen name as a gossip columnist was Suzy Knickerbocker, made the time to recall her friendship with Bunny Mellon; Aileen died in 2016 at age ninety-eight. The ever-fabulous Liz Smith and archaeologist Iris Love provided context and ideas.

Caroline Kennedy graciously sent me the undelivered eulogy that she wrote for Bunny Mellon's funeral and passed along helpful thoughts. Lee Radziwill invited me to her home for conversations that proved useful for this book. Illustrator Cathy Barancik Graham, my friend for thirty years, helped with material on her friend Robert Isabell. Ian Schrager offered up stories about Isabell as well. Novelist Jane Stanton Hitchcock, a friend for a decade, discussed her relationship with Bunny Mellon and her troubling experience with their mutual disgraced financial adviser, Kenneth Starr. Carly Simon, whom I profiled a lifetime ago, added details about Bunny and Jackie Kennedy Onassis.

Retired FBI agent Chuck Stuber, the chief investigator on the John Edwards legal case, spent four hours with me at his office in Raleigh explaining the proceedings. Abbe Lowell, John Edwards's chief defense lawyer, provided his perspective on the trial. John Moylan, a lawyer and supporter of Edwards's presidential prospects, and Josh Brumberger, an Edwards campaign aide, helped with the narrative. Alex Forger, a witness at the trial, described his role and provided closing argument transcripts.

Other writers have been generous in describing their meetings with Bunny Mellon: author and decorator Charlotte Moss, journalist James Reginato, and expert gardening writer Martin Filler. Charlotte also lent me Eliza Lloyd's Foxcroft yearbooks, which she bought at the Sotheby's auction.

William Koch, who bought Bunny and Paul Mellon's estate in Oyster Harbors on Cape Cod, kindly gave us a personal tour of her former home, gardens, and the beach shack where President John F. Kennedy asked Bunny Mellon to design the White House Rose Garden. Bunny Mellon believed in witches, fortune-tellers, and psychics—I do not—but even as a skeptic, I felt historic reverberations while standing at that spot.

Photographer Joshua Greene and his mother, Amy Greene, were tremendously helpful. I am grateful to them for sharing their memories, and especially to Joshua, who spent hours searching his archives for never-before-seen photos that he and his father, Milton Greene, took of Bunny, and then allowing me to use them in my book.

My thanks to Bunny's many employees—some declined to be quoted by name—who recounted their memories, including Dita Amory, Chris Harvie, Lisa Rockwell, Susan Cabral, Ned Crosby, Alison Martin, Nedra Parry, Malcolm Robson, Bob Childs, Bob Hoxie, Inez Setler, Ronald Brumsfield, Linda Evora, and Timothy Patterson. Architect Hugh Jacobsen, hairdresser Maury Hopson, and Bunny's friends Akko Van Acker, Bruce Horten, Beverly Newton, Errol Adels, and Howard Slatkin all made time to speak with me. Retired magazine editor Julie Britt helped with introductions. Sister Parish's daughter Apple Bartlett and granddaughter Susan Bartlett Crater invited me to their home for lunch to discuss Sister's relationship with Bunny.

Lucy Tower, a key figure in my last book on reclusive copper heiress Huguette Clark, was helpful yet again, sharing her Saratoga memories of Paul Mellon and hosting me at her home in Aiken, Georgia, during a trip to interview her friend Louise Whitney Mellon.

Joe Armstrong, the well-connected magazine publisher, aided with this book as well as my first book on Brooke Astor. Staunch friend-to-writers Steve Millington allowed me to linger for hours doing interviews at Michael's restaurant, after all the customers had left.

At Grand Central Publishing, I am grateful to the indefatigable Katherine Stopa, Gretchen Young's assistant, and lawyer Rekha Ramani for vetting the manuscript. One of the advantages of staying with the same publisher is the chance to work with the same top-notch people on a second book: My thanks to hard-working and imaginative publicist Caitlin Mulrooney-Lyski, and eagle-eyed copy editors Carolyn Kurek and Mark Steven Long for saving me from mistakes.

Alyson Krueger, a 2011 graduate of NYU's Arthur L. Carter Journalism Institute, is a classic example of the student who surpasses her teacher. Alyson, who meticulously fact-checked my last book as well as my husband Walter Shapiro's book *Hustling Hitler*, has a vibrant writing career of her own, so I was thrilled and relieved when she agreed to fact-check this book. I am very grateful for her help, but any errors are mine.

I have been blessed with wonderful friends: Jane Hartley, Ralph Schlosstein, Susan Birkenhead, Swoosie Kurtz, Tom Curley, Michelle and Stephen Stoneburn, Mary Macy, Suzanna Andrews, Rita Jacobs and James Wetzler, Judy Miller and Jason Epstein, Mandy Grunwald, Benjamin Cooper, Louise Grunwald, Gail Gregg, Tamar Lewin, Maralee Schwartz, Josh Gotbaum and Joyce Thornhill, Elaine Kamarck, Nancy Leonard and Urban Lehner, Liz Loewy and Paul Giddens, Christine Doudna and Rick Grand-Jean, Joe Klein and Victoria Kaunitz, Michael and Rosina Barker, Caroline Miller and Eric Himmel, Diane Yu and Michael Delaney, Patricia Bauer and Ed Muller, Jill Lawrence and John Martin, Melinda Henneberger and Bill Turque, Nancy and Charlie Kantor, Peggy Noonan, Joanne Hubschman, Brooke Kroeger, Perri Klass, Adam Penenberg, Meredith Broussard, Richard M. Cohen, Margo Lion, Susan Chira and Michael Shapiro, Eileen Kotecki Mancera, Kate Feiffer and Chris Alley, Jonathan Alter, David Ignatius and Eve Thornberg, Julia Baind, Rick Ridder and Joannie Braden, Michael and Kate Walsh, and Kanti Rai.

My world revolves around my husband, Walter Shapiro, who is funny and charming and comforting and smart and even a great line editor. I live for the look on his face whenever he sees me. We've been together for nearly forty years and I treasure every moment. More, please, more.

My parents are remarkable. My mother, Adelle Gordon, now ninety-one, and my father, David Gordon, now ninety-four, have an inspiring zest for life. My mother wants to discuss books with me while my father, attuned to nature, likes pointing to the night sky and urging us to "look at the moon!" I'm grateful for every day, every week, every month, and every year with them.

It's been magical to have little kids in our family: a salute to the irrepressible four-year-old Ozzy Gordon and to two-year-old Sadie

Gordon with her mesmerizing smile. My nephew Jesse Gordon and his wife, Meghan Wolf, Ozzy's parents, and my nephew Nate Gordon and Jenny Rakochy, Sadie's parents, are the lights of my life. I owe a special debt to Nate, a professional photo editor, who designed the photo layout and organized the photographs for all three of my books.

My cousins and their spouses have been there through thick and thin: Debbie and Marty Greenberg, Mindy and Mark Sotsky, Andy and Suzanne Pinkes, Anne Campbell, Jonathan Silverman, Jason Silverman, Joel Silverman and Alba Estenoz, and the memory of my cousin Lynne Pinkes. I miss my brother, Bart Gordon, more than I can possibly say.

Sources

Bunny Mellon cherished her past and saved thousands of documents, including childhood letters; her Foxcroft report cards; letters from her two husbands, Stacy Lloyd Jr. and Paul Mellon; sketches for her design for the White House Rose Garden; and correspondence from such friends as Jacqueline Kennedy Onassis, Hubert de Givenchy, I. M. Pei, the Duchess of Devonshire, and many others.

Her appointment calendars and journals provided a wealth of information. In anticipation of publishing her own memoir, she wrote a series of autobiographical essays and sketched out notes but did not complete a manuscript.

I am very grateful to her grandsons, Thomas Lloyd and Stacy Lloyd IV, her son, Stacy "Tuffy" Lloyd III, and her executors, Alex Forger and Jane MacLennan, for allowing me to read and quote from this trove of material, archived at Bunny's Oak Spring Garden Library in Upperville, Virginia.

Bunny Mellon's voice shines through this book along with extensive context, analysis, and commentary. I conducted interviews with more than 175 people and followed up on multiple occasions with key figures.

At the National Gallery of Art, I read the files on Paul and Bunny Mellon's long-running involvement with the institution. The Smithsonian's Archive of American Gardens provided valuable information on the White House Rose Garden. The State Department's declassified OSS files helped reconstruct the war years of Bunny's two husbands, Stacy Lloyd Jr. and Paul Mellon.

I conducted intensive research using such databases as ProQuest Historical, newspapers.com, newspaperarchive.com, ancestry.com, the Library of Congress's Chronicling America, OldFulton.com, the

New York Public Library's digital archives, and the *Washington Star* archives, available through the District of Columbia Public Library.

In June 2011, I interviewed Bunny Mellon for a story for *Newsweek* and subsequently spoke with her on two other occasions. I remain grateful that I had the chance to hear that inimitable, whispery voice and amused laughter.

The quotes in this book attributed to Bunny Mellon come from her letters, autobiographical essays, journals, and the interviews that she gave through the years. Some family members and friends recalled snippets of their conversation with Bunny, and I have chosen to include their recollections, identifying the sources.

Permission to quote from Bunny Mellon's letters, journals, appointment calendars, and autobiographical essays has been graciously granted by the Gerard B. Lambert Foundation.

CHAPTER ONE. PRESIDENT KENNEDY HAS A REQUEST

Interviews:
Susan Cabral, Ned Crosby, Linda Evora, Chris Harvie, Bryan Huffman, Lisa Rockwell, Sam Kasten, Lee Radziwill

Documents:
John F. Kennedy Presidential Library, Boston; JFK's calendars.
Chris Matthews interview with Bunny Mellon for his book *Jack Kennedy: Elusive Hero*, Simon & Schuster, 2011. Unpublished excerpts.
Jacqueline Kennedy Rose Garden Scrapbook.
Bunny Mellon notes on the Rose Garden, Oak Spring Garden Library.

Articles:
Washington Herald, "Mrs. Andrew Mellon and Her Children," Sept. 15, 1912.
New York Herald Tribune, " 'Richest in U.S.' Doesn't Count Money," Oct. 28, 1957.
Washington Post, "The Equestrian Mellon," by Paul Richard, May 3, 1985.
New York Herald Tribune, "Men Refuse Skull and Bones Honor at Yale," May 18, 1928.
Boston Globe, "Kennedy Lunch with Neighbor at Oyster Harbors," by Frank Falacci, Aug. 14, 1961.
New York Times, "Kennedy and Wife Spend Day on Boat," Aug. 14, 1961.
New York Herald Tribune, "Kennedy Gets Away from It All—For a Few Hours," Aug. 14, 1961.
White House History, Number 1, "President Kennedy's Rose Garden," by Rachel Lambert Mellon, 1983.
Time, "Art: A Portrait of the Donor," by Gerald Clarke, May 8, 1978.

Books:

Katharine Graham, *Personal History*, Vintage, 1998.
Paul Mellon with John Baskett, *Reflections in a Silver Spoon*, William Morrow, 1992.
Richard Reeves, *President Kennedy: Profile of Power*, Simon & Schuster, 1993.

CHAPTER TWO. FIFTY SUMMERS LATER

Interviews:
Bunny Mellon, Bryan Huffman, Thomas Lloyd, Alex Forger
Article:
Newsweek, "Bunny Mellon: The Secret Keeper," by Meryl Gordon, July 25, 2011.

CHAPTER THREE. THE AUCTION OF THE DECADE

Interviews:
Akko van Acker, Deeda Blair, Julie Britt, Mario Buatta, Alex Forger, Hubert de Givenchy, Cathy Barancik Graham, Maury Hopson, Bryan Huffman, Ward Landrigan, Rickie Niceta, Thomas Lloyd, Louise Whitney Mellon, Charlotte Moss, Beverly Newton, Nedra Parry, Babs Simpson, Howard Slatkin, John Saumarez Smith

Documents:
Sotheby's Catalogues: Property from the collection of Mrs. Paul Mellon, 2014.
Eulogy by Caroline Kennedy. Reprinted with permission.
Paul Leonard, "Bunny Dearest," unpublished essay, 2002, courtesy of Valerie Leonard. Published with the permission of Samantha Leonard.

Articles:
New York Times, "Bunny Mellon's Keen Eye is a Boon to Sotheby's," by Carol Vogel, Sept. 12, 2014.
Telegraph, "Treasure Trove of Art and Valuables Belonging to 'Bunny Mellon' to Go on Sale," Sept. 14, 2014.
Pittsburgh Tribune-Review, "Bunny Mellon's Collections, Set to Sell at Auction, a Testament to Elegance, Eclectic Taste," by Natasha Lindstrom and Alice Carter, Nov. 9, 2014.
Bloomberg News, "Bunny Mellon's $250 Million Rothkos Sold in Private Sale," by Katya Kazakina, Sept. 5, 2014.
New York Times, "All 43 Works Owned by Mellon Sell at Auction, Bringing Nearly $160 Million," by Carol Vogel, Nov. 11, 2014.
Financial Times, "A Cultivated Taste: The Bunny Mellon Auction," by Jo Ellison, Nov. 14, 2014.
New York Times, "Inside Bunny Mellon's World," by Guy Trebay, Nov. 19, 2014.
Architectural Digest, "Bunny Mellon's Breathtaking Private Collection on Sale at Sotheby's," by Mac Griswold, Sept. 30, 2014.

Town & Country, "Inside the Auction of the Century," by Meryl Gordon, Dec. 2014.

New York Times, "At Sotheby's Interiors Auction, an Intimate Portrait of an Heiress," by Sarah Maslin Nir, Nov. 21, 2014.

Bloomberg, "Mellon Estate Sale Fetches $218 Million, Led by Rothkos," by James Tarmy, Nov. 24, 2014.

New York Times, "A Thousand Dollars and a Dream," by Steven Kurutz, Dec. 3, 2014.

Time, "Art: A Portrait of the Donor," by Gerald Clarke, May 8, 1978.

CHAPTER FOUR. CHILDHOOD TREASURES: A BOTTLE AND A BOOK

Interviews:

Bryan Huffman, Vernon Jordan, David Fleming, Peter Fleming, Stacy "Tuffy" Lloyd III, John McCarthy Jr., Lily Lambert Norton

Documents:

Bunny Mellon autobiographical essays and letters, Oak Spring Garden Library.

Arthur Lowe letters to Bunny Mellon, Oak Spring Garden Library.

Lily Lambert Norton, "Remembering Mom: The Story of Lily Lambert McCarthy and Her Lifetime of Collecting Admiral Lord Horatio Nelson," interviews with Dr. Chris Howard Bailey, 1994.

Articles:

St. Louis Republic, "At Death's Door: Mr. Jordan W. Lambert Not Expected to Live Long," Dec. 31, 1888.

St. Louis Post-Dispatch, "Jordan W. Lambert Dead: Well Known Citizen Passes Away After a Brief Illness," Jan. 7, 1889.

St. Louis Post-Dispatch, "Death of Mrs. Lily Lambert," March 30, 1889.

St. Louis Republic, "Death of Mrs. Jordan W. Lambert. She Survived Her Husband Only a Few Weeks," March 30, 1889.

Springfield Republican, "The Wellesley Fund Circus," June 10, 1901.

Fitchburg Sentinel, "Notices," Feb. 8, 1908.

Fitchburg Sentinel, "Wanted to Be Married," June 5, 1908.

St. Louis Post-Dispatch, "Wedding of Rachel Parkhill Lowe to Gerard Barnes Lambert," June 25, 1908.

Women's Wear Daily (WWD), Oct. 28, 1932.

Washington Star, "Numerous Luncheons and Teas Are Announced for This Week," Dec. 10, 1933.

New Yorker, "Ahoy, Listerine!" by Jack Alexander, July 16, 1938.

St. Louis Post-Dispatch, "Wooster Lambert Gets Place on St. Louis' Crack Bowling Team," Nov. 21, 1911.

St. Louis Post-Dispatch, "Wooster Lambert, Society Musician, Joins the Union," Dec. 13, 1912.

Morning Oregonian, "Millionaire Buys Luxurious Car to Go to Ball," Jan. 12, 1913.

New York Tribune, "Fined on His Honeymoon: Wooster Lambert Pays Rather Than Part with Bride for Cell," Feb. 1, 1914.

St. Louis Post-Dispatch, "Wooster Lambert Arrested Sixth Time as Speeder," Dec. 10, 1915.

St. Louis Post-Dispatch, "Lambert to Tell Congress of Navy Aviation Needs," Dec. 19, 1915.

Baltimore Constitution, "Seeking Woman in Lambert Suicide," Aug. 8, 1917.

St. Louis Post-Dispatch, "L. J. Lambert Tells of First U.S. Gas Attack in France," Feb. 19, 1919.

St. Louis Post-Dispatch, "Rousing Welcome for Lieut. J. D. Lambert," April 14, 1919.

Washington Post, "West Virginian Buys Historic Burwell Estate," Dec. 7, 1947.

Fort Wayne Sentinel, "Building a Miniature Empire," as described to Louise LeNoir Thomas, April 21, 1917.

Los Angeles Times, "Arkansas Riot-Torn: Whites Battle with Negro Gangs: Shooting from Ambush Is Cause of Race War near Helena," Oct. 2, 1919.

Hartford Courant, "At Least 16 Dead in Race Rioting at Elaine, Ark., U. S. Troops Have Situation in Hand," Oct. 3, 1919.

Washington Post, "Called Out Negroes: 'Paul Reveres' Gave Signal for Attack in Arkansas Riots," Oct. 6, 1919.

New York Times, "Says Negro Union Plotted Uprising: Arkansas Investigation Traces the Trouble to a Young Negro Who Has Escaped," Oct. 7, 1919.

Baltimore Afro-American, "Whites Try Only Colored Men for Recent Race Rioting in Arkansas," Nov. 21, 1919.

Chicago Defender, "Expose New Facts in Ark. Riot Case," Feb. 28, 1920.

Chicago Defender, "U.S. Court Frees Hill," Oct. 16, 1920.

Chicago Defender, "Court Reverses Six Elaine Riot Cases," Dec. 16, 1920.

Washington Post, "Defends Negroes, Ousted, Is Rumor," Aug. 25, 1921.

Anniston Star, "Creeks Run Wild: Seventeen Negroes Perish in Tornado. Arkansas Plantation Cabins Are Swept Away by Storms," May 19, 1930.

New York Herald Tribune, "Col. Lindbergh Buys Site for Home at Princeton. Aviator to have G. M. Lambert, Flight Backer, as Neighbor," Oct. 13, 1930.

Books:

James Crathorne, *Cliveden: The Place and the People*, Collins & Brown, 1995.

Robert Crawford, *Young Eliot: From St. Louis to "The Waste Land,"* Farrar, Straus and Giroux, 2015.

Gerard Barnes Lambert, *All Out of Step*, Doubleday, 1956.

Lily Fleming McCarthy, as told to Lieutenant Commander John Lea, *Remembering Nelson*, privately published in association with the Royal Naval Museum, Portsmouth, England, 1995.

George Pitcher, *A Life of Grace: The Biography of Grace Lansing Lambert*, Princeton University Press, 1987.

Sandra Raphael, *An Oak Spring Sylva: A Selection of the Rare Books on Trees in the Oak Spring Garden Library*, Yale University Press, 1989.

Sandra Raphael, *An Oak Spring Pomona: A Selection of the Rare Books on Fruit in the Oak Spring Garden Library*, Yale University Press, 1990.

Grif Stockley, *Blood in Their Eyes: The Elaine Race Massacres of 1919*, University of Arkansas Press, 2001.

Grif Stockley, *The Encyclopedia of Arkansas History & Culture: Elaine Massacre*, Butler Center for Arkansas Studies, Central Arkansas Library System, 2006.

Ida B. Wells-Barnett, *The Arkansas Race Riot*, Aquila, Chicago, 1920.

CHAPTER FIVE. THE MAKING OF A YOUNG GARDENER

Interviews:

Nancy Collins, Bryan Huffman, David Fleming, Lily Lambert Norton

Documents:

Stacy B. Lloyd and Stacy B. Lloyd Jr. files, Princeton University, Seeley G. Mudd Manuscript Library, Alumni Archives, Boxes 56, 59, 78, 245, and 253.

David Finley letter to Paul Mellon, National Gallery of Art archives.

Bunny Mellon autobiographical essays, journals, and letters, Oak Spring Garden Library.

Arthur Lowe letters to Bunny Mellon, Oak Spring Garden Library.

Lily Lambert Norton, "Remembering Mom: The Story of Lily Lambert McCarthy and Her Lifetime of Collecting Admiral Lord Horatio Nelson," interviews with Dr. Chris Howard Bailey, 1994.

Articles:

St. Louis Post-Dispatch, "Society Notes," Aug. 7, 1921.

New York Tribune, "Two Luncheon Fetes Given at Lenox House," Sept. 22, 1921.

Washington Post, "Wall Street Gossip," March 18, 1925.

New Yorker, "Ahoy, Listerine!" by Jack Alexander, July 16, 1938.

New York Times, "Miss May M. Fine, Educator, Is Dead," Nov. 15, 1933.

New York Evening Post, "Miss Rachel Lambert Is Host to Jolly Group of Younger Set," Aug. 11, 1926.

New York Times, "Children Ride Well in Own Horse Show," Aug. 30, 1926.

Books:

Mary Custis Lee deButts and Rosalie Noland Woodland, *Charlotte Haxall Noland 1883–1969*, Foxcroft School, Whittet & Shepperson, Richmond, VA, 1971.

Gerard Barnes Lambert, *All Out of Step*, Doubleday, 1956.

Lily Fleming McCarthy, as told to Lieutenant Commander John Lea, *Remembering Nelson*, privately published in association with the Royal Naval Museum, Portsmouth, England, 1995.

CHAPTER SIX. TALLY-HO IN VIRGINIA

Interviews:

Apple Parish Bartlett, Nancy Collins, Susan Bartlett Crater, Bryan Huffman, Lily Lambert Norton

Documents:

Foxcroft Tally-Ho Yearbooks.

Bunny Mellon report cards, Oak Spring Garden Library.

Bunny Mellon correspondence with Gerard Lambert and Arthur Lowe, Oak Spring Garden Library.

Bunny Mellon autobiographical notes, dictated to Nancy Collins.

Stacy Lloyd Jr., Princeton University, Seeley G. Mudd Manuscript Library, Alumni Archives, Boxes 56, 59, 78, 245, and 253.

Lily Lambert Norton, "Remembering Mom: The Story of Lily Lambert McCarthy and Her Lifetime of Collecting Admiral Lord Horatio Nelson," interviews with Dr. Chris Howard Bailey, 1994.

Articles:

New York Evening Post, "Vanderbilt Yacht Atlantic Is Sold. Lambert, Pharmacal Magnate, New Owner, Plans to Enter It in Atlantic Race," Nov. 19, 1927.

New York Times, "Famous Atlantic Enters Race: Vanderbilt Schooner, Sold to Lambert for an Estimated $500,000 to Seek Cup. Craft Holds the Record: Crossed Atlantic in 12 Days and 4 Hours," Nov. 19, 1927.

Atlanta Constitution, "St. Louis Stages Big Celebration," May 22, 1927.

New York Times, "Plane Taking Off on Street Hits Girl," June 9, 1927.

New York Herald Tribune, "J. T. Walker, Heir to Millions, Killed and G. L. Lambert, Cousin, Hurt En Route to S. Louis from Princeton," June 25, 1927.

New York Times, "Heir to $5,000,000 Dies in Plane Crash: Princeton Student from St. Louis Killed as Chum's Machine Dives Near Pottsville," June 25, 1927.

New York Post, "Mr. and Mrs. Gerard B. Lambert Will Leave for Bar Harbor This Week on Their Yacht," July 25, 1927.

Boston Globe, "Punta Takes Second from Boston Yacht," July 26, 1928.

Washington Post, "Yacht Race Victors Get Spain's Trophies," July 30, 1928.

New York Herald Tribune, "Princeton Debutante Honored," Nov. 21, 1929.

New Yorker, "Ahoy, Listerine!" by Jack Alexander, July 16, 1938.

New York Times, "Dorothy Kinnicutt Makes Her Debut," Nov. 25, 1928.

New York Times, "Princeton Men Honored," April 21, 1928.

New York Times, "Fliers Up 400 Hours, Two Rivals Killed. George Lambert, Son of Observer at St. Louis, and New Yorker Die in Crack-up," July 30, 1929.

Books:

Gerard Barnes Lambert, *All Out of Step*, Doubleday, 1956.

CHAPTER SEVEN. THE DEBUTANTE DANCES THROUGH THE DEPRESSION

Interviews:

Bryan Huffman, Lily Lambert Norton

Documents:

Bunny Mellon autobiographical essays, Oak Spring Garden Library.

Lily Lambert Norton, "Remembering Mom: The Story of Lily Lambert McCarthy and Her Lifetime of Collecting Admiral Lord Horatio Nelson," interviews with Dr. Chris Howard Bailey, 1994.

David Finley letter to Paul Mellon, National Gallery of Art archives.

Articles:

New York Herald Tribune, "Vacation Period Ended for Many of Princeton Set," Sept. 15, 1929.

New York Herald Tribune, "Society," Sept. 29, 1929.

New York Herald Tribune, "Secretary Adams Will See Navy Team Play Princeton," Oct. 25, 1929.

New York Times, "Stocks Hold Firm in Normal Trading; Pool Still on Guard," Oct. 27, 1929.

New York Times, "Miss Rachel Lambert Presented at Dance. Mr. and Mrs. G. B. Lambert Entertain for Daughter at Their Home in Princeton," Oct. 27, 1929.

New York Herald Tribune, "Ruth Lambert Makes Debut at Princeton: Brilliant Affair Given at Albemarle to Introduce Former Foxcroft School Girl: Notables Attend," Oct. 27, 1929.

New York Times, "Senior Promenade Held at Princeton," Nov. 9, 1929.

New Yorker, "Ahoy, Listerine!" by Jack Alexander, July 16, 1938.

New York Herald Tribune, "Gerald B. Lambert Buys Ancestral Home in Virginia: Princeton Man Purchases Carter's Creek in Tidewater Section," Feb. 23, 1930.

New York Herald Tribune, "Princeton Prom Livens Week End with Gay Activity," March 30, 1930.

Baltimore Sun, "Old Virginia Gardens Open to the Public," May 4, 1930.

Washington Post, "16 Lives Taken When Tornado Hits Arkansas," May 19, 1930.

New York Times, "Brilliant Ball for Miss Hutton," Dec. 23, 1930.

WWD, "Ruffled Themes in Lace, Net, Chiffon and Satin Animate Scene at Barbara Hutton Debut," Dec. 23, 1930.

New York Herald Tribune, "Mr. Whitney and Bride at Their Virginia Home," Sept. 27, 1930.

Palm Beach Post, "Stripes Brighten Style Scene," by Betsy Schuyler, Jan. 26, 1931.

New York Herald Tribune, "Andrew Mellon Buys Rokeby Farm for His Son," March 25, 1931.

New York Times, "Mellon Reaches 76, Buys Stock Farm," March 25, 1931.

Wall Street Journal, "New Gillette Heads: H. J. Gaisman Elected Chairman of the Board, Gerard B. Lambert Named President," May 2, 1931.

Washington Post, "Paul Mellon's Horses Will Be Shown Today: Entries of Secretary's Son to Be Exhibited at Upperville, Va.," June 11, 1931.

Palm Beach Daily News, "Unforgettable Palm Beach: Island Endured Great Depression Largely Unscathed," by Augustus Mayhew, Feb. 21, 2011.

New York Herald Tribune, "Dorothy Kinnicutt Wed at St. George's," Feb. 15, 1931.

Boston Globe, "Secretary Adams Sails the Vanitie to Victory," July 5, 1931.

Architectural Digest, "Delano & Aldrich," by Peter Pennoyer, Feb. 28, 2003.

Books:

Apple Parish Bartlett and Susan Bartlett Crater, *Sister Parish: The Life of the Legendary American Interior Designer*, Vendome, 2000.

Mary Custis Lee deButts and Rosalie Noland Woodland, *Charlotte Haxall Noland 1883–1969*, Foxcroft School, Whittet & Shepperson, Richmond, VA, 1971.

Burton Hersh, *The Mellon Family: A Fortune in History*, William Morrow, 1978.

Richard Jackson Jr. and Cornelia Brooke Gilder, *Houses of the Berkshires: 1870–1930*, Architecture of Leisure series, Acanthus Press, 2011.

E. J. Kahn Jr., *Jock: The Life and Times of John Hay Whitney*, Doubleday, 1981.

Gerard Barnes Lambert, *All Out of Step*, Doubleday, 1956.

Lily Fleming McCarthy, as told to Lieutenant Commander John Lea, *Remembering Nelson*, privately published in association with the Royal Naval Museum, Portsmouth, England, 1995.

Paul Mellon with John Baskett, *Reflections in a Silver Spoon*, William Morrow, 1992.

Daniel Okrent, *Last Call: The Rise and Fall of Prohibition*, Scribner, 2010.

Diana Oswald, introduction by David Patrick Columbia, *Debutantes: When Glamour Was Born*, Rizzoli, 2013.

George Pitcher, *A Life of Grace: The Biography of Grace Lansing Lambert*, Princeton University Press, 1987.

Arthur Schlesinger Jr., *The Age of Roosevelt*, Vol. 1, *The Crisis of the Old Order: 1919–1933*, Houghton Mifflin, 1957.

CHAPTER EIGHT. A COURTEOUS GIRL AND A THOROUGH GENTLEMAN

Interviews:

Nancy Collins, Bryan Huffman, Lily Lambert Norton, Stacy "Tuffy" Lloyd III

Documents:

Arthur Lowe letters to Bunny Mellon, Oak Spring Garden Library.

Bunny Mellon autobiographical essays, Oak Spring Garden Library.

Stacy B. Lloyd and Stacy B. Lloyd Jr. files, Princeton University, Seeley G. Mudd Manuscript Library, Alumni Archives, Boxes 56, 59, 78, 245, and 253.

Lily Lambert Norton, "Remembering Mom: The Story of Lily Lambert McCarthy and Her Lifetime of Collecting Admiral Lord Horatio Nelson," interviews with Dr. Chris Howard Bailey, 1994.

Articles:

Chicago Daily Tribune, "Europa Breaks Record on Maiden Trip," March 26, 1930.

Baltimore Sun, "Berryville Activities," Nov. 22, 1931.

Spur, "The Jock Whitneys Receive," by Taylor Hardin, Dec. 15, 1931.

Baltimore Sun, "Recent Entertainments Take Place in Virginia." Jan. 4, 1932.

New York Herald Tribune, "Members of the Fashionable Set Departing for Southern Climes," Jan. 18, 1932.

Washington Post, "Middleburg Hunter Meet Tomorrow," Feb. 21, 1932.

Philadelphia Inquirer, "Tranquil Isles Now Enchanting Many Travelers," March 20, 1932.

Baltimore Sun, "Races Given at Middleburg," April 24, 1932.

Washington Star, "Jersey Girl Wins Horsemanship Cub," May 10, 1932.

New York Evening Post, "Social Notes," June 7, 1932.

New York Herald Tribune, "Princeton Visitors Join Barge Parties," July 17, 1932.

Lowell Sun, "Gerard B. Lambert, an Official of the Gillette Safety Razor Co. and Mrs. Lambert Today Announced the Engagement of Their Daughter Rachel L. to Stacy B. Lloyd Junior of Philadelphia," Sept. 3, 1932.

Sun, "Berryville Events: Miss Rachel Lloyd Entertains Guests Over Week-end at Summer Home," Sept. 18, 1932.

New York Herald Tribune, "Stacy B. Lloyd Jr. and Miss Lambert Select Attendants," Oct. 24, 1932.

New York Evening Post, "Rachel Lambert to Wed Nov. 26th," Oct. 21, 1932.

Atlanta Constitution, "Arthur Lowe Dies in Fitchburg," Oct. 28, 1932.

New York Times, "Notes of Social Activities," Nov. 8, 1932.

New York Evening Post, "Rachel L. Lambert Is Bride Today of Stacy B. Lloyd Jr. at Princeton," Nov. 26, 1932.

New York Times, "Lloyd-Lambert," Nov. 27, 1932.

Brooklyn Daily Eagle, "Miss Rachel Lambert Bride of Stacy B. Lloyd," Nov. 27, 1932.

Philadelphia Inquirer, "People You Know," Jan. 19, 1933.

Washington Post, "G. B. Lambert Bids 800 to Ball at Carter Hall," Jan. 10, 1933.

Washington Star, "Numerous Lunches and Teas Are Announced This Week," Dec. 10, 1933.

Philadelphia Inquirer, "People You Know," Dec. 28, 1933.

New York Sun, "Miss Lily Cary Lambert the Fiance of William Wilson Fleming," May 7, 1934.

New York Times, "Mrs. Lambert Wed to Dr. M. B. Clopton," July 12, 1934.

Washington Post, "Arthur Whites Are Host to Lord and Lady Dorchester," Jan. 13, 1935.

Charleston Gazette, "Virginia Publisher Buys Jefferson County Papers," June 6, 1935.

Washington Post, "Score of Virginians Cast in Covered Wagon Show Featured at Madison Square Garden," Nov. 10, 1935.

New York Herald Tribune, "Gerard B. Lambert, Yachtsman, Marries Mrs. Lansing Mull," April 11, 1936.

Washington Post, "Recently Wed Couple Visit the Stacy Lloyds," April 26, 1936.

New York Times, "Son Born to Stacy B. Lloyd Jr.," Sept. 25, 1936.

New York Times, "E. B. Morris Dead; Noted Financier. Chairman of the Girard Trust Company in Philadelphia," Jan. 3, 1937.

New Yorker, "Ahoy, Listerine!" by Jack Alexander, July 16, 1938.

New York Hotel Reviews, Volume 16, "Pierre's and the Man Behind Two Ninety Park Avenue."

New York Times, "Sister Parish, Reigning Arbiter of Lovely (and Expensive) Things," by Georgia Dullea, April 11, 1991.

New York Times, "Hattie Carnegie Dies," Feb. 23, 1956.

New York Times, "The Private World of a Great Gardener," by Paula Deitz, June 3, 1982.

Books:

Burton Hersh, *The Mellon Family: A Fortune in History*, William Morrow, 1978.

Gerard Barnes Lambert, *All Out of Step*, Doubleday, 1956.

George Pitcher, *A Life of Grace: The Biography of Grace Lansing Lambert*, Princeton University Press, 1987.

CHAPTER NINE. PAUL MELLON'S REBELLION

Documents:

Foxcroft Alumni Newsletters, 1939–1940.

Chris Matthews interview with Bunny Mellon for his book *Jack Kennedy: Elusive Hero*, Simon & Schuster, 2011. Unpublished excerpts.

Articles:

New York Tribune, "Paul W. Mellon, Son of Secretary, Plans Career as Book Publisher," July 8, 1930.

Associated Press, "Mellon's Son to Learn Handling of Fortune," July 8, 1930.

Pittsburgh Press, "Mellon Scion Goes to Bank Job After Talk with Father," July 9, 1930.

New York Herald Tribune, "Student, Back from England, to Forego Opportunity as Heir to Banking Interest," Dec. 24, 1930.

New York Herald Tribune, "Mellon Son Rises in Bank to Director in 43 Days," Jan. 14, 1932.

Boston Globe, "Started Life with $7,00,000 Each. Mellon's Two Children Have Increased This to $50,000,000—Both Have Midas Touch," March 3, 1935.

New York Times, "Paul Mellon Buys in Virginia," Nov. 28, 1936.

New York Herald Tribune, "This New York," by Lucius Beebe, Feb. 8, 1936.

Washington Post, "Activities Among the Horse-Lovers of Virginia and Maryland," by Nina Carter Tabb, June 1, 1937.

New York Times, "Child for Paul Mellons," Jan. 1, 1937.

New York Times, "Mellon's Funeral Attended by 2,000," Aug. 29, 1937.

Sun, "The Virginias," Nov. 21, 1937.

Washington Post, "New Weekly to Start," Aug. 29, 1937.

Buffalo Courier-Express, "Heir Takes Bride," Feb. 15, 1938.

Washington Post, "The Lloyds Entertain," June 12, 1938.

Saratogian, "The Book Shelf," by Bruce Catton, Aug. 5, 1938.

New York Herald Tribune, "Private Housing Project to Start at Princeton," Aug. 7, 1938.

Sun, "The Virginias," Feb. 19, 1939.

Washington Post, "Mrs. Winmill Serves Dinner," March 5, 1939.

Atlanta Journal-Constitution, "My Day: G.W.T.W.," by Eleanor Roosevelt, Dec. 29, 1939.

Washington Post, "Mrs. Whitney Gets Three Million and Keeps Farm," April 11, 1940.

New York Herald Tribune, "Plan to House 5 Million U.S. Families Urged," Nov. 3, 1939.

New York Herald Tribune, "Red Cross Buys Army Supplies of World War," June 22, 1940.

New York Times, "American Friends of Britain Arrange a Dance," Nov. 17, 1940.

Washington Post, "The Hunt Country," by Nina Carter Tabb, Nov. 24, 1940.

Associated Press, published in *Washington Star*, "Life of Old England Goes On as Transplants of Great Wealth Ride to Hounds Among Romantic Surroundings of Days Before the War of the States," by Barton Pattie, March 16, 1941.

New York Times, "6,000 in Capital at Preview of Art," March 18, 1941.

Chicago Tribune, "Roosevelt Dedicates U.S. Gallery of Art," March 18, 1941.

New York Times, "President Accepts Gallery and Mellon and Kress Art," by John MacCormac, March 18, 1941.

New York Herald Tribune, "Lambert Sells Sloop Yankee to Help British, Gives Schooner Atlantic to U.S. Coast Guard," by William Taylor, April 1, 1941.

New York Times, "Lady Malcolm Douglas-Hamilton, American Who Aided Britain in War, Dies at 103," by Douglas Martin, Feb. 2, 2013.

Washington Post, "Clarke County: Historic Homes and Rolling Countryside Await Virginia Garden Tourists," April 20, 1941.

Washington Star, "Paul Mellon Leaves for Army Duty; Volunteered Service," July 7, 1941.

Philadelphia Inquirer, "Stacy B. Lloyd Dies on Vacation in Maine; Bank President Was 65," July 31, 1941.

New York Times, "Gerard B. Lambert, Yachtsman, Dies," Feb. 26, 1967.

Chronicle of the Horse, "The Chronicle Celebrates 70 Years in 2007," by Jackie Burke, March 23, 2007.

Books:

David Cannadine, *Mellon: An American Life*, Knopf, 2006.

Burton Hersh, *The Mellon Family: A Fortune in History*, William Morrow, 1978.

Paul Mellon, *The Brick House, Upperville, Virginia*, monograph, designed by Bert Clarke, printed by A. Colish.

Paul Mellon with John Baskett, *Reflections in a Silver Spoon*, William Morrow, 1992.

CHAPTER TEN. THE WAR YEARS

Interviews:

John Baskett, Nancy Collins, Bruce Horten, Robin Lloyd, Stacy "Tuffy" Lloyd III, David Fleming, Lily Lambert Fleming

Documents:

Stacy B. Lloyd Jr. letters to Bunny Mellon, Oak Spring Garden Library.

Bunny Mellon letter to Eliza Lloyd Moore, Lloyd family collection.

National Archives. Declassified OSS files on Stacy B. Lloyd Jr. and Paul Mellon.

Bunny Mellon dictated notes to Nancy Collins.

Articles:

Washington Star, "Paul Mellon Made Second Lieutenant," March 27, 1942.

New York Tribune, "Born to Paul Mellon," July 23, 1942.

New York Herald Tribune, "Personal Intelligence," Sept. 21, 1942.

New York Times, "Child to Mrs. Stacy B. Lloyd Junior," Oct. 28, 1942.

Philadelphia Inquirer, "Lloyds at Boyce, Va.," April 2, 1944.

New York Times, "Mrs. L. Fleming to Wed; Will Become Bride Saturday of John G. McCarthy of Navy," May 2, 1944.

Washington Post, "Colonel Lloyd Home," by Nina Carter Tabb, Feb. 25, 1945.

Washington Post, "Col. Jock Whitney, Turf Family Scion, Captured by Nazis," Aug. 30, 1945.

New York Times, "Allies Confirm Escape of Col. 'Jock' Whitney," Sept. 15, 1944.

Washington Post, "Whitney Fled as Allies Raked Prison," Sept. 15, 1944.

Global Research, "Early Psychological Warfare Research and the Rockefeller Foundation," by James F. Tracy, April 29, 2012.

Books:

David K. E. Bruce, *OSS Against the Reich: The World War II Diaries of Colonel David K. E. Bruce*, edited by Nelson D. Lankford, Kent State University Press, 1991.

Nelson D. Lankford, *The Last American Aristocrat: The Biography of Ambassador David K. E. Bruce, 1898–1977*, Little, Brown, 1996.

E. J. Kahn Jr., *Jock: The Life and Times of John Hay Whitney*, Doubleday, 1981.

David Greenberg, *Republic of Spin*, Norton, 2016.

Gerard Barnes Lambert, *All Out of Step*, Doubleday, 1956.

Paul Mellon with John Baskett, *Reflections in a Silver Spoon*, William Morrow, 1992.

Tim Mellon, *Tim's Story*, Mint Leaf Media, 2016.

George Pitcher, *A Life of Grace: The Biography of Grace Lansing Lambert*, Princeton University Press, 1987.

Douglas Waller, *Wild Bill Donovan: The Spymaster Who Created the OSS and Modern American Espionage*, Free Press, 2011.

John Keegan, *The Second World War*, Penguin Books, 1989.

Adam Sheingate, *Building a Business of Politics: The Rise of Political Consulting and the Transformation of American Democracy*, Oxford University Press, 2015.

Christof Wolf, Dominique Joye, Tom W. Smith, and Yang-chih Fu, *The SAGE Handbook of Survey Methodology*, SAGE Publications, 2016.

Robert Eisinger, *The Evolution of Political Polling*, Cambridge University Press, 2003.

Timothy Glander, *Origins of Mass Communications Research During the American Cold War*, Lawrence Erlbaum Associates, 2000.

CHAPTER ELEVEN. MILLIONS OF REASONS TO REMARRY

Interviews:

Bruce Horten, Bryan Huffman, John Loring, Stacy "Tuffy" Lloyd III, Louise Whitney Mellon, Lily Lambert Norton, John Warner, Virginia Warner

Documents:

Stacy B. Lloyd Jr. letter to Bunny Mellon, Oak Spring Garden Library.

Bunny Mellon letter to Huntington Cairns, Library of Congress.

Carl Jung Biographical Archive, Countway Library of Medicine, Boston, interview with Marie-Jeanne Boller-Schmid by Dr. Gene Nameche, Feb. 1970.

Perry Wheeler Collection, Smithsonian Gardens, Archives of American Gardens.

National Gallery of Art, online archives on Mellon art purchases.

Articles:

Washington Post, "The Hunt Country," by Nina Carter Tabb, Dec. 2, 1945.

New York Times, "Mrs. Paul Mellon Succumbs in South," Oct. 12, 1946.

Washington Star, "Memory of Late Mrs. Mellon Honored in Middleburg Race," Nov. 13, 1946.

Philadelphia Inquirer, "Mrs. Paul Mellon," Oct. 12, 1946.

Salt Lake Tribune, "52 Die in Utah Air Liner Crash," Oct. 25, 1947.

New York Times, "Lambert Funeral Tomorrow," Oct. 30, 1947.

New York Herald Tribune, "Dr. Clopton Dies," April 22, 1947.

Washington Post, "Mrs. Mellon-to-Be," by Mary Van Rensselaer Thayer, Oct. 10, 1947.

Philadelphia Inquirer, "Divorce from Stacy B. Lloyd Is Asked in Florida Suit," Feb. 27, 1948.

Associated Press, published in *Philadelphia Inquirer*, "Florida Divorce Given Mrs. Lloyd," March 10, 1948.

New York Times, "Paul Mellon to Marry: Son of Late Financier to Wed Mrs. Rachel L. Lloyd," May 1, 1948.

New York Times, "Paul Mellon Weds Mrs. Rachel Lloyd," May 2, 1948.

Washington Post, "The Hunt Country," by Nina Carter Tabb, Dec. 12, 1948.

New York Herald Tribune, "Mellon Fund Gives Yale, Vassar 2 Million Each for Psychiatry," June 13, 1949.

Washington Post, "Fashion Tea Aids Children's Hospital," April 20, 1950.

New York Times, "Art Sale Totals $50,220," May 7, 1950.

New York Herald Tribune, "Paul Mellon Has Sold Capricorn," June 18, 1950.

Hartford Courant, "Duke's Wife Keeps Fashion Title," Dec. 30, 1951.

New York Times, "Conservation Seashore: Famous Outer Banks of North Carolina Preserved with the Aid of Trust Funds," Sept. 7, 1952.

Washington Star, "Russell Arundel," Oct. 16, 1952.

Washington Post, "Prize Bull Is Bought for $5,300," by Aubrey Graves, Nov. 3, 1952.

Washington Star, "Exclusively Yours," by Betty Beale, Feb. 15, 1953.

Associated Press, published in *Austin American-Statesman*, "No Sand Dunes? He Makes His Own," Aug. 28, 1953.

Washington Herald, "Thanksgiving Hunt Meet Draws Crowds to Foxcroft," by Dolores Phillips, Nov. 26, 1953.

Washington Star, "Hill School Stages Country Auction with City Trappings," Dec. 9, 1954.

Washington Star, "Circling the Countryside," by Dolores Phillips, March 24, 1955.

Washington Post, "Hunt Set Parties at Races," by Kitty Slater, March 28, 1955.

WWD, "Experiences of Smaller Stores; Contact with Capital Society Builds Special Clientele," by Jane Cahill, May 9, 1955.

Washington Star, "Catherine Conover Mellon," by Dolores Phillips, June 16, 1955.

New York Times, "Jeweler Sets Trends with Natural Elegance," Dec. 7, 1960.

New York Times, "Philanthropist, Yale '29, Paul Mellon," Dec. 9, 1966.

WWD, "Schlumberger, The Beauty of Nature," March 12, 1956.

New York Times, "J. Schlumberger Dies in Paris at 80," by Carol Lawson, Sept. 1, 1987.

New York Times, "Books of the Times: How Far an Advertiser Can Go," by Charles Poore, Oct. 27, 1956.

Chicago Tribune, "List Biggest Contributions to Political Campaigns," Oct. 9, 1956.

Washington Post, "New Church in Upperville's Future," June 2, 1957.

New York Herald Tribune, "Miss Catherine Mellon, John William Warner," Aug. 8, 1957.

Washington Star, "Piedmont Point-to-Point Course Will Become Private Airstrip," by Dolores Phillips, Aug. 24, 1957.

WWD, "Remembering Schlumberger," Sept. 4, 1987.

New York Times, "A Modern Medieval Norman French Church in Upperville, Va.," by Nona B. Brown, June 9, 1968.

Wall Street Journal, "The Mellon Millions: How a Wealthy Family Puts Fortune to Work for Benefit of Public," by John Lawrence, Feb. 10, 1964.

Washington Post, "Doyennes of Décor," by Jura Koncius and Patricia Dane Rogers, Oct. 20, 1994.

New York Times, "Sister Parish, Grande Dame of American Interior Decorating, Is Dead at 84," by Eric Pace, Sept. 10, 1994.

Books:

Sherman Adams, *Firsthand Report: The Story of the Eisenhower Administration*, Harper & Brothers, 1961.

Apple Parish Bartlett and Susan Bartlett Crater, *Sister Parish: The Life of the Legendary American Interior Designer*, Vendome, 2000.

Robert Becker, *Nancy Lancaster: Her Life, Her World, Her Art*, Knopf, 1996.

Burton Hersh, *The Mellon Family: A Fortune in History*, William Morrow, 1978.

Gerard Barnes Lambert, *All Out of Step*, Doubleday, 1956.

Paul Mellon with John Baskett, *Reflections in a Silver Spoon*, William Morrow, 1992.

Tim Mellon, *Tim's Story*, Mint Leaf Media, 2016.

Sandra Raphael, *An Oak Spring Sylva: A Selection of the Rare Books on Trees in the Oak Spring Garden Library*, Yale University Press, 1989.

Sandra Raphael, *An Oak Spring Pomona: A Selection of the Rare Books on Fruit in the Oak Spring Garden Library*, Yale University Press, 1990.

John Walker, *Self-Portrait with Donors: Confessions of an Art Collector*, Little, Brown, 1974.

CHAPTER TWELVE. THE BEST-DRESSED LIST

Interviews:

Martha Bartlett, Marion "Oatsie" Leiter Charles, Audrey Greene, Robin Lloyd, Lee Radziwill, Marie Ridder, John Saumarez Smith, Babs Simpson, John Warner

Documents:

Stacy "Tuffy" Lloyd III eulogy, Bunny Mellon funeral, March 28, 2014.

Sotheby's Catalogues: Property from the collection of Mrs. Paul Mellon, November 2014.

Bunny Mellon autobiographical essays, Oak Spring Garden Library.

Bunny Mellon notes dictated to Nancy Collins.

Stacy B. Lloyd Jr. letters to Bunny Mellon, Oak Spring Garden Library.

Paul Mellon letters to Bunny Mellon, Oak Spring Garden Library.

Oak Spring Garden Library website, details of Bunny Mellon's collection.

Articles:

New Yorker, "Pebbles of Verdura," by John Mosher, Geoffrey T. Hellman, and Harold Ross, May 24, 1941.

Washington Star, "Society," by Nina Carter Tabb, Dec. 27, 1935.

Washington Post, "Her Career and Her Dresses Are Both Made-to-Order," by Lucia Brown, Dec. 16, 1949.

Washington Post, "Exciting Trends in Jewelry Mix Diamonds, Colored Gems," May 11, 1947.

New York Herald Tribune, "Schlumberger Designs Garden of Jewels," Nov. 20, 1956.

WWD, "Experiences of Smaller Stores, Contact with Capital Society Builds Special Clientele," by Jane Cahill, May 9, 1955.

Classic Boat Magazine, "Bounty, a Boat with Many Lives," by Robin Lloyd, July 2013.

Washington Star, "Piedmont Point-to-Point Course Will Become Private Airstrip," by Dolores Phillips, Feb. 24, 1957.

Boston Globe, "Visit to Virginia Stables Planned for Queen Elizabeth," by Dorothy McCardle, Sept. 22, 1957.

Washington Post, "Hunt Set Parties at Races," by Kitty Slater, March 28, 1955.

Washington Star, "Catherine Conover Mellon Makes Debut," by Dolores Phillips, June 16, 1955.

Washington Star, "Hill School Stages Country Auction with City Trappings," Dec. 9, 1954.

Washington Post, "New Church in Upperville's Future," June 2, 1957.

Books:

Apple Parish Bartlett and Susan Bartlett Crater, *Sister Parish: The Life of the Legendary American Interior Designer*, Vendome, 2000.

Mary Blume, *The Master of Us All: Balenciaga, His Workrooms, His World*, Farrar, Straus and Giroux, 2013.

Chantal Bizot, Marie-Noël de Gary, and Evelyne Possémé, *The Jewels of Jean Schlumberger*, Harry N. Abrams, 2001.

Burton Hersh, *The Mellon Family: A Fortune in History*, William Morrow, 1978.

Gerard Barnes Lambert, *All Out of Step*, Doubleday, 1956.

Paul Mellon with John Baskett, *Reflections in a Silver Spoon*, William Morrow, 1992.

Tim Mellon, *Tim's Story*, Mint Leaf Media, 2016.

George Pitcher, *A Life of Grace: The Biography of Grace Lansing Lambert*, Princeton University Press, 1987.

Jan Pottker, *Janet & Jackie: The Story of a Mother and Her Daughter, Jacqueline Kennedy Onassis*, St. Martin's Press, 2001.

Sandra Raphael, *An Oak Spring Pomona: A Selection of the Rare Books on Fruit in the Oak Spring Garden Library*, Yale University Press, 1990.

John Walker, *Self-Portrait with Donors: Confessions of an Art Collector*, Little, Brown, 1974.

CHAPTER THIRTEEN. A CONSTANT GARDENER

Interviews:

Martha Bartlett, Deeda Blair, Bob Childs, Frances Fitzgerald, Marion "Oatsie" Leiter Charles, Chris Harvie, Bob Hoxie, Stacy "Tuffy" Lloyd III, Marie Ridder, Lisa Rockwell, Sydney Roberts Rockefeller, George Shaffer, John Warner

Documents:

Bunny Mellon autobiographical notes, calendars, Oak Spring Garden Library.

Perry Wheeler archive, Smithsonian Gardens, Archives of American Gardens.

Chris Matthews interview with Bunny Mellon for his book *Jack Kennedy: Elusive Hero*, Simon & Schuster, 2011. Unpublished excerpts.

Stacy B. Lloyd Jr. letters to Bunny Mellon, Oak Spring Garden Library.

Ferdinand Ostertag horoscopes for Bunny Mellon, 1960, Oak Spring Garden Library.

Articles:

Vogue, "Green Flowers and Herb Trees," by Rachel L. Mellon, Dec. 1965.

New York Times, "Attorney to Wed Miss C. C. Mellon," May 25, 1957.

Washington Post, "Engaged: Catherine Mellon, John Warner Jr.," May 28, 1957.

Boston Globe, "Capital Mirrors: Visit to Virginia Stables Planned for Queen Elizabeth," by Dorothy McCardle, Sept. 22, 1957.

Washington Star, "Betty Beale's Washington," Oct. 9, 1957.

Washington Star, "Betty Beale's Washington," Oct. 11, 1957.

Washington Post, "Most Envied Hostess in Country Today," by Muriel Bowen, Oct. 20, 1957.

Washington Post, "Thoroughbreds Parade for the Queen," by Muriel Bowen, Oct. 21, 1957.

Washington Star, "Middleburg Track Fascinates the Queen," by Daisy Cleland, Oct. 21, 1957.

Globe and Mail, "Queen Likes China Tea," Oct. 21, 1957.

Washington Post, "Washington Scene: Tea Bags Across the Sea," by George Dixon, Oct. 22, 1957.

Anniston Star, "The Smart Set," by Walter Winchell, Oct. 18, 1957.

Long Beach Independent, "The Lyons Den," by Leonard Lyons, Oct. 25, 1957.

Boston Globe, "Paul Mellon Says New Curtains Put Up," by Thomas Winship, Oct. 27, 1957.

New York Herald Tribune, "Awards at Flower Show," March 10, 1958.

Boston Globe, "Kennedy's Wife Loves Campaigning But…," by Mary Cremmen, Oct. 29, 1958.

New York Times, "A Painting That's Modern Art's Story: The Cezanne Masterpiece," by Aline Saarinen, Nov. 2, 1958.

New York Times, "Visitors Throng to Flower Show," March 9, 1959.

Washington Post, "Paul Mellon's Gelding Wins 100-mile Trail-Riding Contest," by Aubrey Graves, April 17, 1959.

Washington Star, "Prince Akihito to Visit the Mellons," May 22, 1960.

Harper's Bazaar, "The Serious Side of Astrology," by Ferdinand Ostertag, April 1960.

Akron Beacon Journal, "Betty Beale's Washington," June 12, 1960.

Associated Press, published in *Washington Post*, "Not Too Reluctant Is Coy Kennedy," by Roger Greene, Nov. 10, 1957.

United Press International, "Jackie Was Cub Reporter," Dec. 31, 1960.

Washington Times Herald, "Girl Reporter Quizzes Crowd at Coronation," by Jacqueline Bouvier, June 1, 1953.

Chicago Tribune Press, "England's Last Queen? This One Is Well Liked," by Jacqueline Bouvier, June 2, 1953.

Newsday, "Heiress Photographer Clicks with Kennedy, Capital's Most Eligible," June 25, 1953.

Boston Globe, "No Time for Ring Yet," by Joan McPartlin, June 28, 1953.

Washington Post, "Jack and Jackie Plan Move," by Dorothy McCardle, Oct. 9, 1956.

New York Herald Tribune, "Antigua Climate Lures Group of U.S. Colonizers," by Teresa Winslow, April 9, 1950.

New York Herald Tribune, "8-Hr. Flight Puts Tourist on Antigua," by W. Storrs Lee, Feb. 12, 1956.

Harper's Bazaar, "Travel Bazaar: Antigua," by Doone Marley, Dec. 1962.

Boston Globe, "Millinery Executives Ask: Why Doesn't Jackie Wear a Hat?" July 9, 1960.

Chicago Tribune, "Mrs. Kennedy Has Full Time Job—as a Wife," July 1, 1960.

Washington Post, "Jackie's Hair-do is 'Le Cygne,'" by Dorothy McCardle, July 31, 1960.

Boston Globe, "How Will the Ladies Rule the Roost? Big Parties or Small in the White House?" by Betty Beale, Aug. 7, 1960.

Chicago Tribune, "The Extraordinary Mrs. Kennedy," by William Moore, July 10, 1960.

New York Herald Tribune, "Mrs. Kennedy Rides Way into Hearts of Hunt Club," by Warren Rogers Jr., Sept. 15, 1960.

Washington Star, "Betty Beale's Washington," May 13, 1946.

Washington Post, "Gardening Wins Out over Politics," by Christine Sadler, March 5, 1955.

Washington Star, "Betty Beale's Washington," Feb. 5, 1956.

New York Herald Tribune, "Kennedys Find an Estate in Virginia They'd Like," by Victor Wilson, Dec. 7, 1960.

Telegraph, "Nancy Lancaster," Aug. 20, 1994.

Telegraph, "Pleaching: The Art of Training Trees," Nov. 26, 2011.

Books:

Hamish Bowles, Rachel Lambert Mellon, and Arthur Schlesinger Jr., *Jacqueline Kennedy: The White House Years*, Metropolitan Museum, Little, Brown, 2001.

Paul Mellon with John Baskett, *Reflections in a Silver Spoon*, William Morrow, 1992.

Tim Mellon, *Tim's Story*, Mint Leaf Media, 2016.

CHAPTER FOURTEEN. THE BEST FRIENDS

Interviews:

Letitia Baldrige, William Brooks, Marion "Oatsie" Leiter Charles, Lily Lambert Norton, Peter Duchin, Valerie Leonard, Stacy "Tuffy" Lloyd III, Marie Ridder

Documents:

Paul Leonard, "Bunny Dearest," unpublished essay, 2002, courtesy of Valerie Leonard. Published with the permission of Samantha Leonard.

Chris Matthews interview with Bunny Mellon for his book *Jack Kennedy: Elusive Hero*, Simon & Schuster, 2011. Unpublished excerpts.

Irwin M. Williams, oral history interview, March 19, 1965, JFK Presidential Library.

Perry Wheeler Collection, Smithsonian Gardens, Archives of American Gardens.

Diana Vreeland letter to Bunny Mellon, Oak Spring Garden Library.

Letters from Jacqueline Kennedy Onassis. Reprinted with permission.

Bunny Mellon dictated notes to Nancy Collins.

Eulogy by Caroline Kennedy. Reprinted with permission.

Frank Langella eulogy, Bunny Mellon funeral, March 28, 2014.

Articles:

White House History, Number 38, "President Kennedy's Garden: Rachel Lambert Mellon's Redesign of the White House Rose Garden," by William Seale.

Pittsburgh Post-Gazette, "Big 2 Urge Sacrifices to Halt Reds. UPI, JFK MacMillan Chart 'New Look' for Free World," April 9, 1961.

Boston Globe, "Mrs. Kennedy Brings Glow to the White House," by Kate Lang, April 23, 1961.

Chicago Tribune, "Mrs. Kennedy Decorating," Jan. 24, 1961.

Washington Post, "It's Paris in Virginia for the First Lady: They All Love Paris—in France or Virginia," June 25, 1961.

United Press International, published in *Washington Post*, "His Job is Staging Society Extravaganzas," by Gay Pauley, July 6, 1961.

Sun, "A Mere Million for Deb Party," by Dorothy McCardle, July 16, 1961.

Pittsburgh Post-Gazette, "Rudolph B. Stanish, 'Omelet King' for the Rich and Famous," by Marlene Parrish, Feb. 12, 2008.

Christian Science Monitor, "Omelet King's Fare," by Marilyn Hoffman, Dec. 29, 1970.

Philadelphia Inquirer, "So Critics Carped at Mt. Vernon Gala," by John M. Cummings, July 17, 1961.

Chicago Daily News, "Kennedy Hears Crisis Details, Then Goes to Sea," Aug. 28, 1961.

Associated Press, published in *Baltimore Sun*, "Horse Balks and Spills Mrs. Kennedy," Nov. 18, 1961.

Knickerbocker News, "Kennedy Song in Play Draws Jackie's Smile," Aug. 18, 1961.

New York Times, "Designer Sets Stage for Royal Visit," by Nancy Tutko, Oct. 6, 1985.

New York Times, "Caroline Foiled in Peek at Tree," by Marjorie Hunter, Dec. 13, 1961.

Washington Post, "Christmas Magic Comes to the White House," by Marie Smith, Dec. 14, 1961.

New York Times, "Charles Ryskamp, Director of Morgan and Frick, Dies at 81," by William Grimes, March 30, 2010.

Books:

Sarah Bradford, *America's Queen: The Life of Jacqueline Kennedy Onassis*, Penguin, 2000.
Alfred Bush, *Charles Ryskamp: 1928–2010*, monograph, Princeton University.
Noël Coward, *The Noël Coward Diaries*, edited by Graham Payn and Sheridan Morley, Little, Brown, 1982.
Katharine Graham, *Personal History*, Random House, 1997.
Frank Langella, *Dropped Names: Famous Men and Women As I Knew Them*, HarperCollins, 2012.
Tim Mellon, *Tim's Story*, Mint Leaf Media, 2016.
Deborah Mitford, Duchess of Devonshire, *Wait for Me! Memoirs*, Farrar, Straus and Giroux, 2010.
Richard Reeves, *President Kennedy: Profile of Power*, Simon & Schuster, 1993.
Arthur Schlesinger Jr., *A Thousand Days: John F. Kennedy in the White House*, Houghton Mifflin, 1965.
Arthur Schlesinger Jr., *Journals: 1952–2000*, Penguin Books, 2007.
Sally Bedell Smith, *Grace and Power: The Private World of the Kennedy White House*, Random House, 2004.

CHAPTER FIFTEEN. A ROSE BY ANY OTHER NAME

Interviews:

John Baskett, Alfred Bush, Amy Greene, Reinaldo Herrera, Lee Radziwill

Documents:

Bunny Mellon autobiographical essays, notes, calendars, Oak Spring Garden Library.
Bunny Mellon letter to Jacqueline Kennedy, JFK Presidential Library.
Irvin Williams, oral history, JFK Presidential Library, March 19, 1965.
Letters from Jacqueline Kennedy Onassis. Reprinted with permission.
Perry Wheeler Collection, Smithsonian Gardens, Archives of American Gardens.
Chris Matthews interview with Bunny Mellon for his book *Jack Kennedy: Elusive Hero*, Simon & Schuster, 2011. Unpublished excerpts.
CBS News, *A Tour of the White House with Mrs. John F. Kennedy*, Feb. 14, 1962.
Frank Langella eulogy at Bunny Mellon's funeral, March 28, 2014.

Articles:

White House History, Number 1, "President Kennedy's Rose Garden," by Rachel Lambert Mellon, 1983.
House & Garden, "The White House Rose Garden," by Rachel Lambert Mellon, Sept. 1984.
White House History, Number 38, "President Kennedy's Garden: Rachel Lambert Mellon's Redesign of the White House Rose Garden," by William Seale.
New York Times, "Aquatic Showplace," Aug. 22, 1954.
New York Herald Tribune, "President's Green Thumb Adds Color to New Garden," May 8, 1962.
United Press International, published in *Washington Post*, "JFK Plants an Idea," by Helen Thomas, May 9, 1962.

Associated Press, published in *Austin American Statesman*, "Gardener JFK Enjoys the White House Plot," May 10, 1962.

New York Herald Tribune, "The First Lady of Fine Arts," June 6, 1962.

Hartford Courant, "First Lady Gives Secret Agent Puzzling Duty," June 6, 1962.

Boston Globe, "President Transforms Rose Garden," by Jerry O' Leary, June 24, 1962.

Washington Star, "Keenly Interested: Kennedy Likes Rose Garden," by Paul Martin, Sept. 8, 1962.

Washington Post, "Paul Mellon Is Elected National Gallery Head," by Jean White, Jan. 31, 1963.

New Yorker, "Paul Mellon," Oct. 5, 1963.

Associated Press, published in *Austin American Statesman*, "Gardener JFK Enjoys His White House Plot," May 10, 1963.

Washington Post, "A President's Love for His City: An Intimate Friend Tells of JFK's Concern for Lafayette Square and Even Trash Baskets," by William Walton, Dec. 1, 1963.

Boston Globe, "Jacqueline Kennedy Garden Once Caused Communication Chaos," by Isabelle Shelton, May 2, 1965.

Washington Post, "Slumbering Gardens Stir," by Mary V. R. Thayer, March 22, 1960.

Washington Post, "Perry Wheeler, Landscape Architect," Aug. 18, 1989.

Books:

Marta McDowell, *All the President's Gardens*, Timber Press, 2016.

William Seale, *The White House Garden*, White House Historical Association, 1996.

William Seale, *The White House: The History of an American Idea*, White House Historical Association, 2001.

Tim Mellon, *Tim's Story*, Mint Leaf Media, 2016.

Deborah Mitford, Duchess of Devonshire, *Wait for Me! Memoirs*, Farrar, Straus and Giroux, 2010.

Richard Reeves, *President Kennedy: Profile of Power*, Simon & Schuster, 1993.

Sally Bedell Smith, *Grace and Power: The Private World of the Kennedy White House*, Random House, 2004.

CHAPTER SIXTEEN. NOVEMBER 22, 1963

Documents:

Bunny Mellon interview with William Manchester for his book *The Death of a President*. Wesleyan University Archives, published courtesy of Gerard B. Lambert Foundation and Wesleyan University.

Paul Leonard, "Bunny Dearest," unpublished essay, 2002, courtesy of Valerie Leonard. Published with the permission of Samantha Leonard.

Perry Wheeler Collection, Smithsonian Gardens, Archives of American Gardens.

Articles:

New York Times, "Vacationing Is Effortless on Sleepy Antigua," by Nan Robertson, Jan. 8, 1961.

Books:

William Manchester, *The Death of A President*, Harper & Row, 1967.

CHAPTER SEVENTEEN. CARRYING ON

Interviews:

Marion "Oatsie" Leiter Charles, Lavinia Currier, David Fleming, Peter Fleming, Amy Greene, Henry Heymann, Bryan Huffman, Valerie Leonard, Iris Love, John McCarthy, Lily Lambert Norton, Lee Radziwill, Marie Ridder, George Shaffer

Documents:

Bunny Mellon autobiographical essays, journals, correspondence, Oak Spring Garden Library.

Robert F. Kennedy letter to Bunny Mellon, JFK Presidential Library.

Bunny Mellon letter to Robert F. Kennedy, JFK Presidential Library.

Bunny Mellon dictated notes to Nancy Collins.

Paul Leonard, "Bunny Dearest," unpublished essay, 2002, courtesy of Valerie Leonard. Published with the permission of Samantha Leonard.

Stacy Lloyd Jr. letters to Bunny Mellon, Oak Spring Garden Library.

Paul Mellon letters to Bunny Mellon, Oak Spring Garden Library.

Kenneth Battelle letters to Bunny Mellon, Oak Spring Garden Library.

Charles Ryskamp letters to Bunny Mellon, Oak Spring Garden Library.

Charlotte Noland letters to Bunny Mellon, Oak Spring Garden Library.

Eulogy by Caroline Kennedy. Reprinted with Permission.

Articles:

House & Garden, "The Jacqueline Kennedy Garden," by Rachel Lambert Mellon, Oct. 1984.

Vogue, "Green Flowers and Herb Trees," by Rachel L. Mellon, Dec. 1965.

United Press International, published in *Chicago Tribune*, "Mrs. Kennedy Reaches Antigua for a Vacation," March 31, 1964.

Washington Star, "Mrs. Mellon's Rose Garden: Setting Does Much for Restless Spirit Political Style of the President," by Doris Fleeson, April 24, 1964.

Washington Star, "Persian Art Exhibit Opened by Shah," by Pat Saltonstall, June 6, 1964.

Washington Post, "Administration Anxious to Save Lafayette Park," by Jean White, Feb. 17, 1961.

Boston Globe, "Mind Not Made Up on VP Bid—RFK," June 8, 1964.

Wall Street Journal, "The Mellon Millions: How a Wealthy Family Puts Fortune to Work for Benefit of Public," by John Lawrence, Feb. 10, 1964.

Hartford Courant, "Inside Fashion: Shining Up the American Image," by Eugenia Sheppard, Dec. 3, 1964.

New York Times, "The Radziwills Give 'Teeny Tiny Party'—for 100 Guests," by Charlotte Curtis, April 21, 1965.

New York Times, "Garden Named for Mrs. Kennedy," by Nan Robertson, April 23, 1965.

Hartford Courant, "Behind a Dark Green Gate," by Eugenia Sheppard, April 7, 1966.

New York Times, "Princeton's Grande Dame Reminisces," Dec. 8, 1974.

Washington Star, "Mellon Shows Art with Humor," by Betty Beale, March 18, 1966.

New York Times, "Guests Flock to National Gallery and Some Look at the Art: Much of Attention Goes to First Lady and the Mellons," March 19, 1966.

Milwaukee Sentinel, "Finds Solace in Art," Oct. 15, 1966.

WWD, "The Morning After," Nov. 30, 1966.

Boston Globe, "Kennedys Go Swimming in Antigua," Dec. 28, 1966.

Washington Star, "Mrs. Kennedy Remains in Seclusion," Dec. 28, 1966.

Palm Beach Post, "The Smart Set," by Suzy Knickerbocker, Jan. 26, 1967.

Associated Press, published in *Palm Beach Post*, "Rich Hermits Pay for Privacy," by Kelly Smith, Feb. 5, 1967.

Chicago Tribune, "Story of Jackie's New Life: Trying to Be Herself," by Liz Smith, Jan. 16, 1967.

New York Times, "Sister Parish Creates Distinctive Interiors by Instinct," by Virginia Lee Warren, May 18, 1965.

New York Times, "Gerard B. Lambert, Yachtsman, Dies," Feb. 26, 1967.

WWD, "Kennedy Day and Night," April 4, 1967.

Time, "Art: The Nation's Grand Showcase," by Robert Hughes, May 8, 1978.

New York Times, "Winter Schedule Planned," Jan. 30, 1966.

New York Times, "Kennedy Candidacy Stirs Wide Interest," by Warren Weaver Jr., Aug. 16, 1964.

Washington Star, "Dr. Lauriston Hardin, 64, Shot While Hunting," Nov. 1, 1966.

New York Times, "Dr. B. Lauriston Hardin, Physician in Washington," Nov. 5, 1966.

Books:

Deborah Davis, *Party of the Century*, Wiley, 2010.

Sarah Bradford, *America's Queen: The Life of Jacqueline Kennedy Onassis*, Penguin Books, 2000.

Paul Mellon with John Baskett, *Reflections in a Silver Spoon*, William Morrow, 1992.

George Pitcher, *A Life of Grace: The Biography of Grace Lansing Lambert*, Princeton University Press, 1987.

Evan Thomas, *Robert Kennedy: His Life*, Simon & Schuster, 2000.

John Walker, *Self-Portrait with Donors: Confessions of an Art Collector*, Little, Brown, 1974.

CHAPTER EIGHTEEN. 1968

Interviews:

Ned Crosby, Richard Giglio, Hubert de Givenchy, Bryan Huffman, Robin Lloyd, Stacy "Tuffy" Lloyd III, Virginia Warner

Documents:

Bunny Mellon autobiographical essays, journals, calendars, Oak Spring Garden Library.

Letters from Jacqueline Kennedy. Reprinted with permission.

A. W. Mellon Foundation, Grants.

Stacy B. Lloyd Jr. letters to Bunny Mellon, Oak Spring Garden Library.

Bunny Mellon letters to Eliza Lloyd, Oak Spring Garden Library.

Paul Mellon toasts and letters to Bunny Mellon, Oak Spring Garden Library.

Articles:

Boston Globe, "A Curl's Best Friend: Men Who Dress the Hair of New York's Best-Dressed Women," by Sara Davidson, March 3, 1968.

New York Times, "Beauty is Big Business to a Lionized Coiffeur," by Marylin Bender, April 30, 1963.

Los Angeles Times, "Troops, Churchgoers Walk in Capital Rubble: Calm Returns to Washington But Curfew Remains, 8 Reported Dead, 4,200 Jailed," by Murray Seeger, April 8, 1968.

New York Times, "62 in N.Y. Delegation Fly to the Funeral with Rockefeller," by Deidre Carmody, April 10, 1968.

New York Times, "TV Memorable Viewing Experience," by Jack Gould, April 10, 1968.

Associated Press, published in *Hartford Courant*, "30 Deaths in Latest Riot Tally," April 10, 1968.

New York Times, "Leaders at the Rite," by Homer Bigart, April 10, 1968.

Associated Press, published in *Chicago Tribune*, "2 Made Widows by Assassins Share Solace Before Funeral," April 10, 1968.

Washington Post, "Congregation Told to Be Tolerant of Other Views," April 22, 1968.

Washington Post, "Susan Stein's Port: Where the Elite Meet," by Beatrice Berg, July 14, 1968.

Los Angeles Times, "Workmen Dig Grave for Senator Near His Brother's," June 9, 1968.

Los Angeles Times, "Nation Pays Homage to Kennedy," by Robert J. Donovan, June 9, 1968.

Los Angeles Times, "Jackie Watching Raised to a Military Art," by Art Buchwald, March 14, 1968.

WWD, "Mrs. John F. Kennedy Has Once Again Changed Her Public Image," April 9, 1968.

Washington Post, "Race Troubles Hunt Country," by Douglas Watson, April 20, 1968.

WWD, "The Best of Everything," by Eugenia Sheppard, May 3, 1968.

WWD, "Inside Fashion," by Eugenia Sheppard, May 15, 1968.

Pittsburgh Post-Gazette, "Eliza Lloyd Weds English Viscount," May 16, 1968.

Washington Post, "Mellon Ceremony Is Like a Gainsborough Portrait," by Nancy L. Ross, May 15, 1968.

New York Times, "Viscount Moore Weds Eliza Lloyd," May 15, 1968.

Austin Statesman, "Own Magical Bedroom Recreated for Bride," by Maxine Cheshire, May 31, 1968.

Washington Post, "Very Interesting People: Is Mrs. Paul Mellon Landscaping a Memorial for Robert Kennedy?" by Maxine Cheshire, June 18, 1968.

Lebanon Daily News, "Walter Winchell" column, June 3, 1968.

Chicago Tribune, "Suzy Says It's Togetherness for Paul Mellons," by Suzy Knickerbocker, June 4, 1968.

New York Times, "Washington's National Gallery Engages Pei for New Building," by Ada Louise Huxtable, July 30, 1968.

Washington Post, "Jackie Watchers Had Better Watch Better the Next Time," by Art Buchwald, Oct. 22, 1968.

Boston Globe, "Gifts of the Golden Greeks," by Fred Sparks, Dec. 15, 1968.

Atlanta Constitution, "Gems for Jackie Dazzle Wedding Party," by Fred Sparks, June 13, 1971.

San Antonio Express, "The Jackie Nobody Knows," by Liz Smith, April 21, 1974.

New York Times, "Designer Sets the Stage for Royal Visit," by Nancy Tutko, Oct. 6, 1985.

Books:

Frank Langella, *Dropped Names: Famous Men and Women As I Knew Them*, HarperCollins, 2012.

Paul Mellon and John Baskett, *Reflections in a Silver Spoon*, William Morrow, 1992.

Laura Jacobs and Victor Skrebneski, *The Art of Haute Couture*, Abbeville Press, 1995.

CHAPTER NINETEEN. PAUL AND BUNNY IN LOVE—WITH OTHERS

Interviews:

Charles Bartlett, Martha Bartlett, John Baskett, Alfred Bush, Marion "Oatsie" Leiter Charles, Lavinia Currier, David Fleming, Alex Forger, Hubert de Givenchy, Amy Greene, Henry Heymann, Bryan Huffman, Vernon Jordan, Kenneth Jay Lane, Valerie Leonard, Stacy "Tuffy" Lloyd III, Pierce MacGuire, Madeline Moses, Lily Lambert Norton, Oscar de la Renta, Marie Ridder, John Warner, Virginia Warner, Liz Winship

Documents:

Bunny Mellon autobiographical essays, journals, and calendars, Oak Spring Garden Library.

Perry Wheeler Collection, Smithsonian Gardens, Archives of American Gardens.

Paul Mellon, speech dedicating Currier House at Radcliffe, Nov. 18, 1970.

Articles:

Washington Post, "Her Career and Her Dresses Are Both Made-to-Order," by Lucia Brown, Dec. 16, 1949.

Washington Post, "Boutique Owner Dorcas Hardin," by Matt Schudel, Jan. 21, 2006.

New York Times, "The House in the Virginia Hunt Country That is Home to the Paul Mellons," by Sarah Booth Conroy, June 1, 1969.

New York Times, "The Horses' Owners Are Ready Too," by Charlotte Curtis, June 7, 1969.

New York Times, "Ailsa Mellon Bruce Dead; Called Richest Woman in U.S.," Aug. 26, 1969.

Washington Post, "Dazzling Gallery Gift," by Paul Richard, Aug. 29, 1969.

New York Times, "Washington Welcomes Devonshire Art and Heir," Nov. 3, 1969.

New York Times, "Jeane Dixon, Astrologist Claimed Psychic Power, Dies," by Eric Pace, Jan. 27, 1997.

Washington Post, "Pat Nixon's Gallery Tour," by Marie Smith, Nov. 21, 1969.

New York Times, "The Mellons Give a Dinner at National Gallery," Jan. 27, 1970.

New York Times, "Glittering Capital Audience Flocks to the Opening of the $70 Million Kennedy Center," by Nan Robertson, Sept. 9, 1971.

WWD, "Eye Too," July 26, 1971.

Washington Post, "Laos: The Question Is How to Get Off the Tiger," by Stacy B. Lloyd, Feb. 6, 1972.

WWD, Eye column, "Bunny Hopping," Sept. 21, 1972.

Washington Star, "Georgetown News," by Suzy Knickerbocker, Sept. 28, 1972.

Books:

Frank Langella, *Dropped Names: Famous Men and Women As I Knew Them*, HarperCollins, 2012.

Tim Mellon, *Tim's Story*, Mint Leaf Media, 2016.

Lee Seldes, *The Legacy of Mark Rothko*, Da Capo Press, 1978.

Sally Bedell Smith, *Grace and Power: The Private World of the Kennedy White House*, Random House, 2004.

John Walker, *Self-Portrait with Donors: Confessions of an Art Collector*, Little, Brown, 1974.

CHAPTER TWENTY. THE SPENDING OF A ROBBER BARON FORTUNE

Interviews:

John Baskett, Deeda Blair, Brita Bonechi, Susan Cabral, Anne Emmet, David Fleming, Alex Forger, Carol Fox, Hubert de Givenchy, Amy Greene, Joshua Greene, Henry Heymann, Hugh Newell Jacobsen, Valerie Leonard, Stacy "Tuffy" Lloyd III, Thomas Lloyd, Marci Nadler, Lily Lambert Norton, Nedra Parry, Oscar de la Renta, Babs Simpson, John Warner, Virginia Warner

Documents:

Bunny Mellon letters to Eliza Lloyd, Lloyd family collection.

Stacy B. Lloyd Jr. letter to Bunny Mellon, Oak Spring Garden Library.

Carol Fox, Oral History conducted by A.C. Viebranz, National Gallery of Art Archives, March 12, 1993.

Articles:

Utica Times Herald, Maxine Cheshire column, March 2, 1973.

WWD, Eye column, "More News from Upperville," Dec. 10, 1971.

WWD, Eye column, "Real Estate," Feb. 28, 1972.

WWD, Eye column, "Jackie O: Fashion's Odyssey," June 12, 1972.

WWD, Eye column, by Kandy Stroud, Jan. 11, 1973.

Washington Post, "Nora McMullen Mellon, Mother of Art Collector," June 1, 1973.

Washington Star, "Russian Art Treasures," by Ymelda Dixon, March 3, 1973.

Vogue, "The Washington Power Pile-Up," by Sandra McElwaine, Oct. 1973.

Washington Star, "At Last! The 20th Century Comes to the National Gallery," Oct. 26, 1973.

Time, "Art: California in Eupeptic Color," by Robert Hughes, June 27, 1977.

Chicago Tribune, "Navy Head and Wife Divorce," Aug. 23, 1973.

Washington Post, "Lloyd-Pepper Vows Exchanged," by Donnie Radcliffe and Tom Shales, Nov. 26, 1973.

Washington Post, "Having a Vail of a Time: Potpourri," by Maxine Cheshire, Jan. 27, 1976.

Washington Post, "Hunt Country's Denizens Live and Behave Well," by Donnel Nunes, July 11, 1976.

Washington Post, "Hunt Country's Industry Is Taxes on Millionaires," by Donnel Nunes, July 12, 1976.

WWD, "Bunny Mellon, Ivy League Eccentric," Nov. 10, 1976.

Washington Star, Betty Beale column, Dec. 26, 1976.

New York Times, "Prayer-Vigil Figure Headed Cult of 200," by Robert McG. Thomas Jr., Dec. 12, 1976.

New York Times, "Cultist Who Tried for 60 Days in '76 to Revive Follower Jumps to Death," by Farnsworth Fowle, April 15, 1977.

Washington Post, "Paul Mellon's Art: The Galloping Anglophile," by Paul Richard, April 24, 1997.

New York Times, "100 Mile Jockey," by Red Smith, May 1, 1977.
Parade Magazine, Walter Scott's Personality Parade column, Dec. 11, 1977.
Vanity Fair, "Power Pei," by Martin Filler, September 1989.
Time, "Art: The Nation's Grand Showcase," by Robert Hughes, May 8, 1978.
Time, "Art: A Portrait of the Donor," by Gerald Clarke, May 8, 1978.

Books:

Apple Parish Bartlett and Susan Bartlett Crater, *Sister Parish: The Life of the Legendary American Interior Designer*, Vendome, 2000.
Lee Hall, *Betty Parsons: Artist, Dealer, Collector*, Harry N. Abrams, 1991.
Burton Hersh, *The Mellon Family: A Fortune in History*, William Morrow, 1978.
Marsha Mason, *Journey: A Personal Odyssey*, Simon & Schuster, 2002.

CHAPTER TWENTY-ONE. THE BOOK STOPS HERE

Interviews:

Dita Amory, Joe Armstrong, John Baskett, Deeda Blair, Susan Cabral, Anne Emmet, Carol Fox, Hubert de Givenchy, Joshua Greene, Genevra Higginson, Jane Stanton Hitchcock, Bryan Huffman, Hugh Jacobsen, Sam Kasten, Ward Landrigan, Valerie Leonard, Robin Lloyd, Stacy Lloyd IV, Thomas Lloyd, Angela Loré, John Loring, Malcolm Magruder, Louise Whitney Mellon, Kathryn Myers, Beverly Newton, Timothy Patterson, Malcolm Robson, George Shaffer, Howard Slatkin, Clarice Smith, John Saumarez Smith, Virginia Warner, Tony Willis, John Wilmerding

Documents:

Bunny Mellon autobiographical essays, journals, and calendars, Oak Spring Garden Library.
Paul Mellon speech to the A. W. Mellon dinner, May 3, 1985, National Gallery of Art archives.
Bunny Mellon letters to Paul Mellon, Oak Spring Garden Library.
Bunny Mellon letters to Eliza Lloyd Moore, Lloyd family collection.
Stacy B. Lloyd Jr. letters to Eliza Lloyd Moore, Lloyd family collection.
Stacy B. Lloyd Jr. letters to Bunny Mellon, Oak Spring Garden Library.
Doris Sanders will, Surrogate's Court, New York, File No. 3108-1999.

Articles:

New York Times, "The Private World of a Great Gardener," by Paula Deitz, June 3, 1982.
White House History, Number 1, "President Kennedy's Rose Garden," by Rachel Lambert Mellon, 1983.
Washington Post, "Mellon Gives 93 Art Works," by Paul Richard, Jan. 28, 1983.
House & Garden, "The White House Rose Garden," by Rachel Lambert Mellon, Sept. 1984.
House & Garden, "The Jacqueline Kennedy Garden," by Rachel Lambert Mellon, Oct. 1984.
New York Times, "Art: Modern Museum Stages Motherwell Show," by John Russell, Oct. 31, 1980.
Washington Post, "Mellon Gives 93 Art Works," by Paul Richard, Jan. 28, 1983.
United Press International, "The House That Jackie Built," by Sharon Hamric, Oct. 1, 1981.
Washington Post, "The State of Cheese," by Walter Nicholls, March 21, 2001.

Washington Post, "Paul Mellon: Reveries and Riches," by Paul Richard, May 2, 1985.
Washington Post, "The Equestrian Mellon," by Paul Richard, May 3, 1985.
New York Times, "Trees Are Us: An Oak Spring Sylva," by Paula Deitz, March 25, 1990.
Washington Post, "Building a Classic Garden Library," by Adrian Higgins, Jan. 12, 1995.
New York Times, "Gardening Books," by Dominique Browning, Dec. 3, 2010.
House Beautiful, "Oak Spring Splendors," by Martin Filler, June 1998.
Library Journal, "An Oak Spring Flora," by Daniel Kalk, Sept. 15, 1977.

Books:

Sandra Raphael, *An Oak Spring Sylva: A Selection of the Rare Books on Trees in the Oak Spring Garden Library*, Yale University Press, 1989.
Sandra Raphael, *An Oak Spring Pomona: A Selection of the Rare Books on Fruit in the Oak Spring Garden Library*, Yale University Press, 1990.
Lucia Tongiorgi Tomasi, *An Oak Spring Flora*, Oak Spring Garden Library, 1997.
Lucia Tongiorgi Tomasi and Tony Willis, *An Oak Spring Herbaria*, Oak Spring Garden Library, 2009.

CHAPTER TWENTY-TWO. ENTERTAINING THE ROYALS (AGAIN)

Interviews:

Akko van Acker, Dita Amory, John Baskett, Sean Driscoll, Martin Filler, Hubert de Givenchy, Bruce Horten, Sam Kasten, Janine La Farge, Malcolm Magruder, Alison Martin, Louise Whitney Mellon, Michael Overington, Timothy Patterson, Malcolm Robson, Ian Schrager, George Shaffer, Clarice Smith, John Saumarez Smith, Lucia Tongiorgi Tomasi, Virginia Warner, Liz Winship

Documents:

Bunny Mellon letters to Eliza Lloyd Moore, Lloyd family collection.
Bunny Mellon letter to I. M. Pei, Oak Spring Garden Library.
Charles W. ("Chas") Freeman Jr., Association for Diplomatic Studies and Training Foreign Affairs Oral History project, interviewed by Charles Stuart Kennedy, April 14, 1995.

Articles:

Christian Science Monitor, "The British Are Coming," by Louise Sweeney, Nov. 8, 1985.
New York Times, "Designer Sets Stage for Royal Visit," by Nancy Tutko, Oct. 6, 1985.
Washington Post, "The Royal Rush Begins," Nov. 10, 1985.
Los Angeles Times, "Charles Hails Welcome Fit for a Princess," by Betty Cuniberti, Nov. 11, 1985.
Newsday, "Caroline's Intended: Intellectual and Down to Earth," by James Revson, May 4, 1986.
W Magazine, "How Bunny Mellon Met Robert Isabell," by Bunny Mellon, September 2009.
New York Times, "Fictions and Facts on Kennedy Wedding," by Michael Gross, July 17, 1986.
Newsday, "Kennedy Nuptials Stir Curiosity on the Cape," by Paul D. Colford, July 18, 1986.
Washington Post, "Jackie Onassis' American Tycoon VIP," by Maxine Cheshire, June 25, 1980.

House and Garden, "Mrs. Mellon's Secret Garden," by Rachel Lambert Mellon, June 1988.

New York Times, "Fire Destroys the Fashionable Kenneth Salon," by Georgia Dullea, May 17, 1990.

Washington Post, "Smithsonian Turns Down Mellon Farm Offer," by Kim Masters, June 20, 1991.

Vanity Fair, "A Cool Mellon," by Martin Filler, April 1992.

New York Times, "He Went into Business for Himself," by Robert Coles, April 26, 1992.

Washington Post, "A Word from Art's Sponsor," by Stephen Birmingham, April 26, 1992.

WWD, "Born with a Silver Spoon," by Susan Watters, April 26, 1992.

Spectator, "Cool, Calm and Collector," by Paul Fussell, June 20, 1992.

New York Times, "It's Time to Say...," July 20, 1992.

Washington Post, "Mellon's Sporting Life Earns Fitting Reward," by Vinnie Perrone, May 2, 1993.

New York Times, "3-Year-Old Gives 85-Year-Old His Derby Dream," by Joseph Durso, May 2, 1993.

Washington Post, "Sea Hero Gives Mellon Thrill of the Race," by Leonard Shapiro, May 13, 1993.

Books:

Paul Mellon with John Baskett, *Reflections in a Silver Spoon*, William Morrow, 1992.

Tim Mellon, *Tim's Story*, Mint Leaf Media, 2016.

CHAPTER TWENTY-THREE. EXITS AND ENTRANCES

Interviews:

Akko van Acker, John Baskett, William Brooks, Ronald Brumsfield, Susan Cabral, Nancy Collins, Ned Crosby, Lavinia Currier, Anne Emmet, Alex Forger, Liz Garvin, Hubert de Givenchy, Chris Harvie, Jane Stanton Hitchcock, Bryan Huffman, Robin Lloyd, Thomas Lloyd, Stacy "Tuffy" Lloyd III, Stacy Lloyd IV, Kati Marton, Louise Whitney Mellon, Earl Powell, Lee Radziwill, Marie Ridder, Lisa Rockwell, Inez Setler, George Shaffer, Carly Simon, Neal Turtell, Virginia Warner, Lilly Wei, Tony Willis

Documents:

Stacy B. Lloyd Jr. letters to Bunny Mellon, Oak Spring Garden Library.

Stacy B. Lloyd Jr., Princeton University, Seeley G. Mudd Manuscript Library, Alumni Archives, Boxes 56, 59, 78, 245, and 253.

Bunny Mellon letters and faxes to Robert Isabell, Oak Spring Garden Library.

Bunny Mellon letter to Virginia Lynch, Oak Spring Garden Library.

Bunny Mellon journals and calendars, Oak Spring Garden Library.

Paul Leonard letters to Bunny Mellon, Oak Spring Garden Library.

Frank Langella letter to Bunny Mellon, Oak Spring Garden Library.

Eliza Moore exhibit catalogue, Virginia Lynch Gallery, "Angels of Light, Portraits of Shadows," by Lilly Wei, May 5, 2002.

Articles:

New York Times, "Jacqueline Kennedy Onassis Has Lymphoma," by Robert McFadden, Feb. 11, 1994.

New York Times, "Jackie Returns to the Social Scene," by Nadine Brozan, March 9, 1994.

Washington Post, "Names and Places," April 18, 1994.

New York Times, "Jackie Kennedy Released from Hospital," May 18, 1994.

Washington Post, "Jacqueline Kennedy Dies at 64," by Malcolm Gladwell, May 20, 1994.

New York Times, "Jacqueline Kennedy Is Buried," by R. W. Apple, May 24, 1994.

New York Times, "Farewell to a Woman of Strength and Grace: The Funeral," by Janny Scott, May 24, 1994.

Washington Post, "The Man at Jackie's Side," by Paula Span, May 26, 1994.

Atlanta Daily News, "Jackie Kennedy Onassis Buried in Arlington Next to Husband John Kennedy," May 26, 1994.

Courier, "Former Editor Dies," Dec. 7, 1994.

East Bay R.I.com, "Admired Art Gallery Owner Virginia Lynch Dies," Dec. 9, 2007.

Time, "Jacqueline Onassis, A Profile in Courage," by Martha Duffy, May 30, 1994.

New York Times, "A Long Time Champion of Culture Turns 90," by John Russell, April 20, 1997.

Christian Science Monitor, "Omelet King's Fare," by Marilyn Hoffman, Dec. 29, 1970.

Pittsburgh Post-Gazette, "Rudolph Stanish: June 14, 1913–Feb. 10, 2008, 'Omelet King' for the Rich and Famous," by Marlene Parrish, Feb. 12, 2008.

Country Life, "A Garden Furnished with Books," by Christopher Ridgway, Dec. 18–25, 1997.

Country Life, "To Walk in a Vision of Economy and Grace," by Christopher Ridgway, Jan. 1, 1998.

Washington Post, "Paul Mellon's Greatest Gift: The Philanthropist Left Behind a Fine Example of the Art of Living," by Paul Richard, Feb. 3, 1999.

Washington Post, "Paul Mellon's Final Gifts," by Paul Richard, Feb. 11, 1999.

New York Times, "Death of a Benefactor," Feb. 3, 1999.

Newsweek, "Paul Mellon: 1907–1999," Feb. 14, 1999.

Wall Street Journal, "A Patron Who Gave As Good As He Got," by Eric Gibson, Feb. 3, 1999.

New York Times, "A Star Floral Designer's Flights of Fancy," by Elisabeth Bumiller, Dec. 22, 1998.

W Magazine, "How Bunny Mellon Met Robert Isabell," by Bunny Mellon, June 2009.

CHAPTER TWENTY-FOUR. ENDURING THE UNENDURABLE

Interviews:

Akko van Acker, Dita Amory, Errol Adels, John Baskett, William Brooks, Diane Brown, Nancy Collins, Ned Crosby, Lavinia Currier, Linda Evora, Martin Filler, David Fleming, Peter Fleming, Alex Forger, Hubert de Givenchy, Cathy Barancik Graham, Henry Heymann, Bryan Huffman, Valerie Leonard, Rickie Niceta, Robin Lloyd, Stacy Lloyd IV, Thomas Lloyd, Beverly Newton, Lily Lambert Norton, James Reginato, Malcolm Robson, Ian Schrager, Babs Simpson, Victor Skrebneski, Virginia Warner, Lilly Wei, Tony Willis

Documents:

Bunny Mellon essays, journals, correspondence, Oak Spring Garden Library.
Bunny Mellon dictated notes to Nancy Collins.

Robin Lloyd, as Executor of the Estate of Eliza L. Moore, v. St. Vincent's Manhattan Hospital, Defendants Ahmed A. Rawanduzy, MD, Case 124120/02 (7-20-2009).

Frank Langella eulogy at Bunny Mellon's funeral, March 28, 2014.

Jamshid Ghajar eulogy at Bunny Mellon's funeral, March 28, 2014.

Eliza Moore exhibit catalogue, Virginia Lynch Gallery, "Angels of Light, Portraits of Shadows," by Lilly Wei, May 5, 2002.

Metropolitan Museum Catalogue: "Jacqueline Kennedy: The White House Years," by Hamish Bowles, Arthur Schlesinger Jr., and Rachel Lambert Mellon, Bullfinch Press / Little, Brown, 2001.

Robert Isabell will, Surrogate's Court of the State of New York, May 21, 2004.

Rachel L. Mellon will, Fauquier County, VA, File CWF2014-62.

Articles:

WWD, "Union Jackie," by Aileen Mehle, April 25, 2001.

New York Times, "Negotiating Among the Powerful at a Gala that Recalls Camelot," by Alex Kuczynski, April 24, 2001.

New York magazine, "All Yesterday's Parties," by Arthur Lubow, Oct. 11, 2009.

New York Times, "Robert Isabell, Who Turned Events into Wondrous Occasions, Dies at 57," by Bruce Weber, July 10, 2009.

W Magazine, "Flower King Robert Isabell," by James Reginato, Sept. 1, 2001.

New York Times, "Paul Leonard Dies at 70, Decorated Famous Interiors," by Mitchell Owens, Nov. 3, 2002.

Vanity Fair, "All the Best Victims," by Michael Shnayerson, Sept. 2009.

CHAPTER TWENTY-FIVE. A PERILOUS POLITICAL AFFAIR

Interviews:

Josh Brumberger, Nancy Collins, Anne Emmet, Kathy Israelian Fleming, David Fleming, Alex Forger, Jane Stanton Hitchcock, Bryan Huffman, Carol Kendrick, Lily Lambert Norton, Rickie Niceta, Stacy Lloyd IV, Thomas Lloyd, Kati Marton, Beverly Newton, James Reginato, Tony Willis

Documents:

Bunny Mellon letters to Bryan Huffman, courtesy of Bryan Huffman.

Bunny Mellon correspondence, calendars, and notes, Oak Spring Garden Library.

United States of America v. Kenneth Starr and Andrew Stein, indictment, May 26, 2010.

Articles:

New York magazine, "All Yesterday's Parties," by Arthur Lubow, Oct. 11, 2009.

New York Times, "Robert Isabell, Who Turned Events into Wondrous Occasions, Dies at 57," by Bruce Weber, July 10, 2009.

New York Times, "He Said It with Flowers," by Christopher Mason, July 19, 2009.

W Magazine, "Flower King Robert Isabell," by James Reginato, Sept. 1, 2009.

W Magazine, "How Bunny Mellon Met Robert Isabell," by Bunny Mellon, June 2009.

Greenwich Times, "Lily Lambert McCarthy," March 11, 2006.

Telegraph, "Lily Lambert McCarthy," April 22, 2006.

Providence Journal, "RISF Receives $1 Million for Lynch Scholarships," by Bill Von Sicler, Oct. 5, 2000.

ABC News.com, "The Many Lives of Rielle Hunter," by Marcus Baram, Aug. 12, 2008.

New York *Daily News*, "Author Jay McInerney, Rielle Hunter's Ex, Takes Swipe at John Edwards," by William Sherman and Celeste Katz, Aug. 9, 2008.

New York Times, "Rickie Niceta and Thomas Lloyd," March 26, 2006.

People, "John Edwards: Sexiest Politician," Nov. 13, 2000.

Washington Post, "Edwards Formally Joins 2008 Presidential Race," by Dan Baltz, Dec. 29, 2006.

New York Times, "Edwards to Continue '08 Bid Despite Wife's Cancer," by John M. Broder, March 22, 2007.

National Enquirer, "Presidential Cheating Scandal! Alleged Affair Could Wreck John Edwards Campaign Bid," by Rick Egusquiza, Oct. 10, 2007.

National Enquirer, "John Edwards Love Child Scandal," by Alan Butterfield, Alan Smith, Rick Egusquiza, John Blosser, Alexander Hitchen, Prakash Gandhi, and Don Gentile, Dec. 19, 2007.

New York *Daily News*, "Ex-Voice of Lois Lane Sues, Calls Adviser Man of Steal," by Jose Martinez, April 17, 2008.

New York Times Magazine, "Rambo Takes a Hit," by Cameron Stracher, March 3, 2002.

Books:

Rielle Hunter, *What Really Happened: John Edwards, Our Daughter, and Me*, BenBella Books, 2012.

Andrew Young, *The Politician*, Thomas Dunne Books, 2010.

CHAPTER TWENTY-SIX. THE FBI MAKES HOUSE CALLS

Interviews:

Josh Brumberger, Nancy Collins, Anne Emmet, Alex Forger, Liz Garvin, Cathy Barancik Graham, Joe Heffernan, Jane Stanton Hitchcock, Bruce Horten, Bryan Huffman, Carol Kendrick, Rickie Niceta, Stacy Lloyd IV, Thomas Lloyd, Chris Matthews, Bunny Mellon, John Moylan, Beverly Newton, Michael Overington, James Reginato, Ian Schrager, Walter Shapiro, Chuck Stuber, Tony Willis

Documents:

Bunny Mellon letters to Bryan Huffman, courtesy of Bryan Huffman.

Bunny Mellon calendars, Oak Spring Garden Library.

Bunny Mellon dictated notes to Nancy Collins.

United States of America vs. Johnny Reid Edwards, Criminal Action No. 1:11CR161. Closing arguments, trial transcript, May 17, 2012.

Chris Matthews interview with Bunny Mellon for his book *Jack Kennedy: Elusive Hero*, Simon & Schuster, 2011. Unpublished excerpts.

Articles:

National Public Radio, "John Edwards Still Has Work to Do," interview with Guy Raz, July 8, 2008.

National Enquirer, "John Edwards Caught with Mistress and Love Child," July 22, 2008.

ABC News.com, "John Edwards Interview," by Bob Woodruff, Aug. 8, 2008.

New York Times, "Eliza Lloyd Moore," May 12, 2008.

McClatchy-Tribune Business News, "Mellon Gave Edwards a Boost," by Mandy Locke, May 3, 2009.

New York magazine, "All Yesterday's Parties," by Arthur Lubow, Oct. 11, 2009.

New York Times, "Robert Isabell, Who Turned Events into Wondrous Occasions, Dies at 57," by Bruce Weber, July 10, 2009.

New York Times, "He Said It with Flowers," by Christopher Mason, July 19, 2009.

W Magazine, "Flower King Robert Isabell," by James Reginato, Sept. 1, 2009.

W Magazine, "How Bunny Mellon Met Robert Isabell," by Bunny Mellon, June 2009.

Philadelphia Daily News, "I am Quinn's Father," by Will Bunch, Jan. 22, 2011.

Daily Beast, "John Edwards' Sugar Mama," by Lloyd Grove, Jan. 29, 2010.

New York *Daily News*, "Starr Fleeced Widow out of Millions over 2 Decades," by Michael Daly, May 29, 2010.

New York *Daily News*, "Bit of Digging Unearths This Real Worm," by Michael Daly, May 30, 2010.

Pittsburgh Post-Gazette, "A Reclusive 'Bunny' Mellon Celebrates 100th Birthday," by Mackenzie Carpenter, Aug. 8, 2010.

Antigua Observer, "Rachel Mellon, Founder of Mill Reef, Celebrates 100 Today," by Martina Johnson, Aug. 9, 2010.

Vanity Fair, "All the Best Victims," by Michael Shnayerson, Sept. 2010.

New York Times, "Guilty Plea in Fraud by Adviser to Stars," by Julie Creswell and Colin Moynihan, Sept. 20, 2010.

New York Times, "A Political Life Filled with Cruel Reversals," by Robert D. McFadden, Dec. 7, 2010.

National Journal, "Don't Ever Go Against the Family," Dec. 6, 2010.

Law360, "Stars Among Creditors in Starr & Co. Bankruptcy," by Dietrich Knauth, Feb. 18, 2011.

Daily Beast, "The Pole Dancer and the Ponzi Scheme," by Peter Lauria, May 27, 2010.

New York Times, "Edwards Case Casts Spotlight on a Long Reclusive Donor," by Katharine Seelye, June 5, 2011.

Newsweek, "Bunny Mellon, the Secret-Keeper," by Meryl Gordon, July 25, 2011.

Books:

Rielle Hunter, *What Really Happened: John Edwards, Our Daughter, and Me*, BenBella Books, 2012.

Andrew Young, *The Politician*, Thomas Dunne Books, 2010.

CHAPTER TWENTY-SEVEN. EVERYTHING SHOULD BE NOTICED

Interviews:

John Baskett, Nancy Collins, David Fleming, Alex Forger, Hubert de Givenchy, Bryan Huffman, Carol Kendrick, Rickie Niceta, Stacy Lloyd IV, Thomas Lloyd, Abbe Lowell, Beverly Newton, Chuck Stuber, John Warner, Roger Whyte, Tony Willis

Documents:

United States of America vs. Johnny Reid Edwards, Criminal Action No. 1:11CR161. Closing arguments, trial transcript, May 17, 2012.

Bunny Mellon, March 28, 2014 funeral, CD courtesy Oak Spring Garden Library. Eulogy by Caroline Kennedy. Reprinted with Permission.

Articles:

CBS News / *New York Times* poll, "John Edwards," April 22, 2012.

Charleston Daily Mail, "Potential Jurors Dismissed from John Edwards Case," by Michael Biesecker, April 17, 2012.

McClatchy-Tribune News Service, "'Sin but No Crimes,' John Edwards' Defense Says," by Richard Simon, April 23, 2012.

Spartanburg Herald-Journal, "Former John Edwards Aide Back on the Witness Stand at Trial," by Michael Biesecker, April 24, 2012.

Los Angeles Times, "Ex-Aide Details Ways He Says John Edwards Hid Affair," by Richard Simon, April 25, 2012.

Spartanburg Herald-Tribune, "Former Aide: John Edwards Denied Knowing of Payoffs," by Michael Biesecker, April 26, 2012.

Los Angeles Times, "Witness Credibility Targeted," by Richard Simon, April 26, 2012.

Spartanburg Herald-Journal, "Former John Edwards Aide: Donors' Cash Went into NC Mansion," by Michael Biesecker, April 27, 2012.

Spartanburg Herald-Journal, "Aide's Wife: John Edwards Knew About Money," by Michael Biesecker, April 30, 2012.

Spartanburg Herald-Journal, "Former Aide Recalls John Edwards' Visit with Key Donor," by Michael Biesecker, May 2, 2012.

Spartanburg Herald-Journal, "Designer Details Scheme to Funnel Money to Edwards with Checks Labeled for Furniture Purchases," by Michael Biesecker, May 3, 2012.

New York Times, "Go-Between for Heiress Details Link to Edwards," by William Dupree and Kim Severson, May 4, 2012.

Spartanburg Herald-Journal, "Donor That Gave John Edwards Millions Told Friend She Felt Used," by Michael Biesecker, May 4, 2012.

Los Angeles Times, "Designer Takes Stand in Edwards Trial: An Elaborate Ruse Disguised Campaign Contributions, He Says," May 4, 2012.

Washington Post, "Choice of Partner Can Tell Us a Lot," by Melinda Henneberger, May 4, 2012.

Daily Beast, "The Man Who Confronted Edwards About His Dangerous Infidelity Game," by Diane Dimond, May 5, 2012.

Sunday Independent, "Edwards Gets Tangled in Forger Cheque," by Sophia Pearson and John Peragine, May 6, 2012.

Spartanburg Herald-Journal, "Librarian: John Edwards Asked Heiress for $3M to Help Hide Pregnant Mistress," by Michael Biesecker, May 7, 2012.

Daily Beast, "Witness Testifies He Took Rielle Hunter to an Airport in the Dead of Night," by Diane Dimond, May 8, 2012.

KeyNews.com, "Obituaries: Andrew Francis Oates Jr.," July 8, 2012.

New York Times, "Kenneth Battelle, 86, Hairdresser to the Stars, Dies," by Douglas Martin, May 13, 2013.

New York Times, "Bunny Mellon Is Thrust to Center of John Edwards Trial," by Guy Trebay, May 13, 2014.

Daily Beast, "John Edwards Defense Gets Off to a Rocky Start," by Diane Dimond, May 15, 2012.

Daily Beast, "John Edwards' Defense Rests After Just over Two Days of Underwhelming Testimony," by Diane Dimond, May 16, 2012.

Spartansburg Herald-Journal, "Closing Arguments Today in John Edwards Trial: Jury Begins Deliberations Friday," by Michael Biesecker, May 17, 2012.

Calgary Herald, "Edwards 'Was Surprised to Hear' About Payments," by Anne Blythe, May 16, 2012.

Daily Beast, "John Edwards Verdict," by Diane Dimond, May 31, 2012.

Spartansburg Herald-Tribune, "John Edwards Acquitted on 1 Count, Mistrial on Others," by Michael Biesecker, May 31, 2012.

Morning Sentinel, "John Edwards Escapes," by Michael Biesecker, June 1, 2012.

Time, "The John Edwards Mistrial: What Went Wrong," by Adam Cohen, June 1, 2012.

Valley News, "Feds Drop John Edwards Case," by Michael Biesecker, June 14, 2012.

Washingtonian, "A Conversation with Abbe Lowell," by Marisa M. Kashinko, June 15, 2012.

New York Times, "Rachel Mellon, an Heiress Known for Her Green Thumb, Dies at 103," by Robert D. McFadden, March 17, 2014.

Washington Post, "Rachel 'Bunny' Mellon, Arts Patron and Confidante of Jackie Kennedy, Dies at 103," by Adrian Higgins, March 17, 2014.

WWD, "Bunny Mellon, 103," by Lorna Koski, March 18, 2014.

Pittsburgh Post-Gazette, "Rachel 'Bunny' Mellon's Millions Distributed in Will," by Tracie Mauriello and Mackenzie Carpenter, March 20, 2014.

Washington Post, "At Bunny Mellon's Funeral, Music from Bette Midler and a John Edwards Appearance," by Roxanne Roberts, March 28, 2014.

Washington Social Diary, "Bunny Mellon's Perfect Funeral," by Carol Joynt, March 2014.

Pittsburgh Post-Gazette, "Rachel 'Bunny' Mellon: Rose Garden Designer and Mellon Heiress," by Mackenzie Carpenter, March 18, 2014.

New York Times, "The Eloquence of Silence," by Charlotte Moss, June 12, 2014.

Wall Street Journal, "Rachel 'Bunny' Mellon's Virginia Estate to List for $70 Million," by Candace Taylor, Aug. 14, 2014.

Washington Post, "Jackie Kennedy's Handmade Scrapbook Offers a Rare Glimpse of the Rose Garden's Birth," by Jura Koncius, July 28, 2015.

Washington Post, "Prized Chunk of Bunny Mellon's Virginia Estate Finds a Buyer," by Emily Heil, Sept. 7, 2015.

Washington Post, "The Fine Art of Renovation," by Ian Shapira, Nov. 29, 2015.

Books:

Rielle Hunter, *What Really Happened: John Edwards, Our Daughter, and Me*, BenBella Books, 2012.

Andrew Young, *The Politician*, Thomas Dunne Books, 2010.

Bibliography

Sherman Adams, *Firsthand Report: The Story of the Eisenhower Administration*, Harper & Brothers, 1961.

Apple Parish Bartlett and Susan Bartlett Crater, *Sister Parish: The Life of the Legendary American Interior Designer*, Vendome, 2000.

Robert Becker, *Nancy Lancaster: Her Life, Her World, Her Art*, Knopf, 1996.

Chantal Bizot, Marie-Noël de Gary, and Evelyne Possémé, *The Jewels of Jean Schlumberger*, Harry N. Abrams, 2001.

Mary Blume, *The Master of Us All: Balenciaga, His Workrooms, His World*, Farrar, Straus and Giroux, 2013.

Hamish Bowles, Rachel Lambert Mellon, and Arthur Schlesinger Jr., *Jacqueline Kennedy: The White House Years*, Metropolitan Museum, Little, Brown, 2001.

Sarah Bradford, *America's Queen: The Life of Jacqueline Kennedy Onassis*, Penguin, 2001.

David K. E. Bruce, *OSS Against the Reich: The World War II Diaries of Colonel David K. E. Bruce*, edited by Nelson D. Lankford, Kent State University Press, 1991.

Alfred Bush, *Charles Ryskamp: 1928–2010*, monograph, Princeton University, 2010.

David Cannadine, *Mellon: An American Life*, Knopf, 2006.

Noël Coward, *The Noël Coward Diaries*, edited by Graham Payn and Sheridan Morley, Little, Brown, 1982.

James Crathorne, *Cliveden: The Place and the People*, Collins & Brown, 1995.

Robert Crawford, *Young Eliot: From St. Louis to "The Waste Land,"* Farrar, Straus and Giroux, 2015.

Mary Custis Lee DeButts and Rosalie Noland Woodland, *Charlotte Haxall Noland 1883–1969*, Foxcroft School, Whittet & Shepperson, 1971.

Elizabeth Edwards, *Saving Graces: Finding Solace and Strength from Friends and Strangers*, Random House, 2006.

Robert Eisinger, *The Evolution of Political Polling*, Cambridge University Press, 2003.

David Edward Finley, *A Standard of Excellence: Andrew W. Mellon Founds the National Gallery of Art at Washington*, Smithsonian Institution Press, 1973.

Timothy Glander, *Origins of Mass Communications Research During the American Cold War*, Routledge, 1999.

Katharine Graham, *Personal History*, Knopf, 1997.

David Greenberg, *Republic of Spin: An Inside History of the American Presidency*, W. W. Norton, 2016.

Lee Hall, *Betty Parsons: Artist, Dealer, Collector*, Harry N. Abrams, 1991.

Neil Harris, *Capital Culture: J. Carter Brown, the National Gallery of Art, and the Reinvention of the Museum Experience*, University of Chicago Press, 2013.

Gregg Herken, *The Georgetown Set*, Knopf, 2014.

Burton Hersh, *The Mellon Family: A Fortune in History*, William Morrow, 1978.

Rielle Hunter, *What Really Happened: John Edwards, Our Daughter, and Me*, BenBella Books, 2012.

Richard Jackson Jr. and Cornelia Brooke Gilder, *Houses of the Berkshires: 1870–1930*, Architecture of Leisure series, Acanthus Press, 2011.

Laura Jacobs and Victor Skrebneski, *The Art of Haute Couture*, Abbeville Press, 1995.

E.J. Kahn Jr., *Jock: The Life and Times of John Hay Whitney*, Doubleday & Co., 1981.

John Keegan, *The Second World War*, Penguin Books, 1989.

David E. Koskoff, *The Mellons: The Chronicle of America's Richest Family*, Thomas Y. Crowell, 1978.

Gerard Barnes Lambert, *All Out of Step*, Doubleday, 1956.

Kenneth Jay Lane, *Kenneth Jay Lane: Faking It*, Harry N. Abrams, 1996.

Frank Langella, *Dropped Names: Famous Men and Women As I Knew Them*, Harper-Collins, 2012.

Nelson D. Lankford, *The Last American Aristocrat: The Biography of Ambassador David K. E. Bruce, 1898–1977*, Little, Brown, 1996.

William Manchester, *The Death of a President*, Harper & Row, 1967.

Marsha Mason, *Journey: A Personal Odyssey*, Simon & Schuster, 2002.

Chris Matthews, *Jack Kennedy: Elusive Hero*, Simon & Schuster, 2011.

Lily Fleming McCarthy, as told to Lieutenant Commander John Lea, *Remembering Nelson*, privately published in association with the Royal Naval Museum, Portsmouth, England, 1995.

Marta McDowell, *All the President's Gardens*, Timber Press, 2016.

Paul Mellon with John Baskett, *Reflections in a Silver Spoon*, William Morrow, 1992.

Tim Mellon, *Tim's Story*, Mint Leaf Media, 2016.

Deborah Mitford, Duchess of Devonshire, *Wait for Me! Memoirs*, Farrar, Straus and Giroux, 2010.

Vicky Moon, *The Middleburg Mystique: A Peek Inside the Gates of Middleburg, Virginia*, Capital Books, 2001.

Diana Oswald, introduction by David Patrick Columbia, *Debutantes: When Glamour Was Born*, Rizzoli, 2013.

George Pitcher, *A Life of Grace: The Biography of Grace Lansing Lambert*, Princeton University Press, 1987.

Jan Pottker, *Janet & Jackie: The Story of a Mother and Her Daughter, Jacqueline Kennedy Onassis*, St. Martin's Press, 2001.

Sandra Raphael, *An Oak Spring Sylva: A Selection of the Rare Books on Trees in the Oak Spring Garden Library*, Yale University Press, 1989.

Sandra Raphael, *An Oak Spring Pomona: A Selection of the Rare Books on Fruit in the Oak Spring Garden Library*, Yale University Press, 1990.

Richard Reeves, *President Kennedy: Profile of Power*, Simon & Schuster, 1993.

Arthur Schlesinger Jr., *The Age of Roosevelt*, Vol. 1, *The Crisis of the Old Order: 1919–1933*, Houghton Mifflin, 1957.

Arthur Schlesinger Jr., *A Thousand Days: John F. Kennedy in the White House*, Houghton Mifflin, 1965.

Arthur Schlesinger Jr., *Journals: 1952–2000*, Penguin Books, 2007.

William Seale, *The White House Garden*, White House Historical Association, 1996.

William Seale, *The White House: The History of an American Idea*, White House Historical Association, 2001.

Lee Seldes, *The Legacy of Mark Rothko*, Da Capo Press, 1978.

Adam Sheingate, *Building a Business of Politics: The Rise of Political Consulting and the Transformation of American Democracy*, Oxford University Press, 2015.

John Saumarez Smith, editor, *A Spy in the Bookshop*, Frances Lincoln, 2006.

Sally Bedell Smith, *Grace and Power: The Private World of the Kennedy White House*, Random House, 2004.

Grif Stockley, *Blood in Their Eyes: The Elaine Race Massacres of 1919*, University of Arkansas Press, 2001.

Evan Thomas, *Robert Kennedy, His Life*, Simon & Schuster, 2000.

Lucia Tongiorgi Tomasi, *An Oak Spring Flora*, Oak Spring Garden Library, 1997.

Lucia Tongiorgi Tomasi and Tony Willis, *An Oak Spring Herbaria*, Oak Spring Garden Library, 2009.

René Verdon, *The White House Chef Cookbook*, Doubleday, 1968.

John Walker, *Self-Portrait with Donors: Confessions of an Art Collector*, Little, Brown, 1974.

Douglas Waller, *Wild Bill Donovan: The Spymaster Who Created the OSS and Modern American Espionage*, Free Press, 2011.

Ida B. Wells-Barnett, *The Arkansas Race Riot*, Aquila, Chicago, 1920.

Christof Wolf, Dominique Joye, Tom W. Smith, and Yang-chih Fu, *The SAGE Handbook of Survey Methodology*, SAGE Publications, 2016.

Andrew Young, *The Politician*, Thomas Dunne Books, 2010.

Index

About the Author

Meryl Gordon, an award-winning journalist, is the author of *Mrs. Astor Regrets*, the *New York Times* bestselling saga about the family fight over philanthropist Brooke Astor, and *The Phantom of Fifth Avenue*, a biography of reclusive copper heiress Huguette Clark. She is the director of magazine writing at NYU's Arthur L. Carter Journalism Institute, and her articles have appeared regularly in *Vanity Fair*, *New York*, and the *New York Times*. Meryl and her husband, political columnist Walter Shapiro, live in Manhattan.